M000250626

Italy Today

"Divided into four major sections devoted to an analysis of politics, economics, society, and mass culture, this book examines a broad range of subjects such as political institutions, parliament, education, trade unions, women, family, the Church, and mass culture, and provides a fascinating account of Italy's overwhelming need for political reform and the repeated failure to achieve it and how Italy has coped or has failed to cope with the challenges of globalization. Mario B. Mignone illustrates how the decline of communism and Catholicism and the surge of immigration are shaping a new national identity for the new millennium. Copiously illustrated and enriched with 'profiles' on various Italian institutions and snapshots on aspects of Italian life, this fascinating and authoritative work is essential for anyone interested in modern and contemporary Italian society and its culture."

Marcello Saija, University of Messina

"Mario B. Mignone's work is a serious and documented panorama of Italy since World War II that is both informative and challenging. It unravels the most complex historical and social problems by approaching them from more than one direction and by using lucid and balanced judgment."

Sebastiano Martelli, University of Salerno

"A framework that courageously builds up the dynamics that gave impetus to the profound transformation of the country. Readers will find it admirable for its mastery of the material and the sobriety of its judgments."

Giuliano Manacorda, University of Rome

Italy Today

Studies in Modern European History

Frank J. Coppa
General Editor

Vol. 16

PETER LANG
New York • Washington, D.C./Baltimore • Bern
Frankfurt am Main • Berlin • Brussels • Vienna • Oxford

Mario B. Mignone

Italy Today

Facing the Challenges
of the New Millennium

REVISED EDITION

PETER LANG
New York • Washington, D.C./Baltimore • Bern
Frankfurt am Main • Berlin • Brussels • Vienna • Oxford

Library of Congress Cataloging-in-Publication Data

Mignone, Mario B.
Italy today: facing the challenges of the new millennium /
Mario B. Mignone. — Rev. ed.
p. cm. — (Studies in modern European history; v. 16)
Includes bibliographical references and index.
1. Italy—Politics and government—1994– 2. Italy—Economic conditions—1994–
3. Italy—Social conditions—1994– 4. Italy—Social conditions. I. Title.
JN5451.M53   320.945—dc22   2007043474
ISBN 978-1-4331-0187-8
ISSN 0893-6897

Bibliographic information published by **Die Deutsche Bibliothek**.
Die Deutsche Bibliothek lists this publication in the "Deutsche
Nationalbibliografie"; detailed bibliographic data is available
on the Internet at http://dnb.ddb.de/.

FSC
Mixed Sources
Product group from well-managed
forests, controlled sources and
recycled wood or fiber

Cert no. SCS-COC-002464
www.fsc.org
©1996 Forest Stewardship Council

Cover design by Clear Point Designs

The paper in this book meets the guidelines for permanence and durability
of the Committee on Production Guidelines for Book Longevity
of the Council of Library Resources.

© 2008 Peter Lang Publishing, Inc., New York
29 Broadway, 18th floor, New York, NY 10006
www.peterlang.com

Printed in the United States of America

TABLE OF CONTENTS

Part 1: Politics and Government

Part 2: Economic and Social Transformation

Part 3: Society

Part 4: Communications and Cultural Changes

Regional Italy since 1919 (adapted from C. Duggan, *A Concise History of Italy*, Cambridge: Cambridge U.P., 1994, p. 197.)

PREFACE

The third edition of *Italy Today* has been recast as a textbook to respond to requests and feedback by colleagues and students who have used this book in their course on post-war Italy. In this new edition, the conventional manner of looking at Italian politics, economics, and society in a linear way, as if history went forward in a consistent manner under the exclusive influence of palpable dynamics, has been broadened to make the fullness of the Italian experience more accessible to the general reader. In the process, I also broadened the cultural context.

The understanding of a country as reflected through its politics, economics, and society will certainly be richer if the assessment is conducted in the wider context of its culture; after all, culture is dynamic; it is both shaped by and shapes society. The word culture here is meant to imply the complex whole that includes knowledge, belief, art, morals, law, custom, and any other capabilities and habits acquired by man as a member of society ("fine arts," "serious" music, philosophy as well as popular music, social rituals, popular traditions, folklore, eating habits, celebrations, and dress codes). These activities need to be understood not just in intrinsic (aesthetic, intellectual, formal) terms but also sociologically and anthropologically in terms of such things as norms of social behavior, the allocation of status and power in society, and the reproduction of values and beliefs. The understanding of a country is richer when we include the study of culture, which stresses heterogeneity, change, intercultural borrowing, and the way people manipulate cultural forms in pursuing diverse and often conflicting interests. Our picture of Italy should include the way Italians use cultural forms as they make daily sense of diverse, often contradictory experiences in social, political, and economic contexts that are in confusing motion.

In this kind of assessment, not only must we rely on the contribution and practice of recent cultural studies, but we must both broaden the focus of our attention and deflate old clichés and perspectives. Anyone who studies Italy comes up frequently against a series of conventional or stereotyped notions about the country, its people, its institutions, both in everyday common sense and in academic scholarship. One of the major problems with the earlier studies was the narrowness of focus. Because of the Cold War preoccupations and Italy being a key member of NATO, most studies were overly focused on politics and tended to assess Italian democracy with suspicion. Another major problem was the assumption about Mediterranean backwardness, which not only inspired the overall focus on family and politics but also played down Italy's history and social and cultural complexity by simply considering the country as an exotic "Other" far removed from the "core" Western reality.

We must also avoid making the mistake of many Anglo-American anthropologists who focused on small communities and tended to treat local cultural forms as homogeneous and fixed. In doing so, we must challenge the classic studies of politics, family, and gender that polarized the opposition between traditional and modern that underlies the Mediterranean perspective. Still persisting today, this perspective has been mainly set in rural or small-town and southern locales. Although the studies were carried out during years of radical social, economic, and cultural transformation, change was rarely built into their representations. Although Italy has changed more in the last forty years than in the previous two thousand, a profound change not experienced by any other nation in a such short time, the studies of culture that were supposed to mirror such changes often treated culture in terms of rigid "codes" or syndromes. Earlier studies also made crude distinctions between elite and grass-roots ideas, failing to consider the role of culture as a means of drawing fine social distinctions in years of great socioeconomic mobility.

While questioning assessments based on the polarized oppositions of *traditional* and *modern,* it is important to see how past and present interpenetrate, how the *traditional* may be formulated as people pursue their own interests in very *modern* circumstances. We should critically discuss the wide claim of Italy as a nation culturally split between north and south, as a country whose inhabitants have a weak national identity and a strong inward-looking attachment to the locality and the family. Moreover, we should identify some distinctive cultural traits, including strong subnational (localistic and regionalistic) identities and preference for personalistic forms of political action, clientelism, and corruption. We should see how and why local specificity is now celebrated.

In trying to define the Italian national identity, it is very important to identify those social problems that tend to be particularly sensitized and important to Italy's national identity. In Italy, national identity in no way may be seen as being reflected through its capitol, as is the case in some other European countries. In France, for example, Paris is the seat of government—it contains the largest concentration of population, and it is the center of the French economy, academic life, artistic culture, sport, and tourism. Italy, by comparison, seems almost centerless. Its financial and commercial capital is Milan. Its industry tends to be concentrated in the north. Florence is at the heart of Italy's language and high culture. Tourists are as likely to be attracted by Florence as by Venice, Rome, Capri, or Taormina.

In the process of questioning old clichés, the fundamental issue of what Italy is as a nation is raised. Is it a social fiction with no fixed identity? Does the fact that a strong civic consciousness and a developed sense of the nation-state, said to be found in the "mature democracies," are held to be lacking in Italy, where "familism" and local identities allegedly hold sway, justify the view that such Italian peculiarities must be pathological abnormalities? The very fact that Italy has remained uniquely plurilingual, with not only a very large number of dialects that are still used by many speakers but also a smaller yet still significant number of minority languages, including Albanian, Greek, German and Ladin, suggests the profound heterogeneity of the country. However, the linguistic diversity of the peninsula and islands, so often interpreted as a sign of a weak national culture, is actually the basis of a rich cultural pluralism.

This book was written under the assumption that the reader has no knowledge of Italy or of Italian culture and history. Of course, the reader who has some acquaintance with the history of fascism or the development of Europe since World War II will be at an advantage, as will the reader who has some grounding in economics and politics.

I have been critical of many things in Italy, but mostly in the way that a progressive-minded Italian might be critical. This book tries to look at Italy from within, more from an Italian than an American point of view, and it takes for granted all that is admirable about Italian civilization. Although I have spent a good part of my adult life in the U.S., I was born in Italy and lived there until I was 20 years old. Since then, I have returned two or three times a year to teach, do research, and see friends and relatives.

A general book such as this has to rely greatly on other people's research; the list of consulted works gives a good indication of my indebtedness. Those scholars have enabled me, through their writings, to come to a better understanding of the complexities of postwar Italy and to substantiate my own assessment. I would like therefore to thank all those who, in one way or another, have contributed to the making of this book: Giuseppe Ammendola, Rocco Capozzi, Alessandro Carrera, Anthony Costantini, Donato Di Bartolomeo, Paolo Giordano, Millicent Marcus, Giuseppe Mazzotta, Fraser Ottanelli, Stan Pugliese, Luca Somigli, Anthony J. Tamburri, Carlo Testa, AnnaLisa Saccà, Senator Kenneth P. La Valle; New York State Comptroller Thomas P. Di Napoli; Franco Borrelli and Stefano Vaccara from *America Oggi,* the American daily in the Italian language, for some of the pictures, ISTAT for statistical data; Margaret Manos for her editorial service; Bernadette Shade at Peter Lang for her exceptional skills and care in the production process; and Chris Myers for having faith in this project.

Stony Brook University
August 2007

Italy and its regions with their capitols. A degree of decentralization of power to the regions was established by the new constitution (1948) but came into force only in the 1970s. Fifteen of these regions have an ordinary statute; the remaining five have a special statute which gives them greater political and administrative autonomy. These are the three border regions of Valle d'Aosta, Trentino-Alto Adige, and Friuli-Venezia Giulia and the islands of Sicily and Sardinia. Each region is further divided into provinces (95 in all), which, in turn, are subdivided into *comuni* (municipalities).

PROFILE OF THE NATION

Official Name: Italian Republic

Location: Southern Europe. A peninsula extending into the central Mediterranean Sea, northeast of Tunisia. Strategic location dominating central Mediterranean as well as southern sea and air approaches to Western Europe

Area: 301,230 sq km, slightly larger than Arizona; about the size of Georgia and Florida combined

Land boundaries—*total:* 1,932.2 km border countries: Austria 430 km, France 488 km, Slovenia 232 km, Switzerland 740 km [Holy See (Vatican City) 3.2 km, San Marino 39 km]

Coastline: 7,600 km

Climate: predominantly Mediterranean; Alpine in far north; in summer, hot, dry in south

Terrain: mostly rugged and mountainous; some plains, coastal lowlands
Elevation extremes:
  lowest point: Mediterranean Sea 0 m
  highest point: Mont Blanc (Monte Bianco) de Courmayeur 4,748 m (a secondary peak of Mont Blanc)

People

Population: 58,103,033 (July 2005 est.) Age structure: 0–14 years: 14.17% (male 4,209,102), (female 3,964,765); 15–64 years: 67.48% (male 19,375,742), (female 19,546,332); 65 years and over: 18.35% (male 4,368,264), (female 6,215,620)

The Italian territory, with the exclusion of Republic of San Marino and Vatican City State, has an area of 301,328 square km with an average national population density of 192 inhabitants per square km. The population density varies much from one region to the other; it is due mainly to the many mountains and hills (76,83%) on the national territory.

According to the last census, carried out in October 2001 by ISTAT (the Central Statistical Office) there are 56,995,744 Italians residing in Italy. This figure has remained quite stable since the previous census 10 years earlier (56,778,031). 26.2% of the population live in north-west Italy; 18.8% in the north-east; 19% in central Italy; 24.5% in the south and the remaining 11.5% on the islands. There are a total of 8,101 municipalities, and those with the highest population are Rome (2,846,804), Milan (1,256,211), Naples (1,004,500), Turin (865,263), Palermo (686,722), Genoa (610,307), Bologna (371,217), Florence (356,118), Bari (316,532) and Venice (271,073). Morterone, in the province of Lecco, is the smallest one, with just 33 residents.

Life expectancy: Male: 76.08 years, Female: 83 years

Population growth rate: 0.07

Ethnic groups: Primarily Italian, but there are small clusters of German-, French-, and Slovene-Italians in the north and Albanian-Italians and Greek-Italians in the south.

Religions: predominately Roman Catholic with mature Protestant and Jewish communities and a growing Muslim immigrant community.

Language: Italian (official), German (parts of Trentino-Alto Adige region are predominantly German speaking), French (small French-speaking minority in Valle d'Aosta region), Slovene (Slovene-speaking minority in the Trieste-Gorizia area)

Cities: *Capitol*—Rome (pop. 2.8 million). *Other big cities*—Milan, Naples, Turin.

Education: *Years compulsory*—8. *Literacy*—98%.

Health: *Infant mortality rate*—5.76/1,000 live births.

Government

Type: Republic since June 2, 1946. Constitution: January 1, 1948.

Branches: *Executive*—president (chief of state), council of ministers (cabinet), headed by the president of the council (prime minister). *Legislative*—bicameral parliament: 630-member chamber of deputies, 315-member senate (plus a varying number of "life" senators). *Judicial*—independent constitutional court and lower magistracy. The Italian judicial system is based on Roman law modified by the Napoleonic code and subsequent statutes. There is only partial judicial review of legislation in the American sense. A constitutional court, which passes on the constitutionality of laws, is a post-World War II innovation. Its powers, volume, and frequency of decisions are not as extensive as those of the U.S. Supreme Court.

Political and administrative subdivisions: 94 provinces, 20 regions.

Political parties: Forza Italia, Democratic Party of the Left, National Alliance, Northern League, United Christian Democrats, Democrats, Italian People's Party, Christian Democratic Center, Socialist, Communist Renewal, Social Democratic, Greens, Italian Renewal. Suffrage: Vote for House: universal over 18; vote for Senate: universal over 25.

Economy

GDP (2006): $1.854 trillion.

GDP—Per capita income (2006): $31,897

GDP growth: 1.9% (2006)

GDP—composition by sector: agriculture: 2.5%; industry: 30.4%; services: 67.1%. Natural resources: Fish, natural gas. Agriculture: *Products*—wheat, rice, grapes, olives, citrus fruits. Industry: *Types*—automobiles, machinery, chemicals, textiles, shoes. **Trade** (2005 est.): $371.9 billion

Exports—$263.6 billion. *Partners*—EU 53%, U.S. 10%, OPEC 4%; mechanical products, textiles and apparel, transportation equipment, metal products, chemical products, food and agricultural products. *Imports*—$254.5 billion. *Partners*—EU 56%, OPEC 6%, U.S. 5%; machinery and transport equipment, foodstuffs, ferrous and nonferrous metals, wool, cotton, energy products.

Labor force: 24.63 million
Labor force by occupation: services: 63%, industry: 32.6%, agriculture: 4.4%

Source: ISTAT

Italy has a diversified industrial economy with roughly the same total and per capita output as France and the United Kingdom. This capitalistic economy remains divided into a developed industrial north, dominated by private companies, and a less developed agricultural south, with more than 20% unemployment. Most raw materials needed by industry and about 80% of energy required are imported.

U.S.-Italy economic relations: The U.S.-Italian bilateral economic relationship is strong and growing. The United States and Italy cooperate closely on major economic issues, including within the G-8. With a large population and a high per capita income, Italy is one of the United States' most important trade partners. In 2002 the United States was the fifth-largest foreign supplier of the Italian market and the largest supplier outside the European Union. Total trade between the United States and Italy was $34.4 billion in 2002. The U.S. ran a $14.2 billion deficit with Italy in 2002.

Significant changes are occurring in the composition of this trade. More value-added products such as office machinery and aircraft are becoming the principal U.S. exports to Italy. The change reveals the growing sophistication of the Italian market, and bilateral trade should expand further. In 2002 the United States imported about $24.3 billion in Italian goods while exporting about $10.1 billion in U.S. goods to Italy. U.S. foreign direct investment in Italy at the end of 2001 exceeded $23.9 billion.

Foreign relations: Italy was a founding member of the European Community—now the European Union (EU). Italy was admitted to the United Nations in 1955 and is a member and strong supporter of the North Atlantic Treaty Organization (NATO), the Organization for Economic Cooperation and Development (OECD), the General Agreement on Tariffs and Trade/World Trade Organization (GATT/WTO), the Organization for Security and Cooperation in Europe (OSCE), and the Council of Europe. It chaired the CSCE (the forerunner of the OSCE) in 1994, the EU in 1996, and the G-8 in 2001 and served as EU president from July to December 2003.

Italy firmly supports the United Nations and its international security activities. Italy actively participated in and deployed troops in support of UN peacekeeping missions in Somalia, Mozambique, and East Timor and provides critical support for NATO and UN operations in Bosnia, Kosovo, and Albania. Italy deployed 1,000 Alpini troops to Afghanistan in support of Operation Enduring Freedom (OEF) in February 2003. Italy also supports international efforts to reconstruct and stabilize Iraq through its military contingent of some 2,800 troops, as well as humanitarian workers and other officials. The troops remain in Iraq under UN mandate and at the request of the sovereign Iraqi government.

The Italian government seeks to obtain consensus with other European countries on various defense and security issues within the EU as well as NATO. European integration and the development of common defense and security policies will continue to be of primary interest to Italy.

U.S.-Italy relations: The United States enjoys warm and friendly relations with Italy. The two are NATO allies and cooperate in the United Nations, in various regional organizations, and bilaterally for peace, prosperity, and security. Italy has worked closely with the United States and other Western nations on such issues as NATO and UN operations as well as with assistance to Russia and the new independent states; the Middle East peace process; multilateral talks; Somalia and Mozambique peacekeeping; and combating drug trafficking, and terrorism.

Under longstanding bilateral agreements flowing from NATO membership, Italy hosts important U.S. military forces at Vicenza and Livorno (army); Aviano (air force); and Sigonella, Gaeta, and Naples—home port for the U.S. Navy Sixth Fleet. The United States has about 16,000 military personnel stationed in Italy. Italy hosts the NATO War College in Rome.

Italy remains a strong and active transatlantic partner which, along with the United States, has sought to foster democratic ideals and international cooperation in areas of strife and civil conflict. Toward this end, the Italian Government has cooperated with the United States in the formulation of defense, security, and peacekeeping policies.

Ethnic makeup: The Italian phenotype is European, but profoundly varied within this context. The history of Italy shows that over the centuries, quite a few non-native ethnic groups have poured into the Italian peninsula and Sicily since Roman times. Almost all of these ethnicities came from Europe with the notable exception of a small number of Arabs who invaded Sicily in the 9th century. The northern Italians of the Po Valley spoke a Celtic dialect and were historically recognized as Gauls (or Celts) by the Romans. The central Italians labeled themselves as Latins and other linguistically related tribes (and may actually be related to the Celts in the north). The main outsiders who came into Italy in the last 3000 years were the Greeks who heavily colonized the southern Italian Peninsula as well as Sicily before the 1st century BC. Then came the Ostrogoths in the 5th century AD, and finally the Lombards in the 6th century AD. Both of these groups were Germanic tribes who had come from the north of Europe seeking land, wealth, and living space. Other later groups such as the Franks, Byzantines, Normans, and the French Angevins ruled parts of Italy but only settled in small numbers throughout the country.

Therefore, the resulting varied appearance of Italians shows that there is no typical Italian 'look' as some claim for other European countries.

Local identity within Italy: From the end of the Roman Empire until the mid-nineteenth century, Italy was not a nation as we know it today. The landmass was fractured into various kingdoms, duchies, and domains. Over the centuries, different dialects and customs evolved as a result of the isolation of the kingdoms from one another and of their being influenced by foreign powers. While all the kingdoms were similar in that they retained basic elements of Roman language and culture, each one built upon this ancient culture to develop their own independent culture and ethnic identity. Even to this day, Italians living in their homeland define themselves by their home region, and most speak both a local dialect and standard Italian.

History

The rise of the Italian city-states: In this climate of political and social fragmentation, individual Italian cities began to assert their autonomy. During the 11th century an elaborate pattern of communal government began to evolve under the leadership of a merchant class grown wealthy in trade, banking, and such industries as woolen textiles. Many cities, especially Florence, Genoa, Pisa, Milan, and Venice, became powerful and independent city-states. Resisting the efforts of both the old landed nobles and the emperors to control them, these communes hastened the end of feudalism in northern Italy and spawned deeply rooted identification with the city as opposed to the larger region or country. The cities were often troubled by violent and divisive rivalries among their citizens, the most famous being the papal-imperial struggle between the Guelphs (supporters of the popes) and the Ghibellines (supporters of the emperors). But despite such divisions, cities contributed significantly to the economic, social, and cultural vitality of Italy.

The Kingdom of Sicily: Unlike the north, with its network of vigorously independent urban centers, southern Italy experienced a significant consolidation after its conquest by the Normans. Bands of these invaders arrived in Italy early in the 11th century. Starting c.1046, Robert Guiscard and his successors expelled the Saracens and Byzantines and carved a powerful domain out of Apulia, Calabria, Campania, and Sicily. Although the Norman territories remained a fief of the papacy, papal overlordship became a mere formality in the 12th century especially after 1127, when Roger II united the southern part of the peninsula with Sicily; he assumed the title of king of Sicily in 1130. While the Normans were consolidating their rule in southern Italy, the papacy and the Holy Roman Empire continued their struggle for dominance in northern and central Italy.

The Italian Renaissance and foreign domination: After 1300 both the papacy and the Holy Roman Empire turned their attention away from Italy. The emperors concentrated on German affairs while the popes met increasing resistance especially from the French as they tried to assert their authority in Europe. For much of the 14th century the papacy was situated at Avignon, in southern France. The weakening of papal and imperial authority accompanied great intellectual changes in Italy. An intellectual revival, stimulated in part by the freer atmosphere of the cities and in part by the rediscovery of ancient Greek and Latin writings, gave rise to the humanist attitudes (Humanism) and ideas that formed the basis of the Renaissance. About the same time, many of the communal governments of the city-states fell under the rule of dictators called *signori* (Signorie), who curbed their factionalism and became hereditary rulers. In Milan the Visconti family rose to power in the 13th century, to be succeeded by the Sforza family in the mid-15th century, a few decades after the Medici family had seized control of Florence. Meanwhile the Este family ruled Ferrara from the 13th through the 16th century. Although they subverted the political institutions of the communes, the *signori* (who became known as *principi*, with royal titles) were instrumental in advancing the cultural and civic life of Renaissance Italy. Under the patronage of the Medici, for example, Florence became the most magnificent and prestigious center of the arts in Italy. During the 14th and 15th centuries, Italian thought and style influenced all Europe. As the larger cities expanded into the surrounding countryside, absorbing many of the smaller cities, they involved themselves in the complex international politics of the age.

The 15th century marked also the beginning and flourishing of the Italian Renaissance, a period characterized by the revival of the economy, resulting in renewed awareness of classical art and a new European focus on humanistic philosophy, quality of life, free trade, university study, literature, music, and art. Florence was the epicenter of the Italian Renaissance, and in fact UNESCO has catalogued that 70 percent of the entire world's art treasures are to be found in Italy.

As the Renaissance evolved to the baroque period, Rome and the Holy See emerged once again as a major power and rival of the merchant city-states. It is fair to say that while Venice and the city-states represent the highest medieval art, Florence represents the height of the Renaissance, and Rome the Baroque period. The church solidified its influence during the Reformation and counter-reformation and remains today very central to the Italian people.

The frequent wars between city-states brought to Italy the mercenary leaders known as the *condottieri* and ultimately resulted in foreign intervention. In 1494, Charles VIII of France invaded Italy, signaling the beginning of a period of foreign occupation that lasted until the 19th century. By 1550 almost all Italy had been subjugated by the Habsburg ruler Charles V, who was both Holy Roman emperor and king of Spain; when Charles abdicated in 1555–56, dividing the Habsburg territories between his brother Emperor Ferdinand I and his son Philip II of Spain, Italy was part of the latter's inheritance. Spain remained the dominant power in Italy until Austria replaced it after the War of the Spanish Succession (1701–14). In the 18th century some areas of Italy achieved independence. Savoy (the Kingdom of Sardinia after 1720) annexed Sardinia and portions of Lombardy; in 1735 the Kingdom of the Two Sicilies became an independent monarchy under the junior branch of the Spanish Bourbon dynasty. Italy itself, however, no longer played a central role in European politics.

Italian unification: In the 18th century, as in the Renaissance, intellectual changes began to break down traditional values and institutions. Enlightenment ideas from France and Britain spread rapidly, and from 1789 the French Revolution excited liberal Italians.

The Napoleonic era in Italy: Europe was soon involved in a series of wars that eventually involved states on the Italian peninsula. Between 1796, when troops under General

Napoleon Bonaparte invaded the peninsula, and 1814 when they withdrew, the entire peninsula was under French domination. Several short-lived republics were proclaimed early in the period. After two decades of Napoleon's modern but often harsh rule, profound changes took place in Italy; many Italians began to see the possibilities of forging a united country free of foreign control. Following the restoration of European peace in 1815, Italy consisted of the Kingdom of Sardinia (Piedmont, Sardinia, Savoy, and Genoa); the Kingdom of the Two Sicilies (including Naples and Sicily); the Papal States; and Tuscany and a series of smaller duchies in north central Italy. Lombardy and Venetia were now controlled by the Austrians.

The *Risorgimento*: The repressive and reactionary policies imposed on Italy by the Austrian leader Klemens, Furst von Metternich, and the Congress of Vienna aggravated popular discontent, and the expansion of Austrian control in Italy stimulated intense antiforeigner sentiment. These conditions gave rise to the Italian unification movement known as the *Risorgimento*. Revolutionaries and patriots, especially Giuseppe Mazzini, began to work actively for unity and independence. A series of unsuccessful revolts led in the 1820s by the *Carbonari*, a conspiratorial nationalist organization, and in the 1830s by Mazzini's Young Italy group, provided the background for the Revolutions of 1848. These affected all major Italian cities and throughout Europe. Charles Albert, king of Sardinia (1831–49), declared war on Austria and along with some other Italian rulers, gave his people a constitution, but both the war of liberation (First War of Independence, 1848) and the revolutionary republics set up in Rome, Venice, and Tuscany were crushed by Austria in 1849. Under the progressive, liberal leadership of Camillo Benso, *conte* di Cavour, Sardinia led Italy to final unification. In 1859, after gaining the support of France and England, Cavour, in alliance with the French emperor Napoleon III (Second War of Independence, 1859), seized Lombardy; in 1860 all of Italy north of the Papal States—except Venetia—was added to Sardinia. Giuseppe Garibaldi, a popular hero and guerrilla leader, led an expedition of 1,000 "Red Shirts" to Sicily in the same year and subsequently seized the southern part of peninsular Italy, which with Sicily constituted the Kingdom of the Two Sicilies. Garibaldi turned his conquests over to Victor Emmanuel, and in 1861 the Kingdom of Italy was proclaimed. Only Venetia and Rome were not included in the new state (the former was added in 1866, through the Third War of Independence, and the latter in 1870). Italians at last had their own country.

The Kingdom of Italy: The new nation faced many serious problems. A large debt, few natural resources, and almost no industry or transportation facilities combined with extreme poverty, a high illiteracy rate, and an uneven tax structure to weigh heavily on the Italian people. Regionalism was still strong, and only a fraction of the citizens had the right to vote. To make matters worse, the pope, angered over the loss of Rome and the papal lands, refused to recognize the Italian state. In the countryside, banditry and peasant anarchism resulted in government repression, which was often brutal. Meanwhile during the 1880s a socialist movement began to develop among workers in the cities. The profound differences between the impoverished south and the wealthier north widened. Parliament did little to resolve these problems: throughout this so-called Liberal Period (1870–1915), the nation was governed by a series of coalitions of liberals to the left and right of center who were unable to form a clear-cut majority. Despite the fact that some economic and social progress took place before World War I, Italy during that time was a dissatisfied and crisis-ridden nation.

In an attempt to increase its international influence and prestige, Italy joined Germany and Austria in the Triple Alliance in 1882. In the 1890s Italy unsuccessfully tried to conquer Ethiopia; and in 1911 it declared war on Turkey to obtain the North African territory of Libya. After the outbreak of World War I in 1914, Italy remained neutral for almost a year while the government negotiated with both sides. In 1915, Italy finally joined the Allies, after having been promised territories that it regarded as *Italia irredenta* (unliberated Italy). The country was unprepared for a major war, however; aside from a few victories in 1918, Italy suffered serious losses of men, materiel, and morale. Moreover, despite the efforts of Vittorio Emmanuele Orlando at the Paris Peace Conference, the treaties that followed the war gave Italy only Trentino and Trieste, a small part of the territories it had expected. These disappointments produced a powerful wave of nationalist sentiment against the Allies and the Italian government.

The fascist period: Plagued by internal political divisions and with an economy devastated by war, the new Kingdom of Italy was no Roman Empire. In 1919, frustrated that Italy had received few gains despite having been a victor in the First World War, a politician named Benito Mussolini launched a movement that called for the restoration of Italy as a great power.

Italy was plunged into deep social and political crisis by the war. Veterans, unemployed workers, desperate peasants, and a frightened middle class demanded changes, and the 1919 elections suddenly made the Socialist and the new Popular (Catholic) parties the largest in parliament. While extreme nationalists agitated for territorial expansion, strikes and threats of revolution unsettled the nation.

The rise of fascism: In 1919, in the midst of these unsettled conditions, Benito Mussolini, a former revolutionary socialist, founded a new movement called fascism. Through a combination of shrewd political maneuvering and widespread violence perpetrated by Mussolini's Blackshirt squads, the fascists gained increasing support. In October 1922, the fascists staged a march on Rome, after King Victor Emmanuel III had named Mussolini prime minister. Within four years, Mussolini had become a dictator, destroying civil liberties, outlawing all other political parties, and imposing a totalitarian regime on the country. Public works projects, propaganda, militarism, and the appearance of order gained Mussolini considerable prestige, and the Lateran Treaty with the papacy in 1929 gave the dictator a wide measure of popularity.

Fascist expansionism: Mussolini spent twenty years consolidating power and building up the Italian economy, bent on the idea of restoring Italy as a great power. Calling himself "Il Duce" (meaning Leader), Mussolini dreamed of leading a new Roman Empire. Mussolini's foreign policy, based on aggression and expansion, moved Italy closer to war during the 1930s. In 1935–36 the Italian army invaded and conquered Ethiopia, and in 1936, Italy sent troops to support Francisco Franco in the Spanish Civil War. Later that year, after Italy had been isolated economically through sanctions issued by the League of Nations, Mussolini and Adolf Hitler, the National Socialist dictator of Germany, established the Rome-Berlin Axis; in 1939, Italy took Albania, and the two dictators then concluded a military alliance known as the Pact of Steel.

When the Second World War broke out, Italy remained neutral at first. However, once it appeared through the Fall of France that Germany would win, in June 1940, 9 months after the outbreak of World War II in Europe, Italy entered the conflict on Germany's side. Mussolini eagerly joined Hitler, a fellow fascist and longtime ally, in the war effort and rushed to invade Greece, the Balkans, and North Africa. Overextended and unprepared for such a large-scale effort, Italy quickly found that it could not maintain its military position and had to ask Germany for help. Before long, Mussolini saw himself losing control of North Africa, the Mediterranean, and eventually his very own country to the Allies. From Fall 1943 to Spring 1945, Mussolini set up a puppet state (The Italian Social Republic) in Salò, Northern Italy, near the Lake of Garda. Abandoned by a disgusted Hitler, Il Duce and his mistress were captured and executed by Italian partisans. After the Second World War, Italy abolished the monarchy and declared itself a republic. With the strong support of the United States, Italy rebuilt its economy through loans from the Marshall Plan, joined the North Atlantic Treaty Organization, and became a strong supporter of what is now the European Union.

Under the 1947 peace treaty, minor adjustments were made in Italy's frontier with France, the eastern border area was transferred to Yugoslavia, and the area around the city of Trieste was designated a free territory. In 1954, the free territory, which had remained under the administration of U.S.-U.K. forces (Zone A, including the city of Trieste) and Yugoslav forces (Zone B), was divided between Italy and Yugoslavia, principally along the zonal boundary. This arrangement was made permanent by the Italian-Yugoslav Treaty of Osimo, ratified in 1977 (currently being discussed by Italy, Slovenia, and Croatia). Under the 1947 peace treaty, Italy also relinquished its overseas territories and certain Mediterranean islands.

Italy's cultural contributions: Europe's Renaissance period began in Italy during the 14th and 15th centuries. Literary achievements—such as the poetry of Petrarch, Tasso, and Ariosto and the prose of Boccaccio, Machiavelli, and Castiglione—exerted a tremendous and lasting influence on the subsequent development of Western civilization, as did the painting, sculpture, and architecture contributed by giants such as da Vinci, Raphael, Botticelli, Fra Angelico, and Michelangelo.

The musical influence of Italian composers Monteverdi, Palestrina, and Vivaldi proved epochal; in the 19th century, Italian romantic opera flourished under composers Gioacchino

Rossini, Giuseppe Verdi, and Giacomo Puccini. Contemporary Italian artists, writers, film-makers, architects, composers, and designers contribute significantly to Western culture.

Source: ISTAT

Fifth Army entering Rome on 5 June only to continue through the city in pursuit of the enemy retreating along the roads north of Rome. During this retreat the Germans were under constant bombing and strafing attacks by Allied air forces. Printed by courtesy of *America Oggi*.

ITALIANS

Who Are They?

When I begin to teach my course on modern Italy or give a lecture on the topic, I ask those present to tell me with what they associate Italy and the Italians. The spontaneous reactions do not change much from situation to situation; responses vary from excitement to bewilderment. "Italians! They have good taste." "Italy is a good place for a vacation; there is sun, spaghetti, and art." "Italians have fine hands; they have a real sense for beauty." Many associate the name of Italy and of the Italians with "Mafia," "pizza," "the Catholic Church," "close-knit families," "political chaos," "the Romans," "fine art," "strikes," and "gusto for life." Anyone with even little knowledge of Italy and the Italians will admit that these clichés refer to a social, political, and economic reality that only partially resembles today's Italy.

Somehow, the American view of Italy is still affected by the memories of Italian Americans whose forefathers had left crushing poverty for a land of opportunity. And although their sons and daughters are corporate heads, sit in Congress and on the Supreme Court, have risen to the top of many professions, and have been economically successful, their success has not completely erased the stereotype of their parents' place of origin as being a poor and underdeveloped country. This image has been reinforced by new situations: a country where the government often falls and is replaced by another with equally poor prospects, where strikes abound, and where people in the 1950s and 1960s were still pouring out of the underdeveloped south to seek work in northern European countries or across the ocean.

The American mass media and the movie industry in particular are keeping alive negative stereotypes and certain pejorative images of Italy. The American media is more interested in Italian passion and sensational events than in representing the country as a whole. In reporting or portraying the persistence of the Mafia and other forms of corruption within Italian political and social life, the American media perpetuate images of Italians that are in line with those portrayed by *The Godfather* and the *Sopranos.*

American attitudes toward Italians have been molded by popular stereotypes which are not uniform. The average American loves Italy's artistic treasures, despises its politics, and envies its gusto for life. Italians are generally perceived to be infatuated with nice appearance, *bella figura,* rather than the intrinsic qualities admired by the Anglo-Saxons. Thus, Italian cars such as Ferraris, Maseratis, Lamborghinis, and Alfa Romeos are admired for their looks, but the admiration doesn't translate into general Italian mechanical reliability. In the world of design, the word "Italian" does connote flair, elegance, and passion, and car makers from Europe, America, and Japan do turn to Italian designers such as Pininfarina to design their cars.

The image of Italy has been positive when it is framed in the artistic achievements of its people. Italy has been a champion of the arts throughout the centuries. Through the works of her artists one can witness the whole spectrum of man's creativity in the last 3,000 years. Because of the high achievements in the fifteenth and sixteenth centuries, Italy has been called the "cradle of the Renaissance." Franklin D. Roosevelt once said: "If we are children of Western civilization, then Italy is our mother."

The skills and genius of Italian artists and writers, builders and thinkers—and the judgment and generosity of their patrons—were crucial to the cultural development of Western civilization. Dante, Petrarch, and Boccaccio molded an Italian literary language from their native Tuscan dialect, but their words, translated into many languages, have become part of the common store of the Western literary heritage. The universal genius of Leonardo da Vinci and Michelangelo sets them beyond the limits of category and chronology. They along with Giotto, Donatello, Botticelli, and Raphael, to name just a few of the greatest artists of the Golden Period, shaped a new image of humanity in Western art. Italy has given to Western thought the ideas of the philosopher St. Thomas Aquinas and the political theorist Niccolò Machiavelli, the spiritual fervor of St. Francis of Assisi, the space revelations of Galileo Galilei, the scientific discoveries of Alessandro Volta and Enrico Fermi, and the musical delights of Palestrina, Scarlatti, Monteverdi, Paganini, Vivaldi, Pergolesi, Donizetti, Rossini, Puccini, and Verdi.

For centuries Italy was the Mecca of the cultured. Many foreign writers and poets have sung of Italy's beauty; from Goethe to Stendhal, from Byron to Ruskin to Henry James, Italy's natural beauty and her people's creativity inspired their works. However, the foreigner going to Italy today is baffled by many conflicting impressions, for Italy is the land of dualities and paradoxes. For example, although Italy houses about two thirds of the world's art—as indicated by a recent UNESCO survey—it is often difficult to appreciate it because a large number of small museums and churches are open for limited hours.

Geography as a Definer of Culture

"Sunny Italy" is not always all that sunny. Situated on the southern border of Europe and stretching from north to south in the Mediterranean Sea for about one thousand miles, the peninsula does not have a uniform climate. Despite its geographical position at the center of the temperate zone (Rome is practically on the same parallel as Boston), Italy has rather variable climatic characteristics but is warmer than expected. This is due to the presence of the Mediterranean, whose warm waters mitigate thermal extremes, and the Alpine arc, which forms a barrier against the cold north winds. Furthermore, Italy is subject to both wet and moderate atmospheric currents from the Atlantic Ocean and dry and cold ones from Eastern Europe. The Apennines chain, confronting the wet winds from the Tyrrhenian, also causes considerable climatic differences between the opposite sides of the peninsula and creates a unique variety of climates for an area that is approximately two-thirds that of California. The Alpine arc has a generally constant rainfall in all seasons, with increased quantities in spring and autumn and much fog in the plain from late fall to the middle of spring. The rest of the peninsula has an irregular rainfall, with the most falling in the winter months. In the southern regions there is a lack of summer rainfall, and in some areas (the Tavoliere in Apulia, southern Sicily, and the Campidano in Sardinia) the scarce annual rainfall often produces serious agricultural problems.

Because of its geographical position, with its surrounding islands almost reaching the coast of Africa, Italy has a particular geopolitical function in the Mediterranean as a European country. Italy has direct contact with the main ethnic and cultural areas of the Old World (neo-Latin, Germanic, and Slav-Balkan), as well as, through the North African countries, with the world of Arab-Islamic civilization.

Consequently, while remaining firmly anchored in the world of Western European civilization, which was the direct heir of the Greco-Roman culture that developed and flourished on this very peninsula for over a millennium, Italy seems to stretch out naturally toward the opposite shore of the Mediterranean, practically dividing its western and eastern basins. Thus Italy can be considered to be the most natural link between Europe and the peoples of Africa and Asia, bordering as they do on the same sea and sharing over many centuries both historical events and cultural influences.

It is true that all Italians, from the Alps to Sicily, love espresso coffee, want their pasta *al dente,* watch the same television programs, follow soccer with the same passion, hum the same pop songs, are equally skillful artisans, and have developed an uncommon proclivity for self-criticism. It is hard to tell northerners from southerners before they speak and reveal their accent or dialect. There are tall, blond Sicilians who look like Scandinavians (after all, the Normans ruled Sicily in the twelfth century), and there are short, chubby, black-haired and dark-eyed Florentines and Mantuans, whose genes may go back to the Etruscans. But there are deep cultural differences that make sociologists question the existence of "one Italy."

One cannot lose sight of the fact that Italy is a relatively young nation. As recently as Metternich's time, Italy was just considered "a geographic expression." Roman law was the widest and strongest historic strand that interlaced the fabric of Italian national identity. However, reminiscences of the Roman Empire and the cultural heritage from the Middle Ages and the Renaissance have always made educated Italians aware, however dimly, of common bonds and common destiny.

The Birth of the Nation on Fragile Foundations

Differences in the social and cultural character of the country persist. During the struggle for liberation from foreign rule and for national unity—the *Risorgimento*—secret societies and uprisings were organized throughout the peninsula but they did not share the same idea on how to politically mold the new nation. Moreover, the *Risorgimento* was in the main a movement of political and intellectual elites. The rest of the population, particularly the farmers, were apathetic and played almost no role in the *Risorgimento*. On the other hand, the social class leading the fight for freedom did not have a united political front either. Giuseppe Mazzini, the founder of the *Giovine Italia* (Young Italy, 1831), a key political organization, was an idealist and republican and had a romantic, almost mystical vision of national unity. For him, Italy's contribution to the family of nations would flow from the resumption of its old role as teacher. His views were opposed by Vincenzo Gioberti, who favored a federation of states under the presidency of the pope. In his book, *On the Moral and Civil Primacy of the Italians,* he attacked the notion of a unitary state and prophesied the difficulties Italy would have under a single statehood. The creation of regions as administrative entities in the 1970s is in a sense the partial realization of Gioberti's plan. Italy was unified according to Cavour's political plan—as the prime minister of the kingdom of Piedmont, he wanted a unified Italy under the house of Savoy. Cavour wanted to unite only northern Italy under a monarchy, and that is what he would have done if Giuseppe Garibaldi, a well-respected general who held democratic principles, had not started his own unification from Sicily and southern Italy and forced the king of Piedmont to come down from the North and "annex" the rest of the peninsula.

Contrary to the myths about the *Risorgimento,* this movement for Italy's resurgence was anything but a popular groundswell; it was Italy's failed revolution. Cavour united Italy under a government guided by aristocratic oligarchs who had a great fear of populism and no intention of sharing the national government with the masses.

In 1870, Italy was a nation of approximately 25 million people. Most Italians were poor peasants who could neither read nor write. They worked long hours in the fields and lived hard, often miserable lives. Few peasants owned their own land, and the labor contracts for sharecroppers and field workers favored the landowners. None of the 20 million of them could vote. Peasants and politicians lived in two different worlds within the same nation.

The new Italy was a centralized unitary state under a monarchy with a parliamentary government. The king had large-scale powers: he could dissolve parliament, appoint and dismiss the prime minister, appoint senators, and issue proclamations with the force of law. The tradition of local government was retained but only in appearance; the limited elected local government was presided over by prefects, administrators appointed by the king. Since everything depended upon Rome, the government was inefficient and soon was perceived as an entity far removed from the people. For most the only contacts with government were tax collection and military conscription. Because of the elitist nature of the new state, the condition of the south worsened after unification. Naples, the largest metropolis in Italy and one of the largest in Europe, lost all its political and economic power. Naples went from being the capital of the south and a very prosperous city—the Bourbons had developed a strong industrial system and prestigious university centers—to being impoverished and losing its luster. Italy had been unified but only as a political entity. Massimo D'Azeglio, a writer and a senator of that time, said "We made Italy; now we must make the Italians." The task proved difficult.

The new Italian liberal state, a constitutional monarchy, had a very narrow electoral basis.[1] Voting eligibility, based on tax payments, restricted participation to certain classes and regions (fewer in the south because of greater poverty). In many areas, especially in the south, deputies were elected to parliament with only a dozen votes. In the years that followed, the suffrage was extended, but even by the 1909 election only 8.3% of the adult population was entitled to vote. Seventy-five percent of the population was illiterate, and the country suffered from a high mortality rate. The new state was dominated by the Piedmontese and had a system of taxation that was repressive toward the south. When the south reacted through mass insurrections or the occasional assassination of prefects and tax collectors, it was repressed by the Piedmontese army.[2] It was clear that the south had been reluctantly accepted into the new state. The anti-brigand campaign army officers and the government understood their opponent predominantly by means of a series of hierarchical binary oppositions, such as between civilization and barbarism, reason and violence, social order and crime.[3] The conceptualization of brigandage as an "Other" was set in the broader frame of an imaginative geography in which the Italian nation is constructed as the opposite of the south;[4] such a conceptualization persists up to today in the debate of north vs. south.

Italy also suffered because it had not been able to solve the "Roman Question." The pope had resisted the new state militarily; after he had been pushed into retreat in the Vatican, he condemned the occupation of Rome as an aggression, declared himself prisoner of the Italian state, and threatened to excommunicate any Italian who would take part in the political life of the country. This position had a profound impact because for many Italians the Church represented the values of authentic Italy.

The separation between the Church and the state did give to the new state the possibility of establishing liberal policies, but it kept the nation divided. Only in 1929, with the Lateran Accords signed between Mussolini and the pope, was the "Roman Question" resolved. Mussolini, however, did not solve the south-north problem ("Southern Question"). Cultural, economic, and social differences between north and south remained. At the end of the nineteenth century and during the first two decades of the twentieth, nationalistic politicians and intellectuals played on Italian chauvinism rather than focus on the nation's north-south tensions. And Mussolini did not improve the situation.

Mussolini and the Struggle for a Unified Nation

Mussolini, the leader of the National Fascist Party, with around thirty deputies in the chamber, took power in October 1922 with the support of the bourgeois and landed interests. The conservative system based on the systematic exclusion of the popular masses from politics was perpetuated. Italy was run by an authoritarian regime of a new type. Although fascist propaganda insisted that the National Fascist Party sought to develop a system that would be neither capitalist nor communist, it did not give any voice to the working class, it kept wages down by destroying free trade unions, and it facilitated the rationalization of Italian capitalism.[5] Unlike Marxism, fascism sought to preserve the capitalist system, neutralizing the internal class struggle by appealing to nationalism as the basis for social harmony. Since the nation was the ultimate good, it was only through the nation that the individual could fulfill his or her potential. By creating the new doctrine "everything within the state, nothing outside the state, nothing against the state," fascism neutralized class struggle and shifted the struggle elsewhere. The concept of Italy as a "proletarian nation" oppressed by the richer, more developed, capitalist nations was skillfully crafted and then embraced by most Italians.

Did Mussolini's regime survive because of popular apathy or because of mass enthusiasm? Mussolini was a charismatic figure who could handle well the power of "words" and had been able to attract strong support from the majority of Italians for his nationalistic policies (strengthening the Italian national identity by instilling pride in the Italian cultural heritage) and for his many popular social initiatives. However, his nationalistic policies did not reduce the south-north division.

World War II: The Beginning of a New Era

World War II did not alleviate the split between north and south; indeed, it exacerbated the rift. For about a year and a half, the country was literally divided in two. The liberation of the country from the south by the Allies and the occupation of the rest of the peninsula (north and central Italy) by the Nazis had a tremendous impact on the evolution of the character of the nation in the democratic era that followed. In that year and half of bloodshed, north and south did not experience the struggle in the same way. The landing of the Allies in Sicily on July 10, 1943, quickly triggered strong reaction against Mussolini, who had entered the war without much support from either the politicians or the populace. In what amounted to a palace coup in Rome, the Fascist Grand Council, including Foreign Minister Galeazzo Ciano, Mussolini's son-in-law, forced the resignation of Mussolini on the night of July 24, 1943 and returned the power of the state to King Victor Emmanuel III. The king had Mussolini arrested and appointed Marshal Badoglio prime minister. Badoglio formed an interim government that dissolved the National Fascist Party, granted amnesty to political prisoners, and entered into negotiations with the Allies for an armistice, which was concluded on September 3, 1943, to coincide with the Allies landing on the peninsula at Salerno. Fearing an invasion by Germany, Badoglio quickly (September 8, 1943) moved his government to Brindisi, far to the south on the east coast, which was then under the control of the Allies. The Germans, who already had nine divisions in Italy, reacted harshly to the news. On October 13, 1943, the Italian royal government declared war on Germany, but the disintegrating Italian army had been left without a commander. Some Italian troops joined the Germans, some the Allies. Others merged with the partisans who had started the resistance in the North. Those who resisted the Nazis with no hope of Allied assistance were massacred. In Cefalonia, south of Corfu, the Italians fought for a week. When they finally surrendered, 4,500 soldiers and officers were shot and their bodies were left in the open.

In the meantime, rescued by German commandos, Mussolini had set up a rival government—the Italian Social Republic—in Salò on Lake Garda in November 1943. In the new government there were the most fanatical fascist elements, who were eager to imitate the Nazis. Ciano and others who were held responsible for Mussolini's ouster were executed. The National Racial Code, unpopular in a country where anti-semitism was virtually unknown when the code was enacted in 1938 to impress the Nazis, was now enforced with terrible exactness in the occupied area.[6] Notwithstanding strenuous efforts of many Italians, about 10,000 Italian Jews perished in Nazi concentration camps.

Because of the stiff German resistance to the Allied advance, hopes for a quick occupation of Rome were disappointed. A battlefront along the Gustav Line during the winter of 1943–1944 engaged the Allies in a bloody standoff. Rome was finally liberated in June 1944 after the breakthrough at Cassino in May. A second German defense line in the north, the Gothic Line, held until the last weeks of the war. When Mussolini was caught on April 28, 1945, he was shot and his body put on public display.

The Resistance Movement: The Struggle for Freedom

In that last year and half, an important role was played by the partisans who fought an irregular war against the Germans and Italian fascists in the north. The Resistance Movement, started in September 1943 as a spontaneous, locally based popular uprising, by the end of the war had a following of 450,000 individuals; 55,000 of them died while about 20,000 remained handicapped from their battle wounds. The *partigiani* excluded no one: rich and poor, professionals and laborers; children, old people, communists, socialists, Christian Democrats, everyone had a significant role.

An especially important role was played by women. Unlike the *Risorgimento,* heroines did not simply serve as "illustrious mothers" and martyr wives. This time they took to the field, too. The women *Gruppi* worked in collaboration, not in contention, with men. The Resistance showed that men and women could pursue the same aims, but it also offered women the opportunity to prove that they were the equal of men, just as enduring, strong, brave, resourceful, and implacable.

The activities of the Resistance varied. Besides engaging several German divisions in the fighting, it provided vital information to the Allies, helped Allied prisoners to escape, engaged in sabotage, disrupted transportation, and organized strikes that slowed down production of war materials. In the last months of fighting the civil war got very brutal. It was a passionate wave of collective hysteria and private vengeance, horrible in its impact but understandable in its context.

The Birth of the Republic

Contrary to what happened in France or Yugoslavia, the Italian Resistance was not led by charismatic figures but instead was organized by political parties: the Communist Party, the Socialist Party, and the Christian Democratic Party. Thus, when the war was over, the only political structures which survived were the political parties. In a popular referendum, held on June 2, 1946, the first universal suffrage, people not only voted to ban the Fascist Party, but also decided to punish the House of Savoy. The monarchy, discredited because it had given in too easily to Mussolini, was abolished and replaced by the republic. Indeed, the king was forced into exile in Portugal, and never allowed to return. His plea to see his homeland many years later, when he was about to die of cancer, was rejected without much public or political debate.

Because the south could not participate in the Resistance on which the Italian Republic was established, it once again found itself obliged after the war to celebrate and mythologize an event not part of its historic experience. The continued support for monarchism in the South and the subsequent powerful attachment to local myths and identities can perhaps be explained by the inability to identify with events and actions that could not be experienced first hand.

The result of the elections confirmed the south-north division. Almost all of the northern and central regions voted for the republic; Rome and the south, led by Naples, voted for the monarchy (79% for the king). The election of the members of the constitutional assembly revealed the same split: the South voted more for the Christian Democratic Party and the center-Right parties, while the North and central Italy voted more for the Socialist Party and the parties of the Left. During this short period, the Communist Party had gained much headway. The leader of the Communist Party, Palmiro Togliatti, played the key role in this transformation. His authority among communist cadres was immense. He was helped in this by the fact that, as the leader of the party, he could enjoy a share of the personality cult that had become established in the communist movement. Undoubtedly the prestige of the U.S.S.R. played a crucial role in this, but so did the fact that the Communist Party had been the leading force of the Resistance. The Communist Party, led by its secretary, participated fully in the drafting of Italy's new constitution. Consequently, next to the principles of liberalism, there were also recognized new "social rights"; freedom of private enterprise was guaranteed but only "as long as it did not conflict with social utility." Since the south did not experience the civil war because it had been quickly liberated by the Allies and had remained under the monarchy, the majority of the people kept their allegiance to the king. The strong emergence of the force of the Left that had been organized during the Resistance to fight Nazis and fascists created such strong fear in the South of a possible communist takeover that Sicily voiced a desire to secede from the peninsula. The political skills of the leader of the Christian Democratic Party, Alcide De Gasperi, and the American political and economic presence in the region, prevented both the secession of Sicily and the takeover of power by the Left. Since no single party was strong enough to capture political power, this had to be jointly managed by the same coalition of parties that had fought in the Resistance: Christian Democratic Party (*Democrazia Cristiana, DC*) 35.1%, Socialist Party (*Partito Socialista Italiano, PSI*) 20.7%, and Communist Party (*Partito Comunista Italiano, PCI*) 18.9%.

Although the Christian Democratic Party was the newest party of the young republic, it became the strongest. Its popularity was facilitated by the fact that it was the heir of the Popular Party, the largely peasant-based Catholic party which had been created in 1919 by Luigi Sturzo, a Sicilian priest, and which had already used the vast machine of Catholic social and political organizations. The *DC* was able to rely on the support of the Church and the mass lay organizations of the Church itself. The weakness of the old Liberal Party, the nearest equivalent to a clearly pro-capitalist party, made the *DC* the only possible choice of industrialists. Because of the kind of base support it had mustered and its ideology, the *DC* also became the only party that the United States came to rely on to lead Italy into the North Atlantic Alliance and the Western camp. It dominated the political landscape throughout the postwar period and ensured a remarkable continuity of governments, leading 49 out of 52 governments until 1993. Because it was always in government and because it tended to be a party that actively encouraged the expansion of the public sector, the *DC* had at its disposal a vast array of jobs that it could offer to those who were politically reliable. Thus, through professional and trade associations and a clientele system of patronage, the *DC* developed a formidable machine, especially in the south where industrial development lagged far behind that of the north. If the *DC* can take most of the merit for the miraculous economic recovery of Italy, it also has to take some of the painful responsibility for the ever-widening economic separation between north and south.

The Recovery from the Ashes

When the country recovered from World War II with surprising speed, foreigners voiced admiration for the Italian miracle. The devastating Allied air raids on industrial centers, railroad hubs, seaports, and eventually on Rome itself, were accompanied by the naval bombardment of Genoa, the loss of a major part of the Italian merchant fleet, and the disaster of the warships sunk in the harbor of Taranto. Furthermore, battles from Sicily to the Po River, with many civilian casualties and innumerable bridges blown up and buildings destroyed, atrocious Nazi reprisals for acts of sabotage and resistance, and hundreds of thousands of soldiers in prison camps, if not dead, left Italy stripped of much of its manpower and infrastructure. All this plus the restrictions imposed by the peace treaty (Paris, February 1, 1947) forced the new Italian Republic to face many problems of material and moral reconstruction.

Italy was devastated by the 1943 defeat, the agony of the ensuing civil war, and the damage to her physical resources. Paradoxically, however, these setbacks proved less destructive in their effects than the "mutilated" victory of 1918. Indeed, in Italy at the end of 1945 there was an extraordinary sense of real hope. After the many years under fascism, a euphoria of freedom gripped the nation. The great event of 1945 was not so much the disappearance of dictatorship, fascism, and the monarchy, but rather the affirmation of those principles that animated the Resistance movement: the sudden awakening of the Italians from the long nightmare of war, and the rebirth of the nation and its immediate concern with the struggle for survival, the restoration of individual dignity. Many Italians saw the Resistance as a new *Risorgimento* because of its struggle against the oppressor and its principles of liberty, justice, and solidarity. It was the Resistance that restored faith in man and his ability to change his own destiny, and it gave rise to the conviction that cultural values could be saved through concrete social and political actions.

The Arts Reflect the New Euphoria: Neorealism

At the end of the war, with the installation of the new democratic government and the elimination of the strictest form of censorship, artists and writers also emerged with a reborn sense of civic commitment. Once the strict censorship of the fascist regime had fallen, they could turn their eyes freely to the observation of reality. The poverty, social disorder, and suffering that fascism had forbidden to be represented, and the humanity ravaged by the war, became their subject matter. The theater, the novel, and the movies became the chief means by which contemporary society was placed under investigation. In the depiction of sociopolitical situations, it was the search for truth that guided the directors and screenwriters in their first neorealist works. Filmmakers wanted spectators to be witnesses to the ills of society in order to raise social and political consciousness. Thus, in their masterpieces, De Sica, Visconti, Zavattini, and Rossellini dealt with the themes of real life, expressing them with deep emotional involvement and consuming lyricism with a clear aim: a naturalistic slice of life and a sociopolitical perspective in which antifascism and class consciousness had to bring action. The intensity and fervor of this discovery rendered the artist inseparable from the man.

The neorealist artist generally took an instinctively populist or Leftist viewpoint, espousing a more or less explicit faith both in the irresistible power of collective action and in Marxist dialectical conflict and the inevitability of historical progress—all supported by a somewhat mystical notion of Christian brotherhood. However, it did not necessarily share the doctrinaire optimism of socialist realism, with its voluntaristic faith in an ultimate, inescapable positive solution to social problems.

The Complex Process of Reconstruction

The process of reconstruction was complicated by the very presence of the Allies. The British favored the strengthening of the monarchy (an authoritarian democratic constitution) and penal peace settlement terms. The Americans, instead, showed a greater degree of understanding. Some Americans were surprised and appalled at the poverty and deprivation they had witnessed in the south, and were willing to give limited tacit support to relatively radical reform programs involving government aid and land distribution. The prospect of a communist takeover in such a strategically significant area for the West was also worrisome.

A policy of reconstruction and economic development was pursued by the various governments in power after 1948, the year in which the *DC* acquired a large parliamentary majority. Initially this took the form of severe anti-inflation measures and then a lifting of restrictions combined with public intervention through a relaunching of IRI, the Institute for the Industrial Reconstruction.

The establishment of the *Cassa per il Mezzogiorno* (Funds for the Development of the South) set in motion a complex series of extraordinary interventions to provide the southern regions with the necessary basic structures (roads, drainage, services, etc.) to assist in economic and, above all, agricultural development. Agrarian reform was particularly necessary in combating the centuries-old feudal structure of the estates of the south. However, because of poor planning, a new and even greater migration occurred, this time not overseas but toward the countries of northwestern Europe (Germany, France, Belgium, England, and Switzerland), where the postwar industrial boom required large quantities of manpower. The movement of population was even greater toward the north of Italy (Piedmont, Lombardy, and Liguria) because of the efforts of private initiative in creating an industrialized climate whose rapid and often disorderly growth came to be known as the "economic miracle."

A Miraculous Economic Recovery

At the beginning of the 1960s, the highest percentage of the work force was employed in the industrial sector, while agriculture continued to diminish and the service industries began their expansion. In the international sphere, with its entry into the United Nations and participation in military alliances and economic agreements with the other western countries (European and North American), Italy began to regain the dignity and prestige that was due its geographical position and the richness of its historical cultural traditions. The Italians once again, like the phoenix, had risen from the ashes. Their innate abilities proved to be their best resource. Their multiform tactile skills and their versatility and mastery in shaping, carving, crafting, refining, drawing, styling, painting, and lettering are part of a long tradition. Today's designers of elegant car bodies and casual wear are heirs to a long tradition that begins with the pottery and tomb frescoes of the Etruscans and embraces the anatomical and engineering drawings of Leonardo da Vinci and a host of celebrated and anonymous artists and artisans going back three thousand years.

Gradually the Italian economy changed beyond recognition and, by and large, caught up with the rest of Europe. In terms of purchasing power and standard of living, the Italian working class closed the gap with Germany, France, and the United Kingdom. The "necessities" of the consumer society, such as remote control color television, multiprogram dishwashers, freezers, cellular telephones, etc., are as available in Italy as they are in the advanced Western countries. Its agricultural population has decreased constantly and so has the birthrate—two other characteristics of major economic powers.

The open market and free enterprise system have played major roles in the diffusion of consumer goods in Italian society. As in the rest of Europe, the state has had to intervene to keep costs of production lower than they would otherwise have been by taking into public ownership some basic production inputs, such as energy, and some basic segments of the infrastructure of the nation, such as transportation, and subsidizing them out of public funds. Furthermore, the state has also had to ensure that minimum standards of health, housing, education, and old age care are maintained. In other words, Italy too became a welfare state. This was achieved and maintained on the assumption that there would be a constant economic growth, which was the case for most of the 1950s and a good part of the 1960s. Problems, however, began to surface in the late 1960s and developed further in the 1970s when the economy slowed down and the manufacturing sector decreased. As a consequence of this condition, the public sector was increasingly less able to sustain a high level of employment and large areas of the private sector succumbed and had to be rescued by the state, which caused high inflation. Italy went through the same phases experienced by the developed West: development of the welfare state, state intervention, and crisis of the welfare state.

A Truly Anthropological Revolution

The major socioeconomic changes began with Italy's opening to the Left, in early 1960, which brought the Socialist Party, previously in electoral alliance with the communists, into a governing coalition with the Christian Democrats, the republicans, and the social democrats. The inclusion of the socialists in government was the first concrete step in a far-reaching realignment of Italy's political forces that was aimed at isolating the largest communist party in the West and forming a stable governmental majority resting on a wide foundation of popular support. The center-Left governments of the 1960s may be criticized for excesses in labor legislation and wasteful public expenditures, but they were the only alternative; a center-Right coalition with the extremely conservative liberals who depended on parliamentary support from the neo-fascists *(Movimento Sociale Italiano, MS1),* might then have polarized Italian society.

Along with the political and economic changes, the rest of Italian life has changed radically, and most of the changes have been for the better. Compared to 1945, the average Italian is better fed, better housed, better educated, more literate, and politically more aware. The enormous gap that existed between Italians and Americans has been practically eliminated. Italians proudly say that "America is here now." That is true on many levels, as we shall see.

After some initial reticence, Italians threw themselves into the consumer society as eagerly as any people in Europe. Some feared that Italy was losing her soul, selling out to an ill-digested Americanization, but most people welcomed this new world of affluence and technology. They were driven by the urge to make money and enjoy the fruits of their labor; like the other losers of the war in Europe, the Germans, they rebuilt and modernized their country through a mixture of technical flair, material ambition, and sheer sustained hard work at all levels, from top manager to industrial worker and farmer.

This postwar modernization has been a powerful, heroic process because it was a leap forward from a backward country to a post-industrial nation. Under the momentum of economic advance, society shifted its equilibrium. There was a massive movement of people from agriculture to industry and service, from the country to the towns. With rapid urbanization, many cities tripled in size, and many provincial towns became vibrant with new activity.

In private and family life, and in purely social relations, Italy has certainly evolved a great deal in the last 40 years. Women have achieved a striking new emancipation. Sexual permissiveness has developed remarkably in the past two decades. Within the family, paternal authority now weighs less heavily and parent/child relations are more frank and equal. In daily life, the pompous use of titles is waning, and home entertaining has become much more relaxed and casual.

Fewer people go to church on a regular basis; more use contraceptives, and more live together without being married. Divorces and abortions are legal while the purchase of pornographic material and the access to risqué movies on television have no equal in the world. The strong presence of the Church and the tradition of puritanical values have not prevented the development of a lifestyle which is, by and large, an adaptation of the many negative aspects of the "American way of life."

A Complex Political System with a Strong Democracy

Italians have a love-hate relationship with the state: they resent it, yet cling to it and expect it to provide endless benefits. In this, as in many other ways, Italy appears to be a country of paradoxes, especially on the political level. The game of musical chairs that cabinet ministers play, the governmental crises, past acts of terrorism in airports and train stations, high inflation, and mega-scandals, which are top news in daily newspapers, have led scholars to depict the country as a democracy headed if not to oblivion then certainly toward some mortal crises. The fact that the Italian government has been very fragile and had fallen until 2001, on the average, once a year, and that in parliament as many as 16 political parties were represented led many political experts, especially Anglo-Saxons, to suggest that the Italian political system was an anomalous democracy that did not deserve to be preserved. On the other hand, Italy has also had one of the most stable democracies in the West; it was the only country in Europe to be ruled by the same party (Christian Democratic Party) for almost 50 years and did not see change in the political elites during that same period. Governing with a multi-party system Italian-style was possible only because of the high skills Italian politicians were able to develop in the post-fascist period. Italians were able to make the business of government an art that constantly requires intuition, creativity, tolerance, endurance, and flexibility. The leading party in power, the *DC*, dealt with the continuous crisis of the country by constantly changing strategies. Not only the nature of its alliance with the political forces had to change, but the nature of each of the political forces with which it had to deal changed. While the *DC* changed by leaning more toward the Left, the Left changed by leaning toward the center. The *PSI* (Socialist Party) changed from being a junior supporter of the *PCI* (Communist Party) in the 1940s and 1950s to becoming a junior partner of the *DC* from the 1960s onward. Rejecting its traditions of a workers' party and becoming more and more a radical party of the center, the *PSI* increasingly espoused the cause of "modernization." By being in power with the *DC*, it obtained a greater share of political and economic resources, and it abused its power. In so doing, it became another party of patronage and clienteles. The *PCI* increasingly abandoned the doctrine of Marxism-Leninism, opened its ranks to people of varying persuasions, including Catholics, accepted with increasing enthusiasm membership in the European Economic Community (EEC) and the North Atlantic Treaty Organization (NATO), disassociated itself from Soviet foreign policy, and supported a *DC* government for nearly three years (1976–1979). By responding to external political conditions and internal pressure and interest groups, political parties changed. Everyone has changed, but everyone has had to pay a price.

In the present era of transnational corporations, of mass international communication systems that penetrate deep into the national culture, and a powerful military system backed by superpower technology, the traditional nation-state is reduced to cosmic insignificance. The shocks of the fall of communism and the collapse of the Soviet Union certainly affected Italian politics profoundly. The disappearance of a political force seen as a threat to democratic stability allowed political parties to disentangle themselves from old alliances. As a result, in 1993, institutional reforms were enacted and a new form of democracy was instituted. The changes were bold and positive, but their success will require more than official reforms. There will also need to be a change in Italian attitudes and a new kind of civic spirit.

The "Southern Question" Is Still Waiting for a Solution

Especially for the south, the reform of institutions will not bring about automatic changes because the performance of institutions depends on their social, economic, and cultural surroundings. We know that if we transplant democratic institutions, they do not grow in the new setting as they did in the old because the quality of a democracy depends on the quality of its citizens. The difference between south and north has to be attributed to the difference in civic attitudes in the two areas and, therefore, the way government is regarded; however, the duality of north and south has become greater because there is a lack of serious initiatives to create jobs on the part of Italy's governing national elite. The Southern Question is an economic question as well as a political one. It is not a matter of simple modernization, or of an increase in state funds. The role of the south cannot even be understood purely in terms of the Italian north; it must be thought of anew in terms of the relations between Italy and the rest of the European Union (EU) and the Mediterranean. Its problems cannot be tackled independently from the north or the rest of Europe because Italian economic development is intrinsically connected to the south. The old solutions have done much damage to the south. For the systematic drainage of the south's sole resource, human labor, the south has been compensated by a constant stream of state funds, which have underpinned the stability of the *DC* regime. This money has not been directed toward "modernization" but has been channeled in a thousand directions under the supervision of all sorts of interest groups including the Mafia. Italy's future depends on its ability to make the south part of the national economic equation.

Despite the southern question and other difficulties such as high unemployment and some unresolved social injustices, I find Italy today a relatively happy and well-adjusted society, perhaps a little cynical and certainly disillusioned with politics and ideologies but no longer daydreaming. At the beginning of the 2000s, Italians finally became aware that material progress had in itself by no means cured all the basic ills of their society. It is a society still segmented, still beset with barriers and inequalities, still attached to a number of outdated structures. There is still much to be done that no government can do by itself, for social change is a matter of habit and psychology more than of politics. As we shall see, the Italians may have changed their lifestyles, but their basic character, built around individualism, social mistrust, and desire for formalism—the desire to present a *bella figura*—remains.

Notes

1. Only 2% of the adult population had the right to vote and, of these, less than 60% actually went to the polls. Only males over twenty-five years of age who were literate and who paid a property tax of forty liras per year could vote. For the election of 1861, the electorate amounted to 1.9% of the entire population, and only about 57% of the electors voted, 240,000 of a population of approximately 25 million. Even the relatively radical reform of 1882, which lowered the age and tax requirements, produced an electorate of under 7% of the population.

2. The main factors behind peasant unrest were economic hardship, the introduction of conscription, and the accumulated discontent caused by the erosion of collective land-use rights. The Piedmontese government associated the social unrest with brigandage and severely repressed it. This aspect of the unification process was one of the darkest sides of that historical period. Without having a definite beginning or end, the war to annex the south continued for a decade, cost more lives than all the battles of unification put together and at its peak necessitated the deployment of about two-fifths of the effective strength of the Italian army at a time when Austria was thought to be a constant danger.

3. Banditry had the entire repertoire of racist imagery deployed against it by the officers of the Italian army: bandits are black, animal, feminine, primitive, deceitful, evil, perverse, irrational. In explaining brigandage with these terms, it was placed beyond explanation in an imaginatively and emotively charged realm of monstrosity. But what is most striking is the use of images of colonialism by the northern establishment: "What barbarism! This isn't Italy! This is Africa: compared to these peasants

the Bedouins are the flower of civilized virtues," writes a government envoy to Cavour from Teano in 1860. In Camillo Cavour, Carteggi: La liberazione *del Mezzogiorno* e la formazione del Regno d'Italia, vol. 3 (October-November 1860) (Bologna: Zanichelli, 1952); letter dated 27 October 1860, 83.

4.   John Dickie, "A World at War; The Italian Army and Brigandage," *History Work-shop Journal,* 33 (1992), 1–24.

5.   Fascism did organize people in associations and enroll people in large proportions in fascist-controlled organizations, but people did not acquire an independent sense of civic responsibility. In this regard, one of the political effects of fascism was to weaken still further the already tenuous links between the individual and organized civic social activities.

6.   See Thomas P. Di Napoli, ed., *The Italian Jewish Experience* (Stony Brook, N.Y.: Forum Italicum Publishing, 2000).

PART 1

POLITICS AND GOVERNMENT

Arch of Constantine in Rome erected in 315 AD. From the private collection of the author.

CHAPTER 1

POLITICAL AND SOCIAL FOUNDATIONS

The Molding of Political Identities and *Immobilismo*

Up to the political earthquake of 1993, Italy constantly attracted negative attention for the way it conducted domestic political affairs; its government was always perceived as faulty and unstable. Until the end of 1980s Italy had many governments and a large Communist Party. The government was massive and omnipresent and the Italian political parties had "colonized" Italian society. Governments did fall constantly; parliaments were dissolved frequently, and worse, every facet of Italian life was politicized. The mere act of joining a trade union or even a sporting club was inevitably a political decision in Italy. Today Italian life is still very politicized. Prospective labor union members still today must choose whether to join the Left trade union, the Italian General Confederation of Labor (*CGIL*), the Catholic union, the Italian Confederation of Workers' Unions (*CISL*), or the politically more moderate union, the Italian Union of Labor (UIL). The whole range of cultural and social organizations, associations, and clubs is not immune to political penetration. Politics has also led to politicization of economic life, particularly in the public sector: state enterprises, banks, credit institutions, television

PROFILE

Giuseppe Garibaldi, The Hero of the Two Worlds

(July 4, 1807–June 2, 1882) was a patriot and soldier of the *Risorgimento*. He personally led many of the military campaigns that brought about the formation of a unified Italy. He was called the "Hero of the Two Worlds," in tribute to his military expeditions in South America and Europe.

In Geneva in November 1833, Garibaldi met Giuseppe Mazzini, an impassioned proponent of the unification of Italy as a liberal republic through political and social reforms. Garibaldi joined the Young Italy movement and the *Carbonari* revolutionary association. In February 1834 he participated in a failed Mazzinian insurrection in Piedmont, was sentenced to death in absentia by a Genoese court, and fled to Marseilles.

From this exile he sailed first to Tunisia eventually finding his way to Brazil, where he encountered Anna Maria Ribeiro da Silva, "Anita," a woman of Portuguese and Indian descent, who became his lover, companion in arms, and wife. With other Italian exiles and republicans he fought on behalf of the separatists of the Rio Grande do Sul and the Uruguayans who opposed the Argentinean dictator Juan Manuel de Rosas.

Calling on the Italians of Montevideo, Garibaldi formed the Italian Legion in 1843. It was in Uruguay that the legion first sported the red shirts, which were to become the emblem of his followers. The formation of his force of volunteers, his mastery of the techniques of guerilla warfare, his opposition to Brazilian and Argentinean imperialism, and his victories in the battles of Cerro and Sant'Antonio in 1846 not only assured the freedom of Uruguay but made him and his followers heroes in Italy and Europe.

Garibaldi returned to Italy amongst the turmoil of the revolutions of 1848. When the Roman Republic was proclaimed in the Papal States, at Mazzini's urging, he took up the command of the defense of Rome. His wife, Anita, fought with him. However, despite their effort, the city fell on June 30, 1849, and Garibaldi was forced to flee to the north, hunted by Austrian, French, Spanish, and Neapolitan troops. Anita died near Ravenna during the retreat. Garibaldi eventually managed to escape abroad. In 1850 he became a resident of New York, where he met Antonio Meucci. For some time he worked as a candle maker on Staten Island.

He returned again to Italy in 1854. In 1859, the Austro-Piedmontese War (also known as the Austro-Sardinian War) broke out in the midst of internal plots at the Sardinian government and Garibaldi was appointed major general, and formed a volunteer unit named the Hunters of the Alps. One outcome of the war, though, left Garibaldi very displeased. His home city of Nice was surrendered to the French, in return for their crucial military assistance.

At the outbreak of the American Civil War (in 1861), Garibaldi volunteered his services to President Abraham Lincoln and was invited to serve as a major general in the Union Army..

After the last military actions he continued doing politics. Then he retired into private life in the island of Caprera where he died on June 2nd, 1882 and where he is buried.

networks, and newspapers are all politically influenced. The great majority of Italians complain about a government that does not work, about political leaders who are crooks, and the related problem of *immobilismo.* Contrary to the perception of the foreign press, they usually do not complain about the constant fall of government; in fact, the complaint is that, notwithstanding the numerous governments and parliamentary elections, the political system remains *immobile,* doesn't change in a profound way. That was true until 1993, when some big political changes were instituted.

In a country where politics is as important as breathing, identities are most commonly defined by political thinking and political practices. Political practices may define people as much as gender, language, religion, and social class. Political behavior is not just an activity delegated to parties and party leaders, but it is also practiced strongly by individual Italians, regardless of other factors that define their life.

Political identity is not simply defined by an individual's sympathies or hostilities toward a given set of parties and political movements but also by social and economic stratifications, as well as professional categories.[1] The rebirth of democratic Italy after the fall of fascism offered the occasion for a reassertion of the political subcultures that had remained dormant under Mussolini's dictatorship (*See Profile on Mussolini, p. 35*).

Political rally in the 1970s. From the personal archive of the author.

The legacy of the war and the Resistance had a markedly different geographical impact on Italy, and, as we saw, this was most clearly demonstrated in the strong support for retention of the monarchy during the referendum of June 1946 in the south and the islands and the overwhelming support for a republic in the center-north. Thus, since its inception, the Italian Republic has been heavily segregated along geopolitical lines, and citizens have displayed a strong loyalty to political parties.

The Cold War as Catalyst of the Electorate

Strong identification with a political party or ideology is typical of those countries where the civic culture is weak; mature democracies are composed of citizens who do not have a priori and fixed political beliefs, and are expected to make the best available choice. However, in Italy, after the war, the specter of fascism and the strident attitude of the Left created a strong identification between citizens and political parties that did not permit people to shift allegiances. The polarized pluralism that resulted from the externally imposed polarities of the Cold War molded a society in which families and individuals were known to have a well-defined political identity, even though the casting of a vote was secret. Political polarization and political pluralism were also the result of the way Italians chose to be governed.

The Italian form of government may have been similar to that of most parliamentary democracies in structure and constitutional principles, but it functioned in a fundamentally different way. The anomalies that characterized it, although subtle, complex, and deeply woven into the fabric of Italian life, are not impenetrable mysteries. If one examines the Italian constitution in its historical context by acknowledging both the important role that it gave to Parliament and the level of democratic pluralism it had desired, then the postwar Italian political history appears less Byzantine, and Italian politicians can be valued for their skills in reaching compromises and for the preservation of a very democratic form of government. One will also be able to understand how the real protagonists, the political parties, developed, monopolized power, contributed to corruption, and affected the general life of the country. One must remember that the postwar period begins with the political parties clearly in charge. They constituted the commanding forces of the Italian Resistance: the Committee of National Liberation (*CLN*) was made up of a coalition of six parties—the partisans were organized on the basis of party affiliation.

The Constitution and Popular Sovereignty

When on June 4, 1944, the Allies entered Rome, Italy was already eager to change its form of government: the Committee of National Liberation demanded a civilian government with clear plans for immediate changes. A six-party coalition government representing the political forces of the Resistance was formed. The temporary government, initially under Ivano Bonomi, had to cope with the disastrous economic legacy of the war and the rehabilitation of the national morale. After moving quickly to suppress the Fascist Party and its dependent organizations and by carrying out an extensive shuffling of prefects (state government representatives in the provinces), Bonomi formalized the Salerno Agreement on July 25, 1944, and established:

- » election by direct universal suffrage of a constitutional assembly,
- » the obligation of the members of the government not to impede institutional reform which was postponed until the liberation of the country,
- » that future ministers must swear loyalty to the nation, rather than to the king,
- » that legislative powers be attributed to the government, by way of decrees approved by the new king, who had been given the title of *Luogotenente generale del regno*.

A provisional decree of March 16, 1946, also established that the "institutional question," the decision to choose between monarchy and republic, had to be resolved directly by the people by referendum.

PROFILE

Benito Mussolini, Il Duce (The Leader)

(Born July 29, 1883—died April 28, 1945) An unruly but intelligent youth, Benito Mussolini became an ardent socialist and served as editor of the party newspaper, *Avanti!* (1912–14). When he reversed his opposition to World War I, he was ousted by the party. This expulsion changed Mussolini's politics radically. He founded *Il Popolo d'Italia* (The People of Italy), a strident news-paper that urged Italy's entry into the war against Austria-Hungary. When Italy did join the war, Mussolini enlisted in the army and served from 1915 to 1917, when he was wounded.

In 1919 Mussolini formed the Fascist Party, called the *Fasci di Combattimento*. The name *fascism* is derived from the Latin *fascis*, meaning *bundle*, a symbol of authority in ancient Rome and representing absolute, unbreakable power. A dynamic and captivating orator at rallies, Mussolini promised to recreate the glories of the Roman Empire in a movement that was nationalistic, anti-liberal, and antisocialist. His movement struck a chord with lower-middle-class people. Supporters wore black shirts and formed private militias.

In 1922 King Victor Emmanuel capitulated to the threat of coup and asked Mussolini to form a government; he was appointed prime minister, the youngest in Italian history. Once in power Mussolini gradually abolished all other political parties and set out to transform Italy into a fascist state. He restored order to the country and introduced social reforms and public works improvements that won widespread popular support. In the process he curtailed individual free-dom, introduced censorship, and limited freedom of speech.

Initially Italians and foreign observers saw Mussolini as a strong leader who brought needed discipline to the economy and social structure of Italy, and he was widely praised for "making the trains run on time."

In the 1930s Mussolini sought to make Italy an international power. In 1935 Italy invaded the East African country of Ethiopia. Mussolini ignored the League of Nations' demand that he withdraw and proceeded to conquer the country. In 1936 he sent Italian troops to support General Francisco Franco's Loyalist Army in the Spanish Civil War. These actions angered France and England who convinced the League of Nations to issue economic sanctions against Italy which led to Mussolini's dependence on Nazi Germany and the disastrous consequences of WWII.

Constitutional Referendum: The Birth of the Republic

In the institutional referendum held on June 2, 1946, the electorate voted in favor of the republic (12,718,641 or 54.26% for the republic, 10,718,502 or 45.7% for the monarchy). Almost all of the northern and central regions voted for the republic; Rome and the South (led by Naples, 79%) voted for the monarchy. After the results of the referendum were proclaimed, King Umberto, who had inherited the throne on the abdication of his father, Victor Emanuel III, left for permanent exile with the royal family. The elections for the constitutional assem-bly, held the same day, saw the clear dominance of the three popular parties (the Christian Democratic Party with 35% of the votes, the Socialist Party with 20% and the Communist

Party with 19%). With this vote two objectives were achieved. First, the Italians had the final word on the institutional question that had divided the country. Second, the way was opened for the introduction of a constitution that was to signal a new political order with the collapse of the fascist regime and the return to democracy. The new constitution was approved by secret

ballot on December 22, 1947, by a vote of 453 to 62, promulgated by the provisional head of state on December 27, 1947, and put into effect on January1, 1948.

By the standards of Italian parliamentary proceedings, or indeed by any standards, the drafting and approval of the constitution was a speedy affair. Yet the work of the constitutional assembly took place in an even more rapidly changing political climate. When the assembly first met, in June 1946, the Cold War had not yet begun and the Italian Communist Party (*PCI*) was still in the government. By the time the constitution was approved, the Left

Marchers in Rome carrying flags of Italy's largest union, March 23, 2002. Photo courtesy of *Indymedia Italy*

had been expelled from the government and Europe was divided into two spheres of influence. Inevitably, the political situation had an influence on the proceedings.

Christian Democrats, communists, socialists, liberals, etc., worked side by side to prepare a governing chart that had to serve the people of the whole nation and that could withstand the weight of time. Since fascism had violated the fundamental rights of individual and collective liberty and had authoritatively centralized all power, the new constitution addressed these issues and emphasized the basic rights of private citizens. Heated debates were inescapable, as were the inevitable compromises. Some of the most passionate discussions centered on the make-up of parliament: the Left preferred one house rather than two. The final approval of the bicameral structure was possible only by giving both houses equal power to legislate as well as to dissolve the government. Another issue that was fiercely debated was the role of the council of misters (the cabinet) and of the president of the council of ministers (the prime minister), especially whether the cabinet had to work as a collective body or be divided along internal hierarchical lines with a strong prime minister. Many issues (such as the establishment of regional administration, constitutional court, the referendum, and the freedom to strike) were not resolved and were left to subsequent decisions.

A Constitution More Progressive Than the American Constitution

Although the framers of the constitution had used the U.S. constitution as a model, they created something unique. In its first part, the Italian constitution reflects the euphoria of newly acquired freedom and the determination never to lose it again. Consequently, it is rich in rhetoric, exceedingly detailed, extremely thorough, and very progressive.

The democratic character of the constitution is evident from Article 1, which states that "Italy is a Republic" and is reinforced by Article 139, which decrees that the republican form cannot be the object of constitutional change. The referendum imposed on the state the character of a republic based on parliamentary democracy. Consequently, political and civil liberties were reaffirmed; the principles of parliamentary government, abandoned under fascism, were confirmed, as was the division of power established by the Virginia Declaration of Rights in 1776. The Republican Constitution, therefore, founded a political and social order based on a pluralistic democracy.

Of essential importance are the affirmation of the political, economic, and social rights and duties of the citizen, the recognition of the role of political parties and trade unions, institutional pluralism, political and administrative decentralization, and protection of minorities. Not only these essential principles of political democracy, but also those of economic and social democracy were considered. The constitution also provides the mechanism by which plural democracy is achieved through political, economic, and social solidarity (Art. 2) and the fundamental equality of citizens (Art. 3).

To Work Is a Constitutional Right

The first article of the constitution gives clear evidence of the strong presence of certain political forces in the constitutional assembly. It states that "Italy is a democratic Republic founded on *lavoro.*" The use of the word *lavoro* (work/labor) sparked much debate. The recognition of human labor as a fundamental value and right is further reinforced later (Art. 4): "The Republic recognizes the right of all citizens to work and shall promote such conditions as will make this right effective." Unfortunately, however, this strong constitutional right has not prevented Italy's excessively high percentage of unemployment! The right to work carries with it considerable implications: representation and trade union protection of professional

Symbol of the center-left coalition of 2006 national elections.

interests, just compensation, equality of treatment, collaboration in management, and social security. In fact, it obliges public powers to stimulate employment and safeguard it at all levels (Art. 35); and it guarantees the fundamental rights of workers concerning equal pay for equal effort, hours of work, weekly and annual paid holidays, equality between the sexes at work, minimum working age, and pension and workers' participation in management (Arts. 36, 37,

38, and 46). The constitution also provides social assistance (Art. 38) for those citizens unfit for work and without private means.

Private and Collective Economic Guarantees

The constitution also recognizes that citizens have certain economic rights: to own property, to take economic initiatives within legal limits, to set aside savings and have them protected. Also relevant is the way the constitution deals with the regulation of private property and wealth: its acquisition, possession, enjoyment, and circulation. Private ownership has legally recognized and guaranteed limits so as to ensure general accessibility and accountability (Art. 42). For example, private lands containing energy resources, or firms producing fuel or providing essential services, may be transferred into public ownership on the grounds of national interest with the payment of an indemnity (Arts. 42 and 43). The law can, in fact, impose limits on ownership and economic initiatives in the name of solidarity and the general social good!

It can, therefore, be said that the economic aspect of the constitution of Italy is based on the following key elements: a mixed economy for ownership and initiatives, central planning entrusted to public authorities, private enterprise encouraged by a series of guarantees, and extensive protection for workers. All of these aspects are aimed at the creation of equally distributed public wealth.

Religious and Ethnic Minorities

Another clear and definitive break with fascism was the recognition and protection of ethnic and religious minorities. Provision was made both for safeguarding linguistic minorities and for the protection of religious worship. Minority rights were then reinforced by way of regional autonomy and investing the first five regions with special status, in particular, the regions of Trentino Alto Adige with its large German-speaking minority and Valle d'Aosta with its French-speaking minority.

Government Structure

Popular Sovereignty

The government of the republic is formed by a system of equal constitutional elements: the president of the republic, the government (cabinet of ministers), the parliament, the judiciary, and the constitutional court. The conformity of the law to the constitution may be subject to verification by the constitutional court, which had not been provided for by the monarchy. The base of sovereignty and, therefore, of constitutional power, rests with the people. Consequently, the Italian people are the holders of sovereign power, which they exercise both directly through voting in elections and referenda and indirectly through institutional representation. Because of this essential principle of political democracy, the right to vote assumes a decisive constitutional significance. By means of a universal, direct, secret vote the electoral body selects political representatives who intervene directly whenever a referendum is proposed; the latter can be used for the abrogation of a law, for constitutional modification, or even for specified regional and local issues that have seen a notable expansion not always provided by the constitution. The constitution thus makes two essential provisions for the execution of popular sovereignty: first, the exercise of democratic representation in Parliament, regional assemblies, and local councils; second, participation through referenda (or direct democracy). Democratic voting and elections are the key elements of political representation and the foundation of legitimate power.

The Legislative Branch: Parliament

Parliament has many important functions and immense political power, primarily in its authority to legislate. Each member of Parliament can promote a legislative proposal. Parliament controls government (the cabinet of ministers), that is, the executive branch, by its power to approve legislation and through the use of the vote of "confidence."

The 1948 constitution established a bicameral parliament (chamber of deputies and senate), a separate judiciary, and an executive branch composed of a council of ministers (cabinet), headed by the president of the council (prime minister).

From 1948 to 1992, members of the chamber of deputies were elected by proportional representation in multi-member electoral districts, except in Valle d'Aosta, represented in the chamber by one member elected by simple majority. Senate elections were held under a system in which three-quarters of the seats were filled in single-member constituencies, provided the winning candidate received at least sixty-five percent of the constituency vote; this requirement did not apply to the Valle d'Aosta senate seat election, which was carried out by plurality voting. Unfilled senate seats were then proportionally distributed in each region. In practice, very few candidates reached the sixty-five percent constituency threshold; consequently, proportional representation was used to allocate nearly all senate seats. The electoral system resulted in a fairly high correlation between the votes obtained by a party nationwide and the number of seats it won in both chambers and was in this sense highly representative of the electorate's political opinions.

Proportional Representation Italian Style

The proportional representation electoral system created by the constitutional assembly (1946–48) reflected the antifascist attitude of its drafters, who tried to limit concentration of power in only one party and in one individual. Unfortunately, by making it easy for relatively small organized groups to win parliamentary seats, it promoted the growth of a large number of parties. This, in turn, produced highly fragmented legislatures (parliaments), and therefore, reduced the governability of the country, since it was difficult to form stable coalition governments: from 1945 to 1993 there were a total of fifty-two governments, which on average lasted less than a year in office. Moreover, Italian voters could never know in advance who was going to be prime minister and/or the type of government they were going to have since coalitions to form governments were formed after the elections. Citizens went to vote without knowing the type of political programs the future government was going to offer because in shaping coalitions after the elections, the leading party and the members of the coalition had to engage in compromises in order to achieve programmatic points of convergence.

In the 1992 legislative elections—the last held under the old proportional representation system—produced a parliament (legislature) in which no single party, or any combination of two parties could command an absolute majority of seats in either house of parliament. The new government could be formed only through a coalition which required negotiations among the sixteen parties represented in the Italian legislature. However, the new government proved to be as shaky as its predecessors, and it lasted just ten months in office.

This situation stood in stark contrast with the outcome of the April 9, 1992, general election in the United Kingdom—held under the first-past-the-post system—in which the ruling Conservative Party, led by Prime Minister John Major, secured an absolute majority in the House of Commons on a plurality vote, formed a new government shortly after the election had taken place, and remained in office for the next five years, despite a seemingly endless succession of adverse developments.

The sharp contrast between the swiftness with which a new government was formed in Great Britain in 1992 and the prolonged Italian governmental crisis did not go unnoticed by public opinion in Italy. Supporters of electoral reform, led by Mario Segni—at the time a leading member of the now-defunct Christian Democratic Party (*DC*)—gathered enough signatures to force a referendum on the issue, which was held on April 18, 1993. Seventy-seven percent of the Italian electorate took part in the vote, in which a proposal to repeal the sixty-five percent constituency threshold for senate elections was overwhelmingly approved, with 82.7% of the valid vote.

While unfavorable comparisons with Britain may have played a part in the outcome of the referendum, a major factor in favor of change was an ongoing, large-scale investigation of corruption at all levels of government in Italy—the so-called Operation Clean Hands—whose findings completely discredited the ruling class and led to the eventual demise of both the Christian Democratic Party (*DC*)—the country's dominant political force since the end of World War II—and its allies, most notably the Italian Socialist Party (*PSI*).

The electoral system that was introduced in 1993 and was used in the 1994, 1996, and 2001 elections was a mixed majoritarian-proportional system. Seventy-five percent of deputies were elected in uninominal districts with the first-past-the-post method. The remaining 25% of the seats were attributed proportionally among those parties which obtained at least 4% of the votes nationwide. This threshold aimed at reducing the number of small parties.

Thus voters cast two different ballots: one for the majoritarian 75% of the seats and the other for the 25% proportional share. In the senate the distribution of the seats on a regional basis in proportion of the population has been maintained. Three-fourths of the senate seats were allocated through in uninominal districts, while the competition for the remaining one-fourth is on the basis of the proportional vote obtained by party lists regionwide.

Parliamentary Organization and Political Pluralism

In dividing the Italian Parliament into two assemblies, the senate and the chamber of deputies, the constitutional assembly was influenced by at least two factors. On the one hand, it considered it appropriate to establish political representation on a balance of power guaranteed by discussion between two assemblies, both of which derived their democratic legitimacy from direct election. On the other hand, it deemed paramount that the procedural considerations of the two chambers allow for a major reflection in the execution of their functions and imposed a need for coordination that would require at least two successive phases of debate.

The structure of the Italian parliament has inherent problems. Constitutionally, the powers of the two chambers are equal and do not represent distinct social or geographic interests. The difference between them is so slight that it is possible to speak of an almost "perfect" double-chamber system. The major difference between them is the functional coordination of the two assemblies; in addition, the age of their members and that of their voters, as well as, until recently, the level of proportional representation, were also different.

Government *all'italiana* means that the more members the parliament has, the better the people are served; so, Italy has more than three times as many members as the U.S. congress, even though the American population is five times that of Italy and has a population make-up that is much more complex. To make the situation worse, members of Italian parliament receive the highest compensation of legislators in the world (more than double that of American members of congress). This kind of self-serving posture by legislators extends to a rich variety of perks without equal in other parts of the world. Consequently, because politicians run a very expensive budget on themselves, each member has a very small and usually ill-informed staff, nothing remotely comparable to the numerous aides and well-staffed offices of U.S. senators and congressmen. One wonders why Italian politicians enjoy such a low esteem among their citizens. In fact, in Italy politicians have been relegated to a class of their own, *la classe politica,* the political class.

Where the structure of parliament is concerned, a general observation can be made that each chamber usually works separately. Only in particular cases, specified by the constitution, do the two chambers unite in common session. This occurs for the election and swearing in of the president of the republic, for the election of the constitutional justices (five of whom are nominated by parliament), for the election of a third of the members of the superior council of the judiciary, and for the president of the council of ministers (prime minister) and his ministers. The affinity of the two chambers and their similar functions, in addition to internal political bickering, make the Italian parliament a very slow-moving body. What made the system Byzantine, as we shall see, is the power that the political parties hold in the parliamentary structure.

Partitocracy Italian Style

The relationship between the parliamentary members and the political party from whose electoral lists they were elected is complex, and attempts at simplification can be misleading. Although the constitution confirms the classical parliamentary principle that members of the chambers represent the nation and exercise their functions without mandatory restrictions and, therefore, parliamentary members are neither the representatives of their electoral colleges nor the mandataries of the political party to which they are affiliated, political parties do exert strong control over them.

Italy has a multiparty system. Italian parties, like those of other Western European parliamentary democracies, are powerful and on the whole disciplined. Citizens vote primarily for parties, not for individual candidates. The party labels are very important to candidates, since a party legislator who antagonizes the party leadership by taking positions contrary to those of the official party line may risk being expelled from the party, making it impossible for him/her to get reelected on the party slate. This explains the much higher level of party discipline existing in Italy than in the U.S., where the individual representative has a greater need to pay attention to interest groups and to please the electorate in his or her district (and this creates a complete new set of more serious problems). Party affiliation is also important when it comes to the assignment of jobs, since it gives more legitimacy to the patron-client relationship.

Italian parties have traditionally reflected the divisions existing in Italian society. Social class, religious belief, urban/rural interests, all play in a different way and to a different degree on an individual relationship with a political party. And Italian political parties, especially the big ones, are well rooted in Italian society due to the networks of subsidiary organizations who are engaged in social, cultural, and recreational activities to a degree that would be unthinkable in the U.S.

The Quest for Stability and the Return to Proportional Representation

The power of political parties was subjected to more control after referenda of 1993. The April 1993 referendum to abolish the public financing of political parties also forced parliament to introduce legislation profoundly affecting electoral campaigns. At present, political candidates and parties have fairly rigid campaign expenditures ceilings, and reporting and control procedures have improved. New legislation has also regulated access to public and privately owned media and has created a supervisory authority.

When Italy adopted its new electoral system in 1993, there were high hopes—both within the country and beyond its frontiers—that the new parliamentary election procedures would lead to a simplified political system, which would in turn produce stable, effective, long-lasting governments. Although the electoral system has led to the rise of two broad electoral cartels on the Right and the Left, which have alternated in power, the party system remains highly fragmented; at the same time, the electoral alliances have proved to be rather fragile, compromising governmental stability in the process.

Back to the Old System with a New Proportional Representation

While many Italians believe the retention of a proportional representation component has led to persistent party fragmentation, the problem appears to originate in the internal agreements reached by coalition partners in order to allocate single-member college nominations: smaller parties usually demand and secure safe seats, as a condition for joining one coalition or the other; rather than risk losing the election, the larger coalition partners usually bow to these demands, outrageous as they may be sometimes. Consequently, small parties often secure parliamentary representation even when they have failed to reach the four percent threshold Although the electoral coalitions appear to give Italian voters the clear choices they were supposedly denied in the days of *DC*-dominated governments under full-blown proportional representation, these alliances have been largely geared to win elections first and sort out policy differences among coalition partners later. However, these policy differences often prove too difficult or impossible to overcome, which makes it difficult for the cartels to hold governments (or even themselves) together.[2]

New Electoral System

In December 2005, the Italian Parliament approved a new proportional representation electoral system, which replaces the electoral system adopted in 1993; the Berlusconi government pushed through parliament legislation to re-introduce proportional representation—with majority prize—for elections to the senate and the chamber of deputies. The new electoral system is based on proportional representation with a series of thresholds to encourage parties to form coalitions.

Both for the lower and higher house of the parliament, Italy will be divided into a certain number of constituencies, in which seats will be distributed according to the share of votes received by a party. In all cases, the list of party candidates is given beforehand, and citizens cannot state a preference for any given candidate: if a list wins 10 seats, its first ten candidates will be elected. The law will officially recognize declared coalitions of parties.

Beginning with the parliamentary election of 2006, Italian citizens residing abroad elected six senators and twelve deputies; the senate seats apportioned among the regions were decreased to 309 while the deputies' seats were reduced to 618.

President: Head of State but Not of Government

The president of the republic is head of state and is not elected by the people. Since Italy doesn't have a vice president, if the president is sick or temporarily incapacitated, the president of the senate takes over the job. If the president dies, a presidential election is held. The president is head of the armed forces and presides over the supreme defense council, ratifies international treaties, and promotes the establishment of peaceful relations with other nations. The president presides over the superior council of magistrature (CSM), the body that guarantees the independence of the judges. He can also grant pardons.

Because the framers of the constitution were charged with creating a parliamentary republic, they were expected also to avoid giving too much power to one individual (as is the case in the presidential republic where the president is head of state and of government). However, even though the president of the Italian republic does not enjoy the power held by his counterpart in a presidential republic, he is not a puppet. The last two presidents have given a clear indication of how powerful the president can be when the executive (government) and legislative (parliament) branches are weak and/or fragmented.

The president of the Italian republic is head of state but not of government, and he represents the nation's political unity and guarantees the constitutional powers. By the power of his message, the president is able to influence political and institutional direction, both from within the institutions and in the country at large. The president has an important role as guarantor and political mediator when a government is being formed following a cabinet crisis. When he is convinced of the lack of "governability," the president is also able to dissolve the chambers early and call for new elections. The head of state in the Italian constitutional model is, therefore, charged with ensuring that the constitutional rules for the ordering of political and constitutional relations between the powers of the state are observed and with intervening to resolve any resulting institutional crises.

The head of state fulfills functions connected with all the constitutional powers of the republic. Where parliamentary and legislative procedures are concerned, the president participates in the formation of laws by promulgation and can send laws back to the chambers for new consideration; he authorizes the presentation of proposed government legislation and indicates political elections and referenda; he can ask for the extraordinary assembly of the chambers and, in consultation with their president, can order its dissolution; and, he nominates up to five senators. In relation to the government and the executive function, the president of the republic is responsible for nominating the president of the council of ministers (prime minister) and, at his proposal, the ministers; he appoints, on the initiative of the government and in those cases provided by the law, the state functionaries; he issues, after government deliberation, decrees having the value of law (legal and legislative), as well as regulations; and he accredits and receives diplomatic representatives.

The head of state, moreover, commands the armed forces, presides over the supreme defense council, and declares the state of war resolved upon by parliament. Also very important is the formal participation by the president in the exercise of several administrative functions:

the recognition of juridical appointments, dissolution of provincial and communal councils, legitimization of natural children, and decisions on recourse to extraordinary administrations and conferment of honors. In relation to the powers of justice, the head of state nominates five justices of the constitutional court, presides over the supreme council of the judiciary, and can grant pardons and clemency.

All the acts of the president, including the exercising of his "own" powers, must be endorsed by the relevant ministers or by the president of the council so that they can assume the political responsibility. Furthermore, the president of the republic cannot be removed from power on the grounds of political irresponsibility. The only political control to which he is subject is that of public opinion and not being re-elected should he choose to stand again for office. However, the force of political interest and the power of the mass media on the president should not be undervalued. The loss of political support, accompanied by unfavorable public opinion, can lead to the president's dismissal from office.

By requiring a minimum age (50 years old), the framer of the Italian constitution clearly wanted a president who had a lot of "tested" experience and who enjoys national respect and authority. Historically all the presidents of the Italian republic have been very old and most of them have been members and leaders of parliament for many years. The previous president, Carlo Azeglio Ciampi, finished his seven-year term at age 85. The present president, Giorgio Napolitano, entered parliament as deputy in 1959, was speaker of the house, minister, and at the end, life senator, began his seven-year term at age 81! It is clear that Italian presidents may not 'use' the presidency for future personal endeavors; in addition, the Constitution states that they automatically may become senators for life and, therefore, brings the experience gained as head of the state to the legislative branch. Undoubtedly this is a clever stipulation in the constitution, however, one may question the intensity of involvement in public life that anyone can give at age 85!

Government in a Multi-Party System

The Executive Branch: The President of the Council of Ministers and His Cabinet

The executive branch is represented by the president of the council of ministers (the cabinet) and their president (prime minister). The prime minister decides the national policy and is the most important person in the government. He is picked by the president of the republic but must receive a vote of confidence by parliament and can be voted out of office by parliament any time. Members of the cabinet are picked by the prime minister, and usually come from the members of parliament. The president of the republic then appoints the members to the cabinet, and they are approved by Parliament. The Italian prime minister and the cabinet are officially called the government. Because the Italian government serves at pleasure of parliament and because of the type of proportional representation system used in electing members of parliament, the composition of government remains fragile. Since no political party can gain an absolute majority in parliamentary elections, the leading party forms a government with the coalition it ran for election.

It is the cabinet of ministers (government) that holds the executive function. According to the principles of "parliamentary government" enshrined in the Italian constitutional model, the government assumes the power of political decision with the consent of parliament, which is expressed by a vote of "confidence" in the government by the two chambers. The nomination process usually begins with a government crisis and ends with the swearing in of the president of the council of ministers (prime minister) and of his ministers by the president of the republic. The second stage is that of parliamentary confidence. It opens with the presentation of the government to parliament, within 10 days of nomination, and closes with a formal vote of confidence by parliament. When a cabinet crisis occurs, the president of the republic, according to a well-established constitutional practice, engages in political consultations with individual state figures (former presidents of the republic, the presidents of both chambers, and former prime ministers) and also representatives and delegations of political parties. At the end of these soundings, the head of state, having judged that the political and institutional conditions exist for forming a government capable of winning parliamentary confidence, will entrust the creation of a cabinet to the designated prime minister. Usually, the latter accepts provisionally until he has established, through consultations with the various political forces, the concrete possibility of being able to form a government that will be supported by the majority of members of parliament. The president of the republic then nominates the president of the council of ministers and, on the latter's proposal, the individual ministers who all then take the oath of loyalty to the republic. Within the ten days allowed by the constitution, the government must present itself to the chambers which, on hearing the declaration made by the president of the council, provide a vote of confidence. The president of the council coordinates the actions of the various ministers and maintains the unity of the general political direction, which is his first responsibility. The council of ministers decides on all the general policies of the government, with specific competence for all the decisions involving the collective responsibility of the executive. Individual ministers join in determining the government's political direction, in participating in the sessions of the council of ministers, and in making the decisions for their respective ministers. Ministers have, above all, a collective political responsibility for all the government's acts and for many of the acts of political consideration that involve the collective responsibility of the government.

The government is in fact the holder of some normative powers: it decides the form in which laws will be proposed to the head of state, which must then authorize their presentation to the chambers. It also approves laws by decree in cases of emergency and legislative decrees on the delegation of parliament. These materially legislative acts are then issued by decree of the president of the republic. Finally, the government is responsible for regulating all the executive activity of the law and the administrative organization. The responsibility can be tested in parliament through the "no confidence" motion, whose approval obliges the government to resign.

By creating a governmental body that had collective responsibility and by giving it a leader who potentially could not assume too much power, the framers of the constitution have spared Italy from the abuses of an authoritative government or leader, but they also gave the country the structure for a political system which, as a consequence of this kind of proportional representation system, proved to be very unstable and would require skillful maneuvering and compromising in order to survive. As the coalition of various political forces, the Italian government was fragmented and fragile. Since the great majority of governments were coalitions of many parties, a spirit of potential conflict and hostility forced a cabinet to fall on the slightest pretext of the leaders of even the smallest parties. The coalition formulas were dictated by possibilities for achieving the required majority in parliament.

In 1992, by the initiative of *DC*, an attempt was made to start to correct one of the major absurdities of the Italian political system, that is, the separation between the legislative and the executive branches. In every democracy, that is the norm, but not in government *all'italiana*. In that year, *DC* established that the offices of government (the cabinet of ministers) and parliament were incompatible in the same person. Consequently, in accepting a post in government, an *onorevole* would have to give up his or her seat in parliament. Aside from being freed from the potentially serious conflicts that would occur by holding positions in two branches of government, the *onorevole* could not vote in parliament

In Italy political campaigns take place also in streets and squares. From the archive of the author.

for or against his own government. Most important, the voting down of governments would not be done lightly because members of government would not automatically return to parliament! The initiative of 1992 remains an isolated decision.

Multi-Party System, Pluralistic Democracy, and Chaotic Proportional Representation

The extended morass of the Italian political system was partially caused by the overly idealistic aspirations of the fathers of the constitution. They rightfully assumed that one of the essential presuppositions to the concept of political democracy was allowing direct political participation to the citizen. To offer a real pluralistic democracy, the juridical channels of consultation, direction, and decision should be many and diverse.

For a country where the specters of fascism were still very much present and the fear of the advent of communism was overwhelming—from the very beginning of the Cold War, Italy was at the frontier of the free world—the presence of a strong political party was scary. The initial proportional representation, without a minimum needed to achieve representation, was intended to foster minority parties and discourage monolithic groups like the communists or the disbanded fascists to take control.

Both the virtues and the problems on which Italian democracy was founded lay in its proportional representation system, which was one of the most representative in the world: the more an electoral system is proportional the greater the tendency for all political forces to be represented. Thus, from the very beginning a fairly wide array of political forces was represented, and it seems that voters responded enthusiastically to this wide spectrum of political choices. Although voting was not mandatory, there was a high level of electoral participation even in local elections and referenda. In fact, the proportion of eligible voters going to the polls in Italy has been the highest in Europe.

However, the system created an unworkable fragmentation of political parliamentary parties: a representation that oscillated between 12 and 16 parties. Moreover, the system did not create among Italians great faith in government. In fact, there is a curious paradox in Italy: a high percentage of voters and a high level of mistrust of government and political institutions. Italy has the lowest index of public satisfaction of any Western European industrial state.[3]

The Ploy of Preferential Vote

In politics *all'italiana,* until 1993, although political parties were at the core of the system, personalities did play a role. For the house of deputies especially, even though many voters simply voted for the party and did not bother to indicate a candidate, voters could express the preference vote. They could favor three or more candidates, according to the size of the electoral district. The personal votes were counted and the candidates of each party were ranked accordingly. If a party won, say, six seats in a particular district, these would have been given to the six candidates with the most preference votes. Candidates could run for election in more than one district (and many leaders did!) and, if they won in more than one, could decide which district to represent. In this case the first of the nonelected obtained the seat that was not filled. The first of the nonelected could also "succeed" a deceased deputy or one who retired during the life of a parliament.

The preference vote system was exploited by the Italian political parties to pull in as many votes as possible. Not only did political parties allow the same very popular individuals to be candidates in more than one district, but they presented lists of candidates that were much more numerous than seats available. Even though some of the names put on the list did not have any chance of winning, they were given a spot for the simple fact that they could attract a certain number of votes for the party.

Rewards for High Preferential Vote

Parties handsomely rewarded those who pulled in votes. There was a constant link between elections, governments, and ministerial appointments. The proportional system was, in a sense, applied to the distribution of government positions and these, in turn, depended to a large extent on the preference system. The preference vote, when sufficiently high, opened the door to the continuous holding of ministerial power. Moreover, as the preference vote was the main avenue for political promotion and, given the clientele nature of the system—more votes were translated into more power of patronage, which returned more votes next time around—campaigns for election did acquire a personal flavor. This system created a high degree of stability: a good preference vote opened the door to a ministerial position, a ministerial position enabled the holder to exercise patronage, and this in turn increased the size of his personal vote. When sufficiently high, the preference vote opened the door to continuous holding of ministerial power, and the system got locked up in *immobilismo*.

Italy's electoral system was geared to a country emerging from fascism into the Cold War. However, even though proportional representation was intended to foster minority parties and discourage monolithic groups like the communists or disbanded fascists, and though it provided a high level of democratic representation, proportional representation Italian style produced several problems. It constantly created unstable coalition governments and an unworkable fragmentation of parliamentary parties—with no fewer than 16 being represented in the early 1990s. It made decision making more difficult and did not offer the electorate a clear-cut alternative between potential governments. In that kind of system, the Italian electorate could only influence a possible coalition by strengthening a particular party's parliamentary representation; it did not vote for a future government.

Although political power remained concentrated in the political parties, and members of the parliament were elected on the basis of party representation, the latter could act independently of the party because they could use a secret ballot through which they were able to avoid party discipline. And many times it was through such independence that governments fell and political crises became more difficult to solve.

In the 1980s and early 1990s, proportional representation *all'italiana* encouraged the proliferation of protest movements, local and one-issue groups which, in the 1992 April national elections, fielded more than 500 slates of candidates. Altogether, a record 16 parties achieved representation in the national parliament, even though only six of them polled more than 5% of the total vote.[4] The complex proportional representation system instituted in 2006 which requires the creation of coalitions before elections gives more stability to governments and offers more political and programmatic transparency to voters.

Partitocracy and the Spoils System

However, one of the major problems of the Italian democracy has been the fact that it is a party-dominated system, sometimes referred to as a partitocracy, *partitocrazia*. In essence, it means that the formal democratic institutions of government and elections play only secondary roles. Parochial interests of the parties were so strong that they determined the creation and the fall of cabinets. It was the strength or weakness of political parties that determined the nature of the coalitions. However, the size of popular support and political influence were not necessarily correlated. To a large extent, the changes in the governing coalition were primarily the result of party politics rather than popular decisions through elections. This could certainly be illustrated by the fact that the Republican Party, with only a popular support of around 5%, shaped many government coalitions, headed many ministries and directed, under its leader, Giovanni Spadolini, the first non-Christian Democratic government in the early 1980s.

Partitocracy degenerated into a system of abuses and an uncontrollable patronage system. Americans are well acquainted with the "spoils system" (President Andrew Jackson once said "to the victor go the spoils"), which enables a newly elected president (governor, mayor, or even county executive, etc.) to replace the appointees of the previous administration with his own handpicked loyalists. The spoils system, Italian style, is inspired by the same principle, but, by force of circumstances, it is far more complex and has a much wider impact on the country.

Until 1994, political appointments were made in every sector of the Italian society, from senior diplomatic posts to positions in education, to opera houses, to the sanitation department, to the health service at the local supermarket. In many cases, political appointments started at the top of the management ladder and continued, less officially, to the bottom. For example, most singers at La Scala were connected with the Socialist Party, because that was the leading party in Milan in the 1980s. The party with the most votes got to dish out the most jobs and favors. The patronage system, called *lottizzazione*, worked just like that.

The political parties claimed that their civil servants, managers, bankers, etc., were qualified and efficient. However, we know that such a system, because of its very nature, does not reward quality and easily suffers from excessive abuse. The national health service, the state-owned television networks, and banks were among the *lottizzazione* monster's favorite lairs. So, too, was government-controlled industry, grouped under three enormous holding companies. The largest, the Institute for Industrial Reconstruction (IRI) was headed by a member of the Christian Democratic Party. The other two, the National Agency for Hydrocarbons (ENI), and the Agency for the Participation and Funding of Manufacturing Industries (EFIM) the manufacturing enterprises, were headed by socialist appointees and had christian democratic vice chairmen.

To correct the problem, some economists and politicians put pressure on government to reduce the public sector through privatization. That is exactly what Italy has done after much political infighting. It has been a heroic decision because the parties wanted to hang on to their quotas of management jobs, known in Italy as *poltrone,* armchairs. To their credit, it must be said that, in spite of the corruption, political parties do not operate in a vacuum. Budgetary problems, the impending union with the rest of Europe, and popular discontent brought them to the realization that changes were in the best interest of both the nation and the parties.

Dilemmas of a Revolutionary Party

Italians have not just been weary of government mismanagement; they have also been weary of most traditional political parties. Indeed, they have grown weary of the *classe politica,* the political class. During the long years of the Cold War they expressed their disappointment by voting communist. This means that many Italians voted communist in those years not because they firmly believed in communism, but because they disliked the other parties. This political behavior had positive, not negative, implications for democratic stability. It gave Italy a political balance and produced profound social reform, most likely unattainable without the presence of a strong Communist Party.

It should be reiterated that the Italian Communist Party was almost unique in its brand of communist ideology. It was in a position quite different from the Eastern-Bloc communist parties that were ousted from power at the beginning of the 1990s. It had deep, emotional roots in Italy as a workers' and anti-fascist movement before, during, and after WWII, and in the 1970s it was the leader in the Euro-communist movement, breaking with Moscow on many policy issues and trying to project Marxism as a valid choice within a democratic society.

Euro-Communism

By rejecting Moscow's direction, Euro-communism was to be understood as an evolution within Western culture rather than as a revolutionary disruption of it. Resonating in Euro-communism was Antonio Gramsci's faith that, within Western culture, the Italian branch of communism was already peculiarly fitted for a humanism of technology and work.

Communists like Antonio Gramsci and Enrico Berlinguer are major historical figures and are even regarded as heroes; many of Italy's top intellectuals, artists, writers, and performers have been communists, and the party generally had the reputation of being more socially active and less corrupt than other major parties.

The Communist Party, too, like other political manifestations, embraced many paradoxes. As the largest, strongest, and in many ways, the most able of communist parties found among democracies, the party not only refrained from any subversive or revolutionary assaults on democratic institutions and processes, at critical moments it even acted unambiguously to support and reinforce them. Despite the Vatican anti-communist crusade, the Communist Party was supported by many practicing Catholics and, contrary to all expectations, it was strongest in some of the wealthiest regions of the peninsula and often weakest in the poorest regions.

Though it regularly claimed one-quarter to one-third of the electorate and had considerable power in local governments, the *Partito Comunista Italiano (PCI),* was never able to lead a national government *(See Profile).* This was due, in part, to an unwritten U.S. veto of

PROFILE

The Christian Democratic Party

The Christian Democratic Party, (*Democrazia Cristiana*), commonly called the *DC*, dominated government for nearly half a century until its demise amid a welter of corruption allegations in 1992–94. The party was in part a revival of the Italian People's Party (*Partito Popolare Italiano*) created in 1919 by the Sicilian priest Don Luigi Sturzo, declared illegal by the fascist regime in 1925 despite the presence of some members in Benito Mussolini's first government.

In the later years of World War II, the Christian Democrats started organizing the party in competition (but also for a time in coalition) with parties of the center and the Left. Breaking decisively with its former Communist coalition partners in May 1947, the party went on to win its greatest election victory in April 1948 with the support of the Church and the United States.

From 1948 until 1992, *DC* was the largest party in parliament, governing in successive coalitions with the smaller Liberal, Republican and Social Democratic parties and, after the 1963, with the Socialist Party. Basing its electoral majority largely on the Catholic countryside, the party moved over time from its reformist origins to a more conservative role. A short-lived *DC* government led by Fernando Tambroni (1960), relying on parliamentary support from the Italian Social Movement, fascism's ideological heir, was disowned by the party following widespread opposition. Later in the sixties, the increased political influence of the Left-wing factions, moved the party to a center-Left strategy based on a coalition with the Socialist Party.

The abduction and murder of Aldo Moro, in 1978 removed one of the party's most highly regarded leaders. At the time, Moro was trying to replicate the inclusion of the socialist party with the communist one, a highly contested maneuver in conservative circles. This policy became known as the historic compromise. However, this policy was discarded after Moro's murder, as the Red Brigades that kidnapped him claimed to be communist, although they did not support the Communist Party.

In the 80s, the *Pentapartito* (five-party coalition) made up of Christian Democratic, Italian Socialist Party, Italian Socialist Democratic Party, Italian Republican Party and Italian Liberal Party was started as a government alliance. Its main aim was to keep the Italian Communist Party away from power. Having ruled the nation for over 40 years with no alternative other than the Communist party, *DC* members had ample opportunity to abuse their power, and undoubtedly some did. With its stronghold in the Italian south, *DC* was the political party most associated with Mafia in the popular opinion. Several leaders were perceived by many to belong to a gray zone between simple corruption and Mafia business.In 1992 an investigation was started in Milan, dubbed *Mani Pulite* (Clean Hands). It uncovered endemic corruption practices at the highest levels, causing many spectacular (and sometimes controversial) arrests and resignations. After two years of mounting scandal and divisions, the party disbanded in 1994.

Some of these politicians were acquitted, and their supporters claim this vindicates them. However, skeptics point out that many times these acquittals are based on the trial exceeding, sometimes narrowly, the statutory time limit.

In January 1994, after suffering many defeats in 1993 local elections, the party changes its name into Italian People's Party. While some the leaders of the centre-right faction of the party decided to launch a new party called Christian Democratic Centre and to make an alliance with the new party of Silvio Berlusconi, *Forza Italia*. Many Christian Democrats decided to join directly *Forza Italia*, and in the years to come *Forza Italia* became the party with more ex-members of *DC* in absolute terms.

a Communist Party rule in a country that was a key NATO member. Without the possibility of being part of a coalition government, the *PCI* remained cut off from Italy's other Left-wing parties, such as the socialists and Social Democrats, both of which were allied with the *Democrazia Cristiana,* to form most coalition governments until the early 1990s. However, as we shall see later, the Communist Party was the most important cultural presence in postwar Italian society, even more important than the *DC (See Profile).*

The Strategy for Success

The Communist Party used a strategy that involved the working-class movement, putting itself at the head of an alliance of social forces that was against monopoly capitalism and the political remnants of fascism and was advancing toward socialism through a combination of legal mass agitations and protests, a full use of the parliamentary and electoral machinery, and a constant effort of ideological penetration and struggle. The strategy was designed progressively to disarm the forces of monopoly and reaction and shift the balance of economic and political power democratically toward the working class and its allies.

The party's postwar strategy was also centered on a cultural policy of the masses. First, it sought to manage its own sector of culture by building its own capillary networks of cultural apparatuses (a party press, publishing houses, libraries, and sites of popular recreation) and thereby penetrate "civil society" at all levels right down to the smallest local area. For the postwar Communist Party, popular culture came to mean largely both autochthonous "folk" and class-based traditions; it was connected with positive notions of popular community, solidarity, and tradition. Second, it sought to win over and mobilize intellectuals, whether "great intellectuals" (leading cultural figures) or middle strata intellectuals engaged in cultural work—teachers, journalists, and workers in the theater, film, publishing, or broadcasting industries. This meant building a party presence in existing cultural organizations by recruiting new members or attracting fellow travelers. Third, the party sought to project a particular set of cultural values and to promote an aesthetic and a morality that were social and collective rather than individualist or private, "progressive" rather than "decadent," outward-looking rather than introspective, and centered upon public civic participation rather than upon private activity and consumption.

While the party created a wide appeal through its cultural programs, it never became convincing enough through its ideology to win over enough voters to become the leading party and take over the government. Certainly, the winds of change that were transforming the communist states of Eastern Europe into democracies had a determining effect on the fate of the *PCI* In 1992 it changed its name, calling itself the *Partito Democratico della Sinistra (PDS),* the Democratic Party of the Left, and reemerged as a new, non-communist entity that hoped to integrate with Europe's social democratic Left and, eventually, come to power. The hammer and sickle that it had held aloft for 69 years was retained, but in a reduced form, submerged beneath the roots of a large, leafy tree that became the dominant emblem. The

Partito Comunista Italiano (PCI)

The Italian Communist Party or *Partito Comunista Italiano (PCI)* emerged as *Partito Comunista d'Italia* or Communist Party of Italy from the secession by the Leninist *comunisti puri* tendency from the Italian Socialist Party *(PSI)* in 1921. During the Cold War it became the strongest Communist party outside the Iron Curtain and China.

The party took part in every government during the national liberation and constitutional period from June 1944 to May 1947. In the first general elections of 1948 it joined the *PSI* in the Popular Democratic Front but was defeated by the Christian Democracy party which was strongly supported by the U.S. and the Church. The party gained considerable electoral success during the following years and occasionally supplied external support to center-Left governments, never joining directly. The party always had its stronghold in Central Italy—particularly in Tuscany, Emilia Romagna, and Umbria (an area that took the name of "red belt"), where it regularly won the local administrative elections—and in some of the industrialized cities of Northern Italy.

The Hungarian Revolution of 1956 and its brutal suppression by the Soviet forces created a split within the *PCI*. After the Athens Colonels Coup in April of 1967, some *PCI* leaders became alarmed at the possibility of a repeat in Italy and the party formally requested Soviet assistance to prepare the party in case of such an event. The KGB drew up and implemented a plan to provide the *PCI* with its own intelligence and clandestine signal corps. From 1967 through 1973, *PCI* members were sent to East Germany and Moscow to receive training in clandestine warfare and information gathering techniques by both the Stasi and the KGB. Shortly before the May 1972 elections, the secretary of the party personally wrote to Leonid Brezhnev asking for and receiving an additional $5.7 million in funding. This was on top of the $3.5 million that the *PCI* was given in 1971. The Soviets also provided additional funding through the use of front companies providing generous contracts to *PCI* members.

However, the relations with the Soviets were not always amicable. In 1969, Enrico Berlinguer, *PCI* deputy national secretary and later secretary general, took part in the international conference of the Communist parties in Moscow, where his delegation disagreed with the "official" political line and refused to support the final report. Berlinguer's unexpected stance made waves: he gave the strongest speech by a major Communist leader ever heard in Moscow. He refused to "excommunicate" the Chinese communists, and directly told Leonid Brezhnev that the invasion of Czechoslovakia by the Warsaw Pact countries (which he termed the "tragedy in Prague") was an act of aggression. At the time the *PCI* was the biggest Communist Party in a democratic state, obtaining a score of 34.4% in the 1976 general election.

Relationships between the *PCI* and the Soviet Union deteriorated more rapidly as the party moved away from Soviet obedience and Marxist-Leninist orthodoxy in the 1970–80s, definitely embracing eurocommunism and the Socialist International. The *PCI* sought a collaboration with Socialist and Christian Democracy parties (the historic compromise). Christian-Democrat party leader Aldo Moro's kidnapping and murder, by the Red Brigades in May 1978, put an end to any hopes of such a compromise.

> During the hot years of domestic political terrorism the *PCI* strongly opposed the terrorism and the Red Brigades, who, in turn, murdered or wounded many *PCI* members or trade unionists close to the *PCI*. The Soviet invasion of Afghanistan led to a complete break with Moscow in 1979. In 1980, the *PCI* refused to participate in the international conference of Communist parties in Paris.
>
> After the fall of the Iron Curtain, in 1991 the Italian Communist Party split into the Democratic Party of the Left (*PDS*) and *Rifondazione Comunista* (Communist Refoundation).

action was not meant to be a "self-dissolution" of the party, or a cutting of the roots; rather, it attempted to give the roots new sap that would lead to a new political formation of the Italian Left that would group communists, left-wing Catholics, greens, radicals, and other reformists and progressive forces.

Old-guard traditionalists, however, felt that Italian communism was not a worn-out relic but still a proud symbol of resistance to fascism and the construction of a postwar democracy in Italy. Therefore, they claimed, changing the party so radically and ridding it of its communist identity would dishonor the Party's past. Representing about one-third of the Party's membership and including key elder statesmen, these people wanted restructuring, but only within a communist framework. They founded the *Partito di Rifondazione Comunista* (Party of Communist Refoundation). They were relics of a political apparatus that had influenced obliquely the course of postwar Italian history and had contributed to the paradoxical "stability within instability" of the Italian political system.

Stability Within Instability

When everything is said and done, Italy's legendary "instability" was an artful illusion in the power game. Despite the air of *opera buffa,* Italian politicians were able, through shrewd maneuverings, to mold one of the most stable democracies in the Western world. Foreigners may have talked about instability, but Italy has had a very stable democracy. What Italy did not have was the alternation in power between different political parties common to other Western countries. This is perhaps the most peculiar aspect of the Italian system until 1994.

In fact, there was a hidden stability in the Italian political instability. Italy actually held two political records. In addition to having had the highest number of governments in the postwar period, Italy is also the only Western democracy in which one political party dominated the government for about 50 years. Italy and Japan were, in fact, the only two industrial democracies in which the same party governed uninterrupted for about 50 years. Alliances and strategies changed, but the Christian Democratic Party remained at the head of 49 of the 52 governments and held the highest number of cabinet posts in all of them.

Photocopy Governments

Stability also came from a second source. The many changes in governments were rarely caused by serious political crises. Much more common in Italy was the "crisis" that was really a disagreement among political leaders or a clash of personalities. This kind of political dispute was fairly easy to resolve. The heads of political parties most often patched up their differences and formed a new government, sometimes in a matter of a few days. Occasionally, the "new" governments were exact replicas of the earlier ones. The Italians called these "photocopy governments." In fact, the recycling of the same people in government after government was another stabilizing element in Italian democracy.

However, the extreme longevity in power of many politicians, while it provided stability, also instituted a kind of dictatorship in a very democratic system. A case in point is the government crisis that occurred in the spring of 1991. Because of disagreements among the parties in the government coalition, Prime Minister Giulio Andreotti resigned. A few weeks later, he was replaced by none other than Prime Minister Giulio Andreotti, initiating his seventh term as the nation's leader. More than any other politician, Andreotti had become the symbol of Christian Democratic permanent power. Andreotti served in the first postwar cabinet in 1946 and remained at the center of power until 1993. Besides being prime minister seven times, he was also minister of defense, minister of the interior, and minister of foreign affairs. Nor is he a unique case; there are several other Christian Democratic notables who had careers of equal longevity.

How did politicians like Andreotti survive so long? Andreotti belonged to a world of compromise, flexibility, pragmatism, shrewd political maneuverings, and ruthless *Realpolitik*. As Andreotti himself observed with characteristic wit: "I am typically Italian, typically Roman and therefore untranslatable and unexportable." In the 1960s he was a leader of the Christian Democratic Right wing, opposing the entrance of the socialists into the government. Then, in the mid-1970s, he headed the first Italian government supported by the Italian Communist Party. He established his reputation as ardently pro-NATO, but began flirting with the Soviet Union long before Gorbachev arrived on the scene. As foreign minister during the *Achille Lauro* hijacking, he allowed the alleged terrorists to slip from Italian custody, presumably because of his design for Italian policy in the Mideast.

Compromise and flexibility were almost a necessity in the first decades of the postwar period. Italy was violently split, with threats from the extreme Right and Left, and the center divided. An American approach of frontal confrontation would have led to civil war in Italy. The *DC* deserves credit for lifting Italy out of chronic poverty and for maintaining democracy. However, the *DC* should be criticized for what it did in the 1980s. It continued to maintain itself through the patronage system and allowed a thin line of demarcation between patronage and Mafia in many areas. Fortunately, with the Cold War over and the dissolution of the Italian Communist Party, part of the rationale for the Christian Democratic power system vanished. It was no longer necessary to tolerate corruption and Mafia influence to assure the triumph of light over darkness, so the calls for serious, systemic change had become deafening in 1992.

Even the ex-president of the republic, Francesco Cossiga, a Christian Democrat, sounded the alarm, talking about scrapping the Italian constitution and writing a new one. "The Mafia has taken effective control over the southern third of the country," said the president, "and Italy's system of coalition democracy has become unmanageable." The revelations of political corruption brought to light through "Operation Clean Hands," as we will see in chapter 3, created such vehemence against the political system by the Italians that political parties could not squabble anymore. Most political leaders had to accept the hard reality that Italy needed to become a "normal" democracy of alternating governments with clear electoral mandates. However, it was not easy to find a credible alternative to the *DC*.

The Italian political system was unquestionably full of paradoxes when it is compared to other democracies. But comparison of one democracy with another can easily lead to misleading evaluations. In doing that, we would be inclined to believe that American or some other brand of democracy is a "template that can be stenciled onto almost any other country and produce similar effects there. We forget the spectacular failures that followed past efforts to export the American-British constitutional formula to Latin American, Asian, and African countries."[5] Moreover, no democratic country will look entirely reassuring when measured against some abstract, idealized conception of a democratic state. But the Italian system did need some profound tuning. In engaging in radical institutional reform to prepare for the "second republic," it is important for Italy not to work in absolute abstraction, even though it has the right because of its history of always being a great inventor in the field of politics. The experience throughout the centuries—from the days of the Roman Empire to the period of the Renaissance city-states, through unification and finally even during the fascist dictatorship—as a laboratory for the political experiments of all Western civilization should not be detached from the learning experience that other modern democracies may offer.

Notes

1. Simon Parker, "Political Identities," in David Forgacs and Robert Lumley, eds., *Italian Cultural Studies* (Oxford: Oxford U. P., 1996), 108.

2. **Chamber of deputies:** Italy is divided in 27 large constituencies. To obtain seats, some thresholds must be surpassed *on a national basis:*

    »   Minimum 10% for a coalition. If this requirement is not met, no seat will be won by any party in the coalition.
    »   Minimum 4% for any party not in a coalition.
    »   Minimum 2% for any party in a coalition.

    The coalition or party that obtains a plurality, but is assigned less than 340 seats, is assigned additional seats to reach this number. This corresponds roughly to a 54% majority.

    Senate of the Republic: For the Senate, the constituencies corresponds to the 20 regions of Italy. The electoral system is very similar to the one for the lower house, but is in many ways transferred to a regional basis. The thresholds are also different, and applied *on a regional basis:*

    »   Minimum 20% for a coalition.
    »   Minimum 8% for any party not in a coalition.
    »   Minimum 3% for any party in a coalition.

Coalitions that win a plurality in a region are automatically given 55% of the region's seats, if they have not reached that percentage already.

3.   Nothing can be compared to the failings of the American system. Presidents and the large majority of legislators are usually elected with the votes of less than 30% of the people eligible to vote. And that cannot be called a mandate. Moreover, of those who do vote, hundreds of thousands of citizens have no real choice of legislative candidates because they live in one of the dozens of districts where the incumbent runs unopposed or faces an opponent so underfinanced that he has no real chance to bring his case before the public.

The fairness of the American elections has been compromised by the enormous advantages incumbents have over challengers in terms of campaign fund raising, access to the ballot, legislative mailing privileges, control of the redistricting process, and ability to dole out "member-item" funds (given to legislators for pet projects in their districts). The increasing ability of incumbents to use the perquisites of power to underwrite their reelection campaigns explains why the incumbent reelection rate for New York State legislators reached 98% during the 1980s.

4.   Italy's dramatic self-renewal transformed the political landscape between 1992 and 1997. Scandal investigations touched thousands of politicians, administrators, and businessmen; the shift from a proportional to majoritarian voting system—with the requirement to obtain a minimum of 4% of the national vote to obtain representation—also altered the political landscape.

Party changes were sweeping. The Christian Democratic party dissolved; the Italian People's Party and the Christian Democratic Center emerged. Other major parties, such as the Socialists, saw support plummet. A new populist, and free-market orientated movement, *Forza Italia*, gained wide support among moderate voters. The National Alliance broke from the neofascist Italian Social Movement. A trend toward two large coalitions—one on the center-Left and the other on the center-Right—emerged from the April 1995 regional elections. For the 1996 national elections, the center-Left parties created the Olive Tree coalition while the center Right united again under the Freedom Pole. The May 2001 elections ushered into power a refashioned center-right coalition dominated by Berlusconi's party, *Forza Italia*. The Olive Tree coalition now sits in the opposition. This emerging bipolarity represents a major break from the fragmented, multi-party political landscape of the postwar era, although it appears to have reached a plateau, since efforts via referendums to further curtail the influence of small parties were defeated in 1999 and 2000.

5.   Joseph La Palombara, *Democracy Italian Style* (New Haven: Yale U. P., 1987), 6.

Bibliography

Allum, P., *Italy: Republic Without Government?* London: Weidenfeld & Nicolson, 1973.

Bull, Martin J. and Martin, Rhodes, eds. *Transition and Crisis in Italian Politics.* London: Cass, 1996.

D'Alberti, M. and Finocchi, R. (eds.), *Corruzione e sistema istituzionale.* Bologna: Il Mulino, 1994.

Della Porta, D. and Vannucci, A., *Corruzione politica e amministrazione pubblica. Risorse, meccanismi, attori.* Bologna: Il Mulino, 1994.

Di Palma, G. *Surviving Without Governing: The Italian Parties in Parliament.* Berkeley: University of California Press, 1977.

Forgacs, D. and Lumley, R. (eds.), *Italian Cultural Studies.* Oxford: Oxford U. P., 1996.

Galli, G. and Prandi, A., *Patterns of Political Participation in Italy.* New Haven: Yale University Press, 1970.

Gozzini, Giovanni and Anderlini, Luigi, eds. *I partiti e lo stato.* Bari: De Donato, 1982.

Guidorossi, Giovanna. *Gli italiani e la politica.* Milan: Franco Angeli, 1984.

http://www.nationmaster.com/country/it/Government

Kogan, Norman. *A Political History of Italy: The Postwar Years.* New York: Praeger Special Studies, 1983.

La Palombara, Joseph. *Democracy Italian Style.* New Haven: Yale University Press, 1987.

Vacca, Giuseppe. *Quale democrazia?* Bari: De Donato, 1977.

Wollemborg, Leo J. *Stars, Stripes, and Italian Tricolor.* New York: Praeger, 1990.

CHAPTER 2

DECISIVE TURNING POINTS AND CONSTITUTIONAL TRANSFORMATION

The Italian political system can be seen as either very chaotic or so stable as to be character-ized as immobile or stagnant. Either way, we must realize that the Italian democracy has gone through an evolution culminating in profound political changes. Although the process has been continuous, we can identify five decisive turning points: the early ouster of the communists from government, the "opening to the Left," the "historic compromise" with the communists, the "fall of communism," and the "Second Republic."

Ouster of the Communists

The expulsion of the communists from government in the immediate postwar period, with American assistance and that of the Church, was probably the most important turning point in modern Italian history. In 1947 the Left was in a strong position as a result of its role in the antifascist partisan movement. This momentum gave the appearance that it could take over Italy in a very few years unless decisive political action was taken. At the time, most Socialist

Party (*PSI*) leaders, prompted by the myth of "working class unity" and by the expectation that the Soviet army would soon become the dominant force throughout Europe, chose to play a secondary role to the *PCI* rather than position their party as a third force between the Christian Democrats and the communists. However America's intervention and maneuverings by some Italian politicians saved Italy from communism, stopping the advance of communism into the rest of Western Europe.

Strategies for Success: The U.S. and the Church

This objective was reached by splitting the Socialist Party. With encouragement and financial support from American labor unions and skillful CIA work, many *PSI* representatives and about one-third of the socialist voters split away to form a Social Democratic Party (*PSDI*) under the leadership of Giuseppe Saragat.[1] The split, finalized early in 1947, a few days after *DC* premier Alcide De Gasperi's return from a visit to Washington, divided the "working class unity" and paved the way for "unloading" the Communists from government. The action also drew the battle lines for the following general election in the spring of 1948: communists and socialists ran on a joint ticket under the label of "People's Bloc" or "Popular Democratic Front," while the Christian Democrats led a centrist coalition that included Social Democrats, liberals, and republicans.

The elections of June 1948 marked a real watershed in the history of Italy. The electoral campaign was incredibly intense and polarized. The Marshall Plan, with its funding of public projects and convoys of food and medicine, was buying a lot of goodwill among the Italian people, and the Christian Democrats, with the help of Washington, succeeded in portraying themselves as the best friends of the United States.[2]

The results of the election went better than expected for the *DC* and its alliance. They came close to polling an absolute majority of the votes, scoring an oversized victory. Millions of Italians, who under normal circumstances would have voted either for some Rightist party or for some moderate left-of-center faction, cast their ballots for De Gasperi's *DC* party as the only available alternative to communism. The new Social Democratic Party got 7% of the votes. Despite the rather poor performance of the republicans (*PRI*) and the liberals (*PLI*) who ran under the label of National Bloc, the centrist governmental coalition won the support of 62% of the electorate, twice as much as the communist-led Popular Democratic Front. The feeling that De Gasperi and the U.S. had saved Italy from communism was widespread even among the representatives of social groups and economic interests that had not voted for the *DC* or had done so with great reluctance.

However, the role played by the Church cannot be underestimated. The Catholic Church had become heavily involved in electoral politics through the actions of the clergy and Church-sponsored lay organizations like the civic committees. It warned Catholics that voting for anti-God parties, or even nonvoting, was a mortal sin. The main priority of the Church was to consolidate support for the Christian Democrats as a bloc against the force of the Left. Catholic unity became a key term in this political discourse, where "Catholic" increasingly came to mean not a general religious identity that was shared by the vast majority of Italians, but a specific political commitment to *DC*. In the polarized environment of the Cold War, both sides defined themselves in opposition to each other, and the ideological connections made between Catholicism and anti-communism are particularly striking. The battle was fought out using all the media: sermons, rallies, radio, cinema, newspapers, and, most strikingly, wall posters. The Catholic Church became both the creator and the defender of the family, and this became a key theme in the ideological battle of the period. More attention was given to the threat posed by communism to the family than any other aspect, real or imagined, of the Left's political program. Family life and values became the crucial ideological terrain on which the opposition between Catholicism and communism was established.[3]

However, the weakened Left still enjoyed the support of a strong labor union. There was deep conviction that unless workers were snatched away from the Leftist labor union through labor issues, the Left could easily regain influence. This led U.S. representatives to press hard for an immediate confluence into a new national union of all workers who were no longer willing to accept the communist-socialist leadership of *CGIL* (Italian General Confederation of Labor), the single, all-embracing labor organization revived during the last year of the war. In the summer of 1948 a new national labor union, *CISL* (Italian Confederation of Workers' Union) was founded to attract Catholic union members. These political events were a major setback for communism in Italy from which the party never regained the power to enter government again.

Political Success Without Social Progress

Notwithstanding the changes, the new government, free of the presence of socialists and communists, was unable to make radical changes. De Gasperi's task in tackling a full spectrum of reforms was difficult because his centrist coalition included both the non-communist Left and the moderate Right, whose views on social and economic issues were far apart. The country needed to implement long overdue tax and land reforms as well as a thorough overhauling of the bureaucratic apparatus and of the economic system itself in order to improve the lot of the most destitute and forgotten groups: farm laborers especially in the South, defenseless against the onslaught of inflation; small industries that had been allowed to wither and die; and labor's stepchildren, the unskilled workers. But political stability turned into stagnation, and reconstruction resulted in the restoration of old economic and social structures.

For the next decade, labor remained Italy's cheapest commodity. . The country continued to be good for the rich and bad for the poor. Economic and political power continued to be vested in few hands: mostly landowners in the south, big business and industrialists in the north. A professional class of politicians, drawn mostly from the swollen ranks of lawyers and

❀ SPIRIT

The Sixties

The sixties were a decade of social turmoil; some regard it as a golden age, others as a time of moral disintegration. In the eyes of the far Left, the revolution was at hand, only to be betrayed by the feebleness of the faithful and the trickery of the enemy; to the radical Right, it was an era of subversion and moral turpitude.

The trends that emerged in Italy from the late fifties to the end of the sixties engulfed the nations of the Western world with striking commonality. Youth culture and trend-setting by young people; idealism, protest, and rebellion; the emergence of rock 'n' roll as a universal language; the loosening of morals; the relaxation of censorship in literature, the media, and ordinary behavior; feminism, gay liberation, and the emergence of 'the underground' and 'the counter-culture' —all were seen optimistically as the dawning of a better day.

The economic miracle (1958–63) launched the economic reconstruction that within twenty years would place Italy among the world's six economic powers. The center-Left government, with the Socialists' entrance in the coalition in 1963, introduced profound changes, including nationalization of some service in the public sector, democratization of the education system, and the beginning of the "welfare state."

Post-war mass education and social affluence gave rise to the unprecedented influence of young people, with youth subculture steadily increasing its impact on the rest of society, through its tastes in fashion, music, and consumer culture. Although youth subculture was not monolithic, it created a vast new market of its own in the merchandise of popular culture. Yet, after the profound student unrest of 1968–69, the years that followed, "the years of the bullet" in Italy, brought terrorism and violence.

The introduction of new technology—television (including Telstar, the first transatlantic transmission being made in 1962), long-playing phonograph records, transistor radios, modernized telephone systems; jet travel; labor-saving products such as refrigerators and washing-machines; the contraceptive pill (first available in 1961)—helped to advance the anthropological revolution. The advent of television, providing unprecedented international cultural influence, played a leading role in social transformation. Massive improvements in material life, so that large sections of society joined the consumer society—which in backward areas of Italy meant the arrival of electricity, together with inside running water—moved many people at the fringe of society into the "civilized world." Italian society, which had been divided for centuries between the agrarian and the urban, also became culturally and socially more homogeneous through internal migration.

The sixties were years of excitement and hope for Italian artistic culture as well. Design culture moved rapidly from design for artisans to design for industry, that is, to "industrial design." The profound cultural and social changes of the period provided the impetus for the nation to enter the even more turbulent seas of international competition. This is particularly visible in the flourishing of Italian movies, which became extremely popular both at home and abroad. Fellini made *La Dolce Vita* (1960). Marcello Mastroianni and Sophia Loren became international stars, while Fellini, Pasolini, Bertolucci, the Taviani brothers, and Scola all became famous as filmmakers.

university professors, provided a parliamentary veneer. The Catholic Church continued to extend its power in every aspect of life. For millions of peasants who toiled in the fields, the only hope for change remained emigration.

Notwithstanding the "economic miracle," by 1961 the discrepancy in the rates of material and civic progress was great. Italy had all the ingredients for a successful democracy, but neither its social and institutional structure nor its administrative practices had been brought in line with those of the modern Western democracies by the 1960s. The country still lacked an equitable tax system, a farsighted approach to land tenure and agricultural problems, antitrust legislation, efficient regulatory agencies in the fields of power, trade, labor relations, etc., and a modern educational system. Under mounting conservative pressure within the coalition not much social progress had been made. Even the great economic expansion of those years, unattended by adequate social progress and institutional modernization, failed to produce political dividends for the government coalition.

A transitional government leaning toward a more stable political solution, approved in parliament with the backing of the neo-fascists, was greeted by bloody riots that swept many parts of the country in July 1960, taking a toll of 11 dead and more than 1,000 injured. The riots indicated the limitations of political choices in a government the Italian people would accept. With the danger to Italian democracy posed by this situation made manifest, this government headed by Fernando Tambroni, which remains the sole "attempt" in postwar Italy of a government supported by the neo-fascist party, survived only two months.

Opening to the Left

From the time of the "economic miracle" in the late 1950s, Italian society had been asking for a profound and sustained process of modernization and secularization. It was not a coincidence that the first center-Left government of 1963 saw the socialists join the executive branch at the same time as organized labor found its voice again after a long period of relative inactivity. Italy's political pluralism had become less polarized and increasingly consensus driven. The sixties were years of profound changes (See Box on p. 64).

The opening to the left in the early 1960s, which brought the Socialist Party of Italy (*PSI*), previously in electoral alliance with the Communist Party (*PCI*), into a governing coalition with the Christian Democrats, Republicans, and Social-Democrats, offered the opportunity for broadening and consolidating popular support for Italy's democratic institutions as well as for her secure anchorage to the West. By 1962 such an opening appeared possible and desirable to the majority of *DC* leaders. Along with an internal evolution, two occurrences outside of the Party made a move to the left possible. First, the accession of Angelo Roncalli to the papacy as John XXIII in 1958 boxed off Right-wing clerics in the Vatican. The new pope had completely different views from those of his predecessor regarding East-West tensions and regarding the Church's adaptation to modern times through dialogue with society's different groups and forces. Second, Pietro Nenni's Socialist Party found itself weakened by its de facto alliance with the communists. The election of John F. Kennedy in the U.S. also helped the move to the Left. John F. Kennedy understood that if the U.S. continued to oppose an opening to the socialists, it would push them back into the arms of the communists. Thus, in February 1962, a new tripartite government of *DC-PSDI-PRI* was formed, supported by the *PSI's* abstention. The "opening" turned out to be the first concrete step in a far-reaching realignment of Italy's political forces aimed at isolating the largest communist party in the West and forming a stable governmental majority resting on a wide foundation of popular support. The new government presented a program whose objectives were the nationalization of the electric power industry, the reform of the school system, the reform of public administration, the establishment of national economic planning, and the reform of urban planning. It was a period of profound changes *(See Box on p. 64)*. The new era of center-Left governments started in 1963 with the Socialist Party (PSI) as full partner of the coalition.

The center-Left government of the 1960s and 1970s may be criticized for excesses in labor legislation and wasteful public expenditures, but it increased democratization in every area of life. A center-Right coalition with the then extremely conservative liberals, and depending on parliamentary support from the neo-fascist *MSI*, would have polarized Italian society and blocked needed social and economic reforms. In fact, the "opening to the Left" was achieved only after the disastrous attempt to seek support from the Right.

American foreign policy, shortsighted most of the time, acted wisely in recognizing these realities and giving the green light to the center-Left in 1961–1963. This reversed the futile policies of Ambassador Clare Booth Luce, who wanted a Christian Democratic alliance with the monarchists, and of Deputy Chief of Mission Outerbridge Horsey, who had considered a government dependent on the support of the neo-fascists a better means of protecting U.S. interests.

Profound social legislation was approved during those years. A major legislative reform was the passing of the Workers' Statute, a body of laws very protective of workers' rights, even by Western European standards.

However, during fifteen years of government, the shortcomings of the center-Left coalitions persistently helped the Communists, not only to keep their role as the main opposition force, but to increase their share of the popular vote from just over 20% in the late 1940s to almost 35% in the mid-1970s.

Historic Compromise

The loss of public support by the center-Left coalition and the strong gain by the communists forced the Christian Democrats to make another turn in their political fight to hold on to power by seeking a *historic compromise* government, which would include the Communist Party. This turning point seemed almost inevitable as the communists gained more popular support due to increasing electoral fragmentation. In the election of 1976, during the last months of the Ford administration, the Communists achieved their all-time high in an Italian election, 34.4% of the vote, and the Left found itself with 47% of the votes. They were extending their hegemony in every important area of Italian life: the schools, the press, the judiciary, the trade unions, and regional and local governments. But the Communist leadership decided that in a climate of economic crisis, with great inflation and budget deficits, and of high tension arising from "red" and "black" terrorist attacks, attempting to form a coalition government of the Left was too risky. Thus *PCI* supported indirectly the newly formed government of Giulio Andreotti by abstaining from voting. It would be a government where abstentions would exceed favorable votes. The possible historic compromise coalition of Communists with the Christian Democrats was perceived as possibly compromising both Italian freedom and the country's support of the Western Alliance.

The U.S. Dilemma

In this atmosphere of crisis, the Carter administration was pressured by both extremes of the U.S. political spectrum. From the Right came demands for the U.S. to take a direct role in stopping the communist threat, through covert operations if necessary. From the Left came arguments that the *PCI*'s accession to power was both inevitable and desirable. The Carter administration gave serious consideration to the counterproductive effects of past covert operations. The communists gave wide publicity to leaks on covert financing operations by Americans and had been very successful in gaining popular support as the defender of the country's sovereignty against "American domination." In addition, incautious statements by U.S. officials during this period appeared to threaten Italy with reprisals if it gave the Communist Party a governing role.

Like its predecessor, the Carter administration was opposed to any formula involving the Communist Party's entry into the government in Italy and was determined to avoid such a development. But there was a clear difference over the strategy to be followed. Ford and Kissinger's strategy was keyed to the concept of trench warfare: hammer away rigidly on American hostility to *PCI*'s participation in the government by means of warnings about the consequences in the international field. Carter's strategy, instead, was built on the concept of mobile warfare: avoid head-on clashes, resort to a more flexible and indirect outflanking maneuver. This had very positive effects in this critical moment in Italian postwar history. The fundamental result of Prime Minister Andreotti's trip to Washington (July 1977) brought about, through an operation quite typical of Andreotti, the apparent reconciliation of two opposed purposes. The premier went back to Rome after having won Washington's approval for a political formula that involved communist cooperation after having persuaded the Americans that he and his party were intransigently anti-communist. The Americans bet on Andreotti's skills as a politician and his ability to keep the communists out of government while governing with their assent.

However, acts of terrorism raised fears of uncontrollable political events. Even though Italian society had shown itself to be remarkably shock-resistant, the continued high level of street violence carried sinister implications for the future. The wave of riots and terrorism was viewed by law-abiding Italians as further evidence of their government's inability to govern and made the communists look increasingly like a party of law and order. The situation required the U.S. to be more explicit on the "communist issue" to underline its "preference" for keeping the communists out of government. Carter, therefore, made public statements that while the U.S. was committed to noninterference in the domestic affairs of any country in Western Europe, it did not want the communist parties to have an influential or dominant role in the governments of those countries. The best way to help assure that communist parties did not come to power in Western European countries was for democratic parties to meet the aspirations of their people for more effective, more just, and more compassionate government. However, the Carter administration's attempts to present its position were distorted in the Italian media. Finally, during a "nonpolitical trip" to Italy, Joseph Califano, U.S. secretary for Health, Education, and Welfare, and the representative of Italian Americans in the Carter administration, stated that "the Americans of Italian origin are increasingly aware of the situation in Italy and overwhelmingly want Italy to be free, strong, and non-communist."

The impact that the U.S. move had on the course of events is hard to gauge. It was certainly a shot in the arm for many *DCs*, socialists, social democrats, republicans, and liberals who looked with dismay at communist participation in the national government, and it gave pause to the political factions in the democratic camp that were ready to underwrite such participation. In any event, its effects were strengthened by an incident instigated by the revolutionary campaign against the state. As has happened many times before, the course of history was changed by actions that had the opposite effect from which they were intended. The kidnapping and assassination of Italian Premier Aldo Moro by the Red Brigade (Ch. 3) were the beginning of the end of any possible historic compromise between the communists and the democratic forces of Italy. The outrage touched the heart and soul of the Italian people, and the elections of that year reflected that outrage.

The Communists Back in the Opposition

By the end of 1978, communist leaders, including Enrico Berlinguer, the top advocate of the historic compromise, decided to cut their losses by taking the party back into the opposition. This precipitated new general elections that were held in June 1979, two years ahead of schedule. The communist share of the popular vote dropped from more than 34% to just over 30%. The myth of the *PCI*'s inexorable, irreversible advance was shattered. In the next several years, the overall communist performance at the polls showed a marked downtrend: by 1988, the party's vote was cut by almost one-third from its 1976 peak.

The government of "national solidarity" with the support of the communists (*PCI*) ended at the beginning of 1979. The United States remained opposed to any entrance of the communists into the government and scoffed at the notion of "eurocommunism" whereby the communist parties of the West could participate in the governments of the region in a manner independent of Moscow.

The 1979 elections paved the way for a new phase of Italian politics that featured a revival of the center-Left coalition. Compared with the government formed after the opening to the *PSI* back in the early 1960s, the reconstituted coalition reflected some significant changes. It included not only a strengthened Republican Party and a Social Democratic Party overshadowed by the newly reorganized *PSI,* but also the liberals were freed from the conservative approach and leadership that over 20 years earlier had set them on a course of strenuous opposition to the center-Left policies. Even more important was the trend toward a more balanced relationship between the *DC* and their lay partners, the socialists first of all. This trend was fueled by the *DC* losses at the polls and the growth of the *PSI* vote. The *PSI* hoped to win a top role in running national affairs by overtaking the fading Communists, developing a "competitive" collaboration with the weakened Christian Democrats, and eventually replacing them as the leading partner in a revamped government coalition.

The Socialists Lead the Government

The election of 1983 showed the dissatisfaction of the electorate against the Christian Democrats and left the door wide open to a government headed by Bettino Craxi, the secretary of the *PSI*. Craxi was premier from August 1983 to March 1987, giving Italy its longest government until that time. Craxi benefited from favorable international economic conditions. The domestic economy, although beset by budget deficits, inefficient public services, and rigid labor rules, nevertheless witnessed low inflation, substantial GDP growth, and a buoyant stock market.

The election of 1987 saw some improvements for the *DC*, while *PSI* progressed, gaining votes over the other lay parties while the Communist Party, hurt by Gorbachev's *glasnost,* lost 3% of the votes. The elections revealed widespread dissatisfaction. The dissatisfaction was most evident by the increasing percentage of blank ballots being cast. This dissatisfaction was highlighted by the strengthening of protest parties such as the radicals, the greens, and the northern regional parties, which shortly thereafter coalesced into the Northern League.

In the 1980s, under Bettino Craxi's leadership, the Socialist Party had put an end to the *DC* hegemony over the government and to the communist hegemony over the Italian Left. The collapse of the historic compromise had given the socialists a new opportunity to perform as the kingpin of Italian politics. Craxi's *PSI* adopted a pragmatic approach to social and economic affairs, wholly discarding the doctrinaire Marxism that had been a persistent yet disastrous feature of traditional Italian socialism. Long before the collapse of the communist block, the *PSI* party symbol was changed from the hammer and sickle to a red carnation. Power-sharing with the communists in local government gradually came to an end. Italy could enter into a new phase of social and economic change without the specter of communism.

The 1980s brought a clear change in political identities. While strong party loyalties were sustained throughout 1970s and 1980s, the nature of this support had changed. Instead of seeing political parties as a collective reality that confers political identity, voters increasingly related to parties as vehicles for representing interests. The growth of the socialists in the south demonstrated that the Socialist Party had become an "exchange party" capable of negotiating with voters as effectively as their Christian Democratic coalition partners.

The Fall of Communism

The fall of communism in the countries of Eastern Europe brought about radical changes in the Italian political system. Before the fall of communism, Italian elections were as dull and predictable as the turning of the seasons. Despite the country's endless crises and revolving-door governments, every election since 1948 had produced the same result: the Christian Democrats came in first, followed very closely by the communists. More than any other country in Western Europe, Italy was frozen into political immobility by the Cold War. Politics had become so stable or "stagnant" that shifts of two or three percentage points were regarded as major electoral changes. The fall of communism changed all this.

After the 1989 collapse of East European communism, Italy began to experience a series of tremors that by 1993 had become a full-scale political earthquake. The changes in Eastern Europe called into question the core of the traditional politics in Italy too. The fall of communism shattered many myths and called for a complete reassessment of political behavior and a new set of myths. As in the rest of the democratic West, Italy experienced a "letdown" that made the Italians more aware of the costs than of the benefits of their victory in the confrontation with the communist East. Mounting frustration and resentment over the apparent failure to reap quick and bountiful "peace dividends" turned into a wholesale indictment of the political and economic groups that had been in control of the nation's affairs in the previous decades.[4]

The collapse of communism completely changed the Italian political landscape.[5] The end of the "frozen party system," therefore, and the surge of nontraditional political groups, did not come as a consequence of the emergence of a new ideology, rather they are the result of the complete collapse of *an* ideology and the change in class structure. Consequently, new political attitudes will have looser ties to political parties and weaker partisan identification. In turn, this means that more Italians are effectively "in the market," shopping around at election time and available to experiment with new alternatives. The consequent broken political system could mean that relatively minor squabbles could provoke the making and remaking of cabinets with minor adjustments and realignments designed mostly to suit factional interests and personal ambitions rather than to reflect policy priorities (see Berlusconi's second government in 2005).

But political engineering is no panacea; it can solve some problems but is not a cure-all medicine. All political arrangements have costs. In politics, too, "there is no such thing as a free lunch."

Aged System: Change or Collapse?

It is important to point out that the erosion of loyalty to the traditional political parties, which shook up the system in the early 1990s, had already been slowly developing with other social and economic changes. The rapid decline of the agricultural sector, the secularization of life and growing liberalism, the occupational and geographical mobility, and the higher education level of most of the population had already affected the way society responded to politics, as is reflected in an increased distrust for the traditional political parties. Although the *DC* and the *PCI* had remained the most important parties until 1991, their percentage of votes had been declining.

The Cold War had caused political immobility. Even as adversaries, the *DC* and the *PCI* had reinforced one another: fear of the communists kept the Christian Democrats in power, and popular dissatisfaction with the government kept the communists strong. There was little room in the middle for the smaller parties, which became satellites of the two big ones. With the collapse of communism, however, the situation became fluid. The fall of communism may have been the catalyst that precipitated all the distrust that had been developing through the years. In fact, the political earthquake recorded in the election of Spring 1992 was mostly the result of anger at the Christian Democrats-led government, long held in check by the fear of communism. According to a 1993 poll, at least 20% of the vote was suddenly up for grabs. Some feared that the new climate of political change might set the stage for a sharp swing to the authoritarian Right. The vacuum created by the collapse of ideologies was filled by a proliferation of special-interest and anti-system parties. There were two different environmen-

tal parties, numerous regional parties, even a hunters' party and a pensioners' party. The real novelty was something called the Party of Love, started by porn star Moana Pozzi, who wanted to follow her friend and colleague Cicciolina into parliament; this was possible in an electoral system that gives representation in parliament even to a party collecting only 1% of the votes. It had been difficult enough to govern Italy with 12 parties represented in parliament; what would happen with a 20-party represntation is unimaginable.

Peace demonstrations always attract thousands of participants. From the archive of the author.

The results of spring 1992 elections provided clear evidence that the old Italian political system could not survive. There were 531 party lists for the chamber of deputies throughout Italy's 32 electoral districts, and 9,742 candidates, an increase of about 20% and 13% respectively over the previous elections of 1987.[6]

"Anti-Party" Political Shock

It was the "anti-party," the Lombard League, that made the strongest showing. Many voted for the League not to approve a set of doctrines or a political program but to demonstrate deep discontent with the traditional political parties and their continuing tenure. The regionally based "leagues" of northern Italy which were then grouped collectively under the title the Northern League, led by Umberto Bossi, have maintained an extreme position that called for the secession of northern Italy from what they saw as the corrupt and Mafia-riddled Roman nation-state. Bossi subsequently invoked federalism. It has been difficult to assess if there is distinctive *Lega* identity in the sense there was one for the communists and one for the Catholics. It has remained difficult to define a *leghista*.

The pressure on parliament to approve electoral reform greatly intensified when the constitutional court approved 10 of the 13 referenda proposed for a vote. Since none of the parties had yet made it clear whether they preferred a majority vote based on a British-style single round or the French system of a second-round run-off when a majority has not been obtained the first time, various measures were submitted to referenda. These included one dealing with the majority-type electoral system that would largely dismantle the proportional system and allow voters to elect their mayors and city administrators directly, wrenching local government from the hands of national party bosses. In the spring of 1993, voters approved by a large margin the eight referenda that were finally put on the ballot: this event certainly marked the end of the First Republic.

Meanwhile, in February 1992, Magistrate Antonio Di Pietro, soon to become a living legend (as we will see in the next chapter) followed by other magistrates, had uncovered a system of contributions to political parties in exchange for the granting of government contracts (called by the press *tangentopoli,* literally "bribesville"), which also permitted some individuals to amass large personal fortunes.

The Second Republic

The new political environment freed the judicial branch from all the political constraints and welcomed a cleaner political system. The consequences were immediate and profound. The widespread revulsion over the mega-corruption of leading politicians that was uncovered by

Italian magistrates in "Operation Clean Hands" and the broader, mounting resentment over the mismanagement of domestic affairs by the mainstream parties, not only rocked the political and economic establishments but forced significant changes in the rules of the political game itself.[7]

In a referendum held on April 18–19, 1993, Italians expressed an overwhelming support for a majority system. Italians wanted clear majorities, tired of the backroom haggling of political power brokers and patched-up coalition governments that lasted one year. The switch to a majority system was backed by large margins throughout the country. The only exceptions were registered in Sicily, notably in some districts of Palermo. Several other referenda likewise showed very large majorities supporting curbs on the powers and privileges of politicians. Public financing of parties was now out, for instance; and three government departments were voted to be dismantled, notably the Ministry for State Holdings, which had become a major source of patronage, abuses, and corruption.

Shift from Proportional Representation to Majority System

The new government formed after the April referendum embodied several new departures clearly in line with the message from the polls. For the first time since the end of World War II, the premier was not a politician: Carlo Azeglio Ciampi had been for 14 years governor of Italy's central bank. With full backing from President of the Republic Oscar Luigi Scalfaro, Ciampi chose the members of his cabinet without going through the customary, lengthy bargaining process with leaders of the parties making up the ruling coalition. One third of the new ministers had no party affiliation.

Upon taking office, Prime Minister Ciampi stated that if parliament did not enact electoral reform along the lines laid down by the April referendum before the summer recess, the government would submit its own bill and ask for a vote of confidence on it. In the summer of 1993 the parliament approved a new electoral system.[8] The reform reflected an earnest effort to reconcile the main benefits of the majority system with some protection on the minor parties' vital interests. It provided for three quarters of the House members (472 out of a total of 630) to be elected on a "first past the post" basis; i.e., along the British and U.S. models. The other 158 seats would be allotted on a proportional basis among all parties polling at least 4% of the nationwide vote. The votes polled by the winners under the majority system would be excluded from the total available to the same parties' candidates to the seats allotted under the proportional system.

These reforms were courageous because with their vote members of parliament not only put on death row some of the small parties that flourished under the old system but also signed their own death warrant since few of those in office were likely to be reelected under the new system.

It was a democratic revolution. Public opinion, which acted as the main engine of change and reform and brought about early general elections in spring 1994, completely changed the political landscape. The Right-wing alliance, led by the media magnate Silvio Berlusconi, won a majority in the lower-house of Parliament and a plurality in the senate *(See Box on p. 78).* The election was a three-way contest involving the Freedom Pole, made up of *Forza Italia,* the separatist Northern League, and the neo-fascist National Alliance; the Center Pole, including the Pact for Italy and the Popular Party made up of former Christian Democrats; and the Left-wing Progressive Pole, composed of the Democratic Party of the Left, the hard-line Communist Refoundation, the Greens, and the anti-Mafia *La Rete.* Official overall election results showed the Right-wing coalition with 366 seats (155 to *Forza Italia,* 106 to Northern League, 105 to National Alliance) in the 630-seat lower house, an absolute majority, leaving its Leftist adversaries a poor second with 213 and Italy's formerly all-powerful centrists with only 46. Five seats went to representatives of smaller parties. In the senate, the Right wing fared less well, winning 155 of the 315 seats. The rejection of the old political structure was so strong that *Forza Italia,* whose name is the soccer chant "Go Italy!" and was founded only three months before the election, was the biggest vote-getter of the coalition. The neo-fascists, who for years hovered on the fringes of Italian politics with 5 or 6% of the vote but no significant representation, emerged with 12% of the votes and 105 seats in the lower house.

The new political stage had very soft ground because the Right-wing coalition did not cement together political forces having a lot in common. *Forza Italia* of Mr. Berlusconi favored tax cuts and a push to sell off Italy's bloated state-owned industrial sector; the Northern League, led by Umberto Bossi, wanted to distance the affluent north from the central government in Rome; and the neo-fascists, led by Gianfranco Fini, wanted a strong central authority while vaguely pressing claims to territory in the former Yugoslavia.

It should be said that Italian democracy was also experiencing the same situation as many other democracies: established political parties were in deep trouble, their legitimacy suspect, and their leader susceptible to attack by populists who preach simple, emotional answers to the complicated questions of the post-Cold-War age. With so much cynicism about conventional politics and politicians around, and with the traditional Left largely discredited after the collapse of communism in 1989, it is hardly surprising that outsiders—many of them self-made businessmen with enough money of their own to run campaigns that defy the long-dominant party machine—popped up. It is going to take some time for the new political forces to clarify their positions.

The success of Berlusconi's *Forza Italia* in the first parliamentary elections to be held under a predominantly majority electoral system suggests that these new political identities are far from solid. The election showed that while there are voters who strongly identify with a particular political formation, there has been the emergence of a large electorate whose sense of political belonging is not a central, important, and conscious feature of their lives. Public disillusionment with the political process as reflected in falling electoral turnout and party membership was symptomatic of a decline in strong political attachments and could be observed throughout the Western democracies in this period. For many, politics as a vocation became politics as spectacle. For the great majority, politics is experienced as an essentially passive activity that is almost dependent on media representations of political monologues or interviews between politicians and journalists. A more independent approach to politics by the voters became evident in the years to come. The outcome of the 2006 national elections, gave troubling results for the future of a stable government: Prodi's L'Unione coalition gained 158 seats in Italy's senate (the upper parliamentary house), compared to his rivals' 156 and won in the lower house (the chamber of deputies) by a mere 25,000 votes, even though it enjoys a wider majority of seats due to the "bonus seats" awarded to the winner.

It is not going to be an easy task for Prodi. He and his allies had promised to get Italy moving and to cut public debt levels that are amongst the highest in Europe. He had planned to cut payroll taxes by five percentage points, saving companies about 10bn euros per year in costs and in theory improving the efficiency of the workforce and making firms more willing to hire new staff.

However, at the behest of the communist parties that make up a key part of Prodi's alliance, they may try to repeal the "Biagi" law (approved under Berlusconi's government) that helped employers use more short-term working contracts and improved labor market flexibility. The far-Left factions of the alliance are also set to complicate any plans to privatize state industries and drive consolidation in areas such as banking. On pensions, one of the few areas that Berlusconi was credited with making some improvements, Prodi's alliance would abolish a law that had raised the retirement age to 60 from 57. Instead it would look for incentives for companies to keep employees working longer—a key factor in a nation where the birth rate is declining and the number of elderly is increasing.

Italy's political parties need to engage in serious dialogue, a real "historical compromise" to solve its problems and that is not going to be easy because political parties today are not grounded in strong political ideologies.

The Political Market-Place

Political parties no longer have the firm grip on cultural, social, and recreational associations they used to have. Not-for-profit organizations independent from the political parties have mushroomed in the last fifteen years. Many traditional party brokers who had turned their districts into personal fiefs are no longer around. With television conferring instant visibility upon those who are more telegenic and master more effectively the soundbite, new political personalities can surface at any time. In Parliament, the influence that political parties exert has diminished. In turn, this has engendered the expansion of the visibility and power of the president of the republic, the presidents of both chambers, judges, and more recently, mayors and governors of regions.

The new electorate has a new basic attitude not only toward politics but also toward the state. For one thing, the welfare state is dead in Italy, as is "liberal fundamentalism." Next to the anti-traditional party attitude there is a new pluralism, which seems to emphasize voluntarism rather than dependency on the state. The rise of a large number of interest groups and self-help associations, new in modern Italian society, indicates that traditional parties are no longer regarded as adequate in defining and satisfying one's needs. Many of these organizations do not have ideological ties or commitments to political institutions, and their members wish to make more "privatized" demands on the political system. For example, the aged are interested in pensions irrespective of their individual political affiliation; the same is true of the handicapped, single-parent families, women, alcoholics and drug addicts, consumer advocates, environmentalists, and many others who are preoccupied with problems of their immediate interest.

Although groups have emerged because of the anger and frustration people share over the failure of the state to deal adequately with problems of health, drug addiction, etc., and therefore should signal a greater predisposition toward self-help as opposed to waiting around for the state to solve problems, the formation of such organizations implies, in the Italian politicized climate, the creation of new political forces. In fact, on closer analysis, what may emerge as the underlying issue may not be an ineffective party system but rather a populace still too dependent upon government action. It often turns out that most of these groups really want governmental authorities to do more, not less. Notwithstanding the apparent lack of confidence in government, government is still expected to solve for society an astounding variety of problems. Italians' anti-government attitude is very complex: when citizen anger is tested on very important issues, the reaction is always pro-government!

In fact, when Italians have been called to vote in a referendum, a formal mechanism provided to the people by the constitution for expressing their judgment on legislative actions by parliament, they have never overturned a law enacted by parliament. It seems that Italians are fundamentally content in the specific sense that they are reluctant to reverse at the polls what their representatives have ironed out through the law-making process. It should also be pointed out that Italians have demonstrated a remarkable capacity to resist using the referendum for narrow self-interest. No better demonstration of this is offered than the 1985 vote on a law that had modified the *scala mobile* (cost-of-living increases based on inflation) to the disadvantage of wage-rated workers. To the surprise of many political experts, especially the communists who had campaigned against the measure, and who had anticipated that the electorate would "vote its pocketbook" as opposed to the "general welfare," the Italians demonstrated a high level of civic and political maturity by refusing to annul the new law. It seems that their dissatisfaction with the system had to do more with the natural attitude of people toward the "other," the abstract institutions, than with a deep-seated political lack of confidence.

However, political practices have changed. Italian politics has become more of a *spettacolo*, of a show. But the Italian political show always had a script. Even during the most chaotic years, Machiavelli was very much alive; political science has always been practiced with the flavor of an art. Political chaos has been avoided because the *spettacolo*, the political show, always has a script with a well established conclusion.

Italian politics becomes more "spectacular" during election time. Public policy often becomes paralyzed, giving way to campaign pontificating and made-for-TV symbolism. Politics *spettacolo* style, fitting very nicely with the Italian character, has become more "spectacular" with the use, misuse, and abuse of television. Indeed, because of the way TV use is manipulated, political discourse has become even more than before like a "show," a spectacle. In the world of "sound bite," where political discourse becomes more uniform, it is difficult for politicians to articulate an ideology to the wider public. Television has created difficulty not only for the parties in power but also for the force of opposition, whose entire outlook on communication had been based on the development of "alternative" information.

Yet, in Italy, the language of politics is still very intense because Italians are still passionately intense in conveying their messages. In the process of changing their political structures, Italians should not copy other forms of democracies. Democracies have to be assessed in their own terms, within their particular social, economic, and historical contexts. A people's history and culture, its economic conditions and social norms, its aspirations and its work-ways, its "national character," will affect the style and structure of its government. Democracy, by its nature, does not have a fixed form; within the same country, it has to be given the freedom to change. Italian democracy is changing to secure more stable governments.

Labor Unions: Crisis of Representation

Even Italy's labor unions, once powerful enough to paralyze the country and make governments fall, have gone through profound changes and are today suffering from lack of public support. A foreign visitor to a major Italian city, seeing streets often filled with demonstrating workers carrying banners with explosive language, might conclude that the unions are still powerful and poised on the brink of insurrection. He would be wrong. These protest marches tend to be little more than remnants of an old ritual, a way of showing the flag and making up for the unions' inability to carry out more effective action. Unions are still strong in public service but have become quite weak in industry and commerce. In the past the organized working class had a strong sense of "them and us," but the decline in trade union membership and the greater importance of nonunionized small firms in the labor market have meant that the workplace solidarity of the 1960s and 1970s has been all but lost. The southern migrant workers no longer form a separate and potentially militant subclass within the industrial cities of the north, and persistently high levels of unemployment, as elsewhere in Europe, have discouraged trade unions from taking industrial action that might result in redundancies or plant closures.

The weakening of labor unions was caused also by the expansion of the service sector, which is very different from the manufacturing industry. White-collar jobs are increasingly dominated by women, few of whom are unionized or in secure full-time employment. The nature of white-collar employment almost invariably requires a face-to-face relationship with managers and employers, and this inevitably results in a greater degree of control over the employees. White-collar workers (in Italy are *impiegati* rather than *lavoratori*) persistently iden-

PROFILE

Silvio Berlusconi

Silvio Berlusconi (born September 29, 1936–) became the new political face in Italy in 1994. His rise in the political arena was rapid. He was elected president of the council of ministers following the March 1994 elections, in which his centre-Right party *Forza Italia* gained a relative majority a mere three months after he founded it. He formed the first unabashedly Right-wing administration in 34 years. However, his cabinet collapsed after seven months, due to internal disagreements. In the 1996 elections, he was defeated by centre-Left candidate Romano Prodi, becoming instead the leader of the parliamentary opposition from 1996 to 2001. In the 2001 elections, he was again elected prime minister and formed his second and third governments, which together lasted five years—the longest in the history of the Italian republic. As leader of the centre-Right coalition in the May 2006 elections, he lost by a very narrow margin and was succeeded once again by Romano Prodi.

Berlusconi's politics are conservative. In economics, he endorsed lowering taxes and placing fewer constraints on enterprise to encourage growth. In foreign policy, his views were strongly pro-American, even at the expense of good relations with other European countries. He supported the U.S.-led 2003 invasion of Iraq by sending Italian troops to join the "Coalition of the Willing" (after the invasion, only for peacekeeping). In social policy matters, the Berlusconi government sponsored stricter laws concerning immigration, artificial insemination, and drug use.

The first of three children, Berlusconi was raised in an upper middle-class family in Milan. His father worked at a small bank. After attending boarding school, he studied law at the Università Statale in Milan, graduating cum laude in 1961. He has five children by two wives. Today Berlusconi owns a business empire that spans media, advertising, insurance, food, and construction. He is the founder and main shareholder of Fininvest. Among the ten largest privately owned companies in Italy, it includes three TV channels that account for nearly half the Italian TV market. After accumulating TV stations, Italy's largest publishing house Mondadori, and the leading daily newspaper *Il Giornale,* Berlusconi's business empire now encompasses nearly 150 companies. He began his business career developing garden apartments in the 1960s. His first entry into the media world was in 1973—a cable television station to service his residential development. He is also the president of A.C. Milan, a prominent Italian soccer team. According to *Forbes* magazine, Berlusconi is Italy's richest person, with personal assets worth $11 billion (USD) in 2006, making him the world's 37th richest person. Although Berlusconi officially resigned from all his commercial group's functions upon entering political office, he is still the largest shareholder and is perceived to have retained control.

Berlusconi elicits strong reactions. Supporters admire him for his tremendous success as a businessman. Detractors say that he concentrates too much power upon his person and attribute his financial success to his closeness to corrupt politicians. Critics say that he overreacts to political opponents, and some suspect that his media empire unfairly slants the news to support his views. Just about everyone agrees that he cares a great deal about his appearance. He is a true showman, with a permanent tan and beaming smile. He has yachts, villas, a glamorous second wife and three young children. His son and daughter from his first marriage, which ended in divorce, help run his companies. The Italians even have a word to describe his flamboyant lifestyle: *Berlusconismo*.

tify with parties of the center and Right rather than with the Left, and their values are highly aspirational: they do not want to overthrow the boss, they want to become the boss.

When life was very politicized, political parties worked to prevent the growth of associations and organized interests that would cut across the political divides. Former resistance fighters' groups, feminists, youth organizations, and all sorts of recreational entities were affiliated to parties. The connection between political parties and interest groups was particularly strong with unions.

Unions' Historical Success

During the years of profound social change, labor unions played a major role because like the trade unions in most European countries, and unlike those of the U.S., they have always been deeply politicized. Political motivation and ideological tradition have been more important than economic structure in determining union membership in Italy—as a result, union membership has greater civic significance in Italy than it might elsewhere.[9] Since the early postwar years, the two major labor confederations, *CGIL* (Italian General Confederation of Labor) and *CISL* (Italian Confederation of Workers' Union), became deeply enmeshed in the struggle between the communists and the Christian Democrats. In 1950, when the two unions were regarded as not offering enough choice, in the spirit of Italian democratic pluralism some of their leaders and workers left and formed a national union of their own, *UIL* (Italian Union of Labor), which made a point of stressing its independence not only from *CGIL* but from *CISL* as well.

The ability of unions to negotiate against employers was limited throughout the 1950s, due to the high unemployment levels. The situation started to change in the early part of the 1960s when labor shortages started to materialize and workers' desire to share in the expanding pie could be more easily met. By 1968, unions had grown dissatisfied with the ability of the center-Left government to introduce social reforms. The workers' and students' movements took to the streets with massive protests. From the "hot autumn" strike wave of 1969 to the mid-1970s, unions, displaying a particularly united front, scored many victories. In addition to getting wage increases that outstripped increases in productivity, the unions obtained the passing of the Workers' Statute in 1970 which, among other things, made laying off workers very difficult, protected student workers, and supported pro-union activities on the job.

By the early 1960s, the three unions had become a very strong political force in the nation and had been able to achieve some important social reforms. Later, in the "hot autumn" of

1969, during a long and bitter confrontation which involved labor, management, and the politicians as well, the unions won sizable wage increases, improvements in working conditions, and promises of concrete progress in availability of decent low cost housing, better schools, hospitals, and public transportation.

By 1969 the unions had forced through the legislature the Workers' Statute, one of the most advanced and, as it was interpreted, radical industrial relations policies ever enacted in the West. Even before this piece of legislation was passed, Italy provided exceptional levels of unemployment benefits and highly attractive compensation at the point of work severance. The statute came close to making the worker untouchable inside the workplace or, for that matter, outside of it. With the help of politically radicalized judges, laborers could be absent from work with impunity and still claim their pay. Job transfers or reclassification simply could not occur without the consent of the party involved. The slightest infraction on the part of management was an almost certain invitation to a work stoppage. Side by side with these guarantees went improvements in fringe benefits that were as costly to employers as they were instrumental in changing the workers' standard of living. In those years, workers came to believe that a steep upward climb in their condition had become a birthright and that even dismissal from one's job for cause was nothing more than a quaint relic of bygone capitalism.[10] Union demands and ideology of those years were based on the assumption that the institutions of government had to assure the equality of outcome rather than equality of opportunity. As Joseph La Palombara indicated, although Italians tend to doubt that all men are created equal, they tend to believe that the state can go a long way to assure equality of results, regardless of the structure of opportunity.[11]

Much additional bitterness and strife developed when the national labor contracts concluded at the end of 1969, and the new legislature had to be implemented at the local plant level. The major labor organizations found it increasingly difficult to deal with the wildcat strikes and the sabotage of production lines carried out by small numbers of workers inspired by radical Left-wing groups.

In the early 1970s, many Italian businessmen thought that the only way to conduct business was to arrange deals with organized labor, which had emerged with a vengeance from an all-too-long condition of weakness in a labor market traditionally marked by chronic unemployment and underemployment. Several of those businessmen engaged in dialogues with communist leaders because the party, which was gaining ground at the polls, maintained a strong hold on the biggest labor confederation, *CGIL*. An accord was negotiated in 1975 by Giovanni Agnelli, president of Fiat and of *Confindustria,* and Luciano Lama, the communist leader of *CGIL* A key clause introduced in contracts was the "rigid and pervasive wage indexation system." Big industrialists tolerated runaway inflation as long as the bill for its magnified impact could be passed on to their customers and to the taxpayers in general.

Labor Unions: Victims of Their Own Success

Labor had achieved such supremacy that in the 1975 agreement between organized labor and organized business it was established that the cost of living would be reviewed on a quarterly basis and wages adjusted upward to keep pace with inflation. The technical basis for making these adjustments, however, was such that, whereas the highest wage earners would just barely stay even with inflation, the lowest wage earners would realize wage improvements slightly above the inflation rate. Without fully anticipating such an outcome, the parties to this agreement put in motion a policy that over time brought about an unprecedented redistribution of income.

By 1980, however, Italian national labor unions were suffering from a self-inflicted mortal wound. The economic crisis of the early 1980s and fundamental changes, such as the downsizing of firms forced by foreign competition and the expansion of the service sector, were also weakening the three unions' positions. In early fall of that year, Fiat management decided to dismiss some 14,000 workers as part of its strategy to cope with a crisis that affected the automobile industry worldwide but which had been exacerbated by recent developments in the national labor field. The unions called a strike that lasted five weeks and was openly backed by the *PCI*. Berlinguer himself (the leader of the Communist Party) addressed the strikers in Turin, Fiat's headquarters, pledging his party's support if they occupied the plants. But the unions' opposition to any compromise collapsed when an estimated 40,000 workers, foremen, and employees marched through Turin shouting "Freedom to work!"

Organized labor had overreached itself and had failed to realize that the tide had turned. Many big and medium-sized industries felt encouraged to follow Fiat's example and started restructuring their plants and calling for sizable payroll cuts. Absenteeism dropped significantly, while production rose. A move away from the rigid indexation of income was undertaken by the Craxi government in February 1984, and the operation of the indexation mechanism was cooled off temporarily by an executive decree. This move was backed by the unions representing Catholic, social democratic, and republican workers as well as by the socialist wing of *CGIL*. But the *PCI* went on the warpath.

It should be pointed out that union membership is much more common in the more civic regions. In fact, union membership is roughly twice as high in those regions.[12]

Today the trade unions are in decline. In the space of a decade, the trade union movement went from a condition of unimagined power to one of precipitous decomposition. Like unions in other Western countries, those in Italy do not know how to adapt to the economic and social transformations that have occurred during the so-called second industrial revolution. The unions also ran afoul of developments that go beyond recession or economic and social change. Their earlier, heady successes contributed to their undoing. The conquests in favor of the working class did not produce a sense of gratitude to the labor confederations that engineered them. In addition, the use of robots operated by engineers in white smocks eliminated thousands of blue-collar workers. Moreover, the decline of the steel and shipbuilding industries and the fall in employment in publicly owned industries, also in trouble, are principal reasons for the erosion in labor's strength. Large-scale industry in general has also declined. Today over half of all workers are found in firms of fewer than 20 employees and such places are notoriously difficult to unionize.

Protests have become fragmented, with sectional interests prevailing. Instead of long strikes, the unions tend to organize one-day token stoppages, which make them appear strong and militant but achieve little; they are a safety-valve for discontent. The old saying "their bark is worse than their bite" well characterizes the labor unions of today. Trade unions have seen their authority increasingly threatened by the rank-and-file organization of separate categories of workers and the strength of the local groups. The *COBAS* (*comitati di base*) have mobilized different groups of workers and of the *ceti medi* (middle classes) with notable militancy, but without the ability to achieve, or indeed even to seek a unifying strategy. The rise of unemployment in traditional labor-intensive industries that once were union bastions and the anti-system mood of the country that has changed the political structure have also affected the once very strong politicized labor unions.

The unions have not been able to suggest acceptable solutions to unemployment, which is one of the most crucial problems of the nation. The claims of some conservatives that the unemployed have little incentive to look for another job quickly because high benefits are breeding laziness, and that many people were earning more on the dole than others in jobs, are certainly unfair. Most recognize, however, that the unemployment crisis is not due solely to outside economic factors; it is also structural, linked to changes in technology. The Italians, like others in highly advanced technological nations, will have to learn to live with a high level of unemployment if some social adjustments are not made. The burden can be shared more evenly by a shortened work week so that more jobs are available. As it is now, rising unemployment has led to less job security and elimination of redundancies.

Notes

1. In the fight against a communist threat in Italy, an important role was played by the Pope family in the U.S. In the immediate postwar period, mainly through the *Progresso Italo-Americano* (the major American daily in Italian language) and the radio station *WHOM,* the Pope family carried on a passionate campaign against a communist takeover of Italy. The *Progresso* organized a letter-to-Italy campaign among its readers and printed a series of alarming articles about the consequences of a possible communist takeover. This resulted in the dispatch of thousands of letters from Americans of Italian origin to relatives and friends in Italy urging them to reject Russian blandishments.

2. Since the PSI and the PCI together received more votes than the DC, they decided to unite in 1948 to form the Popular Democratic Front (FDP). The FDP won the municipal elections in Pescara with a 10% increase in their vote compared to the results of 1946. The new party expected to win the upcoming general elections in a similar manner. The 1948 general elections were heavily influenced by the U.S. as part of their ongoing effort to fight communism. In order to influence the election, the U.S. agencies undertook a campaign of writing ten million letters, made numerous short-wave radio broadcasts of what the U.S. felt would be the consequences of a communist victory. The CIA also funded the center-Right political parties and was accused of publishing forged letters in order to discredit the leaders of the *PCI*. This propaganda campaign proved successful as the Christian Democrats won the 1948 election with

48% of the vote, while the FDP only received 31% of the vote. The communists would never win a general election.

3. Posters from the Cold War period vary a good deal stylistically, from the scatological to the eschatological. The majority contain a very dramatic content, to the effect that Italy must choose between the forces of good and evil in this moment of apocalyptic crisis. This is achieved partly by drawing on images from the Book of Revelation, which deals with the final separation of good and evil.

4. J. K. Galbright, *The Culture of Contentment* (Boston: Houghton Mifflin, 1922); and G. Thurborn, *Why Some People Are More Unemployed Than Others* (London: Verso, 1986).

5. C. Schmitt, *The Concept of the Political* (New Brunswick, N.J.: Rutgers U.P., 1976).

6. David A. Caputo, "Italy's Parliamentary Elections: A New Direction or Only Minor Deviations from the Past?" *Italian Journal,* 6, no. 2 & 3 (1992): 3.

7. The 1992–93 corruption scandals, known as *tangentopoli* ("bribesville"), and the new electoral rules brought about a major realignment in the post-World War II Italian party system: the extent of change was of such magnitude that some historians refer to the post-1993 state of affairs in Italy as the "Second Republic," distinct from the 1946–93 "First Republic."

   Under the so-called "First Republic," Italian governments had been coalitions of the Christian Democrats and one or more of the smaller centrist or left-of-center parties—including the Italian Socialist Party from 1963 onwards—or single-party Christian Democratic minority governments. Unlike in other European nations, there was no alternation in power between Right and Left: instead, all governments were essentially centrist (or center-left) in orientation. This unusual situation resulted from the presence of a very strong Italian Communist Party (*PCI*), which had been the second largest political force in the country since 1948. For a long time, the *DC* and its allies sought to keep the *PCI* out of power because it was regarded as an "anti-system" party, committed to the destruction (or at least a radical alteration) of the existing social and political order. The *PCI*'s attempts to portray a more moderate image were met with skepticism and suspicion about its real goals.

   However, as communism collapsed in Eastern Europe and the Soviet Union, the *PCI* transformed itself into the non-communist *Partito Democratico della Sinistra* (*PDS*; Party of the Democratic Left) in 1991, but this change of name and orientation was the last straw for hard-line communists, who broke away to establish the *Partito della Rifondazione Comunista* (PRC; Communist Refoundation Party).

   The *PCI* was not the only "anti-system" party, as there were several minor political movements to its left, and most importantly, a major neo-fascist party on the far right, the Italian Social Movement-National Right (*MSI-DN*), which had absorbed the Monarchists in 1972. Like the *PCI*, the *MSI* had been regarded as a political pariah, although much more so than the communists, partly because it never had an electoral following as large as the former, but largely because of the historical dimension of its extremist ideological orientation, namely the 1922–43 period of fascist rule in Italy under the dictatorship of Benito Mussolini.

   As a result of the ongoing corruption probes, public opinion quickly turned against the ruling parties, which suffered heavy losses in municipal elections held throughout Italy in 1993.

8. The proportional representation procedures introduced in 1993 differ significantly from the electoral system used from 1948 to 1992, under which members of the chamber of deputies were elected by a two-tier PR system in multi-member electoral districts, formed by groups of provinces—with the exception of Valle d'Aosta, represented in the chamber by one member elected by simple majority. District seats were apportioned by dividing the number of votes obtained by each list by the *Imperiali* quota, calculated by dividing the total number of valid votes cast in the district by the number of deputies to be elected, plus two. Any unallocated seats and unused party list votes at the district level were then collected on a national pool, where the seats were proportionally distributed among party lists with no less than three-hundred thousand votes and at least one multi-member district seat, according to the overall number of unused votes accumulated by each qualifying party list. National pool seats won by a

party were then allocated among its district lists. Party lists were open, and voters could cast preferential votes for up to three candidates until 1991, and for a single candidate in 1992.

Finally, it should be pointed out that while the four percent nationwide threshold reduced to five the number of lists which received proportional seats, the coalition deals within both the House of Freedoms and the Olive Tree allowed the smaller parties affiliated to these cartels to win chamber seats in the single-member colleges—seats they would have had practically no chance of winning by themselves. In this manner, the smaller parties managed to get around the four percent threshold, securing parliamentary representation in rough proportion to their voting strength. In fact, despite the introduction of plurality voting in Italian parliamentary elections, the political party system remains as fragmented as ever.

9.   Salvatore Coi, "Sindacati in Italia: iscritti, apparato, finanziamento," *Il Mulino* 28 (1987): 201–42, quotation from p. 206.

10. For an overview of the labor union achievements of those years, see Tiziano Treu, ed., *L'uso politico dello statuto dei lavoratori* (Bologna: Il Mulino, 1975).

11. La Palombara, 55.

12. Putnam, 107.

Bibliography

Amato, G. *Una politica riformare.* Bologna: Il Mulino, 1980.

Brosio, G. *Equilibri instabili.* Turin: Boringhieri, 1994.

Bufacchi, V., and Burgess, S. *Italy Since 1989—Events and Interpretations.* New York: St. Martin's Press, 1998.

Calandra, P. *Il governo della repubblica.* Bologna: Il Mulino, 1986.

Cassese, S. *Esiste un governo in Italia?* Rome: Officina, 1988.

Cassese, S., and Franchini, C. , eds. *L'amministrazione pubblica italiana. Un profilo.* Bologna: Il Mulino, 1994

Certoma, G. L. *The Italian Legal System.* London: Butterworth, 1985.

Di Palma, G. *Surviving Without Governing: The Italian Parties in Parliament.* Berkeley: University of California Press, 1977.

Duggan, C., and Wagstaff, C. *Italy in the Cold War—Politics, Culture and Society 1948–58.* Oxford: Berg, 1995.

Ferrera, M. *Modelli di solidarietà: politica e riforme sociali nelle democrazie.* Bologna: Il Mulino, 1993.

Furlong, P. *Modern Italy. Representation and Reform.* London: Routledge, 1994.

Galbright, J. K., *The Culture of Contentment* (Boston: Houghton Mifflin, 1922).

Guarnieri, C. *L'indipendenza della magistratura.* Padova: Cedam, 1981.

Leonardi, R., and Nanetti, R. Y. *The Regions and European Integration. The Case of Emilia-Romagna.* London: Pinter, 1991.

Thurborn, G. *Why Some People Are More Unemployed Than Others* (London: Verso, 1986).

Schmitt, C. *The Concept of the Political* (New Brunswick, N.J.: Rutgers U.P., 1976).

CHAPTER 3

DANGERS TO THE STATE

Plots and Terrorism

The Italian state has been under a cloud of suspicion not so much for the kind of system it is governed by as for the kind of people who have been in government and for the presence of organizations that are corroding the social, political, and economic fibers of the nation. Given the fragility of its government and the openness of its political system, Italy became fertile ground for terrorist activity and for political forces from extreme ends of the political spectrum. Contrary to the emphasis on ultra-Left activities by media in the U.S., elements of ultra-conservative groups were also a threat to the Italian state from the beginning of the 60s to the end of the 80s.

Domestic Dangers from the Right

The political terrorism began with the weakening of the political parties that had formed the government coalition up to the beginning of the 1960s and the need to broaden the coalition by including new political forces. With the admission of the socialists into government in December, 1963, and the consequent beginning of a new era of social and economic reforms which caused an artificially created atmosphere of panic, elements of the political forces of the right worked to counteract these changes. Some were definitively unconstitutional.

Probably the most notorious attempt by the Right to overthrow the government was made by General Giovanni di Lorenzo, commander of the *Carabinieri* Corps and a former chief of military counter-espionage (*SIFAR*). He had arranged for the arbitrary arrest and deportation of numerous political personalities by a select group of *Carabinieri* officers. These officers, told to stand by for the order to proceed, had been given to understand that di Lorenzo was acting on personal instructions from the president of the republic—and without the knowledge of the ministers of defense and the interior. The plan would have remained a secret if the magazine *L'Espresso*, did not make the revelation and a parliamentary inquiry into the misuse of *SIFAR* funds and dossiers for political espionage and blackmail was not ordered after a great deal of hedging by the government behind the screen of national security. Although most Italians discounted the possibility of a Right-wing take-over in Italy, they were shocked to realize that, if the political will for such action were forthcoming, the co-operation of the police and the military would not be hard to obtain.

The crisis created by the panic of the entrance of the socialists in government in December 1963 faded quickly. Social reforms were carried out slowly and with moderation until popular pressure for wider social reform became uncontrollable.

The Students Revolt

By the late 1960s, domestic order was challenged on several fronts. As long as the Communist Party had a monopoly on Marxist culture, the state had not had any problems maintaining civil order. But things changed in the late 1960s when that monopoly was seriously challenged and eventually fractured by the student revolts. Extremist groups of the left accused the *PCI* of being revisionist and reformist, authoritarian and bureaucratic in a bourgeois way. The 1968 and 1969 student revolts made the situation worse: anarchist and radical-Left terrorist organizations fomented disorder at several universities and openly clashed on the streets with neo-fascist and far-right groups. This took place in a climate of declining economic conditions and national political stalemate, while various labor unions engaged in strikes and disorders. During the "hot autumn of 1969" the whole Italian society seemed to be in upheaval. The student movement presented a set of political demands that had to be answered by all Italian political parties. It was not just a protest against the alienating character of the capitalist-consumer society but a specific protest against the authoritarian, paternalistic, hierarchical structure of Italian society and of Italian universities, which students took to be mirrors and instruments of the 'system.' The movement became a major political phenomenon and shaped, either directly or indirectly, the crisis of Italian society: from terrorism to the women's movement, from dissent within the

Church to the birth of a host of small Left-wing parties and to the radicalization of large groups of intellectuals and middle-class radicals. The uprisings in southern Italy, the prison revolts, the demonstrations and strikes in the North all owe something to the new spirit of criticism that came out of the universities and the lycées.

The student movement had profound influence. The pressures on government were so strong that many of the reforms the students demanded were granted even before laws were passed. Something radical had happened: once so respectful of authority, so anxious to get ahead with the help of protection and recommendations in a society where influence was all, youth was now questioning the structure of that society. Some of the unionists formed anarchist and radical-Leftist groups similar to those of the students, and these labor extremist groups also engaged the neo-fascists in street battles.

Revolutionary Organizations of the Left

By the mid-1970s many small revolutionary organizations that had emerged from the youth movement entered into a period of crisis. Organizations such as *Avanguardia Operaia* (The Workers' Vanguard), *Potere Operaio* (Workers' Power), and *Lotta Continua* (The Struggle Goes On) had been unable to establish a significant presence in the labor movement. The crisis of these organizations was in large part due to their unsuccessful attempts to subvert the system by using traditional instruments, the political parties. All this was happening while the Communist Party (*PCI*) was anticipating an entrance into government. The intended move was a democratic one: to provide the country with a radical reforming government without pushing a large section of middle-class groups and other social forces into positions of overt hostility. In order to achieve a political majority, the *PCI* sought to forge an alliance with the Catholic masses and enter into a compromise with the Christian Democrats (*DC*). The *PCI* realized that a mere electoral or mathematical majority was not sufficient for its legitimization and that it needed to offer some guarantee that its presence in government would not signify a shift in the balance of forces between East and West to the disadvantage of the West. The flirtation was working well; in July 1976, for the first time since the break-up of the tripartite coalition of 1947 (the first historic compromise), a *DC* prime minister, Giulio Andreotti, appealed to the *PCI* to support his government in Parliament. At the local level, cooperation between communists and Christian Democrats was becoming commonplace, and by June 1977 a wide-ranging government program had been agreed to among the *DC,* the *PCI,* and the other parties.

While engaging in a work of compromise with the *DC,* the *PCI* had to react to the students' unrest. Although its initial response was hostile to the student movement and although one of its leaders, Giorgio Amendola, asserted that it was necessary to fight on two fronts, i.e., against the government and against the students, the party leader, Luigi Longo, was much more flexible.[1] Longo recognized that it was also the *PCI*'s fault if there was such a wide gulf between the party and the students, that the party had become too sectarian and too bureaucratic and that the importance and political autonomy of the student movement had to be recognized. This strategy implied two objectives: on the one hand, the party was trying to fragment the student movement paradoxically by showing sympathy for the student cause; on the other hand, it was sending the message that the only source of legitimate power in Italy was to be found in political parties.

Aldo Moro, secretary of the Christian Democratic Party, found executed by the Red Brigades in Rome. Printed by coutesy of *America Oggi.*

Though not in government, the *PCI* seemed to have become a party of government and, in the eyes of the extreme left, a partner of the established power. For the militant groups, the *PCI* had become a progressive force by betraying its basic revolutionary principles; not only had it sold out by compromising with the *DC,* but it had also entered a policy of complete subordination.

For the ultra-Left, therefore, the *PCI* had become another enemy of the people, and it was their duty to assume the role of defenders of the oppressed. On the other side of the political aisle it was clear that the *DC* had a strategy to transform the *PCI* into a harmless movement for reform, which would bring its supporters and the masses it inspired under the political hegemony of a new governing coalition led by the *DC.*

The radical Left acted to prevent this. From December 1969 to the mid-1980s, politically motivated bombings, murders, and kidnappings became a recurring feature of Italian life. Observers estimated that over 14,000 terrorist acts were committed between 1969 and 1985. Hundreds of Italians were kidnapped, "kneecapped," wounded, or killed. Most affected were those who represented the establishment: university professors, judges, generals, industrialists, politicians.

All terrorist groups of the ideological Left shared the same goal—the overthrow of the bourgeois, capitalist, "imperialist state" and the establishment of the dictatorship of the proletariat. They also tried to bring the *PCI* back into the fold of revolutionary ideology. This was to be accomplished not only through the dissemination of Marxist-Leninist propaganda but also through attacks on the property of industrialists, as well as kidnapping and assassinations.

The Red Brigades

The Red Brigades (or *Brigate Rosse, BR*) were the best known of the Left-wing terrorist groups to operate in those years. To demonstrate their contempt for the democratic state, on March 16, 1978, the *Brigate Rosse* kidnapped Aldo Moro, the party secretary of the *DC* and promoter of the "historical compromise" and, therefore, supporter of communist participation in government. The terrorist group considered Moro nothing more than a tool of the "imperialistic"

American multinationals. The Red Brigades's act was clearly a declaration of war against the state; the state was under siege. As in other critical moments, Italian politicians, through skillful maneuvering, preserved the democracy and defended the state. After intense discussions on how to respond, the government refused to negotiate with the terrorists.

Unfortunately, the mass media became deeply involved in this event. As in many other instances, the mass media played their role as a vehicle for the gathering and diffusion of information, but in this case they also acted as a protagonist that managed to instrumentalize the tragedy to its own purpose. The public and the state learned through the mass media, which like to play on the emotions of people, all the developments of the case. Because of this the Moro case became a memorable example of politics as spectacle. The killing of the five bodyguards in the ambush and the eventual murder of Moro himself, after 40 long days of tension, shook the nation. The explosion of terrorism led the *PCI* to accept new anti-terrorist legislation. Even though the intention was to uphold the democratic principles of the state and of the constitution, the *PCI* could not avoid appearing to the extremist groups as the defender of the entire edifice of the Italian state with its corruption, degeneration, and bigotry. It was accused by many on the Left of espousing anti-libertarian causes purely in order to become part of the government.

Paradoxically, rather than solidify the *PCI* position, the Moro killing put an end to the historic compromise, for the Red Brigades had destroyed the key man who could have paved the way for the entry of the *PCI* into the government. In the wake of the Moro killing, as well as other *BR* murders, 63 members of the *BR* were eventually arrested and put on trial. The Moro experience brought together the political, juridical, and military forces of the nation in a solid bloc which in skillful cooperation mustered one of the most sophisticated anti-terrorist systems in the world.

The first proof that Italy was able to deal with terrorism came in December 1981. The kidnapping of General Dozier, then deputy chief of staff for logistics and administration at NATO Allied Land Forces Southern Europe, headquartered in Verona, was foiled when the State Police arrested the captors and freed the general in a counter-terrorism blitz. By this time the Italian government had created a special force, "the skin heads," to deal with terrorism.

However, other incidents shook up the country before the nation could start to relax. In broad daylight on the campus of the University of Rome, two members of the *BR's* Roman Column gunned down Ezio Tarantelli, a professor of economics. Tarantelli was targeted because he was the author of modifications in the *scala mobile* that the Craxi government eventually adopted as official policy. The "freeze" that Tarantelli's plan placed on wage increases was perceived by the *BR* as an act against the working class. Similarly, Gen. Licio Giorgieri, assassinated in March 1987, was singled out because of his responsibilities in NATO and the space defense program. The victims were individuals who could be associated with the established power structure or its defenders.

The last major domestic terrorist act came in May 1999 with the murder of Massimo D'Antona, an adviser to Italy's labor minister, by individuals claiming to be from the Red Brigades, although the Leftist group had been dormant since 1988. In response, Prime Minister

D'Alema said that Italy had let down its guard on domestic terrorism in the mistaken belief that homegrown terrorist groups no longer posed a danger. He added that Rome was now working hard to identify and neutralize the group that killed D'Antona.

In spite of that attack, Italy achieved some success against domestic terrorism during the 90s. Italian law enforcement and judicial officials arrested and sentenced several individuals tied to terrorist groups, while magistrates requested that many more cases be opened in the year 2000. A notable success for Italian security was a raid against the instigators of the demonstration in May 1999 at the U.S. Consulate in Florence protesting NATO airstrikes in Kosovo. The instigators included several members of the Red Brigades, *Lotta Continua* (The Struggle Goes On), and the COBAS Union.

Right-Wing Terrorists

During the red terrorism described above, the state had also to face the threats posed by neo-fascist Right-wing terrorist groups. These groups were more difficult to deal with because they lacked organizational sophistication and murdered indiscriminately. Since their objectives were to show the weakness of the state in handling violent political crime and social chaos and to create the maximum possible fear, intimidation, and panic, they placed bombs in piazzas, in trains, aircraft, and railroad stations, without making claims for their actions.

Typical of the Right-wing terrorist groups was the Armed Revolutionary Nuclei (*Nuclei Armati Rivoluzionari—NAR*), a neo-fascist organization that authorities have held responsible for major bomb explosions and for the killing of its political opponents. The most terrible tragedy was the carnage caused by a bomb that exploded in Bologna's railroad station on August 2, 1980, killing eighty-five people. This was the peak of the cycle of right-wing terrorism, although not the end to violence. Another neo-fascist group, New Order/Black Order (*Ordine Nuovo/Ordine Nero*), claimed responsibility for a bomb attack on the Milan-Naples express train on December 23, 1984, which killed several people.

International Terrorism

Because of its strategic position in the Mediterranean, Italy also became the stage for acts of international terrorism. The most shocking act was the attempted assassination of Pope John Paul II on May 13, 1981. Efforts to establish the motivation for the plot were inconclusive, but some evidence suggested an attempt by the Bulgarian secret police, presumably acting on behalf of the KGB, to stifle the resurgence of the Roman Catholic Church in Eastern Europe.

Another incident that attracted international attention was the fall 1985 hijacking of the Italian cruise ship, the *Achille Lauro,* while it was sailing the Mediterranean and the murder of

❊ SPIRIT

The Eighties

In the 1980s, the Christian Democratic Party's hegemony as a political force ended. In 1981 Giovanni Spadolini, a member of the Republican Party, became prime minister. He was followed in 1983 by Bettino Craxi, a member of the Socialist Party, who served until 1987. By the end of the 80s the Italian political landscape had changed considerably (thanks also to the collapse of the Berlin Wall in 1989). The old political parties either vanished or changed their names while new political parties emerged. The Northern League made its debut under the leadership of Umberto Bossi and gradually gained power by taking strong federalist positions and an anti-immigrant stand. In 1986 the *Partito dei Verdi*, the Green Party, emerged on the scene.

Meanwhile Italian society had become increasingly more secular. Divorce and abortion were on the rise; so too were civil marriages and instances of unmarried couples living together. In 1984, the Italian government, under Craxi's leadership, revised the Pacts of Lateran with the Church and reestablished the separation between Church and state. However, in this period as well, the veneration for a Capuchin monk, Padre Pio (1887–1968), intensified, reaching a level of worship never before experienced in the twentieth century. His beatification in 1999 and canonization in 2002, and the millions of worshipers who continue to take pilgrimages to his native town (Pietrelcina, Benevento), confirm that the Catholic faith is still strong in Italy, even though obedience to Catholic Church policy and rules may be weak.

At the beginning of the 80s Italy was still recovering from the economic slump of the second part of the 70s and the uncertain political climate resulting from political terrorism. Political terrorism had been brought under control; however, the fight against the Mafia was not successful. Several special prosecutors and judges were killed.

The attention of the general public was directed toward becoming part of the new affluence that was engulfing the country. The big industries, reacting to the high labor costs that resulted from the 1970 workers' statute, opened factories abroad and subcontracted some work to smaller industries (firms with fewer than 15 employees were not affected by the workers' statute). The impact of this approach was profound: it encouraged a new culture of small-scale entrepreneurship, and the family-owned firm became the engine of the Italian economy for the next generation. The previous dream of many Italians, of having a secure job in civil service, became a dream of growing wealthier by taking chances and working harder. The introduction of robots in industry helped to reduce the number of blue-collar workers, which contributed to the weakening of the labor unions. At the same time, as agriculture and manufacturing continued to lose people, the service sector emerged as the largest economic sector.

The pursuit of personal advance reduced citizens' interest in political life and in the common good. Participation in elections and adherence to benevolence associations went down. The faith in a consumer society became connected with a new cult for personal beauty: physical exercise (especially jogging), gyms, fashion, and diet became increasingly popular. Hedonism became almost a new religion.

one of its Jewish American passengers. The incident led to a major international crisis when the Italian government permitted the pro-Palestinian hijackers to escape after U.S. military jets forced the Egyptian plane carrying the terrorists to land at a NATO base at Sigonella, Sicily. The incident also sparked a series of government crises. The moderately independent stand vis-à-vis the United States adopted by Craxi and the Christian Democratic foreign minister, Andreotti, antagonized the Republican defense minister, Spadolini, who adopted a pro-American and anti-Palestine Liberation Organization (PLO) position during the affair. Spadolini also felt he had not been adequately consulted before a PLO official, Abu Abbas (described by American officials as masterminding the hijacking), had been hastily released from Italian custody. For the first time, an Italian government fell largely as the result of an international incident.

International terrorism struck again a few months later, in December 1985, when a pro-Palestinian group fired on a crowd of passengers in the Rome Airport terminal, killing thirteen people.

The Post 9/11 Era

Italy is very much concerned about international terrorism threats coming from the Islamic world and has been playing a strong role in their prevention by trying to find the right balance in being reactive and proactive. While being a strong ally of the U.S., the Italian government is trying to maintain friendly relations with the Middle Eastern countries.

According to the Italian intelligence service, Osama Bin Laden's Al Qaeda organization is moving deep into Italy's organized crime. It is suspected that hundreds of Al Qaeda operatives are being sent to Northern Europe through a maze of safe houses belonging to the Neapolitan *Camorra,* a Naples-based criminal network akin to the Mafia in Sicily.

According to Italian investigative sources, the *Camorra* helps Al Qaeda obtain forged documents and weapons for its operatives, who disembark almost daily from ships connecting Italy to the Arab countries of North Africa: Algeria, Morocco, Tunisia, and Egypt. In addition, in exchange for substantial cargoes of narcotics, these operatives are moved through *Camorra*'s connections from Naples to Rome, Bologna, Milan, and eventually to other major European cities such as Paris, London, Berlin, and Madrid. "The connections are there and real," says Michele del Prete, a district attorney investigating the Algerian Islamic Brotherhood in Italy, "and the exchange currency cementing those trades is drugs." The new Al Qaeda arrivals are swallowed by Naples' intricate network of alleys called *vicoli,* where traditional craft shops and street-level houses mix with computer stores, Chinese bazaars, pizzerias, merchant stalls, illegal casinos, antique boutiques, churches, and museums.

According to a report by DIGOS, Italy's political crime unit, the number of Al Qaeda operatives who have sought refuge in Naples or have passed through the city on their way to Northern Europe in the last five years may exceed 1,000. The magnitude of this convergence has been recognized also by the United States, which recently moved the western headquarters of the Foreign Counter Intelligence (FCI)—the Naval Criminal Investigative Service's office for counter-espionage and counter-terrorism—to Aversa, Italy.

A town outside Naples with a large blue-collar and underemployed population, Aversa in the past has been prime recruiting ground for Italian *terroristi* and political hotheads. From Aversa, FCI now scrutinizes terrorist activities from Scandinavia to South Africa. Italians, in the meantime, are drawing lessons from their fight against the Mafia to devise new ways to combat Al Qaeda in Italy.

Italy has continued its exemplary work against terrorism, disrupting suspected terrorist cells and capturing A1 Qaeda suspects in Milan and elsewhere who were providing support to terrorist operations and planning attacks. An Italian court sentenced members of the Tunisian Combatant Group to prison terms, marking the first conviction of Al Qaeda associates in Europe since September 11, 2001. Members of the New Red Brigades, an offshoot of the once-powerful entity that disrupted Italian life in the 1970s, are suspected of the murder of an adviser to the Italian government in 2004. Other terrorist groups also carried out several small-scale attacks.

The government's various anti-terrorist operations have brought 203 arrests in the last four years and notably included the capture of Hamdi Issac Adus, one of the men charged with being behind an attack on the London bus and subway system in July 2005. On this occasion, the Italian police demonstrated the effectiveness of the investigative measures introduced under new legislation rushed through to combat international terrorism. Specifically, these include the granting of residence permits for foreigners co-operating with the judicial authorities, more powers to interview detainees in relation to investigations concerning terrorism, more stream-lined deportation procedures of those suspected of aiding terrorist cells, and new regulations regarding arrest and detention, proof of identity, and the use of false documents.

The state won the battle against domestic terrorism. In more ways than Italians themselves may have anticipated, terrorism brutally tested the proposition that Italy's democracy, at bottom, is a strong, healthy institution. Because the preservation of high-level democracy in a pluralistic society may require special security measures, Italians have adapted to a new style of living. Whether stoically enduring long lines outside security entrances to state offices, banks, and other public places or voluntarily lavishing money on private security systems, Italians have quickly responded that freedom, whatever the price, has to be preserved.

Ordinary Crime: Too Ordinary

While Italians are justifiably proud of their ability to control terrorism, they are frustrated by the persistence of ordinary crime. However, it must be stated that crime, in general, has considerably decreased in the last five years.

The number of murders over the last four years has been lower than in the two previous four-year periods. Under the Berlusconi government, between July 2001 and June 2005, the number of murders was down by 28.2% compared to the July 1997—June 2001 period. Theft, meanwhile, fell by 4% overall, with car theft down 25.4%, burglary down 33%, pick-pocketing down 11%, and bag-snatching down 22%. Bank robbery dropped by 12.7% and post office robbery by 16.5%.

Before 1969 kidnapping for ransom and armed robbery tended to occur infrequently except in Sardinia, Sicily, and Calabria, but by the mid-1970s it was a serious problem through-out the country and became a major concern for the Italian public. In 1977, for example, over sixty kidnappings occurred, involving members of wealthy families and political figures. In fact, some of the moneyed class moved away from Italy in fear of kidnappings, while others increased personal security through bodyguards and armored vehicles.

The easy availability of heroin from the Mafia network (discussed in the next section) was viewed as a major reason for the upsurge of crime. The Italian narcotics epidemic had become more virulent than in most other European countries. In Rome, considered Italy's drug capital, heroin, marijuana, and hashish could be purchased openly in many streets and piazzas all over the city, and any streetwise teenager knew what the going price was for any illegal drug. Used syringes could be found any day in most parks and along the banks of the Tiber.

People died every month from overdoses, and the authorities seized hundreds of pounds of heroin and other substances. The situation became so critical that in January 1993, to cope with the failure of its tough drug law, which filled prisons with addicts and did little to reduce consumption, the government decriminalized the personal use of drugs. Instead of prison terms, the new law imposed administrative sanctions—including loss of driver's license, gun permits, and passports—for drug users. Today the situation has improved because of the many education programs against drug use run by state and local agencies as well as by private not-for-profit organizations.

Organized Crime: Weak State and Lack of Civic Maturity

Probably the most serious threat to the internal security of Italy is posed by organized crime, as embodied in the Mafia of Sicily, the *Camorra* of Naples, and the *'Ndrangheta* in Calabria. These organizations are not inventions of Mario Puzo, Hollywood, or the mass media. The title of an article, "What Happened to Heroes Is a Crime," that appeared in the Book Review of the *New York Times* on October 14, 1990, is significant: for lack of positive heroes, we create bad ones. Mobsters do not need mystification. Organized crime wields economic and social, as well as political, power, which has a destructive effect on people and their institutions. In areas where the Mafia and other criminal organizations are strongest, the GDP growth rate is the lowest, a testimonial to their sapping effect on entrepreneurship and rates of return.

Mussolini had almost eradicated the Mafia in the 1930s by using draconian police methods such as torture and summary execution. However, in a belief that its power could be used in the struggle against the Nazis, it was reinstated in Sicily during WWII by the American Mafia in alliance with the U.S. Armed Forces and regained its influence not only through the collection of "protection money" for guarding property, irrigation systems, and fishing fleets but also through greater involvement in urban economic affairs. Until the 1970s the Mafia prospered within the *DC* system of power in the south; in turn, it was at the service of politicians. It delivered votes and financed political campaigns. In exchange it obtained local contracts and was allowed to develop protection rackets.[2]

The explosion of social conflict in the late 1960s and early 1970s had an effect on the Mafia's behavior. Since the state was preoccupied with the control of these conflicts and showed signs of weakness, the Mafia seized the opportunity to become an independent economic force and its own master. Old techniques were resurrected in order to finance modern economic activities. Using force, it operated as a parasitic middleman between owners and workers, between producers and consumers, between citizens and the state. Not only did the Mafia gain control of the wholesale market for vegetables, meat, and fish and engage in cigarette smuggling as well as real estate speculation, but it

Terrorists of the Right bombed the Bank of Agriculture in Milan in 1978, causing 13 deaths and almost 100 wounded. Printed courtesy of *America Oggi*.

also attempted to acquire a share of the vast resources the state was sending to the South for economic development in its attempt to face the social conflicts and the wave of terrorism.

However, the decisive factor in the spread of the Mafia was the drug trade, of which it was the primary operator. By the mid-1970s heroin traffic had become an enterprise of authentic multinational dimensions: first opium is imported from Pakistan, Afghanistan and Iran, transformed into morphine in the Middle East and into heroin in Sicily, and eventually transported to the U.S. and other advanced industrial countries. Italy itself, especially wealthy northern cities such as Milan, Turin, Verona, and Genoa, also became a lucrative end market for hard drugs. The enormous profits in successful drug deals provided the Sicilian *mafiosi* and their allies with tremendous influence. The Mafia drug tycoons used their money to buy flashy cars, build sumptuous villas, and enter legal businesses and industries. Many credit institutions in Italy and Switzerland and offshore fiscal havens were only too happy to handle all that cash, thereby becoming instrumental in money-laundering schemes. The expansion of the Sicilian banking system was also linked to Mafia involvement in narcotics. According to most estimates, by the late 1980s, the Italian Mafia earned enough money to have covered Italy's $125 billion debt.[3]

The vast sums of money at stake and the greed of the *mafiosi* brought about a new level of violence. In the old times, a local "honored man" did not very often have to order one of his hitmen to fire the *lupara* at some landowner who would not pay protection money or to eliminate some traitor who had started carrying out robberies on his own. Instead, the Mafia could secure compliance with its orders through a simple warning by a go-between or a more tangible form of intimidation. The organization traditionally preferred to cooperate with local officials rather than oppose them openly or have them killed. Before the late 1960s, attacks on journalists, parliamentarians, police, judges, attorneys, and other representatives of public institutions were unthinkable. Rival Mafia clans instead fought one another; sometimes whole families were wiped out. A kind of Darwinian process regulated their existence. In the 1990s, however, the Mafia entered a new era.

The change came about with the Mafia's entry into the heroin business, and with the streams of billions of liras that the Italian government has been channeling to the Southern regions as financial aid. The attempt to industrialize Southern Italy through large state projects provided both a gold mine for the Mafia and an opportunity for local officials to get heavy bribes. With the sudden influx of wealth, power structures were reorganized; the rules of the game were revised, and the lifestyles of the *mafiosi* changed. The Mafia abandoned its peasant roots. In those years the successful Mafia boss acquired the power of a politician with stable and powerful ties to Rome.

Because of the Mafia, drug use became a bigger problem than domestic terrorism ever was. Solutions are not easy to find because of serious social problems. Increasingly, teenagers become both foot soldiers and casualties in the Mafia's battles. At one time, women and children were off-limits to the Mafia, but that no longer is the case. Juvenile crime has exploded in recent years, coinciding with organized crime's recruitment of youth from local gangs. Some are as young as ten. Possibly to blame is a penal code enacted in 1989 which rules out jail for any minor who commits a crime carrying less than a twelve-year sentence. With unemployment at 20 per cent in the South, many teens either move North or turn to crime. Drug couriers are often paid in heroin, with the consequence that many become addicts and remain slaves of their new-found "work." It is also often impossible for poor teens, once they are recruited and have tasted the glamour and money of organized crime, to free themselves of such servitude.

The Italian court system has had mixed results in responding to the legal challenges posed by the spread of terrorism and organized crime in Italy. On the one hand, even though judges and public prosecutors have often been the targets of terrorist and criminal abuse, they have nevertheless managed to help the government withstand and largely defeat the threat that the Red Brigades and other groups have posed to Italian democracy since the 1970s. On the other hand, the people who make up the judicial corps have themselves occasionally been tainted: some of them have been involved in major scandals, leading to well-publicized resignations and even trials. Many officials of the judiciary were implicated in the "P-2 affair" and had to resign, while connections with organized crime plagued local courts and even the court of cassation, the Italian equivalent to America's Supreme Court.

Sicilian violence reached its worst in the early 1990s. A new wave of assassinations started; during a brief two-week period in the fall of 1988, eighteen people, including a judge, were murdered by Mafia gunmen. Sicily, Calabria, and Campania accounted for 66 per cent of the homicides in Italy, although their populations make up only about 25 per cent of Italy's total. As rival gangs in Sicily, Calabria, and the Naples area started an unending series of murders in their drug-related turf wars, they also killed several magistrates, police officers, and politicians. After each spectacular assassination, high ranking officials of the state government, including the president of the republic and the prime minister, flew to Sicily to attend the victim's funeral and use the occasion to deliver the usual political homilies pledging that the fight against the Mafia would be stepped up. Outraged citizens occasionally responded to these speeches with catcalls and boos. The assassinations of Giovanni Falcone and Paolo Borsellino in 1992, special prosecutors who were successfully prosecuting and jailing hundreds of *mafiosi* in Sicily, outraged the nation.

In response to these brutal attacks, in which powerful bombs were also used to murder the judges and many of their bodyguards, the Italian government took strong measures, including the dispatch of seven elite battalions of troops to assist Sicilian officials and local law enforcement officers. The troops were assigned to protect officials and vital installations, but they were not expected to participate in investigative procedures conducted by traditional police agencies. Most importantly, the government at last committed itself to the creation of a national investigative force, along the lines of the United States' Federal Bureau of Investigation, to fight the Mafia. Known by its Italian initials as the DIA, this force will eventually grow to a strength of 3,000 crime agents.

The government has taken other actions as well. Since the members of *Cosa Nostra,* besides being drug traffickers and racketeers, are also legitimate businessmen and farmers, and therefore are interested in public-works contracts sponsored by local governments, the state has dissolved dozens of local town councils accused of dealing with the Mafia. In 1992 Giuliano Amato's government introduced the first witness protection program and relegated the most prominent Mafia bosses to island prisons, which made controlling their interests back home much more difficult.

Most Italians are upset with the presence of the Mafia in Italy and are horrified whenever television and the newspapers report the latest savagery in gory detail. They frequently organize massive demonstrations to show their outrage. Yet the Mafia continued to flourish until the early 90s. The major problem was that the Mafia lived within the walls of government. Its success had to be attributed to the fact that it had infiltrated or actually controlled the nerve center of regional governments. Its collaboration was considered indispensable at election time, and the more successful candidates did anything to secure it. In early 1984, officials of the Sicilian regional government were forced to resign and were arrested on charges of corruption. In 1991 twenty-one municipal administrations were dissolved because members were found to be connected with the Mafia or *Camorra.*

Serious attempts have been made by individual citizens to create a civic consciousness of the evil of the Mafia. The two most prominent are two writers, Danilo Dolci and Leonardo Sciascia. For many years Dolci campaigned in the slums of Palermo and the little Mafia towns of western Sicily. For a long time he seemed to be making no headway at all, and though his name was widely known abroad, few people inside Italy had heard of him. Again and again, by hunger strikes and other forms of peaceful demonstration, he drew the attention of the outside world to the abuse of the Mafia and the connivance of the Sicilian and the Italian establishment. The task he had set himself was Herculean: nothing less than persuading Italians that things can change simply because enough people—ordinary people without special power and influence—want them to be different. But to do that he had to destroy the ingrained conviction of Italians, northerners and southerners alike, that the only way to get things done is by pulling strings.

The biggest hope, however, has to be found in the collective efforts of southern society, which is giving signs of civic maturity. The structure of the Mafia is classically based on vertical relations of authority and dependence, with little or no horizontal solidarity among equals. Thus it can be demolished only by establishing a pattern of horizontal trust while eliminating the social structure of vertical exploitation dependence that has characterized southern culture for at least a millennium.

The wind of radical political changes, meanwhile, is having an effect also on the Mafia. In response to the massive popular outrage over the assassinations of the special prosecutors, in the summer of 1992, the Amato government enacted tougher measures against the Mafia and other criminal organizations, notably the *Camorra* and *'Ndrangheta*. Thanks to the new legislation and to better coordination between law enforcing agencies, several hundred mobsters have been arrested (including top leaders of the major criminal organizations). Mafia assets totaling over 2.5 billion dollars have been seized.

In the last few years there are clear indications that the government is serious about breaking the organized structure of organized crime. By 2001, over 1,200 *mafiosi*, faced with the threat of very long prison sentences, had turned state's evidence. Many witnesses to Mafia crimes came forward, and tips on where to find Mafia bosses who had eluded capture proved to be ruinous for the organization. By 2001, people imprisoned for organized crime would number in the thousands; it had also become apparent that "Mafia Inc." was facing significant financial difficulties. However, most law enforcement officials believe that the battle against these illegal organizations is not over yet.

White-Collar Crime and the Italian Social System

White-collar crime in Italy attracts attention in the press and in academic studies not only because it is important in itself but also because of what it seems to tell us about Italian society more generally. Widespread corruption has often been seen as confirming a series of related theoretical frameworks which portray Italians as particularly prone to 'favoritism' and 'familism,' perennially subject to pressure to favor their friends and relatives, and incapable of adhering to the impersonal rules of law that characterize a modern state. Because different sets of rules govern the social structures and cultures of different countries, it is difficult to compare the rate of corruption between one country and another. In addition, as Michael Eve rightly points out, before exploring the differences in the social relations involved in 'corruption' in Italy and elsewhere, it is useful to examine the issue of how we come to know about corruption in the first place, how it becomes 'visible'.[4]

White-collar crime is not a classic, clear-cut case of deviance. It has one foot in convention-ality and one foot in deviance; it is usually committed by the affluent in the course of normal business activities. Most people hold the conception that "crime" is what street people, or at least poor people, do. Thus, there is a certain incongruity in seeing an affluent, 60-year-old banker in handcuffs and a prison uniform. With respect to perception and prosecution, evi-dence indicating that a white-collar crime, such as Martha Stewart's insider trading charges, has occurred is often not as clear-cut as in the case of a mugging on the street. Corporate criminals are not heavily stigmatized: businessmen who cheat the government of taxes don't acquire "criminal identities." Relative to the incidence of white-collar crime, arrests are very rarely made. Top management does not have to "get their hands dirty" by directly ordering subordinates to break the law. "It is not difficult" to structure their affairs so that all of the pressure to break the law surfaces at a lower level of their organization or a subordinate orga-nization. White-collar criminals are motivated by two factors: economic difficulty and greed. We all remember the "Savings and Loan Scandal"—the largest monetary theft in history. The total amount of money stolen was six to seven hundred times that which is taken in all the robberies that occur in the United States each year. What happened? The Garn-St. Germain Act of 1982 failed to take into account the human factor of greed. It made the assumption that the entrepreneurs who borrowed money from savings and loans and the officers of the thrift institutions themselves were honest and could be trusted to conduct business on the honor system.[5]

The savings and loan scandal is an excellent example of "heads I win, tails you lose" col-lective embezzlement. It entails the officers of a corporation looting that self-same corporation. The corporation might appear to be the financial institution itself, but in fact, as it turns out, the officers who run and profit from the corporation constitute the corporation. The institu-tion's small investors and depositors are simply unwitting dupes in the creation of a dummy of shell corporation that is set up only to be drained of its assets. The savings and loan scandal of the 1980's cost taxpayers $1.4 trillion. The saying being circulated at that time "The best way to rob a bank is to own one" fully characterized the frustration of people. In U.S. we are fully aware of the corruption in our corporations; Enron and Wall Street frauds are only the tip of the iceberg. Even when occasionally we bring to justice some of the transgressors of the law and we sent them to jail, our culture quickly exonerates them. Michael Milken and Martha Stewart when released from jail, returned to occupy leading roles in our society.

Mass media play an important role in bringing to justice those who commit white collar crimes. The social 'visibility' of an issue often varies greatly between countries because the information we have about a social phenomenon in two different countries is not just natu-rally given but is socially constructed. Because "any social phenomenon, whether rape, child abuse, unemployment, fraud, or corruption, is raised to the status of a 'social problem' only when there are specialists who collect data, classify cases, and interpret evidence, fitting it into patterns," corruption comes to light through the mediation of the law, judges, the police, col-leagues, companies who complain, journalists, and so on. All these institutions and professions operate differently in different countries. Genuinely comparative research needs to be carried out. The search for causes can only be really satisfactory if we are clear as to what it is that is being explained. It is not just 'more' corruption that marks out Italy, but the different context in which it takes place. Yet this does not mean that the special prominence of corruption in Italy is an illusion, merely the result of greater Italian sensitivity to the issue. Again, it is only under certain conditions—fostered partly by the awareness created by newspapers, academics, and political polemicists, by changes in the conceptions of how far it is acceptable for an investigator to go in probing suspicions—that many forms of corruption emerge into the light and are successfully prosecuted.[6]

It should be said that the principal factor behind national differences in the prominence of corruption is not simply a fact of the number of hidden cases which never come to light but in the nature of the rules themselves. Therefore, it is possible that certain actions or decisions may be perfectly legal in a certain country and not in another or be legal or illegal in the same country if the rules change. To what extent are political contributions by companies and lobbying groups perfectly legal? Are not political contributions by companies perfectly legal, and even tax deductible, in many nations? But is it or should it be illegal for the president of the United States to allow to sleep in the Lincoln bedroom of the White House those who contributed at least $100,000 to the Democratic Party national campaign? Should lobbyists be allowed easy access to members of our governments to influence their votes on bills that favor their interests? And should it be legal or culturally acceptable that corporations give any contributions to any candidate or political party? Money does not flow into the coffers of politicians simply for an ideal; it is handed over for a contract, for bending a regulation, for a desired piece of legislation. Even in the culture of gifts there is a problem: although there is no immediate reward, in the long term reciprocity is expected. The differences at issue are differences in the type of social relationships linking firms and politicians. It is certainly noteworthy that relationships between local and national politicians and businesses may sometimes be more intimate in the United States of America than in Italy; indeed, in U.S. they stain our form of democracy.[7] In order to explain why corruption has been such a problem in Italy, it is necessary to grasp the bases of these social relationships, rather than simply distinguishing between corruption on the one hand and respect for the law on the other Rarely, however, a system of *tangenti* is used in a country. That is where Italy went astray and a number of crucial differences had developed between patterns in Italy and those in the United States of America or in Britain.

Change of Political System May Bring Change of Culture

White-collar crimes and political scandals have become very 'visible' in the last few years because of changes in the political climate. A week rarely went by at the end of the 80s and in the early 90s without the revelation that an officeholder, politician, banker, industrialist, military officer, television personality, or even a magistrate had been brought to court or even ended up in jail.

Bribery and corruption infected almost every aspect of Italian life. When a developer, building prisons, was discovered to have handed out millions of dollars in bribes to everyone including the minister of labor, it was dubbed the "golden prisons" scandal by the press. Since then there has been the "golden sheets" scandal, involving lucrative contracts to supply linen for sleeper cars in the Italian railroad, and the "golden bedpans" scandal, in which hospital workers hired to empty bedpans were mysteriously promoted into high-paying administrative positions for which they had no qualifications. Finally, there was the mega-scandal at the end of the 1980s, over bribes offered to political parties. The political scandals reached such proportions as to challenge credulity. Although no party remained immune, the two parties with the most power at that time, the *DC* and the *PSI,* were shown to be the most corrupt.

Many times corruption was more subtle because the relationship between the private sector and the politicians was closer and more symbiotic. The relationship between Fininvest, the group headed by Silvio Berlusconi and whose interests range from television and publishing to urban development and supermarkets, and politicians, especially of the Socialist Party, was so close that reciprocal favors did not seem to have normally flowed down the channel of direct monetary exchange. The Socialist Party seemed to have defended Fininvest's interests by shielding it from effective anti-monopoly legislation in the media industry. In return, Fininvest media gave plenty of interviews with *PSI* spokesmen, with appearances on popular entertainment or chat shows, gave prominent media coverage to issues championed by the party and offered reduced rates for election advertising. In 1994 the formation of a government headed by Berlusconi and containing three former executives of Fininvest as ministers or secretaries of state raised even more intriguing questions regarding relationships between government and industry.

Some suggest that in the 1980s, politicians in Italy routinely stole anywhere from six billion to twelve billion dollars a year. Elections have become so expensive not because running for office costs much more than in France or Germany but because the candidates pocket a lot of money each time the voters go to the polls. One wonders if the frequent fall of governments and the consequent new elections are not part of a political scam. This, of course, must be the reason why so few politicians complain about having to campaign so often. It had become a custom that parties paid their general costs with contract kickbacks and "contributions," while candidates paid for their own campaigns with kickbacks from the families that depended directly on them for jobs.

Bribery had been always associated with southern Italy, and even to some extent with central Italy. The northern part of the country had always been viewed as immune to such corruption. The Sicilians talked about kickback using the word *pizzo* (an old Sicilian word for a bird's beak; by allusion, when it's being dipped in food or water). The Neapolitans said *mazzetta,* which means a small bundle (of money). In the north, Milanese, Venetians, and other cities did not have such a word—not until 1992, that is, when the massive bribery scandal that shook Italy to its core started to unfold in Milan. The scandal not only demonstrated that the North was not ethically different from the rest of the country, but it also showed that the Italian party-dominated system, which has run the country since WWII, was at the core of the corruption.

The investigation, known as *Operazione Mani Pulite* (Operation Clean Hands), showed bribe collection to be one of the most efficient and organized arms of the Italian government. Officials had routinely skimmed from 2 to 14 per cent off government contracts made by the industries of the public sector and for every public service, from airports and hospitals to theaters and orphanages. Politicians had immense power because the government controlled, as we shall see later, vast sectors of the economy, from commercial banking, steel, telecommunications, and energy industries all the way down to ice cream plants, grocery stores, and vineyards. For Italian political parties, such activities were giant spoils machines. Much of the private sector too—from Fiat to small construction outfits—had no choice but to come to terms with *partitocrazia,* or rule by the political parties.

By acting as legitimate democratic intermediaries between the individual citizen and the state, and being essentially vote-getting entities, the political parties had spawned an oligarchy of professional politicians, a *classe politica* (political class) to conduct illegal activities in an almost legal way. The political class for years had relied on graft, or *tangente* (even in this area the Italians try to use some sophistication; they use a neat geometrical term for a kickback).

The scandal of *tangenti* spread rapidly to dozens of other northern cities and brought public disgrace and even jail terms to many top politicians. "Operation Clean Hands hit Italian politics like a cyclone," wrote Giuseppe Turato and Cinzia Sasso. "After this, nothing will ever be the same."[8]

The party-dominated political system was immensely damaging not only because it involved enormous waste but also because it virtually abolished normal politics, as the latter became less and less a question of competition between interest groups and different programs and more and more a struggle for control of a slice of the spoils system.

It is no accident that the scandal came to light in 1992. As we have seen, during the Cold War many Italian voters considered corruption a lesser evil than a government headed by the Communist Party. A majority of Italian voters supported a coalition of parties led by the anti-Communist Christian Democrats and Socialists. But the collapse of communism in Eastern Europe opened a Pandora's box of pent-up frustration and disgust with the Italian political system; voters started to desert the traditional corruption-ridden parties in droves.

The new political climate and the increased European and global competition in the economic system changed also the relation of the Italian business and industrial system with politics. The system of collusion between government and business, which had worked well enough in a relatively closed, protected market, could not continue after 1992 because the onerous tax on businesses made it difficult for companies to compete freely with European and other rivals. The clean up that followed was most welcome. Since most Italians dislike politicians, it was easy for the judges who arrested hundreds of Milanese bureaucrats, businessmen, and politicians, including deputies to the Italian parliament, to become heroes. Indeed, the public response was euphoric. The judge-prosecutor who started the investigation, Antonio Di Pietro, an Abruzzese by birth, suddenly became a national hero and his picture appeared on the cover of most major news magazines. Graffiti writers scrawled "Grazie Di Pietro" (Thanks, Di Pietro) across walls in Milan; Di Pietro T-shirts became the most popular items for teenagers.

In the process, over 3,000 people were arrested or notified that they were under investigation for corruption or illegal acts connected with the financing of political parties. About half of them were economic operators, including top managers of Italy's biggest private corporations (Fiat, Olivetti, Montedison) and state holdings (IRI and ENI). About as many were politicians, including over 150 members of parliament, four former premiers, and a score of former cabinet ministers. By mid-summer 1993, the breakdown by party affiliation showed that every political party was touched.

Such corruption among politicians is symptomatic of a nation with very little resistance to corruption. The central question is why a sense of public morality and respect for the law has been so weak in Italy.

What Does It All Mean?

Judging by the mega-scandals and the wide operations of the Mafia over the entire territory of the nation and the power that the Mafia exercises on Italian institutions, even governmental ones, are we to conclude that Italy has failed as a democratic nation? Should we conclude that Italians don't know how to behave in a democratic system? That civic consciousness is weak in Italian society? Some political experts do think that Italy falls short on many of the measures we use to gauge the health and stability of democratic societies and governments. "Phenomena as various as a proclivity to go through red traffic lights, tax evasion, or the forging of documents to obtain an invalid pension on false pretenses may all be cited as examples of weak internalization of the rules imposed by the national community and a disrespect for the law."(M. Eve, p. 44)

It is important to note in this context that corruption in Italy does not seem to be unambiguously associated with those features we might expect of a 'weak' or even 'absent' state. One of the most persistent paradoxes of Italian society is the coexistence of exceptionally rigorous and detailed laws and administrative regulations designed to prevent the interference of individual interests in public interests. Italian bureaucracy imposes a high number of requirements on those demanding a service or asking for a contract, in the attempt to ensure that those not entitled to the service, not best qualified to receive the contract, will not get it. Unfortunately, while all this inflexible regulation certainly does eliminate some forms of corruption, it often generates new opportunities for it. In Italy in contrast to the U.S. or Britain, much less freedom is given to officials, either in written rules or in conventional working practices that cover the implementation of the rules; hence the kind of minor negotiation that is often possible in other countries is not allowed in Italy, and is classified in the realm of illicit behavior. In fact, the presence of the state is very strong in the economy of the country and we may say that the Italian insistence on universalistic criteria—placing all firms on an equal footing in the competition for a contract—places large areas of behavior out of bounds. Italian legislation attempts to regulate the granting of public contracts with very elaborate measures designed to prevent one firm from gaining an unfair advantage. It is expected that public officials and contractors are two completely separate parties who will act quite independently of each other. In the U.S. and Britain, expectations are lower.

But in the larger picture, lack of loyalty to the national community has to do with the national character. In the Italian social system, loyalties to family and friends, or to the entourage of some influential leader, squeeze out loyalties to the state and the wider community. Hence, when an opportunity arises to favor a friend at the expense of a stranger, a high proportion of Italians will sacrifice the interests of those who are not personally close to them. The problem is a deep-seated cultural and ethical attitude springing from a particular historical experience. The supposedly late formation of Italy as a unified nation is often cited as the background to this weak sense of identification with the national community. An implicit comparison with a type of society that is not particularistic and familistic and where the sense of the state is more deeply rooted in national consciousness will show Italy as being civilly backward.

It should be pointed out that the very democratic form of government with a very "liberal" judicial system makes it difficult for the nation to deal with political opponents of the republic and with those who threaten the stability of the nation. However, we should examine closely how Italy fares in comparison with other Western countries. On the governmental level, Italy can only draw respect. If the Italians change prime ministers more often than do the British, or than Americans change presidents, this really does not mean that Italian democracy is more unstable than the others. If 85–90 per cent of the Italians vote in national elections, as compared with just over half that number in American presidential elections, is it really the case that the Italian and not the American pattern is pathological? As J. La Palombara has made us reflect, "which is a more serious weakness for democracy: the Italian government's apparent inability to bring the mafia to heel in Sicily, or the failure of other democracies to deal with large-scale crime in their major cities? And which kind of corruption is more insidious: the headline-making scandals that fill Italy's daily newspapers or the extensive 'white-collar' crime in the United States that rarely gets any public notice at all."[9]

In talking about Italian crime, scholars and journalists usually use an idealized vision to which they wish the country would live up. The assessment is done by transferring into the conceptual framework all the elements of stereotype attached to the Italian society but without taking into consideration the nature of the 'particularistic' and 'familistic'' fibers of the Italian social system.

So although frameworks that relate particularism to a weak sense of the state are in many ways crucial for the understanding of contemporary Italy, they can be deepened considerably if comparison is made not with a stereotyped and sociologically unrealistic model but rather with the real structures of authority, responsibility, solidarity, and power.

Despite crime (though Italy is certainly not at the top of the list of crime-plagued nations), and despite unemployment and heavy taxes, it seems that life is still good in Italy. In 1989 polls conducted in the French-speaking Valle d'Aosta and in the German-speaking Alto Adige, which was ceded to Italy by Austria after WWI, revealed that although these regions desire greater administrative autonomy, in no way do they wish to secede from Italy. The winds of total autonomy and separatism that are sweeping through Europe are not affecting Italian unity.

Another big challenge that the country will face is the upsurge of regional administrative autonomy that the wealthy northern regions are going to demand. According to the constitution, regions may have their own administration and chart their own destiny. The Christian Democratic governments, or governments of coalitions dominated by Christian Democrats, had, after 1948, refused to implement regionalism, because they rightly feared that it would lead to Communist regional governments. But it steadily became clear that weak local governments, and excessive centralization, were leading to corruption and incompetence. In the years 1968–70 plans were drawn up for fifteen regions, not only on the periphery of the peninsula—like Sicily, Sardinia, the Alto Adige, and the Val d'Aosta, where regional governments already existed—but in the heartlands of the country. The regional councils of these new, large areas were elected in June 1970. By 1980 the regions were spending 18 percent of the entire national expenditure, and at that time the communists were in control of three regions: Emilia-Romagna (centered in Bologna), Tuscany, and Umbria. Communists and socialists together ran Piedmont, Liguria (centered in Genoa), and Lazio. The Christian Democrats, on the other hand, controlled only two, both in the south, but shared power in eleven others. Today the regions exercise wide powers, in fields like welfare and education, and control the expenditure of considerable sums of money. Some of these powers have simply been taken over from the old municipalities, but some, certainly, come from central government. Regionalism has encouraged the growth of grass-roots groups like trade unions and local businesses, but unfortunately in the south it has sometimes made life easier for criminal organizations, such as the Mafia and the *Camorra*. The communist-controlled regions in the north have earned a reputation for being efficient and free from corruption. Nor have they found it difficult to work with big business or the multi-nationals. Bologna, under communist control, had become a symbol of prosperity, efficiency, and civility: it is one of the most prosperous cities in Europe, it is immune from political corruption, and it has escaped the destruction of its ancient beauty.

As the national government continues to be shaken by accusations of corruption, these regional governments, with their inherently closer ties to their constituents, may increase in importance and offer Italy new hope in its quest to combat threats to the nation and maintain its place in the forefront of western democracies.

Notes

1. G. Amendola, "I comunisti e il movimento studentesco, necessita' della lotta su due fronti," *Rinascita*, June 7, 1968; L. Longo, "Il movimento studentesco nella lotta anti-capitalista," *Rinascita*, May 3, 1968.

2. See R. Chinnici, "Magistratura e mafia," *Democrazia e diritto*, 22, no. 4 (July-August 1982), 81. Rocco Chinnici, an investigative magistrate, was killed by the Mafia in the summer of 1983. Other important anti-Mafia personalities had been murdered the year before. On April 25, 1982, the Sicilian communist leader Pio La Torre, who had been in the forefront of the anti-Mafia campaign, was killed with his driver by the Mafia. Later that year, on September 3, the former counter-terrorism chief and then prefect of

Sicily (with special responsibilities for the fight against the Mafia) Dalla Chiesa, was killed with his wife openly in the streets of Palermo.

3.   For a penetrating assessment of the working of the Mafia, see R. Catanzaro, "Mafia, economia e sistema politico," in U. Ascoli e R. Catanzaro, *La società italiana degli anni ottanta* (Bari: Laterza, 1987), pp. 255–79.

4.   "Comparing Italy: The Case of Corruption," in David Forgacs and Robert Lumley, eds., *Italian Cultural Studies* (Oxford: Oxford U.P., 1996), 36.

5.   D. Forgacs and R. Lumley, eds., 83.

6.   There are certainly large international differences in the powers and the expertise of investigating authorities. In Britain and the U.S., where it is the police who have the responsibility for collecting evidence and preparing a prosecution case, resources devoted to fraud and white-collar crime in general, including, therefore, corruption, have traditionally been very limited. Because of the volume of work that fraud squads are expected to undertake, police have remained largely reactive rather than proactive.

7.   A good example, Michael Eve says, is provided by local development agencies such as those organizing urban renewal. In Britain and the U.S., where the idea of private-public partnership in local development has been influential, it has been common to include directors of local companies in publicly funded bodies that have access to substantial government funds and wide powers to decide how development should proceed. Representatives of building companies may thus fit on local development agencies that decide the shape of a local town plan, infrastructures, industrial development, and even allocate individual contracts. Ibid., p. 42.

8.   G. Turato and C. Sasso, *I saccheggiatori* (Milan: Sperling & Kupfer, 1992).

9.   La Palombara, pp. 6–7.

Bibliography

Ascoli, U. and Catanzaro, R., *La società italiana degli anni ottanta* (Bari: Laterza, 1987), pp. 255–79.

Casillo, R., *Gangster Priest, the Italian American Cinema of Martin Scorsese.* (Toronto: University of Toronto Press, 2006).

Chinnici, R., "Magistratura e mafia," *Democrazia e diritto,* 22, no. 4 (July-August 1982).

Della Porta, D., ed., *Terrorismi in Italia* (Bologna: Il Mulino, 1984).

Donati, P. P., *La società civile in Italia* (Milan: Mondadori, 1997).

Eve, M., "Comparing Italy: The Case of Corruption," in David Forgacs and Robert Lumley, ed., *Italian Cultural Studies* (Oxford: Oxford U.P., 1996), pp. 34–51.

Forgacs, D. and Lumley, R., eds., *Italian Cultural Studies* (Oxford: Oxford U.P., 1996).

Gardaphe, F. L., *From Wiseguys to Wise Men. The Gangster and Italian American Masculinities.* (New York: Routledge, 2006).

Sterling, C., *The Mafia* (London: HarperCollins, 1990).

Stille, A., *Excellent Cadavers* (New York: Vintage, 1996).

Turato, G. and Sasso, C., *I saccheggiatori* (Milan: Sperling & Kupfer, 1992).

Watson, J., *The Mafia and Clientelism: Roads to Rome in Post-War Calabria* (New York: Routledge, 1986).

CHAPTER 4

U.S.-ITALIAN RELATIONS

A Strong Ally of the United States

The United States and Italy enjoy warm and friendly relations. The two are NATO allies and cooperate in the United Nations, in various regional organizations, and bilaterally for peace, prosperity, and security. Italy has worked closely with the United States and with its fellow members of the EU on NATO and UN operations as well as on a number of issues including providing assistance to Russia and the new independent states; the Middle East peace process; multilateral talks; Somalia and Mozambique peacekeeping; and combating drug trafficking and terrorism. Italy is a strong and active transatlantic partner and has sought to foster democratic ideals and international cooperation in areas of strife and civil conflict.

In the wake of the tragic terrorist attacks in the United States on September 11, 2001, the two nations have partnered, on the policy level and on the working level, among law enforcement officers and intelligence officials, to work to prevent other attacks. Thus the Italian government has cooperated with the United States in formulating defense, security, and peacekeeping policies. Following the U.S. invasion of Afghanistan in 2001, Italy sent aid workers to assist in redevelopment. After the U.S. invasion of Iraq in 2003, Italy deployed the third-largest troop contingent, and Italian aid, the second largest from a European state, is helping to rebuild Iraq's infrastructure. Under longstanding bilateral agreements flowing from its membership in NATO, Italy hosts U.S. military bases at Vicenza and Livorno (army), Aviano (air force), and Sigonella, Gaeta, and Naples—home port for the U.S. Navy Sixth Fleet. The United States has about 16,000 military personnel stationed in Italy.

New Support for U.S. Policy Positions

In 2001, the election of conservative Silvio Berlusconi as prime minister of Italy presented U.S. President George W. Bush with a rare ideological ally in Europe. Many of Berlusconi's policy positions echoed those of the Bush Administration, and the outspoken prime minister made it clear that he intended to seek a new relationship with the United States. He supported President Bush on some highly contentious issues, from missile defense to Euro-federalism and the Kyoto Protocol on climate change. The Berlusconi government also allied itself with the Bush Administration on the critical issue of missile defense. Asserting that Italy and Europe were as likely to be the targets for rogue state missile attacks as the United States, the prime minister was one of the first European leaders to express enthusiastic support for this Bush military policy. These positions were part of a broader pro-American strategy adopted by the Berlusconi government. The new Italian government looked to America for economic inspiration as well as an ideological counterweight to the preponderant center-Left tenor of the EU and most European governments. The two nations worked together on multilateral initiatives aimed at strengthening civil society in the broader Middle East and North Africa and encouraging democratic governments on the southern and eastern shores of the Mediterranean.

Some Reasons for So Much Agreement

But of course, the two nations agree on so much because they know and trust each other so well. The north of Italy alone is home to over 30,000 U.S. citizens, and 1.5 million American tourists visit northern Italy every year. In addition to the thousands of Italian tourists in the U.S. taking advantage of the "strong euro," 10 per cent of all Americans—almost 25 million people—claim Italian heritage. Thus it is no surprise that there are many Italo-Americans in American government and business and that they constitute a solid bridge between the U.S. and Italy. Each year, the American Consulate in Milan supports the visits of roughly 1,000 VIPs, including many Congressional delegations and numerous state trade delegations. As well, every year thousands of American university students enroll in study abroad programs at nearly every university in Italy; in turn, the U.S. hosts roughly 3,500 Italian students each year. The Italy-U.S. Fulbright Scholarship program has awarded more than 10,000 scholarships since its foundation in 1948.

The U.S. government and Italy's national and regional governments promote and support a lively cultural exchange program. The National Italian American Foundation (NIAF), the Order of Sons of Italy in America (OSIA), UNICO, and many other organizations support Italian culture in almost every city in the United States. Between the two nations there is a constant flow of artistic creativity and human capital, strong evidence of cultural cross-pollination.

To be certain, the relationship faces challenges. Some are short term; others are long term. The United States has changed so completely in the past fifty years that our society may no longer retain its traditional ties with Europe; the fastest growing ethnic group in the U.S. is of people who identify themselves as "multi-racial." However, Americans' celebration of diversity is something that may assist Italy, as it too becomes a more diverse nation through the new immigration.

The American Government's Role after WW II

The U.S. government played an important role in the postwar reconstruction of Italy both through political realignment and economic development. The Marshall Plan provided roughly 1.3 billion dollars in U.S. economic assistance between 1948 and 1952. This sum represented a percentage of the gross domestic product that fluctuated between 2.3% in the late 1940s to 1.6% in the biennium 1951–52. The U.S. also was a major customer of the Italian war industry; U.S. contracts accounted for a total of 540 million dollars between 1952 and 1956 with a peak of 240 million dollars in the months that preceded Italy's 1953 parliamentary elections. Besides supplying money, the U.S. also inspired a new business mentality, resulting in a major productivity drive.

Italy: Dependent Ally or Independent Partner?

Until the fall of the Berlin Wall in 1989, Italian internal political affairs were deeply affected by the U.S. interference in Italy's domestic affairs. The peculiar character of these relations was not based on the existence of any special amicability or feeling of kinship. On the contrary, the singular nature of the relationship was due to America's profound concern about a possible takeover of Italy by its strong Communist party.

U.S.-Italian relations for most of those years were dominated by questions arising from domestic politics rather than international affairs. The critical element in American/Italian relations was the existence, up until 1991, of a Communist Party that was potentially strong enough to share power or even lead the Italian government. From Washington's point of view, such an eventuality would have meant both a political embarrassment for an American president and a risk that Italy might leave NATO or reduce its alliance commitments. The overriding American aim was always to forestall any form or degree of communist participation in the Italian government.

When Jimmy Carter became president in January 1977, Italy was considered the greatest potential political problem the U.S. had in Europe. The Communist Party had recently achieved its greatest gain in an Italian election, 34.4% of the vote. Communists were extending their control in every important area of Italian life: schools, press, courts, trade unions, and regional and local governments. It seemed almost inevitable that they would enter the government in a historic compromise coalition with the Christian Democrats and eventually hinder the country's support of the Western Alliance.

The American Right was putting pressure on the new president to stop the threat of communism in Italy through covert operations if necessary. But Carter rejected that option and decided against the financing of Italian political parties, the manipulation of Italian political events, and the attempt to tell the Italians how they should vote. In making this decision, Carter was influenced by the counterproductive effects of such efforts in the past. As Richard N. Gardner, Carter's ambassador to Italy, pointed out, "early in the Nixon years large sums of money were given by the U.S. Embassy in Rome to the right-wing general who subsequently ran for Parliament on the neo-fascist ticket. Wide publicity was also given in Italy to reports that another covert financing operation was discussed and then aborted in the Ford Administration. Both of these episodes helped the Communist Party to gain support as defender of the country's sovereignty against 'American domination.'"[1]

Italy's political moves had been closely monitored by the U.S. since the end of World War II. During the first months of 1948, Italy was already considered the hottest battleground of the Cold War, and American governments felt free to intervene at every level of Italian domestic affairs.

Much of the intervention went on behind the scenes through covert operations. In the early postwar period the American government had provided encouragement and funding for the establishment of a political party—the Social Democrats—and two trade unions—the *UIL* and the *CISL*. Subsequently the Americans dispensed funds to a variety of individuals, groups, and parties, most especially the *DC* and a Catholic national labor union (*CISL*). The American policymakers did not consider the danger that such moves could turn political stability into stagnation or that the reconstruction drive itself would result in a substantial restoration of old economic and social structures of the prewar era. In seeking their own self-centered aims, the Americans missed an opportunity to broaden the foundations of Italy's democratic institution. Economic and political power had always been in the hands of the few: mostly landowners in the south, big business and industrialists in the north. The predictable results of American intervention were to further strengthen the trend toward stalemate and *immobilismo*.

In the 1950s, America had seen Italy as "an ally in distress" and even wondered whether the country was about to become a "lost ally." The American ambassador to Rome at the time,

Clare Boothe Luce, was concerned that the *PCI* might "take over," or at least gain enough votes to "overtake" the *DC* and become the number one political force in the nation. The fear was so great that U.S. officials in Rome announced that aid might be discontinued if the Leftist parties gained ground in the 1954 election. America let it be known that contracts would be denied to factories where communist-dominated unions continued to poll a majority of the workers' votes. The whole program of economic assistance in Italy became controversial, especially when the spotlight fell on these U.S. efforts to use economic aid to condition Italian domestic developments. Top representatives of President Dwight D. Eisenhower's administration felt that the Italian government did not display the desired vigor in the battle against Italian communism. They suggested, for instance, that the municipal council of Bologna (the biggest communist stronghold in Italy) be disbanded.

America was not concerned that, in 1954, despite a remarkable postwar recovery, Italy was a country where 50 million people were governed by 5,000 in the interest of 500. Mrs. Luce was still toying with the idea that the Right could make a useful and possibly decisive contribution to solving Italian problems. She was worried about Giovanni Gronchi's ascendancy to the presidency and his reported inclinations toward neutrality in foreign affairs and "socialistic openings" in domestic politics, even though he had clearly voiced his support for the Atlantic Alliance and for Western cooperation and solidarity. Gronchi let it be known that he was not happy with the way Italy was being treated in the Atlantic Alliance; he felt that his country was entitled to a more equal standing in an alliance that was practically run by the U.S., Great Britain, and France.[2]

This U.S. attitude toward Italy was not caused simply by fear of a possible communist takeover but also by certain international economic policies with which Italians were having significant success. At this time, the U.S. also had a bitter aversion to Enrico Mattei's initiatives at instigating cooperation with the oil-rich countries of the Third World and to Italy's sharing in the economic development of the underdeveloped countries. In 1953 with the coming to power of the Eisenhower administration in America, many key positions were entrusted to people close to the big oil corporations. Traditional ties to powerful private groups and strong hostility to public intervention in economic affairs prompted large sectors of the U.S. media to sharply attack Mattei and the Italian state oil and gas agency, *ENI*. Mattei was portrayed as procommunist, a typical charge brought against anyone with whom one disagreed in the 1950s. The situation was exacerbated by his ability to achieve significant success in Egypt and other Middle East countries, including Iran, thanks to an approach keyed to partnership with local governments in the oil enterprise. In October 1957, President Gronchi protested to the American ambassador in Rome:

> Quite often the actions of your oil concerns are backed by American diplomatic representatives. We feel that the behavior of these corporations does a great disservice to the United States. Just when the British and French "imperialism" has come to an end in this sector, the "imperialism" of the North American corporations is getting under way.[3]

During this period, the Italian government was trying to be the U.S.'s equal in foreign policy and complained about the Americans' failure to consult with Italy on European and, especially, Mediterranean policy. The U.S. conferred almost exclusively with France and Great Britain, even about the Mediterranean, where the two former colonial powers had lost their clout. Italy, by contrast, had left a good bridge with her ex-colonies and enjoyed a good relationship with most of the Arab world; she felt that the U.S. should have supported her pursuit of political prestige and economic expansion in that part of the world. The Italian government asserted that it was perfectly possible and acceptable for a Mediterranean country like Italy to pursue a policy of friendship with the Arab world while continuing to cooperate with her partners in the Atlantic Alliance. In 1957, the U.S. began to reassess its relationship with Italy. Vice President Richard Nixon, on his trip to Italy in the spring of 1957, stated that it would be useful if in the Middle East the U.S. could act in closer cooperation with Italy and with other major countries more directly concerned. However, it was not easy to change American government attitudes toward Italian internal politics. The historian Arthur Schlesinger Jr., who was to become a high-ranking adviser to President John F. Kennedy, wrote that U.S. policies toward Italy required a thorough updating. In subsequent years, Schlesinger became more and more convinced that the U.S. would greatly benefit, directly and indirectly, from the coming to power in Italy of a coalition based on collaboration between Christian Democrats and socialists. However, many key posts, notably in the State Department, continued to be held or controlled by officials whose ideas about Italy were cemented in the early postwar years. When the shortcomings of the center governments became unsolvable, they tended to look to the Right rather than to the moderate Left.

The U.S. was reluctant to see the Socialist Party in government because its leader, Pietro Nenni, had not dropped his requests for the withdrawal of U.S. forces from Europe and for a neutral Italian position toward the Soviet Union. Despite America's opposition, the leader of the Christian Democrats, Aldo Moro spared no effort to make sure that the dialogue between the *DC* and the *PSI* would make progress. But the center-Left coalition was only possible after a short-lived government had been formed with the support of the neo-fascists, which brought the nation to the brink of a civil war. According to public opinion polls, Italians did not believe that the opening to the Left would bring about a pro-Soviet government.

U.S. Grants Approval to the Socialists in Government

In the early 1960s, the Socialist Party's Pietro Nenni sought to clarify his party's position in order to prepare for its eventual participation in government. He emphasized that Italy's links with NATO represented an irreversible position and that Italy's approach to European integration should be close to that of President Kennedy, which was founded on democratic and supernational principles. Nenni repeatedly stated that his party's objectives were to bring Italy's social and institutional framework in line with the nation's high rate of industrialization and increased production.

The possible participation of socialists in government was not opposed by the Vatican, even though some Italian cardinals did express reservations. Ever since the election of Pope John XXIII, in 1958, the Vatican had adopted a policy of less direct involvement in Italian politics and viewed with benevolent neutrality the flirtation of the *DC* with the *PSI* The Church's position was in line with its new emphasis on the social aspects of its traditional doctrines, as reflected in such papal pronouncements as the encyclical *Mater et Magistra* (Mother and Teacher), 1961.

The gap between Italian political reality and its perception by the U.S. diplomatic corps was narrowed during the first year of the Kennedy administration. As Schlesinger has pointed out, Secretary of State Averill Harriman played a key role in persuading those U.S. officials who had opposed socialist participation in the Italian government to change their point of view.[4] Schlesinger felt that the opening to the socialists provided a good opportunity for both Italian and U.S. interests and, therefore, deserved to be strongly supported by Washington; Italy had to proceed with its plan of social and economic reforms. The American administration's support for the center-Left paid dividends during the 1962 crisis over the deployment of Soviet missiles in Cuba. Nenni did not share the pro-Soviet and anti-American views expressed by the Communist Party and the pro-communist wing of his own. The course followed by the center-Left coalition in international affairs became even more of an asset for the Kennedy administration because of the sharpening differences with France over its opposition to Great Britain's entry into the European Community (EC) and its concept of European unity. American support for the center-Left strengthened the resolve of the Italian government to oppose the Italian conservative forces, in which many U.S. diplomats had long put their faith.

The position taken by the American administration was not followed by most of the American media, which kept repeating old charges and prejudices. Editorials and articles published in the spring of 1962 were a clear reminder of how ill informed and biased the American press was. The slanted reporting of some sectors of the U.S. news media and their inability to understand Italy and Italian politics emerged most flagrantly when the conflicts within the socialist camp led to the failure of Moro's first attempt to form a new center-Left government. The gains scored by the communists at the general elections in spring 1963 were quickly interpreted as a rejection of the coalition of political forces by the electorate. The American press did not realize that the communist gains at the polls had to be interpreted in the context of spreading protests fed by practical rather than by ideological factors and circumstances. Echoing Italian conservative fears, the American press prophesied Italy's near abandonment of solidarity with the West, a free economy, and an open democratic society.

This biased coverage of the Italian political scene was criticized by politicians from the full spectrum of Italian political life. Except for occasional references, the American media did not make real efforts in those years to address the political and economic life of Italy and assess its presence as a modern industrial society. Very rarely did American journalistic reports include insight or analysis of Italy's political, economic, or social conditions and prospects.

Many in the U.S. media, for instance, either failed to understand or badly underrated the significance of the student movement, which in early 1968 was already surfacing as a new and important component of Italian society. A challenge to the entire Italian establishment was naively presented as a simple resentment of an antiquated university system. *The New York Times* (February 12 and March 12, 1968), for instance, stated that the groups involved did not represent any significant percentage of the electorate.

Because there was a complete American media panic on the outcome of the Italian elections of May 19–20, 1968, when the communists scored a big gain, there was a similar overreaction when the *PCI* criticized the Soviet invasion of Czechoslovakia in the same year. The gains scored by the *MSI* (the neo-fascists) in the local elections held in mid-June 1971 unleashed another wave of alarm in the U.S. media. *Newsweek* (June 28, 1971) went so far as to establish a parallel between the social conditions that spurred Mussolini's rise to power and the chaotic state of present-day Italy! Predictions of civil war, impending communist takeover, and/or Rightist coups were often bandied about in the headlines. When *PCI* leaders bid for a deal with the Christian Democrats and probed U.S. reactions in the mid-1970s, the American media reached an advanced stage of reactionary paranoia. Unusual attention was devoted to Italy by the major U.S. media in 1975–1976, which reflected their fears for the *PCI*'s growing electoral strength and prospects.

American interference in Italian domestic politics was used by the *DC* to justify their politics. The Christian Democratic party attributed its policy of slow modernization of the country to the fact that the Party did not have complete freedom. The tendency to use the U.S. as a justification for a whole range of internal political decisions was useful to the *DC*, but it conveyed the perception that Italy was an American satellite.

Writers and other artists, such as the Leftist actor-playwright Dario Fo, criticized the U.S. In Fo's play, *The Lady Is Fit to Be Thrown Away,* the "lady" America is the metaphor for a monstrous machination organized to glorify a system dominated by an obsession with money and the overwhelming power of capital. Like much of the intelligentsia of the Left, as well as radical and Leftist journalists, Fo sought to make real the idea that Italy had been, and still was, a most compliant and exploited "province" of the "American empire."

The covert funding of many activities certainly did not help the American image in Italy. For instance, in 1972 the U.S. provided $10 million to certain political parties to help them in the national election that year. U.S. Ambassador Graham Martin funneled $800,000 to General Vito Miceli, the extreme-Rightist head of Italian military intelligence, without conditions on the money's use. Miceli later became a candidate in the neo-fascist Party. A 1976 report of the U.S. House of Representatives stated that the CIA had disbursed over $75 million to Italian parties and candidates during the preceding three decades.

None of this means that most Italians had become anti-American during this period. Most Italian officials and the majority of the Italian public tolerated such interference with remarkably little resentment. However, respect and admiration for America, which was still more prevalent in Italy than in any other European nation, dwindled in those years.

The Film Industry and American Cultural Domination

Even more than in political and military circles, America has come to be a dominant force on the Italian cultural scene, especially through film. The presence of American film on the Italian peninsula has always been strong.[5] By 1925 some four-fifths of the market was held by American films. Why? The causes were predominantly economic (Hollywood's search for export markets in Europe, Italian exhibitors' demand for popular films), attitudinal (a change in public taste in Italy), and political (inadequate import controls by the Italian government and the American government's drive to promote a certain set of values through the medium of film). The fascist government did very little to combat American domination, either culturally or commercially, presumably because Hollywood was not sending out movies that could be interpreted as critical of the fascist ideology. But the popularity of American films has to be found also in the wealth and organizational maturity of the American film industry—well integrated and geared to making exportable films. The United States was a vast country with many movie houses. A successful American film would recoup its production costs on its first run at home before being exported. This meant that it could be offered to distributors and exhibitors abroad at a lower price than films produced in their own home countries, where they still had to make up their costs.

There was a significant contradiction in the fascist period between official attempts to construct a national culture and the fact that much cultural consumption—both of high culture and popular culture—was of non-national products. The massive preponderance of American films in Italian movie theaters continued until 1939, when more effective protectionist measures were introduced, and for the first time during fascist rule the number of Italian films in circulation exceeded that of American films. The "Americanization" of the cinema in the 1920s and 1930s in turn influenced Italian production because it imposed a commercially popular style that Italian filmmakers were pressured into adopting if they wanted to have a chance of competing at the box office. Effective restrictions designed to limit the amount of foreign material came only during the last years of the fascist regime.

How should the presence under fascism of a large quantity of light entertainment material, much of it foreign, be interpreted? It served a political purpose: it provided a form of escapism. The regime promoted it or was happy to let it circulate, because it fit into a "bread and circuses" policy of keeping the masses happy.

When the Allies landed in Italy in 1943, they brought along a backlog of American films and took over film distribution in the occupied territories. In 1945 the Americans forced Italy to abrogate all the measures that protected Italian films against competition on the domestic market and "dumped" at low prices on the Italian market over 2,000 American films, while Cinecittà (Italy's film studio, located in the outskirts of Rome) was used to house war refugees. After 1945, the movement known as neo-realism attempted to redefine the function of Italian cinema, to introduce to popular audiences a different sort of engagement with reality. The emphasis in neo-realism was on the hidden underside: poverty, unemployment, illiteracy, the legacy of fascist neglect, and the difficulties of postwar reconstruction. But American films continued to be overwhelmingly popular. In the late forties and early fifties, a strong marketing push by American film distributors was abetted by a hostile attitude toward neo-realist films by the center-Right government, much of the press, and Italian promoters eager to get their hands on commercially viable films and make a lot of money. Native filmmakers found it very difficult indeed to get their work financed and shown.

The American supremacy was also a result of advantageous terms the Americans were able to negotiate during the time of Rome's liberation. Thanks to assiduous work by the United States government and the film industry, the wall of protectionism came down, and Italy was inundated by a huge quantity not just of new productions but also of old films and reruns. Ellis Arnall, president of the Society of Independent Motion Picture Producers, reported on a visit to America's President Harry Truman in 1949:

> The president readily agreed that our government has a responsibility to see to it that American-produced motion pictures be utilized to the fullest in carrying the message of Americanism and Democracy to the rest of the world. He expressed these views to the Secretary of State, Mr. Acheson, and requested Mr. Acheson to take such steps as feasible to the end that foreign countries would not discriminate against American-produced pictures and would maintain no unreasonable quotas or unfair restrictions against them.[6]

There was a period in the early 1960s when it looked as if the tide had turned. *RAI*, the Italian state-run radio and television network, was protectionist, and in the cinema the American share of the Italian box office plummeted to less than a third. Italian national production, supported by that of other European Economic Community (EEC) countries, seemed sufficient to satisfy public demand. It looked as if European culture could counterbalance the avalanche of American culture. This proved to be an illusion, however, for while European co-production made economic sense in the cinema, the cultural character of the co-produced films could rarely be described as "distinctively" European. Since the 1970s, Hollywood has dominated Italian screens, especially those of TV. The shows have been for the most part cheap to acquire and undemanding to watch.

The American Myth in Literature

The success of American films in Italy is partly the result of an Italian fascination with America. The Italians perceived America, from the time of its first discovery, as an Eden, a recovery of innocence. Europeans in the age of discovery needed to believe that somewhere there was a land free from the plagues and famines, the dynasties and social classes, and the hypocrisies and cynicism of the Old World. For Italians, America was that land.

Most Italians, unable to visit or emigrate to the U.S., had to be content with an imaginary journey made possible by the accounts and letters of relatives and friends who had made it over. For them, America was a strange, mythical land, whose extraordinary wealth and generosity were often the subject of animated conversation. Giuseppe Berto (1914–1972) wrote about America as the great land of opportunity in his short story, "Aunt Bess, In Memoriam." America was an alluring haven for the hundreds of thousands of emigrants who, during the latter part of the nineteenth century, began leaving Europe en masse for the United States in search of a better life.

The literary experience of the Italians illustrates poignantly the position America enjoyed in the aspirations of those who emigrated to America. Indeed, the Italians, like many other emigrants, built a kind of mythology that remains alive even today; the more ignorant, illiterate, and poor they were, the more they were likely to maintain this dream. The peasant, especially from the south, dreamed of America not because he necessarily hoped to be there, but precisely because America represented something fabulous and, for that reason, consoling. In Italy the myth of America was also nourished by the lack of work and land to sustain its population. The land without products to export exports its own children or else inspires them to fantasize about other lands; the people who do not find in their own country their fulfillment will search for it across the ocean. Poverty does not by itself create a sufficient or even necessary "push" to go elsewhere. But if poverty is combined with personal goals and expectations that are considered unattainable at home, and if a place exists where such hopes appear to have a great chance of realization, the desire to emigrate may become irresistible.

The myth of America in Italian literature is strongly founded in rich popular fantasy. *Fontamara* (1930), by Ignazio Silone (1900–1978), provides one of the best stereotypes of America as the "Eden of the poor." The central characters are a group of peasants in the Abruzzi mountain town of Fontamara whose water rights are stolen by the local fascist landowners in league with the local capitalists. To these peasants, among the most poverty stricken and exploited in Italy, the word "America" has the power of a fetish: it stands simply for the opposite of hunger and deprivation. It is part of their private vocabulary of values and has nothing to do with the real United States. Some of the Fontamaresi, the luckier ones, have made the voyage across the Atlantic and after years of dogged work in America have come back with a little money, which they soon lose cultivating the dry and sterile earth. Their only mistake, it seems, was to come back. After a while, they fall back into the old lethargy, "holding like a memory of lost paradise the image of life glimpsed across the sea." This novel provided the sense of desperation that pushed many southern Italians to emigrate.

Cristo si è fermato ad Eboli (Christ Stopped at Eboli, 1945), by Carlo Levi (1902–1975), offers a more balanced view of America. On the one hand, it portrays the positive views of America held by southern Italian villagers; on the other hand, it suggests the high price of emigration. Influenced by his own experience as an exile in Gagliano in the 1930s, Levi presents a compassionate view of peasants' desire to emigrate, and even a sympathetic view of America as a symbol of prosperity and material progress. A journalist, he records without rancor and almost with a kind of ironic sympathy the fact that Gagliano, in the Basilicata region, had become a cultural colony of America; when he went there in 1935, it had 1,200 inhabitants, and there were 2,000 emigrants from Gagliano in America. However, he treats his material, which is factual, in a novelistic style, and he has a novelist's insight and flair for character. He thus manages to be both objective and personally involved in his material at the same time. He concludes that emigration is not a permanent answer to any problem, either personal or social. Life in America is good, but the price—to be uprooted from your native soil and to lose the source of strength one drew from the earth—is high.

A work by Mario Soldati (1906–1999) provided the first real confrontation between Italian and American culture because he was among the first to combine his intellectual interest with an actual visit to the United States. For Soldati, America was a barbaric country without culture, a fact he particularly noticed in daily American life. His *America primo amore (America First Love, 1935),* the first detailed account of daily life in America, adds new and strikingly different images and interpretations of the New World. It is a novelist's kind of travel book: impressionistic, vivid, and highly personal. The title makes clear from the outset that the author offers the book not as a sociological or political study, but simply as a story of a personal encounter. First loves are ecstatic experiences, but they are also emotional and unrealistic and they frequently end in disenchantment. Throughout the book Soldati's emotional relation to America is obvious; he writes about America the way any sensitive novelist would write about the girl he was in love with when he was 20 and with whom he later became disenchanted. The mood is disillusioned, often ironic, but rigidly honest and never totally hostile.

An interesting dimension can be found in Livia De Stefani's *Passione di Rosa (Passion of Rosa, 1958),* because as a woman writer who spent two years in the U.S., she addresses directly the theme of dislocation to another culture. Her novel communicates the experience of being a Sicilian and a woman in an America free of the male-oriented norms that dominate Sicily. Her book captures the flavor of America as it seems to an Italian in a way few other books do. In addition to her feminist point of view, the other pole of the novel is her birthplace, Sicily. Part of the interest of *Passione di Rosa* relates to the geographical resemblance of Sicily to California; the two regions are physically alike and yet their people and customs are totally different. This difference in the two societies and the effect it has on a young Sicilian immigrant is the focus of the novel. America is presented as in a dream, and as a dream it lasts only as long as it remains a dream; at the first contact with reality it dies. For many immigrants America, too much idealized, became a shattered dream.

Italians continue to wish to encounter America and Americans through writings. This phenomenon happened almost accidentally. The vogue of American literature in the thirties was assisted by a quite incidental fact: that the younger generation of Italian writers, their own creativity discouraged by the fascist regime, turned to reviewing and translation for economic support. A high proportion of these young translators went on to become important novelists and critics. One was Cesare Pavese (1908–1950), who translated Herman Melville, Sherwood Anderson, John Dos Passos, and William Faulkner. His successful translation of *Moby Dick* became for the young Italians of Pavese's generation, more than any other book, what America stood for. Although Pavese never came to America and never even seems to have entertained the idea, in many ways emigration would have been the logical solution to his personal problems. He felt alienated and restless in Italian culture, and from the time of his first poems, he portrayed America as representing a new start, a return to the primitive and genuine. But even if he never considered it as a personal possibility, the idea of emigration always lies just beneath the surface of his writings. Indeed, his first poem, *Lavorare stanca* (Working Is Tiring, 1931), is about the myth of emigration. The protagonist emigrant, drawn from life, is metamorphosed into myth; upon his return, after 20 years of wandering over the world, he tells stories to match those in the *Odyssey*. The emigration theme is further developed in Pavese's *La luna e i falò* (The Moon and the Bonfires, 1949), considered one of the best postwar Italian novels, in which the emigrant, a peasant, returns with two contradictory images of America: the traditional emigrant legend of a land of opportunity and easy riches, and the other, of an America he had discovered in his books—the America of the pensive barbarians, the mythic soil of Walt Whitman, Sherwood Anderson, and *Spoon River Anthology*. It was the example of these writers that led Pavese to search his own native soil for meaning. His protagonist comes to realize that Americans, like Italians, do not know each other and suffer from private loneliness.

Nevertheless, the desire to encounter America is not always felt with the same intensity among Italians. Because of changes in the country's economy, political propaganda about America as a world political and military power, and the perception that America puts money ahead of moral values, Italian interpretations of America have not been uniformly positive.

Therefore, the image of America as home of the violent and land of the gun has also become a popular and enduring one in the minds of average Italians. For years moviegoers have watched massacres of white settlers by vicious savages and the slaughter of unarmed Indians by blood-crazed cavalrymen. They have seen shootouts at the OK Corral and gang warfare on the streets of Chicago. And most prominently, they have witnessed American fighting men from John Wayne to Rambo as they mow down Nazis or Japanese or Vietnamese or some other "enemy." America's glittering image is also tarnished by images that reflect profound social differences in American society. In fact, along with images of mass mayhem, Italians also know visions of skyscrapers, the landing on the moon, the manicured and well-equipped American college campuses, and the mansions of billionaires, as well as the poverty of Harlem and Watts, the kinds of images that reflect the worlds of both the very rich and the very poor.

American Cultural Penetrations: Language and Consumerism

The strongest evidence of the American cultural invasion was the 1958 first rock-and-roll championship in Italy. The event offered a sense of how fast the American cultural penetration was taking place in the young generation. The Italian youngsters were revealing the same behavior and attitudes of their American cohorts: gathering in gangs, wearing jeans and tennis shoes, riding motorbikes, wearing basketball jackets with large superscriptions on their backs.

The strong presence of America on Italian screens has not simply colored the Italian image of America, it has had a profound impact on Italian life. In fact, the 1950s saw the introduction in Italy of American supermarkets, frozen food, electric appliances, jukeboxes, pinball machines, pony tails, and pleated shirts. The American presence was so strong that some film directors felt it as a real cultural colonization and conveyed their message in their movies (Federico Fellini in *Vitelloni,* 1953, and *The White Sheik,* 1952). A number of films of the 1950s, such as *An American in Rome (*1955), simultaneously encapsulate and parody some of these cultural transitions. By the 1960s the model of social behavior and the consumption habits described in American situation comedies was no longer seen as the image of a distant society characterized by great wealth, but one that could be attained by many Italians through the expansion of their market.

The American way of living penetrated especially the Italian working-class house. During the years of the "Economic Miracle"(1958–1963) Italy turned into a consumer society along American lines. Italians sought consumer durables—cars, refrigerators, washing machines, dishwashers, etc.—first as luxuries or providers of social status but then quickly as necessities. The 1950s saw the expansion in Italy of those industries that could supply these goods, while mass market, American-style "women's" and "home" magazines extolled the virtues of the custom-built kitchen and the labor-saving advantage of the electrical appliances, which the Italians called *elettrodomestici.* The ideal home of these years contained a version of the American "dream kitchen" as seen in Hollywood films and American soap operas.

America served as a model of behavior for the younger generation through a specific youth market based on cultural forms such as clothing and music. The profound influence that America had in this area cannot be overstated. Exports by the U.S. to the rest of the world included not only the technical infrastructure for the construction of a youth culture but also the main cultural forms themselves—cheap records, casual clothes, and the know-how to produce them, including the system to transmit via radio and television the new music and the new modes of speech. The formation of this youth culture occurred in the 1960s as television became universal in Italy and as small transistor radios became available at a low price to virtually everyone. In the course of the 1960s in Italy, more than anywhere else, the U.S. cultural form of the youth generation—music, clothes, etc.—was partly integrated by highly politicized forms of protest. This remarkable politicization was more deep-rooted and had a longer lasting effect than the 1968 French student movement, the only other comparable phenomenon in the rest of Europe.

America also had a strong influence on the use of media by politicians. Since the late 1960s, politicians have adapted and packaged their political discourse through various media techniques.[7] Italian politics was already delivered with a high dose of theatricality; television and American influence made the political discourse even more like a show, a spectacle. By becoming more "Americanized," the political discourse became more uniform: all politicians were subject to the same rule.

English has become the lingua franca all over the world; in Italy it is practically the second language. From the schools to the business office, in both scientific and social worlds, Italians are becoming anglophones. This new passion is not so much reflective of a new love as of the necessities imposed by new economic and industrial world realities. The passion has spilled over and has affected the Italian language. English linguistic penetration, or "intimate borrowing," abounds. There has been a more permanent incursion of English terms into the everyday vocabulary of Italian business and technology, where words like marketing, cash-flow, pipeline, design, and fast food have become common currency simply because no one has invented adequate Italian equivalents. The Italian government did not become alarmed at this trend, unlike the French government, which in 1977 made virtually illegal the use of foreign words in advertisements, official documents, and even on radio and television if French alternatives could be found.

The two languages, as is well known, have a common base. Words containing a Latin or, more generally, a romance language base abound in the technical, intellectual, and philosophical discourse in English. Such words most often give rise to loans. Aside from the remarkable number of phonographs (idea, trombone, opera, propaganda, piano, zero, piccolo, chiaroscuro, panorama, etc.) and the quasi-phonographs (umbrella, volcano, tobacco, pantaloons, etc.) to ancient Latinisms and Italianisms, there are also a number of word pairs that differ only in their respective endings (letter-*lettera*, animal-*animale*, second-*secondo*, stories-*storie*, horoscope-*oroscopo*, allergy-*allergia*, solidarity-*solidarietà*, problem-*problema*, govern-*governo*, state-*stato*, comic-*comico*, television-*televisione*, list-*lista*, infinite-*infinito*, deposit-*deposito*, violent-*violento*, brutal-*brutale*, concert-*concerto*) or in the suffixes (-ion and -*ione*, -ty and –*tà*, -ent and -*ente*), which are responsible for the phenomenon of the so-called false friends.[8] Expressions such as "public relations"— *relazioni pubbliche;* "new frontier"— *nuova frontiera*; and "the rest is silence"—*il resto è silenzio*, can be translated almost automatically and are directly responsible for the formation of loan shift. In other cases the "transparency" is such as to make translation unnecessary. For instance, the reference to "palmolive oil" in the American noun "palmolive" works in such a way that "palmolive" is rarely felt to be a foreign word. In fact, even well-educated Italians think of "palmolive" as an Italian word and "palmolive soap" an indigenous product.

English words by the hundreds have entered common speech. It is not unusual to hear in daily conversation words such as OK, babysitter, picnic, barbeque, hamburger, popcorn, fun, rock, tester, shopping, basket, management, manager, business, leader, bus, taxi, shock, show, wham, wow, yippie, and weekend. The use of English abounds in the fields of business, computers, marketing and advertising, sports, tourism, fashion and cosmetics, and news. In fact, the presence of English is so strong that reference dictionaries have been created specifically for English terms used in business.

This ability of the Italian business world to adapt to changing trends highlights the fact that this aspect of life probably represents the best of Italy. No society seems better attuned to the free-enterprise system than that of the Italians; private initiative in many fields has been the secret of the "Italian miracle." Italian cabinet ministers attend international conferences trailed by a score of interpreters: Italian politicians are notorious for speaking no language other than their own. Italian businessmen, by contrast, are proud of their versatility in international communication. Not only do they attempt to minimize the linguistic barriers, but they also try to maximize their understanding of others by getting to know their culture.

Notes

1. In "Foreword" to Leo J. Wollemborg, *Stars, Stripes, and Italian Tricolor* (New York: Praeger, 1990), xv.

2. L. J. Wollemborg, 23.

3. Ibid.

4. A. Schlesinger, *A Thousand Days* (Boston: Houghton Mifflin, 1965), 879.

5. Although Italian movie theaters have been dominated by Hollywood imports for much of their history, Italy's film industry has a history of its own. In the period up to 1915, Italy was one of the world's major exporters of films. Italy became known as a producer of spectacular films on historical themes, and these films were exported partially because of their exotic value. With the First World War, and the rapid growth and organization of the U.S. film industry, Italian production went bankrupt and collapsed. Whereas in 1915 Italy produced 562 films, by 1930 that number had dropped to 12. The fascist government set about reorganizing the industry along more efficient and less wasteful lines, eventually finding itself owning studios, distribution companies, and a chain of cinemas. The Cinecittà studios were built with state money and were taken over by the state: the Centro Sperimentale di Cinematografia, a university-level film school, was established: and the Venice Film Festival was launched as an international showcase for Italian films. In 1938 the state took over the distribution of foreign films in Italy, and in retaliation the eight major Hollywood distributors withdrew from the Italian market. The result was that by 1942 Italy was producing over 100 films a year.

6. Quoted in Thomas Guback, "Shaping the Film Business in Postwar Germany The Role of the U.S. Film Industry and the U.S. State," in Paul Kerr, ed., *The Hollywood Film Industry: A Reader* (London and New York: Routledge and Kegan Paul, 1986), 250.

7. Giovanni Cesareo, "Il 'politico' nell'alba del quaternario," *Problemi del socialismo*, 22, no. 22 (1981): 28–29.

8. For a comprehensive study, see M. Cortellazo and V. Cardinale, *Dizionario di parole nuove: 1964–1984* (Turin: Einaudi, 1985).

Bibliography

Cortellazo, M. and Cardinale, V., *Dizionario di parole nuove: 1964–1984* (Turin: Einaudi, 1985).

Kerr, P., ed . *The Hollywood Film Industry: A Reader* (London and New York: Routledge and Kegan Paul, 1986).

Wollemborg, J. L., *Stars, Stripes, and Italian Tricolor* (New York: Praeger, 1990)

PART 2

ECONOMIC AND SOCIAL TRANSFORMATION

Overview

Italy has a diversified industrial economy with roughly the same total and per capita output as France and the U.K. This capitalistic economy remains divided into a developed industrial north, dominated by private companies, and a less developed, welfare-dependent agricultural south, with 20% unemployment. Most raw materials needed by industry and more than 78% of energy requirements are imported. Over the past decade, Italy has pursued a tight fiscal policy in order to meet the requirements of the Economic and Monetary Unions and has benefited from lower interest and inflation rates. The government has enacted numerous short-term reforms aimed at improving competitiveness and long-term growth. The country has moved slowly, however, on implementing needed structural reforms, such as lightening the heavy tax burden and overhauling Italy's rigid labor market and over-generous pension system, because of the current economic slowdown and opposition from labor unions. But the leadership faces a severe economic constraint: the budget deficit has breached the 3% EU ceiling. The economy experienced no growth in 2005, and unemployment remained at a high level.

Italy will continue to lose market share because of a loss of competitiveness.

" Overall the Italian economy has some serious problems because it has not adjusted sufficiently to the new challenges posed by globalization. GDP growth has averaged only 1.5% a year in the past 10 years compared with almost 2% in the rest of Euroland, including Germany. Italy's biggest problem has been weak productivity growth.

" The weakness of Italian output is primarily related to a loss of competitiveness. Given relatively low productivity growth, Italian wages should be rising less than competitors' if Italy is to maintain unit labor cost competitiveness. Instead, Italian wage growth has averaged 4.9% over the past 10 years vs. 3.5% in Euroland. The rise in relative unit labor cost (ULC) has resulted in Italian exporters steadily losing market share since the mid-1990s.

" Italy's only route to improving its growth performance is to reverse the slide in cost competitiveness. This could arise through faster productivity growth and/or wage restraint. To raise productivity growth, Italy needs to deregulate its product markets, open itself up to competition, and increase spending on education. In the absence of faster productivity growth, Italy needs to exercise much greater wage discipline.

" Demographics pose a further challenge, although rising labor force participation is positive. A more open attitude towards immigration would help to ease Italy's deteriorating demographic profile.

GDP (purchasing power parity): $1.756 trillion (2006)

GDP—real growth rate: 1.9% (2006)

GDP—per capita: purchasing power parity—$30,200 (2006)

GDP—composition by sector: *agriculture:* 2.1%
    industry: 28.8%
    services: 69.1% (2006)

Labor force: 24.63 million (2006)
        Labor force—by occupation:
        agriculture 4.4%, industry 32.6%, services 63% (2006)

Unemployment rate: 7.0% (2006)

Inflation rate (consumer prices): 2.6% (2006)

Budget: *Revenues:* $832.9 billion
        expenditures: $861.5 billion (2006)

Public debt: 107.8% of GDP (2006)

Agriculture—products: fruits, vegetables, grapes, potatoes, sugar beets, soybeans, grain, olives, beef, dairy products, fish

Industries: tourism, machinery, iron and steel, chemicals, food processing, textiles, motor vehicles, clothing, footwear, ceramics

Industrial production growth rate: −1.5% (2006)

Current account balance: −$27.62 billion (2006)

Exports: $450.1 billion f.o.b. (2006)
Exports—partners: Germany 13.6%, France 12.3%, U.S. 8%, Spain 7.2%, U.K. 6.9%, Switzerland 4.2% (2006)

Imports: $445.6 billion f.o.b. (2006)
Imports—partners: Germany 18%, France 10.9%, Netherlands 5.9%, Spain 4.6%, Belgium 4.4%, U.K. 4.3%, China 4.2% (2006)

Persistent problems include illegal immigration, organized crime, corruption, high unemployment, sluggish economic growth, and the low incomes and technical standards of southern Italy compared with the prosperous north.

From an agricultural country before World War II, Italy has changed its base to industry. It ranks as the world's fifth-largest industrial economy and belongs to the Group of Eight (G-8) industrialized nations; it is a member of the European Union and the Organization for Economic Cooperation and Development (OECD).

It is essentially a private-enterprise economy. Lack of natural resources and lack of suitable land for farming make it a net importer. Most raw materials needed for manufacturing and about 80% of the country's energy sources and even food are imported. Italy's economic strength, however, lies in the processing and the manufacturing of goods, primarily in small and medium-sized family-owned firms. Its major industries are precision machinery, motor vehicles, chemicals, pharmaceuticals, electric goods, and fashion and clothing.

Italy has few natural resources. With much of the land unsuited for farming, it is a net food importer. There are no substantial deposits of iron, coal, or oil. Proven natural gas reserves, mainly in the Po Valley and offshore Adriatic, have grown in recent years and constitute the country's most important mineral resource. Italy is in the midst of a slow economic recovery and is gradually catching up to its West European neighbors. In the aftermath of September 11, 2001 and the global economy's tailspin, Italy—like the rest of the EU—saw its economy stumble. The country entered an economic crisis in 2004, with GDP growth at about zero, although GDP started to grow again in 2005. However, statistics as of 2007 show signs of acceleration in GDP growth, estimated at 2% in 2006, a record high since 2000.

Since 1992, economic policy in Italy has focused primarily on reducing government budget deficits and reining in the national debt. Successive Italian governments have

adopted annual austerity budgets with cutbacks in spending, as well as new revenue raising measures. Italy joined the European Monetary Union in May 1998. The national
debt, which stood at roughly 124% of GDP in 1995, declined from 110.6% in 2000 to
107.8% in 2006, as it steadily falls toward the EU-imposed debt/GDP ratio of 60% of
GDP. Italy has enjoyed a primary budget surplus, net of interest payments, for the past
decade. The 1992 agreement on wage adjustments, which has helped keep wage pressures
on inflation low, remains in effect. In the post-September 11 period, imports decelerated
faster than exports, producing an $8.5 billion surplus in 2001, up from the modest 1.8
billion surplus in 2000. With respect to inflation, Italy is now firmly within norms specified
for the Economic and Monetary Union (EMU), a major achievement for this historically
inflation-prone country. Consumer inflation accelerated from 2.5% in 2000 to 2.8% in
2001. Tight monetary policy by the Bank of Italy also has helped bring inflation expectations down. GDP growth decreased from 2001 to 2002 from 1.8% to 0.4%. In 2002 GDP
grew by a margin of 0.4% and increased 0.9% in 2003, and by 1.8% in 2004, supported
by a modest recovery in economic demand.

The deficit in public administration declined to 1.4% of GDP in 2001, down from
1.7% in 2000. The last balance-of-payments data show a current account deficit of 6.8
billion euro in 2006. In light of the stability pact, the EU has been closely watching the
national deficit situation in Italy. The closest trade ties are with the other countries of the
European Union, with whom it conducts about 53.1% of its total trade (2006). Italy's
largest EU trade partners, in order of market share, are Germany (15.5%), France (11.6%),
and the United Kingdom (5.9%).

Small- and medium-sized firms: Peculiar to the Italian industrial system are the "industrial
districts," which are contained in well-circumscribed areas and comprise a tightly woven
fabric of numerous medium-sized and small companies, each specializing in a particular
sector of the production chain. In percentage terms, there are 10% more smaller-sized
companies in Italy than in Germany, almost 20% more than in France, and 25% more
than in England.

Thanks to this model, Italy is one of the countries where entrepreneurial initiative
is most developed, and entrepreneurial autonomy has allowed creativity and the search
for beautiful and tasteful finished products to flourish, making Italian products famous
the world round. This development has historic roots and local manufacturing traditions
dating back to the Late Middle Ages. This structure has meant that Italian industry has
managed to be rapid and flexible enough to respond to the various economic crises that
have hit world markets over the years. This is an industrial system that will have to face
globalization in this new millennium, and which will finally be forced to open up to direct
investments in foreign markets and not limit itself solely to exportation of the finished
product.

Agriculture: Italy's agriculture is typical of the division between the agricultures of the northern
and southern countries of the European Union. The northern part of Italy produces pri-

marily grains, sugar beets, soybeans, meat, and dairy products, while the south specializes in producing fruits, vegetables, olive oil, wine, and durum wheat. Even though much of its mountainous terrain is unsuitable for farming, Italy has a large work force (1.4 million) employed in farming. Most farms are small, with the average farm only seven hectares.

Labor: Unemployment is a regional issue in Italy—low in the north, high in the south. The overall national rate is at its lowest level since 1992. Chronic problems of inadequate infrastructure, high bureaucracy, and organized crime act as disincentives to investment and job creation in the south. A significant underground economy absorbs substantial numbers of people, but they work for low wages and without standard social benefits and protections. Women and youth have significantly higher rates of unemployment than do men. Unions claim to represent 40% of the work force. Most Italian unions are grouped in four major confederations: the General Italian Confederation of Labor (CGIL), the Italian Confederation of Workers' Unions (CISL), the Italian Union of Labor (UIL), and the General Union of Labor (UGL), which together claim 35% of the work force. These confederations formerly were associated with important political parties or currents, but they have evolved into fully autonomous, professional bodies. The CGIL, CISL, and UIL are affiliated with the International Confederation of Free Trade Unions (ICFTU) and customarily coordinate their positions before confronting management or lobbying the government.

Deficit

Years	Millions of Euro	Percent of gross national product
2001	35,963	3.0 %
2002	32,656	2.6 %
2003	37,792	2.9 %
2004	40,877	3.0 %

National debt

Years	Thousand millions of Euro	Percent of gross national product
2001	1384.4	110.7 %
2002	1362.1	108.0 %
2003	1383.1	106.3 %
2004	1429.9	105.8 %

Tax burden

Years	Percent of the gross national product
2003	42.8 %
2004	41.8 %

(Source: ISTAT)

Employment: An employment increase has been registered throughout the country but with some differences. An increase has been registered in the center (+1.6%), while it has been slighter in the northern regions (north-west +1.4% and north-east +1.1%). After the relevant increases at the beginning of the 2000s, the south registered a limited increase of 0.2% in the number of employees in 2005. An employment increase has been registered in all the economic sectors in 2005, except agriculture. The employment rate has registered the following changes in the age group 15-64:

Total		1995: 51.0%	2000: 53.7%	2006: 58.4%
	Females	35.4 %	39.6%	46.3%
	Males	66.9%	68.0%	70.5%
For age group 55-64:				
	Total	28.4%	27.7%	32.5%
	Females	13.5%	15.0%	21.9%
	Males	44.6%	40.9%	43.7%
Unemployment Rate				
	Total	11.2%	10.1%	6.8%
	Females	15.4%	13.6%	8.8%
	Males	8.6%	7.8%	5.4%

Source: Eurostat

U.S.-Italy economic relations: The United States and Italy cooperate closely on major economic issues, including within the G-8. With a large population and a high per capita income, Italy was the United States' eleventh-largest trading partner in 2005, with total bilateral trade of $42.5 billion comprised of exports to Italy totaling $11.5 billion and imports from Italy worth $31.0 billion. The U.S. ran a $19.5 billion deficit with Italy in 2005, up from $17.4 billion in 2004. Part of this imbalance has been due to a strong dollar. Significant changes are occurring in the composition of this trade. Value-added products such as office machinery and aircraft are becoming important U.S. exports to Italy. U.S. foreign direct investment in Italy at the end of 2004 exceeded $33.3 billion.

Introduction

The production and exchange of goods and services, which constitute the basis of economic life, have been evolving since World War II through periods of growth and periods of recession, which in Italy have broadly followed the same patterns as in other industrialized economies in Europe. However, at a more substantive level, the Italian production system has evolved at its own rhythm. Thus we shall first describe the main stages in the evolution of the Italian economic system since World War II and then go on to analyze the changes in the labor force and in the structure of firms. In Italy, these stages are more marked than in other European countries.

The development of production in terms of volume, value, and structure has taken place in two distinct periods, which have radically different characteristics. The first extends from immediately after World War II (the Reconstruction period) up to 1974. During that time Italy experienced unprecedented growth, comparable to that of Japan and West Germany. The second took place in the second half of the 1980s to the mid-1990s with the strong emergence and performance of the small-sized family owned firms. During these periods there were two surprising and striking indicators. First, in the mid-1990s Italy had one of the highest rates of unemployment in Europe, but at the same time, it was achieving one of the highest rates of growth in Europe and a low inflation rate. Second, during the 1980s income differentials increased, thus reversing the trend of three previous decades toward a narrowing of income differentials and more social equality. Despite this, the 1980s were a period of relative social peace, with the lowest number of working days lost through strikes since World War II, again contradicting the perceived idea that Italian people are especially prone to protests.

An Economy with Strong Dualities

The dominant theme in studies of the economy has been that of Italy's dichotomies: first, between one part of the economy that is technologically advanced, with high levels of productivity, and a more traditional part of the economy that is more labor intensive and has low levels of productivity; second, between a part of the economy that used to comprise very large firms and a part that comprises thousands of very small firms, with the absence of much medium-sized enterprise in between; and third, between a rapidly developing north and a backward and underdeveloped south. Of the three aspects of Italy's dichotomies, the territorial divide (between north and south) was for a long time the main focus of academic study. Indeed, *la questione meridionale* (the southern question) has been studied since the beginning of the 20th century and has generated a vast literature spanning various disciplines. The 1980s and 1990s saw the emergence of a revisionist approach to the southern question among historians who argue that the southern question is, to a large extent, artificial. Its origin can be traced to the politics of the late nineteenth century rather than to economic reality, and its continued existence is maintained largely by comparing the south to a level of development normally expected in advanced European democracies. Consequently, all research on the south has been distorted because it has started from these premises. The revisionists' quest is to analyze the south without "meridionalization."

How can these different facets of the Italian economy be reconciled? Is it possible to find a common thread uniting the conflicting trends at work in the Italian economy and the conflicting impressions given by the current situation?

Economic Transformation and Profound Social Changes

At the end of the 1940s, Italy was still basically an agricultural country with a big agrarian society. Now, the great majority are employed in services, and the overwhelming importance of services such as education, commerce, transport, finance, health and communications, in employment and production, is mirrored by changes in the way people consume and the way they organize their lives outside of work. Today around three-quarters of the population live in urban areas and six out of seven are wage-earners as opposed to self-employed workers.

However, these changes cannot be seen entirely as positive or painless. Since the 1980s, unemployment in Italy has only recently dropped below 10% of the working population. Long-term unemployment is a form of permanent exclusion that has created a new category of poor people and families. Many large companies as well as smaller ones continue to reduce their workforces in the name of international competitiveness, and many Italian households either feel excluded from prosperity or experience deep anxiety about an economically uncertain future.

One of the most crucial challenges in the construction of some form of new, post-crisis consensus is posed by the need to reduce the social cost of economic efficiency, especially unemployment, which represents a massive waste. The second challenge is to find a way to reduce the economic gap between the north and the south. The third challenge is to find equilibrium within the open European market and the pressure of globalization. Will the Italian economy retain its specific characteristics that have made the "Made in Italy" tag popular around the world, or will these disappear in a homogeneous European economy? A fourth matter for reflection concerns the future role of the public sector and public authorities within the European Union and the liberalized world economy.

CHAPTER 5

THE ECONOMIC RECOVERY

Today's Economic Challenges

The Italian economy has changed dramatically since the end of World War II. From an agriculturally based economy, it has developed into an industrial state ranked as the world's sixth-largest industrial economy. Italy belongs to the Group of Eight (G-8) industrialized nations; it is a member of the European Union and the Organization for Economic Cooperation and Development (OECD). Today Italy is in the midst of a slow economic recovery and is gradually catching up to its West European neighbors.

From Ashes to World Economic Power

There is no other country in Europe that changed so rapidly in the postwar period. In fact, Italy changed more in the first 40 years after the war than during the previous two thousand.

Compared to 1950, the standard of living of average Italians had changed profoundly by the 1980s. The enormous gap that once existed between Italians and Americans has been closed. Indeed, by the early 1970s many Italians were proud to openly claim that "America is here now."[1]

In the 1980s the British viewed all this with a mixture of envy and admiration. Of course, Italy was starting from a much lower level than Britain and France, and the late industrialization partly explains the high growth rate. But the so-called "economic miracle," in its Italian context, was one of the most remarkable in the world, for it was achieved in the face of Italy's fundamental shortcomings.

Economic development in the postwar era was extraordinary, exceeded only by that of Germany and Japan. As in the case of those two countries, the very scale of the destruction suffered in the war was a blessing in disguise: it brought a chance to make a new start on modern lines. The British, who had the "misfortune" never to be defeated, lacked the same impetus.

Starting from Ground Zero

In 1945, Italy, or a large portion of it, was one of the poorest countries in the West. A land poor in natural resources, with only a quarter of its land suitable for farming, Italy had suffered more from the war than any other Western nation but Germany. In 1947, as one of the war's losers, Italy was obliged to pay, within seven years, $100 million to the Soviet Union, $125 million to Yugoslavia, and $105 million to Albania, besides having to mourn the loss of half a million of its citizens, care for several million wounded, and face the destruction of many factories, the annihilation of the merchant marine, and the loss of one quarter of its railways, 35% of its roads, and thousands of bridges. At the end of hostilities, destitution was widespread, and the population suffered from the classic earmarks of poverty: high illiteracy and infant mortality, poor diet, and limited education. Most housing lacked baths and much of it even running water. Unemployment and underemployment were high; inflation was rampant and taxation regressive. Banditry and black-marketeering had flourished. Panic seized the middle classes, and class hatred or class fear begat hostility to the national environment. A late industrial developer, Italy had only a modest manufacturing sector, which was centered in a narrow area of the northwest and depended heavily on tariffs and state assistance. Merely a third of the labor force was employed in industry; more than half was engaged in small-scale agriculture. In 1945 industrial production was only about 29% of what it had been in 1938, and agricultural production was reduced by about 60%. Per capita income was lower than at any time since unification and half what it had been in 1938.

However, by 1962 Italy was experiencing one of the fastest growing economies in the world. Economists labeled this the "economic miracle." It was a miracle because of the pace with which Italy recovered from a destructive war while lacking natural resources and having a topography that does not favor productive agriculture. By 1970 Italy had become the world's seventh-ranking industrial state (member of the G-7), was a leading international exporter, and held some of the most substantial gold and foreign-exchange reserves in Europe. In the 1980s she had passed England and contended with France for the fourth-ranking world industrial position. Whole new industries, such as steel, chemical, and oil refining, had been established with the most advanced technology and were able to compete with the best in Europe. Old private firms, like Fiat *(See Box on p. 139)*, Pirelli, and Olivetti, had revived to become European leaders in their fields. Unemployment had dropped from over 10% to half that figure. In about 30 years, more than five million agricultural workers had moved into industry, and the farm population had been reduced to about 11% of the total workforce. Italy had passed from an essentially poor rural society to a largely urban one. Italian craftsmanship played an important role in this process as we shall see *(See Box on p. 134)*.

By the late 1980s Italy had become one of the top five industrialized countries in the world. Leaving behind the troubled 1970s, where economic mismanagement and social disorder jeopardized its future, Italy was also named the economic miracle of the 1980s. Today, measured by almost every index of well-being, Italians are better off than most of them ever imagined possible. True, the well-being is not evenly distributed—for the south still lags far behind the north—but things have improved everywhere beyond all recognition.

Progress has been achieved through an economy that is dualistic in character: rich north vs. poor south, private vs. public enterprise, multinational companies vs. small family-owned firms. A study of the relation and change in these areas gives a clear view of how Italy changed in the last 30 years. The amazing growth can best be appreciated when it is related to the low level of available natural resources in the country.

Restructuring Agriculture

In spite of the variety of topographical conditions and the extent of mountainous terrain (80% of the country's area is mountainous or hilly), only 12% of Italian territory (buildings, roads, wasteland, waters, etc.) is actually unproductive. Apart from forests (about 21%) and abandoned and rough ground and service areas (about 9%), the surface effectively destined for annual or stable permanent cultivation amounts to little more than 58% of the entire national territory. Most of this land is owner-farmed (94%) and less than 2% is under the sharecropping system once common throughout most of the country (especially in Veneto and the central regions). Even though much of its mountainous terrain is unsuitable for farming, Italy has a large work force (1.4 million) employed in farming. Most farms are small, with the average farm only seven hectares.

Facing an Ancient Culture

At the end of World War II, Italy found itself in a complex economic predicament. How should she deal with rural laborers' conservatism, which had been a hindrance to solving the problem of land "parcelization"? Fly over many parts of Italy and you will see a crazy quilt

❋ SPIRIT

Craftsmanship in Italy

If we ask someone abroad what is the first thing that comes to mind when they hear the word "Italy," many will surely name one of Italy's famous cars or fashion designers.

Italy has a great design tradition and a vast number of craftsmen specialized in different trades and handicrafts, which often derive from artistic experience passed from generation to generation. Italian craftsmanship is admired around the world, and Italian crafts distinguish and make Italy unique in the world. Among the hand-crafted products which can be readily found in American stores are wood, ceramics, cloth, embroidery, glass and precious metals, as well as the cuisine, which is a form of art with typical hand-made products and local regional productions.

There are also other handcrafted products made by communities, such as Murano glass or Deruta ceramics, which are totally different from items mass produced in a factory.

Italian craftsmen pass their traditions from father to son, jealously keeping the secrets of their particular trade, the fruit of centuries of experience and mistakes, trials and great sacrifices. The values of artisan production keep all this in mind, and when one buys a unique product, one buys the history and tradition of a population along with it.

of thin strips; quite a modest farmer may have several tiny fields, not next to each other but scattered over miles. This is mostly the result of the equal-inheritance laws, as farms have been split up between sons with each new inheritance. Sentimental values remain very strong: how can a farmer give up a field where his father taught him to plough or leave the cherry orchard his grandfather planted? In a nation with so strong a rural tradition, *la terra* can still rouse powerful emotions.

Even after the war the land continued to be split up among a very large number of small farmers, and many of the farms are not big enough to support a family. Three-quarters of the farm holdings are less than five hectares and almost one-third are less than one hectare. Italy has the smallest average farm (7.2 hectares) in the EU, with the exception of Greece. However, the situation is changing. In the last thirty years there has been a drop in the numbers of small farms and an increase in medium to large holdings (20 hectares and more). This trend has been accompanied by fairly limited changes in land ownership and, in the case of small-holders, by abandonment of the land for the town in order to emigrate or, in any case, take nonagricultural employment.

Between 1970 and 1982 the total number of farms dropped by 10% and the cultivated area by 6%. The drop in the number of farms of all kinds and in the land area they cover may be attributed to a number of socioeconomic phenomena acting in different degrees on soil usage according to the country's various regions. A part of the cause is to be found in the persistent decrease in the population of the mountain areas, with a consequent increase in building construction; other causes are tied to the structural changes going on now in the farm sector. For example: the massive exodus of labor from farming, which has encouraged the formation of farms of greater land area; the changes that have taken place in the legal nature of farm contracts (especially as regards sharecropping and colony forms of farming); the different usage of land now; and, finally, the improved configuration of farms, especially in areas that were formerly highly fragmented.

Crop Production

Climate and geology, together with the force of tradition, have determined the yield and kind of crops Italy produces. Italy's agriculture is typical of the division between the agricultures of the northern and southern countries of the European Union. The northern part of Italy produces primarily grains, rice, sugar beets, soybeans, meat, and dairy products, while the south specializes in producing fruits, vegetables, olive oil, wine, and durum wheat. Wheat and maize are the major cereal crops with barley becoming increasingly prevalent, while rice is a specialized crop exported in large quantities. Olive, citrus, and other fruit trees are the commonest and best known, and together with vineyards, they make the country a leader in the Mediterranean and in Europe, though international competition is now strong. Italy is the largest producer of wine and the second largest olive-producing country in the world. The region with the highest production of olives is Apulia, followed by Calabria, Sicily, Latium, and Tuscany. Fruit is also important, particularly apples and peaches. Important also is the production of vegetables (tomatoes, lettuce, beans, cauliflower, and others that are deservedly well known throughout the world), which are grown especially in southern Italy—Campania, Calabria, Sicily, and Sardinia. The fine agricultural products combined with refined cooking skills have brought about the recent resurgent interest in Italian agricultural products and cuisine. The "Mediterranean diet"—lots of pasta, olive oil, little meat, and plenty of vegetables and fruits—has been touted by nutritionists in most economically advanced countries.

Of localized importance is certain tree-type crop production such as chestnut and hazelnut, utilized principally by the confectionery and bakery industries. Among other industrial crops are sugar beets and tobacco. Relatively unknown until World War II, sugar beets have become one of the important Italian agricultural products for industrial utilization.

Floriculture is now expanding rapidly, favored by Italy's mild climate and widespread greenhouse cultivation. An industrial type floriculture has developed to meet the demands of a huge national and international market. Flowers are grown for commercial purposes mainly in Liguria, along the coastal arc reaching from the western Riviera between Ventimiglia and Albenga, and, to some extent, along the eastern Riviera. The crops are cut flowers (carnations and roses especially), bouquet flowers (bulbs, gladioli, chrysanthemums), ornamental plants, and flowers and leaves for perfume manufacture.

Livestock breeding, a traditional agricultural activity, has suffered the effects of the crisis in this sector, as is apparent from underdevelopment in the last few decades. Methods are somewhat backward except in the Po Valley and consequently inadequate to the national demand for meat. Certain old customs, such as transhumance in the Apennines, are now dying out; however in the north, high altitude Alpine pastures are still grazed in the summer.

Agricultural Reconstruction

In the 1960s and 1970s Italian farming went through a real "revolution." In no other aspect of Italian life was change so dramatic or the conflict between old and new so sharp. Farm mechanization changed the landscape of the countryside at every level. The process was not easy: imagine those poor farmers, accustomed to an instinctive rapport with oxen or horses, when they were suddenly confronted with a tractor. The state took several measures to transform the very primitive agriculture that existed.

Shortcomings of State Land Distribution

A series of laws were approved in the 1950s to respond to the revolts of rural laborers of the late 1940s. These laws decreed that large, uncultivated, or badly cultivated estates in huge areas of Sicily, Sardinia, and the mainland South would be expropriated by state agencies. These agencies improved the land and then sold it to landless laborers at low cost and on long-term mortgages. The state also provided, through the *Cassa per il Mezzogiorno* (Agency for the Development of the South), essential services (irrigation, electricity, houses, roads, livestock) at public expense. Similar kinds of state intervention in agriculture had been done during fascism (e.g., the reclamation of the Pontine Marshes), but in the 1950s land was actually expropriated and given to the people.

The land reform had major political consequences. By ending the *latifundium* after more than 2,000 years, it broke the political power of the big landowners, who nevertheless remained economically powerful because they invested the capital they received from the sale of their land in the booming building industry. Land reform also created a "client class" that was dependent on the land agency. The new laborer-owners grew what the agency told them to grow, lived where the agency told them to live (often in houses built by the agency), and sold their produce through agency-run cooperatives. They also voted for the party that ran the agency, usually the Christian Democrats (*DC*). Altogether, about 70,000 families acquired land, but that was only 1% of the rural population.

This program had some shortcomings. Most of the new owners had been landless laborers, inexperienced in farming techniques. Their holdings were normally on poor land and were usually too small to support a family. These failings became more evident in later years with the increasing use of tractors and specialized machinery that are difficult to use on small farms and with increased competition from the north and European Common Market farming. The

☕ *Café* *Wines: Uniquely Italian*

Italians produce high-quality wine and they know how to enjoy it, drinking it with every meal and in between as well. The fruit of the vine has its roots implanted deep in the history of Italy as far back the Etruscan and Roman times.

Grapes are grown in almost every part of Italy, with more than 1 million vineyards under cultivation. Each region is proud of its carefully tended, neatly pruned vines. In some places the vines are trained along low supports. In others they climb as slender saplings.

From the coast to the foot of mountains, the variety of soils and climates in Italy's wine-producing regions ensures an incredible range of wines. Many Italian wines are produced with native grape varieties that aren't as familiar to the international wine market. Varietals such as Nebbiolo, Vernaccia and Trebbiano are little seen outside Italy. Other traditional Italian varieties such as Barbera, Pinot Grigio, and Sangiovese are now gaining broader awareness and recognition in other countries.

Italian wines tend to be acidic, dry, light-to-medium bodied, and subdued in flavor and aroma. Because of these characteristics, Italian wines are, in general, a better accompaniment to food than they are beverages to be enjoyed on their own. From Chianti, dry red wines that are usually best five to eight years after the vintage, typically Sangiovese, to the fresh, white Vernaccia, best enjoyed young, Italian wines offer something for every wine lover.

The main rule to remember about pairing wine with food is that there are no rules: you should drink the wines you like with the foods you like. That being said, there are some basic guidelines that can help you maximize your enjoyment of wine-food pairing.

The Italians are very careful in matching food with the proper wine, that is, matching the weight and texture of the food to the weight and texture of the wine. For example a light-bodied fish like sole works best with a light-bodied white wine like Pinot Grigio, while a heavier-bodied fish like salmon calls for a richer, fuller-bodied white like Aglianico. Italians also like to balance the intensity of flavors in the food and wine. For example, roasted red meat flavored with rosemary could go well with Amarone or Barolo.

They are also very fussy about temperature. Generally, the richer and "bigger" the wine, the warmer it should be served. Thus, red wines such as Amarone, for example, do well at about 63 to 65 degrees, while whites such as Lacrima Cristi exhibit better taste when served at 53 to 55 degrees.

Most winemaking in Italy occurs in modern wineries. However, wine making goes back to the Roman times and some regions have longer traditions than others. Tuscany is the cradle of Italian wine entrepreneurship: the Marchesi Antinori and the Baron Ricasoli are among the oldest businesses in the world.

The Antinori family, coming from a long Tuscan enological tradition, represents the vanguard of "Made in Italy" entrepreneurship. The family justly boasts of its enrollment in the Florentine Winemakers Guild since 1385, and the Antinori have remained leaders for 26 generations, becoming today one of the most prestigious and famous winemakers in the world.

land reform, far from solving the "land question," simply increased the number of poor laborers, who quickly became even more dependent on state subsidy.

In 1970 half the poor landowners of Italy were not full-time farmers; they were forced to
derive much of their income from other sources: industry, commerce, or welfare. Net welfare
payments to small landowners rose from 50 billion liras in 1954, to 245 billion liras in 1960,
to 909 billion in 1968, and to 1,412 billion liras in 1971. By this time, about one-third of the
value of all agricultural production was going to welfare payments, a system that was producing
votes for the Christian Democratic Party (*DC*). Still, Italian agriculture had improved considerably because of direct government intervention. At the end of World War II production was
only 40% of what it had been in 1938, but by 1950 it had surpassed the 1938 figure and by
1960 was 40% above it. The increase continued steadily through the 1960s and 1970s. Food
production doubled between 1950 and 1970. Yields per hectare increased sharply because of
better seeds, mechanization, more fertilizers, irrigation, and technical assistance. Because of
government policies and financial assistance, Italy has become the world's leading exporter of
durum semolina and pasta products and the leading rice producer in Western Europe.

Agricultural Land	Italy	Europe	World
Total cropland (thousand ha) 1999	11,422	307,286	1,501,452
Hectares of cropland per 1,000 population, 1999	199	422	251
Arable & permanent cropland as a percent of total land area, 1998	37 %	13.4 %	11.3 %
Percent of cropland that is irrigated, 1999	23.6 %	7.9 %	18.3 %

Source: www.nationmaster.com

Success Through Technology, Education, and Legislation

Italy's agricultural successes and overall affluence contributed to some unforeseen changes.
The "problem of wheat," so central to fascist policy, especially after the economic sanctions
in 1936, became one of overproduction and underconsumption. People ate less bread and less
pasta, but they consumed more dairy produce. In 1958 imports of cheese exceeded exports for
the first time ever! Italians also ate twice as much meat. Not only was there an increased caloric
intake, but also a rising standard of dietary demands that emphasized meat and other protein
products. However, the gap between meat production and consumption makes meat Italy's
most significant food-deficit item and makes Italy the world's third largest importer of meat and
meat products. Italy has to import half the beef and veal it consumes. For many years, the Italian
economy showed another paradox: Italy was at the same time an importer and an exporter of

PROFILE

Fiat

Founded in 1899 and based in Turin, the Fiat company name is an acronym for *Fabbrica Italiana Automobili Torino* (Italian Car Factory of Turin). In Latin, it means "let there be."

Fiat, best known for Fiat cars, is also a publishing, financial, agricultural, construction, and metallurgy conglomerate. It owns CNH Global, the second largest agricultural equipment manufacturer in the world after Deere & Company, and it is the third largest producer of construction equipment. Fiat also has a stake in commercial vehicles, buses, and firefighting vehicles.

Fiat is Italy's largest industrial concern. It operates in 61 countries and employs more than 223,000 people, 111,000 of them outside Italy. In the 1950s and 60s, by making cars affordable for the working, lower, and middle classes, Fiat played an important role in Italy's post-war economic and social recovery.

There have been some rough times in the last decade. A few years ago, it even looked as though the game might be up for the car group, by then encompassing Alfa Romeo and Lancia, with Maserati and Ferrari also in the greater Fiat empire. The parent company (also called Fiat) considered selling off its auto division—quite a humiliation, and a potential national catastrophe given that Fiat accounts for about 5 per cent of the Italian national income. Since then, however, Fiat has staged a remarkable turnaround. Its European market share is up in 2007, to 8.3 per cent from 7.8 per cent in 2006, and Fiat has returned to a trading profit. Part of the reason for that is their great new automobile model. The 1957 500, a symbol of Fiat's recovery after the Second World War, has been represented in an updated version. The new 500 was developed by the Fiat style centre and will be built in the company's plant in Poland. It's a very small, three-door hatchback—only 3.55m long, 1.65m wide and 1.49m high.

Today Fiat Auto runs well-known firms like Lancia, Alfa Romeo, Autobianchi, Innocenti, Abarth, Fiat, and Maserati. Ferrari is owned by the Fiat Group, but it is run autonomously. Light automobile sales accounted for 46.8% of total revenues during fiscal 2004 (3.2% of which is from Ferrari).

The European Car of the Year award, Europe's premier automotive trophy for the past 40 years, has been awarded eleven times to the Fiat Group, more than any other manufacturer.

meat; it had to export the second cuts of imported meat because Italians ate only first cuts. Since the arrival of American fast food restaurants (for a long time McDonald's in Rome grossed the highest amount of any restaurant in the chain), Italy does not export any more meat!

The introduction of the American system of chicken raising, Perdue style, has also helped to meet the increased national consumption of chickens. At the beginning of the 1960s Italy imported chickens from the U.S., sacrificing quality for quantity; today Italy has become one of the largest producers of poultry meat in the EU.

Italy is the EU's leading producer of fruits and vegetables, which significantly contributes to export earnings. By 1960 Italy was the world's largest producer of wine; it bottled about a quarter of all wine in the world and had improved its quality by putting on the market some of the most renowned wines in the world. By introducing an effective quality control, first by creating the DOC (Denomination of Origin Controlled) wines and later the DOCG (Denomination of Origin Controlled and Guaranteed) for very few exclusive wines, exports increased considerably. Not only did the wines from the more traditional areas of wine country (Chianti and Brunello da Montalcino in Tuscany; Barolo and Amarone in Piedmont; Soave and Pinot Grigio in the Veneto) consolidate their position on the world market, but wines from the south (Taurasi and Aglianico, in Campania; Corvo from Sicily) conquered a good slice of the market reserved for prestigious wines *(See Box on p. 137).*

However, overproduction of wine created serious problems in the EU French farmers resorted to riots in the 1970s to stop the competition presented by some of the more cheaply produced and often more robust Italian wines. The issue was solved when the two nations banned all planting of new vineyards and granted new subsidies for uprooting poor vines. Many producers have now pulled up their vines and changed to other crops with the help of special grants from Rome and the EU.

Through acts of legislature, the government has also been trying to consolidate farm holdings: any time a farmer puts property on sale, by law, the adjacent owners must be informed and must be given preference, if interested, in the sale.

Farmers Achieve a New Social Status

Overall, the government has succeeded in substantially improving the social conditions and status of farmers. In the 1950s the rural laborers still fell into the lowest income bracket; they had the least access to modern conveniences (running water and indoor plumbing) and owned the fewest consumer items (appliances and automobiles). They had the lowest level of education, and their occupation, working the land, was accorded the lowest social prestige. Much of the these workers' apparent resignation had in fact been a result of a long history under a static and feudal system. In the Italian tradition, culture resides in the city, in the *civitas;* life outside of the city lacked any refinement or spiritual fulfillment. Ignazio Silone, in his novel *Fontamara*

(1934) (discussed in chapter 4), represented with somber intensity the life of poverty and sacrifice endured by southern farmers and the scorn to which they were subjected. Farmers used to be considered a social class apart. In the 1960s the situation started to change; since then, there has been a radical change in poor farmers' self-image and in their attitude toward the social system. Improvement in their living conditions, advances in communication (local roads, transport, availability of telephone, special TV programs dealing with

Labor unions demonstrations are numerous and colorful. From the archive of the author.

agriculture issues and farm life), and awareness of the world beyond the boundaries of their own community have made farmers accepted citizens of the wider community.

Traditional poor rural society, once such a strong and picturesque feature of Italy, is passing away, and the new-style farmer is more like a small businessman: he often has a beautiful car and a modern home, and his children are scarcely different from town children. Thus, although the old-style rural worker, semi-literate, living in poor conditions, still exists in some areas, especially in certain areas of the south, a new generation of modern-minded young farmers, with a totally different outlook from their parents, has arisen. They have promoted a new creed, entirely novel in this individualistic milieu: a creed of technical advance, producer groups, and marketing cooperatives. Finally, the old class of *contadini* or *cafoni* (pejorative terms for farmers) has largely become integrated into society.

Unfortunately, as old problems have been solved, new ones have emerged. The Italian government has had to face an aging farm population and an alarming shortage of skilled agricultural workers. Many small farms are in the hands of people who are actually employed in manufacturing or service or are unemployed and who use family farm plots to supplement their food supplies and their incomes. Worse yet, Italian farming is still plagued by a high degree of traditional individualism. Thus, the country has to solve major dilemmas: the old one of how to reconcile the nation's economic needs with the human demands of the family farm, and the new one, shared with the rest of the EU, of how to reduce costly food surpluses without depressing farmers' incomes.

The Changing Face of the Industrial Sector

By the end of 1946 the capabilities of Italian industry were estimated to be approximately equivalent to those of prewar 1938. The rate of productivity, however, could not be increased rapidly because the country was still facing a crippled transportation system and, more fundamentally, the scarcity of raw materials, fuel, and foreign exchange. Confronted with these problems, the economic policy makers of the time broke into two very distinct camps:

- " Those who thought that the reconstruction efforts and the ensuing development had to be centrally planned and directed by the state
- " Those who favored a market-oriented solution, leaving to the free interplay of market forces the most optimal allocation of resources.

The former policy position was favored by the parties of the left, which somewhat paradoxically wanted to use the interventionist economic tools inherited from fascism. They supported the continued rationing of food in order to even out the standard of living among the population and the change of all the currency in circulation so as to identify and tax the holders of large amounts of capital, who in many cases had profited through speculation from the war. The Left also favored very strict controls over foreign exchange transactions and a program of nationalization of the largest industrial groups, connected also to an effective antitrust policy supporting smaller enterprises. On the other hand supporters of free-market and economic liberalization included those who wanted to see administrative controls dismantled and public spending curbed. They opposed the change of currency for its possible negative impact on depositors' confidence and on monetary policy. While accepting the need for expanded debt financing and greater taxes on the largest holders of wealth, they resolutely supported a workers' wage freeze.

Within the governments of national coalition, those in favor of the removal of restrictions to economic activity progressively imposed their views.

Embracing the Western Models

Italy's economic policies were affected by the U.S. presence on the Italian peninsula and its determination to keep Italy in the Western camp. The Marshall plan was not only used effectively to achieve humanitarian objectives, but it was also applied to stop the advance of communism, which had become a big threat to democracy in Western Europe. Government leaders made several policy decisions that profoundly affected the future of the country. Italy became a member of the IMF (International Monetary Fund), which required greater liberalization and stability of the exchange rate; it joined the Organization of European Economic Cooperation (1949); it entered into the European Payments Union (1950), and it was a founding member of the European Coal and Steel Community (1951). This last event marked the beginning of the European integration, which started with the European Common Market (Treaty of Rome, 1957).

The Economic Miracle

In the 1950s Italy's domestic product increased by more than 50%; investments roughly doubled, and exports almost tripled. It was a major achievement for a country that had been devastated during World War II. This dramatic economic growth reached an impressive climax between 1958 and 1963, when GDP grew an average of 7.5% every year. Between 1952 and 1963, per capita income almost doubled. The percentage of workers engaged in agriculture went from 42.2% in 1951 to 29.1% in 1961 while by 1961 the percentage of industrial workers exceeded 40%, up from 32.1% in 1951. The percentage of workers in the service sector increased as well from 25.7% in 1951 to 30.3% in 1961. The profound transformation of Italy into an industrial country was also reflected by the production figures which for the decade revealed growth rates of about 10% yearly in the industrial sector and about 3% in agriculture. This economic growth was accompanied by price stability, high rates of investment, and lack of imbalances in the external accounts. The period 1958–1963 became known as the years of the "economic miracle."

The "economic miracle" was not experienced uniformly throughout the country. The growth was mainly concentrated in the northwest industrial triangle of Genoa-Turin-Milan, an area that became the destination of thousands of emigrants from the south. Between 1951 and

1961 the population of Milan increased by 24.1%, while that of Turin grew by 42.6%. With large masses relocating to the north, the supply of labor became swollen and the bargaining power of unions was considerably less. Italy thus experienced in those years an export boom which was propelled mostly by low labor costs.

The Expansion of the Industrial Sector

The most significant improvement in the Italian economy and society came through a very innovative and largely expanded industrial sector with heavy dependence on imported energy. By the early 1970s manufacturing became the largest sector of the economy, comprising 35% of GDP and employing 30% of the labor force.

The structure of industrial production and service industries is characterized by the prevalence of small and medium-sized companies (94% and 5.6%, respectively), employing 70% of the workforce, with 30% being monopolized by large companies (more than 100 workers) although these comprise only 0.45% of the total. This means that companies are widely dispersed over the whole country, obviously with significant location and concentration of industry, and more than half the industrial companies operate at little more than workshop level, as is seen by the small workforce in each production unit.

There are only a limited number of cooperative companies (food sector and the processing of agricultural products), while large companies tend to become multinational. The presence of companies with foreign capital monopolizing specific commodity sectors (pharmaceutical, photographic materials, electronics, cosmetics, etc.) is far from rare.

One particular kind of development may be seen in medium-sized companies. Frequently these have expanded from small family-run businesses with specialized production technology; through management flexibility and technological innovations they have succeeded in reconverting production and increasing competitiveness. They have penetrated international markets and have contributed to the consolidation of the Italian image and presence throughout the world. It was because of the high productivity of this sector of the industry that in the mid-1980s Italy experienced the so-called second "economic miracle." However, this sector will face big challenges in a globalized economy.

In addressing the specific industrial sectors, the country's economic revival in the immediate postwar period was essentially sustained by development and expansion of the basic industries, particularly the steel industry, itself conditioned by the importation of raw materials such as ores, scrap iron, and coal. Membership in the ECSC (European Community for Steel and Coal) in 1951 enabled the Italian steel industry, which had installed the integral processing cycle, to attain extremely high levels of production, thus satisfying increasingly greater domestic demand, such as that of the engineering industry, as well as the export market. Although this sector is now stagnating, owing to the international economic situation dominated by strong competition from the emerging Asian economies, it gave a strong impetus to the Italian industrial structure in those years of industrial recovery.

Mechanical engineering production became extremely varied and included industries such as shipbuilding, aerospace, car building, etc., with complex work cycles, together with manufacturers of simple tools. Component manufacturing also became well developed and closely allied to companies that produced durable goods not easily classified in any one sector (for example, non-metallic materials used in the car industry: rubber, glass, plastics, etc.). In practice, mechanical engineering, with its diversification and multiple relationships with other industries, is still today considered the mainstay of the national production system in terms of the large workforce employed (over 2 million, according to the 2000 census). Apart from cars and other vehicles, the most highly developed industries are tools, household appliances, electronic equipment, and precision instruments. The industrial machinery sector is particularly active with extensive overseas exports.

Another important change in the industrial sector of the Italian economy was the surge of the chemical and energy industry. The chemical industry is closely linked to mining and quarrying and uses mostly liquid (oil) and gaseous hydrocarbons (methane), from which a high range of materials is produced (rubber, plastics, synthetic resins, synthetic fibers, fertilizers, etc.) in addition to the traditional utilization of heating fuel, engine fuel, etc.

Like the steel industry, the chemical industry went through a critical period because of over-production and problems related to plant modernization. One serious additional shortcoming is the need to resort to large-scale importation of raw materials for transformation, with the consequent submission to fluctuating conditions on the international market.

The Textile Industry

In any discussion of the industrial sectors that spurred the Italian economy, it is important to mention the textile industry. Textiles are the oldest Italian industry. Although widespread throughout the peninsula, they are chiefly concentrated in four regions (Lombardy, Veneto, Tuscany, and Marche) and are linked to the rural community, which provides plentiful low-cost labor. In the postwar period, this sector faced a period of crisis caused primarily by the use of antiquated machinery and inefficient working methods, though also by competition from foreign producers, particularly developing countries, which were already raw material suppliers (cotton, wool, jute, etc.). Because Italy is a net importer of raw material for synthetic fibers and labor cost is very high, its garment industry has been facing big challenges from the invasion of goods produced in China.

Food Industry

The development of the Italian food industry is a direct consequence of the expansion of large urban centers and progressive industrialization. Strictly allied to the primary sector (agriculture and livestock), the food industry nevertheless makes considerable use of imports, the result of insufficient national agricultural and livestock production. A scattering of small artisan-type firms generally oriented toward meeting local demand has now been joined by a number of medium-sized companies operating at a national level, using advanced systems of processing, conservation, and packaging.

The diversification of Italian industry has reached the point where it becomes difficult to classify producers in specific sectors. Certain industries, some traditional, have made a highly important contribution locally or in a specific context to the country's development. One example is the building industry in general (constructions, roads, etc.), particularly the housing sector, which after the depression that affected the whole country between 1975 and 1985, appears to be in a new phase of development. Satellite activities include cement production, with Italian raw materials (lime, marl, etc.), other building materials (ceramics, bricks), and glass manufacture. The woodworking industry, a solid, generally localized industry, uses mainly imported raw materials specifically in the production of household goods and furniture. The manufacture of paper and allied materials has been traditional for centuries and is linked to the production of packaging and particularly to printing and publishing.

Industrialization and State Industries

Lacking basic natural resources to become an industrial nation, Italy had to create a transformational economy much as Japan did. This implied major changes and gambles because Italy became a nation dependent on raw material and a target nation for the export of manufactured goods and, therefore, vulnerable to changes in the international economy. But Italy accepted the challenge and quickly fostered a policy of open economy to stimulate international trade. The major event was the establishment of a European Common Market (Treaty of Rome, March 1957), which opened a larger market for Italian products.

The Italian industrial sector is part of a dualistic economy: private enterprise with a large public sector. Except for agriculture, there are few sectors of the economy in which the state does not operate and several in which it dominated after the war. Not only have many companies had mixed public and private ownership, but all firms, both public and private, are still subject to many legal and financial restraints and carry heavy burdens of social welfare responsibility.

Until the early 1990s, in no other country with a free economy was the government asked to play such an important role in the economy. The Italian government was asked to restructure industry, to improve exports, to make Italy more competitive in world markets, to win it more prestige and respect in international politics, to close the amenities gap between the north and the south, to protect the lira and keep inflation within bounds, to reduce inequality, to provide cheaper energy and curb nuclear power, to take care of every special interest group, and to guarantee everyone work, adequate housing, and health care.

How Government Shaped the Industrial Sector

Today, as we shall see, governments bend to allow more freedom to free enterprise, for the view has gained credence that too much state control puts a damper on private firms' initiative, especially in a competitive free market. This may well be so now. But it does not invalidate the policy of state economic intervention or participation in the earlier postwar decades that was largely a source of strength at a time when private industry was backward or nonexistent and needed a strong lead. In fact, there seems to be no doubt that during that period dynamic state leadership was able to do much for economic development. Governments were able to plan bold new ventures and build up certain key industries.

At the beginning of the 1990s, the government's involvement in the economy was still extensive, especially through state-owned industries. Indeed, the basis for public intervention in the economy was the system of state holdings—regulated by the ministry bearing that name, established in 1956—which represented a necessary tool by means of which the state could exercise control over, and act directly in, the country's development, causing it to attain those results dictated by state economic policy. Initially concentrated in the vicinity of large cities, busy ports, or sources of energy and raw materials, with the declining importance of agriculture, industry moved nearer smaller centers with adequate infrastructures before spreading into the countryside, competing with agriculture for land and changing the face of the country. Nevertheless, in both the north and south the most highly industrialized and urbanized areas are mainly in the densely populated regions.

The traditional industrial triangle (Lombardy-Liguria-Piedmont) has now widened to include practically the whole Po Valley, with the highest concentrations along the foot of the pre-Alps, pre-Apennines, and the Adriatic Coast, as well as the large Alpine valleys. Industry in Tuscany and Umbria is concentrated on the plains and in hollows near the Arno and Tiber river basins: in the Marches it spreads over the whole region, scattered throughout the network of valleys. Industry in Latium and Abruzzo is concentrated in the intermontane hollows and along the coasts as well as around the larger cities.

The distribution of industry in southern Italy, however, follows an irregular pattern, with excessive concentration in certain coastal zones (such as the Caserta-Naples-Salerno belt) or in a number of geographically favorable positions (the Bari-Taranto-Brindisi triangle). Industrial areas on the islands are generally peripheral to port cities.

The Role of the State Holdings

Three state holdings played a very important role in the Italian economic recovery: IRI (Institute for Industrial Reconstruction), ENI (National Hydrocarbons Agency), and EFIM (Agency for Holdings and Financing of Manufacturing Industry). Until the beginning of the 1990s, they covered every sector of the economy, including banking.

IRI had seven sectorial holding companies.[2] Before the privatization process started in the early 1990s, for example, the banking sector of IRI had a large majority of the share capital of such banks as the *Banco Commerciale Italiana*, the *Credito Italiano*, the *Banco di Roma*, and the *Banco di Santo Spirito*. Approximately 90% of the banking activity was in the hands of public sector banks.

Besides the companies headed up by the holding companies and the banks, the group also included a number of firms that were directly controlled by IRI. Among these, the most important were the firms operating in the air transport sector (Alitalia), in the toll-expressway sector (Autostrade), and in the radio-television sector (*RAI*). In 1982, IRI had over 535,000 employees (ranked second in the world, after General Motors, in number of employees). That year it had a turnover of 32.9 trillion liras ($26 billion) and grew to an estimated 47.6 trillion liras in 1989, ranking it fourteenth in the world and third outside the U.S. The privatization that took place in the early 1990s reduced considerably the size of IRI.

ENI, the National Hydrocarbons Agency (1953), was a public holding company whose purpose was to promote and carry out initiatives in the nation's interest in the hydrocarbons and natural steam fields. The group's organizational structure broke down into four main sectors: hydrocarbons (coal, oil), chemical and nuclear, engineering and services, and manufacturing.[3] ENI made a relevant contribution to Italy's economic expansion. Privatization in the 1990s brought this important state holding to its death.

EFIM, the Agency for Holdings and Financing of Manufacturing Industry, privatized in 1992, had as its purpose intervention in the industrial sector to aid further development. Its activities were carried on through firms controlled and coordinated by means of sectorial holding companies.[4] This job was carried out not just through financing but through the performance of services and functions as well, which made it possible for even average-sized firms to get into foreign markets and to make use of more efficient computer and management systems and more effective applied research.

In the 1980s, these state industries became too inefficient and were even considered a liability. Under the new world trade conditions of open frontiers and multinational groupings, the Italian economy can prosper only if it becomes more market oriented and firms cease to rely on state support or protection. Even more detrimental to the national economy was the fact that the big state projects have too often been directed with an eye to political kudos rather than economic usefulness. The public sector had been ruled more by political needs than market demands, and this situation had to change if Italy was going to compete in the open markets of the future.

The Economic Phoenix

Italy's economic development has evolved in several phases and has followed a tortuous road. Economists are in broad agreement that the basis of the launching pad for the economic growth was provided in the immediate postwar period by President Luigi Einaudi's harsh deflation policy, with its tight credit and cuts in government spending that brought inflation under control, stabilized the lira, and won international confidence. The internal policy was supported with aid from the Marshall Plan, which provided a massive infusion of funds to finance vital imports; the discovery of natural gas in the Po Valley, which gave Italy its first indigenous energy source; and a great reservoir of cheap and highly mobile labor. The continuing high level of unemployment was largely caused by the massive shift of population from the south to the north, from rural areas to the cities, and from agriculture into manufacturing and services. Between 1958 and 1963, the number of workers in the agriculture field had declined by 50%. The resulting low labor costs also helped to make Italian goods highly competitive in world markets. In this situation, profits were high and, reinvested in capital stock, produced rapid industrial growth.

With the Italian entry into the European Economic Community in 1957, the country not only gained an expanded market but also was forced into free-market competition in which its products surprised everyone by selling extremely well. In fact, it was exports that led the economic miracle to its heights between 1958 and 1963.

In the early 1960s, many U.S. and other Western observers suddenly discovered the Italian "miracle." They extolled the unexpected developments that seemed to enable Italy to join the leading group of the major industrial nations of the West. Improvements were given additional luster and appeal by a happy season of Italian creativity in such disparate fields as interior decoration, movies, shoes, architecture, and office equipment.

Cheap Labor: The Most Important Ingredient of the Economic Miracle

The economic "boom," as it was also labeled, happened because of the politicians who had fought successfully to replace the protectionism traditionally prevailing in Italy with a wide-ranging liberalization of the country's foreign trade. The "boom" also took place because of the industrialists, technicians, and businessmen who had risen to the challenge by making many Italian products competitive on the international markets. It also took place because of the millions of hard-working and often poorly paid Italians who had played a decisive part in the "quality jump" of the "Made in Italy" label.

The growth was due mainly to low wage rates, which were possible because of high unemployment in the south, weak trade unions, the mobility of the population, and international monetary stability. The exodus from the farms, which gave factories a steady supply of new recruits, with a rural laborer's readiness to work hard for low wages helped to keep down the price of Italian goods and make them competitive on the international market. Another factor that affected the growth in those years was the fact that export prices rose 3.8% per year while the cost of imported raw materials fell on the average of 2% per year. The resulting profits provided substantial capital for investments.

The rapid economic expansion soon brought problems, however, because it ameliorated some of the basic conditions which had helped to spark it—notably the low level of wages and the mass consumption that reflected, in turn, a large and chronic unemployment and underemployment. Too many Italians did not foresee that any sudden speedup in economic growth involves and sharpens tensions, imbalances, and frustrations. In the case of Italy, the costs could be very high because the benefits of the "forward jump" were mostly concentrated in the industrial sector (and did not affect all of it, either) and because the country's administrative, economic, and financial structures were far from adequate for the requirements of a modern democracy.

A Turn in the Economy

In 1963, when the unemployment rate reached a record low of 3.6%, unions started to press for concessions, especially in wages. Gradually these increases went above productivity growth, squeezing profit margins and reducing investments. With more money available, private consumption increased and demands became greater, which resulted in high inflation. The industrial system reacted in its traditional conservative way: lower investments and more utilization of existing labor. As one may expect, the economic crisis brought about a social crisis that then exploded in the "Hot Autumn of 1969" with student revolts.

It is clear in retrospect that, economically, Italy was a puzzle in the 1960s. The country may have had all the trappings of a modern democracy, but neither its social and institutional structure nor its administrative practices had been brought in line with those of the other Western democracies. The country still lacked the facilities to deal with its problems: an equitable and effective tax system, a foresighted approach to land tenure and agricultural problems, antitrust legislation, efficient regulatory agencies in the fields of power, trade, and labor relations, and a modern educational system. At the same time, the tremendous development of television and other communications, although state-controlled, was bringing home to more and more Italians the great gap between the formal ideology that was supposed to guide the country's affairs and their daily experience of the way those affairs actually were conducted.

The Communist Party did not miss the opportunity to exploit this situation and increasingly strengthened its position as champion of social and economic reforms, and fighter against arbitrary authority, public graft, mismanagement, and attempts to hush up scandals and abuses.

The 1960s were years of workers' struggles and political changes. During the recession in 1964, the Socialist Party joined the Christian Democrats in order to form a government based on a program of economic development. This coalition attempted to make the economic system more dynamic by nationalizing certain corporations in the electrical and chemical sectors, including many public services, and started a program for far-reaching reforms and modernization of Italian administrative, fiscal, and financial structures. This economic program was supposed to contain the tools necessary to carry out the reforms required to do away with the chronic geographic and social imbalances and to insure, at the same time, a steady growth. This program was also supposed to render the communist opposition, already weakened by its decision to engage only in parliamentary struggle, completely ineffective.

Social Transformation and Resourceful Italians

By early 1967, it was clear that very little progress had been made in implementing the center-Left's program that was agreed on in 1962–63. The paramount need to avoid an economic slump, following the disorderly boom of the early years, led to the delaying or watering down of the other social reforms originally pledged by the alliance. This had suited most Christian Democrats, who sought to gain votes from the fading parties of the Right. But most socialists, fearful of losing ground on their Left, were pressing again for more vigorous action.

Social Unrest and Students' Revolts

The Italian people, for the most part, had become restless. Unprecedented protests and rebellion by university students represented the most significant challenge to the political establishment and were the most evident symptom of the problems besetting a country that had become one of the seven leading industrial and trading nations but still retained many institutions and administrative practices from the turn of the century (this topic will be treated in greater depth in chapter 9). The student population, which was less than 60,000 in 1935, had now reached almost 450,000. Despite some progress, physical facilities had expanded at a much slower pace, and the number of professors had risen to only 8,000, in comparison to 2,700 in 1935. Moreover, many professors were too busy in politics or business to show up for classes, let alone to devote sufficient attention to their students. University power was still concentrated in a small and self-perpetuating group of deans and full professors. Students demanded a complete

Employment rate by gender and geographic areas (2006)

Geographic areas	Male and female percentage	Male percentage	Female percentage
Total	58.5	70.3	46.7
North	66.4	75.7	56.9
North-west	66.0	75.3	56.6
North-east	67.0	76.4	57.4
Center	61.7	72.4	51.2
Mezzogiorno	46.6	62.1	31.5

Source: ISTAT

revision of the system and wanted their own representatives, as well as those professors of junior rank, to have a voice in running university affairs. Under the leadership of a small group of activists, sometimes self-labeled as "Maoists," "Castroites," or "anarchists," students started a vague but loud and even violent revolt against society. Such a development was taking place just when the center-left governmental coalition had finally presented a reform bill intended to correct at least the most outdated features of the university system.

Similar dissatisfaction was behind industrial and civil servants' strikes and recurrent unrest over such issues as reorganization of the bureaucratic apparatus, modernization of the social security system, and hospital reforms. In those and other fields, the center-Left coalition had achieved more than previous governments, but less than it had pledged or had been thought possible.

A turning point came in the fall of 1969, when workers set in motion a revolution in industrial relations. The delayed effects of the prolonged series of strikes in the industrial sector during the "Hot Autumn of 1969"—which continued well into early 1970 and resulted in sharply higher labor costs and lower productivity—were eventually felt throughout the economy beginning in the late 1970s.

In 1969 the trade unions changed tactics. They became more militant; not only were they asking for better wages and job protection, but they also demanded better working and living conditions. The newly urbanized migrants from the rural south were increasingly dissatisfied with living conditions in the fast-growing cities in the north and demanded better housing, schools, shops, transportation, and health care. The demands were accompanied by frequent strikes and violent demonstrations, besides their increasing support for the Communist Party.

Employed by profession, economic sectors and geographic areas 2006 (in thousands)

Geographic areas	Employed	Self-employed	Total
Total	16,961	6,057	23,018
North	8,833	3,017	11,850
North-west	5,121	1,738	6,858
North-east	3,712	1,279	4,992
Center	3,359	1,292	4,651
Mezzogiorno	4,769	1,748	6,517
Agriculture			
Total	513	506	1,019
North	118	240	358
North-west	54	105	159
North-east	63	135	199
Center	59	79	139
Mezzogiorno	336	186	522
Industry			
Total	5,485	1,489	6,975
North	3,374	822	4,197
North-west	1,955	476	2,432
North-east	1,419	346	1,765
Center	919	316	1,234
Mezzogiorno	1,192	351	1,544
Services			
Total	10,963	4,062	15,025
North	5,341	1,954	7,296
North-west	3,111	1,156	4,268
North-east	2,230	798	3,028
Center	2,381	897	3,278
Mezzogiorno	3,241	1,210	4,451

Source: ISTAT

Social Legislation

Italian society wanted to change and demanded legislative action. One truly startling shift had taken place in Italians' views on such issues as divorce and birth control. In a 1967 public opinion survey, 58.6% of 12,645 Italians interviewed were in favor of legalizing divorce and three out of four favored or accepted birth control. Two out of three said their views or behavior on the subject were not affected by Pope Paul's pronouncement reaffirming the Catholic Church's rigid ban on contraception. Just five years earlier, a similar survey had shown that almost seven Italians out of ten were against the introduction of divorce.

The outcome of the Italian elections of May 19–20, 1968, sent a message of concern to the government. Although the center-Left coalition had slightly increased its share of the popular vote and parliamentary representation, the communists and the extreme Left socialist splinter group scored sizable gains, jolting the governing coalition.

As a consequence of all these manifestations, the Italian government started to plan for radical changes. The early 1970s went down in history as the years when Italy enacted some of the world's most advanced social legislation.

Unfortunately, the quadrupling of oil prices at the same time, beginning in 1973, dealt the Italian economy a tremendous blow. Having to import 80% of its energy needs, Italy was hit harder than any other Western country and had to work feverishly to avoid a complete economic collapse. The combination of wage and oil price increases badly hurt industrial profits and drastically reduced the competitiveness of many public and large private enterprises. Consequently, in 1975 Italy experienced its worst postwar recession.

Unemployment rate by gender and geographic area (2006)

Geographic areas	Percentage		
	Total	Age 15–24	Long period of unemployment
MALE AND FEMALE			
Total	6.9	22.26	3.3
North	4.0	13.5	1.4
North-west	4.2	16.1	1.6
North-east	3.7	10.2	1.1
Center	6.4	21.6	2.8
Mezzogiorno	12.2	35.0	6.7
MALE			
Total	5.6	20.2	2.6
North	2.9	12.1	0.9
North-west	3.2	14.8	1.0
North-east	2.6	8.5	0.7
Center	4.8	19.2	2.0
Mezzogiorno	10.0	30.9	5.4
FEMALE			
Total	8.8	26.1	4.4
North	5.3	15.5	2.1
North-west	5.5	17.9	2.4
North-east	5.0	12.4	1.7
Center	8.6	24.8	4.0
Mezzogiorno	16.0	41.2	9.1

Source: ISTAT

Recession

In the first half of the 1970s there was a significant deterioration in economic performance. In 1975, for the first time since World War II, the economy contracted. Real gross domestic product (GDP) dropped by 3.5%, industrial production fell by 9.5%, and inflation topped 17%, the highest in Europe. Most of these losses were regained in 1976 with a 5.6% increase in GDP and a 12.4% jump in industrial production, but inflation, caused mainly by the demands of militant labor unions, and unemployment remained at high levels. The Andreotti government took steps to restore the economy to steady growth without high inflation. A series of measures to check the growth of government budget deficits and labor costs were adopted, paving the way for a $250 million standby loan from the international Monetary Fund in April 1977 and another $500 million from the European Community. By 1978, these measures, plus favorable exchange rates, had given Italian exports a tremendous boost and moved Italy's current account and even its trade balance firmly into the black, despite the skyrocketing prices of imported oil.

In addition to the increasing energy costs, there were many blunders and actions that hindered company productivity more than was necessary, or possible, in order to reach the desired level of social justice. Many economists link the beginning of Italy's chronic economic troubles of the 1970s to the wage settlements that resulted from the labor unrest that characterized the autumn of 1969. Industrial wage increases averaged 25.5% in 1973 and 24.3% in 1974, while increases in the consumer price index in those years were 10.8% and 19.1% respectively. During the first five years of the 1970s, the consumer price index rose to 171, while on the same scale wages rose to 249. These developments virtually wiped out the low labor cost advantage enjoyed by Italian industries in the late 1950s and early 1960s, which had been a major contributor to the economic boom of that period. More damaging to trade performance were the strikes, absenteeism, and high labor costs that rose continuously throughout the 1970s—accounting for a 40% increase in the price of Italian manufactured goods between 1977 and 1979 alone.

Seeking Solutions to the Economic Crisis

However, employers were able to regain the upper hand. The Fiat strike of 1980 was a major test of strength and a turning point. At Olivetti, Carlo De Benedetti took over an ailing firm and restored it to profitability with an aggressive anti-trade unionist stance. From the end of the 1970s, a prolonged economic crisis and the rise in unemployment had weakened the bargaining power of the unions and pushed them onto the defensive. In 1983–1984 the Craxi government (the first socialist-led government) was able to exploit the new divisions in the union movement to push through anti-inflationary measures. Another factor was the emergence of a self-confident, new-look political center based around Craxi and Christian Democratic Party leader, Ciriaco De Mita. The latter had taken the helm as part of a move to refurbish the Party's image after the damaging scandals of the mid-1970s, culminating in the resignation in 1978 of President of the Republic Giovanni Leone, named in a scandal that involved Lockheed Aircraft.

After 1980, strikes and absenteeism dropped, productivity and capital inflows improved, and profits in many industries soared. Unemployment went from 6.4% in 1977 to 14.2% in 1985, with some three quarters of the unemployed estimated to be persons under the age of 30. In the mid-1980s the Italian economy presented, in short, a bewildering spectacle. It continued to be plagued by high unemployment, high interest rates, high labor costs, high inflation, vast public expenditures, and a staggering public deficit. At the same time, exports were back at an all-time record; some state industry was being restructured and modernized; large private firms were once again European leaders in their fields, the performance of small and medium-sized companies bedazzled observers, and a general sense of prosperity pervaded the country.

Nevertheless, in the early 1990s, the state enterprises still held a strong position. The purely private-sector economy was still proportionately the smallest of major Western industrial countries, accounting for 35 to 40% of Italy's industrial production. This private sector is remarkable for its large number of small producers and its small number of large producers. At least 90% of Italy's industries employ fewer than a hundred workers. The major industries at the top of the pyramidal structure of the private sector are, and have traditionally been, concentrated in remarkably few hands—a narrow cartel of northern entrepreneurs.[5]

The Agnelli family, which owned 40% of Fiat, Italy's biggest private sector company, remained at the center of power. The purchase of Alfa Romeo gave Fiat a virtual monopoly on the production of cars in Italy; it also owned Lancia, Ferrari, and Autobianchi. Fiat had 60% of domestic car sales—a bigger share than any other European carmaker has in its home market. Fiat remains Italy's forte today because it produces a very popular range of smaller family cars that feature low gasoline consumption, thereby maintaining its competitiveness in an oil-anxious age. But Fiat is having a difficult time because of the Japanese imports. Italy is much less competitively placed than Germany to meet the Japanese challenge in other countries, for Italy does not produce the same kind of luxury high-performance cars, such as BMW, Mercedes, and Porsche, which have no Japanese equivalent—the Ferrari, Lamborghini, and Maserati are completely in a league of their own.

Recently, the major firms have changed their character considerably; for one thing they have become increasingly multinational while giving the appearance of shrinking in size.[6] Through mergers, associations with large foreign companies, and restructuring, they have increased international competition, improved productivity, and become financially more solid.

Italian business has long been dominated by a few families. In the past, the power of private business was balanced by a large public sector and strong unions. Today the trade unions are weaker and the public sector has almost disappeared through privatization; there is, therefore, a greater danger that the power of private business will go unchecked.

Notes

1. There is a large body of literature on Italy's economic development and agricultural, industrial, and business structures. The decline in the importance of agriculture in the postwar period is charted in Camillo Daneo, *Breve storia dell'agricoltura italiana 1860–1970* (Milano: Mondadori, 1980), while Russell King analyzes one of the few major reforms of the 1950s in *Land Reform: The Italian Experience* (London: Croom Helm, 1985), and Valerio Castronovo, *L'industria italiana dall'Ottocento a oggi* (Milano: Mondadori, 1980).

2. STET (Telephone Holding Company), whose task was to manage IRI holdings in the telecommunications and electronics fields; *FINMARE,* for shipping company holdings; *FINSIDER,* for steel industry holdings; FINMECCANICA, for machine and mechanical holdings; *FINCANTIERI,* for ship-construction company holdings; *ITALSTAT,* for the urban infrastructures and urban planning sector; and *SME,* the Southern Holding Company, for the food, paper, and automobile sectors in the south of Italy, and for the commercial distribution and promotion of various activities there. To give a broad idea of the level of its presence in the Italian economy, it suffices to say that in the services sector the telephone company SIP (a company belonging to *STET* Group) covers 82% of the Italian *TLC* traffic; Alitalia, 91% of air transportation; *FINMARE,* 21% of maritime transportation; *Autostrade* (a company belonging to the *ITALSTAT* Group), 45% of highways. In manufacturing, *FINSIDER* has 55% of total national production of steel; *FINCANTIERI,* 70% of shipbuilding; Ansaldo, 60% of power supply components; Selenia and Aeritalia, 55% of aerospace; Italtel, 50% of *TLC* switching; SGS, 98% of micro-electronics.

3. Operating in the hydrocarbons sector is AGIP, which oversees various activities from prospecting for coal and petroleum and uranium ores, to mining, and to the distribution of petroleum products. *SNAM,* too, operates in the hydrocarbons sector, carrying on the transport of hydrocarbons and the importing and distribution of natural gas. Another is the Italian Petroleum Products Industry, which operates in the refining and distribution sector. In the chemical and nuclear sector is *ANIC,* which works in the chemicals and refining industry, and AGIP Nuclear, heading up all activities concerned with the nuclear industry. In the engineering and services sector is *SNAM* Progetti, which oversees the study, design, and construction of gas and oil pipelines and of petroleum facilities and petrochemical plants; it also oversees scientific research activities. *SAIPEM* carries on drilling activities and the assembly and construction of pipelines and industrial plants. *TECNECO* sees to both general and detailed development planning for water resources and for developing the territory in general. In the manufacturing sector, textile weaving activities are headed up by the *TESCON* holding company, incorporated to give the management policies of the companies it holds greater coherence and to give them more strength on the financing level. The main companies under *TESCON* are Lanerossi, Lebole, Monti, and MCM.

4. The most important were the Ernesto Breda Holding Company, chiefly concerned in the mechanical sector, instrumentation in particular; the Breda Railway Company, operating mainly in the transport and motor sector: SOPAL (Food Holding Company), which carries on a large-scale activity in sectors running from procuring raw materials for the food industry to their conversion and to the distribution of food products in Italy and abroad. *INSUD* is a holding company that specializes in projects in the south, promoting and carrying out initiatives there in the tourism and manufacturing industry sectors, in combination with Italian and foreign partners. *EFIM* supported. monitored, and coordinated the leader holding companies and operating companies subject to it.

5. Six Italians were listed among *Forbes Magazine*'s annual survey (1992) of the world's richest people. The family names of Agnelli, Benetton, Ferrero. and Ferruzzi, and those of Silvio Berlusconi and Salvatore Licresti, once again made the list of 291 billionaires. Former prime minister Berlusconi is first among the Italians, with an estimated fortune of about five billion dollars.

6. Arnaldo Bagnasco, *Tre Italie: la problematica territoriale dello suiluppo italiano* (Bologna: Mulino, 1977); Michael J. Piore and Charles F. Sabel, *The Second Industrial Divide: Possibilities for Prosperity* (New

York: Basic Books. 1984); Raffaella Nanetti, *Growth and Territorial Policies. The Italian Model of Social Capitalism* (London: Pinter, 1988); Michael Blim, *Made in Italy: Small Scale Industrialization and its Consequences* (New York: Praeger, 1990); Mark Holmstrom, *Industrial Democracy in Italy: Workers' Co-ops and the Self-Management Debate* (Aldershot: Averbury, 1989).

Bibliography

Allen, Kevin and Stevenson, Andrew. *An Introduction to the Italian Economy* (New York: Barnes & Noble, 1975).

Baldassarri, Mario, ed. *The Italian Economy: Heaven or Hell?* (New York: St. Martin's, 1994).

Bufacchi, Vittorio and Burgess, Simon. *Italy Since 1989: Events and Interpretations* (New York: St. Martin's, 1998).

Fauri, Francesca. "The Role of Fiat in the Development of the Italian Car Industry in the 1950s" *Business History* 70 (1996): 167–206.

Mammarella, Giuseppe. Italy after Fascism: A Political History, 1943–1965 (Notre Dame, IN: U of Notre Dame Press, 1966), 344–53.

Petai, Rolf. "Dalla ricostruzione al mercato economico," in Sabatucci, Giovanni and Vidotto, Vittorio, ed. *Storia d'Italia: La repubblica, 1943–1963* (Bari: Laterza, 2002), 361–74.

Romero, Federico. "Gli Stati Uniti in Italia, il Piano Marshall e il Patto Atlantico," in Barbagallo, Francesco, ed. *Storia dell'Italia repubblicana* (Turin: Einaudi, 1995) 1:233–89.

Sechi, Salvatore, ed. *Deconstructing Italy: Italy in the Nineties* (Berkeley: University of California Press, 1995).

Zamagni, Vera. "American Influence of the Italian Economy (1948–58)," in Duggan, Christopher and Wagstaff, Christopher. *Italy in the Cold War: Politics, Culture and Society, 1948–1958* (Oxford: Berg, 1995).

CHAPTER 6

INDUSTRIAL CHANGE AND SOCIAL TRANSFORMATION

The Economic Boom of the 1980s

In the early part of the 1980s, Italy was still victim to the recession largely induced by the oil price hikes of the 1970s and the labor unions' success in having approved protective labor legislation. However, the economic situation changed as a consequence of the greater levels of consumption; the increase in leisure time, which reduced interest in political participation; and labor activism, which ushered in a rediscovered sense of individualism, a new culture of entrepreneurship, and increased secularization of Italian society.

Following massive layoffs by Fiat to meet the crisis affecting the car industry, the unions discovered that the mood of Italians had changed. Workers were not ready to follow their leaders in striking. Unions were also being weakened by downsizing, subcontracting, increasing automation, the increasing importance of service workers in the economy, and the growing numbers of illegal immigrant workers. The increasing acceptance among most segments of Italian society of the Thatcher- and Reagan-inspired ideas on entrepreneurship and risk taking also reflected the changing times.

By the end of the 1980s, Italy had become one of Europe's great success stories. Suddenly it was a land of upward mobility, of vital computerized industry, of bustling young business managers and slick middle-aged tycoons who had abjured their 1960s ideals in the sacred cause of profit. Even the English, long critical of Italy, at the end of the 1980s were saying that the Italians must have been doing something right, and doing it despite a political and administrative system that had remained the least adapted to the requirements of modern, efficient government in Western Europe.

The *Sorpasso*

In 1987, the year of the *sorpasso,* in which Italy actually surpassed Great Britain as an economic power, the government added an extra 18% to its estimate of Italy's national income. Italy's GDP became 10% bigger than Britain's in 1986, and its GDP per capita was 9% larger. These figures shook up the industrialized West. The average Italian was shown to be richer than the average Briton when standards of living were compared using the ownership of consumer goods. In 1987, 76% of households had a car, compared with 58% in Britain; 81% had washing machines and 14% had dishwashers, compared with 77% and 3%, respectively, for British families.

It seems that Italy had understood at the end of the 1970s what Americans had not yet grasped that small firms with highly motivated, skilled workers can be more responsive to market changes than multibillion-dollar institutions with dozens of layers of supervision and hundreds of volumes of operating manuals. Mass production in large American industries had created a monopoly of management expertise at the top, and the polarization of corporate rewards—the top executives who make as much as Madonna, and the unskilled workers who increasingly earn little more than welfare mothers—had corroded the work ethic of the majority who keep the machines working. Moreover, flexible production responds better to rapidly changing consumer markets, because a premium can be put on design and craft, on workers who can take the initiative. Flexibility enables workers to develop craft skills, to reacquire the technical knowledge monopolized by management.

The Second Economic Miracle
Thanks to Small-Sized Firms

In Italy, flexible production stimulated the rise of "SMEs"—small and medium-sized regional enterprises. Emilia-Romagna became the leading area with over 300,000 SMEs; nearly 70,000 were industrial firms. The leading sectors are machine tools, agricultural equipment, ceramics, metalworking, mechanical engineering, garments, and textiles. A lot of the same industries that New York City planners wrote off as too small and too high-cost to compete globally fared very well in Italy. Firms in Bologna, Modena, and Forlì exploited their flexibility; they moved products from design to market quickly. The Italians formed industrial networks: strategic alliances, buyer-supplier partnerships, joint ventures. In the garment industry, they went "upmarket" to

PROFILE

Luxottica: Glasses for Every Occasion and Taste

The history of Luxottica, a small, family-owned firm that became a multi-national eyeglass company, is similar to that of many other Italian firms: it is rooted in the entrepreneurship of family business initiatives.

The company's founder, Leonardo Del Vecchio (b. 1935), was sent to an orphanage at age 7 because his mother could not afford to support five children. At a very young age he became an apprentice at a factory that made molds for auto parts. After mastering the medalist's craft (engraving and striking medals), Del Vecchio decided to open his own shop. Then, with a far-sighted entrepreneurial vision, in 1961 he left the medal-working business to enter the small eyewear metal parts business. He moved his business base to Agordo, in the Province of Belluno, where 95% of Italian eyewear producers are located.

Today he is the chairman of Luxottica, the world's largest producer of eyeglasses. Luxottica owns approximately 5,500 retail stores, including the American chains Sunglass Hut and LensCrafters. It continues to grow: last year it agreed to buy two Chinese retail chains, Xueliang Optical and Ming Long Optical, in Beijing and Guangdong.

The company's strategy to expand abroad kicked off in 1981 with the creation of the first commercial subsidiary in Germany; it was then carried out by opening branches and, in some cases, entering joint ventures.

In ten years' time, Luxottica Group succeeded in creating a huge sales network that presently numbers 38 branches and 100 independent distributors serving 130 countries.

With annual sales of $3 billion, Luxottica Group S.p.A. engages in the design, manufacture, distribution, and marketing of prescription frames and sunglasses in the mid- and premium-price categories. Its brand portfolio includes house brands, such as Ray-Ban, Revo, Arnette, Killer Loop, Persol, Vogue, Luxottica, and Sferoflex; and designer lines, such as Chanel, Prada, Dolce & Gabbana, D&G, Versace, Bulgari, Miu Miu, Salvatore Ferragamo, Donna Karan, DKNY, Genny, Byblos, Brooks Brothers, Sergio Tacchini, Anne Klein, Moschino, Versus, and Adrienne Vittadini. Its wholesale customers include independent opticians, optical and sunglass chains, optical superstores, sunglass specialty stores, and duty-free shops. Luxottica is also active at the retail level, occupying a leading position in the North American optical retail market with more than 2,500 stores, including LensCrafters, Sunglass Hut International, and Pearle Vision. In 2006 Tiffany & Co. announced its entrance into the luxury-eyewear business, signing a 10-year licensing deal with Luxottica Group.

Not bad for a boy who was left on his own at age 7!

escape competition with low-cost producers. These sub-giants formed cooperative networks that compensated for the lack of large sums of capital and were the industrial engine that brought about the resurgence of the manufacturing industry in some cities. The more successful firms invested intelligently in new equipment, pushed productivity up, and gave technical innovation its head. As a result, Italy moved into the forefront of advanced technology, able to export both her products and her "know-how."

Some of Italy's cities, like many American cities, had experienced a big loss of blue-collar jobs in the second half of the 1970s. The emerging Asian competition, rising energy costs, high wages, and rigid union rules caused a decline of the manufacturing sector. To relieve unemployment and replenish dwindling revenues, many cities gave up on industry and looked to services, such as banking and insurance. But bold policies in some cities showed that there was no need to give up on manufacturing. The economic resurgence came about through very small, flexible enterprises organized around multiple-use, automated machinery. The tiny shops became intermediate producers, which linked together in varying combinations and formed networks to carry out complex manufacturing tasks for world markets. Frequent subcontracting within networks made it easy to upgrade product specifications and even change product lines rapidly in response to market signals. Moreover, the small-scale industrial enterprises bridged the distance between artisans and modern production methods.

Local governments encouraged this system of flexible network manufacturing by pitching in with municipal land, credit, child care, public transport, and advanced industrial training. Many municipalities provided affordable workspaces in converted factory buildings and mini-industrial parks. Today, local schools turn out well-trained apprentices and keep shop owners up to date through evening programs. Publicly subsidized research centers provide assistance in product innovation, technology transfer, and export marketing. The emphasis on innovation and quality means that experimentation and education are encouraged. There is continual upward movement as former apprentices open their own firms. The basic features of this Italian industrial system are very much in the American grain. It stresses entrepreneurship, self-employment, the pleasure of making things, creative challenges, and good income.

Decentralization of Production

Luckily for Italy, Italians seem never to lack solutions. Look at how the country reacted to the major crisis at the end of the 1970s. What gave impetus to the second "economic miracle" was certainly the decentralization of production. Such decentralization was mainly caused by the sharply rising labor costs and an expanding social welfare that burdened large companies. Social security contributions and related payments to the state meant that the total cost of labor to an employer escalated to more than double the net salaries. All salaries were linked to inflation, and it was virtually impossible to lay off workers.

By the end of the 1970s, it had become clear that labor union demands and a strong state presence in the economy, which had created the basis for the "welfare state" in the 1960s and 1970s, were now crippling the nation. Lack of vigor in the banking world, an out-of-date fiscal system, poor liaison between pure and applied research, excessive state bureaucratic interference in private industry, all were problems that needed to be addressed. Clearly, the state and the labor unions' strong role in the economy had fulfilled their original mandates, but now their excesses needed to be corrected. Gradual political changes and visionary entrepreneurship brought about a remarkable shift and turnabout in economic direction. The success of the small and medium-sized industry was a blow to the powerful labor unions and served as a clear message to excessive presence of the state in the economy. The "workers statute" approved in the early 1970s affected firms with more than fifteen employees. Smaller firms were free from the "welfare burden." The emerging culture of SMEs must therefore be attributed also to this situation.

The rise of family-owned small businesses became an asset in the Italian economy. This can be seen most clearly in the proliferation of (often family-owned) small firms across northern Italy, many of them grouped in clusters: woolen goods in Biella, cotton textiles in Varese, shoes in Ascoli Piceno, knitwear in Carpi, women's clothing around Treviso (home of Benetton, among others), and so on. At one time these clus-

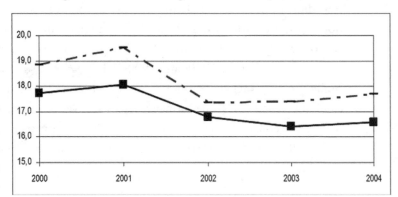

Percentage of GDP of underground economy (2000-2004)

Top line (dashed): maximum estimate　　*Bottom line (solid)*: minimum estimate

Source: ISTAT

ters figured in business-school studies as a key source of Italy's economic strength, especially in the north, now one of Europe's richest regions.

Indeed, Italy as a whole has become a case of study in "small is beautiful." About two-thirds of manufacturing workers are in firms with fewer than 100 employees, compared with 37% in America and 31% in Germany. Italy has more small and medium-sized enterprises than any other country in Europe. For a member of the G-8, Italy has remarkably few big companies.

This small-business sector changed the industrial map of Italy. No longer does the Italian economy entirely hinge on the old industrial triangle of Milan-Turin-Genoa. The new firms are not in large cities but in provincial towns in former agrarian areas. And they have spread from Emilia-Romagna, the Veneto, and Tuscany into the Marches and on to Umbria, Abruzzi, Apulia, and the area south of Rome. They produce clothing, leather products, shoes, furniture, textiles, machine tools, agricultural machinery, toys, car parts, and jewelry. The manufacturing sectors are regionalized: in the northwest there is a large modern group of industries; in the northeast there are small enterprises of low technology but high craftsmanship; in the center and south, the two forms exist side by side. Thanks to the moderate price and high quality of their innovative products, these firms have been resistant to the ups and downs of the international economy.

Among the distinguishing features of these decentralized but integrated industrial districts is a seemingly contradictory combination of competition and cooperation. Firms compete vigorously for innovation in style and efficiency while cooperating in administrative services, raw material purchases, financing, and research. A rich network of private economic associations and political organizations have constructed an environment in which markets prosper by promoting cooperative behavior and by providing small firms with the infrastructural needs that they could not afford alone. These networks of small firms combine low vertical integration and high horizontal integration through extensive subcontracting and the "putting out" of extra business to temporarily underemployed competitors. Active industrial associations provide administrative and even financial aid, while local government plays an active role in providing the necessary social infrastructure and services, such as professional training, information on export markets, and so on. The result is a technologically advanced and highly flexible economic structure, which proved precisely the right recipe for competing in the fast-moving economic world of the 1980s and 1990s. The degree of success of these firms is higher in the Emilia-Romagna region because of the higher level of civic traditions, of contemporary civic community, and of high-performance regional government. Most observers have demonstrated that what is crucial about these small-firm industrial districts is mutual trust, social cooperation, and a well-developed sense of civic duty: in short, the hallmarks of the civic community.

How Did All This Come About?

The legislation approved in the early 1970s that created the "workers statute" was too costly for the industrial system to remain competitive. Big firms, to remain competitive, needed to lower their costs by increasing productivity and/or subcontracting to firms who could produce at lower cost. Many big firms embraced the new culture of subcontracting to smaller firms. In addition, as part of the process, Italy started a program of privatization, following a pragmatic approach in adopting a set of measures: transfer of activities from public sector to private through share offerings; utilization of private companies to manage services previously in the hands of state or local governments; and introduction of a "fee" for services previously offered and financed through taxes. These measures were not entirely based on the standard of what was best for Italy, however. There were some political motives involved, for the center-Right wanted to build up the electoral support of a body of small-scale capitalists who benefited from the liberalization of the market.

At first the privatization programs affected mainly large enterprises. In addition to industrial and financial restructuring, the state giant IRI, in its strategy for recovery, followed the path of privatization and partnership, which means "divestiture of enterprises." It considered putting up for sale three kinds of enterprise: first, marginal ones, which were not integrated with other IRI companies, and therefore had no "mission" to accomplish inside the IRI Group; second, companies that were operating in the red; and third, enterprises, or even sub-holdings of IRI, which were or could be profitable and could even form an integrated whole but did not appear to be consistent with the group's basic long-term objectives. Between 1983 and 1992, over 30 enterprises of different sizes, from big Alfa Romeo to small Ducati (motorcycles), from banks to washing-machine producers, were divested.

Small-Sized Firms and the Underground Economy

In the 1980s, one of the most striking peculiarities of the Italian economy was the remarkable strength of the export sector, which in some ways is a paradigm of Italy's economic performance. In the fashion world, Italian clothing, furniture, and textiles emerged as world leaders, while in some industrial areas, such as machine tools and robotics, Italian products earned an outstanding reputation for quality and won a growing share of the world market.

Because of their exceptional ability to sense changing consumer demand and to produce attractive goods, Italian exporters became highly agile in shifting into new markets and alternative products. The Italian export industry is remarkable for its ability not only to move quickly into new geographic areas but also to change to the production of items for which demand is on the rise.

The achievements in this area are all the more impressive because exporters have rarely received help from the government, either through assistance in penetrating world markets or through export credits. The trade policy, as a result of free-for-all agreements, initially helped the Italian economy.

However, the principal question concerning the Italian economy is how competitive Italian firms are going to be without state protectionism. The successful international performance of Luxottica *(See Box on p. 159)*, Benetton, Stefanel, and fashion designers such as Armani, Fendi, Krizia, Versace, and Valentino shows no signs of letting up. Benetton is recognized as a leader in the "Europreparedness" stakes, having established a vast chain of shops throughout Europe, the U.S., and Asia by the early 1980s. Similarly, Versace went public and thereby raised enough capital to expand its already multinational operation. However, there are serious doubts as to whether the Italian textile industry as a whole will be able to compete with the newly industrialized countries such as Taiwan, Korea, Brazil, and lately China and India which are able to exploit "mature" manufacturing technology with cheap labor. It seems that survival has been found in outsourcing or subcontracting to factories in Asia.

The small and medium-sized firms that were behind the economic boom of the 1980s originally were set up to escape the trade union regulations that followed the "Hot Autumn of 1969" and the "workers statute" of the early 1970s, since firms with fewer than 15 employees need not be unionized or pay standard wages and social benefits. They, therefore, operated at great cost efficiency and high productivity and without risk of strikes. There was still another impetus. Firms with annual incomes below approximately $75,000 were not required to make their books available to income-tax authorities. The astonishing consequence of this was that starting in 1984, fully 95% of Italian firms declared incomes of less than that figure!

Since the production of these small firms escapes official records, the country's real GDP and export statistics are appreciably higher than official accounts would indicate. It is estimated that the "underground economy" employs anywhere from 2 to 4 million persons and helps the economy produce fully 20 to 30% over the official GDP.

Underground Economy and Public Indebtedness

There is no question that the medium- and small-sized industries became the engine of the Italian economy in the second half of the 1980s thanks to:

» creativity
» low product cost
» quick response to market changes
» the creation of a new class of entrepreneurs
» their work as subcontractors to the big firms, and
» the use of immigrant workers to alleviate shortage of labor

The success of medium- and small-sized industries had a positive impact also on the private heavy industry sector, because the industrial giants, by subcontracting to the smaller industries, were able to overcome certain labor demands and, consequently, produce goods more cheaply.

Situations like this could signal serious problems for the average Italian worker. However, in the Italian scene it is always difficult to assess just how changes will influence workers' rights. In economic, as in social, reforms, Italians have gone from one extreme to another, and they are still struggling to find a happy equilibrium. They find salvation in the fact that they are great lovers of drama; whether in opera, politics, or soccer, they swing from the depths of depression one moment to excessive optimism the next. Italians have long proved their ingenuity in the face of apparently insurmountable obstacles.

Italy has long been famed for its hidden economy—that mysterious underworld of tax dodging, illegal employment of foreign workers and students, and civil servants who moonlight in the afternoons when their offices close. Rigid labor laws, high taxes, social security contributions, and a general willingness to break the law are the reasons for the largest underground economy in the industrial world.

Tax dodging is a national problem. Italian wage-earners carry the national fiscal burden. Italian movie stars get in the news because they claim to make less than the sanitation employees; industrial magnates report earning little more than some of their clerks and secretaries; doctors, lawyers, dentists, architects, and accountants report, on average, less income than is paid to skilled industrial workers. The owners of well-known restaurants and cafes regularly report less income than they pay to their chefs, waiters, and dishwashers. Much of this collusion is based on the implicit assumption that the fiscal laws are not fair, that they are not rigorously enforced against everyone, and that the state, in its imperious way, has so defrauded the ordinary taxpayer that it is entirely natural and acceptable that the latter should return the favor. In a nation where the majority of the population regards its democratically elected political leaders as a bunch of *ladri* (thieves), anyone cheating the government may be sure of general benevolence. "None of my money for that rotten system," most of the tax dodgers say. There is something fundamentally democratic about tax evasion in Italy; one way or another, the practice extends to a large proportion of the adult population. It is true, of course, that those on fixed wages and salaries cannot evade, but this applies only to one's first—not second or third—job. Those who are working in the second, unreported economy include hundreds of thousands of blue-collar workers and members of their families, as well as professionals. The practice of auto mechanics, plumbers, carpenters, physicians, dentists, and lawyers wanting payment in cash, and their willingness to be prompt and accommodating when told the customer doesn't need a receipt, is commonplace in Italy. Because of this, wage-earners have a strong resentment toward government.

However, the government has passed stiff laws against cheating on reporting income. Customers by law have to walk out with a *ricevuta fiscale* (register receipt) from any premise where goods are bought or services are rendered, from a cappuccino to a haircut. But, even though fines are heavy and are enforced rigorously, Italians still like to take a chance. In the official economy, the Italian worker is well rewarded with high wages, good benefits, and many paid holidays, but he or she cannot escape from the heavy burden of taxes.

When Bigger Is Better

Can Italy, with its many small firms, survive as an industrial nation in the age of globalization? The problem with having lots of small firms is that globalization and competition from Asia (especially China) have put a bigger premium on size. In the 1970s and 1980s it was enough to supply the home market, or at most reach out to such near neighbors as France and Germany and rely on the local bank for finance. Now to be successful a company such as Benetton has had to grow to the point where it supplies a world market and obtains its products far beyond Italy.

The other problem with Italy's small firms is that too many of them rely on cheap labor for their competitive advantage. The classic example is the textile firms, yet there are many examples of successful Italian firms that have made just such adjustments. Fifteen years ago Benetton produced almost 90% of its clothing in Italy; now the share is down to less than 30%. Geox, an innovative and successful shoemaker, produces most of its products abroad, as

Percentage of underground economy (2000–2004)

Year	Minimum estimate		Maximum estimate	
	Millions of euro	Percentage of GDP	Millions of euro	Percentage of GDP
2000	211.63	17.7	224.513	18.8
2001	225.476	18.1	243.669	19.5
2002	217.535	16.8	224.707	17.3
2003	219.148	16.4	232.411	17,4
2004	230.604	16.6	245.819	17.7

Source: ISTAT

❀ SPIRIT

Tourism: Italy's Big Industry

For the last fifty years, Italy has been one of the five most visited countries in the world. Its more than 57 million tourists annually represent 4.4% of the total travel market, and the numbers are expected to grow in the next few years.

Cultural tourism is at the heart of Italy's attraction. One-third of foreign visitors choose to visit Italy for its artistic and historical attractions, its folklore and traditions, and its religious festivals. Italy's heritage includes 95,000 monumental churches, 20,000 historic town centers, 40,000 fortresses and churches, 56,500 villas and historic buildings, and 4,200 museums.

Italy's ideal location at the center of the Mediterranean, with its beautiful beaches, mountain slopes, numerous lakes, and agreeable and healthy climate yearlong, makes the country even more attractive. The increased attention worldwide to health and wellness makes Italy's thermal resorts and natural spas appealing. Golf, too, offers possibilities for further development of the tourist industry. In 2005 Italy attracted nearly half a million golfing tourists. Most foreign golfers in Italy are from the United Kingdom, Germany, and Northern Europe, typically visiting during autumn and spring to take advantage of the milder weather.

As well, food and wine tourism, though a relatively new activity in Italy, represents a quickly growing market niche with huge potential. The development of itineraries such as "wine roads" and "olive routes," as well as the successful branding of many food and wine districts, testify to the growing importance of this sector. Thanks to Italy's culinary riches and its high-quality food and drink, local people and private companies offer innumerable examples of food and wine tourism. These cover a wide range of experiences involving wine cellars, oil mills, local products and local production workshops, traditional restaurants, taverns, wine shops, farm vacations, hotels in ancient castles and historic houses, as well as wine and farm heritage museums.

Italy's tourism industry is a driving force in the economy, creating 12% of the country's GDP and employing about 2.7 million people. Conference tourism is one of Italy's most dynamic sectors, important both for the number of visitors and for the expenditures of those visitors, considerably more than in the hotel industry overall. In 2002, Rome was Italy's leading conference location, ranking first in both events and number of participants, followed by Milan and Florence.

There is no question that the tourism industry can become even stronger if Italy makes better use of its stunning natural beauty and its artistic, cultural, and historic heritage .

does Luxottica, the world's leading maker of sunglasses. In white goods, Merloni (now Indesit), Europe's third-biggest supplier of refrigerators, stoves, and washing machines, makes almost half the company's products abroad, including in China. Cerutti, a maker of sophisticated printing presses who holds 60% of the world market in printing presses (it supplies many of the newspapers and magazines in Europe, as well as several in America), recently bought a production facility in China. And it has a technical center in India, employing some of the country's finest engineers.

Over the past two decades, in the process of adjustment, some industrial sectors suffered tragically. While Italy's nifty small firms were garnering so much praise, the country lost much of its presence in industries such as chemicals, pharmaceuticals, computers, and food processing. Italy's flagship computer firm, Olivetti, went under in the mid-1990s. But there are some success stories in information technology too—and not only in the north. Near Catania, Sicily, ST Microelectronics, a chipmaker, is part of a vibrant high-tech cluster.

Another problem that Italy must address is investment in research. Italy spends only 1.1% of its GDP on research and development, compared with an EU average of almost 2% and as much as 3.2% in Japan.

Tourism is another area that needs attention in terms of investment and competition. For a country that has so much to offer in terms of culture, nature, climate, and cooking, Italy's tourist industry needs to be developed more *(See Box on p. 166)*.

In 2006 the economic picture of the country looked grim. Italy's average economic growth over the past 15 years has been slow. Its economy is now only about 80% the size of Britain's.

Italian companies, especially the small, family-owned firms that have been the backbone of the economy, are under ever-increasing pressure. Costs have risen, but productivity has remained flat or even declined. Instead of relying on high inflation, high budget deficits, and currency devaluations, it has had to learn to live with low inflation, low budget deficits, and a fixed single European currency. It is not surprising that such a massive adjustment has been painful, and so far remains incomplete. The euro now rules out devaluation, which for many years acted as a safety valve for Italian business. Italy's competitiveness is deteriorating fast, and its shares of world exports and foreign direct investment are small. The economy has also proved highly vulnerable to Asian competition, because so many small Italian firms specialize in such areas as textiles, shoes, and furniture, which are taking the brunt of China's export assault. Today the nation must face the challenges of globalization and of an aging population.

Italy's Economic Problems: It's All About Productivity

With Italian productivity growth slower than in the rest of Euroland, wages should be rising less in order to maintain cost competitiveness. Instead, Italian wage growth has consistently outstripped that of Euroland. Italy's structural problems are founded in its very weak

Percentage of underground economy by economic sectors (2000–2004)

Economic sector	2000	2001	2002	2003	2004
Agriculture	20.5	20.9	21.0	18.3	18.3
Industry	7.1	7.4	6.6	5.7	5.7
Services	15.3	15.8	14.5	13.5	13.4
Total	13.3	13.8	12.7	11.6	11.5

Source: ISTAT

productivity growth. In the last 10 years, trend output per hour has risen only 1.1% a year, compared with almost 2% in the rest of Euroland (including Germany) and 2% in the U.S. As a result, GDP growth has been a disappointing 1.5% a year for the last ten years, on par with Germany, which went through its economically painful post-reunification adjustment, and well below the rest of Euroland and the U.S.

With Italian productivity growth only about half that of the rest of Euroland and the U.S., Italian wage growth should have been constrained accordingly in order to maintain cost competitiveness. The resulting rise in relative unit labor cost (ULC) has led to a steady decline in market share by Italian exporters. Italy's export market share rose sharply following its departure from the ERM in 1992 and has been falling ever since, along with the rise in relative ULCs. Since the peak of the last cycle in 2001, Italian export volumes have fallen 10%, while Euroland exports have risen 9% and Germany's 20%. In an increasingly globalized world with supply of lower-cost labor by the emerging economies, the single most important issue for all of Europe is to raise its output per hour. Without such productivity increases, the rationale for higher cost base—and hence higher living standards—than in the emerging economies will continue to erode.

Why Is Italian Productivity Growth So Low?

Several factors drive labor productivity growth:

» **Too much regulation**. Italy has the most highly regulated product market in Europe. The level of regulation and the degree of protection afforded to incumbent companies play an important role in dictating how quickly countries are likely to improve their productivity rate. With a high degree of regulation and an absence of competition, until very recently, there is less pressure on incumbent firms to innovate or adopt new technologies.

» **Low research investment**. Italy lacks domestically generated technology. Research and development spending play a role in determining the number of industries in which the country is likely to be a market leader. Unfortunately, Italy also scores low in this regard.

» **Education standards are relatively low**. Education plays an important role in determining the speed with which countries adopt new technologies and their ability to develop technologies of their own. Italy also performs relatively poorly in the proportion of science and technology graduates (7.4% vs. 10.9% in Euroland).

An Additional Problem for Exporters: Italy's Industrial Mix.

Italian exports may also suffer because of their concentration in relatively traditional industries such as textiles, leather, and white goods. Apart from Italy's traditional strength in high-end branding, these industries are in direct competition with producers in several developing countries, including China and India. The vulnerability stemming from this was evident when import quotas for textiles and footwear were lifted at the start of 2005: the price of imported garments and other textiles fell 15% in the first months.

Demographics have not played an important role in Italy's poor growth performance relative to Euroland during the last 10 years, although significant differences occurred below the surface. While Italy suffered from slower population growth during the last 10 years than the rest of Europe, it has made up for some of the shortfall through an increase in labor utilization. This rise was primarily driven by a large increase in the unemployment

Italians love public demonstrations because they love to perform life. However, by dramatizing public concerns, "particularism" and "familism" are supplanted by passionate interest in the common good and high ideals. The fight for a global ban of nuclear power is as passionate as the struggle to lessen the hunger in the world. Printed by courtesy of *America Oggi*.

rate, which can be accounted for by an increase in Italy's female participation rate from low levels (the female employment rate rose from 35% in 1994 to 45% in 2004). A similar development has raised overall employment rates across southern Europe.

In addition, Italian households' saving ratio is still higher than Euroland levels, though much less than it was ten years ago. However, government spending has more than compensated for households' thriftiness.

Looking Ahead: What Italy Needs to Do

To improve Italy's structural performance, efforts should be focused on measures to boost competitiveness and productivity. Probably the first step is regulatory reform; productivity growth in a number of Italian sectors has been held back by a prohibitive amount of red tape. In economies (such as the U.S. and Sweden) that have witnessed an acceleration in whole-economy productivity growth in the last decade, this improvement has been driven by just two sectors: high-tech production and retail/wholesale trade. With relatively low levels of high-tech production, Italy is unlikely ever to be a major beneficiary here. However, with the right policies, Italy could boost productivity growth in its wholesale/retail sector.

Another important step is to raise the level of education attainment. Some efforts have been made: the length of compulsory schooling has been raised from 10 to 12 years, and changes have been made to the structure of primary and secondary education. However, it will be some time before these measures have an impact on productivity growth.

The Italian economy would also benefit from other measures not directly related to improving productivity:

» Establishing greater wage differentiation: The level of productivity in the south was only 80% of that of the north and 85% of that in the center in 2003. However, wage differentiation is not present. This is partly because collective contracts for a particular sector are binding for workers even if they do not belong to a union. As a result, unit labor costs are too high in the south. Increasing the differentiation of wages according to productivity may help improve the competitiveness of the economy as a whole.

» Improving the demographic situation: Italy has witnessed a substantial increase in immigration in the past decade. However, immigration has generally occurred despite rather than because of the efforts of Italian authorities; much of the immigrant population in Italy remains illegal. Italy would benefit from opening its markets to the ten new EU members immediately rather than waiting the maximum allowed time of seven years.

» Regaining cost competitiveness: Italy has no other option than to regain long-term cost competitiveness

Labor Market and Pension Reform

Italy has been taking important steps in the labor market by passing some pension reforms.

» A more flexible labor market improves the capacity of the economy to respond to shocks and helps increase Italy's participation rate, which is one of the lowest in Europe (61% of working age population in 2002 compared with 76% in Germany and 70% in France).

» Italy is one of the fastest-aging countries in Europe. Government spending on pensions is currently around 15% of GDP and is set to increase in the next few years. Controlling spending on pensions is essential to setting government debt on a downward trend again.

» Recent labor market reforms have already had some positive effect in employment growth. The more flexible regulations on part-time work were definitively positive. The percentage of part-time workers remains one of the lowest in Europe for both males and females (4% and 17%, respectively, in 2002, compared with 5% and 30% in France, and 6% and 39% in Germany). A lifting of the obligation for a company with more than 15 employees to rehire workers laid off when hiring needs reemerge has already increased the participation of women in the labor market. These measures are important as Italy is likely to suffer from unfavorable demographics over the next decade. Higher participation of women in the labor market should partly offset the negative effects on trend growth from a rapidly aging population.

» Meanwhile, Italy should be commended for its pension system reform. Since the 1990s, various Italian governments have designed and implemented far-reaching reforms of the government pension system. When the effects of these reforms kick in,

Italy's Pay-As-You-Go (PAYG) system could well be ranked among the most sustainable in continental Europe:

» The 1995 reform improved considerably the long-term sustainability of the pension system by linking the benefits to the economic performance of the previous five years and making the system actuarially fair (i.e., making benefits match contributions). However, this reform only applied to young workers. Workers with over 18 years of seniority who were currently in their mid-forties or older (i.e., the baby-boom generation) were exempt from the reform! This means that the reform did not help reduce pension payments in the most difficult time of demographic transition.

» In 2004, after a lengthy period of social unrest, the government managed to push through further reforms. The new legislation increased the minimum age for seniority pensions: currently, when people have contributed towards social security for 35 years, they can retire at age 57. The minimum age rises for men to 60 in 2008, 61 in 2010, and 62 in 2014. These reforms allow Italians to collect full pensions at a much younger age than the present 65 years and 6 months in the U.S.

» The government has also instituted a tax-free bonus for people who postponed their retirement until 2008.

These reforms are very good moves, but their timing means that Italy's spending on pensions, which is one of the highest in Europe (the latest available data suggest that the new system—PAYG— spending was nearly 15% of GDP in 2001 compared with 13% in Euroland), will continue to rise in the next few years and will prevent government debt from resuming a downward trend.

Other Serious Problems

Although the Berlusconi government was quite bold in dealing with pensions and the labor market, the problems persist. By raising the retirement age, cutting pension values, and encouraging private pension funds, Italy has done more than some other EU countries to tackle the looming problem. However, given its demographic outlook, Italy still needs to do more to reduce its formidable pensions burden. Reforms in the labor market have been even more striking. The Biagi law exempted many new jobs from rules that required most work to be full-time and permanent. This has led to a boom in temporary and part-time posts. The privatization of labor exchanges and changes to apprenticeship contracts will inject even more flexibility into the Italian labor market. Although unemployment went down as a whole, now just under 8%, and is relatively low by European standards, it remains high among the young (almost 23%) and in the south. However, Italy's strong employment record has a downside: zero or even negative productivity growth as more marginal and less productive workers have been brought into the workforce. It is the combination of poor productivity growth and rising wages that has caused Italy's unit labor costs to rise so much faster than those in other EU countries in the years since the euro came into use in 1999.

Another big problem is that there is not enough competition in services in general, which matters because the share of services in the Italian economy, as elsewhere, is going up—services now account for two-thirds of GDP. Small shops, taxi firms, pharmacies, notaries, tradesmen: most are protected from competition by special rules, often administered by local authorities.

One problem is that the whole notion of service is rather undervalued. Indeed, Italy often seems to suffer from a pervasive anti-business, anti-customer culture. Italians may be entrepreneurial and creative, but they are by no means pro-market. The political and religious (the strong presence of the Catholic Church) cultures have showed disdain towards profit. Italians tend to look more for favoritism and protectionism than to serve the customer better.

In the early 1990s, public services represented the most dismal feature of the Italian economy because they reflected and compounded, more than other sectors, the still partially solved problems besetting a nation which, only recently and very hastily, has become affluent and demanding. Public services in such key areas as health care and railroads, social security, the postal service, the court system, schools, and airports needed profound changes. By and large, these services are more expensive than in many other Western countries; they often operate at a loss; and their performance is generally well below the standards required by a modern democracy.

Although Italy has a marvelous highway system, its rail system is still being modernized. This situation may not be important for passenger transportation—because Italians love their *macchina* (car)—but it spells trouble for the effective transportation of goods. The state railroads' freight service is so unsatisfactory that today less than one-eighth of all goods moving in Italy are shipped by rail. Trucking in Italy costs three times as much as shipping by freight train, but farmers and manufacturers usually put up with this increased expense for the sake of speed and reliability. Southern fruits and vegetables cannot be sent by rail to northern markets because the trip may take three weeks!

Mail service, notwithstanding recent improvements, is still a serious problem. It may take half an hour to buy stamps at the postal office, and it may take a week to send a letter across Rome. These difficulties persist despite a slackening demand brought about by the increasing appeal of fax machines and e-mail.

What Can We Expect in the Immediate Future?

Italy's governments have generally been made up of coalitions that do not necessarily agree on specific policy measures once they are in power. This can be more of a problem towards the end of the term of office as each party within the coalition prepares for the elections ahead. It is hoped that the center-Left Government (2006) will make serious efforts at putting government debt on a downward trend.

History tells us that when the government and the people have been forced to make hard choices, the response has been effective and people have demonstrated extraordinary resilience.

When Italy had to respond to the requirements set by the Maastricht Treaty (1992), in establishing a monetary union in Europe, the response was admirable. On the other hand, Italy did not have any choice if she wanted to continue to belong to the European Union. The European linkage, first of all, meant a commitment to a sound economic system that is in tune with the EU and the international market. To meet Italy's commitment and to ensure the country's continued participation in the EU's economic unification program, and the monetary union in particular, the government had to reduce the budget deficit to 3% of GDP, and the national debt to under 60% of the gross domestic product. These were difficult goals to achieve because accomplishing them would create hundreds of thousands of additional jobless workers, on top of an already high 11% unemployment rate.

To respond to the gravity of the situation, the Italian parliament supported for prime minister Giuliano Amato, a socialist and a graduate of Columbia University law school, a man of integrity, intelligence, and character. He had to head the first Italian government after the collapse of communism in Eastern Europe and and had the thankless job of steering an economic course for the country that would allow it to comply with EU requirements for continued full membership after the single European market was established on January 1, 1993. Premier Amato's task was to form a government that promised less to its citizens and at the same time asked more from them.

The government engaged in a policy that would wage war against tax evasion and the growth of public debt, while attempting to hold inflation to a level close to the rates prevailing in the most stable European economies. It also made recommendations on how to improve the efficiency and productivity of public services. The package of economic measures consisted of three separate areas. The first, dealing with fiscal policy, outlined ways to raise $26 billion through tax and excise increases and the imposition of 0.6% levy on all monies held in bank deposits and on residential real estate. The second set of measures was designed to save the Treasury tens of billions of dollars by raising the retirement age for workers covered by the government's nationwide pension plan to 65 years for both men and women. At the same time, the Treasury's support of Italy's universal health care system was cut. Third, the government would speed up the privatization of three Italy's public sector companies, IRI and *ENI*, and *EFIM*. The government proposed also to privatize the *Istituto Mobiliare Italiano*, the country's oldest and most powerful merchant bank, as well as *Banco Nazionale del Lavoro*, a commercial bank.

Italy, through the bold measures of its government and the sacrifice of its people, was able to meet the requirements set by the Maastricht Treaty and participate in the creation of Euroland. There is no doubt that the nation will be able to meet the new challenges posed by globalization.

Between EU and the Regions

Probably the bigger issue is how Italy is going to take advantage of the opportunities offered by the EU and how the EU is going to evolve. Since Europe does not want to remain the offshore battleground of the consumer superpowers of Asia and the U.S., it is forging a single consuming and producing entity that can offer the world a third alternative. In this struggle Italy has to raise itself to a level that will enable it to play a primary role. The success or failure of the challenge is like life and death.

However, the road to European integration is full of obstacles. One of the principal impediments is the fact that, within the borders of the 25 EU member countries and their non-EU neighbors, hundreds of years of social, cultural, and moral differences seethe. Some, such as language, are profound; others, such as ritual lunch hours, can be downright amazing.

Geographically, two countries, the United Kingdom and Greece, do not even touch any other EU member's borders, although the U.K. is connected with France via the Channel Tunnel. One nonmember country, Switzerland, drives a geographical wedge into the EU between Germany to the north and Italy to the south. The U.K. and Ireland, alone among the EU states, drive on the left-hand side of the road. Work habits also differ sharply. The Germans arrive early, take a short break for lunch at noon, and leave the office at 4:00. By contrast, in many parts of Italy, most stores close for the midday meal from 1:00 to 4:00 P.M. and then do not shut their doors until 8:00 in the evening. Public offices in Italy operate in an even less efficient way: most of them close for good at 2:00 P.M.!

The EU has to break down centuries of physical and cultural barriers. Besides the hard obstacles—which include the different and, at times, conflicting laws, procedures, and administrative practices that dominate each individual country—the EU also has to solve soft obstacles, which encompass the cultural and social methods, morals, and mores that have kept Europe a patchwork of separate states since the decline of the Roman Empire. Interestingly, the EU finds the soft issues the hardest to address.

No less important, certainly, is how Italy continues to delegate power and authority to its 20 regions. The constitutional reforms enacted in October 2001 define the areas where the state has exclusive legislative powers. Among these are foreign policy, defense, customs, financial markets regulation, public order, immigration, judicial system, social security, environmental protection, statistic collection coordination, and state tax system. Among the legislative powers to be shared with the regions (the state establishing the principles and the detailed legislation to be shared with the regions) are international relations (including those with the EU), foreign trade, the local banking system, scientific research, education, health protection, and emergency services. However, the social, economic, political, and cultural contexts into which the new institutions were implanted differ dramatically.

Some regional governments have been consistently more successful than others—more efficient in their internal operations, more creative in their policy initiatives, and more effective in implementing those initiatives. The regions in the South have been less effective. We agree with Robert D. Putnam that the main reason for the lower level of effectiveness must be found in the lower level of civic virtues in southern society. The fact that southern Italians tend to pursue personal interests and to be less civic minded makes the south less successful in its quest for socioeconomic modernity. The same attitude makes it easier for criminal organizations, the Mafia and *Camorra,* to enter the government.

Nevertheless, the Italian south has to find new energy and resources in the new wave of regionalism. Of course there are dangers in the process of regionalism. The individualistic character of the Italians could certainly create parochialism and entrenched local autocracy. The regions are now competing more vigorously with each other—not just by lobbying for favors from Rome, as in the old days, but by seeking their own solutions. The new system can in time produce a new and dynamic generation of younger local leaders and could provide a lively new focus for local loyalties and energies. While this seems to be a positive factor, there is a danger that more force will be expended on local issues than on the larger, national scene. Another problem is that poor regions may fall further behind. It will be up to the state to provide them with good roads, telecommunications, research centers, and so on, and then hope that the new industries will develop of their own accord.

Overall, the process is positive, for it releases new local energies and may allow Italy to capitalize on the richness of its diversity. The drawback is that the competition could lead to some waste and duplication of effort and that it could accentuate the disparity between the rich dynamic regions and the poorer ones. Decentralization has created new vitality and self-awareness in many towns and their regions. The cultural revival of many towns has been striking: new theaters, concerts, and art galleries help to make life more exciting, and the influx of new populations has created a more open and varied society.

Thus, economically and socially, Italy has gone through a profound change. The percentage of those employed in industry and agriculture in Italy has decreased, while the tertiary sector has grown to include half the working population. The numerical importance of the working class is in diminution, and Italy is fast becoming a "post-industrial" society like other advanced Western countries. However, in Italy there remains the issue of an astronomical public debt, a corrupt political class, and the problems associated with full participation in the EU. Underneath all of these difficulties lies an even more serious obstacle to Italy's future success. It is an issue that differentiates Italy from every other European nation and we will deal with it in the next chapter.

European Union

Although the EU is not a federation in the strict sense, it is far more than a free-trade association, and it has many of the attributes associated with independent nations: its own flag, anthem, founding date, and currency, as well as an incipient common foreign and security policy in its dealings with other nations. In the future, many of these nation-like characteristics are likely to be expanded.

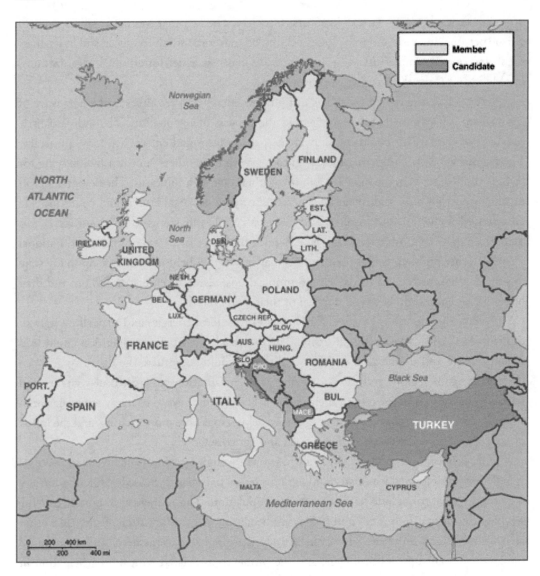

The evolution of the European Union (EU) from a regional economic agreement among six neighboring states in 1951 to today's supranational organization of 27 countries across the European continent stands as an unprecedented phenomenon in the annals of history. Printed from Wikipedia.org.

Background

Following the two devastating World Wars of the first half of the 20th century, a number of European leaders in the late 1940s became convinced that the only way to establish a lasting peace was to unite the two chief belligerent nations—France and Germany—both economically and politically. In 1950, the French Foreign Minister Robert Schuman proposed an eventual union of all Europe, the first step of which would be the integration of the coal and steel industries of Western Europe. The following year (1951) the European Coal and Steel Community (ECSC) was set up when six members, Belgium, France, West Germany, Italy, Luxembourg, and the

Netherlands, signed the Treaty of Paris. The ECSC was so successful that within a few years the decision was made to integrate other parts of the countries' economies. In 1957, the Treaties of Rome created the European Economic Community (EEC) and the European Atomic Energy Community (Euratom), and the six member states undertook to eliminate trade barriers among themselves by forming a common market. In 1967, the institutions of all three communities were formally merged into the European Community (EC), creating a single Commission, a single Council of Ministers, and the European Parliament. Members of the European Parliament were initially selected by national parliaments, but in 1979 the first direct elections were undertaken and they have been held every five years since.

In 1973, the first enlargement of the EC took place with the addition of Denmark, Ireland, and the United Kingdom. The 1980s saw further membership expansion with Greece joining in 1981 and Spain and Portugal in 1986. The 1992 Treaty of Maastricht laid the basis for further forms of cooperation in foreign and defense policy, in judicial and internal affairs, and in the creation of an economic and monetary union—including a common currency. This further integration created the European Union (EU). In 1995, Austria, Finland, and Sweden joined the EU, raising the membership total to 15.

A new currency, the euro, was launched in world money markets on January 1, 1999; it became the unit of exchange for all of the EU states except the United Kingdom, Sweden, and Denmark. In 2002, citizens of the 12 euro-area countries began using the euro banknotes and coins. Ten new countries joined the EU in 2004—Cyprus, the Czech Republic, Estonia, Hungary, Latvia, Lithuania, Malta, Poland, Slovakia, and Slovenia—and 2 additional ones, Romania and Bulgaria in 2007, bringing the current membership to 27. In order to ensure that the EU can continue to function efficiently with an expanded membership, the 2003 Treaty of Nice set forth rules streamlining the size and procedures of EU institutions.

An EU Constitutional Treaty, signed in Rome on 29 October 2004, gave member states two years to ratify the document before it was scheduled to take effect on 1 November 2006. Referenda held in France and the Netherlands in May–June 2005 that rejected the constitution suspended the ratification effort. Despite the expansion of membership and functions, "Eurosceptics" in various countries have raised questions about the erosion of national cultures and the imposition of a flood of regulations from the EU capital in Brussels. Failure by all member states to ratify the constitution or the inability of newcomer countries to meet euro currency standards might force a loosening of some EU agreements and perhaps lead to several levels of EU participation. These "tiers" might eventually range from an "inner" core of politically integrated countries to a looser "outer" economic association of members.

People

Population: 490,426,050 (July 2007 est.)

Age structure: *0–14 years:* 15.72% (male 37,208,905/female 35,254,445); *15–64 years:* 67.17% (male 154,439,536/female 152,479,619); *65 years and over:* 16.81% (male 31,515,921/female 45,277,821) (2007 est.)

Population growth rate: 0.16% (July 2007 est.)

Birth rate: 10 births/1,000 population (July 2007 est.)

Death rate: 10.1 deaths/1,000 population (July 2007 est.)

Net migration rate: 1.6 migrant(s)/1,000 population (July 2007 est.)

Sex ratio: *under 15 years:* 1.06 male(s)/female; *15–64 years:* 1.01 male(s)/female; *65 years and older:* 0.69 male(s)/female; *total population:* 0.96 male(s)/female (July 2007 est.)

Infant mortality rate: *total:* 4.8 deaths/1,000 live births; *male:* 5.3 deaths/1,000 live births; *female:* 4.3 deaths/1,000 live births (July 2007 est.)

Life expectancy at birth: *total population:* 78.7 years; *male:* 75.6 years; *female:* 82 years (July 2007 est.)

Total fertility rate: 1.47 children born/woman (July 2007 est.)

Religions: Roman Catholic, Protestant, Orthodox, Muslim, Jewish

Languages: Bulgarian, Czech, Danish, Dutch, English, Estonian, Finnish, French, Gaelic, German, Greek, Hungarian, Italian, Latvian, Lithuanian, Maltese, Polish, Portuguese, Romanian, Slovak, Slovene, Spanish, Swedish; note—only official languages are listed; Irish (Gaelic) became the twenty-first language on 1 January 2007.

Source: www.cia.gov

Government

Union name: *conventional long form:* European Union *abbreviation:* EU

Political structure: a hybrid intergovernmental and supranational organization

Capitol: Brussels, Belgium; *note:* the Council of the European Union meets in Brussels, the European Parliament meets in Strasbourg, France, and the Court of Justice of the European Communities meets in Luxembourg

Member states: 27 countries: Austria, Belgium, Bulgaria, Cyprus, Czech Republic, Denmark, Estonia, Finland, France, Germany, Greece, Hungary, Ireland, Italy, Latvia, Lithuania, Luxembourg, Malta, Netherlands, Poland, Portugal, Romania, Slovakia, Slovenia, Spain, Sweden, UK; note—Canary Islands (Spain), Azores and Madeira (Portugal), and French Guyana, Guadeloupe, Martinique, and Reunion (France) are sometimes listed separately even though they are legally a part of Spain, Portugal, and France; candidate countries: Croatia, Macedonia, Turkey.

Independence: 7 February 1992 (Maastricht Treaty signed establishing the EU); 1 November 1993 (Maastricht Treaty entered into force)

National holiday: Europe Day 9 May (1950); note—a Union-wide holiday, the day that Robert Schuman proposed the creation of an organized Europe

Constitution: based on a series of treaties: the Treaty of Paris, which set up the European Coal and Steel Community (ECSC) in 1951; the Treaties of Rome, which set up the European Economic Community (EEC) and the European Atomic Energy Community (Euratom) in 1957; the Single European Act in 1986; the Treaty on European Union (Maastricht) in 1992; the Treaty of Amsterdam in 1997; and the Treaty of Nice in 2001; note—a new draft Constitutional Treaty, signed on 29 October 2004 in Rome, gave member states two years for ratification either by parliamentary vote or national referendum before it was scheduled to take effect on 1 November 2006; defeat in French and Dutch referenda in May–June 2005 caused a suspension of the ratification process

Suffrage: 18 years of age; universal

Executive branch: *chief of union:* President of the European Commission

> *Cabinet:* European Commission (composed of 25 members, one from each member country; each commissioner responsible for one or more policy areas) *elections:* the president of the European Commission is designated by member governments; the president-designate then chooses the other Commission members; the European Parliament confirms the entire Commission for a five-year term; election last held 18 November 2004 (next to be held 2009)

> *Legislative branch:* Council of the European Union (25 member-state ministers having 321 votes; the number of votes is roughly proportional to member-states' population); note—the Council is the main decision-making body of the EU; European Parliament (732 seats; seats allocated among member states by proportion to population); members elected by direct universal suffrage for a five-year term *elections:* last held 10–13 June 2004 (next to be held June 2009)

> *Judicial branch:* Court of Justice of the European Communities (ensures that the treaties are interpreted and applied correctly)—25 justices (one from each member state) appointed for a six-year term; note—for the sake of efficiency, the court can sit with 11 justices known as the "Grand Chamber"; Court of First Instance—25 justices appointed for a six-year term

Flag description: on a blue field, 12 five-pointed gold stars arranged in a circle, representing the union of the peoples of Europe; the number of stars is fixed

Economy

Economy—overview: Domestically, the European Union attempts to lower trade barriers, adopt a common currency, and move toward convergence of living standards. Internationally, the EU aims to bolster Europe's trade position and its political and economic power. Because of the great differences in per capita income (from $10,000 to $28,000) and historic national animosities, the European Community faces difficulties in devising and enforcing common policies. For example, both Germany and France since 2003 have flouted the member states' treaty obligation to prevent their national budgets from running more than a 3% deficit. In 2004, the EU admitted 10 central and Eastern European countries that are, in general, less advanced technologically and economically than the existing 15. Twelve EU member states introduced the euro as their common currency on 1 January 1999. The UK, Sweden, and Denmark do not now participate; the 10 new member states may choose to adopt the euro when they meet the EU's fiscal and monetary criteria and the member states so agree.

GDP—purchasing power parity: 13.08 trillion (2006 est.)

GDP—real growth rate: 3.2% (2006)

GDP—per capita: purchasing power parity—$29,900 (2006)

GDP—composition by sector: *agriculture:* 2.2%; *industry:* 27.3%; *services:* 70.5% (2006 est.)

Labor force: 222.7 million (2005 est.)

Labor force—by occupation: agriculture 4.5%, industry 27.4%, services 66.9%; *note:* the remainder is in miscellaneous public and private sector industries and services (2006 est.)

Unemployment rate: 8.5% (2006 est.)

Oil—production: 3.115 million bbl/day (2005)

Oil—consumption: 14.68 million bbl/day (2005)

Oil—exports: 5.322 million bbl/day (2001)

Oil—imports: 15.69 million bbl/day (2001)

Oil—proved reserves: 7.294 billion bbl (1 January 2002)

Source: www.cia.gov

Notes

1. Mark H. Lazerson, "Organizational Growth of Small Firms: An Outcome of Markets and Hierarchies?" *American Sociological Review* 53 (June 1988): 331.

2. Patrizio Bianchi and Giuseppina Gualtieri, "Emilia-Romagna and Its Industrial Districts: The Evolution of a Model," in Robert Leonardi and Raffaella Y. Nanetti, eds., *The Regions and European Integration: The Case of Emilia Romagna* (New York: Pinter, 1990), 83–108. See also Robert N. Putnam, *Making Democracy Work* (Princeton: Princeton U.P. 1993), 159–162.

3. See especially Pyke, Becattini, and Sengenberger, eds., *Industrial Districts and Inter-firm Co-operation in Italy* (Geneva: International Institute for Labor Studies of the International Labor Organization, 1990).

4. "High Pay for a Short Week in Seven Industrialized Countries," *Italian Journal*, 6 no. 4 (1992): 57.

5. The establishment of the regions did not make the Italian system of government fully federal, for the constitutional and political status of the Italian regions is less autonomous than, for example, the American states or the German Lander.

6. Putnam, *Making Democracy Work*, 8.

Bibliography

Becattini, P. and Sengenberger, eds., *Industrial Districts and Inter-firm Co-operation in Italy* (Geneva: International Institute for Labor Studies of the International Labor Organization, 1990).

Ginsborg, P., *Italy and Its Discontents—Family, Civil Society, State: 1980–2001* (New York: Palgrave Macmillan, 2003).

Lazerson, M. H. Organizational Growth of Small Firms: An Outcome of Markets and Hierarchies?, *American Sociological Review,* 53 (June 1988).

Leonardi, R. and Nanetti, R. Y., eds., *The Regions and European Integration: The Case of Emilia Romagna* (New York: Pinter, 1990).

Mershon, C., *The Micropolitics of Union Action: Industrial Conflict in Italian Factories,* Ph.D. diss., Yale University,1986.

Nannetti, R. Y., *Growth and Territorial Policies: The Italian Model of Social Capitalism.* New York: Pinter, 1988.

Nannetti, R, Y. and Robert Leonardi, eds., *The Regions and European Integration: The Case of Emilia-Romagna.* New York: Pinter, 1990.

Putnam, R., *Making Democracy Work* (Princeton: Princeton U.P., 1993)

CHAPTER 7

THE TWO ITALIES AND THE SOUTHERN QUESTION

The North-South Divide

One of the biggest challenges Italy faces is the north-south divide. While Italy, as a nation, is Europe's fourth largest economy, life in the *Mezzogiorno,* the south, remains as tough as it's always been, if not tougher. Instead of catching up with the rest of Italy, the region seems to be falling farther and farther behind. If southern Italy were an independent state, it would be the poorest of the EU's 25 members, in per capita income; Northern Italy, by contrast, would be the richest. The divide is not new; nor are the resentments of northern Italians toward the south for holding down Italy as an economic power. From the Unification of Italy (1861) until the present day, the *questione del Mezzogiorno,* the "southern question"—primarily, the issue of what to do about the persistent underdevelopment of the south vis-à-vis the north—has been at the center of intense debate.

The South and Its Representation as "Other"

The recent debate on the role of the South in the development of the Italian state and Italian society has tended to draw heavily on a series of well-worn stereotypes that equate the

🏵 SPIRIT

The South and Magna Graecia

It is sometimes hard to remember that southern Italy was virtually part of Greece for hundreds of years before the Roman conquest and has a long history of high culture and prosperity. Southern Italy was called Magna Graecia (Latin for "Greater Greece"), and many Greek legends actually have their setting in southern Italy.

Building large urban centers and religious shrines, Greek settlers established a brilliant civilization and founded towns that became the centers of a new, thriving Greek territory. Many place names on both coasts, from the Bay of Naples and the Gulf of Taranto southward, are of Greek origin, including Naples, derived from *Neapolis,* a Greek word literally meaning new city; Naxos (Giardini Naxos); Catana (Catania); Syrakus and Zankle (Messina) on Sicily; and Rhegion (Reggio Calabria) on the mainland.

With this colonization, Greek culture, with its ancient dialects, its religious rites, and its traditions of the independent *polis,* was exported to Italy. An original Hellenic civilization soon developed, later interacting with the native Italic and Latin civilizations. The most important cultural transplant was the Chalcidean/Cumaean variety of the Greek alphabet, first adopted by the Etruscans, which subsequently evolved into the Latin alphabet and went on to become the most widely used alphabet in the world.

The Greek thinkers Pythagoras, Herodotus, Aeschylus, Euripides, and Plato all visited what is now called the *Mezzogiorno,* much as artists visit central Italy today. The philosopher Empedocles belonged to the ruling clan of Akragas. Archimedes, the greatest mathematician of antiquity, was a native of Syracuse. Magna Graecia was the center of two philosophical groups in the 6th century B.C., that of Parmenides at Elea and that of Pythagoras at Crotone. Through Cumae especially, the Etruscans of Capua and the Romans came into early contact with Greek civilization.

Some of the most splendid remains of Greek temples in the Mediterranean are in southern Italy: at Paestum, near Salerno; and at Agrigento, Syracuse, and Segesta, in Sicily. The *Valle dei Templi* ("Valley of the Temples," a misnomer, as it is a ridge, rather than a valley) is in Agrigento. The only words to describe the temples of Agrigento are "magnificent works of art." Ancient Greeks built these temples on an acropolis, surrounded by olive trees and almond orchards with a view fit for the gods. Although many of the temples are in ruins, they are stunning by day or night. The temples served purposes similar to what churches do now. In Europe, churches and temples are usually placed relatively higher than everything else and people go inside to worship. In Greek temples, however, only the priest or religious figure was allowed inside. All public events, including sacrifices, took place outside the temples to the east. The Greeks sacrificed animals, usually bulls, but only partially: they ate the rest, in a sort of ancient barbecue.

The Valley of the Temples comprises a large sacred area that includes seven monumental Greek temples in the Doric style. Now excavated and partially restored, they constitute some of the largest and best preserved ancient Greek buildings in the world. The best preserved are two buildings traditionally attributed to the goddesses Juno Lacinia and Concordia (though archaeologists believe this attribution to be incorrect). The Temple of Juno also is called the Temple of Hera, after the wife of Zeus, the goddess of fertility. While weddings were held at this temple, it also served women who had trouble in marriage, relationships, or getting pregnant. Perhaps most beautiful is the Temple of Concordia, after the Latin word for peace and unity. The city of Agrigento and the western town of Marsala still celebrate peace and unity with almond festivals on the first Sunday in February.

Source: www.wikipedia.org

south with forms of social and economic backwardness, delinquency, organized crime, and political corruption. The old resentments of the prosperous north toward the less developed south have acquired such dimensions as to generate serious concerns. Many northerners like to think of themselves as closer to the European continent than to the peninsula. They feel that the southerners have ruined their dream of being the richest country in Europe. There is good reason to reflect, therefore, on the historical accuracy of these images and indeed to look more closely at the assumptions that have equated the history of southern Italy over the last century with the "southern question."

We should start by asking what is meant by the south. The answer is problematic because in the overcharged anti-south rhetoric, the south has no fixed boundaries. The boundaries of Umberto Bossi, the leader of the Northern League, have shifted over time and include an area that has no historical precedent as a political entity. They include an imagined area that extends as far as wealth and supposedly perfect government extend or where rising crime, Mafia influence, clientelism, and a dysfunctional state begin. Such a representation has found expression in graffiti slogans and journalistic and academic discourse as well as in heated political debates. Today's political and scholarly views of the south as a "problem," as if it were a colonial or backward and underdeveloped country resistant to modernization, have their roots in views that were first articulated at the birth of the nation.

Today's Stereotypes Go Back to the Unification

Stereotypical representations of the *Mezzogiorno* are a persistent feature of Italian culture at all levels. In an interesting and persuasive article entitled "A World at War: The Italian Army and Brigandage 1860–1870," John Dickie analyzes these stereotypes in the post-Unification period, when the *Mezzogiorno* was widely seen as barbaric, violent, and irrational, an "Africa" on the European continent. Drawing on recent theories of "Otherness" and national identity, Dickie shines new light on the origin of the stereotypes used to illustrate the divide between South and North.

John Dickie claims that the south was transformed into an "Otherness" against which the new Italian state and society sought to define itself.[1] Even the "question of brigandage" in southern Italy during the most critical years of Italy's unification was identified with a "southern problem." The so-called brigand war lasted for about a decade, cost more lives than all the battles of unification put together, and at its peak required the deployment of about two-fifths of the effective strength of the Italian army.

Many historians have argued that the "bandits" were not simple outlaws and have questioned if in the process of unification the south was "liberated" or "annexed" or "subjugated." In 1860, the lands belonging to the Kingdom of the Two Sicilies, which became part of the new united nation, were in a weak position and were obliged to measure themselves against cultural and economic models based on profoundly different societies. The south's identity was in fact based on negation, on what it lacked in relation to the ideal model as represented by the Kingdom of Piedmont, the unifying state. The ruling class of the north showed a total lack of understanding of the culture and institutions of the south in establishing its hegemony on the rest of the peninsula; in the process, any resistance was met with force. John Dickie claims, with a convincing argument, that the Piedmontese establishment was able to mold a negative image of the south to consolidate its authority without conceding any social change.

We know that the main factors behind peasant unrest and brigandage were economic hardship, the introduction of conscription, and the accumulated discontent caused by the erosion of collective land-use rights. In the period between 1860 and 1864, the large bands of "brigands," often numbering in the hundreds and with varying degrees of popular support and motivation, attempted to spark popular uprisings. In 1860–1861, particularly, some towns were briefly taken over and troops and national guard units were engaged in direct battles.

Many historians, in representing brigandage, mask or even misrepresent peasant unrest and the strong element of social protest by focusing their attention on the criminality of the unrest, reflecting the authorities' view of the phenomenon. The authorities certainly did not see the peasant revolts and the support given by the so-called bandits as a form of class mobilization, "the extreme, armed manifestation of a movement of revenge and protest which reaches the level of crude forms of class struggle."[2]

It should be remembered that the first historians of the conflict were almost all army officers who had fought in it. In the anti-brigand campaign, army officers and the government

Family average net income by geographic areas–2006 (in euros)

Italy	28,950
North-West	32,084
North-East	32,613
Center	31,150
South	23,965
Islands	22,861

Source: www.eu.org

understood and portrayed their opponents predominantly in the form of a series of hierarchical binary oppositions, such as between civilization and barbarism, reason and violence, social order and crime. A government envoy writing to Cavour (prime minister of Piedmont) from Teano in 1860 stated: "What barbarism! This isn't Italy! This is Africa: compared to these peasants the Bedouins are the flower of civilized virtues."[3] Nino Bixio, an officer in Garibaldi's army and then a deputy in the Italian Parliament, writing to his wife while working with the parliamentary commission of enquiry into brigandage, exclaimed, "in short, this is a country that should be destroyed or at least depopulated and its inhabitants sent to Africa to get themselves civilized!"[4] A young Italian officer wrote to his father in November 1861 that: "The brigands are like the Arab Phoenix; everyone says they exist, no one knows where they are; and I am beginning to believe that their existence is only the product of the over-active imaginations of these people."

Banditry had the entire repertoire of racist imagery used against it by the officers of the Italian army: bandits were "black," "animal," "primitive," "evil," "perverse," "irrational." In defining banditry this way, the Piedmontese establishment placed it beyond explanation in an imaginatively and emotively charged realm of monstrosity. The conceptualization of brigandage as an "Other" is set in the broader frame of an imaginative geography in which the Italian nation is constructed as the opposite of its south.

In the nation-building process, the "Other" was used as a negative term of comparison, i.e., as representing those cultural and ethical traits—much nearer to the Arab than northern European countries. The more general perception of the region was of a foreign and barbaric land that the young nation should strive *not* to imitate. The south was a cauldron of images of the Mafia and *Camorra*; brigandage and feudalism; indolence, illiteracy, superstition, and magic; cannibalism and corruption; dirt and disease—coupled with pastoral beauty and tranquility.

If banditry is constructed as the very antithesis of law, civilization, and reason, as 'occult, invisible, secret,' and if it extends throughout the social fabric and even into the "instinct of the people," then to combat it the army must have an unrestricted mode of operation. The use of unconstitutional measures to combat banditry becomes not only justifiable but ethically imperative. And that is exactly the way the government allowed the army to operate. Because of the social and political unrest, large parts of the south spent the first five years after incorporation into the new state under different forms of what was essentially a military regime. The use of summary execution and collective punishment began with the first entry of Piedmontese troops and the first signs of peasant unrest. A "state of siege," which was declared when Garibaldi landed in Calabria in August 1862, officially suspended constitutional guarantees and allowed the use of summary execution, detention without trial, collective punishment, special tribunals, and the widespread use of the death penalty.

In fighting brigandage, as an invisible "monstrosity," as an "Otherness," the government could go as far as to establish (through the approval of appropriate laws) that any band of three or more people caught in the countryside with arms of any kind (including agricultural tools) could be accused of brigandage. If one now tries just to visualize or imagine the kind of agrarian society that existed at that time, one can understand how easy it was to accuse people of brigandage, and, therefore, to crush any social unrest. In this way, the social features of banditry could be intentionally wiped out. Thus the construction of the south, *Mezzogiorno,* as "Other" within an imagined nation, had its origins in its incorporation into the Italian state.

The issue of brigandage and the way it was treated by the political establishment sheds some light on how the "southern question" came into being and how the south has been perceived almost exclusively in these terms. If everything in the south is related to brigandage, then brigandage becomes the key to understanding the south. Just as the army represents and embodies Italy, so brigandage is seen to embody the *Mezzogiorno.*

The Pervasive Ethnocentrism

At the superficial level of the kind of images evoked, one can find the same ethnocentric themes across a century of Italian history. Today's perception of the south has its roots in the construction of the "otherness" defined at the dawn of the nation. Indeed, references to the south are described mostly as an Italian problem, a problem that emerges through the construction of the "other." Even the rise of the Northern League and the League's attitudes toward the south are built on the concept of "other." The League has managed to get people to think that national political and social problems are territorial, that is, coming from some "other" place.

The wastefulness and degeneration of the Italian state can be selectively blamed on the presence of southern workers in state jobs, and on *assistenzialismo* (public assistance) and clientelism in the south, all of which are seen to contrast with the image of a widespread self-reliance in the north. Vague aspirations to a European identity can be seen simultaneously as a move away from "Africa," as Umberto Bossi commented just after the general election of 1992: "The North has chosen federalism and Europe, the South has chosen Fascism and Africa." The ethnocentrism of the Northern League is tied into an exclusive, centrifugal regionalism; it functions for the construction of a regional political identity. Although the League has argued for various forms of political separation from the south, it still needs the south, in the sense that it is dependent on the otherness it projects onto the south to mobilize its supporters.

However, the Northern League's thinking of political problems in geographical and ethnic terms not only is not new, but today is used to sharpen the political rhetoric of separation or, at least, to promote federalism. This rhetoric needs contrasts: the more we loathe an "Other," the more we need that loathing. Therefore, for political geographic areas that would like to shape for themselves a new identity, the construction of a negative "Other," from which they want to separate, is very appealing. In this case the League's rhetorical intent toward the south, referencing powerfully charged emblems of threats, is evident: rising crime, social decay, and the drug trade can be considered entirely the product of the Mafia—which comes from the south.

However, ethnocentrism has been used by southerners in turn to define their distinctive characteristics and to shape their images of diversity. For example, at a time when the process of nation-building was being defined in antithesis to social and cultural traits attributed to the south *en bloc,* Neapolitan culture was busy retreating into mythical and self-contained worlds, constructing its own positive stereotypes *(See Box on p. 188).* Neapolitan writers have had a difficult time redefining Naples outside of its traditional image as portrayed especially in many films and songs. This is a problem because only through culture can the south be freed of the endless images of abnormality and diversity under which it suffocates. The cultural concepts of *napoletanità* and *sicilianità,* and the concept of *meridionalismo,* which have supported for so long the myth of diversity, are sustained by this broad social and political base.

Certainly the use of the south as a metaphor to represent national ills and problems has contributed to the reinforcement of old stereotypes because the metaphor can be turned into a scapegoat—in other words, from the south as a symbol of social and political ills that characterize Italian society as a whole, to the south as a geographical area where such ills originate and are to be found. This degeneration of the south from metaphor of the nation to scapegoat for the nation parallels the degeneration of the south as "other," which, from being seen as an integral part of the process of nation building, becomes the sick limb that needs to be cut off from the healthy body.

The images that identified the south with backwardness, barbarism, primitiveness, crime, and violence amount to no more than ill-informed and prejudiced northern perceptions, which in the last ten years have been a central target of a lively revisionist historiography. Some sociologists have focused on social constraints on growth. Carlo Triglia, for example, has recently reexamined Gramsci's insistence on the "disaggregation" of society in the south, to argue that the failure to develop forms of horizontal social mobilization comparable to the trade union and cooperative movements in northern Italy have been central barriers to economic growth and social change in the south. In the absence of alternative forms of collective organization, primary social institutions retained their primacy in ways that inhibited the emergence of small-scale entrepreneurship and encouraged the persistence of clientelist politics.[5]

An American Study That Reinforced the South-North Divide

We should point out that Italy's south-north dualism was reinforced after WWII by the American scholar Edward C. Banfield as the U.S. was shaping its aid policy to the war-torn economies of Europe. In Italy, U.S. influence was of considerable importance in the development of state intervention in the south. It operated at a theoretical level through the example of Roosevelt's "Development areas" and in practice through the consultancy of American experts, on loan first to SVIMEZ *(Associazione per lo Sviluppo dell'Industria nel Mezzogiorno)* and then to the *Cassa per il Mezzogiorno.* Banfield confirmed one of the many stereotypes about the *Mezzogiorno:* that of its immobility and exclusion from history. For Banfield, who spent several months in a small village of Basilicata in 1955, the backwardness of the south was explained by a "traditional" ethos, which he called "amoral familism."[6]

≋ **PLACES**

Naples

Naples (from Greek νεπολη < ναπολις *Néa Pólis* 'New City') is the largest city in southern Italy and capital of the Campania region and the Province of Naples. The city has a population of about 1 million. By one count the metropolitan area of Naples is the second largest in Italy, after that of Milan, with more than 4,200,000 inhabitants. The inhabitants are known as *Neapolitans, napulitane* in Neapolitan, *napoletani* or poetically *partenopei* in Italian. Naples is located halfway between the volcano, Vesuvius and a separate volcanic area, the Campi Flegrei, all part of the Campania volcanic arc.

Naples is a city where life is lived in the streets and squares. In fact the street is where Naples happens, in all its chaotic glory. In addition to excitement, Naples also has beautiful architecture, a thriving port area, and frequent ferries out to the lovely islands of Capri and Ischia; and the ancient world lies just out of town in the shape of Pompeii, Herculaneum, and their ruins. Neapolitan (*'o napulitano*) is the colorful, rich Romance language that has been a trademark of southern Italy ever since the period of the Kingdom of Naples and the Two Sicilies. Everything in Naples—the buildings, museums, and even the language spoken by the natives—bear traces of all the periods in its history, from its birth as a colony of ancient Greece until the present day. This history, coupled with its size, has given Naples the unofficial status of being the capitol of the south.

Over the centuries Naples has played an important and vibrant role in music not just of Italy, but in the general history of western European musical traditions. This influence extends from the early music conservatories in the 1500s through the music of Alessandro Scarlatti during the Baroque period and the comic operas of Pergolesi, Piccini and, eventually, Rossini and Mozart. The vitality of Neapolitan popular music from the late 19th century has made such songs as "O sole mio," "Santa Lucia," "Torna a Surriento" and "Funiculì Funiculà" a part of musical consciousness all over the world.

By tradition Naples is the home of pizza. It is the birthplace of the *Pizza Margherita,* which is made with mozzarella cheese, *pomodoro* (tomato) and basil—representing, respectively, the red, white, and green of the Italian flag. The pizza was named when it was served to Queen Margherita during a visit to the city. *La vera pizza* ("true pizza") is made in a wood-burning oven. There is a certification body that issues recognition to pizza places around the world that have been deemed to make true Neapolitan pizza. Another traditional Neapolitan favorite is *Melanzane alla parmigiana,* baked layers of fried slices of aubergine (eggplant, very often coated in egg and flour, or in a light batter), alternated with mozzarella, tomato sauce, and parmesan (*parmigiano*) cheese (a less common version does not include mozzarella).

Naples offers several kinds of unique pastry, the most famous of which is the *babà,* followed by *choux* (Neapolitans write it as *sciù*) and the *Pastiera,* a cake prepared for Easter. The *babà* (also known as *savarin*) is a mushroom-shaped piece of leavened sweet paste, soaked with an orange flavored mixture of rum and water. *Choux* is a small "bubble" of leavened paste stuffed with light cream, usually coffee or chocolate flavored. The *Pastiera* is a cake with a complicated recipe, varying by the county in which it is prepared. The ingredients are typically annealed grain, eggs, and sometimes cream (it is sometimes made with boiled rice instead of grain in the area of Salerno), in a sort of short-crust pastry with strips of pastry on the top making a sort of grid. Another typical Neapolitan pastry is the *Sfogliatella* (*riccia* or *frolla*).

Lemons from Sorrento and from the Amalfi Coast—famous worldwide as an essential ingredient for *limoncello*—are very different from traditional lemons: they are larger, have a strong aroma, and have a thick peel and juicy pulp. The terraces where this special type of lemon is grown have been part and parcel of the landscape on the Sorrento peninsula and Amalfi coastline for centuries.

In Naples coffee is a ritual you just should not miss. It was once made with the traditional Neapolitan coffee-maker made famous by actors Edoardo De Filippo and Totò in their plays and films. Today coffee is made with the Italian *moka* espresso coffee maker following a few technical tricks that all Neapolitans know perfectly. First of all, the *moka* should never be washed with soap but rinsed with warm water only. The secret of a good cup of espresso consists in not pressing down the coffee grains in the filter too hard, and in turning the flame down to a minimum as soon as the coffee starts to "gurgle," leaving it for a few seconds before taking it off the hob and serving.

The term "amoral familism" designates a form of behavior directed solely toward the pursuit of the good of the family. It implies an endemic inability to act for the common good—what is popularly called a lack of civic consciousness. It is often associated with centralized and authoritarian states that discourage the growth of intermediate institutions of government between state and citizens. In Banfield's view, "amoral familism," stripped of its descriptive content, came to mean simply the tendency of southerners to favor the family group; as such it was identified as one of the major causes of patronage in the south. The strength of the family was linked to the persistence of "tradition," and tradition, in turn, to the extended patriarchal and patrilinear families. Thus southern society, already considered "backward" and "traditional," now also becomes patriarchal. At the same time, this stereotyped perception has coincided with another, which is closer to Banfield's original idea: that of a fragmented south, lacking valid principles of social organization, dominated by extreme individualism, riven by the war of "all against all," incapable of creating permanent group identities.

The history of the concept of "amoral familism" illustrates well the processes by which the image of the *Mezzogiorno* has been constructed. The image of backwardness has been adopted both within and outside the south. The falsity of the concept may be quickly detected when an identical phenomenon, the patriarchal family—commonly associated with underdevelopment—goes unnoticed if it relates to a society in the north. Thus the representations of patriarchal families in the Veneto or Tuscany are neutral facts unworthy of mention, while similar images referring to the south make a powerful impression on public opinion and confirm the mental model. It must also be underlined that the patriarchal family is not supreme in the south; women have a "traditional" power there, which is unquestionably greater than that of other Italian women—division of wealth between the sexes according to an equitable method, careful protection of the dowry throughout a woman's life and its direct inheritance by the children, enormous moral and contractual power within the family, and so forth.

In the discussion of the conflict between north and south, it should also be pointed out that there is a considerable integration between the two areas: one need only consider all the intermarriage between northerners and southerners, the assimilation into the northern cities of several millions of southern migrants in the 1950s and 1960s, and the high number of southerners amongst the Italian ruling class (in Milan and Turin, for example, there is a substantial group of company directors who were born in the south and graduated there).

In the early 90s, Banfield's less-than-happy concept of "amoral familism" found new energy through the studies of American political scientist Robert D. Putnam, who revived the old argument that the divergence between north and south is rooted in the absence of a civic tradition in the south. He tried to breathe new life into a thesis of cultural determinism that extends from the Middle Ages to the present.[7] *(See Box on p. 192)* Directly or indirectly, these two scholars have contributed to the perception that:

> »   Southern Italians have a reactive rather than proactive approach to government and living conditions.
> »   Southern Italians have a pathological distrust of the state and authority.
> »   The rulers of the south systematically promoted mutual distrust and conflict among their subjects, destroying horizontal ties of solidarity in order to maintain the primacy of vertical ties of dependence and exploitation.
> »   There is a direct link between civic community and economic development of the regions.
> »   Southern Italians have achieved less economically and politically because of their cultural pattern of rooting themselves in the neighborhood they worked to create.
> »   Family interests are more important than the common good.

The Historical Division

What is the south (*Sud, Mezzogiorno, Meridione*) in geographic terms, anyhow? It is difficult to define because, as we have seen, it is much more than a geographical area; usually it is a metaphor that refers to an imaginary and mythical entity, associated with both hell and paradise.[8] Since it is usually defined or molded through a comparison with the north by scientific paradigms and preexisting stereotypes, the boundaries that separate the two areas depend on how northerly one's vantage point may be.[9] The south cannot even be defined easily in economic terms because, as recent studies show, the area is not economically uniform or undifferentiated. If one accepts the well-established geographic division of Italy in three parts (north, center, and south), the south includes the five southern regions of the peninsula (Molise, Campania, Puglia, Basilicata, and Calabria) and the surrounding islands, including the two major islands (Sicilia and Sardegna).

In ancient times the south was the most prosperous part of the peninsula *(See Box on p. 192)*. Under Roman rule it became an area of enormous farming estates, the *latifundia,* where a slave population worked the soil, enabling the absentee landlords to regale themselves in Rome. Then came raids and invasions by Germanic tribes and centuries of domination by Byzantines and Arabs, and by Norman, German, French, and Spanish rule.

It was during the domination of the Normans, at the court of Frederick II in Palermo, that the first Italian literary school, *La Scuola Siciliana* (the Sicilian School), started to produce a literature with a national character (1220–50). The *Scuola Siciliana* preceded the well-recognized Tuscan school, *Il Dolce Stil Novo* (the Sweet New Style), by about half a century.

Refugees from other Mediterranean areas have also played a part in the southern culture. There are twenty-six Albanian villages that originated from Mehemet II's invasion of Albania after he had taken Constantinople in 1453.

Between the fifteenth century and the *Risorgimento* of the nineteenth century, the south was subjected to foreign rule and exploitation numerous times. Colonialism imposed a strong tradition of strict class structure that was reinforced by the presence of a powerful and oppressive feudal organization, which was abolished much later than those of other European countries, creating certain sociocultural barriers to development.

With the unification of Italy things did not improve. Count Camillo Benso di Cavour, the diplomatic architect of Italy's unification, was not interested in liberating the south or making it part of Italy. Since Garibaldi's march from the south made this an accomplished fact, Cavour did not have a choice in the matter. However, as prime minister of the Kingdom of Piedmont, Cavour never even bothered to visit the south.

Consequently, southerners quickly gained the feeling that they were not citizens of a new Italian state with the same rights and opportunities as the northerners but instead had become subjects in a colony. The new institutions, laws, and economic policies were generally alien to the customs and contrary to the interests of the south. Taxes on agriculture became ruinous, while the industrialization of the north perpetuated and even deepened the division. Some southern intellectuals did react persuasively to the damage that was being inflicted on the south.[10] In government, the strongest defense of southern interests came from Francesco Saverio Nitti. His theory was that Italian unification had been created at the south's expense, by squandering its immense financial resources and thus preventing it from developing independently through its own energies. He was convinced that the state had to intervene strongly with an industrial policy in order to compensate for the imbalance that had been created. Nothing happened. Economic conditions were so hard that in the 50 years before World War I, roughly half of the southern population—5 million people—emigrated.

The fascist regime not only did not take important initiatives in the economic development, but it also contributed to remodeling the image of the south on old stereotypes. In fact, despite some spotty reforms, under fascism the south was still regarded as a "no man's land" and it continued to lag behind. The fascist regime carried through some of the land reclamation projects they had devised, but instead of using them for a radical transformation of the south's industrial infrastructure, the land reclamation for the generation of energy and industrializa-

≣ **PLACES**

The Roots of the Two Italies May Go Back to the City-States

Some scholars argue that the roots of the southern question and the differences between the "two Italies" may derive from the fact that the south never enjoyed the experience of city-states as it was enjoyed by central-north Italy.

Italy between the 12th and 13th centuries was vastly different from feudal Europe north of the Alps. The peninsula was an assortment of political and cultural entities rather than a unified state. Probably geography determined the history of the region because within the Italian peninsula there is great physical diversity. Italy is cut into numerous small regions by mountains, which until the last century made inter-city communication very difficult. Because an attack across the Alps was very difficult, German princelings could not exert sustained control over their Italian vassal states, and thus Italy was substantially freed of outside political interference. So no strong monarchies emerged as they did in the rest of Europe; instead there emerged the independent city-state with republican sensibilities. The civic culture that arose from this was remarkable.

By the late 12th century, a new and unique society had emerged: rich, mobile, expanding, with a mixed aristocracy, interested in urban institutions and republican government. During the 11th to the 13th centuries big changes took place: a rise in population with the emergence of huge cities (Venice, Florence, and Milan, had over 100,000 inhabitants by the 13th century, and many others surpassed 50,000, such as Genoa, Bologna, Verona); the rebuilding of great cathedrals; a substantial migration from country to city (the rate of urbanization reached 20%, the most urbanized society in the world at that time); an agrarian revolution; and the development of commerce.

This expansion of society was fuelled by rapidly expanding commerce. By the 13th century, northern and central Italy had become the most literate society in the world. Fifty per cent of the male population could read in the vernacular (an unprecedented rate since the decline of the Roman Empire), as could a small but significant proportion of women.

In the thirteenth century, Europe in general was experiencing an economic boom. The trade routes of the Italian states linked with those of established Mediterranean ports and eventually with the Hanseatic League (an alliance of trading guilds that established and maintained a trade monopoly over the Baltic Sea and northern regions of Europe) to create a network economy in Europe for the first time since the third century. The city-states of Italy expanded greatly during this period and grew in power independently of the Holy Roman Empire. During this period, the modern commercial infrastructure developed, with joint stock companies, an international banking system, a systematized foreign exchange market, insurance, and government debt. Florence became the center of this financial industry and the gold florin became the main currency of international trade.

This produced a new mercantile governing class, who won their positions through financial skill, adapting to their purposes the feudal aristocratic model that had dominated Europe in the Middle Ages. A feature of the High Middle Ages in northern-central Italy was the rise of the urban communes that had shaken off control by bishops and local counts. In much of the region the landed nobility was consistently poorer than the urban patriarchs in the High Medieval money economy, whose inflationary rise left land-holding aristocrats impoverished. The increase in trade during the early Renaissance enhanced these characteristics. The decline of feudalism and the rise of cities influenced each other; for example, the demand for luxury goods led to an increase in trade, which led to greater numbers of tradesmen becoming wealthy, who, in turn, demanded more luxury goods. This change also gave the merchants almost complete control of the governments of the Italian city-states, again enhancing trade. Trade increased social mobility, hence the emergence of the merchant bourgeoisie that affected the political system and increased a civic culture. Freedom of thought and entrepreneurship in an open society advanced also artistic creativity and intellectual thinking.

Unfortunately, the south did not experience the life of the city-states and its civic culture. For some scholars the lack of this experience created a divider between the center-north and the south that characterizes differences that remain strong even today.

tion was transformed into land reclamation for ruralization. Whereas in the north the fascist regime played a modernizing role, in the south the message was populist and ruralist. During the economic crisis of the late 1920s, as had happened before in the history of the south, capital flowed back to the north, along with control of the economic system. The south's dependence on the north increased.

Another evidence of how Mussolini regarded the south as a "no man's land" may be found in the fact that when fascist authorities wanted to dispose of "dangerous" individuals, they would exile them to the south. And it is from one of these experiences that writer Carlo Levi, while in Basilicata, wrote a stunning book, *Christ Stopped in Eboli* (1945), in which he represented the primitive society and pattern of life he found in a land that he felt Jesus (i.e., civilization) had never touched. Ignazio Silone offered another stunning representation of the precarious conditions of the southern peasants at that time in his novel *Fontamara* (1949):

> The same earth, the same rain, wind, the same feast days, the same food, the same poverty—a poverty inherited from our fathers, who had received it from their grandfathers, and against which honest work was of no avail. The life of men and beasts, and of the land itself, revolved in a closed circle. . . . There has never been a way out. At that time, a man could perhaps save twenty or thirty soldi a month, and in summer perhaps even a hundred, so that by the autumn he had thirty lire. They disappeared at once—in interest on some loan, or to the doctor, the pharmacist or the priest. And so one began again, the next day. Twenty soldi, a hundred soldi.[11]

In the same book, Silone gives an ironic picture of the hierarchy of a region still pervaded by strong feudalism:

> At the head of everything there's God, the master of Heaven.
> That everyone knows.
> Then comes Prince Torlonia, the master of the land.
> Then come the Prince's dogs.
> Then come the Prince's guards.
> Then nothing.

Then, still nothing.
Then come the *cafoni* (the peasants).
And that's about all.(p. 29)

Fontamara eloquently represents the hopeless world of the southern *cafoni*. *Cafone,* explained the author, means "flesh accustomed to suffer" (p. 43). Silone was well aware that the name *cafone,* in Italy, was an insult. "But [he says] I use it in this book in the certainty that when in my country suffering is no longer something to be ashamed of, it will become a title of respect, perhaps also of honor" (p.6).

Works such as these began to have a profound impact and generated debate on the theme of economic backwardness. Economists and sociologists were brought in to define the economic features of the south. The debate was on how to trigger development in a society that was considered to be at zero. The south was once again a land without history, in a state of nature. Writings by Carlo Levi, Ernesto De Martino, and Rocco Scotellaro, although very different from one another, had in common the desire to interpret the popular culture of the south. The poor laborers of the south became a uniform category and were made into a symbol of pain, suffering, and oppression. However, those studies were important attempts to understand a culture from within and restore a measure of dignity to it. Some of postwar Italy's leading writers—Domenico Rea, Leonardo Sciascia, Saverio Strati—were also publishing eloquent novels on the plight of the south. These authors understood better, felt more deeply, and conveyed more powerfully than the politicians and anthropologists what life there was really like.

Modernization Without Much Economic Change

The south was not considered an area that had to be industrialized after WWII; the new government planned to continue the same policy of the prewar governments, that is, to keep the south agricultural.

In fact, the first attempt to institute reforms came as a consequence of the 1949 southern laborers' takeover of some of the *latifondi,* or large estates. At that time over half the population of the south—compared to a third in the rest of Italy—earned its livelihood from the soil as small holders, tenant farmers, or day laborers. These workers barely made a subsistence living. In the face of spreading discontent, the new republic undertook to solve the "southern question" with one of the largest and most ambitious regional development programs in Western Europe, a land reform program to buy-out large estates and sell the land to the workers. The single most important institution in this process was the Fund for the South (*Cassa per il Mezzogiorno*), created in 1950. Its main source of funding was state revenue, but it also drew on foreign loans. During the first dozen years, from 1950 on, the government, through the *Cassa per il Mezzogiorno,* concentrated its efforts and roughly 78% of its money on agriculture, with most of the remainder going to related infrastructure. Land reclamation, construction of dams, irrigation, aqueducts, and a vast extension of the road network gradually changed the face of the south. Technical experts introduced new farming and marketing methods. Malaria, which had afflicted the fertile lowlands in many parts of the south, was finally eradicated. State intervention contributed to the end of the *latifundia* system and to the birth of a new small-owner class.

However, when the program was largely completed in 1962, a mere 1.5 million acres had been transferred to some 85,000 farmers and laborers. For many, especially in the mountainous areas, the redistribution amounted to no more than a small plot of poor soil, insufficient to maintain a family. In the south as a whole, land holdings—half the average size of those in other Common Market countries—were too small to achieve fully modern and low-cost production. The real income of the average farmer did not increase much. As a consequence, the share of those employed in agriculture in the south declined from 57 to 27% of the workforce. Soon enough it became clear that efforts to improve agriculture had not reduced unemployment, raised incomes, or narrowed the overall gap between the south and the rest of Italy.

For about fifteen years the *Cassa per il Mezzogiorno* built up the infrastructure of the South and created incentives for the development of the new industrial sectors. There is no question that the *Cassa* contributed significantly to the region's high growth rates in this period. But there were costs: The *Cassa*'s Rome-centered, highly discretionary approach left little room for holding local authorities responsible and making public choices accountable. These turned out to be very serious flaws, especially in the south, where neither local nor state officials were trusted.[12] Members of the local ruling class, mostly acting as mediators for decisions made in Rome, were delegitimized as providers of public goods. In the eyes of many southerners, local politicians and administrators were exploiting local offices for personal advantages.[13]

In the mid-1960s, it became more apparent that major mistakes were being made in the allocation of resources. Lack of accountability increasingly allowed public authorities to be captured by private interests. The negative economic effects were immediate: the income gap between north and south stopped dropping. The flight from the land intensified. Tens of thousands continued to leave the farms and pour into the labor market in the cities both in the south and the north. As in the previous hundred years, state intervention in the south was subordinated to the interest of the industrial economic groups.

In fact, the massive migration from the south, which could supply cheap labor for the north, was not the result of "natural" causes but was politically determined. Angelo Costa, president of the Italian Employers' Confederation (the *Confindustria*), in the course of an investigation conducted by the government explained that he thought that adopting policies to localize industry along the U.K. model would be detrimental to the Italian economy. He asserted that it would be preferable to "move people" rather than things.[14] In other words, Costa was in favor of internal migration rather than the location of industry in the south. This implied that the role of the south in postwar reconstruction would be that of providing the northern industries with a necessary supply of low-cost labor. The development of the north and the so-called "economic miracle" was thus financed by the systematic drainage of the south's sole resource: human labor. In exchange, the south was given a constant stream of state funds to support public projects and develop a welfare system. This policy was spearheaded by the *DC*, the leading party in the government, because, through the process, it could establish a strong patronage system that would underpin the stability of its regime. The Christian Democrats followed the plan outlined by Costa, who accepted the need for public works programs in the south provided that the wages in the southern public-sector programs would be inferior to wages in the industrial northern sector in order not to compete for labor with private industry. Thus, there was a conscious political decision to intervene where private industry is reluctant to intervene and to do so on the basis of a low-wage policy.

Costa's plan of assuring cheap southern labor for the north was sustained by a consciousness that the southern Italians, unlike workers in other underdeveloped countries, had a cultural level, however low it might have appeared to some, already structured by the ethics and the mentality of the technological world. It was this cultural aspect that permitted the transformation of the southern laborer into a high-productivity, assembly-line proletarian in a couple of weeks, a transformation that is unthinkable in a similar space of time in the majority of under-developed countries.[15] Thus government policy protected a section of the southern population and more or less forced the rest to seek a life away from the land.

The *DC* agrarian reform and creation of the *Cassa per il Mezzogiorno,* while intended to restrict the numbers of absentee landlords, created a large class of small land-owning farmers and united them in a political bloc that stopped the communist advance in the south. However, it would be difficult to demonstrate that the lack of industry in the south was part of a *DC* political design to keep the conservative land-owning poor farmers from becoming progressive urban proletarians; it is a fact that the great majority of southerners who became northern factory workers became communists.

Poor State Planning: Cathedrals in the Desert

When the agrarian reform began to be criticized for its failures, the *Cassa* embarked on large-scale projects to create infrastructures. The strategy of public works programs, which was in the hands of the *Cassa* and other state agencies, was to consolidate the infrastructures, strengthen the agricultural sector, and develop tourism. These kinds of state interventions could be accepted by the north because they developed a market in the south for northern produce without increasing the competitiveness of southern industry. The *Cassa* obtained the favor of southern political and business leaders because it helped to expand the building industry, sustained a vast network of small farmer properties, and created a sector of dependent public employees. In fact, through the development of the state sector, a large class of white-collar workers was also created, which with time became a clientele system for the *DC*.[16] However, in reality, government action in the south helped the north more than it did the south: first, by increasing southerners' income through a public works program, it expanded the market for northern industry; second, the monies spent on the infrastructure (e.g., highways) helped northern industries both directly and indirectly.[17] Moreover, in the process, the *Cassa* programs created a sector of marginalized workers who were marginally trained. Those who had left their land to work in one of the *Cassa* projects could not return to it when the project was terminated;

they, too, had to move further north. The massive decrease in employment in agriculture was partly due to the change in emphasis in the direction of state intervention in the agricultural sector. This became clearer with the second Green Plan (1966): small farmers were discouraged, and public intervention went increasingly toward electrification and irrigation projects that were meant to favor existing entrepreneurs in rural areas rather than the marginal farmer.[18]

Many experts had insisted all along that only rapid industrial development would create the jobs and prosperity needed to break the vicious cycle of unemployment and poverty. Put simply, industry was to be moved to the area of surplus labor rather than labor's moving to the area of industrial activity. The shift of state investment funds from agriculture to industry would have paved the way for a serious attempt at the industrialization of the south.

The *Cassa's* spending on infrastructure was therefore cut from 42% in 1957 to 13% in 1965, while assistance to industrial enterprises was stepped up from 48% to 82%. To encourage private investment, the government offered generous credits and tax incentives. It also required the state holding companies *IRI* and *ENI* to invest increasing amounts of capital in the south. *IRI,* the major investor, injected over $20 billion into the south between 1963 and 1978.

The industrial policy for the south had two political motivations: first, to enable local entrepreneurs to become full-fledged industrialists instead of remaining craftsmen or farmers; second, to attract northern investment. The state intervened with large public projects through its enterprises: *Istituto per la Ricostruzione Industriale* (*IRI*) established giant steelworks near Taranto while *Ente Nazionale Idrocarburi* (*ENI*) located large petroleum refineries in Sicily. In this way came about a steel industry (at one time the most modern in Europe) at Taranto, an Alfa Romeo plant near Naples, and giant petrochemical factories in Sicily and Sardinia. The volume of industrial development in the south during this period was remarkable.

However, even though some of these investments were productive and profitable, the all-out heavy industrialization program did not turn out to be the magic solution to the south's problems. The new industries were not labor intensive and created relatively few jobs. The managerial and technical personnel were recruited from the north and later returned there, leaving the south without an indigenous managerial and technical class. And the industries themselves were subsidiaries of northern companies that never developed links to the local economy. These large-scale, technologically advanced plants had no connection with the rest of the southern economy. They were a sort of colonial enclave with little or no contact with the small local firms. They did not generate ancillary small and medium-sized enterprises in their areas; on the contrary, they maintained a direct connection with the north. Moreover, the *Cassa* began to finance basic large-scale enterprises, both private and public: electricity, steel, paper, chemical, gas—all industries that are fairly capital intensive but contribute little to employment.[19] Italians speak of the solitary industrial giants in the south as their cathedrals in the desert. Some factories in the south were apparently built only to collect the state subsidies for economic development in the region. Furthermore, many firms from the north were able to obtain considerable funds from the state in the form of subsidies, low-interest or interest-free loans, as well as direct grants as a part of invested capital. Consequently, the investments of the *Cassa* often went back to the north. Northern firms got subsidies for starting up factories in the south and then went bankrupt and re-exported their machinery to the north.

Bad Planning, Bad Economics, and Bad Politics

Often these new southern industries could not compete in the international market or withstand changes in economic trends. The steel plants at Taranto and Naples-Bagnoli were dragged down by the decline of the entire European steel industry in the 1970s. The huge petrochemical plants on the coasts of Sicily and Sardinia were based on cheap petroleum supplies; after the price increase in 1973 they, too, failed.

Overall, by 1980, the old south was changing. About 2,400 new factories employing over 305,000 persons had settled in designated industrial estates. However, new industrial jobs were concentrated in a limited number of sectors; 73% of southern factory employment in 1980 was in the chemical, mechanical, or metallurgical industries. Most of the firms in these sectors were large, state-controlled, capital-intensive units. In 1982, *IRI* accounted for 52.5% of employment in southern manufacturing plants with more than 1,000 workers. Other state holding companies represented another 11.5% of employment compared with 36% for the private sector.

However, at the beginning of the 1980s the problem continued: industrial development in the south was confined to specific geographic regions. The bulk of development was concentrated in three main areas: Naples and its neighboring areas, the Bari-Brindisi-Taranto triangle, and the Syracuse-Augusta axis of eastern Sicily. Eighty percent of the funding of the *Cassa* went to only four regions: Puglia, Sardinia, Sicily, and Campania. Spending was also extremely concentrated within the regions. For example, two-thirds of the Puglia investments were directed to Taranto.

The government had enacted laws in 1971 and 1976 requiring the *Cassa* to concentrate on a new range of intersectorial and interregional projects. These included the further development of industrial infrastructure, the exploitation of natural resources, social projects in metropolitan areas, water-reclamation projects, cleaning the Gulf of Naples, extending the road network into remote mountainous areas, reforestation, and promotion of citrus fruit production. Many of these programs had to be scaled down or scrapped as a result of the economic crisis following the oil price increase after 1973. Some of them were gigantic fiascos.

Emphasis then shifted to the selective encouragement of small- and medium-sized firms, which in the early 1980s accounted for over 90% of the projects and 85% of the investment of the *Cassa.* Unfortunately, this met with limited success. Only Abruzzi and Puglia witnessed the growth of a dynamic sector of small firms similar to those that have developed in northeastern and central Italy.

As a result, the private investment that was to follow the development initiated by the state never came. Private investors had to cope with the so-called southern Italian risk, that is, worker absenteeism, low productivity, labor unrest, low labor mobility, and organized crime.

A concrete example of such "risk" was the Alfa Romeo plant constructed near Naples in 1972. It was so afflicted by labor strife and absenteeism that it ran up losses of $700 million, which had to be covered by the parent company in the north. For many years, every "Alfa Sud" car on the road was sold at less than its production cost.

Potential investors, Italian and foreign, consequently often decided that the south was too great a hazard, and in fact, in the late 1970s and 1980s there was a net decline in foreign companies investing in the south. Even the investment that did occur in the south did little to reduce unemployment, because industrialization and employment were not entirely compatible goals. This problem was typically faced by the expansion of the bureaucracy and on the public purse.

Economic development had been the victim of bad planning, bad economics, and above all, bad politics. The shift from agriculture to infrastructure development, to large industry, to small and medium-sized industry, and back to agriculture reflects the lack of conviction in bringing real prosperity to the south. Fiat president Gianni Agnelli's remarks at a conference of southern experts in 1980 expressed well the problem: the development process of the south went ahead "either in the good faith of error" or in "the bad faith of political 'necessity.'" By the mid-1980s the government had created an economy grounded on this weak base:

»   The industrialization attempts through direct use of public funding had created a protected sector in the economy which was established on clientele relations and would not stand up against competition.

»   The welfare state had built a bloated class of white-collar workers through a big expansion of the bureaucratic apparatus.

»   The welfare state was providing assistance to hundreds of thousands of citizens through disability pensions.

In the early 1980s, the south did not derive any particular benefit from the effects of the decentralization of production toward the hidden sector, which permitted Italy to achieve a growth-rate higher than most industrial nations. The small and medium-sized firms of the hidden sector were located, on the whole, in the center and in the north, with very few in the south. Therefore, when the larger firms, both public and private, decreased the rate of growth of their investments, the south was hit harder. The state resources that could have been used otherwise had to be directed toward enabling existing firms to pay their debts or reorganize existing plants.

By the early 1990s the state had poured into the *Mezzogiorno* an estimated $150 billion of public funds. Approximately two-fifths of this expenditure went to public works, the remainder being allocated primarily to investments in agriculture, industry, and tourism. Some tangible accomplishments were evident. Thousands of miles of new streets and hundreds of bridges, many new schools, universities, and hospitals, and a network of modern hotels, restaurants, and service stations were built. Running water, electricity, and telephone service were brought to even the smallest hamlet, and a few large, new industries, like the Taranto steel mills and the petrochemical complexes at Brindisi and on Sicily's east coast, were built. Infant mortality declined by three-quarters, and illiteracy among youngsters has been practically eradicated as well, and while the overall character of the south has remained rural, its principal cities have greatly expanded. Their historic cores are now surrounded by vast belts of condominiums and new housing projects. The countryside is also full of elegant new housing.

Surprisingly, however, the economic gap between the *Mezzogiorno* and prosperous northern and central Italy has continued to widen. The problem of the "southern question" has been exacerbated by the combined effects of the deep recession of the early 1990s and the liberalization of the Italian economy. Liberalization and privatization have resulted in the gradual termination of subsidies to state industry in the South, a drive to reform a welfare state that used disability pensions in the South to disguise long-term unemployment, and the winding up of the "Fund for the South" *(Cassa per il Mezzogiorno)*. Connected to these effects are the problems posed by organized crime in Naples (the *Camorra*), Calabria (*'Ndrangheta*), Apulia (*Sacra Corona Unita*), and Sicily (Mafia and *Cosa Nostra*). The fact that the south is lagging so far behind the north needs additional explanation.

By the early 1990s the South—an area the size of Greece, with 40% of the country's land area and 30% of its population—accounted for only 20% of GDP and had an official unemployment rate of nearly 20% of the labor force, against 5% in the North. The per capita income in southern Italy was still barely 60% of the average in the rest of Italy, while the per capita income was more than 80% in the north. Today the overall picture remains grim: 7.3 million residents in southern Italy still make less than 521 euro a month (however, because of the prevalence of the underground economy, real figures are hard to find), and half of those live on less than 435 euro per month, according to ISTAT, Italy's national statistics institute. Reportedly, there are hotels in the south that can demand 500 euro a night, with families living on less than that per month just a few kilometers away.

No one denies that southern development, despite a number of isolated successes, fell short of all its original expectations and goals. Economists and political scientists have given many possible reasons:

>> Physical disadvantages of the south, including distance from markets, unfavorable terrain, and lack of natural resources
>> Misguided government policies
>> A culture of patron-clientelism
>> Lack of civic traditions

But the south has suffered mainly because of its own faults. The southern elites have failed to establish greater autonomy. Because of the vulnerability of the southern economies, the south remained more dependent on state intervention. In contrast to northern and central Italy, the bureaucratic state was an older historical reality in the south, whose importance grew in direct proportion to the failure to develop more robust and spontaneous forms of economic growth. In the *Mezzogiorno,* the observation made by Pasquale Villari in 1883—"One feels too much the 'I' and too little the 'we'"—is still valid.[20] Civic traditions and civic engagement alone do not account for the big difference between north and south, but their weak presence in the south has made a profound difference. Civic traditions help explain why the north has been able to respond to the challenges and opportunities of the twentieth century so much more effectively than the south. The most relevant distinction is not even between the presence and absence of social bonds but rather between horizontal bonds of mutual solidarity and vertical bonds of dependency and exploitation. The southerner has sought refuge in vertical bonds of patronage and clientelism, employed for both economic and political ends.

The Dawn of a New Era

Although the *Cassa per il Mezzogiorno* was formally dissolved in 1986, its true dismantling was delayed by the network of private interests that it created. Finally, in 1992, the pressure of European integration made it impossible for Italy to persist in implementing clearly anti-competitive policies. The top-down approach to policy-making for the south was abandoned. And one year later, the process of privatizing state-owned enterprises was launched, bringing "compensatory investments" in the south to a halt.

At the same time, popular resentment of the state's role in the south, long repressed in the center and north, came to the surface with the rise of the Northern League. As a result, the issue of the *Mezzogiorno* disappeared from the political agenda of all parties. Since no alternative economic policy was implemented, public investment in the *Mezzogiorno* started dropping even more than in the economy as a whole. Only in one policy area was the central government more active than in the past: law enforcement. After the assassination in 1992 of the two most prominent members of the anti-Mafia pool (see Chapter 3), measures in favor of collaborators (*pentiti*), from family protections to reduction in sentences, were taken with unprecedented results.

In 1993, a crucial event enabled new local leaders to emerge, enhancing the responsibilities of the local authorities. A reform in the electoral system of municipal governments made it possible for citizens to vote for city mayors (before they were voted by city councils). Since then the strength and the increased personal responsibility of mayors have created the incentive and the means necessary to modernize administrations and to restore the historical centers of many towns in the south. The direct election of mayors has brought stability to municipal administrations and opportunities to implement serious economic plans. Likewise, regions gave their citizens the right to elect their leaders (governors) and consequently enter an era of stable governments that have the authority and ability to deal with state and European Union funding. Endowed with strong power and direct accountability, the new "governors" have much stronger incentives to enact public investments with long-term effects and to modernize their administration accordingly.

After 1995, the positive results were evident: the turnover rate of southern nonagricultural enterprises—the number of new businesses opened, minus the number of those shut down—

started to rise; by 1997, it had become higher than in the center-north. The region's lively entrepreneurial climate led to the strengthening of many local agglomerations.

At the end of the 90s, southern regions launched serious initiatives for economic growth especially by focusing on the development of cluster firms. Hoping to create a permanent incentive for local entrepreneurs to create businesses and for foreign business to move into the area, developers worked to improve relations between firms within the clusters and take better advantage of the large reservoir of unemployed youths with university educations. This latter potential asset has already been fully exploited by a few high-tech firms—Bosch, Getrag, and ST Microelectronics, for example—that have invested in university areas.

In the 2000s the southern economy suffered a setback, parallel to that of the rest of Italy and Western Europe. However, the changes registered at the end of the 1990s support four provisional conclusions:

»   Reform can take place even in the Italian *Mezzogiorno*. With its age-old traditions and idiosyncratic culture, the *Mezzogiorno* can move away from its historical backwardness if its heritage of hospitality, curiosity, and open-mindedness is fully exploited by the appropriate institutional design.

»   Local administration efficiency became possible only after Rome reduced its top-down policy-making: the resulting increase in local responsibility looks like the main driving force for change.

»   The key changes have involved a more efficient exploitation of resources peculiar to the *Mezzogiorno:* the natural resources of the Apennine mountains and the coast lines; the region's cultural heritage and supply of previously underutilized human capital, both intellectual and manual.

»   The economic and social turnaround is not yet fast and strong enough to reverse long-held prejudices and redirect national and international capital to the area. Changes affect only a few areas and sectors and are often quite small. And the state has been slow to adjust: increasing municipal and regional efficiency has not yet been matched by the state's ability to increase the efficiency of its apparatus and to plan and implement those public investments that are called in by market awakening.

It is abundantly clear that a policy aimed at increasing territorial competitiveness must be centered on the potential competitive advantages of the region: the *Mezzogiorno*'s human capital; its existing networks of firms; its unique cultural and natural resources. At the moment, these assets are far from being adequately exploited. The south needs to better utilize the underexploited natural resources and promote better the region's cultural resources. Its natural and cultural resources ought to make the *Mezzogiorno* a major tourist destination. To achieve this goal the government must invest in the restoration of archaeological sites, fortresses, and monuments, the creation of attractive museums, and the protection of natural areas. It also must improve transport to these sites and set aside areas to develop appropriate hospitality services for all type of tourism.

Let's Not Despair

The future of the south lies in its ability to become a mature civic society and in the prospect of seeing the younger generation fully integrated into a productive Italy and Europe.

Throughout the history of modern Italy, southern Italians have demonstrated their competence in many fields. They make clever lawyers, able administrators, sharp police investigators, and consummate diplomats; they excel in philosophical speculations and mathematical theory. The plays and novels of Luigi Pirandello, Sicilian Nobel Prize-winner for literature (1934), continue to offer penetrating psychological insights into the south.

Beyond any doubt, the south has been transformed and the social changes are very striking. The *Mezzogiorno* is no longer isolated; southerners have gradually gone through a process of "Americanization" or modernization. Their outlook and mores—the secularization; the standards of consumer society, with all its defects; the social values—have come close to those of the northerners. The south is now linked to the rest of Italy not only through radio and television but also through one of the most advanced networks of roads and highways in Europe and a web of economic relationships.

Thus, in the new millennium, the "southern question" is not a matter of simple modernization, or of an increase of state funds. It cannot be addressed by pointing fingers at southern shame or northern guilt. The "problem of the south" cannot even be understood purely in terms of the Italian north, but must be thought of anew in terms of the relations between Italy and the rest of the EU and the Mediterranean.

So, we are left with two final questions. Is it possible to free the south of all metaphors of evil and otherness, from the stereotypes, both positive and negative, endogenous and exogenous, that contribute to its isolation? What, if any, is the real identity of the south, and who should carry out such a complex cultural and ethical project?

Notes

1.   John Dickie, "A World at War: The Italian Army and Brigandage 1860–1870," *History Workshop Journal* 33 (1992): 1–24.

2.   Franco Molfese, *Storia del brigantaggio dopo l'Unita'* (Milan: Feltrinelli, 1964), 342.

3.   In Camillo Cavour, *Carteggi: La liberazione del Mezzogiorno e la formazione del Regno d'Italia*, vol. 3 (Oct.–Nov. 1860) (Bologna: Zanichelli, 1952); letter from Farini dated 27 October 1860, p. 208

4.   *Epistolario di Nino Bixio*, vol. II (1861–1865) (Rome: Vittoriano, 1942); letter dated 18 February 1863, p. 143.

5.   Carlo Triglia, *Sviluppo senza autonomia* (Bologna: Il Mulino, 1992).

6.   Edward C. Banfield, *The Moral Basis of a Backward Society* (Glencoe, Ill.: The Free Press, 1958).

7.   Robert D. Putnam, *Making Democracy Work. Civic Traditions in Modern Italy* (Princeton: Princeton U.P., 1993).

8. F. Barbagallo, "Il Mezzogiorno come problema attuale," *Studi Storici,* 31 (1990): 587–89.

9. Some of the Legua representatives have sought to explain what the north is by reference to ancient invasion by northern peoples or to a mixture of historical and ethnic traits that produce a "non-Mediterranean" mentality. It is, however, a well-accepted fact that the most politically significant aspect of the imagined north is the hostile forces seen to lie beyond it.

10. A few southern economists dissented from the northerners' view of the south and put forward alternative interpretations and solutions. Napoleone Colajanni, for example, argued that it was precisely the supremacy of the bureaucracy, an uncontrolled power, that generated corruption. He criticized what he defined as "fiscal inequality" and claimed it was caused by the state, which "because of its absurdly centralized organization, acts on the periphery like a suction pump, which only returns a tiny part of what it absorbs." In *Sicilia* (Rome, 1894), 42, Gaetano Salvemini (a federalist) and Guido Dorso (an autonomist) were both convinced that the south could only reassert itself by being autonomous from central government, and it was the duty of political activists to make sure that the southern upper and middle classes would push for progress. These classes had the extremely important historical task of completing the "unfinished revolution of the Risorgimento" and thus of bringing about a real unification of the country, one which involved the mass of the people.

11. *Fontamara* (Milan: Mondadori, 1974), 7–8.

12. How could they be trusted? In a European contest, if the average GDP in the European Union in 1991 equaled 100, the GDP of northern and central Italy was 122, that of the south, 68.9. Indeed, northern and central Italy had a higher per capita GDP than Germany (113.8), France (108.9), and the UK (106.3). In the same year, if the south received 53% of the capital transfers from the Italian state, it only paid 20% of the national direct tax revenue, 29% of all indirect revenue, and 16% of national social security contributions.

13. Robert N. Putnam, *Making Democracy Work,* 158–159. For a good assessment, also read Gianni Toniolo, *An Economic History of Liberal Italy: 1850–1918,* trans. Maria Rees (New York: Routledge 1990); Vera Zamagni, *Industrializzazione e squilibri regionali in Italia: Bilancio dell'età giolittiana* (Bologna: Il Mulino, 1978.

14. In L. Villari, ed., *Il capitalismo italiano del Novecento,* vol. 2 (Bari: Laterza, 1975), 486–87.

15. Marcello De Cecco, "Lo sviluppo dell'economia italiana e la sua collocazione internazionale," *Rivista Internazionale di Scienze Economiche e Commerciali,* October 1971, 982.

16. Mariano D'Antonio, *Sviluppo e crisi del capitalismo italiano 1951–1972* (Bari: De Donato, 1973), 236.

17. Guido Fabiani, "Agricoltura e Mezzogiorno," in AA. VV. *Lezioni di economia. Aspetti e problemi dello sviluppo economico italiano e dell'attuale crisi internazionale* (Milan: Feltrinelli, 1977), 158.

18. Giuliano Amato, *Economia, politica e istituzioni in Italia* (Bologna: Il Mulino, 1976), 52.

19. Vittorio Valli, *L'economia e la politica economica italiana* (Milan: Etas Libri, 1979), 107.

20. Pasquale Villari, *Le lettere meridionali* (Florence: Le Monnier, 1875).

Bibliography

Ascoli, R. A. and Von Henneberg, K., *Making and Remaking Italy—The Cultivation of National Identity around the Risorgimento*. Oxford: Berg, 2001.

Banfield, E. C., *The Moral Basis of a Backward Society*. Glencoe, Ill.: The Free Press, 1958.

Barzini, L., *The Italians*. New York: Atheneum, 1965.

Bollati, G., *L'italiano: Il carattere nazionale come storia e come invenzione*. Turin: Einaudi, 1983.

Bonomi, A. *Il capitalismo molecolare*. Turin: Einaudi, 1997.

Bull Cento, A. and Giorgio, A., eds., *Culture and Society in Southern Italy, Past and Present*. Supplement of *The Italianist*, No. 14, 1994.

Dickie, J., "A World at War: The Italian Army and Brigandage 1860-1870," *History Workshop Journal* 33 (1992).

Ginsborg, P.,ed., *Lo stato dell'Italia*. Milano: Mondadori, 1994.

Ginsborg, P., *Italy and Its Discontents—Family, Civil Society, State: 1980-2001*. New York: Palgrave Macmillan, 2003.

Levy, C., ed., *Italian Regionalism—History, Identity and Politics*. Oxford: Berg, 1996.

Putnam, R. D., *Making Democracy Work. Civic Traditions in Modern Italy*. Princeton: Princeton U.P., 1993.

Silone, I., *Fontamara*. Milan: Mondadori, 1974.

Triglia, C., *Sviluppo senza autonomia*. Bologna: Il Mulino, 1992.

Verdicchio, P., *Bound by Distance—Rethinking Nationalism Through the Italian Diaspora*. Madison, N.J., Fairleigh Dickinson UP, 1997.

Viesti, G. F., "Che succede nell'economia del Mezzogiorno? Le trasformazioni 1990-1995," *Meridiana*, nos. 26–7 (1966).

Italians are masters in preserving antiquity while embracing modernity. Naples, for example, is experiencing a renaissance after years of decay. While new, attractive buildings are being erected, old parts of the city, neglected for years, are being claimed as important cultural areas. Scores of neglected churches, museums, and palaces in dilapidated districts have been reopened and are attracting large numbers of visitors. The cultural renaissance not only has given Neapolitans the opportunity to rediscover their identity, but it has also made Naples one of the most attractive Italian cities again. Printed courtesy of *America Oggi*.

CHAPTER 8

EMIGRATION, MIGRATION, IMMIGRATION, AND SOCIAL TRANSFORMATION

In Search of a Better Life

A complete knowledge of the development of postwar Italy is not possible without an understanding of the significant demographic changes that have occurred through emigration, internal migration, return migration, and immigration into the country. Because Italy in the mid-1950s was still, in many respects, an underdeveloped country, Italians, mainly from the south, were still emigrating by the thousands in search of a better life. Emigration was still a way of life for many, just as it had been for the previous three or four generations. Emigration had a profound impact on the economy of large areas of the country, on family life and structure, and caused the socio-transformation of many villages and small towns.

The Causes of Mass Emigration

Italy never colonized parts of America as did Spain, France, and England. Rather, many Italians started coming to America in the 1880s to escape poverty at home. Emigration became

From the Autobiography of an Italian Immigrant

We reached New York on a Saturday, but when the health officer saw those poor Greeks with their skin covered with abrasions, he decided that there were cases of an infectious disease on board. So the ship was held in quarantine. We came very close to having a revolution on board and we all tried to explain that it was not an infectious disease. It was because of fleas, that's why those poor wretches were always scratching themselves.

The snow fell and Saturday and Sunday passed. All of us were visited. Finally, Monday, around noon, we began to go ashore. Those we traveled with had already gone. Me and Gennarino were kept in a room with a card on our jackets that prevented us from leaving. When I tried to protest, an immigration officer fixed his eyes on me and asked, "Do you know where you are going?"

I immediately: "We're going to Meadville."

And he, losing his patience a little: "This is New York."

· · · · · ·

So, after twenty-one hours on the train, we arrived at Meadville. I left home at night, fifteen days before it was time to harvest grapes, and I arrived at night where it was all snow. It was six in the evening. At the station Gennarino found an uncle who was waiting for him. I found nobody. It was dark and cold out. I thought, "I'll go with them this evening, they're not going to close the door on me I hope." I was about to go up to Gennarino's uncle and ask if I could go with them, when I thought I heard someone call me. I turned without believing it. But then I heard again. Someone really was calling me and, blindly, without realizing it, I cried out in response, "Minicuccio."

In fact, it was him. I no longer recognized him, but it was him. Laughing, he took my bag and asked me, "How are you?" And without waiting for me to reply, he continued, "Come and stay with me and we'll live like tramps."

· · · · · ·

By now I had a steady job and Michele advised me to send my father the one-hundred and twenty-five lire of collateral, without guessing that the money would have stirred up a revolution back home:

"Just arrived and he's already sent money?"

"How much?"

"A lot . . . a hundred . . . a thousand."

Until finally, to calm everybody down, my father had to show the money order and explain that it was to pay back the amount we had borrowed. But few believed him.

On the job there was one accident after another. One of the guys from our team ended up with a leg in a tub of sodium hydroxide. It ate up the entire calf. He did not die, but he was dismissed from work. One of the most distressing accidents I remember was that of Francesco the Marcianisan. He was a little over thirty years old and was very pleasant. A certain John Green, a mulatto, ran the crane and Francesco was his assistant. That day Francesco went to hook up the crane-car to an open car and he got his head caught in between. Blood came out of his nose, his ears, and his eyes. When we tried to console him, he said to us, "the trouble isn't so much dying as living poorly."

He ended up simple-minded. When he returned from the hospital, they put him on clean-up for a few days. Then one of the bosses came up to him and asked if he had received anything for the accident. When the poor guy shook his head, which was always hurting him, the man said to him, "Sign here and I'll see that you get something." He got a hundred dollars. The document he signed was a receipt that exonerated the company from any responsibility. But he did not know this. A friend whom he called on later told him after he had been fired. In his condition he could not find another job and so he went back home to his wife and children living in Marcianise.

[The author emigrated to the U.S. in 1907]

The Discovery of America, an Autobiography, by Carmine Biagio Iannace

a mass phenomenon, but it continued to be motivated more by the desire to find a place to work than a search for a permanent home to live. Between 1898 and 1914, approximately 750,000 Italians emigrated each year. The agricultural system of Italy was not modernized, and it was hurt both by a disease that destroyed grapevines and by the increasing number of products from America invading Italian markets. The price of wheat and other agricultural produce fell. Thus, the primary motivation for Italian emigration was economic rather than political or religious. But to emigrate people need also guts, a sense for adventure, and an innate Ulyssesism or burning desire for discovery; that is why not all poor people emigrate (*See Box above*).

The invention of the steamship certainly gave impetus to the movement across the ocean and made emigration a big business. Agents acting on behalf of steamship companies or foreign employers were eager to enlist laborers. Moreover, the small-town "political class" had a vested interest in emigration because it was an important unofficial source of income. Lawyers, teachers, politicians, and travel agents were all involved in arranging for passports, booking the passages, lending the money for the fares (often at usurious rates), and finally selling off the poor laborers' land and houses. Such "businessmen" were often not much more than venal speculators and traffickers in human flesh. By the 1890s, the southern middle class was busy enrolling poor laborers, hiring ships, and making money on those whom it had previously been exploiting the most. Sometimes it even managed to export its social dominance across the Atlantic, to reappear in America as "bossism."

For millions of Italians, especially from the south, America, as a dream land, offered hope for a better future. Close examination of the choices made by the various regional groups reveals that southern Italians generally preferred to go to North America while those from northern regions favored Latin America. Ligurians and Piedmontese, for example, constituted a significant presence in Argentina; Venetians went mainly to Brazil. These choices were influenced by three factors:

» Previous immigrant flows

» Information from the "new countries"

» Job opportunities and their correspondence to the emigrants' personal skills and experience

Although the new Italian immigrants were unfamiliar with some of the new occupations they found in America, they predominated in those with which they were already familiar. They worked in mines, lumberyards, quarries, tunnels, and railroads. Thus they constituted a strong presence as masons, stonecutters, barbers, and shoemakers. In particular, more than half of all masons who immigrated to the U.S. were Italian; they took pick-and-shovel jobs, entered the building trades, provided manpower for the waterfronts, and worked for municipal sanitation departments. Some managed to scrape together enough money to open small restaurants or groceries. The women became seamstresses in the sweatshops and factories of the garment industry.

The length of the projected stay abroad frequently influenced the choice of occupation, because the immigrant could decide either to leave Italy at once, taking his family with him, or to emigrate alone and work intensely in the new country for some months in order to maximize his savings. This typical feature of migration especially relates to travel to South America; because it was reminiscent of the seasonal trips of migratory birds across the hemispheres, it was whimsically referred to as "The Little Swallow." Emigration based on temporary mobility characterized the initial life of Italian immigrants in the host countries in a way that was different from the other immigrant groups who made a clear break from their country when they left. Letters and literature written by immigrants reveal a strong nostalgia for Italy and a strong intent to go back home after building a comfortable savings.

Many immigrants who had left their families behind dreamed of going back to the old village one day to buy a piece of land that would give them independence. Quite a few did go back, sometimes 20 or more years later, when the children they had last seen as infants were adults. Most, however, changed their minds about returning and had their wives and children join them in America. Although the bulk of these immigrants were originally from rural areas, in the U.S. they tended to cluster in cities and suburbs, forming "little Italies."

Most of the immigrants from the south were virtually illiterate, and their country's cultural heritage had no meaning for them. In a sense, many of them had left Italy before becoming Italians. If this situation contributed to a negative impression of Italians abroad, it did not really matter to the United States because the growing country needed large numbers of sturdy laborers for the heavy construction work. Southern Italians played a key role in building America, for they dug the ditches, toiled in the mines, laid the rails, and carried the bricks and mortar. They gave their sweat and blood to lay the material foundations of America.

Overcoming Domestic Obstacles

Those Italians who stayed behind generally welcomed the exodus because they considered it a remedy to social problems at home. In the 1890s, Prime Minister Francesco Nitti described emigration as a "powerful safety-valve against class hatred." Sidney Sonnino, another prime minister of the exodus period, maintained that to prevent emigration would be a clear attack on the poor. Nevertheless, emigration was restricted in some areas of the south where the big landowners controlled local government and wanted to preserve the system of exploitation. There were others who were opposed to emigration because of the way the emigrants were being treated abroad. Edmondo De Amicis (1846–1908), a socialist, aroused much indignation by representing emigration as shameful in his moving book, *Sull'oceano* (*On the Ocean,* 1889). The Catholic Church, too, initially did not support emigration because of its effect on family life (families were split for many years; very often they were never reunited) and on religious belief (thousands of emigrants to America became Protestants, often Pentacostalists). In fact, Protestant groups in the U.S. actively conducted missions in an effort to convert Italians. At one time there were almost 300 Italian Protestant missionaries engaged in full-time work. Prominent figures like Leonard Covello, Fiorello La Guardia, Ferdinand Pecora, and Charles Poletti were Protestants.

Nationalists were also opposed to emigration because they worried that Italy was losing too many of her potential soldiers; they believed that southern overpopulation should have been remedied by colonies in Africa, not through emigration to America. Thus, after 1907 the debate on emigration gradually changed and was combined with imperialistic ideas. In the 1930s, stories about America in the depths of the Depression certainly weren't favorable to emigration, and the fascist regime also did its best to keep people at home by making emigration regulations more bureaucratic. Mussolini wanted to build up the male population to fight his wars and had to increase the overall population to justify his colonial expansion and his imperialistic dreams. The "great safety valve" had suddenly been shut. Not only was emigration discouraged, but during the Depression Mussolini was sending ships to New York to pick up any Italian who wanted to return to Italy. Depressing accounts of those Italians who came back thinking to escape the American Depression are given in novels mentioned earlier, *Cristo si e' fermato ad Eboli* (*Christ stopped at Eboli,* 1945) by Carlo Levi and *Fontamara,* 1933, by Ignazio Silone.

Peculiarities of the Italian Immigration to the U.S.

Italian migratory waves to the U.S. can be outlined in some general trends.

» Immigrants were not an undifferentiated mass; they represented specific regional and occupational groups.

» A peculiarity of the Italian migrants was that although most of them lived in the countryside in Italy, once in the U.S., they became urban dwellers. Most Italians lived especially in the big cities in the Northeastern U.S., because they did not have enough money to move further inland.

» Italian enclaves often occurred in the U.S. Called "Little Italy," these neighborhoods still exist in many cities today. Unlike the Irish, the Jews, the Germans, and the Poles, who dispersed themselves among other immigrant groups, the Italians for the most part remained in their clusters: Mulberry Street in lower Manhattan, South Philly in Philadelphia, North End in Boston, the New Westside in Chicago, the port area in Baltimore, "Dago Hill" in St. Louis, North Beach in San Francisco, and New Orleans. In addition to clustering into particular neighborhoods, new immigrants clustered into groups according to their place of origin. Thus the Sicilians resided in New Orleans; the Neapolitans and Calabrians were in Minnesota, and the northern Italians went to California.

» Italians adapted more slowly to the new country than other immigrant groups, such as Irish and German, because many of them came to the U.S. intending to return home. Their adaptation in the U.S. was slower than those emigrants who went to South America where they found a culture and a language closer to theirs.

» To understand why Italians were so clearly divided into different groups, one needs to remember that until 1861, Italy was not a consolidated state. Only when Italians arrived in America did they realize what the concept of nation meant. "They became Americans before they were ever Italians." Italians came from a nation that struggled to become a state. They lacked political consciousness, because they lacked national consciousness. Sicilian peasants especially identified more with their village than with Italy. The center of the migrant's concern remained his *paese* (hometown). No matter how long they lived in the host country, they continued to think of the problems and needs of their home town as paramount.

» Another factor that distinguished the Italian emigration was that the number of men who left Italy was much higher than the number of women.

» Italian men came to America just to earn money, rather than to settle and begin a new life. Eventually many Italian men decided to settle permanently in America, so their wives and children joined them. As a result, the image of Italian families became more common in 19th century America.

Postwar Rural Exodus

After World War II the exodus resumed, especially from the south, and it lasted until the beginning of the 1970s when economic and industrial crises changed production processes and patterns, defining a different allocation of activities and labor. And it was again a consequence of deep disillusionment, and this time probably also of impatience.

In the 1951 census, agriculture was still by far the largest single sector of employment; it accounted for 42.2% of the working population nationwide, including 56.9% for the south. But the agriculture was still rudimentary and the livelihood it provided, especially in the south, was still very poor: in 1950 the income per capita was about 60% that of 1924! Fully aware of their social situation and the prospect of better conditions in the urban industrial world, farmers flooded the cities of their own country. Those who were more adventurous and could not be absorbed by the expanding Italian economy went abroad. Emigration was again an escape from crushing poverty, but now it took different forms. People left the countryside by the thousands: some came to the U.S. and Canada, many went to Australia, but most of them remained in Europe.

Southern emigrants moving to northern Italy. Courtesy of *American Oggi*.

Between 1951 and 1961, about 1.75 million people left the south; this number increased to 2.3 million in the following 10 years. (These are net figures and do not include seasonal workers.) The figures of total emigrants that include those who returned to the home areas are understandably much higher: 7.5 million emigrated from 1946 to 1976 (net emigration of 3.5 million). One shocking statistic is that Italy is the only country of the advanced industrial world that suffered massive emigration while sustaining rapid economic growth. The most dramatic form of emigration was overseas, to the Americas and Australia. Between 1946 and 1957 the numbers of those leaving Italy for the New World exceeded by 1,100,000 the number of those returning: 380,000 had remained in Argentina, 166,500 in Canada, 166,000 in the U.S., 138,000 in Australia, and 128,000 in Venezuela. They were for the most part artisans and poor proprietors rather than landless laborers; nearly 70% were from the south.

The new flow of Italian emigrants to the Americas and Australia included a high percentage of people who were much better educated and highly skilled than the previous generation of emigrants. As Europe struggled with unemployment and lack of food following World War II and the devastation of the European economies, the American economy began to boom and there was an impetus to increase immigration. In 1947, Canada removed the "enemy alien" designation for Italians. The Italian government supported emigration and, in 1948, the Canadian government opened a Rome embassy. In the U.S. emigration was reopened in 1953 on a "quota basis." With these actions the two nations also aimed to strengthen the western alliance in the fight against the Communist threat at the start of the Cold War. This is a fascinating shift in the rationale for promoting immigration: the view that overpopulation meant poverty for a great many Italian people, which consequently could have constituted a large recruiting ground for the Communist Party, spurred U.S. and Canadian willingness to open the doors to additional immigrants. The unemployed in Italy in November 1948 num-

✵ SPIRIT

Causes of Southern Emigration

The big Italian migration at the end of the 19th and beginning of the 20th century was largely the result of the severe economic crisis in many regions of Italy after 1870. Although northern Italy experienced hardship, causing many northerners to emigrate, nevertheless southern Italians comprised about 80 per cent of Italian immigrants to the United States. The exodus reflects the extraordinary miseries of the underdeveloped and overpopulated *Mezzogiorno* which includes southern Italy and Sicily.

The poor economic conditions of southern Italians were both natural and man-made. Southern Italy is ill suited for agriculture, as it is formed largely of rugged hills and mountains and contains relatively little good arable land. The summers are hot and extremely dry, and drought is the norm. Malaria was another big problem. At first, it only struck in the coastal areas, but this changed as deforestation, erosion, and flooding enabled it to spread. The forests were largely communal and the continued exercise of common rights worked to their destruction. The deforested hillsides were unable to retain water when it rained, while the plains were marshland, in many areas infected with mosquitoes and ridden with malaria, until Mussolini drained them. Although feudalism had been officially abolished in the early 1800s, it was the unification of Italy that broke down the feudal land system that had survived in the south, where land had been the inalienable property of aristocrats, religious bodies, or the king. The breakdown of feudalism, however, and redistribution of land did not necessarily lead to small farmers in the south winding up with land of their own. Many remained landless, and those who became small land owners watched their plots grow smaller and smaller (and, thus, more and more unproductive) as land was subdivided among heirs. Many farmers worked small plots of land with short-term leases that encouraged the overexploitation rather than the improvement of properties. It was no help that their methods of cultivation were hopelessly antiquated.

The southern Italian economy deteriorated industrially and agriculturally after 1870. Because of the abandonment of protectionist policies following Italian unification, the underdeveloped southern Italian industries were unable to compete with their more developed rivals in northern Italy and abroad. Southern Italy was thus flooded with cheap industrial manufactures. During this time, Italian agriculture was hurt by the increasing amount of products from America that invaded Italian markets. The price of wheat and other products fell, and unemployment increased as landowners and rural laborers and farmers no longer could profitably trade. In the late 19th century southern Italian agriculture, including Sicilian wheat production, declined sharply in the face of challenges from the economically and technologically more advanced North Atlantic world. The lemon and orange growers of Calabria, Basilicata, and Sicily could not compete with those of California and Florida. And southern Italian wine production was terribly affected by the *pronospera*, a disease that decimated grape wines, while its export was affected by trade barriers that were raised by several countries, especially France. In addition, during the last decades of the nineteenth century the technologically outmoded Sicilian sulphur industry succumbed to foreign competition.

The general rule that "emigration from cities was negligible" has an important exception, and that is the city of Naples. The city went from being the capital of its own kingdom in 1860 to being just another large city in Italy. The disruption encouraged unemployment. Also, in the early 1880s, grave epidemics of cholera struck the city, causing many people to leave. The epidemics were then the driving force behind the decision to rebuild entire sections of the city to make them more livable, an undertaking that lasted until World War I. That process of tearing down and rebuilding also disrupted urban life and became another reason for many to leave the city.

bered almost two million. Any increase in emigration to the U.S. and Canada would have been of practical help to Italy in tackling her gravest problem. It would also have been a small but distinctly American contribution to strengthening the democratic 'Western' government and in making less likely its replacement by Communists or by extremists of the right. Initially (1946–1954) there was a certain balance between emigration toward other European countries and other continents, but after 1955 Italian emigration was essentially European.

Emigration to Western Europe

In a silent mass migration that made no headlines either at home or abroad, six million southern Italians—nearly one-third of the population of the *Mezzogiorno*—moved northward. Between 1946 and 1957 the numbers heading to northern Europe exceeded by 840,000 the numbers of those who came back: France took in 381,000, followed by Switzerland with 202,000 and Belgium with 159,000. The emigrants to these countries tended to go for short periods, six-month or one-year contracts, and regarded work abroad as a temporary rather than a permanent solution to their problems.

After 1955, emigration from the rural south was directed both toward the countries of Western Europe and to the urban areas of northern Italy, which by now had taken their place among the world's advanced industrial centers. The movement became easier in 1968, when citizens of the EC were given the right to free movement within EC boundaries; however, migration to Europe had already peaked in 1961. In northern Europe, the emigrants provided manpower for large and small industries, went down into coal mines, worked as ditch-diggers and bricklayers, as hotel maids and waiters, as cooks and dishwashers. Many made good quickly and became foremen in factories and construction firms, or opened their own pizzerias or restaurants.

This export of labor continued until 1973. In that year, for the first time in the history of modern Italy, more Italians returned home than left: between 1973 and 1978 the "balance of labor" showed a gain of nearly 68,000 people.[1] In fact, starting in the early 1970s and until 1981, repatriation was proceeding at a higher level than emigration. The return of Italian emigrants was mainly due to the international economic crisis that hit construction and manufacturing, particularly assembly-line work in the car sector. This led countries such as West Germany to "unload" some surplus laborers by sending them back.[2]

The emigration to Western Europe is notable for some peculiar features. Not only were emigrants disposed of like any other surplus goods, but the host countries were mostly saved all the expense of educating the imported workers and providing social assistance for their families. Since many had come when they were young and able-bodied and without their families, the host country was spared the expenses associated with schooling, pensions, health services, and so on. In other words, foreign workers put into the economy far more than they got out of it in terms of social services.[3]

Internal Migration and Regional Identities

During the period of the "economic miracle," many southerners migrated to the north of Italy. This internal Italian migration acquired, from the very beginning, a form of permanent migration. This was a new phenomenon; until the mid-1960s migration was still illegal. According to fascist laws still on the books, migrants needed a job to get housing and housing to get a job: this had been the fascist way to preserve social stratification. But with the new laws, Italian citizens could move freely both geographically and between categories of work. The workers who left the countryside for the northern industrial triangle of Milan-Turin-Genoa had citizenship rights equal to those of the local people. Unlike Italians emigrating abroad, these could not be discriminated against politically, isolated by language barriers, or expelled.

Facing the Same Prejudice at Home

However, the problems of adjustment and integration were not less severe. Many southerners met the same unfriendliness, slights, and hostility in the north as did those who emigrated abroad and, as we shall see later, suffered some form of racist prejudice. In Italy's north, the standard disparaging nickname for any native of the *Mezzogiorno* became—and still is—*terrone,* a word derived from *terra* (soil). *Terrone* suggests less a yokel than an uncivilized but cunning fellow, an individual who is clannish and anti-social. For northern Italians, the *terroni* are the causes of all Italy's ills. Northerners' antipathy for southerners has found increasingly less subtle expression, especially in the northern news media. Newspapers in Turin, Milan, Venice, and Bologna often make a point of noting that an arrested robbery, burglary, or murder suspect was born in Palermo or some other place in the South. Northerners do not hesitate to openly accuse the bureaucrats in the nation's capital and the southerners of stealing and squandering the tax money they contribute from their efficiency and hard work.

The adjustment to the northern environment has been difficult for southerners of every age group. Even for the youngster, for whom social and cultural adjustment is normally easier, integration was difficult. A very perceptive representation of that condition has been given by many artists in their films and literature. *Rocco e i suoi fratelli* (*Rocco and His Brothers),* by Luchino Visconti, a movie released in 1960, focuses upon the migration of southern Italians to northern industrial areas and the struggle to survive in an environment that demands profound adjustments. Visconti concentrates on the dramatic clash of differing value systems, that of the traditional southern family of poor laborers and its archaic code of honor and family loyalty on the one hand, and a more individualistic and contemporary morality that reflects industrial society on the other. Although Visconti omits much of what a historian or a sociologist would consider essential to a discussion of urban migration in Milan—unions, strikes, racism, crime, and so forth—he does give a penetrating picture of the effects of rapid cultural change upon the ancient values of traditional southern Italian families.[4]

For southern Italians, the absence of collective festivals, of the piazza as a meeting place, of street-living and inter-family visits had a profound impact. On the one hand, families suffered in the stifling atmosphere of a shanty-town; on the other hand, each nuclear family unit tended to be more closed in and less open to community life or to forms of inter-family solidarity. The problems and inadequacies that emerged from these environmental and familial shortcomings were not to be underestimated.[5] Certainly, the younger members of the family found greater opportunity for social pleasures in the new urban settings. Bars, dance halls, soccer matches, etc., did offer new freedoms and pastimes. Moreover, authority structures within the family became less rigid, as did paternal control over family finances.

Unlike the emigrants to Germany and Switzerland, the southerners who emigrated to northern Italy brought along their families, their demands, their claim of the right to influence political organizations and trade unions, and, in 1969, they would be in the forefront of the events leading to the "hot autumn." With emigration, the "southern question" was not solved; indeed, it became more complex. Its reserve army of labor fed the Italian "economic miracle," and when this came to an end the tension remained, grew, and exploded.

Cost and Benefits of Emigration

In a sense, migration worked. Besides relieving rural overcrowding, the prosperity of immigrants and repatriated emigrants and the substantial remittances received from relatives who had emigrated had a strong impact on the economy. Locally, the remittances of emigrants have been responsible for the rapid rise in the standard of living of many. Both those who have migrated and those who have stayed behind have been affected positively. Indeed, it could also be said that the most visible economic and social changes in the south came through emigration. At last, the poor became upwardly mobile; unfortunately, the change came about through becoming outwardly mobile. Despite the often appalling conditions of emigrants' life and work, however, it was better than staying at home. Moreover, migration served to expose more and more Italians to life beyond the village. Returned migrants brought back new ideas and new ways of looking at the world. Those who remained were not forced to unacceptable terms of sharecropping. The huge disaffected rural proletariat, the *braccianti* (day laborers), could find work at last and make demands.

Unexpectedly, there were also some ecological benefits. The abandoned hills began to revert to pasture and forest, just what Italy needed. After years of deforestation and reclamation, mountains and hills were increasingly surrendered to nature and were spared from the constant dangers of landslides and erosion.

However, emigration also had a profound negative effect on the social structure, which was more apparent in the towns than in the countryside. The cities became overcrowded. Turin, for example, had to cope with 700,000 immigrants in fifteen years, and by 1970 had more southerners than any other city except Naples. Rome, with 1.1 million inhabitants in 1936 and 1.6 million in 1951, passed the 2 million mark in 1960 and had over 3 million at the end of the 1970s. Dreary tenement housing arose everywhere in city outskirts, most of them hastily erected without benefit of planning and often without adequate roads, schools, electricity, or even sewage systems. Parks and open spaces were destroyed. The hapless immigrants were often put into huge blocks of flats, with densities of 500 people per hectare in some parts of Rome. In short, Italian cities became "Americanized."

Since most of the immigrants to northern cities were southerners, they aroused much resentment and even racial hostility among locals. The immigrants, as usual, were blamed for crime, illiteracy, sponging off welfare, and overloading the public services—transport, housing, schools, hospitals, etc. Because of the new political and social awareness, the immigrants did not accept tacitly the negative reactions to their presence and responded by voting communist at the general elections.

All this was part of the cost of "making Italians." Millions of southerners were being assimilated into northern cultural values, although the process must often have seemed to be working the other way around.

The cost to the emigrant and the community that was left was higher than that incurred by those who hosted them. The cultural shock for the emigrant on entering a new way of life was considerable. Considering the fact that most emigrants were moving from an agricultural to urban setting, the adjustment process usually called for a complete change in life, from habits, to customs, to traditions, and use of language. The separation from home and family created serious psychological as well as social problems for many: the problem of identity, the price of assimilation, the pain of discrimination.

A film directed by Franco Brusati, *Pane e cioccolata (Bread and Chocolate,* 1973), captures these problems in poignant images. The protagonist, Giovanni Garofali, a "classical" southern Italian worker in Switzerland, is pathetically out of place in his "guest-country." The clean, tidy, but cold nature of Swiss culture is juxtaposed to the more exuberant and humane, although somewhat tacky, Latin culture. The urban life, with its rules as well as its social benefits, is in marked conflict with the old habits enjoyed in the rural setting, which is more relaxed but always accompanied by deprivation and suffering. Every time Giovanni starts home toward southern Italy, the sight of singing immigrant workers on the trains turns him back to Switzerland. It is a desperate situation, one experienced not only by hundreds of thousands of Italians abroad but by millions of others in Europe as well: forced to leave their homeland and their cultural roots, these workers fail to discover anything abroad to replace their old values and attachments. Like Garofali, they are trapped between a world that forces them to leave to escape poverty and a world where prosperity is given at the cost of identity.[6]

The reversal of emigration, with a strong pattern of repatriation, began in the 1970s. The Italian Population Census of 1981 showed a continuous increase of returns with a concomitant decrease of departures and the first significant arrival of foreign people. These factors worked together to produce the first positive demographic balance of the migratory patterns, generating a positive difference of about 270,000 people. It must be noted that emigration has not stopped completely; today there is a strong flow of people with high skills who are moving abroad. The situation, defined in some Italian newspapers as "hemorrhage of brains," reflects the inability of Italy to deal with a society that has high skills and does not want to do manual work. Italians with university degrees and high skills are going abroad, and immigrants with low skills and willingness to do manual work are entering the country.

Immigration

Because of the economic success that Italy was achieving, a strange turnabout was soon to take place in the matter of Italian emigration: immigration. By the early 1980s, Italy had ceased to be a net exporter of workers: there were an estimated 800,000 immigrants (mostly illegal, called *clandestini*) in Italy; by the early 1990s, the number had gone well over one million. The real "explosion" of immigration occurred during the early 1990s, because of the geographic position and political role that Italy played in the European setting at the end of the century. For as a result of the sudden lack of a political and socio-economic balance in the Balkans, and the progress made in the ongoing process of political and economic unification of Europe (i.e., European Union), Italy became a safe haven and a gateway into Europe. Immigrants mainly came from Romania, Albania, and the former Yugoslavia. Thus, new national and ethnic groups joined the "traditional" foreign presence in Italy, which up to that point had consisted mainly of African and Eastern Asian citizens who were coming from sub-Saharan Africa (Ethiopia, Somalia, Nigeria, Senegal, Cape Verde), the Middle East (Iran, Iraq), Asia (India, Sri Lanka, China, the Philippines), and Latin America (Brazil, Peru, Argentina).

Crammed into precarious boats, hundreds of refugees, mainly African, land regularly at Licata in Southern Sicily and on the nearby tiny island of Lampedusa. The most remarkable fact about these arrivals is how unremarkably they are received by the Italian media and the public in general. The fact is that hardly a week goes by without a boat depositing its human cargo on Sicily or Lampedusa.

Most immigrants are from other parts of Europe, however, with the majority from Romania, which had sent 240,000 immigrants to Italy by 2004. Also by 2004, Italy counted 227,000 Moroccans and 51,000 sub-Saharan Africans from Senegal, according to the Catholic organization *Caritas*, which is involved in assisting immigrants. According to its findings, by 2004 Italy had over 2.6 million legal immigrants and another 200,000 to 800,000 *clandestini*.

The total number of recent immigrants amounts to no more than 4.5% of the Italian population, a smaller percentage than the average of Western Europe (5.2%) or especially that found in Germany, France, or Britain (40% Europeans, 28% Africans, 20% Asians, 12%

Americans, 48% Christian, 37% Muslim, 7% other religions) *(See Box on p.223)*. However, their presence has caused a degree of social alarm that can only be explained by taking into account the historical circumstances in which the immigration has taken place. Finally in 2004, the Italian government successfully negotiated with the authorities of some of the nations with the largest flow of illegal emigrants to put an end to departures from their ports. But these measures did not stem the tide, according to SISMI (Italy's equivalent of the CIA), which estimates that about 1.5 million potential immigrants are waiting their turn to reach the Italian coast. Despite the hardship of getting there, daunting bureaucracy and paperwork, as well as unavoidable prejudice, thousands of immigrants continue to risk their lives to get to Italy. As the years go by, these new members of Italian society are becoming assimilated. Although it is still rare to see an immigrant working in a bank or holding a civil service job, many are emulating the entrepreneurial Italians by starting their own businesses. By mid-2004, there were 71,843 immigrant-owned firms on record.

Immigration has generated heated debates; most people don't want it, but they are aware that they cannot do without it. Increasingly, the Italian economy, like the American economy, is a gray market, a place of cheap deals and skirted regulations. Like Americans, Italians understand how they benefit from illegal immigration and how dependent they have become on cheap labor:

» Immigrants perform work that most Italians do not want to do.
» They work hard for a low pay and Italians are willing to hire them.
» With their work, they add value to products or services, but they are not paid as much as the value they add. The surplus is profit for the business, which goes into taxes, shareholders, and investments.
» They keep the labor supply up and wages down.
» The gray market that results often ignores government regulations that control product safety, working conditions, business licensing, and taxes.
» In a global economy, cheap labor is the most competitive tool.

However, there is a cost:

» Employers skimp on employee salaries and benefits.
» Workers live in overcrowded homes
» Laborers who are injured on the job are dropped off at emergency rooms where they must be treated for free.
» Social tensions exist between illegal immigrants and local people.

The Plight of the Immigrants

Since returning Italian emigrants are not willing to take low-paying jobs, immigrants from the Third World are allowed to fill them. Immigrants have been taking the same type of jobs and finding the same obstacles as the Italian emigrants did when they landed on the shores of the Americas. They have been finding jobs in the informal labor market—picking tomatoes for the southern canning industry, working as domestic servants for Italian families, and taking on jobs in dangerous and polluted work environments such as chrome or tanning factories in the building industry. Others have become street-peddlers or wash car windshields at the traffic lights as they wait for a job. Their most visible activity, dominated by the Moroccans, is the selling of poor-quality clothes, bags, and trinkets on streets and beaches up and down the peninsula. The humiliation and suffering of the Italians in northern Europe in the 1950s and 1960s are now those of the Africans in Italy.

Until recently, the word "immigrant" bore connotations of refugees from the Third World. But with the upheavals in Eastern Europe and, more particularly, in the Balkans, Italians had to face a new tide of economic refugees from across the Adriatic Sea. The flood of Albanians strained Italy's self-image as a land of tolerance for immigrants and of welcome and benevolence toward the dispossessed.

But the new immigrants, for the most part, come from far away and are non-European; about 50% of them are women, many come from cities, and up to half have at least a secondary school diploma. Although most immigrants are in regular work, there is no doubt that many of those without work are sucked into illegal rackets: drug-pushing, prostitution, and managing teams of young peddlers. In Turin it has been estimated that nearly one thousand Nigerian and East European prostitutes work under threat of violence and in particularly brutal conditions. There are also large numbers of Moroccan (male) child and teenage peddlers. Half the inmates of Turin's young offenders' prison are immigrants, imprisoned for drug-peddling or petty theft.

Because a relatively high percentage of crime in the country is committed by poor illegal immigrants, racism (xenophobia) has emerged as a serious problem.

Immigrants are easy scapegoats for whoever wishes to avoid tackling the structural reasons for the persistence of widespread corruption and crime.

The drug traffic existed long before the arrival of the new immigrants, as the Turin prefect was quick to point out after public protests in the main Turin street market. The immigrants, he said, could not be blamed for the disorder there. They could be seen doing a hard and honest job washing down the pavements or preparing the market for the next day. Thirty years ago there were southern Italians on the pavements, now they were behind the stalls.[7] If the flow of illegal immigrants can be curbed, there will be less chance that these minority groups will be singled out for negative reasons like committing crimes, because foreigners in the country legally will be able to get normal jobs.

The changing demographic structure of the Italian population, the community life of the different cultural, linguistic, and religious groups, intercultural living and spatial segregation, the changing job markets in the context of the globalization process—these are all issues that need to be explored and scrutinized in order to gain a wider understanding of the broad situation. Although Italy has a long history marked by migratory experience, immigration generates a forum where the most heated debate takes place today.

It appears from a study on attitudes toward the immigrants in the north that southern-ers with an experience of emigration are no more favorable than others to the settlement of non-European immigrants. This is probably related to the fact that although many of the first-generation southern immigrants consider themselves integrated, they are still more vulnerable than other groups and occupy a lower position in the labor market.

Ethnicity, Racism, and the Process of Industrialization

The Northern League, a political party in northern Italy, has been engaged in strong anti-immigrant campaigns and has often been described as a party with a racist or quasi-racist ideology, although it has systematically rejected such accusations. The League's president, Umberto Bossi, admitted in his autobiography that the Northern League exploited anti-southern and anti-immigrant feelings in order to gain attention from the media and from the public.[8] Bossi seemed to be saying that although the Northern League itself was not racist, quasi-racist sentiments were diffused among northern Italians and provided the stimulus for the rise of the League.

The League espouses a complex form of racism that arises from a specific society and economy, one that can be defined as tightly communitarian. It is complex because, whereas Northern League racism can be partly explained by the recent wave of extra-European immigration, this explanation does not hold for the anti-southernism of the League. To a large extent anti-southernism and anti-foreign immigration can both be linked to the ethno-regionalist aspirations of the party, but this still begs the question of why a pseudo-Lombard ethnicity has achieved political prominence at a time when linguistic and cultural differences within Italy are on the wane. The 1992 political program of the Northern League states explicitly:

> Our party's strongly critical attitude toward migratory policies stems from our specific concept of mankind. A human person is not simply an economic agent: s/he is also made up of affections, cultural values, and identities which can find their best expressions in separate historical and environmental communities. Immigrations, having a purely economic value, break up this equilibrium which forms a vital part of human nature. The theorization of a "multiracial society" as the predestined future for mankind is both vain and openly instrumental *(Lega Nord-Legs Lombardo, 1992)*.

This process of racialization has a subtext: southern Italians have been associated with a specific, negative image (which can be subsumed under the term *mafiosi*) whereas the other ethnic immigrants are seen to possess potentially threatening but as yet unidentified and undefined cultural labels. The Northern League's position is that of other right-wing extremist parties in Europe who believe that all ethnic groups should live in their natural environment. Whereas the French politician Le Pen discriminates on the basis of skin color (his racism is more openly based on skin color; the main targets of the French National Front are immigrants from North Africa), Bossi discriminates on the basis of cultural differences. Therefore, while he discriminates against Arab fundamentalists and Maghrebians two non-assimilatable groups, the target for Bossi's party is also the southern *mafiosita*.

PROFILE

Muslims in Italy

Muslims first came to Italy in the 9th century: Sicily, Sardinia, and some regions in Peninsular Italy were part of the Muslim *Ummah* between 828 (the Muslim conquest of Sicily) and 1300 (the destruction of the last Islamic stronghold of Lucera in Puglia). Muslims were almost entirely absent in Italy from the time of the country's unification in 1861 until the 1970s, when the first trickle of North African immigrants began to arrive. These North Africans, mostly of Berber or Arab origin, came mainly from Morocco. They have been followed in recent years by Tunisians, Albanians, and to a lesser extent Libyans, Egyptians, Pakistanis, Somalis, Middle Eastern Arabs, and Kurds.

The number of Muslims in Italy today probably surpasses the one-million mark, though only 60,000 or so Italian citizens are Muslim, foreigners who have obtained Italian citizenship and native Italians who have converted to Islam. According to the latest statistics, Muslims make up about 37% of the 2,400,000 foreign residents living in Italy. To these 820,000 foreign residents of Muslim heritage legally residing in Italy, another 100,000–150,000 should be added, as Muslims represent, according to the widely accepted yearly estimates of Italian association Caritas, about 40% of Italy's illegal immigrants.

Despite their minority status among illegal immigrants, Muslim immigration has become a prominent political issue, as reports of boatloads of illegal immigrants or *clandestini* dominate news programs.

However, many of the people who land in Italy are only using Italy as a gateway to other EU nations, where economic opportunities are greater. Even so, to some Italians, there is a sense that a constant wave of arrivals has placed the nation under siege—the foreign customs and practices of these new immigrants are alien to many who have lived their entire lives in an almost homogeneous Italo-Catholic environment and have no memory of the history of Muslim expansion into Italy. Muslims represent 1.4% of Italy's population, a percentage much lower than that of other EU countries, and still slightly lower than that recorded in Italy between the middle of the ninth century and the end of the thirteenth century, before the removal of the last Muslim strongholds in Puglia in 1300. While in medieval times the Muslim population was almost totally concentrated in insular (Sicily, Sardinia) and southern (Calabria, Puglia) Italy, it is today more evenly distributed, with almost 55% of Muslims living in the north of Italy, 25% in the center, and only 20% in the south.

The relatively small size of the local Muslim community means that Islam has yet to make a significant impact on public life, but there are signs that this is changing. Recent points of contention between native Italians and the Muslim population include the presence of crucifixes in Italian state school classrooms and hospital bedrooms. Adel Smith, a Muslim convert of Scottish ancestry, attracted considerable media attention by demanding that crucifixes in public places (i.e., schools, hospitals, and government offices) be removed. However, many other Muslims have stated their opposition to removing the crucifixes, noting that in many countries with a Muslim majority, it is common to find arrow-signs in hotel rooms indicating the direction of Mecca, and that this is not made an issue by non-Muslims.

The whole racist discourse of both Le Pen and the League is also based on the construction of myths. Le Penism treats national identity as a given and thus creates a myth out of French ethnicity that is totally devoid of content, so much so that among the threats against French identity, the party program cites fast food and the Americanization of the French language. Departing from the view of the socioeconomic homogeneity of the north (nothing is more false: the north has seen countless invasions, immigrations, and occupations, and it has a highly variegated regional and linguistic culture and highly contrasting economic activities), the League has invented a Lombard ethnicity that in reality had to be created, a sense of imagined community ex *novo*. The myth of Lombard ethnicity is built around a core of fairly specific cultural characteristics: a strong work ethic, entrepreneurship and personal risk-taking, a spirit of sacrifice, a high propensity to saving, as well as trust, solidarity, and law-abidance. These civic virtues that are preferred in every society are contrasted with vices that are present in today's societies but are isolated in southern Italians and immigrants.

It is clear that the League does not accept traditional modernization theories, which argue that the process of industrialization would be accompanied by the related phenomena of urbanization, political mobilization, and cultural uniformity. According to these views, these processes would dissolve "tribal" affiliations in favor of new attachments at the national level. Urbanization would lead to a convergence of economic and social systems toward a global pattern, consisting of a comparatively small number of relatively homogeneous nation-states.[9]

The Socioeconomic Roots of Racism

The northern Italian economic system developed geographical concentrations of small manufacturing units operating in close-knit communities characterized by an overlapping of business and family ties, low social and political polarization, and a high degree of entrepreneurship. The socioeconomic characteristics of this system are primarily the preservation of the family as an economic unit and the protection of primary ties and localistic, community based allegiances.[10] The process of industrialization of these regions with a strong political subculture rests on the preservation of a tightly communitarian society. In the community of small-scale industries, trust and solidarity are born out of living in the same village, speaking the same dialect, and sharing family as well as business ties. Trust and social cohesion are viewed as part of a dual process of inclusion/exclusion. Therefore, when trust and solidarity are community-based, the community becomes racialized; a sharp division exists between those who are seen as belonging to the community and those who are considered outsiders; it is Us against the *Other*. Northern racism is, therefore, built into the local socioeconomic structure. The League has exploited racist sentiments that are already present in the population, particularly in areas of diffused industrialization. Having taken over from the old Christian Democratic Party (*DC*) the representation of the interests of the local small business, the Northern League has been able to translate the xenophobic and inward-looking culture of the Lombard communities of small firms into the myth of Lombard (and northern Italian) ethnicity.

But besides the problem caused by northern racism, there are complex general national problems. Italy has been caught totally unprepared politically, psychologically, culturally, and bureaucratically in its attitude toward immigration. Moreover, job-seeking immigrants overlap with 2 million Italian unemployed. Italians have long prided themselves on being less racist and less anti-semitic than other nationalities and consider themselves to be politically progressive and tolerant, but some Italians are falling short of civil expectations as they confront immigrants who, not being provided with proper housing and work, appear to be idlers, thieves, and a nuisance to the community. After all, 15% of Italy's prison population is made up of immigrants, of whom 52%, many of them North Africans, have been convicted of selling drugs.[11] Tolerance and open-heartedness are being put to the test.

The Political Debate on Immigration

Italians are struggling to determine which party or political coalition can best deal with immigration. In this political debate the rhetoric is not transparent.[12] The Left focuses on the poor living conditions of immigrants. It argues that immigrants—particularly illegal immigrants—accept wages and working conditions that Italian citizens, even poor citizens, would not. It also argues that the government should enforce legal protection for immigrant workers that are enjoyed by Italian citizens. The center-Right, on the other hand, has been more cautious and has been pressing for more control of the flow of illegal immigrants into the country. It maintains that the low-skill immigration of recent years has been a mixed help to the economy of the country; it has helped a few businesses that have profited from the supply of cheap labor, leaving the community at large to pick up the social costs. The Right also argues that what most immigrants pay in taxes, when they work legally, covers only a fraction of the services they receive; moreover, it claims that the downward trend in immigrant skills has been accompanied by an upward trend in their use of public assistance: immigrants compete with citizens for drastically reduced public services. The Right further argues that no immigration policy can remedy the failures of other nations to meet the needs of their poor, so it is both sensible and moral to base Italy's national policy primarily on the needs of the country: generating an economic revival and raising the standard of living of the nation's poorer citizens. However, the center-Right appreciates the fact that immigrants arrive with a high level of desire and drive, so much so that their basic contribution can be felt in the stimulation of the natives to do better. Immigrants usually live, at least in the beginning, in areas where the lesser achievers live; their presence may become a social and economic reawakening force.

Most Italians understand that emigration today is part of a global phenomenon, entwined with the global economy, and therefore different from previous emigration movements. It must be seen as a phenomenon of mobility, part of an age in transformation. Immigrants enter countries today with a different set of expectations and a predisposition to contribute to the multiculturalism of the host country. In the age of Internet and satellite television, immigrants may remain culturally attached to their country of birth and well informed about life at home. Therefore, not only may they remain more detached from the culture of the host country, but they also may have a strong impact on the local culture.

Thus, many Italians are genuinely concerned about the impact of the flow of immigrants on Italian culture—in its psychological, social, and anthropological dimensions—since the immigrant groups are characterized by ethnic, linguistic, and religious diversities that pose completely new cultural and social problems. For example, Islam has become the second religion in Italy, and Rome is the home city of the largest mosque in Europe. Considering the large number of races, languages, and dialects that make up the people coming from the very same country (e.g., Ethiopia, Senegal, Nigeria), some Italians perceive in the immigration flux a potentially explosive mixture, especially where conflicts present in the country of origin are transplanted in Italy. The biggest change is likely to happen once the second generation of immigrants grow up. In September 2004, some 300,000 children from 90 different nations were attending Italian schools. Will Italy's melting pot bring about a fusion of diversity?

Legalizing Immigrants While Facing Terrorist Threats

One tactic the Italian government has used to get immigrants out of hiding is to hold amnesties for any illegal immigrants, a time where they could apply for Italian citizenship and not get punished for having been there illegally. This worked on one level, since it reduced the number of workers in the underground sector, thus reducing the size of this unrecognized economy. Between 1986 and 1998, the Italian government held 4 amnesties, granting citizenship to about 700,000 people. In 2002 the Italian government passed a law to formalize the presence of so many illegal immigrants in the country. Cosponsored by *Lega Nord* party leader Umberto Bossi and the *Alleanza Nazionale* Party's Gianfranco Fini, the Bossi-Fini law offered a general amnesty to non-European Union immigrants provided they had a job, decent housing, and no criminal record. Those that met the test would receive a *permesso di soggiorno,* or residency permit, that allowed them to live and work legally in Italy and eventually be eligible for citizenship. More than 700,000 applied and about 650,000 were accepted. The Bossi-Fini law also gave new powers to Italian naval forces, allowing them to turn away any vessels carrying presumed illegal immigrants to Italy. Those caught would be expelled, as would any *clandestini* discovered already living in Italy.

But this did not solve the problem; it actually ended up attracting more migrants. Italy's labor force fluctuates, and, like many other countries, it needs foreigners to work in its factories. Unfortunately, not only did these amnesties cost the government a lot of money, they made Italy's immigration policies appear lenient. This in turn has made even more foreigners want to move there, and since there is so much red tape involved with getting legal citizenship, many choose to enter the country illegally. At the moment, Italy's policy is that if foreigners want to find work in Italy, they must go to an Italian consulate to have their names put on a list. Italian employers then go to labor offices to hire people off these lists, which can take a while, sometimes a couple of years.

While Italian communities deal with the problem of assimilating these immigrants and their children who don't speak Italian and are not Catholic, the Italian government must face the problem of terrorists entering the country disguised as illegal immigrants. There is a widespread conviction among Italians that after the terrorist bombings in Madrid in 2003 and

London in 2005, Italy is next. A poll in the *Corriere della Sera* newspaper during the 2005 summer revealed that 82% of Italians saw "a serious risk" of terrorist attack.

In January 2005, the Italian police arrested 29 immigrants suspected of being Al Qaeda recruits. The immigrants had been brought over from North Africa, paying between 500 to 1,500 euros for their passage. Those who refused to work for Al Qaeda were sold off to other criminal organizations.

In response, the Italian government passed a new antiterrorism law with measures that include increasing the power of the police to stop, search and arrest terrorist suspects as well as take saliva samples for DNA identification. Those found carrying false identity cards or passports now face a four-year prison sentence. It is also now illegal in Italy for women to wear a *burqua* or *chador* that entirely covers the face.

Catholic Charities Filling the State Shortcomings

In many ways the state government has fallen short in meeting the needs of immigrants However, as usual, state failures are compensated for by individual inventiveness. There is a growing tendency among the public to promote a culture of acceptance. This attitude of acceptance animates the work of numerous voluntary associations that have either sprung up to offer help to immigrant workers or existed before the influx of foreigners and have subsequently changed their priorities. Among these last there are widespread national service networks, of a religious or trade union character, which operate all over Italy and involve the immigrants themselves. The most supportive organizations are the efficient Catholic charities, especially Caritas. Quite often the initiatives of Catholic charities, trade unions, or other voluntary organizations are coordinated with those of the local authorities whose decisions anticipate or go beyond those of the central government. A first wave of Catholic or municipal reception centers and services for immigrants was reinforced with the help of immigrant leaders and associations, and by a second wave of voluntary initiatives that promoted the perception of immigrants as people who, on the one hand, were being denied their civil rights, but who, on the other, were contributing something of value to Italian society. Immigrants were not just "people needing help." Now there are groups for the legal defense of immigrants—immigrant cultural associations, groups to promote multicultural education in schools, trade union offices for immigrants, and so on. It is sometimes pointed out that the effect of immigration on the economy is positive given the low Italian birth rate and the aging native population.

The speed, generosity, and highly articulated nature of the voluntary effort to meet the immigrants' needs and to reduce the impact of any racist backlash have few parallels in other European countries. As a result of Italy's generally liberal immigration policy, there is concern in many European nations that with the free movement throughout the European Community that began in January 1993, Italy will serve as a port of entry for an influx of illegal immigrants from Asia, Africa, and South America. The Italian government would prefer to see uniform European immigration laws, but it may soon be forced to institute visa requirements. As the overwhelming demographic and economic disparities between Europe and the developing nations grow, the movement of desperate job-seekers will certainly increase; so too, however, may the series of violent acts against immigrants.

The argument of the positive economic impact of immigrants remains the strongest persuasive explanation. Many economists and most people feel that the recent influx of immigrants has helped fuel much of the economic growth during the past decade. And, while some perceive foreigners as taking jobs away from native-born Europeans, those who have studied the matter say recent immigration has had little impact on the employment opportunities of people born there. New immigrants, these experts say, tend to go into low-wage industries, where native-born groups don't usually compete for jobs.

Other Positive Impacts of Immigration

Italian law may be cracking down on illegal immigration, but the manpower immigrants represent could help break Italy's long-held world record for zero-population growth, the lowest in the world, and put much-needed funds into government coffers. In less than 10 years, Italy's immigrant population has more than tripled. ISTAT, the Italian government statistics bureau, reports that in 1996 Italy had 737,800 immigrants; in 2000 the figure was 1.27 million and by 2005 the number had risen to 2.6 million. As a result, in 2004, Italy's total population, including legal immigrants, stood at 58,463,000—the first time since 1992 that its population had risen, not fallen. Also that year, 1.2 million immigrants paid taxes to the Italian government—twice as many as the previous year. By 2023, Italy's immigrant population is expected to grow to 6.5 million, or 11% of the population. According to INPS, Italy's national social security institute, one in ten legal workers is now a foreigner.

The transition from legal immigrant to voting citizen in Italy is arduous. Six years after obtaining their hard-earned *permesso di soggiorno* (residency permit), foreigners must apply for a *carta di soggiorno* (permanent residency papers). To become a full citizen with voting rights they must live in Italy for 10 years. However, people coming to Italy from nations within the European Union receive Italian citizenship after four years of residency. Anyone who marries an Italian citizen becomes a citizen after three years.

Italy is facing a brand new problem: immigration. A flood of over a million immigrants in the last decade is producing radical tensions that Italy has never known. In March of 1991, nearly 24,000 Albanians arrived at the port of Brindisi in the southern region of Apulia. Many Italians fear that the thousands coming from Albania, Morocco, Algeria, Somalia, and the former Yugoslavia may be just the forerunners of waves of wildcat immigration from less prosperous nations. Printed by courtesy of *America Oggi*.

Is Racism Going to Fade?

One of the consequences of immigration has been some racist feelings, directed mainly against the immigrants of color. This has been fueled above all by rising unemployment. It is all very sad and perplexing, because the Italians always enjoyed the reputation of being less color-conscious than most Western Europeans and, in another respect, a good deal less nationalistic and chauvinistic. Their legitimate patriotism has taken on a more modern flavor; except at international soccer matches, it is difficult to see Italians displaying their flag as an expression of passionate nationalism. And the sight of that flag never creates tears in the eye or vibrates strongly nationalistic heartstrings. Italians are less insular than the British and less chauvinistic than the French. Italians have traditionally been less xenophobic toward other people and more open to outside influences, more aware of belonging to a wider community. Clear evidence of this may be seen in news coverage by the national media. Whereas the British media tend to under-report international sporting events, and the French tend to cover international sports matches only when the French are also involved, in Italy they get much fuller coverage. The Italians do seem to think of themselves in terms of a wider community, and in conversation will often talk of "we in the West" or "we in Europe," where an Englishman may still say "we in Britain."

Therefore, apart from the very few isolated incidents of antagonism against immigrants, Italians do not have discriminatory feelings. In the same vein, Italian attitudes to the Third World are rather positive. Italy today spends large sums on overseas aid, and the Italians are at least as ready as most other European nations to play their part in helping poorer nations.

Notes

1. Claudio Calvaruso, "Rientro dei migranti e condizione delle collettivita' italiane in Europa," *Civitas* 31, no. 1 (1980): 34.

2. In 1982 there was a total of 601,600 Italians in West Germany; 41,400 Italians entered West Germany, and 81,800 left that country. A favorite destination from 1950 to 1980 was Switzerland, which in 1982 had 233,100 Italian workers with annual contracts, who with their families totaled 412,000. In 1982 some 11,800 Italians entered Switzerland, and 20,200 Italians with annual permits left that country. France had attracted migrants early, and in the 1940s and early 1950s became, along with Belgium, a major target. In 1982 France had 136,800 Italian workers and 441,000 Italians, including family members. Rinn-Sup Shinn, *Italy, A Country Study* (Washington: The American University, 1985), 110.

3. Bruno Trentin, *Da sfruttati a produttori* (Bari : De Donato, 1977), xi.

4. Peter Bondanella, *Italian Cinema: From Neorealism to the Present* (New York: Ungar Publishing Co., 1983), 199.

5. For a valuable assessment of this phenomenon, see L. Balbo, *Stato di famiglia* (Milan: Mondadori, 1976).

6. The plight of emigrants has also been repeatedly represented in compelling literary works by Rocco Scotellaro, Mario La Cava, Nino Palumbo, and especially Saverio Strati.

7. B. Frandino, "Così sistemerò Porta Palazzo," *La Repubblica,* 30 April 1994.

8. Umberto Bossi (with D. Vimercati), *Vento dal Nord* (Milan: Mondadori, 1992).

9.   A. H. Richmond, *Immigration and Ethnic Conflict* (London: Croon Helm, 1988).

10.   A. Cento Bull and P. Corner, *From Peasant to Entrepreneur. The Survival of the Family Economy in Italy* (Oxford, Providence: Berg, 1993).

11.   In 1992, one-third of Rome's criminals were said to be immigrants, with an overwhelming majority of them born outside the European Community. The foreign-born criminals, who in that year numbered about 1,000, were not spending time in jail for having committed a violent crime. Rather, of the approximately one thousand, 543 were jailed for drug-related charges, and 339 for petty theft. Most of the criminals were arrested in the city's historic center, particularly in the area surrounding the train terminal. For a comprehensive understanding of Italian immigration, the following scholarly works provide an excellent presentation:

Graziella Parati, ed., *Mediterranean Crossroads: Migration Literature in Italy* (Madison, N.J.: Fairleigh Dickinson UP, 1999).

Graziella Parati, *Migration Italy: The Art of Talking Back in a Destination Culture* (Toronto: University of Toronto Press, 2005).

Matteo, Sante, ed. *ItaliAfrica: Bridging Continents and Culture.* Stony Brook, NY: Forum Italicum Publishing, 2001.

12.   Bergamo. "A Few Bad Apples." *Economist.* 13 January 2001: 50.0keth, Kenneth. "Undocumented Immigration Haunts Italy's Ruling Coalition." 1 Nov, 2003. *Migration Information Source.*

Bibliography

Cento Bull, A. and Corner, P. , *From Peasant to Entrepreneur. The Survival of the Family Economy in Italy.* Oxford, Providence: Berg, 1993.

Franzina, E., *Gli italiani al nuovo mondo—L'emigrazione italiana in America 1492–1945.* Milano: Arnaldo Mondadori Editore, 1955.

———, *Dall'Arcadia in America—Attivita' letteraria ed emigrazione transoceanica in Italia (1850–1940).* Torino: Edizioni della Fondazione Giovanni Agnelli, 1996.

Gabaccia, D., *From Sicily to Elizabeth Street—Housing and Social Change Among Italian Immigrants, 1880–1930.* Albany: SUNY Press, 1984.

Martelli, S., *Il sogno italo-americano—Realta' e immaginario dell'emigrazione negli Stati Uniti.* Napoli: Istituto Suor Ordola Benincasa, 1996.

Massara, G and Bove, A., *'Merica.* Stony Brook, N.Y.: Forum Italicum Publications, 2006.

Parati, G., *Migration Italy: The Art of Talking Back in a Destination Culture.* Toronto: University of Toronto Press, 2005.

Pozzetta, G. E. and Ramirez, B., *The Italian Diaspora—Migration Across the Globe.* Ontario: Multicultural Society of Ontario, 1992.

Richmond, A. H., *Immigration and Ethnic Conflict.* London: Croon Helm, 1988.

Sante, M., ed., *ItaliAfrica: Bridging Continents and Culture:* Stony Brook, N.Y.: Forum Italicum Publications, 2001.

Trentin, B., *Da sfruttati a produttori.* Bari: De Donato, 1977.

PART 3

SOCIETY

Introduction

The years since World War II have seen deeper and more rapid social changes in Italy than any time before. In the last 50 years the exodus from the countryside has been strong. Most Italians now live in town, and those who remain in the country have seen their lives transformed by the provision of public utilities and the modernization of agricultural methods., Meanwhile, town and country have been brought closer together by vast improvements in the infrastructure of public transport and telecommunications. The nature of work has changed, as has the composition of the workforce; the age structure of the population has altered and, with it, people's aspirations and expectations. The social structure of the prewar period, with its seemingly rigid divisions between *borghesia* (bourgeois), employed in the city, and the significant number of *contadini* (farmers), or people working on the land, has been profoundly altered by the disappearance of the traditional working class that was composed of male industrial workers and their families, and the concomitant growth of service sector employment, the largest occupational sector. Mass secondary education and the mass media have undoubtedly had a homogenizing effect; the cultural specificities that were attached to earlier social divisions, with distinguishably different bourgeois and working-class cultures, have practically disappeared. At the same time, other forms of cultural diversity have emerged, which are based on regional, generational, gender, and ethnic differences, the latter enriched by the surge of immigration.

The motor of these changes has been economic and political as well as cultural. As described in Part 3, the Italian economy experienced unparalleled growth during the 30 years following the war. The consumer society arrived in Italy in the 70s with an impact that was rendered all the greater by the dramatic contrast it created with the relatively low living standards of the prewar period. But in embracing consumerism and the "affluent society," Italy has also lost many of its distinguishing characteristics and has become more like other Western European countries. Side by side with economic convergence has been a political normalization, as described in Part 1, together with a sustained effort on the part of Italian leaders to promote European integration. The content of politics has become national and European, encouraging convergence with the remainder of Western Europe.

This evolutionary process has not proceeded smoothly. Two periods of social change may be noted whose separation is marked by the student unrest at the end of the 1960s. The first was a period of modernization that accompanied the high economic growth of the "economic miracle." Living standards improved dramatically and the advent of the consumer society brought with it changes in habits, lifestyles, and expectations. Physically, Italy was transformed by massive programs of building and renovation. The second was a period molded by the revolt of students and workers and the pressures of the labor unions. The strikes and demonstrations lasted for many months and affected industries, businesses, and public services. Banks, broadcasting, and transport were all affected alongside the education system and the manufacturing industry. Although the political revolution, led by workers and students, did not overthrow the government, it did have a profound social impact. Social and industrial relations changed for good: the old hierarchies and the old paternalism were replaced by the more relaxed, flexible, and nonhierarchical forms of institutional and interpersonal relations that are common today. This was evident in all kinds of ways, from the widespread use of the *tu,* "you," the familiar form of address, to the clothes worn to school and in the street, to eating habits, as well as in the adoption of participatory management in industry and in public institutions such as universities.

With the start of the 1970s, Italian society ceased to be bent on unquestioned modernization. For as long as families had been inadequately fed and housed it had seemed obvious that modernization should have as its object the provision of basic amenities and a decent standard of living for all. Qualitative considerations began to replace quantitative calculations, so that the consumer society, for example, was not universally seen as a good thing. Criticism of consumerism is, of course, the luxury of affluence, but it was none the less real.

The 1970s marked the beginning of the second period of social change. The effects of the first oil crisis caused the first interruption in rapid growth since the war and led to a less rapid expansion of living standards; however, it was a great period of social reform. Virtually all the popular demands of the 1960s and early 1970s were embodied in social legislation, bringing Italy into line with other Western countries. Contraception and abortion were legalized; equal opportunities legislation was enacted, and paternal authority was reduced.

But this social modernization also reflected a shift in the debate about social inequalities. Until the end of the 1960s, social policy was implicitly underpinned by a model of a society based on the division into classes. This meant that the process of social change was directed at integration, at incorporating the less privileged workers and rural laborers into the national community by offering them comparable living standards and the social protection available to the middle classes. From the middle of the 1970s onward, however, other forms of social grouping, based on factors such as sex and age, rather than class only, were recognized as significant, and legislation was directed at ensuring equal provision of benefits and amenities for such groups. Individuals rather than the family became the focus of social and economic change. Thus, women, for example, achieved equal rights but forfeited the expectation that they would be supported and cared for by father or husband. In all this, mass education played an important role: it affected family structure, women's role in family and society, religious belief and practice, the Church's role in society, and the Church's relation with the State.

By the 1980s, Italian society had changed profoundly. The pages that follow will discuss the major social changes that have taken place in Italy since World War II and will examine some of the factors of convergence and division.

Monument to the Unknown Soldier. One of the imposing landmarks in Rome. From the archive of the author.

CHAPTER 9

DEMOCRATIZING THE EDUCATION SYSTEM

Education Profile

Number of students enrolled in the system: 7,742,000 (2006–2007 school year data) 960,984 boys and girls were enrolled in nursery schools; 4,216,668 in compulsory schools (2,515,219 at primary school and 1,701,449 at lower secondary schools); and 2,442,575 at upper secondary schools.

Number of schools: 10,788 schools.

Number of teachers: approximately one million people are employed in schools: head-teachers and teachers (permanent and otherwise) and technical, administrative and auxiliary staff.

Budget: In 2006 the State spent $82.53 billion (not including university) on education.

University funding: According to a survey carried out by ISTAT, the funds available to the university system in 2006 amounted to approximately 11.6 billion euro, the majority of which is government funding (74.5 per cent).

Faculty: In 2006 the number of teaching staff, both permanent and otherwise, amounted to a total of approximately 74,000 people.

Universities: The number of universities increased from 82 to 109 during the 1990s. Since the 1992–93 academic year, the year that university certificates (splitting of shorter undergraduate degree and the creation of specialization programs) were instituted, the number of short-term courses has almost tripled, while there has been an increase of approximately 50% in long-term courses.

In the 1999–2000 academic year there were 2,946 courses of study in degree, certificate and specialized programs. University education has also been enriched in terms of the variety of subjects on offer, with 206 new types of university courses.

Nevertheless, the number of secondary school graduates who go on to university (the number of enrollments for every one hundred students who have obtained an upper secondary school diploma) dropped from 73% in 1993–94 to 65% in 1999–2000. This overall decrease in the number of enrollments is entirely due to "long university cycles." In fact, a decrease of 6.6% was registered in 1999–2000 enrollments in these courses as compared with the previous academic year, while those enrolled in "short university cycles" have increased by 13.5%.

In terms of both compulsory and higher education, Italy is currently undergoing a period of transition through which the basic structure of the state system, as a whole, is being overhauled. These changes are designed not only to bring Italian education in line with the rest of the European Union but also to create a more flexible system, which better and more broadly educates those choosing to study in Italy. In March of 2003 a law on school system reform introduced important innovations.

Age group
» Under 3 years: Day nursery (*Nidi d'infanzia*)
» 3 to 6 years: Nursery school (*Scuola materna*)
» 6 to 10 years: Elementary school (*Scuola elementare*)
» 11 to 14 years: Middle school (*Scuola media*)
» 15 to 19 years: Upper secondary (*Scuola secondaria di II grado*):
> Classical (*Classica*)
> Scientific (*Scientifica*)
> Technical (*Tecnica*)
> Vocational (*Professionale*)
» Higher education (4 to 6 years duration): Universities (*Università*)

School system
» The state school system is currently divided into **nursery school**, **primary school**, **lower secondary** and **upper secondary school**.
» **Nursery school**: 3 year duration and attended by children from 3 to 6 years of age. It is not compulsory.

» **Primary school**: 5 year duration and concludes with a state examination. On passing this children obtain their primary school diploma. The school is attended by children from 6 to 10 years of age and is compulsory. The study of a foreign language begins in first grade and it is mandatory.

» **Lower secondary school**: 3 year duration. It is attended by boys and girls from 11 to 13 years of age and concludes with a state examination. On passing it the pupils obtain their lower secondary school diploma.

» **Upper secondary school**: set up for different streams, some of which have different specializations.

The upper secondary schools specializing in the humanities and scientific fields have a 5 year program, and conclude with a state examination. On passing it the students obtain a classical or scientific upper secondary school diploma. The technical category also lasts 5 years and is divided into various specializations (chemistry, mechanics, electronics, etc.), ending in a state examination to obtain the technical school diploma. Then there are vocational schools whose duration varies depending on the specific specialization. At completion of the program, students obtain a certificate. Finally, the artistic category is divided into two types: artistic lyceum and arts institute. Students obtain a high school diploma.

The new law requires that everyone leave the system with some sort of diploma or qualification. There is more flexibility in choosing qualification because the new law mandates complete transferability of credits between different kinds of institutions. There will also be a work-study/formal apprenticeship program, in which on-the-job experience can be translated into scholastic credits and, again, transferability between this and classroom programs is supposed to be guaranteed. In practical terms, this will be difficult to accomplish. Even the "experimental" *liceo artistico* now has a curriculum heavy with academic subjects such as physics; how could a student transfer from an apprenticeship program into a *liceo* without the background courses needed to keep up with the current year's work?

University system: Reforms currently taking place represent a general restructuring of the higher education process. Italian universities have adopted a '3 cycle system':

» The first cycle, 3 years in length, will be focused on a curriculum with a professional training bias and will culminate with the awarding of a first level degree as defined earlier, *Laurea*.

» The second cycle will last 2 years and will end with the awarding of a *Laurea Specializzata* (master).

» The third cycle lasting between 1–3 years will earn a student either a doctorate or a postgraduate specialized degree.

Students are admitted to the first degree program with a high school diploma and finish with a degree. The degree provides access to two-year courses aimed at giving students an advanced level of training. These courses result in a specialized degree (our masters degree). After this degree, students can go on to complete specialization courses, first and

second level masters (which are additional specialized graduate courses), or research doc-
torates (our Ph.D.). All courses must be based on the European system for the transfer of
academic credits (ECTS) as provided for in recent agreements reached at the EU level.

Study abroad as visiting student in EU: Erasmus/Socrates Programs: Italian students, like
all the students within the European Union, may study abroad through the Erasmus and
Socrates Programs sponsored by the European Union. Going to Italy to study, as a foreigner, under these programs:

» A foreign student can benefit from the support offered by his or her home
institution;

» Application to university courses is simplified and speeded up;

» There tends to be a strongly positive attitude towards Erasmus/ Socrates students in
Italy;

» Such students receive an elevated status and operate, in most cases, within a more
organized environment.

Source: ISTAT

Reforming an Education System
That Was Only for an Elite

Like every other institution and aspect of Italian life, education has drastically changed in
postwar Italy and, like everything else, it had to be rebuilt in every aspect. Because of the
sociopolitical changes caused by the war, the new government faced a situation that demanded
a restructuring and revamping similar to that needed after the unification of 1870. Education
under fascism and under the liberal regime that preceded it was the ideological and cultural
reproduction of a narrow ruling class.[1] Not only was an elite student body taught by an elite
teacher corps, but the education system was built in such a way that it preserved the established
social class structure. The new constitution provided the basis for social equalization through
equal opportunities in achieving higher education.

To achieve this goal Italy put in place a centralized and public system, financed by the
government through taxation, that provides the same quality of education to everybody, socially
and geographically. (This system is clearly different from that of the U.S., which is a prevalently
decentralized and private system, with public education mainly financed at the local level and
more students going to private schools.)

Given this characterization, an Italian family at a low level of income should receive the
same level of education available to a higher income family. It would seem reasonable to pre-
dict for Italy a more compressed distribution of human capital investments (and therefore of

incomes) matched by a higher likelihood of upward mobility for poor families. However, that is probably not the case. While Italy seems characterized by less income inequality than in the U.S., for instance, standard measures of social mobility through occupation and education indicate that poor and non-educated families are less likely to invest in the education of their children and to move up along the occupational ladder. Even though the Italian centralized public education system offers equal education opportunities gographically and socially, it does not produce a society with great social mobility because motivation to support and to take advantage of the education system is not part of the public political discourse or of the general popular culture. Therefore, as we will see, notwithstanding the democratic approach to achieving social progressive goals, the system has not realized the potential of those at the bottom of the social ladder.

World War II Offered the Opportunity to Make the Initial Changes

The destruction brought about by the war demanded and, ironically, permitted a complete reshaping of that system. Not only was it necessary to rebuild the physical infrastructure, but everything else, including the outline of the studies, curricula, syllabi, teaching methods, school management system, and the responsibilities of the administrative offices and operators at all levels had to be profoundly transformed. At the end of the war most of the school buildings were severely damaged, if not destroyed; the classrooms that were available were crowded, had no heat and little furniture, and lacked proper sanitary conditions. In some areas of the country, especially in the south, many children could not attend school because they lacked proper clothing. In mostly agricultural areas of the south, many parents were still keeping their children on the farm to help with daily tasks. There is a moving scene in the Taviani brothers' film *Padre Padrone,* set in the 1950s, when an authoritarian shepherd comes to school to physically remove his son from the classroom. Based on a true story, it gives a stark picture of the Sardinian families so completely dependent upon their herds that their children must be kept home to help with the work.

A Democratic Education System to Create a Democratic Society

As late as 1951, as many as 5 million people (about 10% of the population) were still illiterate! The new democratic government had the overwhelming task of rebuilding the infrastructure and of reorganizing the system on a democratic base; that is, giving all citizens the right to reach the highest levels of education, whatever their financial means. The changes involved included reshaping the attitude of teachers, making them more conscious of the need to keep up to date and of the necessity of continually improving their professional knowledge and, therefore, the progress of their schools.

Changes were possible across the country because the system was highly centralized. The Ministry of Education had, and still has, central control of curricula, syllabi, hiring and payment of teachers, and much of the financing. By the early 1980s, the system had completely changed its

PROFILE

Scuola Normale di Pisa

The *Scuola Normale Superiore di Pisa*, also known in Italian as *Scuola Normale* (Normal School), could be considered the Harvard of Italy. Founded in 1810, by Napoleonic decree, as a branch of the *École Normale Supérieure* of Paris, its first goal was to produce the best college and high school teachers. It has since become a prestigious research institution with a highly selective admissions procedure.

Recognized as a "national university" in 1862, one year after Italian unification and named during that period the "Normal School of the Kingdom of Italy," it obtained its administrative autonomy in 1936, during the fascist regime. Since then, the Normal School has become an entity separate from the University of Pisa, with complete administrative, didactic, and regulative freedom. The Scuola, together with the University of Pisa and with Sant'Anna School of Advanced Studies, belongs to the Pisa University System. Professors, researchers, and students all work together as one, teaching and studying, in classrooms as in laboratories, developing cultural activities and experimental initiatives together. The greatest resource of the Scuola Normale is the quality of the students who come there. Entrance to the Scuola Normale can be obtained only by competitive exams in which a committee of internal and external professors evaluate candidates' overall capacities: basic knowledge of the subject area to be studied, solid general education, aptitude for research, and critical capacity. Once admitted, students live and study in a completely free system; they receive free tuition, free housing, free lunches and dinners, and a monthly salary. (The Italian government pays most of the costs.)

They absorb the natural mixture of experience, research, in-depth analysis, and intuition that characterizes the environment at the Scuola Normale.

The Scuola does not host a full program of undergraduate and graduate studies; instead, students follow the ordinary courses at the public University of Pisa and complement them with additional classes and seminars taught by the professors of the Scuola. The *normalisti* are required to score high marks in their exams at the public university (average marks of at least 27/30 and no mark below 24/30) in order to maintain their grant. The Ph.D. program is separate and completely independent of the one hosted by the University of Pisa. The Ph.D. course is called *corso di perfezionamento,* and the students are called *perfezionandi.*

Some of the alumni of the *Scuola* have had an international impact:

» Enrico Fermi, physicist and Nobel Prize winner
» Carlo Rubbia, physicist and Nobel Prize winner
» Giosuè Carducci, poet and Nobel Prize winner
» Giovanni Gentile, philosopher and politician, minister of education during the fascist regime.
» Guido Fubini, mathematician; in 1939, because of fascist anti-Semitism, Fubini moved to the Institute for Advanced Study in Princeton
» Ennio de Giorgi, mathematician
» Vito Volterra, mathematician
» Luigi Bianchi, mathematician

> » Carlo Azeglio Ciampi, economist and politician, lifetime senator, former prime minister of Italy, former president of the Italian republic, former governor of the Banca d'Italia
> » Massimo D'Alema, politician, present Italian minister of foreign affairs, former Italian prime minister
> » Giovanni Gronchi, politician, former president of the Republic of Italy
> » Fabio Mussi, politician, present Italian minister of the university and research.

character. The expansion of education not only increased the number of educated young people but also changed qualitatively, *not always uniformly,* the education system in Italy.

In few other areas has Italy advanced more since the war than in its progress from a poor to a relatively modern educational system, one in which practically everyone goes through the upper school, and a very high percentage continues to the university. However, despite these advances, much remains to be done.

Radical Reforms

In the immediate postwar years, reforms were still conducted conservatively. Although there was clearly a need for a profound change from the lowest to the highest levels of education, the changes made during the first 15 years were just window dressing.

The first substantive reform came about with the establishment of compulsory secondary schooling until the age of 14 and the establishment of a single system of middle schooling. The basic reform law that triggered this transformation process, approved in 1962, abolished the old lower secondary school *(scuola media),* which was attended by students intending to continue their studies, and the secondary technical school *(avviamento),* attended by those intending to enter the job market as soon as possible. It instituted a single lower secondary school *(scuola media unica)* that was equal for everyone. It was an important reform socially and democratically, since it enacted the constitutional norm, which established a period of equal compulsory education for at least eight years for every student. It also tried to ensure that another constitutional norm was applied, whereby the most able and deserving were entitled to reach the highest levels of education by assuring that everyone enjoyed the same opportunities at the outset. The two main aspects of the new system, training and guidance, were an attempt to achieve greater social justice.

However, the reform was slow to succeed because many middle-school teachers remained hostile to the new law, claiming it watered down the curriculum (Latin became optional) and threatened discipline; implicitly, the teachers did not want to see the old elite middle school "destroyed." Consequently, to a certain extent, the curriculum remained archaic until the end of the 1960s, when radical change swept through the entire academic system. However, in bringing to eight the number of mandatory school years, the state made a heroic effort to make education accessible to everyone, including the children of farmers who, for economic, cultural, and social reasons, had stayed away in large numbers. In the 1960s and 1970s the government spent billions of dollars in this effort; schools were built in even the most remote hamlets, sometimes serving only a few dozen children. With these new schools came all the other supportive facilitation: roads, telephones, electricity, and free transportation.

Consequently, the number of students and the make-up of the student population changed radically. For the first time in Italian history children from every social background had the same opportunity for a basic education. The impact of the changes brought about a cultural revolution. Indeed, the material bases of the explosion of protest in the Italian universities and high schools of the late 1960s are to be found in the education reforms of the early 1960s. The mandatory reforms for the middle school opened the road to demands for mass education beyond the eighth grade. The student body, whose number increased rapidly, for the first time included a high percentage of girls and children from the low, middle, and working classes. Many of them, especially from the middle classes, decided to continue their studies and go on to the university. Legislation of the 1960s made this easier: in 1961 access to science university programs was opened to students from technical high schools (institutes), and in 1965 entrance to the university by examination was abolished. By 1968 the number of university students totaled over 450,000, compared to only 268,000 in 1960. The number of female students had doubled in the same period, but in 1968 still constituted less than a third of the new students beyond the mandatory years. But by the academic year 1991–2 a historic *sorpasso* (overtaking) had taken place: the number of women enrolled in Italian universities exceeded for the first time the number of men. The slow but steady growth of educational qualifications, and especially the increase of women's education, made their influence felt in every Italian family, for its composition, structure, size, and life outlook.

However, as we shall see, a lot remains to be accomplished. If the disparity of gender had been solved, those of geography and, above all, of class had not. In the 1980s in Italy 55.6 % of children from families of professionals, managers, and entrepreneurs gained an upper secondary school diploma. The corresponding figures of children of workers in industry and services were only 20.8 % and 2.1 %. The family of origin was still by far the largest single determinant of educational opportunity.[2]

There Can Be No Democratization Without High Standards

Primary and secondary schools have been democratized, but quality education has been sacrificed. Curricula were reformed not only because of the emergence of new fields—aeronautics, electronics, marketing, computer science, linguistics—but, above all, because the middle-class values of the system did not match those of many of the users. The school had to respond to the problem of how to equalize educational opportunities for all children, regardless of their socioeconomic background. The new breed of students during the militancy of the early 1970s had engaged in a sociocultural revolution. They not only asked for curriculum reforms but also questioned the old methods of teaching based on *nozionismo* (notions), the accumulation of knowledge without relating it to a practical context. Reformers also declared that a less authoritative teacher in the classroom would make the learning process more effective. In a series of memos written after 1968, the government's education authorities directed high school teachers to take into consideration the entire personality, intellectual commitment, and mental process of a student, not his or her performance on a specific test. This was an implicit rejection of *nozionismo,* and it encouraged students to cultivate the old Italian penchant for rhetoric. The testing, mostly through oral exams throughout the whole educational system, certainly allows the teacher and pupil to cover more ground, since speaking is obviously so much faster than writing, and if the student's thinking is woolly, the teacher can question more searchingly. It should also be said that in Italy, personal communication has always been highly prized, and therefore Italian students have much better oral communicative skills than American students. Because of their long experience in oral exams, in general Italian students have quicker reflexes and are better prepared to engage in argumentative discussions.

The new method of student assessment replaced the progress reports based on numerical markings with brief analytical reports. Moreover, in planning class activities and programs, teachers were asked to take into account not only the needs of the group but also of individuals. In this regard, it should be pointed out that special efforts have been made to integrate handicapped children into regular classes in elementary and lower secondary schools. Special education was seen as demeaning and negatively affecting the potential learning abilities of students; therefore, it was limited to the severely physically and mentally handicapped. Consequently, remedial teaching activities for pupils with problems, foreseen by law, were reinforced and provided through the support staff properly trained in two-year specialization courses. It must be said that the situation of these experiences is not uniform throughout the country owing to the diversified social context in Italy. While some special education programs are well advanced, others are facing difficulties and contradictions. This process of integrating the handicapped into normal classes would seem to be irreversible and is no longer questioned. However, there is still some discussion on how to achieve this integration, that is to say, on how to plan teaching activities and how to organize all the other aspects connected with the presence of a handicapped child in the class. Certainly, the handling of "special students" is done much better in Italy than in the U.S., where school districts inflate the number of students needing "special education" because of the large amount of money available for such students from the federal and state governments.

The Evenness of the System

The evenness of the quality of the system is guaranteed by the fact that public school teachers are considered state employees and get their jobs through state competitive exams, *concorsi,* administered by the ministry of public education. They are assigned or transferred without consideration of the exigencies of the individual schools. In Italian public schools, teachers cannot choose the schools they prefer, and no school can choose its own teachers. Contrary to the American system, which is classist (separatist) because of the close connection of real estate value with school district prestige and the internal selection of students in each school through the creation of honor sections, advanced placement (AP) courses, etc., the Italians do not use a tracking system. Italian educational authorities feel that students tend to stay in their track throughout their school years and that remedial students develop poor self-images and are alienated from schooling.

Students in a tracked system do not learn better, and the content and quality of education offered in each track are very different. Students form self-concepts, social relationships, and aspirations that reflect the status of the track in which they are placed. In America, this problem is alarming because the racial and socioeconomic makeup of students in different tracks tends to mirror the race and social class stratification of the larger society. In Italy, on the whole, everyone from the son of the doctor to the daughter of a waiter mixes in the same classroom. However, this does not mean that elitism has been completely eradicated. The most prestigious high school is still the *liceo classico* which, notwithstanding all social changes, still attracts for the most part children from an educated background. Indeed, some educationists criticize this system. However, Italy has understood that in today's high-tech world of work, countries cannot overemphasize college and demean technical training. Italian school officials help the non-college bound students to pursue a more demanding curriculum than the "general" course so many American kids choose. It spares Italian industries and businesses from spending more money on training workers, and it spares colleges from spending so much on the remediation of ill-prepared freshmen who may not belong in college at all. The question remains: who is going to professional technical schools? The great majority are children from working class families.

In addition, the democratization of the system did not eliminate gender preferential divisions that are determined by tradition and social predeterminations. As most studies show, girls are very selective in the choice of the type of school they attend. Their number is greater than that of boys in those professional schools that lead to elementary school teaching careers (girls comprise 90% of the total enrollment in these schools), in art schools (64%), in technical schools that prepare for clerical occupations (53%), and even in those schools for children of the upper and upper-middle classes. Girls are more numerous in the classical lyceum, *liceo classico,* centered around literature and philosophy (53%), than in the scientific lyceum, *liceo scientifico,* based on mathematics and natural sciences (38%). The same situation can be found at the university level, where girls account for only one-third of the enrollment in medicine, economics, and law, one-fifth in physics and chemistry, less than 10% in engineering, but 60% in biology and 75% in literature and philosophy.

Flirtation with educational practices that skip rudiments, inflate basic concepts, and hurry to get results has had detrimental effects. Secondary schools have been moving toward the American school model, where fun-and-games, talk-ins, and so-called self-expression take the place of real intellectual training. Experimental teaching methodologies aimed at finding ways to make learning less laborious and demanding abound, while the use of audio-visual machinery has become more desirable than subject matter. As in everything else, Italy has been looking at the U.S. for an improvement of its education system; unwittingly, it has been looking at a system that has been in search of its own easy fix!

On the positive side, when compared to other countries, Italy presents some favorable aspects in the academic picture. Italy has 210 class days, compared to 180 in America. It has the lowest teacher-to-student ratio in Europe; between 1980 and 1992, the enrollment in the first eight years went down by almost one and a half million students while the number of teachers grew by about one hundred and thirty-five thousand. Parents still play a key role in the learning process at home. Another important feature of the elementary school is the inclusion, among the new subjects, of foreign languages as a means of understanding and comprehension and as part of the overall framework of linguistic education.

Teachers Must Be Accountable

Many teachers and parents alike are simply left bewildered by the spate of often contradictory reforms and tinkering over the past 30 years and are skeptical as to whether any reform will succeed. But it is clear that no new system or reform will ever work effectively without a more flexible commitment and generous attitude on the part of the teachers. In and out of class, they are the key to the whole problem. They have certainly evolved since the late 1960s in terms of more relaxed human contact with their students. But one of their handicaps is still their lack of up-to-date training: they were taught to instill academic virtues, and few of them have much knowledge of modern teaching methods, or of what might be called "education for civics and leisure." But the teachers' attitude is the most serious problem. The majority of teachers are not ready to put their hearts into the kind of work usually accepted as a basic part of the job in Britain or America. It is the usual Italian problem: teachers complain about state control but then have no idea how to use their freedom when they get it. Many of them lack any initiative, except that of protest, and some of the protests are justified because Italian teachers are the lowest paid of any economically advanced nation. No educational system can attract quality faculty if it must indiscriminately pay its teachers/professors the same regardless of talent, potential, or performance.

Like any professions, the teaching profession includes three general groups: the excellent, the good, and the bad. Since unions bargain for pay increases as if all teachers performed at the same levels, excellent teachers become consistently underpaid while poor teachers are over-remunerated for their professional service. The cost of carrying poor teachers falls on the backs of the large middle group of good teachers. If the unions supported a merit pay structure, as is done in some of the U.S. university systems, they would lose their clout overnight. Unions argue that since teaching is a subjective art that cannot be accurately measured, a merit system could not possibly work. The argument may be sound, logical, and fair, but it completely misses the point. All institutions, both public and private, in a free market system evaluate performance on subjective as well as objective bases. Politicians win elections; executives capture promotions, and consumers buy goods and services, not just because they meet strictly measurable standards, but because people vote, work, and spend their money by whim and perception as much as by fact. Periodically, the education process itself looks rather subjective from the students' point of view. Grades, test scores, and most evaluations reflect subjective criteria to some degree or another. To improve quality in a real sense, schools should be allowed (the impossible dream) to ruthlessly expel teachers who do not perform to set standards. Doing so would traumatize a system that has long protected and promoted its incompetent labor force, but in the long run, such paring of the inferior will better prepare the system, its teachers, and students to compete in the age of a global knowledge network.

The situation has been changing. On the one hand, the ministry of education has been trying to overhaul teacher training, making it less purely academic, with a new stress on modern pedagogic techniques. On the other, the education system has reacted positively, showing great reserves of vitality. There is a growing awareness at the grassroots level that billions of euros alone cannot improve the quality of a democraticized school system. High academic achievements and a relevant education are achieved through revised course content and updated teaching methods, which must be carried forward by the teachers themselves with the full involvement of the community and individual parents. But in the politicized Italian world, such a transformational process from the grassroots level has raised some concerns: the Left has raised the smoke of the inequalities that such initiatives may cause. That is to say, while such initiatives toward reform are developed in some areas where the situation is favorable, they may be lacking in others. Here lies perhaps the most important challenge facing the government and school administrations in the coming years. Instead of imposing new profound reforms from above, the ongoing reform process should be better monitored and guided at the local level.

A Democratic System Failure

Notwithstanding the democratization process and good goals set by the various governments, the percentage of students from the lower rungs of the social ladder who graduate and pursue higher education is relatively low. Probably one factor is the lack of self-confidence and the conviction of the lower social classes in the social transformational power of education. The other factor is at the democratic base of public education systems that can be thought of as being motivated, among other reasons, by the goal of increasing self-confidence in poor groups so that talented but poor children may reach higher education levels and skilled occupations. The way to achieve this goal is generally to offer a uniform quality of education to all citizens, so that poor families have the same opportunities as rich families to invest in the education of their children. But an offer of equal educational opportunities may not necessarily generate more mobility if the incentive to use education as a way to climb the social ladder is low. Under plausible conditions, even if the quality of education offered to poor population by the state system is higher than the quality offered by a private system, the investment in education may be more attractive for poor people in the private system because there is some personal commitment in the process of social change.

The quality of Italian education varies very much. Italian elementary schools are often of excellent standards, with a long tradition of dedicated female teachers. Secondary education is much more patchy; the reform of lower secondary schooling, one of the achievements of the center-Left governments in the 1960s, proved a great disappointment. Upper secondary schooling boasts some excellent *licei* and technical institutes in the major cities, but overall it is disappointingly archaic, with scant attention paid to languages and sciences. Secondary schooling is largely populated by a demoralized staff lacking incentives. One of the major problems is that secondary schools have limited powers of decision-making, with a top-heavy centralized administration. Local-level impotence also makes itself felt in the limited degree of participation of families in school administration through community committees. A system of participation had been laboriously worked out in the 1970s, but it proved a substantial failure. Percentage turnout of parents for the election of their representatives was very low and reflected the fact that a majority of parents did not identify with their children's schools or feel that their presence in school administration could really change anything.

How to Educate Immigrants with Radical Expectations?

The integration of Islamic immigrants into Italian society raises thorny problems for the education system. In 2005, a Milan high school announced that in the fall it would have a first-year class composed only of Muslim students, at the request of their parents. These students had completed eight years at a private Islamic school in Milan. (This school is not accredited by the Italian education authorities, so the question raised by many was, why were 400 students allowed to attend it? By law, all children resident in Italy must attend regularly-licensed state or private institutions.)

In the past, students of this Islamic school would either stop at 8th grade (also illegal in Italy, which until 2004 was requiring school through age 15), return to their countries of origin, or continue their studies with private tutors. Their parents asked a local social organization to help create a special section in a regular Italian high school where the kids could continue their studies, be kept together as a group, and the girls (17 of the group of 20) could wear the veil. The principal of a social sciences high school and the Italian social workers saw this as a step towards integration for these kids, who come from rigidly religious families that will not allow them to mingle with Italians.

Protests were immediately raised by both political extremes, the Left denouncing the initiative as racist, while the real racists of the *Lega Nord* thundered that this was a very dangerous step towards the Islamization of Italian society, and a deep wound to the profoundly Christian roots of their collective religious and cultural identity. The educational authority for the region of Lombardy decided then that separating students on the basis of religion was unconstitutional, and the project was halted. The Italian constitution (modeled on the American one) insists on the separation of church and state, and especially the secularity of public schools.

It's a difficult issue. There is no question that it would be better to take a step, however small, towards the social integration of these kids—although segregated in the classroom (by their parents' insistence), they would surely still manage some contact with other students in the school. Following a standard Italian curriculum with Italian teachers and in Italian would also help them to integrate. And ensuring that they continue their education is preferable to letting them drop out, especially the girls. For women, the best road out of oppression is education: educated women are far more able to stand up for themselves.

On the other hand, it is a serious risk to set a precedent. "Separate but equal" was proven a failure in the U.S. 50 years ago, and separation of Islamic students has already been tried and abandoned in other parts of Italy. The Milanese experiment certainly would have been a step in the wrong direction.

We are sure of one thing about this situation: the Italian education system is very good at social integration. If anything, it sometimes goes too far in keeping all children in the same classroom, no matter their language handicaps (e.g., brand-new immigrants) or learning disabilities. These kids don't always get the help they need to truly integrate, and some simply get left behind. But most of the time integration works. The schools place particular emphasis on the class functioning smoothly as a social unit, which forces the kids to rub along together. In fact, acts of verbal or physical violence as caused by ethnic friction in Italian schools are rare.

The students in Milan's Islamic school were being allowed to study in an apparently illegal situation which is handicapping them for life in mainstream Italy and bypassing the social integration function of a normal (public, or properly licensed private) Italian school. This was wrong. The parents, whatever their religious beliefs, have made a choice to immigrate to Italy, and are therefore obliged to live by Italy's laws, including those regarding their children's schooling. Allowing them to form Islamic ghettos creates misunderstanding and conflict and allows them to avoid truly coming to terms with the country they have chosen to live in. It's up to the Italian government to enforce the law and get these kids into regular schools, to the long-term benefit of all.

The Transformation of the University System

The student generation that started higher education in the 1960s entered a university system that was still terribly antiquated. The expansion of infrastructure carried out in secondary schools had not been continued at the higher level. The number of universities had remained the same and all had maintained their essentially feudal structure. Worse still, many of the professors were rarely present in the university. Their obligations to the universities were limited to 52 hours of teaching per year; once their obligation had been satisfied, they could attend to their "main" profession, that of being doctors, lawyers, engineers, architects, chemists, and, above all, politicians. There were no seminars, no tutorials, and no faculty-student contact. Not surprisingly, the number of students who failed their oral exams was very high. In 1966, 81% of those with a secondary school diploma went on to university, but only 44% succeeded in graduating. In such a situation, the students coming from the lower social classes faced the worst odds of success. Even worse, most of the sons and daughters of the "new" university society who graduated, mostly from the expanding urban middle classes, suffered a series of disillusionments when trying to enter the job market. It seems that the university continued to operate a particularly subtle form of class-based selection. The Left in government had succeeded in opening up the doors of the university to everyone but had not been able to prepare the system for the new student population.

This kind of environment, nourished by ideological issues that were brewing in many parts of the world, led to the student revolts of 1967–1968. Many students of the mid-sixties were doubtful of the values that had become predominant in the Italy of the "economic miracle": individualism, the exaltation of the nuclear family, and consumerism. Education had made the students more critical of society's failures and more interested in social justice. The dream based on achieving success through talent and hard work was revealed to be just a myth for many students coming from the lower classes. Social status and connections (whom you know) seemed to be the biggest factors for success. A lack of social status was considered the major constraint on upward mobility. Although the university door was open, the effects of social origin on academic success and occupational achievement and mobility remained significant. Students questioned this situation by leaning on current Catholic social doctrine and Marxist thinking; values of solidarity, collective action, and the fight against social injustice and social division were juxtaposed with the individualism and consumerism of "neo-capitalism."

Some world events certainly had their impact on this situation in ferment. The Vietnam War changed the way a whole generation of Italians thought about America: the image of an America that offered opportunity and a realizable dream, in the 1950s, had been replaced by that of a powerful and destructive America. The Cultural Revolution in China in 1966–1967 was interpreted in Italy as a spontaneous, antiauthoritarian mass protest movement; Mao's invitation to Chinese youth to "open fire" on headquarters was interpreted in Italy as a cultural revolution against the "establishment" that had to be carried out from below. Finally, there were the teachings of radical South American priests who sought to reconcile social Catholic doctrine and Marxism. This explains why the first university revolts took place in strongly Catholic institutions. The explosion that started in the autumn of 1967 (long before the French unrest) at the University of Trento, followed by those at the Catholic university at Milan and at the public university at Turin, set the stage for a cultural revolution that swept through the nation. Students questioned not only what was being taught, the "canon," and the way the mental process was put to work but also the individualistic ways of presenting one's image. Students changed the way they dressed and looked. Men let their hair and beards grow and abandoned jackets, ties, and somber-colored clothes in favor of jeans and other casual attire; women abandoned make-up, dresses, and high heels in favor of jeans, pullovers, and boots. The movement reached its climax in fall 1969 but continued throughout the 1970s.

Enrolled students by disciplines and gender at university (Academic year 2005/2006)

Disciplines	Number of Students	% of Male	% of Female
Scientific: Mathematics & Physics	10,933	75.4	24.6
Chemistry and pharmaceutical	13,125	37.8	62.2
Biological sciences	19,193	38.7	61.3
Medical school	26,454	36.3	63.7
Engineering	33,891	81.6	18.4
Architecture	16,399	51.7	48.3
Agrarian	7,702	56.9	43.1
Economy/Statistics	45,199	51.7	48.3
Political and Social Sciences	39,878	38.7	61.3
Law	38,566	41.3	58.7
Literature/Humanities	28,886	34.1	65.9
Languages and Linguistics	19,251	18.2	81.8
Education	16,038	10.3	89.7
Psychology	10,873	21.1	78.9
Physical and Sport Education	5,129	68.7	31.3
Police and Public Security	423	83.5	16.5
Total	**331,940**	**44.2**	**55.8**

Source: ISTAT

The most unfortunate aspect of the democratization process was the deterioration of quality education. The open-enrollment policy aimed at eliminating the privileged situation of some schools (*licei*) was supposed to be temporary. The awaited reforms at the upper secondary school level and those undertaken in universities were supposed to bring some balance to the system. The extended period of open enrollment has had profound effects on the entire university system. The open enrollment policy instituted in 1969 proved to be only a ploy of the Left to demonstrate another victory for the masses, without in reality providing a real gain in professional success. The democratization of the school system transformed the system from a university for the elite into a university for the masses, but the transformation has taken place more to satisfy a political necessity than to prepare a society of highly educated and skilled citizens; it was done more to fulfill a political agenda than to raise the level of education of the nation.

In the mid-1970s, when the welfare state was being instituted in a most bizarre way, the education system was experiencing the same turmoil as the rest of Italy's institutions. The

Rate of employment right after graduating high school and after completing college (2004)

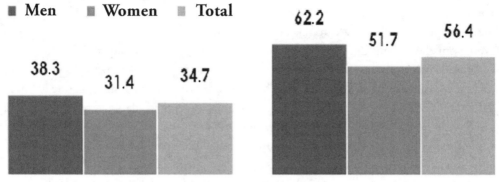

Source: ISTAT

Unemployment rate of college graduates by gender and discipline (2004)

Discipline	Total	% of Male	% of Female
Scientific: Mathematics & Physics	14.0	9.8	18.9
Chemistry and Pharmaceutical	9.2	7.1	10.6
Biological Sciences	20.3	13.7	24.3
Medical School	8.3	7.9	8.7
Engineering	4.8	4.5	6.3
Architecture	9.8	7.6	11.9
Agrarian	15.2	10.2	21.8
Economy/Statistics	11.4	10.1	12.8
Political and Social Sciences	10.8	9.8	11.4
Law	27.1	20.6	31.6
Literature/Humanities	21.6	16.7	23.0
Languages and Linguistics	19.0	14.1	19.4
Education	12.8	6.7	13.3
Psychology	16.0	10.6	17.1
Physical and Sport Education	4.6	4.3	4.7
Total	**14.5**	**10.2**	**17.9**

Source: ISTAT

principles at the base of the workers' statute and other social insurance laws that were aimed at bringing about considerable equality of conditions were also at the base of the democratic reforms in education. In education, too, equality of opportunity was meant to be also equality of results; in the democratic spirit, regardless of how well-prepared students were, everyone was expected to pass, and students were expected to graduate as a matter of right. Thus, great pressures were placed on professors to relax the stringency of the oral examinations that prevailed throughout the system. During those chaotic years, not only did the quality of students and academic standards decline, but those who taught moved to make their own jobs permanent as a matter of law. Several legislative reforms had the effect of granting tenure, in one fell swoop, to thousands of academics, irrespective of their qualifications as scholars and teachers. Although not all of these got to be full professors (*professori ordinari*), they all joined the ranks of millions of other public servants in public service jobs who had lifetime job security.

The state also responded in a confused way to meet the serious problems created by overcrowding. Although the state opened many more universities throughout Italy, this new generation of university students entered a system that was still grossly inadequate.

Overcrowding strained all academic facilities. In the 1991–1992 academic year, the state universities in the three largest Italian cities (Rome, Milan, Naples) enrolled over 40% of the total university population; nine university centers throughout the country are so overcrowded that each enrolls more than 40,000 students. In the mid-1980s, the University of Rome, "La Sapienza," had an enrollment of 160,000 on a campus built for about 33,000. Some professors lectured to audiences of more than a thousand students. Rome's medical school was supposed to train 23,000 students concurrently; many of them never made it to the anatomy laboratory. To secure a library seat, students had to line up early. However, most Italian students (especially in the humanities and social and behavioral sciences) did not bother to go to classes; they expected to accomplish more by studying in the comfort of their homes rather than in a classroom where seats were scarce and professors frequently canceled classes. As some form of standards started to be reapplied, not surprisingly, many students failed their exams, with the complaint from the Left that the reforms had not satisfied the aspirations awakened by the social changes. Indeed, the Italian university system unintentionally began to operate a subtle form of class-based selection; while it was supposedly open to all, the odds remained heavily against students from lower social classes earning a degree or finding a job.

Italy's university system is not preparing the new generation for employment. After three years from graduation only 62% of graduates are employed with an average pay of 21 thousand euros (ISTAT). Certainly, given the low percentage of college graduates that Italy produces, the problem cannot be attributed to a surplus of college graduates that the economy cannot absorb. Italy's big university problem is that everything is run on a democratic basis: the president of the university *(rettore)* and the deans *(presidi di facolta)* are elected by faculty and representatives from the staff; academic changes are under the jurisdiction of faculty council (*consiglio di facoltà*), whose power is in the hands of full professors (*professori ordinari),* who for the most part are old and want to preserve their power. This basically means no substantial change in the curriculum. On the other hand professors don't have to worry not having students in their program; programs are not abolished in Italy for lack of students, as in the U.S.!

The Italian university system needs a built-in system of competition. Funding should be diverted to those programs and universities that are "producing" graduates prepared to bring skills and creativity to the evolving new world. The Berlusconi government was promoting the creation of some private universities to inject some form of competition into the system and the first signs were positive. Unfortunately, the new center-Left government has announced that education will remain public (and, therefore, return to the status quo). An additional solution would be to grant total academic and financial autonomy to each university and allow each to prosper or sink as a result of their own decisions.

Ideology and Academic Freedom

Like everything else the system has been highly politicized. Politics seeps into every area of the educational system—from bottom to top, from nursery and elementary schools to the high schools and universities. Schools actually produce in some students and reinforce in others clear-cut political predispositions.

Needless to say, university student bodies are politicized as well. In the late 1960s and early 1970s, they represented the prime recruiting ground for political terrorist organizations, particularly those of the Left. Several founding members of the Red Brigades were contemporary students of sociology at the University of Trento. Even the most "normal" organizations are typically organized along the same lines that define Italy's political parties. In this sense, Italian student organizations are in line with European student practice. They are vigorously active bodies with, very often, formal ties to the political parties within which many students will pursue political careers or from which they intend to seek support when they go out to look for jobs. Italians rarely can conceive of student organizations American style, that is, ones having just social and cultural aims.

Unfortunately, many students become professional students who, supported by political parties, make a living out of being political agitators. The system is so absurd that in theory it is possible for a student to spend up to 25 years getting a degree. Not surprisingly, only one-third of all students who enroll in Italian institutions of higher learning ever graduate; the other two-thirds remain "professional students," eventually dropping out to look for a job or swell the unemployment lines. It could be argued that in the Italian university system, as in all industrial countries, further education is probably encouraged as an alternative to unemployment. The system gives hundreds of thousands of young people a chance to educate themselves and a sense of belonging to society. The Italian government has come to understand that it is cheaper to pay for an education that is a "parking place" than to be forced to pay for other social services or even detention institutions as a consequence of the lack of employment.

Besides being political and social, the problem is also ethical. Even though the prospects of finding a job with a degree in the humanities are remote, the largest percentage of students enroll in those disciplines because they are easier than the sciences. Very few enroll in physics, notwithstanding the high demand for physicists and other scientists. Physics still enjoys the reputation of being the heir to an illustrious tradition but also produces statistics that are unattractive to students who are not highly motivated: of those who enroll, only about 30%

graduate and most of them take five or six years instead of four. The enrollment in medicine is also very high in spite of the vast number of doctors scrambling for jobs. Italy has the lowest ratio of doctor to inhabitants in the EU.

Since Italian life is politicized at every level, changes cannot be implemented easily and in some cases are even impossible. The answer seems to lie in a selection system for applications for enrollment, as well as in a suitable strengthening of structures and premises that should also be evenly distributed throughout the country. The state has tried to respond to the overcrowding by opening new universities, including several private universities.

Although the number of universities increased by about one third between 1970 and 1990 (30 new universities were opened in that period), the overcrowding in the old centers was not alleviated. Most students preferred to enroll in institutions with a tradition and associated with the scholars and scientists who have had a long-lasting impact in many fields throughout history. No one can convince students that a degree from a new university such as that of Calabria is worth as much as that of a university with an illustrious past, such as the University of Bologna or the University of Pavia. Students are also very aware that the new centers attract only the young professors who accept those first appointments as a "parking place" while they wait to move to an older university as soon as the opportunity presents itself. In a country where traditions are still highly prized, it becomes even more difficult to reduce their significance when they are attached to a glorious past. Italy has the oldest university tradition in the world. Salerno was the first, founded in the ninth century by "four masters": a Jew, a Greek, a Saracen, and an Italian. By the twelfth century, before Oxford or Cambridge colleges had even been founded, Bologna University, founded in 1088, had ten thousand students. The University of Padua was founded in 1222, Naples in 1224, Rome in 1303, Pisa in 1342, Turin in 1404, and Catania in 1444. Some of these are among the most distinguished in the West, boasting centuries of humanistic and scientific achievements. Even today, despite the intrusion of politics into the system, several universities remain islands of intellectual rigor and innovation that rival similar institutions anywhere else in the world.

Today, however, the troubles of the system stem from the strong power achieved by the students and by the old autocratic faculty system. Students have become so powerful, or the government has conceded so much power to them, that effective reforms have been difficult to come by. When in November 1984 the prefect of Rome suggested that all universities should limit enrollment in the medical schools to 70% of the previous year's number, there was such a political uproar that no one who had been contemplating the measure was willing to support it (however, medical schools now have reestablished a limit on the number of students accepted). In 1985, in reaction to a proposal by the Minister of Public Education to increase tuition by about $100, the students of the Left organized such a general protest that the government backed off. The problem was not that Italians were overburdened by the cost of higher education (today even the poorest university student spends $100 in a weekend out for pizza) but that students assumed the position that education should be completely free. On that occasion, the lack of students' political maturity and their politicized positions became more evident than ever. No student organization leader responded to the government with a counterproposal or with a constructive critical assessment of the university system and how it should be improved in order to justify the additional fees. No student group suggested that the extra $100 would be palatable provided it were spent in the university system, perhaps to improve the service of libraries, which at the time were a disgrace.

When another attempt was made to reform the system in spring 1990, the universities were practically shut down for almost two months. Reaction to a proposed law that would give individual campuses more autonomy to set course requirements than they had under a highly centralized system, and which would also have allowed individual universities to sign contracts and started joint research projects with private companies, brought back memories of the late 1960s and mid-1970s. Students worried that big corporations may be given a free hand to reshape the country's schools to fit their own needs. While the sciences and engineering were likely to get adequate financing, they argued, the liberal arts would fall by the wayside.

In American universities, good science departments, through the grants they bring to the campuses, often enhance the life of the humanities and arts divisions. Usually, real scientists support university policies to share the "indirect costs" charged by the universities on grants with every academic area of the campus: a good comprehensive university needs humanists and artists to prepare a more "humane society," especially in a scientific age. In Italy, however, laboratory researchers joined the protests because they also felt that they would lose their independence and become tools of industry. Large companies, it was also argued, are more likely to invest in the well-developed Italian north, further widening the considerable gap with the relatively poor south. Not coincidentally, the campus protests first erupted in Palermo, where the unemployment rate was over 20%, four times that in Turin. Objections to the plan reflected widespread cynicism about the concentration of economic and political power in the hands of a few industrialist titans.

However, today's students are very different from those of the late 1960s and 1970s. Protest may flare up over specific grievances, but gone is the old political idealism. The vast majority share the current Italian disillusionment with ideologies; those who are politically active are either on the extreme Right or extreme Left and keep political activism alive on campuses, as we shall see later.

How Democratic Can a System Be in the Hands of *Barons*?

As we have previously mentioned, one of the major problems of the Italian university system, like the entire education system, is the high level of politicization. Professors are openly concerned with politics and are openly lined up with political parties. Despite arguments about the importance in a democratic society of intellectuals remaining relatively autonomous, aloof from political parties, in order to remain honest critics of social and political arrangements, in Italy the situation is completely the opposite. "By and large, Italian intellectuals not only shun any such effort; they thrive in political works. Far from being the critics of political parties and party factions, they are often the latter's major spokesmen. Far from seeking a modicum of space, in a politicized society that admittedly offers very little of it to anyone, they hanker after the rewards, including public offices, that the parties can distribute to the faithful."[3] That is true today as it was in the years of strong ideological beliefs.

What is even more damaging to the entire system is that the universities are firmly in the hands of autocratic senior professors, unfondly called *baroni*. As La Palombara underscores, the Italian "barons" are not just playing academic politics; they are intricately a part of the bigger political game as well. In the bargains, the "barons" strike; in the trade-offs, they concoct; and in the "balance," they seek to establish, within the university community, political and ideological considerations that reflect the politics of the nation. The political coloration of the competing professorial candidates weighs at least as heavily as their professional qualifications, and sometimes more (Ibid., p. 72). So, despite appearances to the contrary, professors practice the same division of the spoils enjoyed by the political parties in the patronage system, which almost brought Italy to ruin. Italian professors are known as *baroni*, not only for the prestige they enjoy and the influence they exercise, but also for their authority and independence. Still today, they can choose the date of when to begin the academic year; they can delegate their work to a host of assistants; and until recently, they could freely take up another post at another university. Efforts have been made to induce professors to devote less time to their private affairs and more to their academic duties. For instance, if a professor is elected to parliament or receives another important public appointment, it has been established that she or he will be placed on leave of absence from the university. However, efforts to induce professors to hold one position, to reside in or close to the cities of their chair, and to teach and undertake research in their universities have been only partially successful. It is not uncommon in Italy for professors to reside two or three hundred miles away from the university where they teach!

Moreover, as in most universities throughout the world, there are no tests on the actual ability to teach or lecture. It is inconceivable that an Italian university professor would allow students to evaluate classroom experiences the way we practice and value it in the American university system.

A law was passed in 1980 to restructure the ranking of the academic body and to create some 45,000 new positions. These would be divided into three categories. The *ricercatore*, "researcher," the lowest position, is appointed through a *concorso*, a state competitive examination and assessment of publications, and three years teaching experience. The next stage, *professore associato*, associate professor, can lead to the third and last stage, full professor, *professore ordinario*; both stages are achieved through a national competition. These changes, which were meant to break the feudal system, have met with only partial success because through manipulation of the system nepotism and clientelism are still very much alive. Notwithstanding the many attempts by the government to break the culture of nepotism and clientelism, the "baroni" still succeed to manipulate hiring procedures in favor of candidates who are highly "connected." This situation has been worsened by government decisions to encourage older professors to remain on the job in an attempt to reduce the deficit of the pension plans.

Another big issue is commitment to teaching. As in the American university system, there is an overemphasis on research and a corollary distaste for teaching. Unfortunately, as in the U.S., some of the research is "make believe scholarship," which can be confirmed by how infrequently a researcher's work is cited by others within five years of publication. In the sciences, fewer than half the articles published were cited in that period of time. In the social sciences the "uncitedness" index rises to 74.7%, in religion to 98.2%, and in literature to 99.8%! It's not difficult to conclude that much research is self-defensive and self-indulgent.

Today there persists much controversy about what role a university should play. Do we still believe that in a university:

» We learn how to learn;
» We teach and learn how to question;
» We teach and learn how to be analytical;
» We create new knowledge;
» We prepare to get a job and/or be functional in society?

Should the university be primarily for research or for teaching? Can the university still fulfill the Renaissance ideal of producing the well-rounded, cultivated individual? Or, in this age of the masses that is also an age of specialization, should the university become more vocational? Should it teach for "culture" or for professional ends? There are many who believe that it can and should do both, but that its courses should distinguish more clearly than at present between these two ends, instead of blurring them. On the whole, Italian universities emphasize culture, and the classical tradition is still strong.

The most serious problem that the Italian university system faces, and one that has slowed down any reform because of its implications, is that not enough independence is permitted as an institution. The question is: "should the constitutional norm, which recognizes the right of universities to be autonomous organizations, be applied in a complete way?" It is, in fact, obvious that the problem of autonomy for universities is connected with innovation and the development and programming of university studies. The very future of the university lies in finding the balance that permits accessibility and affordability while providing a sound education.

Probably the university system is one of Italy's weaker educational institutions, with the highest drop-out rate in Europe, no time limits set upon the completion of courses, and students graduating with painful slowness, usually in their mid- to late twenties. The reforms of the early 1990s, which created a greater degree of autonomy for universities from central government, had been a step forward in theory but not in practice. Starved of adequate central government funding, the new autonomy seemed mainly synonymous with cuts. One of the gravest consequences of this short-sighted containment of spending was the exclusion of a whole generation of young and brilliant students from the prospect of continuing their studies beyond the doctoral level.

In the public institutions there are almost no funded jobs for the new generations, not even on limited-term contracts. This forced exclusion of youth from the teaching corps of the universities, presumably one of the key groups in the formulation of national culture, is pregnant with consequences for the country's future. The situation will not get better if the government continues with the present policy of encouraging old professors to continue to teach so that they will not collect pensions.

In this bleak picture, probably too severe, there are some bright spots. It is possible to find centers of excellence in Italian universities, as elsewhere in the Italian education system. The *Bocconi,* a private university in Milan, enjoys world prestige, especially for its program in Business and Economy. Another outstanding institution, *the Scuola Normale Superiore di Pisa,* a public university (with free tuition, room and board) where students have access by competitive exams, has produced scientists of world fame *(See Box on p. 240).* In addition, a small number of Catholic universities enjoy prestige in the humanities and social sciences (Sacro

Cuore, LUMSA). But these small centers are often deprived of the possibility of developing lasting traditions of research and scholarship.

Student Life Today: Less Political but Not Civic Oriented

Incidents of the last few years indicate that students are very different from those who stormed the barricades in the late 1960s. Protest may flare up over a specific grievance, but it is not the old political idealism. The vast majority share the current Italian disillusion with ideologies; the few politically active ones are usually extremists.

As individuals, Italian students are hard-working, serious, and worried about their own futures; they are not indifferent to the world's problems, but they are skeptical and have lost faith in the ability to improve even their university or school environment, let alone society. Significantly, only a small percentage of university students even bother to join a student union. And a severe setback to the 1969 ideal of participation is the fact that very few students vote in the new university elections or come forward as candidates. So students stay quietly in the background, their noses in their textbooks, obsessed by the hunt for diplomas (*laurea*) that may stave off unemployment.

Even in their leisure time many feel isolated, for Italian universities and secondary schools are not warm, club-like communities, as is often the case in America. Unlike in Britain and the U.S., the tradition is that students go to their local university; therefore, the great majority live at home, where they at least have the comfort of family and a nucleus of existing friends. But others, whose homes are too far away, live in rented rooms or dormitories, and here they can be very lonely.

The scarcity of clubs and organized social life has always seemed to Americans and Britons a striking feature of Italian universities, which have no equivalent to the big American "student union" building, a focus for community. Many large universities do not even have a student drama group or orchestra, and attempts to start them have been growing ever rarer now that students are so preoccupied with work, exams, and job prospects. Consequently, students seldom show any enthusiasm for their university or school. The Italian education system, especially the universities, does not attempt to create a community spirit, a binding glue among the students themselves or between the institution and its students. In America all this becomes part of an "identity," of having been and remaining part of a group, the alumni of an institution, a strong patrimony for both. American institutions work hard to keep alumni attached to their universities: alumni contribute millions of dollars to their "alma mater" every year!

Why is all of this weak or nonexistent in Italy? It is not altogether the students' fault. The building of campuses has not helped. Until the late 1960s nearly all universities were situated downtown. Here the students crowded the local café, deriving some warmth from the town and adding to its liveliness in return. But, with the growth in numbers, many departments are now scattered throughout the cities or have been transferred to big new campuses on the outskirts. Some of these are quite attractive, and they have eased working conditions, but the students are now more isolated than ever. For both universities and secondary schools, the problem is still institutional. Neither local faculties nor the state ministry have made much effort to turn the school or university into more of a real community—a focus for loyalty and a social place for students to stay around when classes are over. That is not the Italian tradition. Schools, and to a large extent universities, are facilities for the transmission of knowledge and the passing of exams, and nothing more. There is nothing like the student organizations and athletic teams of American campuses. Photography clubs, drama societies, concerts, plays, recitals, sport events, and other cultural or recreational events are unheard of in most Italian universities. The ministry of education pays lip service to the need for more out-of-class activities, but in practice puts them near the bottom of its budgetary priorities.

If out-of-class activities such as clubs are so few, it's also because so few teachers are prepared to stay on after hours to help organize them. Teachers do not see this as part of their job; in fact, most likely they belong to a union that militantly opposes this kind of unpaid overtime. The average professor/teacher regards the school as a kind of office job: one arrives, holds classes, maybe with donnish brilliance, then goes home. The students' out-of-class lives are not their business. This attitude is changing a little among younger teachers, but it is still widespread. School/university activities are considered marginal to the academic life. Real life for students is what they get from outside travel, television, friends, and family.

Training in democracy, leadership, and civic feeling helps American students feel part of a living community and allows them to share responsibility for it. But in Italy, tradition holds that it is the family's responsibility, not the school's, to build character. It could be that parents look on school as an academic utility that should not compete with them as a center of loyalty; and if a school were to attempt training in leadership or civic responsibility, this would be resented as an intrusion into their own sphere. From an Anglo-American point of view, this leaves a void in the youngster's full education.

In conclusion, it is easy to be impressed by Italian students' resilience and their apparent ability—helped no doubt by their home background—to survive the system to which they are subjected. Yet, one is equally sure that a system that would attend to the formation of a social conscience might go a long way toward healing the maladjustments in Italian society and Italian public life. This is true of secondary schools; it is even more true of the universities.

A System in Need of a Fix, Notwithstanding the Many Reforms

If we accept the premise that one of the goals of a democratic public education system is to favor equal opportunities of social mobility, the Italian schooling system is not fully achieving this goal, and no system can do that. The centralized and public structure of education financing in Italy has indeed ensured a substantial uniformity of the quantity and quality of education offered to both rich and poor families, but despite this offer of equal opportunities, Italy, in comparison to the U.S., displays lower intergenerational mobility not only in terms of occupations but also in terms of education levels.

The fact that family background is a more important determinant of individual social fortunes in Italy than in the U.S. is particularly puzzling given that in the U.S. a large fraction of the expenditure for education is financed locally through real estate taxes, bringing it close to a private system. Indeed, because of local financing, the quality of education in the U.S. is significantly different according to the (perhaps implicit) price paid for it; and the quality of the education provided to the child is decided by the parent on the basis of this cost. In the U.S. the quality of the pre-college education is significantly different in different neighborhoods, and it has an implicit price in the property tax paid by residents and in the higher price of the houses in the best neighborhoods. The choice of residence is clearly in large part a choice about the education that will be provided to the child. However, motivation may be more important than equal opportunity. Therefore, even if in Italy moving up the social ladder should be easier, the incentive to move may be lower, making mobility less likely.

A Reform That Works

Because of the needs posed by social changes, pre-schooling was instituted and, as the industrialization level of the country increased, gradually expanded. However, nursery school, *asilo nido,* and kindergarten, *asilo infantile,* for children from 3 to 5 years of age are only optional since they serve more as preparation for the compulsory school, though both are of special social importance, providing as they do babysitting service for working parents. Since it is not mandatory, such service is not funded by state government but is run either by the municipalities or by private bodies; therefore, once again, it becomes available either privately to those who can afford it, or publicly by only those municipalities that are financially stable. Public nursery schools are in short supply, and even those run by the local public administrations can be expensive to support. Therefore, children of mothers who have jobs are given preference. In urban centers like Milan and Rome, more than one-third of the demand is unsatisfied. The lack of state, regional, and municipal support in this area, as we shall see in Chapter 11, is one of the major factors of Italy's low birth rate.

However, at this level, Italians have produced some outstanding models: the *Reggio Emilia* and Montessori (*See Box on p. 261*). Both have received worldwide praise. In the *Reggio Emilia* system, departing from the basic concept that each child is unique and different, the system works on the assumption that in pre-school, teachers should only be concerned with the physical, emotional, and social aspects of development and should provide children with a rich and stimulating environment that is, at the same time, warm, loving, and supportive, and create in them a solid sense of security, positive self-esteem, and a long-term enthusiasm for learning.

The program is designed to foster young children's learning, representation, and expression through exploration and mastery of many symbolic media. *Reggio* educators believe children have preparedness, potential curiosity, and interest in constructing their learning, in engaging in social interaction, and in negotiating with everything the environment brings them. Creativity is seen not as an exceptional occurrence or a separate mental faculty but as a characteristic

PROFILE

Maria Montessori

Maria Montessori (1870–1952) was a physician, an educator, a philosopher, and a humanitarian. Her philosophy on how best to educate children from birth to adolescence is in use today in schools, both public and private, around the world.

Montessori was the first woman to graduate from the University of Rome La Sapienza Medical School in 1896—in other words, she was the first female physician in Italy. As a member of the university's Psychiatric Clinic, she became intrigued with trying to educate the "mentally retarded" and the "uneducable." Because of her success with these children, she was invited to start a school for children in a housing project in Rome. *Casa dei Bambini,* or Children's House, opened on January 6, 1907. Its success sparked the opening of many more like it, and the Montessori method of education was born.

The basic Montessori concept holds that children teach themselves. Montessori schools operate according to the following principles:

» The teacher must pay attention to the child, rather than the child paying attention to the teacher.
» Children will proceed at their own pace in an environment controlled to provide the means of learning.
» Children are competent beings and are encouraged to make maximal decisions.
» Curriculum is developed through observation of the children in the environment.
» Children learn best in the most natural and life-supporting environments. These small, child-sized environments must be continually adapted in order that children may fulfill their greatest potential—physically, mentally, emotionally, and spiritually.
» Imaginative teaching materials are the heart of the process.
» Each method is self-correcting; children proceed at their own pace and see their own mistakes.

A 2006 study in *Science* magazine demonstrated the efficacy of Montessori's teaching methods. According to the study, Montessori children had improved behavioral and academic skills compared with a control group from the mainstream system. The authors concluded that, "when strictly implemented, Montessori education fosters social and academic skills that are equal or superior to those fostered by a pool of other types of schools."

Despite much initial criticism, the Montessori method of education was ahead of its time. It is now applied widely and successfully on six continents and throughout the United States.

In the 1990s, until Italy adopted the euro, Maria Montessori was pictured on the 1000-lira bill (by far the most common one), displacing Marco Polo.

way of thinking, knowing, and making choices.[4] Children's work is not casually created but rather is the result of a guided exploration of themes and events that are relevant to the life of the children and the larger community. Classwork is organized around themes that allow children to learn a variety of skills and help them understand their world. What looks like art, for example, is actually a science, math, and art lesson. The classroom space is utilized in a manner that encourages creativity and individual freedom.

These schools are tax-base supported; however, families with children enrolled in the childcare (*asilo nido*) pay a monthly fee of no more than $300 (and sometimes quite a bit less), based on the family's ability to pay. Disabled children and single-parent children are admitted automatically. Other admissions are based on interviews.

Many features of the *Reggio Emilia* pre-school reflect Italian values. The relationship that is created between parents and teachers is similar to the roles played by the Italian extended family. Parents, teachers, and other members of the community work together to produce a unique pre-school/day-care program that proves that children learn and grow in a social atmosphere outside of, and in addition to, the home. The emphasis on the arts and aesthetic insights expresses an appreciation of detail and a sensitivity to design that is in the mainstream of the Italian creative tradition. And so, amid endless debate, the struggle goes on to find solutions to the educational problems of a new age.

Notes

1.   G. Vacca, *Quale democrazia?* (Bari: De Donato, 1977), 168.

2.   See the important essay by A. Schizzerotto, "La scuola e' uguale per tutti?," in Paul Ginsborg, ed., *Stato dell'Italia* (Milano: Mondadori, 1994) 558–61. His figures are of 1985. In the early 1990s 56.6 per cent of Italian families declared that they had fewer than twenty-five books in their homes, and 23 per cent none at all; T. De Mauro, *Idee per governo. La scuola* (Bari: Laterza, 1995), 9.

3.   La Palombara. *Democracy Italian Style* (New Haven: Yale U. P., 1987), 68.

4.   For an informative report and assessment of the *Reggio Emilia* preschool system, see: R. S. New, "Excellent Early Education: A City in Italy Has It," *Young Children* 45, no. 6 (1990): 4–10; "The Ten Best Schools in the World," *Newsweek,* 2 December 1991. 50–58; P. Hinckle, "A School Must Rest on the Idea That All Children Are Different," *Newsweek,* 2 December 1991; D. Newbold. "A State Nursery School That Is Simply the Best," *Time Educational Supplement,* 14 February 1992, 15; B Rankin, "Inviting Children's Creativity: A Story of Reggio Emilia, Italy. *Child Care Information Exchange,* vol 85 (1992): 30–3.

Bibliography

S. Cassese, ed., *Ritratto dell'Italia* (Bari: Laterza, 2001).

C. Ceolin, ed., *Università, cultura, terrorismo* (Milan: Franco Angeli, 1984).

T. De Mauro, *Idee per governo. La scuola* (Bari: Laterza, 1995).

P. Ginsborg, ed., *Lo stato dell'Italia* (Milan: Mondadori, 1994).

P. Ginsborg, *Italy and Its Discontents* (New York: Palgrave Macmillan, 2003).

J. La Palombara. *Democracy Italian Style* (New Haven: Yale U. P., 1987).

G. Vacca, *Quale democrazia?* (Bari: De Donato, 1977).

S. Vertone , ed., *La cultura degli italiani* (Bologna: Il Mulino, 1994).

CHAPTER 10

SECULARIZATION OF STATE AND SOCIETY

Religion Profile

Religious demography: Italy is an overwhelmingly Catholic country (Catholics make up 87% of the population, with 36% considering themselves practicing Catholics and 30% attending church every Sunday).

The religious composition of the Italian population (58,751,711—2006, estimated) is the following:

» Christians: 53,500,000 (91.1%)
» Catholics: 51,600,000 (87.8%)
» Roman Catholics: 51,500,000 (87.6%)
» Eastern Catholics: 100,000 (0.2%)
» Italo-Albanians: 60,000 (0.1%)
» Others (Romanian Catholics, Ukrainian Greek Catholics, Armenian Catholics, etc.): 40,000 (0.07%)
» Other Christians: 1,900,000 (3.2%)

- » Protestants: 1,200,000 (2.1%)
- » Evangelicals and Pentecostals: 550,000 (0.94%)
- » Assemblies of God: 400,000 (0.68%)
- » Others: 150,000 (0.25%)
- » Jehovah's Witnesses: 500,000 (0.85%)
- » Waldensians and Methodists: 35,000 (0.06%)
- » Seventh-day Adventists: 25,000 (0.04%)
- » Latter-day Saints: 22,000 (0.04%)
- » Others: 80,000 (0.14%)
- » Baptists: 20,000 (0.03%)
- » Brethren: 20,000 (0.03%)
- » Anglicans: 15,000 (0.03%)
- » Lutherans: 8,000 (0.01%)
- » Others (Disciples of Christ, Reformed, Presbyterians, Mennonites, etc.): 15,000 (0.03%)
- » Eastern Orthodox: 700,000 (1.2%)
- » Greek Orthodox: 180,000 (0.31%)
- » Romanian Orthodox: 150,000 (0.26%)
- » Others (Ukrainian Orthodox, Moldovan Orthodox, Serbian Orthodox, Russian Orthodox, etc.): 370,000 (0.63%)
- » Muslims: 850,000 (1.4%)
- » Buddhists: 110,000 (0.2%)
- » Hindus: 70,000 (0.1%)
- » Sikhs: 70,000 (0.1%)
- » Jews: 45,000 (0.1%)

Immigration—both legal and illegal—continues to add large groups of non-Christian residents, mainly Muslims, from North Africa, South Asia, Albania, and the Middle East. Of 2.9 million immigrants, an estimated 1 million are Muslim, primarily Sunnis. Islam is Italy's second religion today. Today Rome besides being the seat of the Vatican is also the home of the largest mosque in a non-Muslim country.

Legal status of Church and religion: There is no state religion. There is freedom of religion and separation of Church and state. However, the Roman Catholic Church enjoys some privileges, stemming from its sovereign status and its historical political authority as an independent state in Central Italy until the Unification.

Legal relations with the Catholic Church are regulated by the Pacts of Lateran, signed in 1929 and amended in 1984, which make provision, among other things, for the Catholic religion to be taught in state schools to those pupils who so request.

Relations between Church and state: The "Roman question": Before the Unification of Italy, the central part of the peninsula was part of the papal State. Therefore, the process of unification included fighting the papal army and annexing the Papal territory to the new nation.

Despite the guarantees immediately provided by the Italian state to the pope for the free exercise of his functions as leader of the Catholic Church, set forth by the guaranty law of 1871, Pius IX refused to recognize the new political and territorial arrangement. Thus, the "Roman question," which prevented both a normal relationship between the Vatican and the Italian government, as well as active participation of the Catholic world in the political life of the country, remained unresolved.

The 1929 Pacts of Lateran, signed by Mussolini and Pope Pius XI, solved the long-standing disputes stemming from the dissolution of the Papal States in 1861. With that accord, the Church and the Italian state brought to an end a conflict that had begun with the unification of Italy. Italy had been unified on liberal, secular principles and, in keeping with Cavour's famous principle of "a free church in a free state," most of the Church's legal privileges had been abolished. When Italian troops entered Rome in 1870, the pope ceased for the first time in centuries to be a temporal sovereign. In anger he shut himself into the Vatican as a self-proclaimed prisoner of the Italian state. The Church refused to recognize the new state, excommunicated its monarch, and forbade the faithful to hold public office or vote in national elections. In assuming such a position, the Church not only fostered a widespread popular alienation from the state but also isolated itself and its faithful from the vital forces of society.

The problematic solution of the Roman question with the Pacts of Lateran: The Roman question was not settled until Mussolini saw an advantage in gaining Church support and was willing to pay a high price for it. The Pacts of Lateran, which solved the Roman question, were in three parts:

» One was a treaty creating an independent Vatican city-state of 108 acres and giving the Holy See possession of a number of churches and palaces in Rome; a papal summer residence at Castel Gandolfo, on the outskirts of Rome; basilicas at Padua, Loreto, and Assisi; and custody of all catacombs in Italy. The pope was recognized as juridical sovereign, and the Vatican was accorded the attributes of a sovereign state, with the authority to maintain its own police, postal system, bank, and radio enterprises. In return the pope recognized the Italian state and renounced the Vatican's claim to the former papal territories. With mutual agreement, crimes committed on Vatican soil would be tried in Italian courts and be subject to Italian legal penalties.

» A second accord was a concordat that established Catholicism as "the sole religion of the state" and gave the Church sweeping privileges in civil affairs. Catholic religious instruction was compulsory in both elementary and secondary schools. Church marriages were deemed legally valid and did not have to be followed by a civil ceremony; their dissolution was solely the responsibility of ecclesiastical courts. Religious institutions were authorized to hold property and were exempted from taxes. Seminarians and priests were exempted from military service, and those expelled from the priesthood were banned from teaching, government employment, and any position that brought them into contact with the public. Priests were also banned from party membership and political activities. The state was given the right to approve the appointment of bishops.

» A third accord dealt with the financial settlement that gave the Holy See more than 750 million liras, plus an additional one million liras in Italian state bonds, as compensation for the loss of the pre-1870s territories; this huge indemnity, in time, became the basis of a financial empire, first in Italy and then abroad. Moreover, in its few years in office, Mussolini's government increased clerical salaries, granted several million liras for damaged churches, restored the crucifix in classrooms and law courts, rescued the (Catholic) *Banco di Roma* during the Depression, and closed down all brothels and anticlerical journals. It also set up a national examination system to enable Church school students to graduate on an equal footing with those from state schools and recognized degrees given by the new Catholic University of the Sacred Heart in Milan.

Unquestionably, Mussolini did settle the Roman question, but he settled it at the expense of the separation of Church and state, which had been at the core of the *Risorgimento*. But for all the legal concessions, the fascists did circumscribe the activity of the Church in civil life, with the result that relations between the Church and the government were at times strained. For example, under fascism there was great hostility to Catholic Action because it was regarded as a vocal alternative to, rather than a support of, the regime. Many leading Christian Democrats such as Aldo Moro, Amintore Fanfani, and Giulio Andreotti were closely linked with the Church and had been leading members at the time Cardinal Montini, who later became Pope Paul VI, had an influential role. With the fall of fascism, and the supremacy of the Christian Democrats in political affairs in the immediate post-war period, the Church became very powerful politically and established a strong grip on every aspect of Italian life. Its activities were facilitated by the fact that the constitutional assembly, by a vote of 350 to 149, supported the incorporation of the Lateran Pacts in the new constitution. That decision, in fact, set the stage for the subsequent course of Church-state relations: a nearly organic relationship, almost in symbiosis, between the Church and the Christian Democrats.

Farewell to the Catholic State

By the beginning of the 1980s Italian society had changed so profoundly that the 1929 concordat had become a relic of the past. The time was ripe for a new agreement. A 1984 revision of the Concordat formalized the principle of a secular state but maintained the practice of state support for religion—support that also could be extended, if requested, to non-Catholic religious nominations. It was signed in February 1984 by the Vatican Secretary of State Agostino Casaroli and by Bettino Craxi, the Italian prime minister, the first from a party of the Left. In the three most important articles—dealing with marriage law, religious instruction in public schools, and tax exemption of Church organization—the Church did not retain much power. Although a religious wedding retained its validity in civil law, the act of marriage had to conform to the legal requirements set by the Italian laws. Marital annulments by ecclesiastical courts were subject to approval by Italian courts. Religious instruction in public schools was made purely voluntary. The Vatican had for years claimed exemption from taxes both on the property of Church organizations and on the Vatican's shareholdings in Italy. When under parliamentary pressure it was forced to pay taxes, the Vatican sold off its Italian stocks, but it continued to lobby for tax-exempt status for some 50,000 ecclesiastical organizations and properties that were used at least in part for commercial purposes, such as monasteries that rent rooms to tourists. At the end it was agreed that only Church properties of a strictly religious nature would retain their tax exemption. The stipend to the clergy (which amounted to $175 million in 1984), as well as funds for the construction of churches, was phased out by 1990, leaving the Church dependent on voluntary contributions, which are tax deductible as in the United States.

The most difficult problem to resolve was finding a way to control the activities of the Vatican bank, which operates as a normal commercial bank for depositors of the ecclesiastical order, and has always been very secretive about every aspect of its affairs. Not being subject to Italian banking regulations and exchange controls, the bank has operated freely. Until the end of the 1960s, the bank's investments were in a broad range of Italian industries and in vast real estate holdings. With the taxation pressure on its stock dividends from the Italian government, in 1968 the bank moved its assets into financial shareholdings outside Italy, especially in the U.S. In transferring these funds, the bank's president, Archbishop Paul Marcinkus, an American with no financial experience, depended heavily on the assistance of two Italian bankers, Michele Sindona and Roberto Calvi. The two bankers turned out to be first-rate financial swindlers who brought embarrassment and huge financial losses to the Vatican.

Since the 1960s, most bishops have assumed a conciliatory position in political ideology. However, the bishops and the curia maintained the firmest links with the *cattolici popolari,* the descendants of the old *DC.* The bishops knew that the *cattolici popolari* needed Catholic electoral support as much as ever, but they recognized that each side could do less for the other. The Church's interest in politics and its influence on them have declined. Although remaining an important factor in national life, the Church can no longer command the allegiance of the majority of Catholics on any issue of public life. In practice, the area in which the Church and state interact has steadily diminished and is now quite small. What has evolved is a Church-state relationship of the sort Prime Minister Cavour originally intended back in 1870.

State Relations with Other Religions

The 1984 revision of the concordat formalizing the principle of a secular state maintained the practice of state support for religion—support that also could be extended, if requested, to non-Catholic denominations. In such cases, state support is to be governed by legislation implementing the provisions of an accord (*intesa*) between the government and the religious confession. An *intesa* grants ministers of religion automatic access to state hospitals, prisons, and military barracks, allows for civil registry of religious marriages, facilitates special religious practices regarding funerals, and exempts students from school attendance on religious holidays. If a religious community so requests, an *intesa* may provide for state routing of funds through a voluntary check-off on taxpayer returns, to that community, a privilege that some communities initially declined but later requested. The absence of an *intesa* does not affect a religious group's ability to worship freely; however, the privileges granted by an *intesa* are not always granted automatically, and a religious community without an *intesa* does not benefit financially from the voluntary check-off on taxpayer returns. Government units provide funds for the construction of places of worship as well as public land for their construction, and they help preserve and maintain historic places of worship that shelter much of the country's artistic and cultural heritage.

In 2001, the Campania regional administration approved the request for approximately $3.1 million (2.6 million euros) to build a mosque in Naples despite the absence of a formal *intesa* between the state and the Muslim confession.

Influential Role of the Catholic Church Today

While Roman Catholicism is no longer the state religion, its role as the dominant religion occasionally gives rise to problems. The Catholic Church's influential role in society has led to controversy when Church teachings have appeared to influence Catholic legislators on matters of public policy.

In 2004, Parliament passed legislation favored by the Vatican that equates an embryo with a human life, prohibits the use of donated sperm for artificial insemination, restricts the production of embryos, and limits scientific research on embryos. The legislation drew support from Catholic legislators across the political spectrum, while secular conservatives and communists joined to oppose it. In January 2005, Camillo Ruini, president of the Italian Bishops' Council, urged Catholics to abstain from voting for four referenda to abolish parts of the new fertility law; this sparked strong reactions from some Leftist leaders who accused the Catholic Church of inappropriate interference in the political process. The June 2005 referenda failed when only 26% of the required 50-plus percent of the population voted. The low turnout reflected a variety of factors, including Church opposition, the ambivalence of most secular politicians, and voter apathy on a summer weekend. Another issue of contention is in asserting that the draft European Constitution should include language recognizing Europe's Christian heritage.

Constitutional Tests in Courts

The continuing presence of Catholic symbols, such as crucifixes, in courtrooms, schools, and other public buildings has drawn criticism and has led to a number of lawsuits. In 2003, President Ciampi had argued that the crucifix was a symbol of national identity and not only a religious emblem and was praised by several politicians and intellectuals for his position. In December 2004, the Constitutional Court ruled that, based on a technicality, a 1928 regulation that provides for the display of crucifixes in public classrooms is constitutional. A mother in Venice, who asked that the crucifixes be removed, brought the case. In April 2005, a court ruled that crucifixes do not have to be removed from polling stations, as requested by the president of a small Islamic association. In March, Interior Minister Pisanu had argued publicly that the crucifix was a symbol of great value that represented 2,000 years of civilization and culture.

Religion Perceived as an Obstacle to Integration

Increasing immigration, from Eastern Europe, Africa, China, and the Middle East, is altering demographic and cultural patterns in communities across the country and has led to some anti-immigrant sentiment. For the country's Muslim immigrants, religion serves as an additional factor differentiating them from native-born citizens. Interior Minister Pisanu ordered his prefects to reach out to moderate Muslim communities to enhance their integration into society. In December 2004, the Minister of Equal Opportunity created a new national Office to Combat Racial and Ethnic Discrimination to monitor and prevent discrimination and assist victims with legal assistance.

However, some members of the Northern League political party asserted that practices present in many Islamic societies, notably polygamy, some elements of Islamic family law, rules governing the role of women in society, and the lack of separation between religion and state, rendered many Muslim immigrants incompatible for integration into Italian society.

Italy is a land of contrasts:

» Perhaps the most Catholic politician in Italy is not a conservative, as might be expected in America, but Romano Prodi, the former European Union chief and prime minister of the present center-Left government.

» Italians routinely ignore the conservative popes in matters of private morality, such as contraception, divorce, and marriage (far fewer Italians are marrying, in the Church or out), but they admire the popes deeply for their stand on issues such as caring for the poor and their outspoken opposition to warfare.

» Crucifixes may hang in public schools, but they do not have the heavy political over-tones that come with displays of, say, the Ten Commandments in public places in America.

» The splintering a decade ago of the Christian Democratic party, often seen as a main route for the Church's influence, along with Europe's deepening secularization, helped make Italy more like other European nations. Despite the teachings of the Church against contraception, Italy has one of the lowest birth rates in Europe. Divorce and abortion became legal in the 1970s despite strong opposition from the Church.

» Abortion is a non-issue and is perhaps the best example of the more civil tone, in Italy, of the debate over religion and state. It seems less an argument than a very long conversation.

» Some conservative politicians and the Vatican lament the decline of moral values and religion, some wondering whether Italy and Europe have lost touch with their Christian roots at a time when, as some see it, the West is facing a deep challenge from Islam.

» On the more secular Left, many leaders lament the lingering influence of the Church among politicians, who they say pander to the Vatican.

» But many Left-wing politicians have their own strong ties to the Church. Even more secular ones find allies in the Church on issues like helping the poor and the recent immigrants.

In the rest of Europe, this mix of church and state is often regarded skeptically. But, paradoxically, Italy has in many ways less religious zeal than the United States, where the lines between church and state are much more sharply drawn, but where personal religious conviction (self-made religion) can be stronger.

And so, like urban architects who struggle to make Rome a modern city without destroying the ancient, Italians maneuver deftly around their heritage—granting both Church and state a more equal share than do many other countries, and with greater equanimity.

The Catholic Church: The End of Its Hegemony Within Italian Society

Rooted in a peasant society and culture, Italian Catholicism changed profoundly with the rise of industrialization, economic development, and the emergence of the welfare state. In assessing the status of religion in Italy, the most evident peculiarity is Italians' widely diffused propensity to deviate from full Catholic orthodoxy. While the Catholic Church has maintained its preeminent position in Italy's internal religious market, it has lost ground in recent decades and at present must reckon with a considerable lack of both vitality and orthodoxy. There is no question that one of the most radical changes that Italy has undergone in the last 25 years is the secularization of every aspect of life and the consequent change in the relationship between state and Church. However, while the authority of the Church as an institution has diminished, a new-style, liberated spirit of religion is very much alive.

The Strong Role of the Church until the 1960s

At the end of the 1950s, the Italians' outlook toward the Church and religion was basically that of many centuries before, reflecting a primarily agricultural society. The Church's centuries-long role on the Italian peninsula as a religious, political, cultural, and social institution was still strong in the early 1960s. The Vatican was an Italian institution and the pope himself was bishop of Rome and primate of Italy. Italy was still the geographic center of the Catholic world. By the terms of the Italian constitution, the Church enjoyed privileges unique among democratic countries. Catholicism formed a profound and natural part of the nation's social fabric; it permeated every aspect of Italian cultural life; it had a position of overwhelming dominance within Italy and generated an enormous variety of cultural forms. Catholic values had played, both anthropologically and culturally, a decisive role in shaping individual lives and collective behavior. Church ceremonies were both social and religious events, and Italians were passionate about professing their faith. Religion, in the form of adoration of a host of local saints in a widely diffused pagan religiosity, offered peasants, in particular, a sustaining refuge from the harsh realities of life.[1]

The Church's presence in the lives of citizens was strong at every level also because of its education and welfare activities. The parish priest was the center of community life—he was lawyer, adviser, teacher, psychologist, and social and spiritual healer. He was responsible for the local nursery schools, bible classes, oratories, the parish library, and more. Over many decades the Church had built up an impressive network of hospitals (the most popular bearing the name *Fate bene fratelli,* or "Do Good Brothers") and nursing and old people's homes staffed by various religious orders. Most private schools and universities are still Catholic. In addition, the POA *(Pontificia Opera di Assistenza,* The Pontifical Welfare Agency) organized a large number of educational and recreational institutions. These varied from seaside and mountain camps to kindergartens, to *doposcuole* (afternoon activities for six-to-twelve-years olds), to *case del fanciullo e della fanciulla* (homes for boys and girls) for runaway teenagers. In the absence of state provision for old people, families turned with gratitude to Catholic welfare institutions. The Catholic agency Caritas even today is the strongest provider of social assistance to Italy's legal and illegal immigrants.

Religion as Cultural Pillar

In understanding how Italians live their religion(s), it is important to look at Italy's cultural tradition and to weigh the different experiences that constitute it. Although the Catholic Church endows some people with authority to assure the authentic practice of religion, Italians have developed particular practices and beliefs (from baptism to the invocation and veneration of saints) that show clearly that religion can be very personal and is a continual process. In dealing with this process, the Church constantly struggles to achieve and defend its hegemony within Italian society.

Church teaching provided many of the basic conceptions in a cosmology of ideas about human agency, natural forces, fortune, and misfortune. God's grace was invoked when the priest made the annual blessing of all the houses of his parishioners before Easter and later blessed the fields of the village. A whole range of practices grew up to deal with misfortune, from the ringing of church bells to avert storms, to exorcism, to the invocation of particular saints specializing in helping with bodily illness. The celebration of the mass was no more important than the use of a religious amulet as protection against the evil eye. The blessed olive branches on Palm Sunday and other objects blessed on other occasions, together with religious formulas

Processions carrying statues of Christ or Mary to celebrate major holidays in the liturgical calendar, or of local patron saints on their feast day, are still popular practices notwithstanding the big drop in church attendance. Printed by courtesy of *America Oggi*.

and imagery, were used by laity faced with misfortune in private acts of divination and curing. In part these practices slipped out of the control of the clergy, and magical practices and their interpretation have been controversial. Certainly there are parallels between these practices and those of non-Catholic peasantries; some have their roots in a pre-Christian culture that the Church has been unable to eradicate. However, far from being survivals, some of these magical practices show a fundamental continuity with central parts of Catholic theology, for example with the rite of exorcism that is part of baptism.

Being a Catholic meant to be shaped and identified by specific social practices. Catholics, when they are baptized, receive a baptismal name chosen from the calendar of saints, and that saint's name day (*onomastico*) is celebrated by everybody who carries that name. Catholic identity is also based on territory. Many Italians have a strong sense of pride and identification with their town or village of birth; there are names and stereotypes for these regional and local identities, and in a number of areas it was the Church that provided the focus for the large-scale activities that brought a village together as a collective entity. The village patron saint, with its statue, cult, and processions, provided one way in which a village's collective identity was articulated.

Impact of Church on Civic Consciousness

In the 1950s Italian parishes were spilling over with activities. Almost 70% of adults said that they attended church regularly. The great number of masses, confessions, and communions in each parish each week testified to the Church's vigorous state of health. So too did the number of organizations associated with parish life, especially Catholic Action, which represented the civic face of Italian Catholicism. However, Catholic Action was two or three times stronger in the civic, more association-prone regions of the north than in the less civic areas of the south. In Italy, as Robert Putnam demonstrated, organized religion was an alternative to the civic community, not part of it. Vertical bonds of authority were more characteristic of the Italian Church than horizontal bonds of fellowship.[2]

The vertical bond that the Church developed with its followers created a psychological predisposition to a kind of civic behavior that proved to be negative over time, as society evolved. Especially in southern Italy, where the Church had a stronger bond with people, the culture of clientelism and dependency persisted when the economic system changed. Living in an agrarian society where the state was absent and people lived *on* and *from* the land at the mercy of nature, religious belief in supernatural forces that controlled drought, floods, hail storms, and any natural cataclysm was a natural option. Guided by the Church, people lived with hope in a world pervaded by danger and uncertainties. Religion offered belief in the efficacy of magic and devotion to saints and Madonnas, along with a basic indifference to and distrust of government.

From statistical studies of the cult of the saints in Western Europe, it is clear that Italy has "produced" more saints than most other European countries. The Italian predisposition to "create" saints is matched by a similar tendency to "create" Madonnas. Thus, while the official Church may maintain that there is only one "Mary," the fact is that Italy has long been a land populated by a plurality of Madonnas, each of whom is venerated separately, usually in association with a particular image at a particular location, and each of whom is seen as independently power-ful. When Italian Catholics want help for their crops, or a miraculous cure for themselves or members of their family, or protection from dangers, both seen and unseen, they appeal to their preferred Madonna or saint. Consequently, Italy has hundreds of churches that

Immigration into Italy has had a profound social and cultural impact. Islam has become the second religion in Italy and Rome is the home of the largest mosque in Western Europe. Printed by courtesy of *America Oggi*.

house (or have housed) a miraculous image. Sometimes people travel to these churches as pilgrims seeking cure for an illness; more commonly, as the painted *ex voto* at these shrines indicate, people travel there *after* having confronted some great danger and having been deliv-ered from that danger by appealing to the image resident there.

Historically Italians have had strong, realistic sense of religion. Until recently faith was professed with fervor and an irrepressible expressiveness. Their faith was guided by an innate urge to externalize and materialize spiritual impulses in art, architecture, music, and elaborate

✺ SPIRIT

Jews in Italy

The Roman Jewish community is the oldest Jewish community in the West. Large numbers of Jews lived there even during ancient times, and for some centuries the whole of Italian Jewish history coincided with the history of the community in Rome. Jews were among the many Greek-speaking people who came to Rome as merchants during the second and first centuries BC, as Rome increased its dealings with the eastern Mediterranean.

However, the uniqueness of Italian Jewish history does not lie in its ancient roots; rather, it is in the religious toleration Jews enjoyed in Italy compared to the rest of Europe. In 1859, 12,000 Jews fought with Garibaldi. Thereafter, Italian Jews became senators and generals and considered themselves fully integrated in Italian society. At this time, northern Italian Jewish communities were cosmopolitan, non-religious, and highly assimilated. In Rome, on the other hand, many religious Jews continued to live within the confines of the old ghetto. The Jewish communities and fascism worked well together until the end of the 1930s. Although Mussolini later adopted Hitler's anti-semitism, originally he maintained the traditional equality between Jews and Gentiles. In his first government, Mussolini appointed Jews to three key positions. In 1931, 39,112 were counted in Italy; by 1938 the number was 47,252, as Jews from elsewhere in Europe found haven in Italy.

In 1938, however, after signing the Rome-Berlin Axis Pact with Germany, Mussolini declared the Italians to be part of the "pure race" along with the Aryans. Jews were expelled from all public services, such as the army and the public schools. At this point many Jews decided to leave Italy. In 1943, the German army occupied Italy and the Nazis sought to deport the Jews. Consequently, despite the fascist government's initial refusal to deport Jews to Nazi death camps, about 20% of Italy's Jews were killed. Southern Italy, under the Allies, took in many Jewish refugees from Nazi Germany and other parts of Europe. After the war, many Jews left Italy for the newly formed nation of Israel while others stayed to reconstruct their communities.

Today there are over 40,000 Jews in Rome and Milan alone; the total population is close to 50,000.

ceremony (which clashed mightily with the religious habits of both Protestants and other Catholics); Italians demonstrated their highest level of inspiration in sacred art. There is a rich tradition of piety centered in the privacy of the home. Saints' pictures and crucifixes decorated homes; votive candles flickered before homemade shrines to saints, the Virgin Mary, and Christ. The rhythms of family life followed the liturgical calendar, with appropriate foods prepared and prayers said for the feast days of important saints. The private religious life was complemented by the public *festas.*

Saints and Madonnas were (and to a certain extent still are) worshipped through many social contexts, both inside and outside the walls of the churches, in streets and squares in a variety of ways. The external and exuberant religious practices clashed with the reserved and internal Anglo- and Irish-American practices when Italians came to America. It is not at all surprising that the Irish-American Catholics would view as "flamboyant paganization of true Christianity" the public *festas* (feast days), processions, and pageants in honor of various saints and Madonnas. It must be understood that the "civil" part of the *feste* was mere amusement, an occasion to show collective love for "show"; food, music, companionship are a public expression of joy and thanks for the "protector."

Especially among Southern Italians the veneration of saints and Madonnas is imbued with a high dose of paganism. Sacred images are often seen with such superstitious symbols as *il corno* (twisted horn), worn to ward off *il malocchio* (the evil eye); rituals are performed to ward off the evil spirits. Although there are some who might eschew the *corno* in favor of the scapular, the cross, or the religious medal, often it is possible to see Italians wearing a combination of secular and religious items.

Catholicism Italian Style

Catholicism as professed especially by some southern Italians includes elements that are clearly off the parameters of the Catholic faith as defined officially by the Catholic Church. Catholicism, Italian style, is also characterized by the following:

Sharp distinctions between the "sacred" and the "profane" are rejected.

» Religion is seen at its base as "existential," a matter of experience, rather than being just "doctrinal."
» Religion is contoured to the demands of the family.
» Religion is mediated through vehicles that are personal, concrete, immediate, and situational.
» Religion is both pragmatic and this-worldly and lacks any "surrender" to the transcendent.

It must be stressed that popular religion is seen as emerging from the mutual intersection between distinct social groups, each of which is associated with a different variant of Catholicism. The basic idea here is not entirely new. Quite some time ago, Antonio Gramsci, an intellectual and co-founder of the Italian Communist Party in 1921, suggested that :

> Every religion, even Catholicism (in fact especially Catholicism, precisely because of its efforts to maintain a superficial unity . . .) is really a multiplicity of religions that are distinct and often contradictory: there is a Catholicism of the peasant, a Catholicism of the petty bourgeoisie and urban workers, a Catholicism of women, and a Catholicism of the intellectuals.[3]

Gramsci's insight suggests that the particular form of Catholicism embraced by Italians is shaped by the needs and desires that emerge in us as the result of our being members of a particular group. Still, the needs and desires that arise from group membership, and that shape the Catholicism a group embraces, can change over time. In the end, the emphasis on group intention and on adaptation to changing conditions has fostered a more creative view of popular Catholicism.

PROFILE

Città del Vaticano

Vatican City is a walled enclave within the city of Rome. At approximately 100 acres, it is the smallest sovereign state in the world. It was created in 1929 by the Lateran Treaty as a vestige of the much larger Papal States (756 to 1870) and is ruled by the Bishop of Rome—the pope.

Popes ruled much of the Italian peninsula for more than a thousand years until the mid-19th century, when most of their territory was seized by the newly created Kingdom of Italy. Between 1861 and 1929 the status of the pope was referred to as the "Roman Question." The popes were undisturbed in their palace and given certain recognitions, including the right to send and receive ambassadors. But they did not recognize the Italian king's right to rule in Rome, and they refused to leave the Vatican compound until the dispute was resolved in 1929. Vatican City attests to the great history of the Catholic church. At its center is St. Peter's Basilica, with its double colonnade and a circular piazza in front and bordered by palaces and gardens. Its dome is also a dominant feature of the Roman skyline. Possibly the largest church building in Christianity, it covers an area of 5.7 acres and has a capacity of over 60,000 people. One of the holiest sites of the Catholic tradition, it is believed to be the burial site of its namesake Saint Peter, who was one of the twelve apostles of Jesus, first Bishop of Antioch, and later first Bishop of Rome. Tradition holds that his tomb is below the baldachin and altar; for this reason, many popes, starting with the first ones, have been buried there.

Construction on the current basilica, over the old Constantinian basilica, began on April 18, 1506 and was completed in 1626, the fruit of the combined genius of Bramante, Raphael, Michelangelo, Bernini, and Maderna. Bramante was entrusted in 1506 with the construction of the new San Pietro basilica, the renovation of the facade of the Apostolic Palace, completed by Raphael in 1519, and the construction of the massive wall and the three raised terraces between the Palace and Belvedere.

In 1546 Michelangelo started planning the complex of the three apses and the dome. At the time of his death in 1564 the left apse and the drum, which would be vaulted in 1585, were completed. In 1612 the facade of the church was erected and Pope Paul V Borghese could finally declare the conclusion of the whole project. Bernini completed the sumptuous decoration of the basilica (the Baldacchino of the High Altar and Saint Peter's Chair) and the brilliant, grandiose arrangement of Piazza di San Pietro (1656–66).

A big interest for visitors of the Vatican are the Swiss Guards who give a touch of color to St. Peter's Square: in their Renaissance costumes, with puffed sleeves and knickerbockers striped red, blue and yellow, they stand on either side of the basilica, guarding the gates into Vatican City. When the company was founded, in 1505, the soldiers wore simple tunics, but in 1548 the present uniforms were adopted. A long-standing tradition holds that they were designed by Michelangelo, but there is no foundation for this belief. As well as their everyday costumes, the Swiss Guards have suits of armor, with swords weighing thirty kilos, but these are used only for escorting the pope during special ceremonies in St. Peter's. The force currently numbers 107: the commander, five officers (including a chaplain) and 101 soldiers, all of Swiss birth. Until about 30 years ago, only citizens of the German-speaking cantons were eligible for admission to the company, but in recent years there has been a dearth of candidates and now French- and Italian-speaking nationals can also enroll. They must be Roman Catholics, unmarried, between 18 and 25 years of age, and they must also be good-looking. Officially they are supposed to be over 1.74 meters tall, but nowadays this regulation is not enforced too strictly. Their pay is not very high—the equivalent of just over 1,000 U.S. dollars per month, paid in Swiss francs—but they are given full board and lodging.

The Vatican Museums are comprised of the papal apartments of the medieval Apostolic Palace decorated with frescoes during the Renaissance, the Sistine Chapel, the exhibition rooms of the Vatican Apostolic Library, and the museums themselves. The decoration of the palace and of the adjacent Sistine Chapel constitutes a unique ensemble of the pictorial art of the Renaissance.

The Cult of Saints and Madonnas

In Italy, both the cult of the saints and the cult of Mary remain more popular than the cult of Jesus Christ. In part, this is the result of a sustained belief that the saints and the Madonna are more accessible and receptive to human needs. Italians relate only marginally to Jesus Christ. With the exception of Christ child adoration (which also features the grieving Madonna), Jesus is generally seen as too abstract a figure to correlate with everyday existence. Michelangelo, with his Pietà, focusing on the grieving mother, reinforces this popular belief.

An extraordinary number of religious rituals revolve around the Madonna, especially in southern Italy, where she is one of the principal religious forces in the life of the people. Southern Italy's strong attachment to the Madonna is related by and large to the matriarchal character of its peasant society. Historically, and to this day, southern Italian mothers have played focal familial and social roles; popular veneration of the mother of Christ is a natural phenomenon there. In the eyes of many, Mary is the strongest advocate for petitioners, for she alone can plead their cases directly to her son, the God-made-man Christ. She is called upon for her capacities to grant favors and perform miracles. Of course, there is only one mother of Christ, but for Italians, the Madonna has many identities and titles, which differ based on her numerous abilities and her special relations with people in various locales. Hence, distinctive devotions call upon her specific titles and attributes.

The popular religiosity of many saints, which includes allegiance to saints of particular regions, is another characteristic of Italian Catholicism. Saints are models of a perfect life to be emulated, and because of their ideal life they enjoy a special relation with Jesus and God and therefore may act as intermediaries for those who ask for help and spiritual guidance.

Probably the best known of southern Italian saint-related traditions are the feast days, on which people come together for a shared celebration and commemoration of their village or city patron. On the feast day, a saint or the Madonna is honored through all manners of rituals, as family, friends, and *paesani* skip everyday activities to demonstrate their individual and group devotion. Though it is a religious event, the essence of the *festa* is its merging of the sacred and the secular ("religious" and "civil") programs of activities. Among the activities are a procession in honor of the saint, the carrying of lighted candles as a sign of devotion, and the recitation of prayers. Even the Italian men, whose socialization fosters resistance to more formalized aspects of Catholicism, are happy to immerse themselves in feast activities and express devotion to a saint in the process. Year after year, at various intervals during the year, the *feste* serve as a periodic divergence from the monotonous routine imposed by work and as a mechanism to reconnect people, collectively, to the Church and their faith.

The 60s Bring a New View and Rapport with Religion

The old religious world largely vanished in the course of two decades or so.

The drastic population shifts from the land to the cities and from the south to the north destroyed the centuries-old social order. The secularization of society was one of the most dramatic effects of the process of urbanization and industrial development. Migration, especially, had such a profound impact because there was a marked difference between northern and southern religiosity. Southern migrants missed the local customs, patron saints, and feasts of their village churches and could not reconcile themselves to the somewhat barren and arid life of the northern churches. Some northerners denounced the southerners for living their religion in a superficial way, more as magic and bigotry than in a truly Christian manner.[4] Moreover, as the growth of the welfare state made state and local authorities more responsible for social services, which for years had been the prerogative of the Church, the social functions of the Church contracted remarkably. Not less important, the American model of a consumer society unquestionably helped to erode Catholic values. Political parties, clubs, social circles, and sporting associations could provide outlets for a host of activities that were once primarily centered around the Church.

How extensive and how fast was the secularization process? In 1956, 69% of the population attended mass regularly; 20 years later the figure had declined to 37%, and by 1985 it had fallen to 27%. In a 1974 poll, 59% of those questioned characterized themselves as "indifferent" to the Church's calls and 11% in "opposition" to it. Only about 30% described themselves as practicing Catholics. Another indicator was the number of couples who had only civil, as opposed to religious, marriage ceremonies. Before 1970 there were very few of them; by 1980 the figure had reached 10% and in Rome 25%. The number of abortions soared during this period as well. A 1980 survey by the Diocese of Rome on sexual morals, abortion, and divorce showed that even among practicing Catholics, 60% approved of divorce, 47% of abortion, and 52% of birth-control methods. More surprising were the results of a poll conducted in 1984 by the Regional Episcopal Council of Piedmont. It showed that only 9% of the Catholics in the region attended Mass every Sunday, with another 21% going to church at most once a month. Although 89% had a religious wedding and 92% had their children baptized, only 12% shared the views of the Church on sexual morals and a mere 6% opposed abortion. In step with the times, in 1970 the constitutional court annulled a law making adultery a crime and several months later canceled the prohibition against contraception and the dissemination of birth control information.

The process of secularization is also evident in the rapid decrease in the number of clergy. Between 1961 and 1981, while the population increased by about 2%, the number of priests declined from 43,000 to 40,600. In 1961, 601 persons took holy orders; in 1980, the number was down to 347. Not only has it become increasingly more difficult to recruit new priests, but the diocesan clergy has become an aging body ever less able to cope with a growing and changing population. Today the priest is no longer the center of the community as he once had been; in a society in which roles are more diverse, he can easily be lonely and isolated.

Nuns constitute more than three-quarters of the ordained or consecrated Church personnel. From a total of about 155,000 nuns in 1971, the figure had declined to 26,000 in 1991; meanwhile, the male clergy had fallen to 25,000 in 1991. In the south and on the islands, there is one nun for every 300 women over the age of 20; in the center-north the ratio is one for every 150. Two-thirds of the nuns in the center-north are engaged in hospital work, teaching, and social assistance. To fill the vacuum being created by the fall in number, some religious orders are recruiting novice nuns in Africa and Asia.

In the face of these deep social and ecclesiastical changes, Catholic bishops have shifted their attention to pastoral matters, in particular religious renewal at the diocesan and parish levels.

A Self-Made Religion

Although the Italians have hardly given up their Catholic identity, most live a subjective religion which in many cases is far away from Church doctrine. However, the subjective nature of their religion cannot be seen as a rejection of Church belief.

The most startling indication of the changes in religious belief is the public's stand on abortion. In 1978, Parliament enacted a liberal abortion law. Despite a Catholic campaign against it, abortion became widespread. It is calculated that in the 1980s the abortion rate was 800 for every 1,000 live births. When the pope and the *DC* forced a popular referendum on the issue, in May 1981, merely 30% voted to repeal the liberal abortion law. To the surprise of everyone, women in the conservative south voted to retain abortion by roughly the same proportion as those in the north. In the 80s it became clear that religion had become more homogenized geographically and socially and that Italians had taken more liberty in molding their "own" religion, accepting from the Church what they saw fit in their new prosperous and materialistic life:

> » In a 2004 poll, just 32 percent of Italians surveyed said it was right for religion to have an influence on the laws of the state. Yet crucifixes hang in public schools, and most Italians accept their presence.

» Abortion is legal in Italy and is not much debated anymore. Yet, religious sentiment runs deep. One study, in fact, showed that 27 % of all protagonists on public television are priests, nuns, or saints (though it is also hard to ignore that other large percentage on Italian television, of near-naked women).

All this might sound like fertile ground for a war of culture and values similar to the one raging in America, but in Italy, the European nation where religion and state have mingled most, the disagreements are somehow less bitter and absolute than in the United States. It is not that the debate over religion's influence in political life has ended, nor that Italy is exempt from a counterpoint argued angrily these days in Europe: whether the Continent has actually become so secular that it is now outright hostile to religion.

However, it may be accurate to say that, in a nation with a Christian heritage stretching back to the Emperor Constantine's conversion early in the fourth century, the debate over Church and state has not stopped for 1,700 years. Those years seem to have lent enough time and hard experience for Church and state to settle into an almost indistinct whole, where the very real secularization in Italy in the last few decades is balanced by its history, culture, architecture, and, even though church attendance has declined significantly, faith. Paul Ginsborg, a prominent historian, described the overall atmosphere, in Italian, as *"la religione diffusa,"* the religion of everyone or, in his loose translation, "It's in the air."

A preliminary explanation of the self-made religion spreading in Italy in the last decades can be found in the "post-monopolistic" religious market, which continues to be dominated by the influence of the Church in society. Although many people have an outlook on life that is in contrast with the teaching of the Roman Catholic Church, they maintain their Catholic identity, though they integrate it with new elements. Why this free-spirit attitude when dealing with religion? The interest in differentiating between religious beliefs and acts derives from the implicit risk that what religions promise for the afterlife is not 100% certain. It seems that by adapting a "self-made religion" in dealing with the "rules" of the Church, Italian Catholics are able to harmonize the theoretical perspective of religion as a meaningful and rational strategy with needs of modern life. It is clear that "self-made religion" is a remedy for the crisis caused by modernity in relation to religious discourse.

Panoramic view of Rome.. From the archive of the author.

Two main aspects of this crisis can be identified:

» The first is the more open attitude toward other religions, which are very popular in Italy. To many it seems today that Catholicism is just one possible way of explaining the supernatural. Empirical research reveals, for instance, that for most Italians different religions are equally useful to obtain eternal life. This new tendency not only is not a deviation from the Roman Catholic Church; it also represents an effort to harmonize one's own religious beliefs with the new conditions of globalization.

» The second point concerns the crisis of the traditional supernatural representations of the body, health, and sexuality. The secularization of society has caused traditional religions to give up their direct influence on many aspects of everyday life, and various sciences such as medicine and psychology have substituted for religion. For instance, the Church no longer interferes with Catholics' sexual life, as it did in the past. The public discourse on sexuality is now under the authority of the secular experts such as doctors and psychologists and dispersed by mass media.

In Italy many people manifest a growing trust in a Church that espouses traditional moral values. However, many in this same group do not accept that the Church has the authority to interfere with their personal choices, mainly those having to do with sexual issues. The position of the Church on sexual issues contrasts with the leading values of Italian society, according to which every person should be free to make his or her own decisions. As a result of this loss of credibility of official Church discourse, many people prefer to modify Church doctrine individually, rather than accept the demoralizing condition of the sinner.[5] Consequently, previously condemned behavior becomes acceptable within a new ethics in which traditional values, such as the authority of the Church, are reconciled with the contemporary belief in the priority of individual choice. In this new setting, the Church preserves its role as rule-maker, but it is the individual who has the ultimate power to make decisions. These re-interpretations of the role of the Church aim to solve the contradiction between the subjectivity that characterizes modern religiosity and the interest of individuals to preserve cultural and religious inheritances. On the one hand, believers maintain their feeling of belonging to an institution that is strong and offers a contrast to the moral relativism of contemporary society. On the other hand, believers do not give up their subjective way of living the faith. For many Italians there is no contradiction in such behavior.[6]

Such Catholicism, determined by a "practical logic" (as illustrated by Pierre Bourdieu), creates an individual religion that always acts in compliance with one's specific needs, although one may not take a public stand against the Church. Therefore, this behavior should be considered an effort to adjust the Catholic religious code and make it function better, but it should not be considered an indication of a lack of interest in the religion. It is clear that Catholics deviate from Church doctrine but generally are not attracted by alternative beliefs. If they do approach alternative ways of believing, they tend to adjust them according to the traditional Catholic code. This kind of assessment clearly reveals the diminishing influence of the Catholic Church on Italian society. However, the end of its domination does not mean that religion does not have a role in the culture and structure of society.

Catholic culture is still very much alive today. However, when we pass into the realm of practicing faith, for the most part, religion is no longer a matter of social convention but of real conviction, and so it is now more sincere. A young person's faith is no longer so "protected" by the environment of family and parish. It has to pass through the ordeal of contact with atheism, and if it survives, it may be more real than in the old days. While social action continues, if less widely than in the 1960s, simultaneously those who practice their faith are now turning back to the true spiritual sources of Christianity, to the fundamentals of prayer and worship. In some cases this is due to a feeling that social action for its own sake had gone too far and that Christ was in danger of being forgotten. It may also be caused by the fact that in this new anxious age people feel a greater need for spiritual consolation. At any rate, the trend is widespread. Again, it does not take the form of a return to traditional church services. Like some other countries, Italy has seen the rise of the so-called charismatic movement, whereby informal groups meet regularly for prayer and discussion, often in private homes. It is all vaguely revivalist, very different from old-style Catholic worship. Often no priest is present. Prayers are spontaneous and expressed in everyday language, a complete break with the ritual rosary-type prayers of Catholic tradition.

Therefore, a number of religious communities have also arisen, often formed by laymen who find the traditional parish context inadequate. These are not enclosed and tightly disciplined centers like the old monasteries, but informal meeting places where laymen can come together in their leisure time, maybe under the guidance of a priest or maybe not. These groups represent a new desire of laity and priests alike for more self-expression, for finding their own ways to God and to Christ.

The Church hierarchy in Italy has reacted warily to the new trends. On social issues the Church projects, sincerely, a liberal image. At the same time, it is now outwardly adopting a much tougher line on access to abortion, birth control, pre-marital sex, and divorce. Its problem is that its doctrines are no longer in tune with the actual behavior of the majority of Catholics. The Church may preach against birth control, yet most younger Catholics practice it and do not find it inconsistent with their Christian faith. Again, this difference may not signify any waning of real Christian belief, but it does have serious implications for the relationship between the Church hierarchy and the laity.

Evolution of the Church

In the face of radical social and cultural changes, the Church could not remain entrenched in its old rigid dogmatic positions. It had to evolve with society if it wanted to remain a valid voice on moral, ethical, and religious issues. That evolution is clearly evident as society changes.

Church Strategies and Changes During the Cold War

Twice in the postwar period, the Church developed new strategies in the face of major social changes. The first time, it defined true Catholicism in terms of obedience to the political directives of the clergy; the second time, it modernized its liturgy and priorities in relation to the secular forces within Italian society. However, neither shift prevented the loss of parishioners nor the loss of the Church's status as the state religion. At the end of the 1940s, the hierarchy of the Church identified itself closely with the upper-bourgeois ruling class and protected its interests by defending the social status quo. In rural areas, priest and gentry were natural allies. Although the Church was anti-temporal, it did meddle in politics. Priests took an oath to devote their lives to the re-Christianization of the working class. Many Catholics, especially younger ones, felt that it was time for the Church to broaden its role and to share in building a better world, and with ardent faith they set about this task. Strong faith, they claimed, was necessary to defend belief from the possible influence of satanic political doctrines (such as communism).

The Cold War had a profound impact on Italian Catholicism and Church relations with its faithful and redefined the characteristics of Catholic identity. The 1948 election was fought not just for control over the state but also to determine the position Italy was to occupy within the emerging world order. The Church committed itself totally to this political contest, and its organizational and ideological support was crucial to the victory of the Christian Democratic party (*DC*). The battle was fought using all the media: sermons, rallies, radio, cinema, newspapers, and, most strikingly, wall posters. The iconographic tradition representing good (the Archangel Michael and other figures of strength and purity) and evil (the Angel of Death, masked devils, demons, and monsters) had a center stage. In this ideological battle even the concept of family became a means. The Church was the creator and defender of the family, recognizing its unique and sovereign status, whereas under communism the moral and sacred ties of family life were destroyed; people's loyalty and allegiance were to the state; divorce and free love were encouraged. In representing the Cold War as part of the eternal struggle between good and evil, the Church was conducting a struggle for the soul of Italy which had to be defended from the barbarian hordes: Catholicism was a central component of Italian identity, communism was an external threat.

This evolution of Italian Catholicism had its own dynamic. Communism could be fought by creating a society consistent with Catholic doctrine, and to achieve that the Vatican, the hierarchy, and the laymen's organizations had to work together to mold Catholics into a political bloc and to tie that bloc to the *DC* as a necessary alternative to the dreaded Communist Party. At election time, the Church, from pope down to the parish priest, stated that it was a religious duty to vote for the *DC*. The *DC* was greatly helped by Catholic Action, or *Azione Cattolica (AC)*, an organization based on the parish and not on the party. It was open to members of both sexes, but women always prevailed: in 1946, *AC* had 151,000 men and 370,000 women; by 1969 it had 183,000 men and 459,000 women. Church and *AC* provided the strongest basis for women in the *DC*.

If one looks closely at any of the grass-roots movements of postwar social reform, in nearly every case one will find that some nucleus of Catholic militants played an important role. The new militant social Christian action took many forms but always with the purpose "to build the Kingdom of God on earth," something the Church, it was claimed, never used to care much about. The Church had also developed a political ideology known as the social doctrine, a fairly vague set of principles that could be used for social and political activity and that could be constantly reinterpreted by the Church. Its central idea was class reconciliation.

Pope John XXIII

Pope John XXIII was seventy-seven years old when he was elected to lead the Catholic Church in 1958. Although Vatican watchers expected a short reign and few changes during his papacy, Pope John XXIII radically changed the direction of the Catholic Church. This pope came from a different social mold. The fourth in a family of 14, his family worked as sharecroppers, a striking contrast to his predecessor, Pope Pius XII, who came from an ancient aristocratic family, long connected to the papacy. Pope John XXIII's personal warmth, good humor, and kindness captured the world's affections in a way his predecessor, for all his great learning and personal holiness, had failed to do.

Pope John XIII stressed his own pastoral duties as well as those of other bishops and the lesser clergy; he was active in promoting social reforms for workers, the poor, orphans, and the outcast; and he advanced cooperation with other religions: among his innumerable visitors were many Protestant leaders, the head of the Greek Orthodox Church, the archbishop of Canterbury, and a Shinto high priest. In 1958, in the first official acts of a pope away from Vatican territory since 1870, he visited children suffering from polio at the Bambino Gesù hospital and then visited Santo Spirito Hospital. The next day he visited Rome's Regina Coeli prison, where he told the prisoners: "You could not come to me, so I came to you." These acts, which reflected a new openness in the Church, created a sensation. His 1961 encyclical *Mater et Magistra* was a vigorous document, advocating social reform, assistance to underdeveloped countries, a living wage, and support for all socialist measures that promised real benefit to society.

Pope John XXIII changed the hierarchy of the Church. He almost doubled the number of cardinals, making the College of Cardinals the largest in history to that point. In January 1959, he quietly announced his intention to call an ecumenical council to consider measures for renewal of the Church in the modern world, promotion of diversity within the encasing unity of the Church, and the reforms that had been intently promoted by the ecumenical movement and the liturgical movement. The convening of the council in October 1962 was the high point of his reign. From the Second Vatican Council (colloquially known as Vatican II) came changes that reshaped the face of Catholicism: a comprehensively revised liturgy, a stronger emphasis on ecumenism, and a new approach to the world.

John XXIII's pontificate, which lasted less than five years, presented him to the entire world as an authentic image of the Good Shepherd. Meek and gentle, enterprising and courageous, simple and active, he carried out the Christian duties of the corporal and spiritual works of forgiveness: visiting the imprisoned and the sick, welcoming those of every nation and faith, bestowing on all his exquisite fatherly care.

In 1962, Pope John XXIII was named *Time Magazine's* Man of the Year.

His heartiness, his overflowing love for humanity individually and collectively, and his freshness of approach to ecclesiastical affairs made "Good Pope John"—as he was called—one of the best-loved popes of modern times.

Italian society was further polarized when on July 13, 1949, Pope Pius XII issued a decree that prohibited Catholics from joining the Italian Communist Party (*PCI*), and from writing, reading, publishing, or distributing any communist literature. Those engaging in any of these activities could be excommunicated and would not receive any of the sacraments. Two weeks later the Vatican explained that excommunication would apply not only to those who joined or supported the Communist Party but also to any of its associated organizations or allies, including the trade union *CGIL* and the Socialist Party. The actions of the Church legitimated a policy of excluding the Left from positions in the state, and, in the hands of the local civic committees, were designed to marginalize non-Catholics in all spheres of public life. This was an alienating message for many Italians who had been hoping for big social changes through political changes. Most of them were neither atheists nor devotees of free love. They had married in Church, baptized their children, placed a high value on family life, and participated in many of the same devotional practices as other Italians. Yet now they were being defined as not true Catholics and were being asked to choose between Church and party.

All this had a deep impact on Italian society. By injecting itself into every aspect of civil life and dividing the political world into saints and devils, the Church reinforced the country's historic problem of social division. As La Palombara commented in his book, by separating "loyal Catholics" from other Italians, the Church's massive political intervention had the same effect after 1945 as immediately after Unification.[7] Some broke with the Church and no longer recognized its authority in any domain of life. A larger number recognized it only in a restricted domain of religion and personal morality, separate from the social and cultural domains. Pius XII's action did not stop the growth of the Left over the next 40 years, nor did it prevent the rapprochement between the *DC* and the *PSI* in the 1960s. Indeed, the conservative position of the Church up to the end of the 1950s had no positive results either on the spiritual or the political level.

New Pope Brings New Direction in the Church

The election in 1958 of Angelo Roncalli as Pope John XXIII signaled the desire of the Church to move with the times *(See Box on p. 284)*. The new pope had an acute sense of how fast the world was changing and how important it was for the Church to understand and adapt to this change. In his brief papacy he dedicated himself to an *aggiornamento*, a modernization of the Church.

The process, begun in the early 1960s, had as a most significant development the gradual transformation of the Church from a Eurocentric body, in which Italy was the leading country, to an international body whose center of interests spread throughout Europe and to the Third World, particularly Latin America. In 1958, the College of Cardinals had 55 members, of whom 18 were Italian, and Europe had the highest number of baptized Catholics in the world. After the mid-1960s, the size of the body was expanded and the number of Italians in it declined through attrition. By 1971 there were 120 cardinals, of whom only 28 were Italian. For the first time the Italians were not a majority in the Church hierarchy.

At the same time, Pope Paul VI (in office 1963–1978) had reduced the importance of the Italian hierarchy in other ways. In the second half of the 1960s, the Italian dioceses were consolidated and the number of bishops reduced from 315 to 270, still a disproportionate number when compared to France's 88 and Spain's 65. This change was accompanied by an effort to place some distance between the Vatican and the Italian ecclesiastic hierarchy. With the pope as primate of Italy and the curia essentially Italian, the Vatican and the Italian Church had always been interconnected. In 1966, for the first time in Vatican and Italian history and about one hundred years after similar bodies had been established in other countries, an independent conference of bishops, the *Conferenza Episcopale Italiana (CEI)*, was established. When John Paul II was elected in October 1978, the College of Cardinals had doubled in number (110), with 56 non-European cardinals, 44 of whom came from the Third World, and Latin America had the highest percentage of Catholics (40%). Therefore, the election in 1978 to pope of Karol Wojtyla, archbishop of Krakow, the first non-Italian to ascend to the throne of Saint Peter since 1522, although somewhat dramatic, was not unexpected. The election of a Pole to pope also implied that the Church was going to play a much less important role in Italian affairs than in the past and that the time was approaching for a renegotiation of the relations between state and Church. The election of Joseph Cardinal Ratzinger from Germany to Pope Benedict XVI in April 2005 was not a surprise either.

Where Pius XII had tried to erect barriers, John XXIII sought to open doors. As a first step he designed a strategy to revise Church relations in three areas: (a) toward Eastern Europe; (b) toward non-Catholics, including Marxists; and (c) toward capitalism.

Certainly, the political changes in Eastern Europe were just as important. Historians will eventually assess the kind of direct and indirect role or influence the Church might have played in the fall of communism in Eastern Europe at the end of the 1980s. The process of detente with Eastern Europe was initiated with a series of symbolic acts. Pope John's meeting with Khrushchev's daughter and son-in-law, in March 1963, was symptomatic of that new mood.

While the pope himself began to look at the larger world picture, Italian political affairs were being delegated to the Italian bishops. As a consequence of this change, the Church intervened more, not less, in Italian politics. In May 1960, in a leading article in the *Osservatore Romano,* the official Vatican daily, the Church hierarchy attempted to establish its supremacy in Italian affairs by making some "basic points":

» The Church must guide the faithful in both ideas and practice;
» The Church cannot be politically neutral;
» The Church must be the judge of whether political cooperation between the faithful and the nonbelievers was permissible;
» The Church cannot allow believers to cooperate with Marxists.

Meanwhile, however, the pope was making some very radical pronouncements. In the encyclical letter *Mater et Magistra (Mother and Teacher,* 1961), he began to question the support given by the Church to capitalism. Concentrating on the social teachings of the Church, he rejected the free play of market forces, emphasized the need for greater social justice, and called for the integration of the disinherited into the social and political order. This position coincided not only with the debate on the modernization of the Italian economy but also with the debate on the constitution of a center-Left government of the *DC* in alliance with the *PSI.*

The 1963 encyclical *Pacem in Terris (Peace on Earth)* called for international conciliation based on the neutrality of the Church and its refusal to accept the barriers of the Cold War. The encyclical was addressed to "all men of good will," not just to Catholics, and argued the need for cooperation between people of different ideological beliefs. In addition, the encyclical stressed the need for the betterment of the economic and social development of the working classes, the entry of women into public life, and the justice of anti-colonialist struggles in the Third World. The possibility for a dialogue between the Catholic and Marxist worlds had been opened. The repercussions in Italy of *Peace on Earth* were very strong, for in practice the pope had given his blessing to the new coalition.

The changes in the Church were also underlined by the papal decision to convene an ecumenical council (the twenty-first in the history of the Church and the first since 1870). The Council, known as Vatican II, was called to modernize the Church as an organization, develop better relations with other religions, and face the problems of modern society. In political terms, it was seen as an "opening to the Left": the campaign against communists was lifted while support for the *DC* continued.

Vatican II opened in October 1962 and closed under Paul VI in December 1965. It represented a renewal of the Church, an attempt to respond to the forces that were changing society and to reconsider the position of the Church in an evolving international context. As a result of the Council, the position of the bishops was considerably strengthened by instituting synods of bishops to be elected by national churches. The distinctive contribution that the laity could make to the Church was recognized and encouraged. But the most striking changes came in practice and emphasis: the introduction of the vernacular, instead of Latin, into the celebration of the sacraments. For the first time during the Mass, the priest was speaking the same language as the laity, and this together with other changes in the ritual reduced the distance between the two. The use of deacons from the laity to read the lessons, the addition of choral singing, the offer of wine as well as the wafer to communicants, all these increased the level of participation by the faithful in the service.

Bringing the Church Closer to Christ

Vatican II, besides reducing the distance between laity and clergy, also changed the prevalent conception of God as a remote figure. Emphasis shifted from God the judging Father to God the loving Son who makes himself available to believers through the sacraments and can be approached through prayer and good deeds. This also involved a reminder of Christ's commandment to love one another and a reaffirmation of Church belief that a Christian life is lived not just through private acts of devotion and the sacraments, but in acts of love, charity, and fellowship with other human beings.[8] These shifts of emphasis to the teachings of Jesus Christ and his sacrifice, which are at the core of religious life, have been called Christocentric. The external cults that focused on the power of the mediating figures, Mary and the saints, were devalued. Local clergy also began to withdraw their support from many popular forms of celebration, including the procession with a saint's statue or other religious images, which often included a great deal of locally generated ritual and symbolism.[9] Church leaders were concerned

A *Carnevale* float in Viareggio. From the archive of the author.

that parishioners were participating in the events more out of social convention and tradition than for their spiritual significance. Nevertheless, these kinds of celebrations lost much of their significance for people who migrated because the village that provided a bond, and a stable community did not exist anymore. Therefore, forms of Catholicism that had permeated and shaped many social identities and that had operated through ritual acts and symbolic forms, lost their resonance and were replaced by a view of religion that was concerned essentially with the spiritual aspect. There was a general shift away from traditions, which were embedded in particular social contexts whose existence was normally unquestioned, to a more universalistic ethos based on individual conscience. These kinds of changes in religious practice also found better reception with middle-class values.

Paul VI continued the policy of detente with the East and vigorously pursued a policy of dialogue with the Third World. As the Vatican became more international in body, it also became less of a Christian Democrat support system. The important encyclical *Populorum Progressio* (*Progress of the People*) (March 26, 1967) stated that Christian principles were incompatible with a political system that put at the base of everything the pursuit of private profit and competition and the absolute right to private property. The encyclical also asserted that, even though revolutionary insurrections can be evil, they may be necessary in exceptional circumstances, such as in the struggle against a permanent and cruel form of despotism.[10] In the *Octogesima Adveniens* (May 14, 1971), Paul VI asserted in stronger terms his belief that no social system could be derived from the "social doctrine" of the Church. If there was no "Christian political thought," then it followed that there could be no "Christian political party." This meant that Catholics could be active in all political parties.[11]

Seeking to Be an Autonomous Voice in Political Matters

The implications for the Italian political scene were obvious. After 1968 some clergy had already started to assume political aims; they felt that Christianity needed to be liberated from the Church, which they regarded as a tool of the bourgeoisie. Social issues became their main focus. "Priests don't talk about God any more, they talk about the housing crisis," was an often-heard complaint of many older Catholics.

The autonomous role of the Church in political affairs was parallel to the autonomy declared by the lay Catholic organizations. Organizations such as the Association of Italian Christian Workers *(ACLI)* and Catholic Action *(AC)* officially cut their political affiliation with the *DC* When the *DC* sought to abolish the divorce law through a popular referendum, expecting the Vatican's support, the Vatican delegated to the Italian bishops the anti-divorce campaign. The attitude of the Vatican could not but encourage Catholic dissent in Italy. The youth branches of *ACLI* came out in favor of divorce; *ACLI* itself refused to take a position and so did a number of leading bishops and some important cardinals. Many Catholic intellectuals fought openly on the side of the divorce parties, and during the campaign loosened their ties with the *DC*. For some of them the difference created such an emotional and ideological split that in the next political campaign they ran and were elected to parliament as candidates on the Communist Party (PCI) or Socialist Party (PSI) lists. In the referendum held on May 12, 1974, the opponents of divorce were able to muster only 41% of the vote.

The *DC* had come to rely on the formidable organization of the Church and, through it, had established a presence in virtually all sectors of society, but by 1975–1976 the *DC* had lost its monopoly over Catholic representation. The Church and the DC, the two institutions that dominated postwar Italian society, had lost their power; a decisive majority of Italians had stated implicitly that religious doctrine was not to be the basis of the country's laws or social life. The 1970s were, in fact, a traumatic period for Catholics in Italy and the world. As a result of the cultural crisis of the 1960s, the end of the economic miracle, the workers' unrest, the growth of political dissent, the students' movement, the birth of feminism, and the changes within the Church itself, young Catholics became attracted by new forms of internationalism and, particularly, by the new theology, or liberation theology, coming from Latin America, as well as by new anti-authoritarian forms of organization. At the base of these radical forces there was both an anti-establishment attitude and an inner desire to improve the world. Many of the groups were community based and active in helping those who were at the fringes of society, like the handicapped or drug addicts; others assumed more of an international posture and campaigned for world peace, antinuclear policies, and economic assistance to the Third World.

The largest renewal movement in contemporary Italy is *Comunione e Liberazione,* founded in 1969 in Milan. This organization of devout laity has spiritual leadership from powerful sections of the hierarchy. It emerged first on the political scene as a radical force, bringing news of the liberation struggles of Catholic poor farmers in Latin America and denouncing the corruption and loss of spiritual purpose in the Italian political establishment. At the grass-roots level, Communion and Liberation is strongest in the north and in the cities, and especially in the universities, where it has eclipsed the Left as the major political force. For young students leaving their homes in rural areas and villages, Communion and Liberation offers a network of assistance and welcomes recruits into wholesome social activities, parties, outings, and music, and all are pervaded by an active Christian evangelism.

Another Catholic lay organization that assumed an important active secular and political role is the *Movimento Popolare* (Popular Movement), founded in 1976, which represents a more militantly political Catholic element that is ready to oppose the Left, take part in demonstrations, and heckle at communist meetings. With the intent to work at the sociopolitical level, the members of the Popular Movement have worked to take control of student assemblies in schools and universities and have created hundreds of cultural centers. Although fervent Christians, they are an independent community.

The Conservative Voice of Pope John Paul II

Ambiguity, conciliation, and passivity were not the traits highly prized by the Polish John Paul II, and in the course of the 1980s a change of style and direction in the papacy became increasingly evident. From the start, the hallmark of his office was the affirmation of a monolithic, authoritarian, and aggressive church. Appalled by Western secular and materialistic values, he pursued a mission of promoting traditional—and conservatively interpreted—social and ecclesiastical values.

The pope was very critical of the Italians' religious practice: a secularized society afflicted by a "de-Christianization" of mentality and morals caused by a "practical materialism" that was abetted by atheistic ideologies. The substance and manner of John Paul's approach contrasted starkly with the conciliatory stance of the majority of the hierarchy. For the first time in modern history there were substantial differences between a pope and most Italian bishops, and it wasn't just that they did not speak the same language! The central disagreement was over the Church's political and social engagement. It is very important to make clear the difference between the Vatican as the center of the world organization and as the Italian Church. In the past, this distinction hardly seemed to exist. Although the ultimate head of the Italian Church is the pope, it is the cardinal who presides over the Italian Episcopal Council and who has the day-to-day responsibility of running the Italian Church. The new system, almost fifty years old, originated with John XXIII and gives the Italian Church its own identity, similar to the French, Spanish, German, American, or any other national Church.

The Church remains a strong presence in Italian political life, with its approximately 28,000 parishes performing about 160,000 Sunday services that are attended by several million people. Its cultural apparatus is responsible for producing several hundred books every year, as well as a daily paper, *Osservatore romano,* over 50 weeklies (one of these, *Famiglia cristiana,* is still the largest circulation weekly in Italy), well over 200 monthlies, and several hundreds of parish bulletins.

A *New Modus Vivendi*: Pluralism and Cohesion

Practicing Catholics are now a minority of only 27% in Italy. In today's increasingly urban society, the struggle is between faith and apathy. There is a lack of interest in religious problems and there is a kind of independence from the Church's teaching. The weakening of the traditional faith is partially the consequence of a cultural crisis, the result of the shattering of many successive illusions in the last two hundred years, from the eighteenth-century faith in Reason, to that in Progress, Nationalism, and Development. And the fall of Marxism, for many, was the fall of yet another god.

However, among those who do practice their religion, there has been a reexamining and sharpening of faith, and a major shift of emphasis away from old-style pious liturgy and toward social action and private prayer. Moreover, although most Italians do not go to church on a regular basis and regard Church laws as any other laws, which means, therefore, they can be broken (contraception, divorce, abortion), it must be stressed that their spiritual adherence to Christian teaching is still very strong. They have an almost innate sense of what is right or wrong and a capacity to view everyone as people with individual souls, to feel that there may, perhaps, be a purpose in this life because it leads to another one. The Church has helped to give Italians much of their humanity, their balance between spontaneity and restraint. In every village, the Church and its bell tower *(campanile),* dominate the town square, looking down from above like a guard guaranteeing order and calm. In fact, the Italian word *companilismo* means local patriotism, love of one's village. In times of joy, it functions as a place of welcome, crowded with celebrants of christenings and weddings; in time of sorrow, it is like a black hearse, followed by weeping relatives to the tolling of a bell.

The Church's worldly role today is mainly helping those in trouble. Not merely providing handouts for the poor, or sustenance to immigrants, the Italian Church and Italian Catholics are involved in many projects to assist the needy and those living on the fringe of society, such as drug addicts and homosexuals. The Church still staffs hospitals, schools, old people's homes, mental asylums, and homes for the handicapped. The *ACLI* still runs universities and trade unions, while the *Movimento Popolare* finds work for its members and runs centers selling food at a discount to poorer people. The Church involvement in Italian society still stirs an active conscience both in the individual and in society.

Notes

1. The various cults of the South, from the *tarantismo* (dance of the spider) that is analyzed by the famous Italian ethnologist Ernesto De Martino to the "festivals of the poor" described by Annabella Rossi, were different expressions of an autonomous culture, separate from the structure and social doctrines of the Catholic Church. This was a world that offered the possibility of trance and release, of mass pilgrimages and miraculous cures. E. De Martino, *Sud e magia* (Milano: Mondadori, 1959), *La terra del rimorso* (Milano: Mondadori, 1961); and A. Rossi, *Le feste dei poveri* (Bari: Laterza, 1969).

2. Robert Putnam, *Making Democracy Work,* 107.

3. Antonio Gramsci, *Il materialismo storico e la filosofia di Benedetto* Croce (Turin: Einaudi, 1966 (1948)), 120.

4. Church-going plummeted, especially on the peripheries of the big cities where the new urban population was most concentrated. See A. Monelli and G. Pellicciari, "Comportamenti di voto e pratica religiosa," in Pellicciari, ed., *L'emigrazione nel triangolo industriale* (Milano: Mondadori, 1970), 334.

5. Very enlightening are the research of two important scholars in the field: Abbruzzese S. "*Secolarizzazione e consenso religioso,*" in: L. Diotallevi (a cura di), *Chiesa e società in Italia* (Milano: Cens., 1995), 167; I. Diamanti , "Il Dio relativo degli Italiani," *La Repubblica,* 22 giugno 2003.

6. Cesareo V., Cipriani R., Garelli F., Lanzetti C. e Rovati G., *La religiosità in Italia* (Milano: Mondadori, 1995), 261; and Hervieu-Léger D. *Religione e memoria* (Bologna: Mulino, 1996).

7. La Palombara, *Democracy Italian Style,* 60–65.

8. In view of these changes, some priests took a more radical view of their society and their role: worker-priests and organizers of community initiatives amongst the deprived.

9. Processions carrying statues of Christ, Mary, and patron saints to celebrate major events in the liturgical cycle remained an important part of Italian religious practice, especially in the south. The processions clearly reveal the relationships between the human and the divine, and at the same time establish various social identities.

10. For more on this encyclical see Lucio Lombardo Radice and Luigi Pestalozza, "Intervento sulla Populorum progressio," *Problemi del socialismo,* 9, no. 18, (May 1967): 78–92.

11. Gianni Baget-Bozzo, *Il partito cristiano e l'apertura a sinistra. La DC di Fanfani e Moro 1954–1962* (Florence: Vallechi, 1979), 128–29.

Bibliography

G. Baget-Bozzo, *Il partito cristiano e l'apertura a sinistra. La DC di Fanfani e Moro 1954–1962* (Florence: Vallechi, 1979)

A. J. Beckford, *Religione e società industriale avanzata* (Roma: Borla, 1991)

E. De Martino, *Sud e magia* (Milano: Mondadori, 1959).

V. Cesareo, R. Cipriani, F. Garelli, C. Lanzetti e G. Rovati , *La religiosità in Italia,* (Milano: Mondadori, 1995).

T. P. Di Napoli, *The Italian Jewish Experience* (Stony Brook, N.Y.: Forum Italicum Publishing, 2000).

L. Diotallevi, *Il rompicapo della secolarizzazione italiana,* Soneria Mannelli: Rubettino, 2001).

G. Filoramo, *Millenarismo e New Age* (Bari: Dedalo, 1999).

F. Garelli, G. Guizzardi, E. Pace (ed.), *Un singolare pluralismo. Indagine sul pluralismo morale e religioso degli italiani* (Bologna, Il Mulino, 2003),

L. Iannaccone, *Rationality and the Religious Mind* in "Economic Inquiry" (1998) 36, 3.

L. Iannaccone, *Rischio razionalità e portafogli religiosi* in "Inchiesta" (2002) n° 136.

C. Levi Strauss *Il pensiero selvaggio* (Milano: Il Saggiatore,1990).

P. Lucà Trombetta *Il bricolage religioso. Sincretismo e nuova religiosità,* (Bari: Dedalo, 2004).

E. Pace, *Credere nel relativo: persistenze e mutamenti nelle religioni contemporanee,* (Torino: UTET, 1997).

A. Rossi, *Le feste dei poveri* (Bari: Laterza, 1969).

J. Varacalli, S. Primeggia, S. LaGumina, D. D'Elia (ed.*), Models and Images of Catholicism in Italian Americana: Academy and Society* (Stony Brook, N.Y.: Forum Italicum P., 2005).

J. Varacalli, S. Primeggia, S. La Gumina, D. D'Elia (ed.), *The Saints in the Lives of Italian-Americans* (Stony Brook, N.Y.: Forum Italicum Publishing, 2003).

CHAPTER 11

FAMILY

Tradition and Change

Family Profile

Demographic situation: As of 31 December 2003, 57,888,215 people lived in Italy (28,068,608 males and 29,819,637 females), of which 26,100,554 (45%), lived in the north, 11,124,059 (19.2%) lived in the center, and 20,663,632 (35.7%) lived in the south.

The Italian population is getting older and is now the oldest in Europe. Today 18.9% of the Italian population is over 65 years of age. The number of young people under age 14 has also decreased and now accounts for approximately 13% of the population. The ratio between the population aged 65 and more and the population aged 0–14 reached 135.4% on January 1, 2004 (in other words, for every 100 young people aged 0–14, there are 135.4 old people in the territory).

Age structure: *0–14 years:* 13.9% (male 4,166,213/female 3,919,288) *15–64 years:* 66.7% (male 19,554,416/female 19,174,629) *65 years and over:* 19.4% (male 4,698,441/female 6,590,046) (2005 est.)

Median age: *overall:* 41.77 years *male:* 40.24 years *female:* 43.35 years (2005)

Population growth rate: 0.07% (2005)

Birth rate: 8.89 births/1,000 population (2005)

Death rate: 10.3 deaths/1,000 population (2005)

Net migration rate: 2.07 migrant(s)/1,000 population (2005)

Sex ratio: *at birth:* 1.07 male(s)/female *under 15 years:* 1.06 male(s)/female *15–64 years:* 1.02 male(s)/female *65 years and over:* 0.71 male(s)/female *total population:* 0.96 male(s)/female (2005)

Infant mortality rate: *total:* 5.94 deaths/1,000 live births; *male:* 6.55 deaths/1,000 live births; *female:* 5.29 deaths/1,000 live births (2005)

Total fertility rate: 1.28 children born/woman (2005)

Fertility rate: Italian women's fertility rates show a slight increase; 1.27 children per woman were registered in 2003, in comparison with 1.26 children per woman in year 2001 (Source: *Annuario Statistico Italiano* 2004, pp 31–33). As of the 31st of December 2003, 71.5% of the communes (5,792) had up to 5,000 inhabitants and 18.1% of the population lives in these communes.

On the other hand, 0.5% of the communes (43) have more than 100,000 inhabitants and 23.1% of the population lives in these communes. Altogether, the most relevant share of the population (almost 30%) lives in communes with 5,001 to 20,000 inhabitants; these communes are a little more than 22% of the Italian communes (Source: *Annuario ISTAT* 2004, pp. 39–40).

Family size: Italy has more families today than ever before, but the families are smaller.

While the number of families is rising (21,503,088 compared with 19,909,003 in 1991), their average size is falling: from 2.8 members in 1991 to 2.5 today. The biggest reduction has been in the north-east: at the end of World War II, the average family consisted of 4.2 members. The number of families with one member only is also on the increase: in 2000 there were 700,000 more singles than in 1995. This phenomenon is present in all the regions and is caused in part by the gradual aging of the population. Finally, Italy's birth rate is one of the lowest in the European Union: the number of births per 1,000 inhabitants is 10.6 in the EU, while in Italy the figure is 9.6.

Marriage: Italy has seen a collapse in marriage, a reduction of 23.5% in the last 25 years. Today there are 62 % more divorces than in 1982.

Abortion: Italy is in 3rd place, after France and the U.K., in abortion rates. On average, an abortion is performed every 30 seconds in Italy. As well, fewer babies are born out of wedlock; only 14.9% in Italy as opposed to 55.4% in Sweden, 45.4% in Denmark, 45.2% in France, and 42.7% in the U.K.

Life expectancy: Male: 76.08 years, Female: 83 years (2005 est.).

The number of people over the age of 65 is increasing and has come to represent 18.9% of the population, but this figure is likely to go up to 34.4% by 2050. Those over 80 account for 4.4% and, again by 2050, that figure will probably reach 14.2%. For every 100 children between the ages of 0 and 14, there are 130 old people. This percentage is the highest in Liguria (241) and the lowest in Campania (78).

Population density: The Italian territory, with the exclusion of the Republic of San Marino and Vatican City State, has an area of 301,328 square km with an average national population density of 192 inhabitants per square km. The population density varies much from one region to the other; it is due mainly to the many mountains and hills (76,83%) on the national territory.

Population mobility: Finally, it is worth mentioning that overall internal mobility in Italy (from the south to the north) has decreased from the 1960s onwards; however, starting from the beginning of the 1990s, the opposite trend has been registered, together with an increase in international mobility. (Source: *Annuario ISTAT 2006*).

Crisis of the Institution

Older Italians often complain that modern times have changed Italy's family structure and family values. The traditional picture of the Italian family as the place where people go for consolation, help, advice, provisions, loans, weapons, allies, and accomplices, remained unchanged for centuries. However, in modern times, as Italy has changed, the stability, effectiveness, and social values of both the extended and the nuclear families have changed as well. After Italy became a welfare state, in the 1970s, the family world described by Luigi Barzini as a closely knit community held together by emotional attachments and material interests, ever ready to form a common front against all outsiders and to take care of its own, could not avoid being affected by all the social changes.[1] No question: the family has consistently acted as the pillar of Italian society and the gauge to measure everything in that society. It has always been one of the most important metaphors in assessing Italy's moral, social, and economic situations. In Italy it is not the state or any social organization that provides examples or models for the family; it is the family that provides metaphors and role models for society and the state. In a nation whose other social institutions are notoriously brittle, the family has indeed long functioned as the sole unit that, rock-like, withstands all adversities.

That image accurately described, to a large degree, the Italian family until the early 1960s. Since then, economic, social, and cultural factors have affected the structure of the family and its role in society. There is, for example, a definite link between the socioeconomic characteristics of a region and the living arrangements found within that area. In fact, the changes are more profound going from the agricultural to the artisan and from the small-industrial to the industrial areas. In the urban areas, which are industrially dependent, it is more common to find permanent, relatively atypical family structures that are very similar to the pattern of the "modified extended family." Areas of small land ownership and micro-artisan and industrial enterprise display models of family organization based on the extended family. However, the traditional Italian family has usually been defined by the following characteristics:

> » extended and patriarchial;
> » unbreakable and relatively large;
> » largely determined by agrarian conditions;
> » structured vertically;
> » built on Catholic faith and values;
> » highly suspicious of the outside world.

In the early 1940s, when Italy was still predominantly a rural and small town nation, there certainly existed in many parts of the south and the islands those social structures that American anthropologist Edward Banfield found in Basilicata: nuclear families, the size of which were largely determined by agrarian conditions, by the strips of land on which the poor farmers had to make a living. In those years southern and central Italian families were large and usually multiple and vertical in structure, in the sense of having more than one married couple and more than two generations living under the same roof. Hierarchies within the families were clearly established (in the center more than the south). The male head of the household had sole control of the family's money and took all responsibility for relations between the family and the outside world. The senior female figure, usually his wife, also exercised considerable power within the domain of the household and over the other women of the family. Lack of

Marriages per 1000 inhabitants (1993–2003)

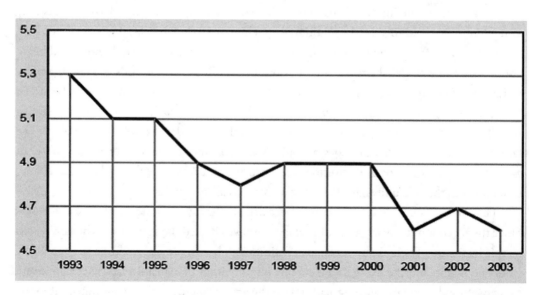

Source: ISTAT 2005

trust amongst the poor farmers, in addition to lack of associationism, fatalism, and despair were also prevalent.

It is important to notice the link that bound Italian families together through their inter-generational solidarity. Grandparents, parents, and children often lived close together and in daily contact one with the other. Grandparents remained closely involved in the care of grandchildren, and they in turn received considerable assistance and company, especially from the female members of the younger generations, in their old age. Today, that picture is a thing of the past.

The New Family Structure

The family has become both numerically restricted and chronologically protracted. It is "longer" and "thinner" in the sense of increased longevity and contact between the generations, accompanied by a decrease in the number of children and the complexity of the family structures; there is a decline in the number of marriages, an increase in illegitimate births, and a rise in the number of divorces and legal separations. Census figures also show that a sharp decrease in the "extended family" (consisting of a married couple with children and other relatives in the same household). There is an increase in households made up of only one person, of childless couples, of couples whose children have left the home, of couples living together without being married, of families with one parent, and of families that have been reconstructed, as by a second marriage after a divorce. While before World War II, thanks to high fertility and death rates, families had, on the average, large numbers of children and tended to be rather young, today, because of the low birth rate and increased longevity, families are older. Yet, in Italy this process of individualization has not, by and large, led to family ruptures, estrangements, or distances between parents and children. On the contrary: a process of negotiation, of mutual tolerance and appreciation has allowed children and parents to continue to live under the same roof.

The most radical changes have taken place in the last 35 years not only because of industrialization and more women entering the workforce but also because of the legalization of divorce and abortion. In 1970, the average number of children per woman was 2.42 (the same as the European average); 20 years later, in 1990, the average had gone down to 1.27, which is the lowest among the members of EU. The big change is the emergence of the "prolonged family," due to the fact that a very high percentage of adult children, mostly unemployed (and this is the main cause of the change), continue to live with their parents, even though they enjoy a high degree of independence and have developed their own network of social relations.

Changes in the family structure are uneven. In 1951, nuclear families, composed only of husband, wife, and children, formed 55.7% of the total number of Italian families; 20 years later they formed 54.1%; today that percentage has not changed much. In the same period, extended families declined more rapidly, from 22.5% to 16.9% of the total, with percentages for the south much higher. In the last 20 years, however, there has been a considerable increase in "non-family" households (of only one person); a steady increase, although more limited than the preceding one, in "married couple" households; a slight decrease in nuclear households; and a big decrease in extended households. From a general point of view, these figures confirm that the structure of the Italian family tends to be moving toward a prevalence of the conjugal or nuclear pattern. Because of industrialization and the mobility imposed on working individuals, the extended family has registered increasing numbers of breakups.

In 1971, households comprising five or more members were nearly twice that of one-person households. Between 1971 and 1981, one-person households increased by 5%. Households made up of six or more persons went down from 9.7% to 5.4% of all households. As might be expected, in the north one-person households are now twice as common as large households. In the last two decades, 1987–2007, there has been a considerable increase in the number of non-family households, a smaller increase in married couple households, a slight decrease in nuclear households, and a large loss of over 10 percentage points in extended households.

The main change since World War II is that the focus of loyalty has been steadily narrowing from what sociologists call the extended family to the nuclear family: from the big multi-generation clan to the immediate home cell of parents and children. The trend varies from social class to social class. In the property-less lower bourgeoisie, the nuclear family has long held more importance than the clan, but now even in rural areas the big patriarchal poor laborer families have been losing their influence as the young drift away to the town. In the upper bourgeoisie, as property gives way to income, as family managements disappear and sons disperse to new salaried careers in other parts of Italy, the tight network of the big family gathering has become less necessary for the individual's future and security and also less easy to maintain. Many younger couples are today likely to prefer pleasure traveling or a weekend cottage shared with a few close friends to the traditional big family reunions on Sundays and in the summer.

Although the structure of the Italian family has changed in the last two decades, as has the interrelation among its members, the family, as the basis of human relations, is as strong as it was 2,000 years ago. The dynamics of Italian families can easily be compared with those in most Western countries, which have been influenced by a process of progressive nuclearization of family forms over the last couple of decades. Still, in its percentage of extended families, the Italian situation markedly differs from other countries with an equal degree of economic development. For one thing, while economic development has undoubtedly contributed to modify the family unit for a considerable part of the population, it has not caused traditional structures to disappear. Moreover, the social and economic changes have not changed family values. Though clan loyalties towards more distant relatives may be waning, an adult's ties with his or her own parents and with *their* parents often remain remarkably close. If many younger people are today trying to lead more emotionally independent lives, it is often not without a sense of guilt or an awareness of the pain it causes their parents, who cling to a different family tradition. This may be so in any country; it is especially sharp in Italy.

"Particularism" and "Familism"

When we talk about the Italian family, we usually fall into the trap of terrible generalization and, therefore, equally terrible misrepresentations, because it is easier to deal with general characterizations. Although *the* Italian family has *never* existed, because even before the postwar anthropological revolution, the structure of Italian families differed according to geographic areas, social classes, and urban/agrarian societies, the notion of the Italian family as social unit became popular thanks to Edward Banfield's controversial and hotly disputed thesis of amoral familism. Indeed, North American anthropology of Italy became almost obsessive in its focus on this debate in the period before the 1970s, to the neglect of researching other important areas.

Banfield claimed that southern poor farmers and laborers were relegated to poverty by a traditional ethos that made them maximize the material, short-run advantage of the nuclear family, thereby inhibiting the cooperation and solidarity basic to modern political and economic life.[2] He stated that the backwardness of Chiaromonte in Basilicata was caused by "the inability of the villagers to act together for their common good, or indeed, for any good transcending the immediate, material interest of the nuclear family." His theory implied, therefore, an endemic inability to act for the common good—what is popularly called a lack of civic consciousness. It is related to societies where the fundamental unit is the nuclear family and more complex forms of social organization are absent. It is associated with centralized and authoritarian states that discourage the growth of intermediate institutions of government between the state and its citizens. This was "amoral familism," and Banfield claimed that such crippling and exclusive concentration on the family did not apply just to the village he had studied but to many other parts of the rural south. Banfield's theses were heavily criticized by some scholars, but the term familism lived on. It did so because in all probability it struck a resonant chord, not simply as a description of attitudes in the backward and primitive south of those years but also for Italy as a whole. The concept was extended to the rest of Italy to demonstrate that because of the high degree of individualism that characterizes Italians, Italian families do not interact well with the social structures at large, and in fact, the Italian familial institution has been the cause of negative social, economic, and political development of the country.

Banfield did not address some important issues:

» What form of family favored a fruitful relationship between individuals and civil society?

» What type of society, and even more so civil society, could exercise a benign influence on families?

» What actions of the state could foster both less familist families, and the burgeoning of a modern civil society?

Banfield's idea of familism was challenged in 1968 by Sydel Silverman, who saw southern poor farmers' exclusive attachment to their nuclear family as an effect, not a cause, of their poverty. Rural laborers were unable to support the large families that were to be found in areas of farmer ownership and long-term tenancy, such as central and northern Italy.[3] Paul Ginsborg, in his *Italy and Its Discontents: Family, Civil Society, State: 1980–2001,* gives a coherent interpretation and approach to issues raised by interweaving them with the whole cultural and economic history of the country. He states:

> Civil society is composed primarily of individuals, not families. A successful relationship between family and civil society would be one in which family members were encouraged, both by their family background and by the wider society of which they are part, to participate in the activities of civil society as individuals and equals, to become citizens and not just voters. The form of the family (its openness or closeness, its gendered hierarchies or lack of them) and the possibilities of politics are thus intimately linked.[4]

Familism is also connected with nepotism, the practice of favoring relatives in the conferring of public offices and contracts. Within the framework of a set of relationships between family, civil society, and the state, characterized by strong and cohesive family units, a historically weak civil society, and scant respect for a negligent state, it was to expected that individual families, both powerful and powerless, would view the public sphere as a plundering ground.

Strong familism, whether conceived as moral or amoral, also characterizes other societies around the Mediterranean. Domineering patriarchs, clinging matriarchs, and relatives who stick together to defend and further the interests of the family or the clan can be found among Spaniards, Greeks, Turks, and Arabs.

Historical Roots of "Familism"

In the case of the Italians, the causes of familism are mostly attributed to historical circumstances. In his *Prison Notebook,* Antonio Gramsci lamented the negative effects of the exclusion of the lower classes in the passive revolution that brought about the unification of Italy in 1870 and the failure of the ruling elite to integrate the popular classes into the new state and to establish their own hegemony. The passive revolution, by its exclusive nature and repressive tendencies, accentuated the antagonism of the Italian lower classes toward the state and their propensity for autonomous organization; it also made them less open to class ideologies, whether Marxist or anarcho-syndicalist.[5] It should be pointed out, however, that in the Italian lower classes, familism did not originate with the unified state, though it may well have been intensified by it. The origins of such attitudes should be sought in the effects of centuries of foreign domination, with the consequent destruction of any *fede pubblica* and the influence of Catholic teaching on the family, with its emphasis on the natural law that determines the preeminence of the family in civil society and its separation from the state.[6]

One can say, however, that after unification, in the absence of almost any adequate structures, apart from repressive ones, linking civil society and the state, the mass of Italians concentrated their attention on the single structure in civil society over which they could exercise some control—the family. The family became the epicenter of life, the only moral force, so much so that for some observers, like Pasquale Villari, the relationship between individual and community, between family and collectivity, seemed not to exist at all.[7] Luigi Barzini used to say that the true patriotism of Italians is loyalty to their own families.

Certainly the Church played a major role in shaping the moral and social core of the Italian family. The weekly magazine *Famiglia Cristiana,* which had its largest circulation in the 1950s and 1960s, was one of the best media reaching the Italian family in preaching the sanctity of the Christian family and the primacy of the family in civil society.

The *Enciclopedia Cattolica* (1950) stated that "the precedence of the family over society is above all temporal; the family was the first form of social organization, the first school and first temple." Furthermore, in a hierarchy of values, society was subordinated to the family "since society is a means to assure to the family and through it the individual that which is indispensable for its [family] self-realization."[8] In family-state relations, the emphasis is on the need to protect the family from external control. Again the *Enciclopedia Cattolica* stated that "the state must recognize the family as it has been constituted by God" (pp. 994–95). The state's duties were, therefore, to protect the family and to enable it to "accomplish its mission"; only if the family failed in this task did the state have the right to interfere. Tullio Goffi made a similar point in saying that "the family enjoys a pre-eminence over civil society in an ordering of ends . . . family duties, founded on piety, love and unity, are of a superior essence, although less defined and distinct, than social duties, which emanate from justice."[9] In the relationship between family and collectivity, the Christian family thus had many more

Civil and Religious marriages (1993–2003)

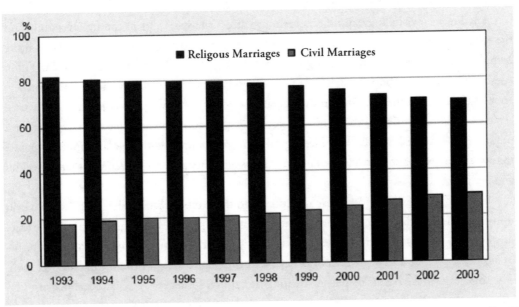

Source: ISTAT 2005

rights than duties. The family's duties were primarily internal, not external. Such an ideology could be accused of catering to familism, of isolating the family from society, of stressing private rather than public virtues.

If this was the predominant view of family-society relations, it should be stated that Catholic social teaching, as we saw in the preceding chapter, balanced the picture by placing the family in a wider social context. The Catholic family had to be defended against the Communist menace and the threats of modern society. It could only do so if it emerged from its isolation.

The prime mission of the family within the Church was to link with and help others: community spirit over individualism. Therefore, there was a permanent tension in the Catholic view of the family. On the one hand, there was the tendency to stress the family's internal values, its primacy over society, and the need to protect it from a hostile world. On the other hand, there was the desire to overcome the family's isolation, both with relation to the Church and society.

Family and Associational Life

There is no question that families have determined the political and economic history of Italy. Countless small- or medium-size businesses that have boosted the Italian economy are family enterprises, or started as such. There have been places and periods when family strategies have acquired an overridingly private dimension and the collective aspect of social life has become secondary. The decline of collective values and the vigorous new emphasis on the material prosperity of the individual family unit have led to a new age of familism: Families have become ever more concerned with their own well-being and less with the collective problems of society as a whole (a trend dominant in the 1980s).

Anyone who visits Italy and has occasion to assess the workings of the Italian family and the relationship between the family and the community will return with a view that is more complex and less one-sided than that presented by Edward Banfield and another scholar Tullio Altan. The family has both contributed to, and worked against, collective action; the furtherance of the family can lead both toward greater solidarity and away from it. In other words, attachment and devotion to the family do not necessarily carry the negative social connotation of familism. It is the historical and ideological context in which working-class families operate that to a great extent conditions the degree of nonsociability and exclusiveness of family values and actions.

It might be expected, given these structures and the extent to which the family was a world unto itself, that Tullio Altan's Albertian family reigned supreme. This was only partly the case, however, for side by side with these attitudes, we also find the greatest mobilizations in terms of land occupations and outbreaks of dissent that the inland areas of the south had ever seen. The southern rural laborers displayed a strong horizontal solidarity. The habitual distrust and ingrained individualism of the south were eclipsed by those elements that prompted solidarity among these workers.

Indeed, collective consciousness and a strong sense of community did exist in the life of poor farmers during these years. They were based on a complex system of favors and exchanges, and on a social network that was almost exclusively confined to the neighborhood; family and collective action related in a variable and complex way and certainly not in a simple polar opposition to each other. The core of collective consciousness, the focal point of action, was the *paese* (village) itself, with its closed concentrated formation and its *piazza* (square). The dimension of the *vicinato* (neighborhood), of face-to-face relations, had fundamental importance; it was the basic element of aggregation. Faced with the uncertainties of work, with the particular harshness of life on the plains (the miles and miles covered on foot or on bicycle, the risk of malaria, the difficult relationship with the landowners), the *paese* was the symbol of peace, of solidarity, of physical rest and recovery, of affections, of friendship. The *paese* offered *civiltà*, culture. People used to sit outside their doors, on chairs and stools, chatting away. Allegiances developed between families as well as amongst kinfolk. Even in the agrarian society, where farmers operated in social isolation and the family's binding internal structures would make one expect the degree of contact and cooperation between neighbors to be very limited, the Albertian concept of familism does not reign supreme. Italian literature gives ample testimony to this cooperation and collective work efforts—especially at crucial periods in the agricultural calendar. Giovanni Verga's narrative, for example, provides some classic examples of certain collective practices (the salting of anchovies, for example) in Sicily.

Number of marriages celebrated in Italy and main characteristics of marriages (2005)

Geographic areas	Total number of marriages	Marriage rate per 1000 inhabitants	Civil marriages per 100 total marriages	Marriages with at least one spouse in his/her second marriage	Marriages with at least one foreign spouse	Average age of brides at their first marriage	Average age of grooms at their first marriage
North-West	58,674	3.8	42.4	16.3	16	32.8	30.1
North-East	41,809	3.8	45.4	16.1	18.6	33.1	30.3
Center	51,382	4.6	35.2	14	18.7	33.1	30.5
South	68,581	4.9	17.9	6.5	5.6	31.1	28.3
Islands	30,533	4.6	23.2	9.3	4.2	31.3	28.5
Italy	250,979	4.3	32.4	12.2	12.5	32.2	29.5

Source: ISTAT 2006

Sharecropping families had, for example, developed a rich network of exchanges and mutual aid. The exchange of labor between families at crucial moments in the agricultural calendar, such as at threshing and harvest times, and other seasonal farm work drew families together with a spirit of generosity and strong cooperation.

On a cultural level there was also the important practice of the *veglia*. During the long winter evenings, families would gather in the kitchens of the farmhouses to play cards and games, to knit and to mend, to tell stories and to listen. Participation in the *veglia* was not segregated family by family, but involved rotating hospitality and a varied system of visiting. *Carnevale,* which culminated with *mardi gras,* was the time of maximum community interaction.

One cannot forget the strong Catholic tradition of collective action and solidarity, of mutual aid and cooperative societies that affected the life of every family. We cannot underplay the influence of Catholic ideology and leadership on the relationship between family and collective action, especially in the south and in the northeast, even though Catholic teaching asserted the primacy of the family in civil society and the need to protect it from the interference of the state. On the other hand, the Church's strong emphasis on the internal morality of the family—on its indissolubility, on the responsibility of the parents to educate their children in a Christian manner—had its impact. The approach was essentially defensive and inward looking. The Christian family had more rights than duties in a hostile world from which it had to be safeguarded. However, as mentioned in Chapter 10, we cannot ignore the important historical experience of Catholic social activism in Italy.

On the political level, the Christian Democrats were concerned with the lack of social activism of Italian families, and at the first Congress of the party in April 1946, Guido Gonella, the party secretary, made a strong plea to Catholics to emerge from the shell of the family:

> It is an illusion, and the women present should understand this better than the men, to try to defend the family from inside the family. The state with its wars will tear away from you your husband or your brother, and atheist education or the corruption of the streets will steal the soul of your child. The family is a fortress which cannot be defended from inside the fortress. Certainly we must build up its internal strength, but we must also issue forth and fight the enemy in open battle.[10]

Family and collective action combined in a crusading spirit, which was not to be transformative of social relations but was to defend the Christian family from the Marxist and atheist threats.

Sociability was certainly higher in the working class of the urban areas than in the agrarian South. Italian housing, with long balconies on each floor looking over the street or inwards onto a communal courtyard, facilitated dialogue and human connection. Even in the working-class quarters on the periphery of the great cities where housing usually took the form of flats in tenement blocks, isolated from the rest of the city, a strong sense of community developed, as did solidarity between families. They were based on a complex network of favors and exchanges, on a sociability that was almost exclusively confined to neighborhood, and on the powerful political culture of socialism and Christian solidarity.[11]

Urbanization and New Family-Based Communities

Looking at Italy as a whole in the 1940s, we must not idealize the relationships that existed between family and collective life at that time. In reality there was nothing idyllic about rural life or relationships in the south. Nor was there a linear passage anywhere in Italy from the existence of compact communities based on mutual aid to the destruction of communities brought on by modernization.

The next two decades, when Italy underwent a most profound social revolution, with a mass exodus from the rural areas toward the cities and from the south to the north (between 1952 and 1962, more than 15.5 million Italians changed their place of residence), had a profound effect on the family and its relation to the community. The mass urbanization that was the product of individual family strategies (the young who went first used kinship and sometimes village networks in order to survive the first impact and to find work and housing; then they brought other members of the family) certainly reshaped the structure of the traditional family.

As families began to put a new emphasis on home-centered living and consumption, so the family and especially the woman's role within the family changed. In the 1960s, more Italian women than ever before became full-time housewives. Theirs was the responsibility to care for children who were leaving for school later than ever before. Theirs too, especially in the north, was the task of looking after the needs of a husband whose workday often lasted 12 to 14 hours. The women's magazines and the television advertisements of the time exalted this new figure of the modern Italian woman.

The material improvement in living conditions also had an impact on leisure time activities, which were also radically changed. The television set was the most important innovation of these years. At first television was both a socializing phenomenon and an object of political division. People, especially youngsters and adult men, gathered in bars and in their political party's section headquarters to watch favorite programs.

Gradually, however, the collective and habitual way of television viewing disappeared as more and more families bought their own sets and each family watched television in its own apartment. This startling development increased the tendency toward passive and familial use of leisure time and decreased drastically other more participatory and collective pastimes.

At the same time, people from the Italian popular classes became more mobile. The Fiat *Seicento* and *Cinquecento*, because of their relatively low cost, made it possible for people not only to travel out of the *vicinato* but to do so on their own, as a family, rather than on bus or train with others. Sunday outings by car became popular.

The amount of paid holidays increased slowly but significantly, as did the tendency to travel further. The car and the television further encouraged an essentially private life and familial use of leisure time. All this had an impact on the life in the courtyard and with the extended family. The role of the family unit became even more important. The new urban structures served to isolate families, which were decreasing in size, in small but comfortable living quarters, and provided few spaces for collective gatherings or community life. Women became the principal target of the new consumerism, and the increased emphasis on their service role within the home intensified their isolation. The economic miracle (1958–63) increased the atomization of Italian civil society; it linked rising living standards with accentuated individualism and introduced into Italy a new model of urban social integration.

The Cultural Ferment of 1968 and Its Aftermath: New Forms of Associationism

The Italian student rebellion of 1967–1968, which was seen as a rebellion against all authority and the dominant ideology, was also against the individualist and atomizing values of the economic miracle, against the individualism of the new Italy. The extraordinary flourishing of collective action of these years in the major cities, especially in the industrial north, must also be viewed in this context. During these years, for significant numbers of people, time at work, but free time even more so, was filled with meetings, mobilizations, demonstrations, and discussions. The activities led to new networks of friendship and solidarity, to contacts between intellectuals and workers, and to a minor cultural revolution.

How did this ferment of collective action in the new, urban Italy relate to the family? Families were drawn out of their isolation and found a new common purpose. It was noteworthy that women played a greater role than ever before. Collective action and sociality often took priority over family needs.

Conversely, however, the most significant development of these years was that some sections of the collective movement called into question the very structure and bases of the family. The critique of the family took various forms, some of which found widespread support. The need to introduce divorce, to allow the family to be dissolved, won majority support in Italian society, as the outcome of the referendum of 1974 showed.

The attempt by the women's movement to combat patriarchy and change the traditional roles within the Italian family also made significant inroads in changing Italian society. The most radical critics wished to attack the very existence of the nuclear family. Attempts were made to find alternatives to this family unit and to substitute communal living for family life. Such experiments, though, rarely extended beyond radical student groups in the major cities.

In central Italy, where sharecropping families started small family businesses, the 1970s witnessed the extraordinary growth of family capitalism, of decentralized and small-scale industrialization, and family structure and familism remained strong.

In the south, in the rural areas, the agri-towns ceased to be the centers of solidarity. With the great exodus, the class structure was modified irrevocably. No longer was the population divided into the small elite of landowners and the mass of the rural poor and working class in a cooperative effort. Although the class structure had become more varied, human relations deteriorated. In whichever direction they went, the potential for collective action in the rural south had been destroyed. Some evidence of collective action could be found in the industrial working class only. However, the dominant trend in the south was an economic growth and development that was chaotic, unstable, precarious, and mainly without respect for any order or civic discipline.[12] In the interstices of this vital but chaotic growth, criminal organizations like the Mafia in Sicily and the *Camorra* in Naples increased their networks of influence and protection. Society was divided against itself, and each family fended for itself as best it could. Narrow municipal or corporate or criminal rivalries flourished, leaving little possibility for the sort of solidarities that had existed before the "democratic" chaos controlled by the Christian Democrats. The political class of the south, corrupt and clientelistic, presided contentedly over this spectacular free-for-all.

Notwithstanding all this, today students and parents have become active in school councils; some neighborhood and block associations have sprung up, and new environmental and consumer groups are active. In Sicily, churchmen and schoolteachers are taking an active part in the fight against the Mafia. The continuing and rising importance of associational life suggests that Italians are drawn together for other reasons than work and consumption. Associationalism (since Tocqueville's time, long considered an index of any civilized democracy) actually increased by 2% in the early 1990s as compared to the mid-1980s. No fewer than 21% of adult Italians belong to an association of one kind or another and more than half of these participate in voluntary groups. Another important observation is that, while in the past such voluntary activity had been almost exclusively organized by Catholic organizations, in recent years the ideological motive has been replaced by a desire to contribute to the life of the community outside the confines of formal politics and work life. Contrary to what one might imagine, the volunteers tend to be reasonably high-earning males in early middle age. This suggests that Italy is witnessing the steady abandonment of strong, party-based political activity in favor of a much weaker, more varied, and dynamic form of social self-realization.

The continuing impression of a national political class operating under conditions of imminent and often actual crisis does nothing to encourage the renewal of political life in Italian civil society itself. But despite the decline in traditional forms of political activity, there has been no appreciable drop in public participation in citizens' initiatives—ranging from support campaigns for the victims of civil war in Bosnia to the victims of the 2004 tsunami in South East Asia, to the rather less edifying neighborhood protests at the presence of clandestine immigrants in larger Italian cities.

Italy is undoubtedly on the road toward democratic maturity, and its people are becoming increasingly involved in public affairs.

Divorce and New Family Structures

The long debate that accompanied the introduction of divorce into Italian legislation is closely related to the issue of the solidarity of family ties. The fear of jeopardizing the strength of this network of relationships was one of the main reasons for the opposition campaign of the anti-divorce front.

Although the Christian Democratic party and the Catholic Church opposed it, divorce was introduced in 1970 when the Left-wing parties and the small anti-clerical center groups in Parliament surprisingly mustered enough votes to overcome the opposition. True, the new rules called for a five-year waiting period from the moment a married couple had formally separated. Nevertheless, the old principle that an Italian marriage was indissoluble—save through annulment by state or Church courts—had been scrapped. The Christian Democrats remained nearly isolated in the senate and chamber of deputies in their defense of the old, rigid legislation; they were joined only by the neo-fascists.

Although militant, outraged Roman Catholics collected enough signatures to request a referendum aimed at repealing the divorce statute, and the Church hierarchy and the Christian Democrats staged a nationwide anti-divorce crusade, the law was not repealed. The referendum of 1974, in which 59.1% of the electorate upheld divorce, dealt a humiliating blow to the Church and the *DC*. Even many Italians who attended mass every Sunday voted for divorce, proving that they, like Roman Catholics in other countries, were selective in obeying the teachings of their Church.

Many married couples who had been living apart were at last able to have their collapsed marriages lawfully ended and to remarry. But the large, general rush into divorce that adversaries of the reform had predicted did not occur. In 1987 the legal waiting period between separation and divorce was reduced to three years. By then it was estimated that one out of every fifteen new marriages would end in divorce—a far lower divorce rate than in France, Britain, or certainly the United States, where one out of every two marriages does not last.

Despite almost 60% support for divorce at the referendum in 1974, and the fact that divorce has been legal since 1970, the Italian divorce rate remained low until the early 1990s. Even with the legal right to divorce, Italians hesitated to dissolve their family units. In 1981, only 13,000 couples were divorced in Italy. Not only does the Italian bureaucracy make divorce onerous, it is a slow process: three years of separation are required before a divorce, and that's if the partners agree; if one partner opposes the divorce, the required period of separation is five years. The influence of Catholic morality on the customs and choices of married life for Italians also seems to be considerable. There are also important economic reasons arguing against divorce. The old-fashioned housewife status of a considerable portion of Italy's female population, for example, has acted as a check on the divorce rate until recently. The lack of economic independence, along with the poor protection the law offers to the weaker partner, undoubtedly represents an efficient impediment to the decision to proceed with a request for

Number of legal separations and divorces (1999–2003)

Years	Separations	Divorces
1999	64,915	34,341
2000	71,969	37,573
2001	75,890	40,051
2002	79,642	41,835
2003	81,744	43,856

Source: ISTAT 2005

separation. There are also cultural reasons, including the domestic topography to which Italians feel so attached. They cannot separate from a host of friends, from a part of their own lives. But, most of all, the welfare and advancement of children comes first, as always. The situation, however, has changed since, with education, women have become more economically independent, and equally important, there are fewer children around to worry about.

Some Italians seem to need the thrills and stress of adultery. Playwright Luigi Pirandello, Benito Mussolini, the leader of the Italian Communist Party, Palmiro Togliatti, film directors Vittorio De Sica and Roberto Rossellini, and thousand of prominent citizens have had well-publicized extramarital affairs.

Indeed, adultery and unfaithfulness have always been major themes in Italian life and art. From Dante, Boccaccio, and Machiavelli to many modern writers, these themes have provided fertile ground for the imagination of artists. However, despite the fact that the most celebrated works are family tragedies, erotic and adulterous entanglements have mostly been farcical in the eyes of Italians.

Today, even though divorce is legal and marriages are not "arranged," infidelity has not diminished. In fact, with more free time and the increase in travel and other leisure activities, infidelity, especially among the bourgeoisie, has increased. The culture is such that, even though prominent individuals are having extra-marital affairs, the press doesn't give them any attention: the public does not care. Many government ministers and other public figures with mistresses are not chased by *paparazzi* because a public man's private life is considered to be his own business so long as he is discreet and does not step outside the law. Thus, despite this behind-the-scenes activity, the majority of Italians have always tended to be exceptionally discreet about their love affairs.

Notwithstanding all these changes, there exists one of the most absurd paradoxes of the Italian mentality: the obsessive preoccupation that Italian males, especially those in the south, have with a woman's faithfulness, while they themselves are engaging in extra-marital affairs. There is no worse insult to a man than calling him *cornuto* (cuckold). The Italian male seems to want his right to stray from the strict marital path, and he knows in his heart and from frequent sociological studies that adultery is not uncommon, but he is obsessed by the fear of being cuckolded, of having his own wife be unfaithful.

Fragmentation and Continuity

Contraception and abortion were legalized in the 1960s and 1970s after lengthy campaigns in both cases. The concern with population growth did not abate after the Second World War. The belief in the intimate relationship between demography and power was extremely strong during fascism, which colored the terms in which social policies on sexuality and the family were discussed and enacted. During this period having a large family was presented as a way to support national unity and the future of Italy.

In the 1960s, the development and popularization of the contraceptive pill gave added weight to demands for repeal of laws against contraception. Demographic data revealed that

☕ *Café* *Momism*

One stereotype has it that young Italian men are "Mamma's boys." There is even an Italian word for it: *mammoni.*

There is some truth to this stereotype. The facts seem to confirm the idea of Italian sons so dependent on their mothers that they just cannot bear to leave the home. The classic Italian *mamma* pampers her boy, telling him over and over that he is *bello* (handsome) and *bravo* (clever). According to a 2005 study, an increasing number of Italians are living with their parents well into their 30s, and sons linger much longer than daughters, with 36.5% of men aged 30 to 34 remaining at home, compared to just 18.1% of women. The number of marriages has fallen as well; 257,880 couples tied the knot in 2003, fewer than half the number in 1971. However, the poll also found that one in three married Italian men still see their Mommys every day. An Italian mamma is glad to press her married boy's shirts, cook his favorite dishes, and discreetly and sympathetically listen to his progress, even his sentimental tales.

"Mammoni" cling to their mothers' apron strings partly because of the economy: Some of the young men polled said that they couldn't afford to leave the nest, and in fact, a high level of unemployment for college graduates and soaring costs of living since the introduction of the euro are partly behind the trend. However, another reason is surely cultural. After being coddled by their families from birth to adulthood, many Italian men simply do not feel the need to lead their own lives. They enjoy being with their parents and siblings and they like living with them. They like the home-cooked meals and the free laundry and housekeeping services. Their parents are happy to have them; Italian parents do not think giving the children wings and teaching them to fly is an appealing idea either. To make sure the problem is even more difficult to solve, Italian universities do not have campuses to house students from far away, and thus there is no enticement to go to school in other parts of the country. Instead, most students live at home during college while their parents foot all their expenses. By the time they graduate at 25 or after, the comfortable routine is set; the men end up seeking jobs near home so they can continue to receive the comfort they are accustomed to, and the parents continue to provide the care without a thought.

The term "mammoni" is applied to men only, because while Italian women strike for the independence their mothers did not experience, Italian men hold Mom to the traditional role into which she was born. To stay at home and have Mom cook their meals, wash their clothes, iron their shirts, and make their bed? That's a normal, acceptable, and even encouraged behavior for this amorphous generation.

a large number of brides were pregnant at the time of marriage, and surveys showed that third and subsequent children were often unplanned or unwanted. Thus, the case for legalizing contraception was made on the basis of family planning, which would allow couples to choose when to have their children and how many to have. The decision to legalize contraception was not made on the basis of any principle of sexual freedom, and it was not until the mid-1970s that contraception became widely used among young people.

The change in sexual attitudes in the last few years, as has occurred in most industrial countries, has certainly had an impact on family structure. It is important to remember, however, that the Italy of the economic boom was still a society full of taboos about sexual behavior. The restrictive codes of official morality were deeply intertwined, especially in the south, with codes of honor, and sexual mores were to change more slowly than anything else.

Old Bonds and New "Familism"

Notwithstanding the changes, a few characteristics of the traditional family ethos do remain. Curiously, after a tense period of transition, the past few years have even seen a new strengthening of the links that bind the nuclear family. In the late 1960s and early 1970s, Italian teenagers shook off the reins of traditional parental authority. This was a blow to the nuclear family. But today, having asserted their right to independence, young people are moving back to closer emotional ties with their parents on a basis of greater equality than before. So the family today is united less by constraint and convention than in the old days and more by genuine need and affection. The autonomy of much of northern youth and its partial challenge to the family in the late 1960s and early 1970s have given way to a new attachment to the family unit. The generational conflict has subsided now that youth has won its rebellion. Whereas the youth of the 1960s rejected the values dictated by their parents, today's adolescents are turning again to the family as a defense and a source of comfort since they no longer find solid values in the public world. The fears created by rising youth unemployment have increased this homing trend. Grown-up children tend to stay at home well into adult life.

Some of the traditional intra-family links such as the mother-son relation remain untouched by modern changes. The self-admiring Latin lover is to some extent a product of such momism. *(See Box on p. 310)* In the dynamics of Italian family life, father-daughter relations also are close. The new family is geared to the production of income and the meeting of needs through the activity of each of its members.

With women's work outside the home increasing noticeably in the eighties, the family is usually living on two salaries. It also has access, thanks to the reforms of the 1970s, to a far wider range of state services than ever before. Consequently, family savings have risen markedly since 1970, as has the overall standard of living. In their lifestyles and in their culture, average Italian families have come a long way.

In the center and northeast, where small family-owned businesses are widespread, extended families appear more frequently than in other regions, though obviously not as abundantly as the earlier sharecropping families of the agrarian society. In these regions a very strong work ethic, geared to the making of family fortunes, allows self-exploitation and the exploitation of one's relatives at levels that are no longer accepted elsewhere in Italy. There is thus less leisure time and less mobility here than in the working-class families of the north. It is hardly surprising to find that the strong, collectivist subculture of these regions has been severely affected by such developments. Political and Catholic associationism have suffered but, as indicated before, a new form of associationism has emerged. The ex-communists, now *DS,* attract people to their cultural events in decreasing numbers. The secularization that necessarily accompanied urbanization realized the fear of the Church that with the decline of rural communities there would naturally occur a weakening of the links between the family and the Catholic religion.

In the urban south, the majority of lower-class families are nuclear in structure and have significantly more children than those of the north or center. In 1971, the average Neapolitan family included 4.7 persons, compared to 3.3 in Bologna. These larger families have to survive in a period of deepening gloom in the labor market. Southern urban families also have to survive in a situation where the services offered by the state are less efficient than the services offered in the center or the north. In the southern cities the state pays out a high number of invalid and social pensions (i.e., poverty pensions) for old people who have never been employed in regular work.

Family or Money?

Despite the recent changes in Italian kinship structures, millions of families throughout the country continue to function in the traditional way of providing warmth, security, moral and economic support, and assistance in crisis. Hundreds of thousands of such self-supportive families have also become successful businesses. Countless small or medium-size businesses that have boosted the Italian economy are family enterprises, or started as such; the outstanding case history is the Benetton family.

There are hundreds of families in Italy who dream that their entrepreneurial ventures may one day take off the way the Benettons' did. Yet, as Italian capitalism matures, and with fewer brothers, sisters, and children of business clans available or willing to pitch in, outside managers, financiers, and corporate raiders are more likely to get into the act. The decline of the large, close-knit business family is also likely to transform the country's economic landscape.

At the same time, it remains true that most of Italy's privately owned, large industrial companies have retained some features of a family enterprise. Outside the hefty state sector, which now is shrinking, Italy has many fewer corporate giants than do the other leading industrial nations; the largest is Fiat, and it is still, in effect, the family holding of the Agnellis of Turin.

There is, however, plenty of evidence that family bonds are loosening or even breaking apart. Good times seem less favorable to kinship solidarity than bad ones. Marital and monetary conflicts have bedeviled many families. Conflicts over inheritance have been divisive for many families. Scores of ordinary Italian families with sons and daughters estranged from their parents, siblings locked in bitter lawsuits and no longer on speaking terms, and aged widows and widowers abandoned by their children or relegated to old-people's homes with perfunctory visits or occasional telephone calls do exist.

The New Family

The early 1960s saw the first stirrings of a new moral outlook. Timid discussions of pre-marital sex appeared in some women's magazines; one weekly (*L'Espresso*) even published an investigation of infidelity levels amongst Italian wives. Profound changes began to occur in the 1970s. For one, the pill was made available everywhere, and the whole ferment of the late 1960s and early 1970s had revolutionized sexual mores. Results can be seen in the population figures and family size today. Population growth is approximately zero, which is lower than Great Britain and much lower than France. The number of families with several children has rapidly diminished. Italy now has one of the lowest birthrates in Europe, Naples today produces proportionately fewer infants than Stockholm. The legalization of abortion and the availability of more reliable contraceptives, including the pill, have certainly had an impact on the population growth. Because many women feared the side effects of the pill, in 1980s abortions became the most widespread form of birth control—more than 360 abortions per 1,000 live births. The abortion rate in Italy is the second highest within the EU, and illegitimate births are, therefore, low.

Certainly, the 30% who remain practicing Catholics must be influenced by the pope's adamant refusal to countenance any variation on the Church's teachings on chastity and contraception. However, as we have seen in the previous chapter, here again we are faced with Italian flexibility and spontaneity.

Italian families are, thus, getting smaller and more nuclear and continue to be cohesive. Even in urban contexts, Italian grandparents remain closely involved in the care of grandchildren; it is still common to see in a public park a child kicking a soccer ball with his *nonno* (grandfather). Nevertheless, some fundamental shifts have occurred in the roles and needs of individuals within the family. There has been an ever-increasing process of individualization within the family, of demarcations of activity and consumer rules by age and by sex; women have redefined their roles and responsibilities; youth have increasingly sought their own activities and space at an ever younger age; and individual members of the family relate more and more to their peer groups and the outside world.

The amoral familism raised by Banfield in the 50s is not an issue anymore. The recent changes in family forms in Italy are slowly pushing family-civil society relations

The Italian Catholic tradition is that on Christmas Eve you are supposed to eat different kinds of fish. "Fish" generally encompasses all types of seafood and includes (but is not limited to) scungili, crab, lobster, clams, scallops, cod, and scampi. Source: Wikipedia.org.

closer; as gender relations change, and individuals become more free within the family, it is possible that citizenship will grow more outside of the family. Yet the legacy of the past, while not a uniform one, weighs heavily upon these prospects. Families in Italy have become accustomed to developing defensive, cynical, and even predatory attitudes towards much of the outside world, towards the institutions of the state, towards those wider loyalties that transcend kinship or narrow local networks of friendships.

Causes for Small Family

As we shall see in the next chapter, the size of the Italian family has been mainly affected by the changing status of women in society. The decline in the fertility rate, undoubtedly the most relevant factor, is part of concomitant changes in Italy's cultural mentality that have emerged in the last two decades:

» The change from an agrarian, to an industrial, to a service society.

» The shifting view, as an increasing number have moved to the city, of children less as an economic asset (helpful labor on the farm, for example) and more as an economic liability, especially considering the lack of space and high cost in cities.

» Increased education, especially of women.

» The difficulty women have in attending to both motherhood and their careers.

» The high unemployment rate among 18–30-year-olds.

» The later age for leaving home and prolonged period in school.

» The secularization of society.

» Changes in work law that have created greater insecurity.

» New priorities in a materialistic society.

» The popularity of birth control (91 percent of married women report using some form of contraceptive).

» The impact of mass communication—radio, movies, and especially television—[that] speeds up the substitution of the traditional family model by a modern one (single parent, few children, unmarried couples living together, etc.).

» The lack of state and public agency assistance for young families with children.

» The decrease in the share of child benefits in the total security budget of Italy over the last few decades—child benefits went from 13.3% in 1970 to 3.9% in 1992.

» The deferral of child-bearing to an older age.

Since 1931 (when the first statistical information concerning the fertility of the privileged became available), a strong and inverse relationship has been clearly established between the level of fertility and the 'standard of life' of the family. Studies show that birth rate declines with affluence. On this subject, Antonio Golini, professor at the University of Rome, says:

> Affluence plays a considerable role. Today's affluence pushes people to consume more, have an expensive car, and take a vacation abroad. Subsequently, in some cases, a child or a second child is placed as an alternative to having these things. And therefore some couples decide to have a vacation to the islands and postpone having a child to the next year. But the following year something else happens and they postpone again. It's a fact that couples who have one child or two children are economically penalized when compared to a couple without children. Being childless has an economic advantage. Babies are expensive and there is no social help for couples with children. (PBS, 2003)

In addition, increasing affluence is associated with better medical services and a resultant decrease in infant mortality (8 children in every 1,000 births die), leading people to bear fewer children with the expectation that most of them will survive.

The Troubles Created by a Graying Population

Italy's low birthrate is a serious problem. According to United Nations projections, over the next 50 years Italy's youngest generation (0–14 age group) will drop by 14%, the working population (15–64) will fall by 44%, while the population over 64 will rise by 50% and the group composed of those over 80 years of age will increase in size 160% *(See Box on p. 317)*. If it were not for the fact that people live longer and immigrants keep coming into the country, the population would be decreasing rapidly. Italy's population looks like a reversed pyramid (some economists like the metaphor of a pear): a smaller, younger population at the base sustains a much larger population at the top. That creates many problems. Of more immediate relevance to Italians, however, are the unique social and political problems created by a graying population. Central to this problem is the pressure it places on a social welfare system for the elderly, which is generally financed by the (shrinking) adult population. In 1950, for example, the population of those aged 65 and older within Italy was 8.3 percent of the total population—in 1995, it was 16.8. As a result of these changes, the potential support ratio for Italy has declined from 7.9 persons aged 15–64 for each person aged 65 or older in 1950 to 4.1 in 1995. The picture has worsened in the last ten years. It thus becomes difficult for fewer workers to support a very large population that is retired, especially in a socialist nation such as Italy.

A contracting labor force will undoubtedly limit Italy's potential for economic growth. This prospect has already alarmed some European companies. European countries are already trying to buy up American banks or companies, because they will not have a customer base with affluent population decreasing. European enterprises have a graying, diminishing customer base. Italy is responding to the challenges posed by a shrinking work force and the increasing cost of pensions simply by increasing the age of retirement. The Berlusconi government, in 2004, changed the minimum retirement ages to 57 for males and 56 for females.

In the midst of these reforms, the economic and age diversity of Italy should be kept in mind. Presumably, those in the lower economic strata of Italy's population will have begun working at an earlier age, and so any change in the retirement age must take these workers into account. Additionally, there exists a subtle pressure on employers to hire younger workers in the new, knowledge-based economy. For this reason, policies preventing the displacement of older workers are also needed.

As the first country in human history where the number of people over the age of 60 is greater than the number of young people under the age of 20, Italy is suffering from a shortage of young workers. As a result, the nation finds itself increasingly challenged economically. Compared to the U.S. and India, for example, Italy's prospects for a prosperous future are challenging; Indians are being trained in excellent educational systems, and they are excellent mathematicians, engineers, and statisticians. Therefore, the large software companies are now going to India to recruit from a young, well-prepared workforce. In this way, Italy's aging population has serious implications for the nation's ability to compete on the world market.

Many of the economic and social consequences of a shrinking population are offset in Italy by immigration, primarily from sub-Saharan Africans and Arabs. These immigrants are also the ones who pay into the Italian social security system, creating a sensitive cultural situation due to their potential to transform Italy's indigenous culture. Oftentimes, however, this cultural sensitivity arrives in opposition to Italy's social, political, and economic needs.

However, the most striking feature of the debate about population growth in developed nations, especially those, like Italy, approaching zero population growth, is the lack of consensus on whether continued population trends are desirable or not. Italians currently face a collective ambivalence on the issue; while these trends mean that Italy is putting less stress on the world's environment and other resources, they also mean social instability and a potential increase in the erosion of traditional Italian culture. For these reasons, many Italians continue to clamor for increased population growth. The other extreme is to simply accept increased immigration, revised pension systems, a less potent young work force, and many other social and cultural compromises. Is there a middle road?

If they hope to increase population growth rates, developed countries like Italy also need to revise their gender roles. Men need to take a greater role in child-rearing, so as to make the possibility of an Italian family with two working parents and multiple children more feasible. Central to any discussion of future policy on population in Italy is a contradiction: while Italy's declining population creates a number of problems for its citizens, the nation is also a member of the global community, which suffers from *over*population. As such, there remains no clear decision as to what direction Italy should take in regards to the population question, although the general consensus appears to favor a low population while safeguarding Italy's economic and social health. Right now these challenges are being offset through two routes: foreign investment and increased immigration.

The Problems of an Aging Society

With life expectancy in Italy climbing to 79 years for women and 72 for men, families must deal with the prolonged lives of their senior relatives. In all social classes, couples no longer accept so readily that an elderly widowed parent should come to live with them: *nonno* and *nonna*—grandpa and grandma—are now expected to stay in an apartment of their own. It is estimated that about one-quarter of elderly Italians live by themselves. Since in many families both junior spouses work, there is no alternative. This has caused a good deal of heartache.

In the absence of family-centered care, the state has begun to realize the necessity to help the elderly, and society is finally accepting that its elderly are no longer solely a family responsibility. In recent years shelters and recreational facilities for the elderly have been opened—a new departure for Italy. However, although public *case di riposo* do exist, they vary greatly in number and quality, depending on the town. In many northern towns there are well-developed services for old people, including libraries, places for film viewing, and general recreation.

☕ *Café* — *The Oldest Population in the World*

Until recently, Italy had a young population. In the past thirty years, however, the population structure has reversed: today Italy has the oldest population in the world and, after Spain, the lowest birth rate. In a population of 58 million, 13.8% are 14 years old or younger, 66.5% are between the ages of 15 and 64, and 19.7% are 65 years or older. Italy's declining birth rate and increased longevity have led to a progressive increase in its older population.

In the town of Laviano, outside of Naples, the effects of the declining birth rate are symptomatic of the general Italian condition. Just thirty years ago, Laviano, which now has a population of 1,500, saw as many as 70 babies born every year. In 2002, there were only four births. In Vastrogirardi, another southern Italian village, only two babies were born in 2002, and none at all in 2001. These devastating statistics have been repeated in many of the 40,000 towns and villages across Italy. Even the affluent provinces have very low birth rates. In Ferrara, a northern city, the annual birth rate has been under 0.9 every year since 1986. (It must be pointed out that in the last few years a small increase has been registered. As of 2007, the birth rate had moved to 1.29 per woman (compared to 1.21 in 1990). However, the boost was mainly due to the increased immigrant population, which tends to have a much higher percentage of children than Italian citizens.)

The population decline is causing a major problem for Italy's economy: there are 22 million pensioners and only 21 million in the workforce. If the trend continues, in the next decade 25% of the population will be over sixty; by 2040 the elderly will make up 40% of the population. State and local governments have responded to the crisis by giving bonuses of 1,000 and 2,000 euros to families for each child born: a small bandage to cure a severe hemorrhage!

Unfortunately, private rest homes are out of reach for many people, for their cost is equivalent to a worker's monthly pay. The state of desperation of many elderly has caused a big increase in the suicide rate of people over age 65. To see how serious the problem is, you only have to watch what happens to the elderly during the summer months when many are left behind by their children who depart on vacation. The chronic-disease wards of Italian hospitals fill up every summer with elderly patients; their relatives park them there for several weeks so they can enjoy their vacations.

Municipalities do offer many other kinds of aid and assistance. There are discounts for old people on buses and at cinemas, and inexpensive lunches are provided. Some municipalities organize mini-vacations to the sea or mountains. These services are more common in the north; the further south one goes, the weaker the central organization and the more the family takes its place.

An interesting development for old people, mainly in large cities, is the establishment of the *Università della terza età* (The University of the Third Age). Anyone over 40, whatever their education, can sign up for courses. Courses are usually on subjects of local interest and are taught mostly by professors from local universities, who sometimes donate their time.

Whatever the actual effectiveness of the various services, Italy is confronted with a new phenomenon that has social dimensions that cannot be easily solved by institutional services. Centuries of family tradition make people reluctant to depend on anything less personal. The average Italian still believes that the best social worker is a relative. In general, there remains a deep-seated moral obligation of children to parents, and in this, as in many other situations, the Italian family and its traditions continue at the center of all social intercourse.

Notes

1. L. Barzini, *The Italian* (New Yoek: Hamish Hamilton, 1964).

2. After the war, the U.S. also sponsored research projects, mainly in the south, as part of the U.S. plan of capitalist reconstruction of Italy. E. Banfield, *The Moral Basis of a Backward Society* (Glencoe, Ill.: The Free Press, 1958).

3. S. Silverman, "Agricultural Organization and Social Structure, and Values in Italy: Amoral Familism Reconsidered," *American Anthropologist,* 70 (1968): 1–20.

4. P. Ginsborg, *Italy and Its Discontents—Family, Civil Society, State: 1980–2001* (New York, Palgrave Macmillan, 2003).

5. A. Gramsci, *Selections from the Prison Notebooks,* eds. Q. Hoare and G. Nowell-Smith (London: Lawrence and Wishart, 1971), 52–120.

6. Paul Ginsborg, *Daniele Manin and the Venetian Revolution of 1848–49* (Cambridge: Cambridge U. P., 1979), 371.

7. P. Villari, *Le lettere meridionali e altri scritti sulla questione sociale in Italia* (1885: reprint, Naples: Guida, 1979).

8. See the entry "Famiglia," *Enciclopedia Cattolica,* vol. 5 (Roma, 1950), 994.

9. T. Goffi, *Morale familiare* (Brescia, 1962), 264.

10. "La DC per la nuova Costituzione," in *I congressi nazionali della Democrazia Cristiana* (Rome: Arti Grafiche Italiane, 1959).

11. A. Gribaudi, *Mondo operaio, mito operaio* (Turin: Einaudi, 1987).

12. M. Rossi-Doria, "Dopo i fatti di Battipaglia," in *Scritti sul Mezzogiorno* (Turin: Einaudi:1984).

Bibliography

Banfield, E., *The Moral Basis of a Backward Society* (Glencoe, Ill.: The Free Press, 1958).

Baranski, Z.G. and Lumley, R. (eds.), *Culture and Conflict in Postwar Italy* (London: 1990).

Barzini, L., *The Italians* (New York: Hamish Hamilton, 1964).

Gambino, R., *Blood of My Blood* (Garden City, NY: Doubleday, 1974)

Ginsborg, P., *Daniele Manin and the Venetian Revolution of 1848–49* (Cambridge: Cambridge U.P., 1979)

Ginsborg, P., *Italy and its Discontents—Family, Civil Society, State: 1980–2001* (New York: Palgrave Macmillan, 2003)

Gribaudi, A., *Mondo operaio, mito operaio* (Turin: Einaudi, 1987).

Hofmann, P., *That Fine Italian Hand* (New York: Henry Holt and Co., 1990).

Rossi-Doria, M., "Dopo I fatti di Battipaglia," in *Scritti sul Mezzogiorno* (Turin: Einaudi, 1984).

Silverman, S., "Agricultural Organization and Social Structure, and Values in Italy: Amoral Familism Reconsidered," *American Anthropologist,* 70 (1968).

CHAPTER 12

WOMEN AND GENDER RELATIONS

Profile of Women

Population: About 29,500,500, or 51% of the country's population. There are 94 men for every 100 women.

Age structure: *0–14 years:* 13.9% (male 4,166,213/female 3,919,288); *15–64 years:* 66.7% (male 19,554,416/female 19,174,629); *65 years and over:* 19.4% (male 4,698,441/female 6,590,046) (2005); more than 1 in 5 of the population is now over 65.

Median age: *total:* 41.77 years; *male:* 40.24 years, *female:* 43.35 years (2005 est.) Population growth rate: 0.07% (2005). According to current estimates, there will be 14 million fewer Italians by the year 2050.

Birth rate: 8.89 births/1,000 population (2005)

Death rate: 10.3 deaths/1,000 population (2005)

Sex ratio: *at birth:* 1.07 male(s)/female; *under 15 years:* 1.06 male(s)/female; *15–64 years:* 1.02 male(s)/female; *65 years and over:* 0.71 male(s)/female; *total population:* 0.96 male(s)/female (2005)

Infant mortality rate: *total:* 5.94 deaths/1,000 live births; *male:* 6.55 deaths/1,000 live births; *female:* 5.29 deaths/1,000 live births (2005)

Life expectancy at birth: *total population:* 79.68 years; *male:* 76.75 years; *female:* 82.81 years (2005)

Total fertility rate: 1.28 children born/woman (2005)
   The country spends just 3.8% of its GDP on child-related social spending compared with an EU average around 8%.

Legislation affecting women: 1861: Publication of Salvatore Morelli's *La donna e la scienza o la soluzione del problema sociale.*
   1864: Publication of Anna Maria Mozzoni's *La donna e i suoi rapporti sociali.*
   June 25, 1865: Civil code of the Kingdom of Italy: women under the marital authorization of men, the 'head of the family.'
   1869: Publication of John Stuart Mill's *The Subjugation of Women.*
   1919: Universal male suffrage at age 21.
   1925: Women given the right to vote in local administration.
   1925: Creation of National Agency for Maternity and Infancy.
   1929: Decree for the protection of employed women during pregnancy period.
   1930: Law in the penal code dealing with "Offense to Protect Honor."
   1942: The civil code reaffirms husband's position as "head of the household."
   1945: Universal female suffrage.
   1956: Equal pay for equal work.
   1958: Abolition of legal prostitution.
   1963: Law extending female employment in practically every sector, including the judicial system (but women are still excluded from police and military).
   1970: Legalization of divorce.
   1971: Law for the protection of employed women who become mothers.
   1974: Referendum to repeal divorce law: 59.3% votes for "no" against 40.7% with a participation of 87.7%.
   1975: Legal equality of husband and wife (abolition of law making husband "head of the household."
   1977: Equal rights on work issues.
   1978: Legalization of abortion.
   1981: Women accepted in the police force.
   1981: Referendum to abolish legal abortion defeated by a vote of 21,505,323 to 10,119,797.

1981: Abolition of the law that protected the "delitto d'onore," a violence against a woman who committed a sexual transgression.

1991: Law to promote female entrepreneurship.

1993: Law to promote female employment in public administration.

1996: Rape considered as offense against the "person" and "morality."

1998: Law against the exploitation of prostitution, pornography, child molestation.

Source: ISTAT 2006

The Central Role of Women in the Traditional Family

Women's roles have changed profoundly in Italy both as members of the family and as individuals in society. A revolution in education and work began with the modern feminist movement of the 1970s, and the revolution is now so great that, year after year, more women than men graduate from college, and there are more job openings for women than for men. The changing status of women has been accompanied by a decline in fertility and has not been followed by the new concept of parenthood as a task that applies equally to mother and father; as a result women find it difficult to attend to both motherhood and their careers. Worse yet, the state and other public administrations are not meeting the new needs of working families.

Historically, the division of labor and space, the importance of women's networks, the centrality of children in the family and of food in defining membership within the household, contributed to making women and especially mothers central to household organization and family life. Until recently, the mother has played a strong central role in the Italian family. The mother in the Italian household is an archetype whose model is the Virgin Mary: the supreme example of purity, a symbol of motherhood defined by pain and sacrifice born of wisdom, a model of humility and forgiveness, and a key mediating figure in Catholicism, interceding between God the Father and God the Son. It is not by chance that Italians in their exclamations of pain or distress exhort interchangeably "Madonna mia!" or "Mamma mia!" Italian mothers are special because of the amount of inter-generational care they shoulder, the intensity of their attachment to their sons, the reverence they receive, and the dependency they create.

Until the end of the 1950s, the role of women in Italian society was generally defined in terms of the institution of the family. Urban women were primarily caretakers of the house and of the home and held a subordinate position to men. The situation was different in the agrarian society, which had a more complex family structure. In the south and in the rural and semi-rural areas of the north and the center, where the extended family was the prevailing feature of the social structure, there wasn't a sharp division between the sphere of production and that of domestic life; women held a very active role in productive activity. As in other countries with a pre-industrialized society, the wife had considerable power owing to her productive role in the family economy. In pre-industrial society, familial and work activities overlapped and the family formed the basic economic unit, making it difficult to characterize family structure and domains; families were patriarchal as much as matriarchal. This was the dominant structure in Italy until the end of the 1950s when Italy ceased to be an agricultural society.

The subordinate role of woman as homemaker, mother, and wife was regulated by laws and encouraged by the Church, against the democratic and liberal views of some prominent intellectuals and civic and political leaders.[1] Mussolini had certainly circumscribed the position of women. Fascism had actively discriminated against women in the matter of right to work by limiting access to jobs and careers and by mandating separate pay ranges according to sex.[2] Fascism succeeded in promoting sex-role stereotypes that permeated popular mores and behavior, education, and culture in general. In everyday life, for the majority of Italian women—particularly for lower-middle-class women—this meant confinement to menial household chores, made still more difficult by general economic hardship. Under fascism, the state sought to organize the subordination of women around their central role of devoted spouse and exemplary mother. Women were to be guardians of the hearth and subject to the legitimate authority of the husband; they were regarded as mothers whose duty it was to produce soldiers and workers for the state. *Il Duce* went as far as to state that "War is to man what motherhood is to woman."[3]

The Struggle for Identity

In a 1954 article, Gini and Caranti observed that "the existence of a genuine difference of position of the man and woman in marriage and in social life" constituted a fundamental presupposition of the stability of the Italian family.[4] Since then this difference between the roles of men and women has been steadily disappearing. In its transition from a traditional agricultural to a modern industrial society, Italy has also witnessed a significant redefinition of the role of women. Women have made major strides toward fuller emancipation and legal, professional, and sexual equality. The political action of the women's movement, the changes in lifestyles caused by economic changes, as well as extensive legislative decrees, have all favored the acknowledgment and affirmation of the social condition of women and the formal equalization of the sexes. Along with the quantitative growth of the number of women attending school, there came a "historically" significant change in the labor supply, especially from the start of the 1970s. It was only at this time that significant changes began to appear, and there are reasons for these delays:

»   The latent *machismo* of Latin society;
»   Catholic traditions and culture that encouraged particular roles for women;
»   Lack of accessibility to education in an agrarian society.

It is curious that Italian women themselves, whose social role has always been so strong, did not show much interest in legal equality or in sharing a man's privileges, at least until recently. Before the 1970s and the modern women's movement, Italian women seemed to feel they had enough space and power in their traditional roles. When necessary, they chose to use their "feminine charms" to win their way.

Church and Women

Until the early 1960s, the Church was also very direct in forging the social functions of people, especially women. In a 1931 encyclical, "Casti connubi," in unison with the fascist policy, Pope Pius XI continued to reinforce the traditional role of women as primarily loving wives and caring mothers. The position of the Church did not change with the fall of fascism and the end of the monarchy. In 1946, Pope Pius XII confirmed the previous position of the Church:

> Every woman is destined to be a mother . . . For true women, all life's problems are understood in terms of the family . . . Equality with men, outside the home where she is queen, subjects the woman to the same burdens the man has. The woman who goes to work outside the home . . . dazzled by the tinsel of a counterfeit luxury, becomes greedy for unworthy pleasure.[5]

The Church's position began to change with the election to pope of Giovanni Roncalli. In 1960, John XXIII declared that women's lives pivoted on "two centers, two nuclei; those of the family and of work." He implied that in a post-masculine society women had to be given the opportunity to harmonize family and work lives.

Equal but Different

It is also relevant to point out that socially, women in Italy have rarely been segregated or treated as inferiors. The Italian woman regarded herself, and was regarded, as the equal of man—equal, but different. Until the late 1960s, given an opportunity to play the same role as a man, she often shied away in fear of losing her femininity, and men cheered her for it. Probably this perception is best reflected in a popular saying that I heard many times when I was growing up in Italy: *Il padrone sono io, ma chi comanda e' mia moglie* (I am the boss, but my wife is the ruler). An Italian woman traditionally viewed herself in relation to the family, where her role was powerful, in every age and in every social class—and in relation to individual men, rather than to other women or to the community as a whole. So it is not surprising that the modern feminist movement in its more militant form was marginal in Italy, and has been generally unpopular. However, in the past dozen years or so a milder and different kind of feminism has taken root among the new generation. Italian women today expect equality of rights and career prospects, equal personal freedom (sexual and other), and equality in marriage: they no longer expect their husbands to make all of the decisions and share none of the chores. They resent, and fight against, *machismo*. But in Italy, men and women alike have a fear and contempt for "bossy" women, and the Italian women who emerge as public figures are usually extremely feminine people, such as Nilde Jotti and Irene Pivetti, ex-presidents of the chamber of deputies, or the six women ministers of the present government.

The Road to Emancipation

Italian women today have emerged from a transitional phase. From the old dependence on a man's world they have moved toward real emancipation. However, the road to full emancipation has been tortuous for the average woman. Because one can speak more of urbanization than of actual industrialization—given a real exodus from the land to the urban areas, and a peculiar mix of development and underdevelopment, tradition and modernity, economic and geographic dualism—the redefinition brought about by the transition has peculiarities that are typically Italian. The process of cultural unification that has taken place, largely because of the spread of the national education system, the diffusion of mass media, and the intense internal and international migrations, has reduced differences in behavioral patterns but not eliminated them.

The separation of home and work brought an end to the family economy and an end to the prevailing family bonds. No longer did the entire family work together, but instead the husband left home early in the morning to go to the factory or office and returned late in the evening.

Economic Miracle and Internal Migration

The move toward full emancipation was slow. Notwithstanding the social changes and the economic boom of the early 1960s, women did not enter the workforce en masse; indeed, the number actually went down. The 6,500,000 women at work in 1959 declined to 5,110,000 by 1972—a unique development in Western nations, where the numbers of women in the workforce had been mounting. There are several reasons why industrial employment for women remained relatively low in Italy compared to other well-advanced European countries:

» In Italy there has never been a condition of full employment for men, and in Italian society, male unemployment is considered a greater evil than female unemployment;

» Wage differentials between men and women are less marked in Italy than in other Western countries, and employers have, therefore, little incentive to hire women because their work is not significantly cheaper;

» Labor legislation for the protection of women workers during pregnancy and in the period following each childbirth is progressive in Italy, but this very fact produces serious obstacles to the employment of married women.

» Employers tend to avoid hiring workers who are likely to be absent from work for prolonged periods of time and who show a high rate of absenteeism, yet who cannot be fired due to the legal protection accorded to motherhood.[6]

» Another factor no less important is the fact that the relocation of a considerable part of the population from the backward regions of the south to the industrialized regions of the north radically changed the family's needs and often profoundly weakened kinship alliances.

The lack of enough public facilities for child care such as kindergartens and nursery schools, the fact that full-time schooling has been practically nonexistent, and the demise of the extended family make it extremely difficult for many mothers to have full-time employment.

However, the official data do not tell the whole story about female employment. Because of the peculiar industrial development and the widespread system of black labor—of work not officially registered as such and for which employers evade paying for social security and other kinds of benefits—there is a much higher percentage of working women than is indicated by the statistics.

In the early years of the new industrial Italy, not only were families restructured—e.g., the average number of extended family members declined drastically—but the roles of their members were redefined. The role of the husband and father was to be the wage earner, while the wife's responsibility involved the "preservation of familial unity in terms of love, personal happiness, and domestic felicity."[7] The wife became the proud *casalinga,* the housewife.

For many women, especially those who moved north from the south or to the urban centers from the countryside, life in a comfortable and secure setting meant progress in a real sense. For the husband, too, having a wife at home who was the "queen" of the house meant real success. To return for vacation to the south or to one's rural areas of origin and be able to boast about a "well-kept" wife meant a profound social improvement for the new urban man. The transfer to the cities gave married women less freedom from traditional family hierarchies and less autonomy, but younger women in the north who came from agrarian societies where the extended family was a common structure enjoyed a greater freedom. The new idealized confinement not only intensified the isolation of married women but also acted to enclose them in a purely private dimension and to remove them even more than previously from the political and public life of the nation. The nuclear family, which was seen as the normative family form in modern industrial society, was not the means toward self-realization that women had hoped for. Instead, the family fettered women, trapping them in the private sphere of the household and in the role of housewife.

In the urban society, the *casalinga* was subordinated to her husband economically and legally. Until the mid-1970s, the husband was defined as the "head of the household" by Italian civil law. By implication, women had a secondary role in every aspect of Italian society. For instance, before 1969, adultery by women (but not by men) was a crime, with stiffer penalties than rape. Rape was considered merely a temporary possession of the female body, while adultery was theft not only of the body but also of allegiance, of the whole woman, love, "soul," honor, and pride. In 1961, the constitutional court defended Article 559 of the penal code, which stated that adultery of the woman could be punished with a prison sentence, whereas that of a man was not a criminal offense. The court maintained that this did not contravene the sex equality article of the constitution because a woman's adultery was an act of "different and greater entity" than that of man. The court changed its mind only in December 1981.

Women in the Students' Movement

The Italian political tradition did not offer much to women. In the marketplace of ideologies, Marxism, in spite of the enrichments brought about by thinkers such as Antonio Labriola and Antonio Gramsci, was still concerned essentially with the forging of alliances between social classes that were organized as specific political parties and not with improving the lot of women. For the millions of party members, communism was an alternative Italy within Italy. The party offered the abstract utopian hope that, one day, all Italy would be communist and, thus, all women would be equal to one another.

As with so many other things, the place and role of women in society started to change with the student movement that began in the fall of 1967. This movement was, among other things, the expression of a social conflict that could not be defined in terms of class, but it was also a movement that critiqued authority and accepted forms of organization and behavior while reproducing, within itself, the subordination of women. Thus, those radical women who were attracted to the politics of the students' movement perceived fairly early on the marked contradiction between the goals of the movement in general and its patriarchal form of organization. Even though in the first several months women did not play a strong role (indeed, they experienced considerable ambivalence in their attitude toward the movement), more young women took part in politics than at any time since 1945. Although most of them remained subordinate within the movement, unable to express their own needs and desires, there were strong positive elements of new political commitment and an extraordinarily intense sociability. These were important years of fermentation, culminating in the formation of several women's groups, which by 1975 constituted a strong national women's movement, a movement that was mostly political rather than intellectual.

Women's Movement

While some of the impetus for the women's movement in Italy came from the student protests of the late 1960s, it mainly grew out of the small feminist groups that were formed by mostly middle-class women at the beginning of the 1970s in major urban centers. Though certainly a consequence of the many economic, social, and cultural changes that had been transforming Italy, during the 1970s the movement took on a life of its own. It became an important interlocutor of political parties, trade unions, and social movements. In the first stage, the movement found its propulsion mainly in the American women's movement, with its emphasis on separatism and gender consciousness-raising. However, the impact of inflation and the stagnation of the economy, caused especially by the oil crisis, cannot be underestimated either. Working-class women especially found it increasingly difficult to balance family budgets. Their own potential for contributing to their families' resources through paid work was constantly menaced by the economic crisis. Political action to meet specific social needs became their initial primary demand.

Contrary to the American counterpart movement, which was for the most part elitist and engaged in having token women appointed to top, visible positions, the Italian movement attracted most of its adherents from the middle and lower classes and worked to develop a collective consciousness. Italian women became involved in social struggles on an unprecedented scale. The battles for housing and for improved services in the neighborhoods, among others, saw women emerge from the private sphere and take a leading role in collective action. Interested in dealing with their experiences in a man's world (patriarchal, fraternal, etc.) that was hostile to them, women worked together to analyze their own sexuality and their oppression by men and to formulate demands that were less for parity than for women's rights. Italian feminists wanted a loose and non-authoritarian organization of all forms of institutions. In a sense, the movement sought to discover and affirm female subjectivity. Whether or not it proved possible to do away with the mediation of men, women within the movement saw themselves as women, laying claim to a gendered identity and seeking to understand and live out that identity. Women worked with men to pass legislation that affected the lives of women in the private sphere and in the social and global environment.

The Emergence of Different Women's Groups

Different groups in the Italian women's movement raised different demands and issues. *Lotta Femminista* (Women's Struggle) raised the slogan of "wages for housework"; the issue, which touched all classes, was meant to equalize the household environment and provide a healthier context for decisions on procreation and sexuality and to improve the poor relationships between men and women, which the group attributed to women's economic dependence on men. The UDI, *Unione delle Donne Italiane,* the traditional movement of communist women, put more emphasis on the intervention of the state to relieve women's oppression, while *Rivolta Femminile* denounced marriage and the family as the site of male domination. One of the most influential groups was the *MLD, the Movimento della Liberazione delle Donne Italiane* (Movement for the Liberation of Italian Women). *MLD* combined demands for equality—the elimination of gender discrimination in the schools, of sexual discrimination at work, etc.—with those that would increase women's autonomy, such as the right to control their own bodies through free contraception and the liberalization of abortion laws. In 1975 the *MLD,* with the support of the small Radical Party, organized the collection of signatures for a referendum on the abortion question. Five hundred thousand signatures were needed; 800,000 were collected. Women's mobilization on this issue transformed it from an important civil-rights question into a wide-ranging discussion on woman's position in Italian society.[8]

About 35 years or so have elapsed since the birth of the new feminism in Italy. There is no doubt that it has scored some remarkable successes both in the domain of ideas and institutionally. Nevertheless, it has changed its approach for changes. The women's movement of today has come to understand that it needs the cooperation of men on the political level to create enough mass support to bring women's issues to the forefront. This generation of young women generally welcomes men into the movement. Feminists do not speak in terms of "us" vs. "them" but of cooperation and of natural and social relationships. They recognize that men are basic to women's life as women are basic to men's, and young women have been able to create a discussion about men's stake in the women's movement and reasons that men should contribute to social and political change. Italian men have come to understand that the solution of women's issues directly benefits them too.

Moreover, the number of grassroots groups has grown larger, especially women's networks in various sectors of professional life. The same is true of women's cultural centers, resources, and support centers, which have opened in various larger and middle-size towns, with the purpose of providing counseling on matters of sexual violence, battering, harassment, etc., or advising women on issues of professional and work discrimination.

New Legislation

Pressures from the women's movement were also a determinant in bringing women legally on a par with men. In 1971, women obtained equal rights of guardianship to their children in the case of separation or divorce. In 1975, a long-awaited reform of the family law established parity between the two partners in marriage. Previous insistence on the supremacy of the male head of household and of the right of the husband to control his wife's behavior and activity was abandoned definitively. The new laws also stipulated that the housewife share equally in family property, thus acknowledging the contribution represented by domestic work. In 1977, men and women were given equal status at work, including equality of pay for the same kind of work, regardless of the value of the product, and retirement rights at 60. A wife now also retains personal ownership of any property she has brought to the marriage, while women working in the civil service can get a pension after fifteen years if they have one child. Of particular interest is the recognition of the right of fathers as well as mothers to be absent from work in order to look after children—and not just children by blood, but adoptive children and other children for whose care the worker is responsible are included.

A change has occurred in the area of sexual crimes, where in the past a man facing assault charges got away scot-free if his victim was unwed and he then married her in what was known as a "reparative marriage." Today police investigators and magistrates are showing greater respect for victims of sexual violence than they did only a few years ago, although rapists often still receive lenient sentences, which may be even further reduced on appeal. Nevertheless, between 1979 and 1980, the criminal code dealing with rape, sexual violence, and extenuating circumstances by reasons of "honor" came under scrutiny, and an all-encompassing and radical reform bill was introduced in Parliament, thanks to the efforts of women's groups. The cases of extenuating circumstances on account of "honor" were repealed in 1981; "crime of passion" vanished from the criminal code.

As late as the 1960s, the old moral codes of this Catholic society remained in force. All evidence suggested that Italian unmarried girls generally, especially in the south and in the provinces, were among the most virginal in Europe. Until the 1960s virginity in unmarried women was still highly prized by many Italians despite the changes in sexual mores. When a nationwide sample of 1,000 people of both sexes was polled in 1977, 57.1% were found to attribute prime importance to female virginity before marriage. Predictably, the strongest response against premarital sex for women came from the south.

New Behavior

However, following the lead of the Nordic countries, in the 1970s sexual freedom had finally begun to spread. Parents were more willing to allow their daughters to go out more freely with boys; young people had more leisure and money for going off together. At the beginning, the new freedom was welcomed with mixed feelings: on the one hand, they welcomed the growing climate of frankness between the sexes, on the other, they felt uncomfortable without any form of convention.

The major shift in values in the 1970s was due to several factors: foreign influence, the freeing of legal controls over contraception, the steady decline in the role of the Church. The majority of teenagers are now promiscuous for at least a while. Sex in this phase is rarely linked with love: it is simply a means of communication and self-discovery. For most teenagers, virginity is no longer considered a virtue. It should be pointed out that, once again, such liberalization is far less evident in small towns or rural areas than in large urban centers. Some social classes, too, remain more strict than others. Working-class families tend to retain a more stringent sense of morality, a tighter watch over their daughters, than the middle class. But overall, a father cannot expect to bring to the altar a virgin daughter, and the groom, after having slept with so many girls, cannot expect to marry a virgin.

Despite the new sexual freedom and equality, traces of the old Latin mentality persist, at least among the over-40 crowd. Even today, a woman must not be too brash or assertive, she must use guile to achieve her sexual ends, or she will be considered unattractive, and what she treasures above all is male appreciation of her femininity. This she is given abundantly. The Italian male's demonstrative pleasure in female company gives to relations between the sexes a certain romantic tenderness and intimacy not always equaled in countries with an older tradition of emancipation. In spite of his egotism, and partly to flatter his own vanity and sense of sexual power, the Italian man is more sensitively concerned than most males to see that his woman, too, is fulfilled.

All these changes have also had an impact on the political behavior of women. Education and work opportunities have freed many women from the pervasive electoral influence of the pulpit. This is especially notable in the south and in the northeast, traditionally Catholic regions where the *DC* enjoyed until very recent years its most impressive bedrock strength. In fact, in these regions, electoral shifts away from the Christian Democrats could not have occurred or would not have been as strong were it not for some radical changes in the voting patterns of women.

Legalization of Abortion

Until the early 1960s birth control was almost as taboo in public discussion in Italy as it was during the fascist period. (Hypocritically, on the pretext that they limited syphilis, male condoms had always been freely on sale in drugstores.) Abortion was legal only when the mother's life was in danger, and most doctors interpreted this with a religious literalness. Consequently, death from clumsy self-abortion ran into several thousand per year. Certainly, rich and informed women avoided these problems by traveling to private doctors in Switzerland or England. But millions of working wives, faced with raising a large family in cramped Italian housing, came to regard sex and their husbands' desires with panic. Reform had been blocked mainly by Catholic opinion, but the 1960s saw a steady change of heart among fervent Catholics, including, even, the clergy. The campaign of a few pioneers forced a breach in the curtain of social prejudice and brought the whole issue into the open. The prejudices waned first in the middle class; working-class wives remained reticent far longer. It seems there was a political element here, since official communist policy for many years was to oppose birth control as a capitalist trick to reduce the numbers of the proletariat. But beginning in the early 1970s the *PCI* swung in favor of contraception, as well as for abortion, and this change in attitude paved the way for a steady change in working-class attitudes.

As with birth control, the government for years was afraid of legalizing abortion for various political reasons. Not only was the opposition from the Church and traditional Catholics far stronger in this case, but there was a clear hostile majority among the pro-government parties in parliament. The current law gives women, married or single, the right to claim an abortion within the first 12 weeks of pregnancy; after this, termination can take place only if there is medical evidence that there is grave risk to the health of the mother or the child, verified by two specialists. There are some other restrictions: minors (under 18) must obtain parental consent; a woman must first be interviewed by a psychiatrist to establish that the abortion is psychologically sustainable. Abortion is not free, but it is covered within the social security system, which reimburses a percentage of the cost. So today, women don't have to go abroad or resort to the back-street hacks; the situation is certainly helped as well by the continuing spread of contraception. However, problems do exist, caused partly by a shortage of hospital facilities and especially by the fact that many doctors, nurses, and hospital directors are refusing to cooperate. Medical personnel who are practicing Catholics have the right to invoke a conscience clause.

The belated legalization of contraception, and then of abortion, has been a major factor behind women's great leap forward over the past decades. Psychologically and practically, these changes have liberated women in many ways. These shifts are the basis of their new pre-marital sexual freedom, and inside marriage women are now more able to order their lives as they would wish. But these advances are still contested by many Catholics. Still in the moral Catholic context, in 2003 Italian lawmakers enacted rules that limit reproductive scientific applications. The law bans the use of donor sperm, eggs or surrogate mothers and restricts assisted fertilization to heterosexuals.

Marriage

Over the past 25 or 30 years, because of divorce and new sexual behavior, the number of first-time marriages has been going down while the number of consensual unions, as a flexible alternative to marriage, has grown. However, the development of cohabitation in Italy differs not only quantitatively from that of other European countries but also in its essence. In 1996, 45% of all Swedish women aged 20 to 24 were cohabiting. The corresponding percentages for women in this age group for the Netherlands and Germany were 17% and 16%, respectively. In contrast, rates of non-marital cohabitation are very low in Italy and in several other Mediterranean countries (Spain, Portugal, Greece) as well as in Ireland. Although cohabitation figures have begun to rise in Italy, in 1996 only 4% of Italian women aged 30 to 34 lived in an informal union and much lower rates were identified for younger age groups. Within Italy there is a high degree of regional heterogeneity. In 2001, 3.6% of all Italian couples were living in cohabitation. In the northern regions, especially in Valle d'Aosta and Emilia Romagna (which are also the regions with the lowest fertility rates in the country), the proportion was between 5% and 8%. In the south of Italy the figures are below 2% (*ISTAT 2001, Censimento*). When it comes to the diffusion of the different stages of non-marital cohabitation—cohabitation as an avant-garde lifestyle, as a preliminary stage before marriage, as a socially accepted living arrangement, and as a partnership equal to marriage—in Italy in relation to Europe, again Italy is different. In the Nordic countries, non-marital unions are socially accepted as alternatives to marriage. In Italy, in contrast, cohabitation remains a precursor in the transition to marriage. There are two reasons for this difference: Catholic upbringing, and, most of all, lack of stable job opportunities for the age group 18–30. On the issue of marriage, it is interesting to take a look at the mixed marriages *(See Box on p. 332).*

Although the prospect of finding part-time and temporary contracts for full-time jobs has increased, the economic uncertainty of young adults has increased additionally. Under these circumstances young adults are not able to form autonomous households. Furthermore, the structure of the housing market is very rigid: most people own the property in which they live— renting an apartment is highly uncommon and very expensive. Another factor influencing the transition to non-marital unions is the family background. Women coming from families with more highly educated fathers tend to be forerunners in the development of informal unions in northern Italy. Women with two highly educated parents as well as women with mothers who have a higher level of education than does the father are significantly more likely to enter such a union.

Women in the Work Force

The last fifteen or twenty years have brought about a significant transformation in the social identity of Italian women through employment. The shift in the Italian economy—the growth of the service sector, and especially the growth of public welfare services in the late 70s and early

Café   *Mixed Marriages Booming*

The recent influx of immigrants has caused a surge in mixed marriages in Italy. In Italy such interracial marriages are quite a new feature compared with the United Kingdom or France, which have a richer history of colonialism and contacts with a variety of nations; so, although they are still not very common, they are on the rise.

The number of marriages between Italians and foreign natives living in Italy has increased tenfold in the past 15 years.

According to ISTAT, a statistic agency, mixed marriages are up from 60,000 in 1991 to 600,000 in 2006. In the last 10 years there has been an increase of 300%. In 2004, 10.4% of Italian marriages were between mixed couples.

Italian men appear to prefer Filipino, Romanian, Peruvian, and Albanian women. More than three quarters of Filipino women in Italy have married Italians, while 67% of Romanian immigrants have tied the knot with Italians. About 60% of Peruvian and Albanian women have Italian husbands.

Italian women, by contrast, appear to prefer North Africans. 75% of the Senegalese have Italian wives. Tunisians come second with 72%, followed by Moroccans with 53%. The Chinese are more likely to marry someone from their same ethnic background: more than 84% of Chinese in Italy marry other Chinese.

Geographically, prosperous northern Italy leads the way in mixed marriages. Even so, mixed marriages are more likely to last in the south as opposed to the north. In addition, the number of children of mixed marriages has risen 22% in the last six years, and 10% of marriages are now between Muslims and Catholics. In the vast majority of such cases, the children are raised as Muslims. If the wife is Catholic, statistics show that she is likely to convert to Islam. Given the profound cultural differences, it is not surprising that these mixed marriages are fragile—although there too the figures show a geographical difference. The average Catholic-Muslim union lasts just 5 years in the northern city of Milan, and 13 years in southern Lecce.

80s—offered possibilities for women's employment that previously had not existed. Women were able to grasp these opportunities for a number of reasons:

» They were better educated than ever before;
» Equal opportunities legislation (especially the laws of 1977 and 1991) had opened up areas of the labor market previously excluded to them;
» They were having fewer children, though whether this was the cause or the consequence of increased women's employment is debatable.

Traditional patterns of gender differences were interrupted. The image of the man as better educated, as the principal breadwinner, as the family figure with exclusive access to the public world of work, and that of the woman as having less education, as mother and housewife, became blurred. Women were moving out, making contact with a wider world, and few aspects of modernity were to produce so great a feeling of liberation as well as so much anguish.

Working life has been regulated by sweeping pieces of legislation. Legislation hinged on the idea that women's basic rights—the right to work and have economic independence—should not be infringed by childbearing. Starting in the 1960s the Italian Parliament protected motherhood with very progressive laws. Maternity leave now lasts five months (two before giving birth and three after) at 100% salary for employees and 80% for the self-employed; an additional six months of unpaid leave are available, with the right to return to the same job afterwards. The constitutional court has issued a ruling that in the absence of the mother due to death, disease, or other serious cause, the father may make use of the leave after childbirth, thereby guaranteeing child care by a parent. The laws also provide for optional leaves in the event that the child is sick or handicapped.

The concept of the "social value of motherhood" also fueled a drive for kindergartens and day-care centers. In 1968, kindergartens (for children from age three to six) came to be part of the educational system in many towns and cities; the system has expanded somewhat over the past years, in spite of much criticism of the schedules, which often do not meet working women's needs.

To accommodate the new role of men and women in the family, the pension system has also been changed so that a pension plan can be transferred not just from a husband to his widow but from a wife to her widower. The most important instrument of change was Bill 903 of 1977 because it eliminated all discrimination in hiring practices, promotions, salaries, and social security.

As a result of the progress women have made, women's roles in society and their relation to those roles have become increasingly complex. Because women are no longer defined exclusively or even primarily by family but instead by work, it is important to see women in the job market.

Italian women's entry into the world of work occurred at a much lower rate than that of other Western countries. Although women were given the chance to obtain the same education as men, as we have seen, there are many reasons why in Italy women have not been competitive with men in the labor market. Nevertheless big changes did take place.

In 1961 the rate of female activity in Italy (the number of women working or actively seeking work as a percentage of all women able to work) stood at a lowly 22%; by 1991 it had risen to around 30%. At the same time the female labor force in Italy had reached 37.2% of the total labor force.

The modest numerical change hides a profound social change. There was, for instance, a spectacular rise in the female presence in some high-status professional jobs: for example, the number of female prosecutors and judges doubled between 1985 and 1992. Above all, women workers became visible in great numbers: there were women working on construction sites, collecting garbage, policing streets, inspecting tickets on trains. To the casual eye, it became evident that the habitual gender division of work, so heavily centered in the past on the public–private divide, had been radically transformed.

When the "miracle" was over, women began to return to the labor force, but they tended, on the whole, to take jobs in the so-called hidden economy of casual labor and small family firms. Women workers can stay at home and look after their children and at the same time contribute to the family income. But many factors have influenced the entrance of women into the job market. It seems that women born between 1936 and 1946 who were adolescents during the emergence of the culture of consumption and the availability of washing machines, refrigerators, cars, and televisions, moved into the labor force in large numbers in the mid-seventies, after they had raised their children. Women born between 1947 and 1957, who experienced the political turmoil and changes of the late 1960s and early 70s and faced gender debates and changes (including the legalization of abortion and contraception) at the onset of adulthood and their first adult choices—marriage, childbearing, and holding or giving up a job—were the first to enter the labor force in great numbers and to remain in it after marrying and having children. Women who entered adulthood in the middle 80s, born between 1962 and 1968, seem to have a different social identification from older women because they have greater equality with men and have benefited from the gains that the preceding generation obtained. However, these women no longer have a sense of collective identification and goals as the previous generation had.

Anomaly in Today's Labor Force

There is an anomaly in the Italian labor force: the low participation rates of married women in the labor market together with low birth rates among these same women. The explanation for this apparent anomaly involves the Italian institutional structure, particularly as reflected in rigidities and imperfections in the labor market and characteristics of the public-funded child care system. These rigidities tend to simultaneously increase the costs of having children and discourage the labor market participation of married women. (The Italian labor market is highly regulated. Strict rules regarding the hiring and firing of workers, in addition to high wages for entry-level workers, severely restrict employment opportunities for labor market entrants. These regulations have been largely responsible for the official high unemployment rates of women and youth and their consequent widespread employment in the underground economy.) Empirical results show that the availability of both child care and part-time work increases a woman's probability of working and of having a child. Policies that would provide more flexible working hours and greater child care availability would help reduce the financial burden of children. The fact that part-time employment was extremely rare in Italy until the Biagi law was passed in 2001 is an important factor in accounting for the low employment rates of married women, particularly those with children. Married women who choose to or must work tend to have full-time work commitments, which are less compatible with having large numbers of children. Moreover, even married women who do not work tend to limit their family size, at least in part due to the characteristics of the labor market. Because entry-level positions are so hard to find, many young adults live at home until they find their first "stable" employment, which often doesn't happen until they are in their early 30s. The Berlusconi government revised some labor laws to create more part-time jobs, and the results were positive. However, the center-Left government led by Prodi is committed to revising the law.

The public child care system does not provide much assistance to families. In particular, while the quality of publicly-provided child care services is very high in many regions in Italy, there are a limited number of slots available, and the hours of child care are typically compatible with full-time working hours in specific public employment sectors (e.g., teaching or public administration). The availability of family support, both in the form of transfers and in the form of grandparents, increases both the probability of market work and of having children. But that support has waned during the last fifteen years.

A survey taken in the mid-1980s showed that 22.5% of Italian women had full-time jobs, 5.8% had casual employment, and 71.8% did not work. However, it is difficult to have exact figures in this area because many Italian women carry on industrial production in their living rooms, ranging from knitting and sewing clothes to making electronic components. It is estimated that women make up 70% of the unofficial labor market.

If we examine women's employment in various categories of the service sector we find that, without exception, women tend to be concentrated in the lower-paid jobs, although there has been a marked improvement since the 1980s. Women's increased entry into the civil service occupations occurred concurrently with a lowering in the prestige of such occupations. It has been found that women, unlike men, are attracted to civil service jobs not because of status but because of the security of tenure of work and welfare benefits as well as the formal criterion of "equality of opportunity." Women make up 66% of the education work force: 79.4% of elementary school teachers, 63.7% of middle-school teachers, 49% of high-school teachers, and 21% of university professors are women. The health profession also has a strong presence of women; 22% of physicians and over 65% of nurses are women.

Unquestionably, women in their mid-20s now entering the job market experience a greater equality than their mothers did, both legally and in their daily practices and behavior, although these experiences vary according to social contexts. Young women enter the job market with the same expectations as young males; they sometimes want to work throughout their adult lives without leaving their jobs to get married or have children. In addition, the mothers of these young women support their daughters' plans to find a job and keep it throughout the years of raising a family. Work for women is increasingly viewed as valuable for reasons of personal autonomy, as family insurance in a time of insecure employment, and as personal insurance, perhaps against the hazard of divorce.

The less a job offers them rewards, the more likely it is that young women will perceive marriage and motherhood as the only place to find a sense of self-worth. Certainly, women's lifestyles and desires depend also on the level of education achieved and the urge to prove themselves. Indeed, education was a key factor in changing the role of women in Italian society. Studies have shown that a woman's education is consistently and strongly related to gender-role attitudes. Formal education is a means of social mobility, and the right to an equal education has made women more competitive with men. Education has empowered the process of change in women's roles in Italy, but this process has met with definite constraints. Women must confront the problem of the outside labor market while trying to assure that the family organization functions adequately.

Women in Political Life

Women's participation in political life has had a determining effect on the Italian democracy. Since they were given the right to vote in 1946, women have always participated in elections in numbers that exceed 80%. Even so, there are still few women in public office. In the administrative elections in 1990, 8.5% of the candidates elected were women; in the political elections in 1992, that figure rose to 10.2%. Although these figures appear very low, they are not when viewed in comparison to other countries. In the parliamentary elections of 2006, more women than ever were candidates for office and more than ever were elected (109 of 630 equal to 17.3 % in the lower house; 44 of 315 equal to 13.7 % in the senate); six were appointed ministers in the new government.

However, it is in participation in social life through volunteer associations that the number of women becomes predominant. Women volunteers are trying to use traditional values to change society and the condition of women from outside the political system.

Women in Literature

Another important development in the sphere of culture has been the growth of women's writing, in a range of forms, from narratives to diaries to journalism. This new output draws on a long tradition of women's participation in literary work. When the modern women's movement was at its height, in the 1980s, there was a great flowering of women's writing and feminist writing, born of the sense that women now had the chance to produce and express new forms of thought. Female voices came from the experience of consciousness-raising groups, from the pages of the new women's periodicals *(Effe, Sottosopra, Differenze),* and from feminists' encouragement to one another to take their old writings out of the closet or to embark on fresh ones. At the same time, women's literature showed itself more and more aware of its cultural context and its new character. There was a complex interplay between these dimensions, a matter not of casual relationship but of common participation in the process of creating language, values, and consciousness. In the 1980s, women's literary and autobiographical writing continued to grow in energy and in quantity, engendering whole series of works, publishing houses, and bookshops, and giving rise, too, to a body of critical and reflective commentaries. Feminist publications celebrated the discovery of other women, of their speech and their bodies. As women made their presence felt in the world of publishing, the boundaries of gender shifted in the cultural sphere and a huge new market was created. All of these developments, by highlighting the growing creativity of women, highlighted also the contradictory fact that women received little institutional recognition; it fostered closer ties between members of the same sex, but it sometimes sharpened conflicts between women and men in the public sphere.

The New Complex Role of Women

Younger Italian women have more education and enjoy equal social status to men and full emancipation. At the same time, women's lifestyles and life strategies have become explicitly more diversified, as resources and options have opened up. Childlessness, celibacy, divorce, and remarriage increasingly are acceptable options. At the same time, the social competence women show (and are expected to have) in dealing with social institutions on behalf of themselves and their families is significantly changing the public/private boundaries, creating new resources for social relations and self-definitions and perceptions. It should be clear that class differences matter a great deal in the analysis of women's changing roles in Italy.[9]

Many young women still think that marrying someone they love and are loved by, and having one or two children, is the most valuable option they can choose. More often such a woman is found where there is no rooted tradition of women's work, such as in the south. An increasing number of young women, however, do not focus on marriage and motherhood as an important goal in their near future. Rather, they see having a family as a potential burden for their career and as a hindrance to having a "full life," in terms of pursuing their interests and their social relations. Although they do not reject the possibility of a family, they put it off into an indefinite future.

Moreover, the decline of the extended family and the lack of support from grandparents to help rear children have put an additional burden on women. The growth of the welfare state did not compensate for the service that the extended family was providing. "The services of the welfare state are available only if there is an individual who is prepared to engage in the necessary bureaucratic practices needed to obtain these services" (Sassoon, p. 103). This job falls in the laps of women, who must also compensate where public services fail. Moreover, the extension of the consumer society and the constant and dramatic decrease in the self-sufficiency of the household (compare a rural laborer family with an urban family who must purchase virtually everything it needs) add another task for women: the purchase of private services. Regardless of their occupation, employed women spent on average 2.5 to 3 hours more per day on housework than employed men.

By entering the male working world, women have gained freedom of movement in society, but they have also brought to their lives a burden: the splitting of their roles and identity. Many young wives have found it a great strain, both physically and psychologically, to combine a career with running a home, especially in the north where the tempo is so fast and standards so exacting: office hours are long, bosses are demanding, and a husband will expect everything just perfect when he wants to entertain. Women continue to readjust and redefine their role and the roles of other family members. Nevertheless, what is considered appropriate for a woman is less and less dictated by tradition and more and more by the ideas of the highly educated career woman.

To sum up, women work before they have children, then either abandon or continue their work while they raise their children. Thus, mothers must function as the agents of the welfare state within the family, as the agents of the consumption sector of the economy within the family (purchaser of private services). Furthermore, they must also compensate for the deficiencies of the welfare state. They are citizens of two worlds: they have full-time responsibilities in both, family and work. Not only do they assume two roles, they also belong to two complex social systems that are interrelated, yet separate, and they have full-time responsibilities in each. Working women generally have a different experience from working men, because the latter do not have full responsibility for the everyday maintenance of the family and, therefore, are not penalized by society for their reduced participation in it. Compared to women's lives, the life of the man is a rather simple one.

In the process of female emancipation, married women have found the new life style especially difficult also because their husbands, with their *machismo*, have found the adjustment hardest. Traditionally, in this Latin society, women exerted their greatest power within the family or in relation to one man, or to individual men, such as their brothers and fathers, rather than to the community. Pleasing a man lets a woman remain queen of the house. Italian men, notoriously egotists, have exploited their advantage both emotionally and in practical ways, down to refusing to help with the chores because it is thought unmanly.

This has been the general pattern, but in the past 20 years Italian women, mainly younger ones with a college education, have rebelled against it. These are the generations influenced by British and American societies via the media. Today, if her man behaves with thoughtlessly arrogant *machismo*, a woman will simply walk out on him. She expects the same degree of sexual freedom as a man, and, conversely, the same degree of fidelity from a man. Inside marriage, she demands equality of decision-making and equal control over shared finances, and she insists that her own leisure interests and her own cultural or other needs be taken as seriously as her husband's. Younger men generally adapt easily because the egalitarian experience of their student days is carried on into marriage.

Homosexuality and Individual Difference

The 1970s were crucial years for the history of gender relations in Italy. Long-standing tensions and dynamics came to the surface, expressing themselves both in legislation and in the sphere of symbolic representation, and this led to far-reaching changes in the ways people spoke and behaved. Today, there is greater freedom for lesbian and gay male relationships. Women have become more visible in a range of places and situations and more visible to one another.

Legislation on sexual matters, as on matters concerning the family, has been brought into line with advances in medicine and with common practice. The pro-abortion campaign, in particular, brought together demographic pragmatists, those campaigning for greater social justice, and those who believed in the freedom of the individual and refused the right of the state to regulate this private domain. At the same time such campaigns were being organized by women to defend and promote what were essentially seen as women's rights, campaigns were launched to secure equal legislative treatment for homosexuals. The homosexual movement echoed many of the practices of feminism: the collective-based structure, the emphasis on beginning with the personal, the critique of psychoanalysis, the celebration of the body and sexuality, the critique of the bourgeois family and of formal politics. The campaigns focused on matters such as attempting to secure harmonization of the age of consent for homosexual and heterosexual acts.

From June 1972, FUORI (*Fronte Unitario Omosessuale Rivoluzionario Italiano*, The United Italian Homosexual Revolutionary Front) published its monthly magazine of sexual liberation, also called *Fuori!*, which means "out." In its pages we find all these themes, addressed in direct, impassioned, and unsparing words and images. The movement embarked on a "critique of normality" based on a critical consciousness that went well beyond the problem of homosexuality. This consciousness drew upon the tradition of Leftist intellectual culture and referred, in a more or less critical spirit, to the works of Marx, Freud, Adorno, and Sartre. The movement proclaimed the New Revolutionary Homosexual, the man who, while he criticized the limited nature of class politics, preferring a trans-class approach, nonetheless emphasized economic and social oppression and paid attention to such questions as homosexuality in the factory. *Fuori!* offered a generalized critique of the violence of the capitalist world.

The question of homosexuality was brought into sharp focus by the AIDS epidemic. Italy has one of the largest AIDS populations in Western Europe. Hitherto these cases have been mainly confined to the male homosexual population, particularly middle-class males between the ages of 25 and 45 who live in large urban centers. A significant number of hemophiliacs have also been infected with HIV by contaminated blood, and, as elsewhere, HIV is spreading to the heterosexual population. The relatively large number of cases may reflect more efficient notification and better facilities for treatment. In the absence of a vaccination against HIV or a cure for AIDS, there has been considerable resistance to proposals for mass testing, together with a reinforcement of measures to ensure that those infected with HIV do not encounter discrimination.

Like many governments in the West, the Italian government is dealing with proposals to grant homosexual couples legal status. In 2007 the debates started at a time of increasing tension between conservatives and secular groups in Italy. Prime Minister Romano Prodi's government proposed allowing civil unions, called DICO *(diritti di coppie conviventi)* in Italy, in February 2007. The planned law, which would also give unmarried heterosexual couples more rights, met with strong opposition from conservatives and centre-Left Catholics in Parliament. Several members of Prodi's own centre-Left governing coalition are opposed, including a senator and member of the conservative Catholic group Opus Dei who has been a prominent figure among Left-wing Catholics who consider DICO a political provocation and unfair competition to marriage. This debate is taking place while the annual number of marriages in Italy fell from 419,000 in 1972 to 250,000 in 2005. The number of children born to unwed parents has doubled in 10 years.

Notes

1.   Already during the *Risorgimento*, in the pursuit of a just unification of the country, Giuseppe Mazzini was proclaiming the parity of women: "Cancel in your minds every idea of superiority over women. You have none whatsoever." D. Meyer, "Sex and Power." *The Rise of Women in America, Russia, Sweden and Italy* (Middletown, CT: Wesleyan U. P., 1987), 141.

2.   The fascist legacy in matters of pay differential between men and women ranged in 1945 between 30% and 50% in manufacturing as well as in services. In the textile industry, where women made up 75% of the workforce, they were paid from 20 to 40% less than men for the same work.

3.   As reported in M. Clark, *Modern Italy 1871–1982* (New York: Longman, 1984), 276.

4.   C. Gini and E Caranti, "The Family in Italy," *Marriage and Family Living,* 8 (1954), 354

5.   G Ascoli. "LUDI tra emancipazione e liberazione (1943–1964)," in *Problemi del Socialismo.* Oct.–Dec. 1976. 119.

6.   E. Lupri, ed., *The Changing Position of Women and Society: A Cross-National Comparison* (Leiden: The Netherlands: E. J. Brill, 1983), 5.

7.   G. Filippini, "Movimenti femminili, femminismo," in *Istituto Gramsci, La crisi della società italiana e gli orientamenti delle nuove generazioni* (Rome: Edizioni Riuniti, 1978), 110. A. Cavalli. "The Changing Role of the Women: The Case of Italy," in E. Lupri. Ed., *The Changing Position of Women in Family and Society* (Leiden, Netherlands: Brill, 1983). 183.

8.   The first major demonstration of the women's movement, some 20,000 strong, took place in Rome on December 6, 1975. Throughout the following years the women's movement developed rapidly. Women had become the center of political controversy. Another good indication of changes is provided by the 1976 general elections, for here, for the first time, every political party felt the need, in its campaign, to address itself specifically to the female electorate, to include many women in its lists of candidates to Parliament; and, finally, to manage to have them elected with an unprecedented number of votes. Women had become social actors and, probably, a social force in their own right.

There were also some structural preconditions behind the women's movement, such as an increase in female education; it would make women more competitive with men in a number of occupations. Another consequence was a decrease in the birth rate. As a result women were anchored to domestic chores for a shorter period of time.

As the women's movement gained momentum, the two leading parties increasingly cultivated women's support. Although the *PCI* had always had a smaller proportion of women members than the *DC*, it certainly did more to promote the advancement of the women in their party than did the *DC*. In the chamber of deputies that was elected in 1983 19.9% of *PCI* deputies were women (38 out of 198) against 2.6% for the *DC* (6 out of 255) and 1.4% (1 out of 73) for the *PSI*. The total of women corresponded to 7.9% of all deputies', more than twice those in the British House of Commons or the American Congress. The highest office in Italian politics ever held by a woman was held by Nilde Jotti, a communist leader, when she became president of the chamber of deputies in 1979 and held the position until 1992. Another woman, Irene Pivetti, filled that high position in government for a shorter period.

9.   See Alessandro Cavalli, 186–189.

Bibliography

Accati, L., "Explicit Meanings: Catholicism, Matriarchy and the Distinctive Problems of Italian Feminism" in *Gender and History,* 7 (1995).

Baranski, Z.G. and W.Vinall, S., eds., *Women and Italy: Essays on Gender, Culture and History* (London: Macmillan, 1991).

Bono, P. and Kemp, S., eds., *Italian Feminist Thought: A Reader* (Oxford: Blackwell, 1991).

Bono, P. and Kemp, S., eds., *The Lonely Mirror: Italian Perspectives on Feminist Theory,* (London: Routledge, 1993).

Cavalli, A., "The Changing Role of the Women : The Case of Italy," in E. Lupri. Ed., *The Changing Position of Women in Family and Society* (Leiden, The Netherlands: Brill, 1983).

Cicioni, M. and Prunster, N., eds., *Visions and Revisions, Women in Italian Culture* (London: Berg, 1993).

Clark, M., *Modern Italy 1871–1982* (New York: Longman, 1984).

Gini, C. and Caranti, E., "The family in Italy," *Marriage and Family Living,* 18 (1954).

Lazzaro-Weis, C., *From Margins to Mainstream: Feminism and Fictional modes in Italian Women's Writing 1968–1990* (Philadelphia: University of Pennsylvania Press, 1993).

Lupri, E., ed., *The Changing Position of Women and Society: A Cross-National Comparison* (Leiden, The Netherlands: E. J. Brill, 1983).

Meyer, D., "Sex and Power." *The Rise of Women in America, Russia, Sweden and Italy* (Middletown, CT: Wesleyan U. P., 1987).

Miceli-Jeffries, G., ed., *Feminine Feminists: Cultural Practices in Italy,* (Minneapolis and London: University of Minnesota Press, 1994).

Panizza, L. and Wood, S., eds., *A History of Women's Writing in Italy.* (Cambridge University Press, 2001).

Piccone, S. and Saraceno, C, *Genere: La costruzione sociale del femminile e del maschile.* (Bologna: Il Mulino, 1996).

http://digital.library.upenn.edu/women/eagle/congress/salazar.html

http://www.columbia.edu/~mjw2023/1Cultural.html (For a good comparison of Italian families with the rest of the world throughout the past 100 years): *http://www.unu.edu/unupress/unupbooks/uu13se/uu13se02.htm*

http://www.tcd.ie/erc/activ/Newslett/NLissue4.pdf

PART 4

COMMUNICATIONS AND CULTURAL CHANGES

Introduction

The old concept of culture exclusively identified with education, literacy, and "print culture," as well as with the high arts, began to change in Italy at the end of the 1960s, much later than in other Western nations. A number of reasons may explain the resiliency of the old concept:

- » the combination of restricted access to institutions of higher learning and low national rates of literacy, particularly in rural areas;
- » the prestige and durability of a humanist intellectual tradition—the neo-idealism associated particularly with the philosophers Benedetto Croce (1866–1952) and Giovanni Gentile (1875–1944)—which identified culture with intellectuals and cultural history with intellectual history;
- » the international prestige enjoyed by the "high" arts.

Today, however, the prevalent concept of *cultura* among Italian intellectuals is very broad and encompasses many social manifestations. It seems that Italians have also come to accept the view that identity is molded by consumption, that there is something one could call consumer identity. The term commodity aesthetics, referring on the one hand to beauty as an appearance appealing to the senses, and on the other hand to a beauty developed in the service of the realization of exchange of value, has had an impact on Italians' view of culture and how it is produced. The creation/production of culture as a product is part of the system of selling and buying of aesthetic illusions, of commodities bearing value and, therefore, the use of values. The more affluent a society is, the broader and stronger are this culture and the cultural phenomenon.

This new view of culture was influenced by the economic development and rapid urbanization which was accompanied by a remarkable rise in living standards as reflected in consumer modes, lifestyles, and leisure activities. From the new fad for designer clothes to the kinds of vacations they take, Italians have become more able and willing to spend more euros, to be more mobile, open, and socially homogeneous.

The passion of the Italians for good clothes and anything that displays good taste is well known, as is their leading role in the fashion world. Although Milan has become the unquestioned world fashion center, trend-setter, and a Mecca for foreign talent, the whole country is rich in high-level designers. The new fashions have for many years been quickly copied and mass produced for the major stores at prices within the reach of all strata of society. Today, the ordinary woman dresses more elegantly than she did 30 years ago and not much differently from those in wealthier families. Fashion magazines and television have drummed notions of elegance into the heads of ordinary Italian women who, as a general breed, have always had a special claim to being very well dressed.

Popular magazines and television can also take some of the credit for improvements in housekeeping, personal appearance, and especially hygiene. New campaigns brought about a rise in the sales of detergents, deodorants, toothpaste, and a big variety of shampoos and cosmetics. Modern techniques of advertising and public relations arrived late in Italy but then swept through the land with torrential force. In the process, the experts decided that Italians could be conditioned to accept a commodity as new and smart if it were given an English name; therefore, the clothing and cosmetics worlds virtually adopted English as a lingua franca.

Such social transformation was not separate from the cultural modernization of the country. In many of their leisure habits (discotheques, weekend pleasure, sports and various entertainment activities), as in so much else (the spread of television, personal computers, stereos, cellular phones), Italians have surpassed most industrialized nations. The cinema was the first area to incorporate a new cultural style. Immediately after the war, directors of the "neorealistic" school, such as Roberto Rossellini, Vittorio De Sica, and Luchino Visconti, focused on contemporary Italian problems and characters taken from ordinary life and made the Italian film world famous. The neorealist cinema had a greater commercial and artistic impact abroad than in Italy, which remained dominated by Hollywood productions. Even after 1951, when a U.S.-Italy accord curbed imports and allowed more Italian films to be exported to the U.S., American films predominated at the Italian box office; nevertheless, Italian neorealist works had a lasting cultural influence in the cinematic field.

In the 1960s new artists emerged who represented life from different angles and through different "lenses." Directors such as Federico Fellini, Mario Monicelli, and Pietro Germi brought to the world films that opened new approaches for the representation of different levels of reality. In the 1970s, the crisis that struck Italian society affected the film industry as well. Italian filmmakers explored alienation in modern life and political issues of concern to Leftists of that period. Directors such as Michelangelo Antonioni, Pier Paolo Pasolini, Bernardo Bertolucci, Lina Wertmuller, Elio Petri, Ettore Scola, and Francesco Rosi became famous all over the world.

Cinema is an important art form for understanding the evolution of any society. In the case of Italian cinema, we also see how rapidly the culture of the country changed and how culture is consumed. One of the most striking aspects of these changes is how stars are "produced" and "consumed." The star phenomenon is not strictly Italian. Stars arise in societies that are democratic, capitalist, predominantly urban, and at least moderately prosperous and in possession of an extensive network of mass communications. However, in Italian culture there is something more: the cult for *bella figura*. And the *bella figura* must be seen in relation to the role of *piazza* (square) in Italian life, the architecture of buildings, the role of bar/caffè in daily life.

The social, economic, and political changes discussed in the previous chapters were accompanied by a dramatic decline in illiteracy; the surge of mass media brought about for the first time in Italy a uniform, nationwide mass culture. New interest in books and cultural products has also had profound effects on every aspect of literary culture in Italy. Everything surrounding the actual literary texts has been affected too—production, distribution, sales, and, above all, the reading public. Changes in all these areas in turn have had their effects on writing itself, on its general role and status in society, and on the role of those who write. At the same time, traditional practices and long-standing social factors have continued to play an important part, exerting a conservative, braking pressure on the drive toward innovation and expansion.

The Colosseum, the largest amphitheater ever built in the Roman Empire, is one of the greatest works of Roman architecture and engineering. Originally capable of seating around 50,000 spectators, it was used for gladiators' contests and public spectacle. From the archive of the author.

CHAPTER 13

CULTURAL MODERNIZATION

Changes and Conflicts

New Consumer Modes:
Literary Culture and the Reading Public

Language Changes

In the profound socio-cultural changes that took place in Italy after WWII, the Italian language, its dialects, and everything related to printed material experienced intense transformation. The changes were due to many factors, including education; internal migration; the construction of superhighways; the arrival and popularity of mass media, especially radio and television; and urbanization.

Standard Italian (*italiano*) is a Romance language.[1] Out of all the Romance languages, Italian is generally considered to be the one most closely resembling Latin in grammar, vocabulary, and pronunciation. Since about sixty percent of English words derive from Latin, anyone studying Italian enriches tremendously his or her English vocabulary. Most of the dialects spoken by Italians, like standard Italian, derive from Latin.[2] In fact, standard Italian is the evolution of the Tuscan dialect, one of the dialects of central Italy that imposed itself as the literary language in the thirteenth century.[3]

Dialects

Many of the so-called dialects of Italian spoken around the country are different enough from standard Italian as to be considered separate languages by most linguists and by some speakers themselves. It can be said that they are separate Romance languages and differ from each other as much as French differs from Spanish. They differ from each other in phonology, grammar, and vocabulary. It should also be said that many dialects have a long-standing and rich literary tradition, in many cases going back to the Middle Ages. In fact, they are part of the Italian literary tradition. We should also underline that what we call Italian literature finds expression, up to the sixteenth century, mainly in two languages, Latin and its vernacular, and from the beginning of the sixteenth century a third medium was added, dialect. Dialect literature is of course not the same as popular literature and normally belongs to a sophisticated level of elaborate, self-conscious high culture, rather than to spontaneous popular culture.

How many different dialects are spoken in Italy? The question is problematic; just as it is difficult to assess the number of languages in the world, so it is difficult to assess the number of Italian dialects. Linguists agree on about fifteen main dialect groups, clearly different from each other and roughly corresponding to the traditional subdivisions into regions. But it is clear that often there are noticeable differences between neighboring towns, and even within the same town. The issue of the dialects is separate from that of *linguistic minorities*. These are enclaves of speakers of foreign languages, often established in Italy for many centuries.[4]

The attempt to establish how the use of dialects has changed and/or how many people use Italian and how many use dialect poses considerable difficulties. Only since 1951 do statistical data distinguish between literates and semiliterates. The census of 1951 revealed that 12.9% of Italians over the age of six were illiterate; in the south the illiteracy rate reached 24%. We must remember that, at this time, Italy had been unified for less than 100 years. Having been dominated by so many diverse countries and cultures, there were dozens of dialects still in common use immediately after WWII. In addition, until recently the agrarian and laborer population was largely illiterate. This situation has changed greatly in the last forty years, but many old people still usually speak a dialect.

In 1862, it was estimated that the number of people in the country who could speak Italian (i.e., either the old Florentine-based literary language or the dialects of Tuscany and Rome that were close to it) was between 2.5% and 10% of the population. In other words, the national language was not used by at least 90% of Italians. Italian was essentially a written language that had yet to enter into common spoken use. Even when it did, it would take several generations to start supplanting the dialects.

In more recent years the figures, as we may expect, are very different:

Usage in the family	1974	1982	1988	1991
dialects with everyone	51%	47%	40%	36%
Italian with everyone	25%	29%	34%	34%
Usage with friends and colleagues				
Only or mainly dialect	42%	36%	33%	23 %
Only or mainly Italian	36%	42%	47%	48%

Source: ISTAT 1993

The data are not based on direct observation of linguistic behavior, which would be extremely difficult to assess but on answers given by 2,000 adults to a questionnaire concerning linguistic behavior. The questionnaire asked whether the informant spoke Italian, or a dialect, or both (a) in the home or (b) with friends and colleagues. Since, in general, more prestige is attached to the use of Italian, it is possible that the answers were biased in that direction. The figures are also interesting when they are interpreted analytically. There are proportionally more dialect speakers among women than men; among older than younger people; in the south and the islands than in the center and north; in the country than in the urban centers; and in the lower than in the middle and upper classes. These data obviously show a fall in the use of a dialect and a rise in the use of Italian. Italy today is a largely bilingual country where the standard language is much more used, whereas before the 1960s it was effectively a monolingual one, consisting of dialect speakers.

Use of language by persons 6 years and older according to the living contexts (percent)

	In family				With friends				In formal situations			
	Mainly Italian	Mainly dialect	Both Italian and dialect	Other language	Mainly Italian	Mainly dialect	Both Italian and dialect	Other language	Mainly Italian	Mainly dialect	Both Italian and dialect	Other language
1987/1988	41.5	32.0	24.9	0.6	44.6	26.6	27.1	0.5	64.1	13.9	20.3	0.4
1995	44.4	23.8	28.3	1.5	47.1	16.7	32.1	1.2	71.4	6.9	18.5	0.8
2000	44.1	19.1	32.9	3.0	48.0	16.0	32.7	2.4	72.7	6.8	18.6	0.8
2006	45.5	16.0	32.5	5.1	48.9	13.2	32.8	3.9	72.8	5.4	19.0	1.5

Source: ISTAT 2007

Dialects are generally not used for general communication but are limited to groups of people who can actually speak them and to informal contexts. Speaking a dialect is unfortunately often frowned upon in Italy as a sign of substandard education. Younger generations, especially those under 25, speak almost exclusively standard Italian in all situations, usually with a slight local accent.

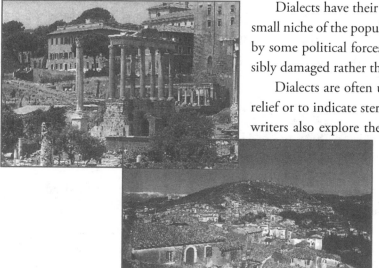

Regardless of where one goes in Italy, over two thousand years of past history are visible and may be appreciated in many human manifestations. Large cities, small villages, and countrysides constantly offer a reminder that the present is the evolution of a most fascinating past. Printed by courtesy of *America Oggi*.

Dialects have their share of enthusiasts, but this is a small niche of the population. The promotion of dialects by some political forces such as the *Lega Nord* has possibly damaged rather than promoted their status.

Dialects are often used in movies to provide comic relief or to indicate stereotypes. However, many screenwriters also explore the more expressive and spontaneous features of a dialect, often to challenge the common clichés and present a richer, less explored reality.

The main processes leading to the diffusion of a national standard language (in reality, a set of regional and social varieties of Italian) were mass urbanization, geographical mobility, schooling, conscription, and the mass diffusion of radio and television. Radio and television certainly had the major impact because they touched in the same and more direct and profound way every citizen.

Although schools could be important sites for disseminating the national language and acquiring literacy, one must not assume rigid and automatic correlations between state education, the learning of the national language, and literacy. While it is true that most illiterate people spoke only their local dialect and were not speakers of Italian, the converse did not necessarily hold. That is to say, a person who learned to understand and speak a form of Italian did not necessarily acquire literacy skills. Illiterate or semiliterate people could learn Italian through social contact, for instance in the labor migrations to the cities or the mass conscription of rural workers into the army, and later through radio, sound films, and television. The printed media (books, newspapers, and periodicals) have a lower impact because of social barriers. For the rural and blue-collar working population, with its lower levels of literacy, lower incomes, and lack of free time, the print media have always had only minimal impact.

Although it is an indisputable fact that the number of people who use Italian rather than a dialect has grown a lot, some linguists question the sort of Italian the masses speak. Many linguists, especially on the right side of the political spectrum, feel that Italian has entered into "mass" use by acquiring many colloquial structures from the most popular dialects. The complaints are, of course, not maliciously concocted; they are based on the fact that many more people than before go to high school and university and come from more varied social backgrounds. As a consequence, there are many more students than in the past who, at the level of secondary education, and even at the university level, make elementary grammatical mistakes; a sizeable proportion (particularly among those who come from the more disadvantaged

Knowledge of foreign languages and type of languages by gender (2006)

	At least one foreign language	English	French	Spanish	German	Other language
Male	59.2	45.7	28.0	7.0	5.7	4.1
Female	54.7	41.6	30.2	6.1	6.1	4.0
Male and Female	56.9	43.6	29.1	6.5	5.9	4.0

Source: ISTAT 2007

socioeconomic groups) do not have a full command of the traditional literary idiom. What we are witnessing is the emergence or the establishment of varieties of the standard language that have been called popular Italian, regional Italian, and media Italian. In this process one can observe a slight narrowing of the gap between spoken and written usage, with the penetration of certain features of the former into the latter. One has the feeling that written Italian is becoming less formal and elaborate than it used to be. The notion is a positive one because it carries progressive and democratic connotations: popular Italian is a symbol of the social, economic, and cultural achievements of the working class.

Some linguists establish a connection between the emergence of this brand of Italian and media Italian.[5] On the one hand, it seems clear that television has played a crucial role in spreading the knowledge of Italian; on the other, one would need detailed studies providing serious evidence for the specific influence of television in modifying the grammar of modern Italian. Most people complain about the negative effects of television, of the impoverishment it has brought to the language; rather, this attitude indicates confusion between the low intellectual level of much that appears on television and linguistic impoverishment.

Italian has been changing, and the gap between high and low levels is closing. The question is desirability: whether the gap should be bridged by lowering the high level or by raising the low level, or by making them move toward each other.

Political Cultural Strategies:
Books as Cultural Commodity

The process of language change and the increase in the literacy rate affected literary art and the related industry starting in the late 1950s. It resulted in the overall expansion of book production and sales of the large-scale best-seller, including works of contemporary Italian fiction. The first of these was *Il gattopardo* (*The Leopard*) by Tomasi di Lampedusa; it sold an unheard-of 100,000 copies in the 12 months following its publication toward the end of 1958. Similar sales were achieved in the early 1960s by various novels of Carlo Cassola and Giorgio Bassani. By the early 1970s it was possible in a few cases for a best-selling paperback to reach sales of a half million or more. The best example was *La storia* (*History/Story*) by Elsa Morante, which within a few months of its appearance in 1974 sold over 600,000 copies. Today many novels go over one million copies sold.

In this process of accessibility to literary work and change in literary tastes, once more the 1960s were a turning point in Italian affairs. This was the decade during which the economy took off; consumerism was born; education spread; culture found new markets, and social tensions exploded. Inevitably literature, too, was deeply affected.

Probably, the new appetite for the book would not have reached such levels so quickly if it were not for well-orchestrated marketing strategies on the part of the publishers. By the end of the 1960s, book publishing had become a business like any other. In the process of expansion and reorganization by the major publishing firms, one important step was the introduction of the modern paperback. Cheap series had already been introduced in the 1950s, most notably the *BUR* (*Biblioteca Universale Rizzoli*); it included a wide range of Italian and foreign classics. But the more attractive paperbacks did not appear in Italy until 1965, partly because publishers were not as aware of potential markets as they would later become. When Mondadori launched its *Oscar* series in that year, there followed a paperback boom, which gradually drew in the other principal publishers, including those which initially felt that, with the paperback, literature was being all too blatantly made into a commodity. In fact, that was what Mondadori was doing with some force; this aggressive publishing enterprise was looking for new markets among the mass of habitual non-readers.

By the mid-1970s sales of books had increased tremendously; however, the expansion had limits. Although there had been a significant change in the volume of publications, the reading public was still concentrated in particular areas of society. The sale of about 140 million books in the mid-1970s, an average of three books per inhabitant per year, did not mean that every Italian read a few books: rather, it meant that large sections of the population read a great deal, while others read hardly anything. The reason has to be found mainly in the literariness of Italian prose. In fact, even commercially successful narrative prose is commonly a good deal more refined than is the case with its American or British equivalents. In creative writing there has been a remarkable survival of a highly literary style. Italian discursive prose, as it is used for historical, sociological, philosophical, and critical writing, has remained remarkably complex and abstract in vocabulary, Ciceronian in syntax, and conceptually sophisticated. The positive result of all this is that the intellectual and stylistic level of Italian writing has been high; the negative result is that it has maintained a barrier between insiders and outsiders.

Partly because of a new concept in mass culture and partly because of the arrival of a new intellectual sophistication—semiotics, post-structuralism, modern Marxist thought, and new theories of psychoanalysis quickly penetrated Italian literary culture—there developed a shift away from conventional fiction. In the non-homogeneous literary culture, there emerged two main bodies of fictional writing, elitist and non-elitist. The elitist, restricted to a small reading

public, has consistently positioned itself against the established order and against the consumerization of literature. Its overwhelming tendency has been to denounce, from a variety of points
of view, the new industrialized and consumerized Italy as a physical and moral wasteland to
which alternatives must be found. The non-elitist writing has been more accepting of the social,
political, and economic order of the country. Whatever its critical position, it has inevitably
been deeply involved in the commercialization and consumerization of literature, and it has
been commonly perceived as providing consolation or escape for its readers.

By the beginning of the 1980s, in Italy more people were engaged in services than in the
production of industrial goods. In the 1981 census, the service sector emerged for the first
time as the largest broad occupational category, employing 50.2% of the active population,
followed by industry with 36.8% and agriculture with 13%. The respective figures for 1987
were 57.4%, 32.2%, and 10.4%.[6] In 2005, agriculture accounted for 2.5 percent of the GDP,
while industry and services accounted, respectively, for 30.4 percent and 67.1 percent of the
GDP. The agricultural labor force is steadily diminishing (down to 3.5 percent of the total
workforce in 1999), and industrial employment is also shrinking due to the impact of the new
economy to 32.6 percent. The service sector employs the largest percentage, 63.9 percent, of
the Italian workforce. Like other advanced economies, Italy had evolved from an industrial
society to a post-industrial society, with the difference that the change in Italy was rapid: the
changes from pre-industrial to industrial to post-industrial have been concentrated in the space
of less than two generations.

As we have had occasion to note, the entry into a post-industrial era has not meant that
the manufacturing economy has become unimportant, or that there are no longer depressed
regions. The term post-industrial is mainly equated to an information society in the sense
that the majority of the working population is engaged primarily in the handling of information communications, computer data, and cultural services. All of them have characterized
important changes in production and distribution and the organization of the labor process.
Certainly one can say that the development and marketing of telecommunications and information technology, together with other changes in the economy, education, and social habits,
have profoundly restructured Italian society and culture over the last generation.

In fact, Italy's formation as a post-modern nation encompasses profound cultural changes
especially in the area of mass culture. The development of industries engaged in the production,
reproduction, and distribution of cultural products brought in their wake an anthropological
revolution, a break-up of old ideologies and class identities, and a new cultural homogenization around a petty-bourgeois consumerist ethos.[7] The industries that produce or reproduce
and distribute books, newspapers and magazines, films and radio and television programs were
central to these changes.

To fully assess the change in the country, therefore, one cannot forget to consider the
impact of modern cultural industries on Italian society as it unevenly developed and the
development of mass audiences and markets.[8] In so doing, a clear synchronization should be
established between cultural and political changes, and an attempt should be made to measure
the degree of political influence upon culture. However, we have to keep in mind that although

cultural industries operate within political constraints, they are not driven by political interests alone. There tends always to be a reciprocal play of interests between cultural entrepreneurs and political forces. And we cannot ignore the peculiar nature of the relation of cost/consumer of the cultural products. Despite the fact that modern cultural artifacts (newspapers, magazines, films, records, television programs, etc.) possess the unusual character of commodities, we cannot neglect the relevance that such production acquires in the realm of mass culture and in the economy.[9]

The Homogenization of Culture and Challenges from the Left

In judging modernization and how the consequent advent of mass culture has affected Italian society, the following questions may be raised:

»   Did modernization "denature" Italian culture by breaking up its traditions of regional differentiation?

»   Did it bring a beneficial transformation?

»   Has it standardized and "leveled" cultural consumption?

»   Or has it brought new forms of cultural "distinction"?

»   How have contemporaries viewed these changes in the supply and consumption of culture, i.e., in the prevalence of popular genre cinema, the continued predominance of film imports, the development of popular magazines and strips, and the development of television?

The most typical approach in the 1950s and 1960s was to interpret these changes largely in negative terms as the advent in Italy of a low-quality, Americanized mass culture. The conservative minority lamented this cultural leveling. Most Left-wing critics tended to interpret the cultural changes, which began in the postwar reconstruction period, as one-dimensional: as functional only to a politics of conservative legitimation. Mass culture, in their view, was simply a fabrication, part of an ideological operation. These critics lamented above all the alleged dismissive attitude toward the annihilation of popular culture by the political class in power. Thus, the Left interpreted mass culture in an overtly political manner and as a more or less direct agency of class domination presided over by the Christian Democrats with the support of the Americans. The political forces of the center and of the Right correctly argued, on the other hand, that cultural products do not have the same meaning for everyone and that mass cultural forms may assume complex and diverse meanings for different individuals and social groups.

In general, it is hard to make such a view of the connections between cultural modernization and political domination fit the facts. The advent of mass culture seems to have contributed to socially liberal forms of consumerism and to a revolution of rising expectations. For example, it brought about the formation of a cultural youth market (records, scooters, fashion) which probably helped to catalyze, by the later 1960s, the first substantial rejection of the styles of an older generation.

Nevertheless, political presence was very strong in Italian culture and had a profound effect on the changes of mass culture and culture in general. In this regard, the primary role played by the Communist Party cannot be underplayed. The *PCI*'s influence was particularly strong and important in the first thirty years of the postwar period.

In the first few years after World War II the *PCI* tended to identify culture largely with print culture, to associate it with books and education. In this respect, of particular importance were the Communist Book Clubs and reading groups that sprang up at the end of the war. They provided a form of public, civic participation in an associative, collective cultural activity outside the home, and they linked to education and the development of public forms of political consciousness. One went to the *Centro del Libro Popolare,* just as one went to the *casa del popolo* or to an education class at the party club; the culturization charged with political consciousness was implicitly confrontational in nature.

The confrontational attitude of the party, as one may expect, was strong also toward the film industry because the party claimed that 'the vulgar commercial film production' pandered to the most facile tastes of the public, avoided films of ideas, and therefore denied cinema its natural cognitive and formative function.

The communist party tended to view masses as possessing cultural aspirations that needed to be satisfied by recommended reading of progressive books or films that presented an authentic reality. The masses allegedly needed to be protected from the aspirations created by American films and the *Reader's Digest,* which pushed them into a "world of dreams" and tried "to make them forget the problems that assail the working class."

In all this, the concept of the intellectual having to have common utility was very strong. Such a concept was Gramscian but by no means exclusively so. The notion that culture resides within intellectuals was part of the legacy of idealist thought. Benedetto Croce had viewed culture as a patrimony of educated elites acting as the motor forces of history, and this notion was to a large extent reproduced by Gramsci, despite his much broader and more democratic conception of the intellectual's role. This explains the cross-fertilization between idealist and Marxist thought in postwar Italian cultural theory. In this period, the idea that the intellectual had to go through a process of proletarization and complete assimilation into the vanguard class in order to be useful to the service of truth acquired a stronger significance. Because ideal service to humanity is always produced together with those forces that are really operative in the concrete situation, the intellectual can operate properly and effectively only in full contact with the people's life.

Literary Representation

It is this kind of thinking that was behind the promotion of a cultural system centered upon realism and collective solidarity and a corresponding critique of decadence. Realism or neorealism, as it reemerged after the war at the level of artistic practice and aesthetic evaluation, was associated with engagement or commitment rather than detachment, with the involvement of intellectuals in the working-class movement as opposed to ivory-towered intellectualism, with the concrete versus the abstract, with clarity of expression against stylistic preciosity and difficulty. Art, literature, and cinema were valued only when they could be interpreted in a realist or a socially committed key. Otherwise modernist works tended to be consigned as cultural waste and labeled as formalist, decadent, abstract, irrational, sterile, snobbish, or bourgeois. The truth and sincerity of realism were opposed to the supposedly phony commercial tinsel of the Hollywood entertainment film. The social dimension of realist art, its essential mass, popular nature, and its human warmth were opposed to the minority appeal and arid intellectualism of the avant-garde.[10] Realism became, in its appropriation by the forces of the Left, a slogan heavy with connotations, one in which many new meanings and oppositions were condensed.

Neorealist writers focused on the years of the Resistance and the German occupation of Italy. Cesare Pavese's *La casa in collina* (1947–1948), Elio Vittorini's *Uomini e no* (1945), Beppe Fenoglio's *Una questione privata* (posthumously published in 1963 with the title *Un giorno di fuoco;* the definitive edition appeared in 1965), and Italo Calvino's *Il sentiero dei nidi di ragno* (1947) are the novels that have come for many to represent the writing of this period.

The realist aesthetic strongly favored an art that was social, public, and political as opposed to one that dealt with the personal, private, or inner life. In this aesthetic, there was a noticeable anti-Americanism. Although there was a positive critical evaluation of some aspects of American culture—for instance, the films of Charlie Chaplin and the social fiction of novelists John Steinbeck, John Dos Passos, and others—there was a strong deprecation in the postwar period of what America represented in terms of mass culture and cultural imperialism. In the Cold War climate new vigor was also given to the idea of the dominance of an essentially decadent and bourgeois culture. In a sense, during the Cold War, the Left made and associated the concept of a progressive national tradition with itself and the working class as its legitimate standard bearers; at the same time, it reinforced the idea of a decadent culture as belonging to American and capitalist society.

During the same period, the Christian Democrats tried to popularize their democratic views by linking them with corporate collectivity, the family unit, the rural hinterlands, the Catholic tradition, the economic reconstruction, and the new industrial civilization. They identified democracy with property rights, a *laissez-faire* economy, freedom from totalitarianism, in short, with the American way of life. Consequently, they, too, pushed neorealism as a democratic form of artistic expression and carried out their own strategy with regard to the spread of popular culture. However, in the first decade of economic recovery, the acculturation of the masses was not taking place through the printed medium. In 1956 merely 5,623 books were published in Italy, including original works, translations, new editions, and reprints. And in 1957 40.8% of Italian families, according to official figures, did not habitually read printed matter of any kind.

The cultural strategy of both the Communist and Christian Democratic parties came to a crisis with the rapid rise of living standards, the spread of consumer culture, and increasingly centralized ownership and control of the cultural industries. The strategy of capillary penetration in a democratic society through the level of popular culture did not make sense with the introduction of new forms of popular culture mediated by mass communication technologies.[11] Italy was also going through a profound change that involved interrelated trends: a shift in occupational patterns resulting in a gradual decrease of blue-collar workers; a relatively fast growth of tertiary (service) sector jobs within the labor market as a whole; and an increase in the number of people trained to enter the professions (teachers, doctors, lawyers, journalists, civil servants, etc.). These changes were connected with the downward social mobility of intellectuals that reduced them to the status of salaried employees (in the professions and the fast-expanding cultural and communications industries), to intellectual workers on a par with other workers. All these changes were bringing to a crisis the notion of the national popular culture and the outlook that had sustained the neorealism concept in the critical discourse of the Left.

Therefore, although the cultural and ideological significance of neorealism within postwar culture should not be undervalued, it was a relatively short-lived movement, undermined by three important developments in Italy's economic and cultural life as a whole:

» the shift in attitude toward historical events, World War II in particular;

» postwar economic growth, which created a climate favorable to new writing practices; and, significantly,

» a change in the critical understanding of neorealism as exemplified by one of its most famous practitioners, writer Italo Calvino.

First of all, there was the question of attitudes to the country's recent history. In addition to the neorealist narrative of the 1940s and 1950s that featured the partisans ultimately as history's victors, who entered the national consciousness as patriots and heroes, gradually there was greater readiness to listen to the quiet inflections of the victims of war and the defeated—the Jewish communities, women, children, civilians in general. In 1962 Giorgio Bassani's *Il giardino dei Finzi-Contini* was published. Primo Levi wrote remarkable documentary narratives, *Se questo è un uomo* (1947) and *La tregua* (1963).

The second factor that contributed to the undermining of neorealism was the accelerated growth in the postwar economy that was to bring about a shift from a predominantly rural farmer to a neocapitalist society. At the same time a new generation of writers, most of whom had been educated after the fascist period, launched a confrontational attack on neorealism and its aesthetics, who became known as the *Gruppo 63* or the neo-avant-garde.[12]

The writers and critics of the *Gruppo 63* were concerned not with mimesis but with exploring the formal resources of language. The 1960s saw writers exploring new paths largely in response to changes in the society in which and for which they were writing. Put in general terms, this meant that a great deal was written that attempted to interpret the reality of the new Italy and, in some cases, to act upon it. But it also meant that new areas of language and new techniques were investigated, often on the basis of advanced theories of literature. Indeed, experimental modernism became one of the strongest trends in both the verse and prose of the 1960s, but even poets and novelists, who were more cautious, found themselves modifying and modernizing the way in which they wrote.

By the early 1970s the *Gruppo 63* and the *neoavanguardia* (neo-avanguard) were expiring. Today they no longer have imitators among young writers, and their leaders have mostly ceased producing novels. In the academic world, from the *licei* to the universities, their names rarely appear among the authors who are recommended. So what has the *neoavanguardia* achieved? Some critics feel that it has been useful as a language laboratory in the search for new forms of literary representation. For others, its influence seems to have been mainly negative in its passion for nonsense. For some years the *neoavanguardia* used their influence over the younger novelists, making them feel unable to write in a traditional manner.

Today their particular brand of nonsense is no longer much in vogue, and the Italian novel is returning to humanist values. In fiction today there is no dominant school or trend at all. A few modestly successful writers have emerged. With the waning of the experimental novel, the literary trend now is back to books that tell stories and develop characters. But there has been a burgeoning of critical forms to the detriment of creative ones; a takeover of the literary heritage by pedagogues, linguists, and psychoanalysts has stifled the literary spirit of adventure, the ambition and taste for imaginative writing. Yet, it is remarkable how few of these deal squarely with themes of contemporary Italy. Serious writers seem to prefer to set their books in the past, their childhood, or abroad, rather than to analyze Italian society today. They are not concerned with exploring the social tensions or crude consumerism of modern Italy; instead they concentrate on private life and the refinement of style. So the novel survives as a fragile, anemic creature, cut off from the mainstream of life. It is a pity, considering that Italy's society has been going through so fascinating a period of change that the novel has virtually abdicated its classic role as chronicler of that society.

Who are the new novelists, poets, playwrights, and thinkers who have emerged in the last twenty years to make any lasting impact? There are several names: Franco Fortini, Andrea Zanzotto, Mario Luzi, Dacia Maraini, Leonardo Sciascia, Roberto Galasso, Enrico Palandri, Gianni Celati, Andrea Camilleri, Vincenzo Consolo, Melania Mazzucco, Roberto Saviano. The intense interest after WWII in Alberto Moravia and Cesare Pavese, the growing reputation of Italo Calvino, the success of Dario Fo, the impact of the ideas of Antonio Gramsci, and the reception of Umberto Eco's outstanding work in semiotics testify also to the Italian presence in the international literary and intellectual circles. Their works also reflect accurately the social and cultural transformation of Italy after the war. In their work, from different and changing perspectives, what has been happening in the country is articulated, interpreted, and in some cases resisted and denounced. And despite the particularity of the Italian situation, their interest is not purely local. For in their work the general problems of literature and of articulate understanding of advanced capitalist society in general achieve intense, sometimes brilliant formulation.

These are authors who recognize the widespread sense that the boundaries of literature are shifting, that new demarcations are in the process of being drawn between literature and history, between literature and ideas, between one form of writing and another.

Again, this panorama confirms the fact that in literature, more than the other arts, this is an age of criticism and documentary rather than of high creativity; consequently the novel suffers, in Italy more than in Britain and the United States. One could say that the Italian novel has either grown stale through remaining too conventional or has suffered from the terrorism of the avant-garde and its technical experimentation with language and form.

The Emergence of Women Writers

In the 1970s, women emerged in large numbers on the literary scene. Although many women participated during the Resistance movement, they showed a muted response to the war. One explanation as to why women did not contribute to stories of the Resistance is provided by the nature of the genre itself. The Resistance, as it was relived in the collective imagination, shared many of the attributes found in the world of boys' adventure stories where life is lived, often literally, in the wild, beyond the reach of home and family. Missions have to be carried out, dangerous open spaces crossed, enemies killed. Conventions of the genre were established very rapidly, and they excluded women.

In fact, a substantial body of women's fiction was produced during the years of neorealism: in the decade from 1943 to 1953 there were publications by, among others, Elsa Morante, Gianna Manzini, Anna Maria Ortese, and Anna Banti alongside Maria Bellonci, Natalia Ginzburg, Lalla Romano, Livia De Stefani, Alba De Cespedes, and Milena Milani. Many of their narratives did not address either fascism or the war.

In the 1970s a generation of women writers emerged whose writing took three forms: the testimony, autobiographical narrative, and fiction. One of the most noticeable features of what otherwise manifested itself in a diversity of narrative practices was their constant recourse to first-person narration. To understand the nature of this public position, one has to con-textualize what became for a while a culture industry for and by women, often conducted in separatist bookshops and publishing houses. In the early 1970s a number of women, many of them associated with radical groups, realized that neither these groups nor the *PCI* appeared to have an interest in women's issues. It was a decade when, as part of the general process of modernization that the country was undergoing, social legislation began to catch up with the demands of a modern industrial state.

Born of the need to document, in one sense these books continue with the project, pre-sented in the first instance by realism and later by neorealism, of unveiling Italy's hidden face, this time by creating a space for the marginalized to speak for themselves. They speak only for themselves, of experiences that are uniquely theirs. The public's continuing desire for documen-tation about the realities of Italy is reflected in the fact that these testimonies were published, in paperback, by mainstream houses. Important narratives were produced by Gabriella Para (*Voci dal carcere femminile,* 1973), Armanda Guiducci (*La donna non è gente,* 1977), Dacia Maraini (*Memorie di una ladra,* 1972; *Donna in Guerra,* 1975), Francesca Sanvitale (*Madre e figlia,* 1980; *Il figlio dell'impero,* 1993), and Natalia Ginzburg (*Caro Michele,* 1973). To reject memory is to reject one's own experiences and the ability to connect self to other, life to history, present to past. The project of so much postwar writing by women writers in Italy is to salvage and make sense of experiences that otherwise will be lost, forgotten.

One important novelty in the Italian literary landscape is the appearance of literary works by immigrants.[13] Small publishing houses tend to publish the texts in this growing genre, and many are not widely available. These works have been published in the last few years, and thematically they all concern, however loosely, the immigrants' experience in Italy. The structure and format of these texts, though, vary: from diary format, to collections of transcribed oral narratives, to a novel-like text that includes a glossary and exercises about immigration and racism.

The Arts and Intellectuals: Low Creativity

In Italy's postwar cultural modernization and democratization process, more than in most Western countries, the performing arts have displayed a lively activity in collective cultural manifestations rather than high creativity by the individual. In fact, much of the best creativity has been not by the solitary playwright or sculptor, but by little groups of actors, dancers, and musicians, or workshops of sculptors, decorators, weavers, video directors, all in close touch with their public and very much part of society. It is a kind of culture that is less philosophical and spiritual, in many ways more ephemeral, and certainly much more social.

The revival of the performing arts, and popular enthusiasm for them, began soon after the entrance of the socialists into government in 1963. The renaissance of theater, especially in the provinces, was followed by the reemergence of musical activities. Museums and art exhibitions, too, have attracted big new audiences. This widespread thirst for culture was not balanced by a high creativity of the first rank by many writers, painters, and playwrights. Even the cinema, except for the heyday of neorealism and a few individual works, has not maintained a high level of creativity; and the music revival, fecund in performance, has yielded little as yet in the way of gifted new composers.

In philosophy and literature, Italy no longer appears as the great champion of Western thought and creativity. Italian thought and humanism have lost their old radiant universality and have yielded to the arid form of today's critical inquiries and the loquacious void of the *pensiero debole,* weak thinking (Gianni Vattimo).

The decline of creative writing has been even more apparent in the theater. No new playwrights of any great substance have arisen in the past 20 years to take the place of the Ugo Betti, Diego Fabbri, Eduardo De Filippo generation; and in most Italian theaters, nearly all the good plays are foreign imports, revivals of classics, or free-wheeling adaptations. So, today it is commonly said that the Italian theater is moribund. However, this is not a fair assessment; it has been still lively, innovative, and international. This is due above all to the exceptional creativity of some outstanding directors—Orazio Costa (1911–1999), Paolo Grassi (1919–1981), Giorgio Strehler (1921–1997), Luigi Squarzina (1922–), Carmelo Bene (1937–), Eugenio Barba (1923–), Franco Zeffirelli (1923–), Memé Perlini (1947–)are among the big names—

who become the real stars of the plays, more than the actors or the playwrights. For better or for worse, they impose their own personality on the texts, often reworking them totally. This is a new theater of gesture, lighting, and movement, more than, in many cases, of the spoken word.

The commercial theater has been kept alive, together with the state repertory companies that attract younger audiences and can afford to experiment with the help of government subsidies. The major subsidized theaters are *teatri stabili* because of heavy state patronage and hence present a picture of greater success. With the help of generous subsidies (for example in 2005, the Piccolo Teatro di Milano, Teatro Stabile di Torino, Teatro di Roma received, respectively, 3,910,000, 2,300,000, and 2,090,000 euros), these theaters have been able to pursue a policy of low prices and build an audience very different from that of the prewar period students, young intellectuals, even some workers who would never dream of rubbing shoulders with the elite for a repertory that today continues to mix the Italian classics with a few modern or foreign plays but with the accent on stagecraft.

There is a clear difference between the American, British, and Italian stages. Classical revivals apart, New York's and Britain's forte is the craftsmanlike production of well-written new plays; Italy's accent is on the fireworks of experimental *mise-en-scène*. What good new playwrights, if any, have emerged in the past thirty years? Not many. Young playwrights find it hard to get a break; private theaters are wary of taking the financial risk of presenting a serious play by an unknown writer, while the big national theaters make far less effort than their British and American counterparts to seek out new talent. So Italy fills up its stages with revivals and imports. English and American plays are in vogue with the public. Many producers and actors feel that foreign playwrights, far more than Italian ones, provide them with meaty subjects and strong acting roles that relate to the real modern world. As in the case of the novel, too many new Italian plays are about the hang-ups of writing a play or some equally hermetic theme.

Yet there may also be quite another explanation for the dearth of new talent. This lies in the dominance, during the 1970s especially, of a school of clever and fashionable directors who have an entirely different concept of doing theater. They are simply not interested in receiving a text from an author and then faithfully staging it, like a kind of publisher. To them a live author is a potential nuisance, an impediment to their creative fancy. They prefer either to reinterpret the plays of dead authors or else to devise their own texts.

Some directors have been taking literary texts or political ones and working them into a kind of play. Even more controversially, some of these new star directors apply their creative gifts to reworking the classics. The intent is to give a modern force, a twenty-first-century resonance to the old texts. However, one could easily say that the classics have been put under torture as they have been chopped up, rearranged, reworded, and re-plotted.

What are the reasons? It could be argued that the arts and ideas, in Italy and elsewhere, flourish best either in times of settled prosperity, or under oppression and austerity, but not in an in-between period of industrial transition and social changes when the nation's energies are elsewhere. Unquestionably, the politicization of the arts was damaging to cultural creativity, and so was the attitude of artists and intellectuals toward society. Many intellectuals, being mostly from the Left, not only disliked a capitalist regime but also felt embittered frustration at the rise of a new way of progress that brushed aside their own theories and precepts. How could they reconcile the fact that a cookbook sold more than a good novel?

There is another explanation for the status of Italian performing arts. The Italians have a tradition of promoting the arts, and in the welfare state, Italian-style, that means funding comes from the state. In the original government plan to support the arts there was undoubtedly the element of national prestige but also the strand of socialist idealism, the desire to popularize the arts and bring them closer to people's daily lives. The thought was that a better cultural climate might stimulate new creative work and revive the flagging Italian genius. Moreover, at the basis of the government thinking was that *all* the arts matter, even minor ones, and that culture must be truly popular. So state patronage was extended to many spheres previously neglected by it.

But like every other aspect of Italian life where the state is involved, the arts and cultural manifestations in general were not immune to political muddling. Financial support for the arts, therefore, easily became part of the clientelistic system which, as we know, is very politicized. Unfortunately, for the Italian artist, the dependence on state money is particularly acute because private philanthropy for the arts has been practically unknown in modern Italy.

By heavily subsidizing the arts, the government increasingly made political decisions and allocated funds on the basis of straightforward political criteria. In the 1970s, theatrical companies made it to the stage only if they were supported by one or more political parties. Visual artists, too, were unlikely to go far unless they received the blessing of a political party or an interest group associated with a political party. Parties had their favorite painters, sculptors, filmmakers, writers, poets, dance groups, musicians, art galleries, photographic studios, and so forth.

Parties sought out these symbols of culture in order to demonstrate that leading exponents of the fine and visual arts were located in their ranks or approved their programs. The Communist Party boasted of having among its members some of the most prominent painters, sculptors, architects, filmmakers, musicians, writers, actors and actresses—Luchino Visconti, Federico Fellini, Roberto Rossellini, Pier Paolo Pasolini, Vittorio De Sica, Franco Zeffirelli, Claudia Cardinale, Marcello Mastroianni, Ignazio Silone, Giacomo Manzù, Renato Guttuso, Curzio Malaparte, all were members of the *PCI*. Because so many of the obviously outstanding artists were long associated with the Communist Party, it and the Left in general counted on a good portion of available patronage.

In such a situation, the basic understanding was that for any creative person in search of support, the right political party connection was as important as sheer talent. Awards were almost never made without regard to the applicant's ideological or political coloration. As one may expect, intellectuals were concerned even more with politics and were openly lined up with political parties; indeed, many of them held prominent roles in all levels of government. It was rare to find intellectuals or artists who were relatively autonomous or distant critics of social, political, and economic structures. As a group, they have been engulfed by politics and happily have thrived in it. Because they knew it was risky to be independent, artists got trapped in a vicious cycle: once a person became a slave of the political system, he or she could not survive without it. The reasons for this are easy to understand.

Certainly the emphasis today, as we have seen, is on success, enjoyment, and quality of life, and culture plays a sizeable role in this new leisure world and will continue to do so under any regime. But whether it will lead to any upsurge of real individual creativity, especially in literature, is still far from certain. Of a revival of serious literature, or playwriting, there is not much sign. In fact, a discernible trend in Italian culture as a whole over the past decade or so is that its emphasis has become less solemn and cerebral, more colorful and amusing, or in some cases, the pretentious gives place to the superficial.

Cinema: Ups and Downs

In the mass culturization process of the country, cinema also played an important role and, as one may expect, was even less nationalistic in character than TV, as we shall see, mainly because of the excessive presence of American imports.[14]

Notwithstanding the excellent Italian film tradition, cinema did not become a mass cultural phenomenon until the end of the 1950s. The Catholic Church was instrumental in the creation of over 5,000 parish cinemas, often in rural areas, and the whole Italian industry expanded both in production and exhibition, so that by the late 1950s we can identify films as directed toward the more rural south, and we can find the box-office returns for Italian films coming as much from provincial and rural cinemas as from the urban ones.

The Italian production sector picked up gradually during the late 1940s also for other reasons. Some films of the period dealt in a remarkably realistic way with the social and political conditions of Italian life in the aftermath of the war and established a movement that became known as neorealism. In its short period of popularity, neorealism began to find a warm response in the art cinema circuits abroad by redefining the function of cinema and introducing to popular audiences a different sort of engagement with reality: Rossellini's *Rome Open City* (1945), De Sica's *Bicycle Thief (See Box on p. 367)* (1947), Zampa's *Living in Peace* (1947), and De Santis' *Bitter Rice* (1949). All the stress in neorealism was on the hidden underside of Italian life—poverty, backwardness, the legacy of fascist neglect, and the difficulties of postwar reconstruction.[15] It should be pointed out that just as fascist cinema tried to ignore the Depression, so the postwar cinema seemed oblivious of the economic miracle that was gathering pace throughout the 1950s.

But ignorance of what was occurring in the economic lives of Italians was not the most obvious defect of Italian cinema. It is particularly in representations of the sexual question that Italy fell out of step not only with America but with much of the rest of Europe. Although Italian films of the 1950s were more sexually explicit than American films of the period, their morality remained conservative. Not only did Italian law not recognize divorce, but the subject was virtually taboo. It was not until 1961 that a film such as Pietro Germi's *Divorce Italian*

Café   *The Spaghetti Western*

Spaghetti Western is a nickname for a broad sub-genre of Western film that emerged in the mid-1960s, so named because most were produced by Italian studios. Originally they had in common the Italian language, low budgets, and a recognizable highly fluid, violent, vivid and minimalist cinematography that eschewed many of the conventions of earlier Westerns—partly intentionally, partly as a result of the work being done in a different cultural background and with limited funds. The term was originally used disparagingly, but by the 1980s many of these films were held in high regard, particularly because it was hard to ignore the influence they had in redefining the entire idea of a Western.

Many Spaghetti Westerns were shot in the Spanish desert region of Almería, which resembles the landscape of the American Southwest. (A few were shot on Sardinia.) Because of the desert setting and the readily available southern Spanish extras, a usual theme in these movies is the Mexican Revolution, Mexican bandits, and the border zone between Mexico and the U.S.

The best-known Spaghetti Westerns were those of Sergio Leone, whose Dollars Trilogy, consisting of *A Fistful of Dollars* (1964), *For A Few Dollars More* (1965), and *The Good, the Bad, and the Ugly* (1966), featuring Clint Eastwood, came to define the genre.

A Fistful of Dollars was the first of the trilogy. All the actors spoke their lines in their native language (Eastwood was the only English-speaking actor in the film), and English was dubbed in for the American release. This movie was unique in its treatment of the hero: the "good guy" wasn't always good, but he was "human," and in comparison to the "bad guys" he was the hero—not because of his outstanding moral character but by default. The violence in these Westerns was intense; the landscapes were harsh; the dialogue was minimal; and the often discordant music (scored in all three by Ennio Morricone) added to the suspense of the unusual camera angles. Spaghetti Westerns were a visual and aural experience unlike any other movies of the time. Critics didn't give them high marks but the American audiences were enthralled; Clint Eastwood became a superstar almost overnight.

In contrast to the Euro-Westerns that preceded it, from the opening credits of *A Fistful of Dollars,* Leone demonstrated that he wasn't interested in simply imitating American Western conventions. The film opens with a hazy white spot on a blood-red screen, creating an almost psychedelic effect and immediately setting the tone for Leone's fantasy vision, with one foot in history and the other in Hollywood dreams. The title sequence resounds to the sound of gun-shots and Morricone's distinctive music, strikingly different from the orchestral scores and hokey renditions of folk songs that had characterized the soundtracks of American Westerns up to that time. Drawing on sound-effect experiments he had been conducting, Morricone incorporated gunshots, cannon fire, whip-cracks, chanting, whistling, and watch-chimes into his soundtracks for Leone's first three Westerns. The attention-grabbing music proved an ideal complement to Leone's baroque imagery and playful use of genre iconography.

A Fistful of Dollars begins with Clint Eastwood's character approaching a well in a sun-baked landscape of harsh light and white-washed stone buildings. Whereas many Spaghetti Westerns sought to make their Spanish locations look as much like the American-Mexican border region as possible, Leone's expansive wide-screen vistas highlight the landscape's slightly alien feel, creating a setting that certainly doesn't look European but doesn't quite look American either. Leone was a great admirer of surrealist art, and it is perhaps no coincidence that the Spanish locations of his Westerns are the same arid dreamscapes Salvador Dali employed in many of his nightmarish images of the 1930s. Leone was to later comment that the cinematographer Tonino Delli Colli filmed the desert sequence in *The Good, the Bad and the Ugly* "in a way that was worthy of the great surrealist painters."

Style could be produced. Italian marriage law was only one aspect of sexual double standards that went uncriticized in Italian films until the 1970s.

The Christian Democrats, who had practical control of the government until the 1960s, exercised a rigid control on cinema as well as on TV. They did not attempt to dictate what the cinema should be but took active steps to ensure that it did not become anything they did not want it to be. The postwar Christian Democratic governments were in fact more repressive toward the cinema than the fascists had been, but then they had to be. Whereas the fascists could rely on general quietude and an ignorance of the formative role of cinema in popular ideology, the Christian Democrats saw that they had a real struggle on their hands, not only to establish a national cinema competitive with Hollywood but to ensure that this cinema expressed a concept of Italian nationality they approved of rather than the variant of the "national-popular" espoused by the Left and expressed through neorealism.

Another factor influencing the protection of many films in the early postwar period was a strong public interest in comedy, inspired, in large part, by the great vaudeville tradition of comic persona and performance. One of the major stars of this type of films was Totò; he entertained audiences in dozens of films and became one of the great comedic performers of the twentieth century.

In fact, one cannot help being struck by the extent to which comedy has always been a staple of Italian cinema, a comedy that is built around a comic actor of a certain kind, the clown. Erminio Macario was the little man lost in a world too complex for him to understand; Totò was the Neapolitan clown turning the world upside down in the anarchic expression of his vitality.

At the beginning of the 1960s the Italian film industry needed to expand production, and in the absence of a large pool of untapped creative talent waiting to be exploited, imitation and repetition offered a way of achieving this. In 20 years some 450 "spaghetti westerns" were produced, most of them shot in Spain and distributed also abroad *(See Box on pp.364–365).* Sergio Leone's film, *Per un pugno di dollari (A Fistful of Dollars,* 1964), cost 200 million liras to make, and netted over fifteen times that amount worldwide. This genre was very successful and lucrative. At the same time, however, Italian cinema was building for itself an international reputation for art cinema, films whose origins lay in the ideas and artistic creativity of their directors. They were viewed by sophisticated, middle-class audiences in Italy, in art cinemas of the major cities of the world, at film festivals, in universities, and in film clubs and societies. The reputation created by the neorealist films was reinforced by the films of Federico Fellini, Michelangelo Antonioni, Pier Paolo Pasolini, Bernardo Bertolucci, Liliana Cavani, Ermanno Olmi, Lina Wertmuller, Elio Petri, Marco Ferreri, Marco Bellocchio, and the brothers Paolo and Vittorio Taviani. Probably the most innovative was Antonioni.

Characteristically the typical Antonioni character is economically secure and emancipated from Catholic morality but troubled by neurotic anguish and doubt. Sexual relations provide little fulfillment but a certain limited consolation to individuals oppressed by the techno-bureaucratic machine. For Antonioni the modern world is an already realized Eutopia with its bad consequences, and his images of unpleasant modernity are merely the veneer of the sentimental portrayals of Italian backwardness elsewhere in the cinema.

The vigor of the Italian art cinema in the 1960s, relying on the creativity of great directors, depended on the general vigor of the Italian production sector, particularly at the popular level, supported by ticket sales of 700 million a year and plentiful American investment in production. There was a brief period in the early 1960s when it looked as if the tide had turned. *RAI* television was resolutely protectionist, while in the cinema the share of Italian box-office receipts obtained by American films plummeted to less than one-third. Italian national production, supplemented by that of other EU countries, seemed to be sufficient to satisfy public demand, prompting the illusion of a European cultural revenge against America. In fact, the idea of a shared European culture turned out to be most illusory. While European co-production made economic sense in the cinema, the cultural character of the co-produced films could rarely be described as distinctively European. The cultural contest therefore remained to be between Italian and American products, with a handful of nebulously European films and television programs playing a marginal role.

In the mid-1970s American finance was withdrawn, and the reorganization of distribution led to rapid drops in ticket sales. This change was escalated by the arrival of television in Italy; television replaced the routine of cinema-going, and with this contraction of the base, higher-quality film production became starved of financing. Between 1950 and 1969, Antonioni directed 12 films; between 1970 and 1990 he directed just four. From an annual output of up to 300 films in the late 1960s and ticket sales of over 700 million, more than half of them to Italian films, annual production dropped to around 100 films in the mid-1990s. Ticket sales fell to just over 100 million, with 80% of the money going to U.S. films.

As with popular culture in general, cinema and TV became Americanized by default. To compete at the box office Italian films were forced to imitate American models, which they did fairly well. But it was American films that seized the popular imagination, and it was not long before the Italian film industry reestablished itself in a role very similar to the one it had assumed in the fascist period, supplying cut-price versions of popular American genres, though with a distinct national inflection. The return of American cultural products is one of the significant features of the media explosion of the 1970s and 1980s.

☕ *Café* *The Bicycle Thief*

(1948) New York Film Critics Circle Award: Best Foreign Language Film—1949
Golden Globe Award: Best Foreign Film—1950

The Bicycle Thief is Everyman's search for dignity. Set in post-World War II Rome, it tells a simple story, relying for its impact on coarse realism and emotional reality. There are no subplots, just a few key characters. The dialogue is the day-to-day talk of poor people struggling to survive.

Director Vittorio de Sica pioneered a lean, stark presentation with nonprofessional actors. The style, with its subject matter based on hard postwar life, epitomizes Italian neorealism. The spectator follows the fortune of Antonio, a family man whose wife pawns their household linens so that they can reclaim from the same pawnshop a bicycle that is required for a job he has been offered. Jobs are scarce and the family is poor; much depends on possession of the bike.

The bicycle is stolen on Antonio's first day at work and he and his young son Bruno search the streets of Rome in hopes of recovering it. A series of frustrating episodes mark the day, tension and desperation growing as chances for recovering the bicycle, and with it, their dashed hopes, fade. The events of the day—from a confrontation with a suspect and his neighbors, to a brief stop for a restaurant meal that they can't afford, to a visit to a fortune teller—have a cumulative effect, deepening the spectator's understanding of, and feelings for, the father and young son. And then, in the closing sequence of the movie, Antonio, in an act of desperation is tempted to steal a bicycle himself without succeeding. Even an honest man like Antonio, under the duress of desperation, could become a thief! Compassion prevails and he is allowed to walk home, humiliated also by the presence of his son.

In the 90s, even though American films are maintaining their traditional dominance, a new generation of directors has helped return Italian cinema to a healthy level since the end of the 1980s. The sign-bearer for this renaissance is *Nuovo Cinema Paradiso*, for which Giuseppe Tornatore won the Oscar for Best Foreign Film in 1989. This victory was followed two years later by another, when Gabriele Salvatores's *Mediterraneo* won the same prize. Another exploit was in 1998 when Roberto Benigni won three oscars for his movie *Life Is Beautiful* (*La vita è bella)* (Best Actor, Best Foreign Film, Best Music). In 2001 Nanni Moretti's film *La stanza del figlio* (*The Son's Room*) received the Palme d'Or at the Cannes Film Festival. Other recent films of note include: *Jona che visse nella balena* directed by Roberto Faenza, *Il grande cocomero* by Francesca Archibugi, *Il mestiere delle armi* by Olmi, *L'ora di religione* by Marco Bellocchio, *Le fate ignoranti*, *La finestra di fronte* by Ferzan Özpetek, *La bestia nel cuore* by Cristina Comencini. In 1992, for the first time in years an Italian movie, *Johnny Stecchino*, starring and directed by Roberto Benigni, outran star-laden American imports to earn the biggest profits (it grossed $25 million) ever recorded for a movie in Italy. Moreover, Italian movies brought home coveted foreign prizes the Cannes Grand Jury Prize for Gianni Amelio's *Ladro di bam-*

bini (*Stolen Children*). In 1996, *Il postino* (*The Postman*) was up for several Academy Awards. These honors are signs of new vigor for what was once Europe's most robust movie industry. Clearly, this success, attributed to the emergence of a new generation of actors, directors, and scriptwriters, remains overshadowed by the unanswered question of how public tastes, attuned to television, will affect the reviving movie industry; after all, the public at the movies is a public that was formed in the bosom of television.

These events come after three decades in which the Italian movie industry generally followed a downward curve, both in theater attendance and in quality. In the fabled year of 1955, Italian movie theaters sold a record 819 million tickets, more than eight times the present-day figure. Not only that, the number of movie theaters had fallen from 7,500 at the beginning of the 1980s to around 3,500 at the end of the 1990s. Only 1,200 of them qualify as active theaters, and, in any event, such are the peculiarities of the Italian movie theater season that they are open for an average of only 240 days a year. For many Italians, the lure of television sitcoms and game shows remains irresistible.

Car design belongs to the rich Italian tradition of crafts and creativity. From Wikipedia.org

The Italian film industry also cannot rely on the American market. For directors who work in foreign languages, America today has scant appreciation of foreign movies. Few foreign-language films are released in the U.S. these days, and those that are attract fewer viewers. Americans, absorbed in their junk culture, are shuttering a window to the rest of the movie world.[16]

On the cultural level, regardless of what will happen to the movie industry, Italy will always enjoy a prominent position in the world. Italy's main cultural export is itself. It has enough heritage not to need a heritage industry. So long as the tourists can be packed into the Uffizi or the Sistine Chapel, or the Pantheon or the Arena at Verona, or the ruins in Pompeii, the other Italies where American soap opera, the imitations of American game-shows, and American movies top the ratings can be ignored.

Notes

1.   The other Romance languages are French, Spanish, Portuguese, and Rumanian. Italian is the official language of Italy and San Marino, and it is an official language in the Ticino and Grigioni cantons of Switzerland. It is also the second official language in Vatican City and in some areas of Istria in Slovenia and Croatia with an Italian minority. It is widely used by immigrant groups in Luxembourg, Germany,

Belgium, the United States, Canada, Venezuela, Brazil, Argentina, and Australia, and is also spoken in neighboring Albania. It is spoken, to a much lesser extent, in parts of Africa formerly under Italian rule such as Somalia, Libya, and Eritrea. It is widely known and taught in Monaco and in the neighboring island of Malta and served as an official language of the country until English was enshrined in the 1934 Constitution.

2.   Italian dialects identified by the Ethnologue are Tuscan, Piemontese, Abruzzese, Pugliese (Apulian), Umbrian, Laziale, Central Marchigiano, Cicolano-Reatino-Aquilano, Molisan, Neapolitan, Sicilian, and Sardinian. Other dialects are Milanese, Brescian, Bergamasc, Modenese, and Bolognese.

3.   The dialect of Tuscany became the basis for what would become the official language of Italy, by way of the famous Tuscan authors Dante Alighieri, Francesco Petrarca, and Giovanni Boccaccio. Alighieri and other Tuscan poets were inspired by the Sicilian koinè used by the Sicilian School under Holy Roman Emperor Frederick II. His project (in which Giacomo da Lentini invented the sonnet) was accomplished by enriching the Sicilian language with new words adapted from French, Latin, and Apulian. The Sicilians produced a collection of love-poems which can be considered the first standard Italian ever produced, though it was only used for literary purposes until Guittone d'Arezzo. When the Svevs dynasty ended, the Tuscans and Dante re-discovered it (see the *Devulgari Eloquentia* and *Vita Nova*) and integrated the Sicilians into Florence's linguistic heritage.

     Dolce stil novo, the platonic school of courtly love, can be considered the link between the old southern school and Tuscan poetry, which aimed to express the new intellectual sensibility and fervor of the newly-born city-states, such as Florence. Dante's work, *Divina Commedia,* was the first of its kind to be written in a dialect (though sensibly enriched compared with its spoken counterpart), as opposed to the traditional Latin. The success of his work spread the Florentine dialect and gave it prestige and acceptance. For this he is referred to as the father of the Italian language.

     By the time Italy was unified 1861 and Rome was annexed in 1870, the Italian standard had further been influenced by Florentines through the work of the Accademia della Crusca (Cardinal Pietro Bembo and followers). Bembo laid the foundation for what is today's modern standard. But Bembo was a purist and had accepted no other influence than that from Dante, Petrarca, and Boccaccio. As time went on, the language was losing touch with linguistic change and could not keep up with technology and science. The much-needed update would have to wait a little longer—for what is probably the masterpiece of Italian literature, *I Promessi Sposi* (*The Betrothed*) by Alessandro Manzoni. (Alessandro Manzoni further refined his widely read novel by "rinsing" it in the waters of the Arno [Florence's river], as he states in his 1840 Preface.) However, Manzoni refused the Crusca's purist, written, Florentine-only attitude and admitted a certain influence from other dialects, though he reduced it as compared to the first edition of 1821. After unification the huge number of civil servants and soldiers recruited from all over the country introduced many more words and idioms from their home dialects, in fact confirming Manzoni's linguistic views.

     Tuscan has thus become one of the twenty official dialects of Italy. Though technically speaking the division between dialects and language is purely conventional, it has been used by scholars, for example Francesco Bruni, to distinguish between the languages that made up the Italian koinè and those that had very little or no part in it, such as Albanian, Greek, Südtirolean, Ladino, Friulian, and Occitan, which are still spoken by small ethnic minorities.

4.   From current literature the following list emerges, with the estimated (and very hypothetical) number of speakers in brackets. There are small historic relics, often going back to the fifteenth and sixteenth centuries: Greek (30,000) and Albanian (100,000) in several villages in Southern Italy; Catalan (15,000) in Alghero, Sardinia; German (13,000) in small communities in Piedmont and in the Veneto; Croat (3,000) in the Molise; Occitanic and Franco-Provencal in small colonies in Southern Italy. Stronger groups, adjacent to bordering foreign countries are German (280,000) in South Tyrol; Occitanic and Franco-Provencal (115,000) in Piedmont; Slovene (53,000) in the Veneto. There is a large group of recent immigrants (estimated to be about 1,000,000), mostly from North and Central Africa. It is dif-

ficult to evaluate how far these will become part of the permanent population and whether they will preserve their original languages.

5.　Tullio De Mauro, *Storia linguistica dell'Italia unita* (Bari: Laterza, 1976), 430–59

6.　*Le regioni in cifre,* (Rome: ISTAT, 1988), 92.

7.　See Pier Paolo Pasolini, *Scritti corsari* (Milan: Garzanti, 1978), pp. 50–81 and *Lettere luterane,* (Turin: Einaudi, 1976), 77–91.

8.　An interesting and informative discussion of this issue can be found in Silvio Lanaro's *L'Italia nuova. Identité e sviluppo 1861–1988* (Turin: Einaudi, 1988).

9.　It is very expensive to make the first copy, but once these first-copy costs have been recovered, it is relatively cheap to run a few hundred more copies. This impels cultural firms to go for large runs and to create large markets. It also encourages them to take control of distribution, because it is with mass distribution that big profits and high returns on economies of scale are made.

10.　For a useful general discussion of realism in the *PCI*'s cultural policy during this period, see Nicoletta Misler, *La vita italiana al realismo. La politica culturale artistica del PCI dal 1944 al 1956* (Milan: Mazzotta, 1973).

11.　Francesco Pinto, *Intellettuali e tv negli anni '50* (Rome: Savelli, 1977).

12.　Although *Gruppo 63* and the *Neoavanguardia* faded from sight quickly, in their heyday they caused more journalistic ink to flow than they deserved in terms of achievement. They were never really a school, for their leading exponents were quite different from each other and frequently quarreled; yet they did have some things in common. The most obvious shared feature of their work was an obsession with the rejection of the moralistic or social-commentary conventional narrative and an attraction for minute, physical description, whether of objects or sensations, to represent a much dehumanized situation. Their semi-scientific approach to literature had a clear link with structuralism, emerging at about the same time.

13.　Some of the titles are: Mohamed Bouchane, *Chiamatemi Alì*, eds. Carla De Girolamo and Daniele Miccione, (Milan: Leonardo Editore, 1990); Giuliano Carlini, ed., *La terra in faccia: Gli immigrati raccontano* (Roma: Ediesse, 1991); Nassera Chohra and Alessandra Atti di Sarro, *Volevo diventare bianca* (Rome: Edizioni e/o, 1993); Amelia Cristiano, ed., *Ho trovato l'occidente: Storie di donne immigrate a Palermo* (Palermo: La Luna, 1992).

14.　In the period up to 1915, Italy was one of the world's major exporters of films. A few large production companies had grown up, and around them there existed a multitude of smaller companies. Italy became known as a producer of spectacular films on historical themes, and these films were exported partly because of their exotic value. With WW I, and the rapid growth and organization of the U.S. film industry, Italian production went bankrupt and collapsed. Whereas in 1915 Italy had produced 562 films, by 1930 that number had dropped to twelve. The fascist government set about reorganizing the industry along more efficient and less wasteful lines, eventually finding itself owning studios, distribution companies, and a cinema chain. The Cinecittà studios were built with state money and were taken over by the state; the Centro Sperimentale di Cinematografia, a university-level film school, was established; and the Venice Film Festival was launched as an international showcase for Italian films. The result was that by 1942 Italy was producing over 100 films a year.

15.　This is a departure from the tradition. One of Italy's most successful exports before WWI was the historical genre, representing great moments in Italian medieval or Renaissance history. It should be said, however, that Italy never abandoned completely this genre of film, which adopted a pose of cultural dignity and which had the virtues of being spectacular, of reinforcing nationalist notions of Italy's great past, of inviting comparisons between the politically righteous and the dissolutely opportunist.

16.   What did go wrong? In the 1950s and 1960s the allure of foreign language film was twofold—they had class and they had sex.

Bibliography

Baranski, Z. and Lumley, R., (eds.), *Culture and Conflict in Postwar Italy* (New York: St. Martin Press, 1990).

Baranski, Z. and West, R., (eds.), *The Cambridge Companion in Postwar Italy* (Cambridge: Cambridge UP, 2001).

Bondanella, P. *Italian Cinema: From Neorealism to the Present* (New York: Continuum, 2001).

Carlini, G., ed., *La terra in faccia: Gli immigrati raccontano* (Roma: Ediesse, 1991).

Chohra, N. and Alessandra Atti di Sarro, *Volevo diventare bianca* (Rome: Edizioni e/o, 1993).

Cristiano, A., ed., *Ho trovato l'occidente: Storie di donne immigrate a Palermo* (Palermo: La Luna, 1992)

De Mauro, T., *Storia linguistica dell'Italia unità* (Bari: Laterza, 1976).

De Mauro, T., *Idee per il governo. La scuola* (Bari: Laterza, 1995).

Lanaro, S., *L'Italia nuova. Identità e sviluppo 1861–1988* (Turin: Einaudi, 1988).

Marcus, M., *Italian Film in the Light of Neorealism* (Baltimore: The Johns Hopkins U.P., 2002).

Misler, N., *La vita italiana al realismo. La politica culturale artistica del PCI dal 1944 al 1956* (Milan: Mazzotta, 1973).

Pinto, F., *Intellettuali e tv negli anni '50* (Rome: Savelli, 1977).

Sciolla, L., 'Identità' e mutamento culturale nell'Italia di Oggi,' in Cesareo ed., *La cultura dell'Italia contemporanea,* q.v., pp. 35–69.

Testa, C. *Italian Cinema and Modern European Literature, 1945–2000* ((Westport, CT: Praeger, 2002).

www.modaitalia.net

www.lifeinitaly.com

www.bookrags.com

www.radioliberty.com

http://www.italiaplease.com

http://www.dialettiitaliani.org

The Roman Forum was the political and economical center of Rome
during the Republic. In imperial times, the importance of the Forum as
a political center diminished, but it remained a center of commerce and
religious life. From the archive of the author.

CHAPTER 14

COMMUNICATIONS REVOLUTION AND CULTURAL CONSUMPTION

Communications

The severe destruction of World War II, combined with Italy's backwardness, meant that the nation not only had to rebuild its traditional means of communications, including its transportation system, but also develop and adapt to new electronic communications systems. The process was systematic and profound and covered many areas:

» a comprehensive highway system (*autostrade*),
» easily accessible technological mass media, such as radio and television,
» the popular print media, especially newspapers and magazines, and
» in time, the Internet.

Since only 20% of Italy is flat, communication had been difficult before World War II. Of course, communications had improved dramatically with the advent of the railways and the construction of roads to serve them. Even so, many rural areas were practically inaccessible, and it was not until the war that many people traveled more than a few kilometers beyond their native village. Because World War II and particularly the invasion of the Allied armies and the retreat of the German forces had caused so much damage, in the 1950s and 1960s the roads system was entirely reconstructed and modernized. Italy's impressive highway system, *autostrade,* was matched in Europe only by Germany. There was a strong rise in public and private motor transport as well as the beginning of tourism in private motor cars, fostered by the publication of road maps and the creation of the *Michelin Guide.* Private car ownership grew significantly, as manufacturers like Fiat developed popular models like the Fiat 600 and 1100 to make car ownership available to the working classes. After a slow start in the second half of the 1950s, television became a feature of most Italian homes during the 1960s, with nearly 80% of households owning at least a black and white television by the early 1970s.

The decades of the 1970s and 1980s witnessed a qualitative transformation of communications in Italy, based in many cases on the application of new technologies to existing systems. In 1970, only 11% of Italian households were equipped with a telephone. Today, of course, 99.3% of Italian homes have a telephone, and most Italians, including children, have cellular phones. In the 1970s the telecommunications system eliminated lengthy waiting lists for telephones, created a network of public telephones, and introduced fully automated connections for national and international calls. Other Western countries similarly modernized their telecommunications systems in the 1970s and 1980s, but in Italy the process was both exceptionally rapid and extremely thorough. By the end of the 1980s, Italy had acquired one of the most advanced telecommunications systems in the world.

The rail network did not undergo a similar transformation because Italy put its focus on developing its highway system. However, the development of a high-speed train system today is radically reducing travel time throughout the peninsula and bringing together people from different parts of the peninsula at a faster pace. The Internet has certainly had a profound impact. A study conducted by the Bocconi University in Milan revealed that Italians, especially the younger generation, make a wide use of the Internet (entertainment, communication, financial and banking, working, and buying activities online, distance education, use of e-mail, interpersonal relationships) above the Western European average. The online activities, in many ways, like people in other countries, have brought people closer.

Thus, in the space of a generation, the individual's relationship to and perception of space has been profoundly transformed in Italy. Greater possibilities for rapid transit combined with highly developed *in situ* communications have made it possible to access information sources from around the world. The accompanying cultural revolution is much greater than that brought about by the railways in the nineteenth century. The psychological impact of such changes is hard to overstate.

Television: A Revolutionary Cultural Medium

Of all the media, probably the advent of television had the most profound impact on every sector of the population after World War II, and it was most responsible for the cultural revolution that took place in those postwar years. The development of a mass television audience predated mass ownership of sets because of the widespread practice of public viewing in bars and other public locales. Collective viewing was more widespread especially in the lower-class and working-class neighborhoods, where television functioned as a "social cement." By 1964, a decade after regular transmissions began, there were 5.22 million television sets, of which 95,200 were in public places, and the average audience between 9 P.M. and 10 P.M. was estimated at between 12 and 13 million.

In its first decade, the one-channel television had a profound impact on the life of the country. In 1951 the government granted *RAI* a monopoly on all radio and all future television broadcasting services. The license lasted until December 1972. Television was required to inform, entertain, and educate; at the same time it was expected to reflect the ideas of the political majority. Because television was state owned, the Christian Democratic-led governments made it essentially an instrument for holding power by controlling public opinion. People were fed programs that were in line with the cultural policy and ideology of the government. For the first decade of its existence, *RAI* was slavishly Christian Democratic in its politics and piously Catholic in its cultural values.[1]

As one may expect, during the first phase of expansion, television was not supported by many intellectuals; it was criticized and rejected by the Left and suspected by the Church. It was a matter of elite culture rejecting popular culture, either because (in the case of Leftist intellectuals) television was considered a diabolic invention of the corrupt capitalist West or because (for Catholic and conservative intellectuals) television threatened to undermine traditional religious and ethical values. Both sets of critics saw television as the bearer of a mass culture, a commodification of art; they felt it lowered the status of the intellectuals who wrote for it. There is no question that television had a noticeable impact on the life of the average citizens, leading to:

» an increase in family life and a decrease in social activities,
» a decrease in outdoor life, including the amount of time spent in the piazza or dedicated to the *passeggiata,* and
» a tendency to isolate individuals as passive subjects.

But television also contributed to the creation of a more culturally unified nation, by:

» closing the cultural gap between social classes and between urban and agrarian society,
» encouraging linguistic unity, and
» molding the national character.

In the 1960s state television perfected its educational model and reacted to some of the criticism by adding another channel and increasing broadcasting hours with informational, cultural, and school programs. *RAI* 1 would "represent" the government view from the Christian Democrats' perspective, *RAI 2* would "represent" the government view from the socialist perspective. Even with these changes, no channel had complete freedom to take its cameras out into the streets to make probing reports on controversial topics by actually asking people what they thought about any particular issues. All of the political parties considered this kind of freedom far more dangerous than safe studio talks with party "representatives." Certainly, the two channels offered more variety of views than the previous monolithic network had. This change, however, did not neutralize the criticism of the political parties, who could not completely control the flow of communications to both the general public and specific constituencies.[2] Nevertheless, the polarization of the political and cultural climate, and the ability of political parties and the Catholic Church to shape the cultural formulations of their followers through state-run television, started to come to an end.

In evaluating the first phase of Italian television, that is, the period of *DC* control, it must be said that Italian television quickly became noted for its fine programming. The state gave the needed support to create an Italian BBC; and the system did acquire the prestige or self-confidence that is essential for creating the standards and attracting the talent required for good programs. In fact, the state financed the system very generously while it was a state monopoly and even afterward; thus some very good productions went on the air.

Indeed, the brighter side of the coin was that in the Christian Democrats' days, Italian television at least tried to keep up a certain cultural tone. State monopoly offered the advantage that there was no need to compete with commercial television for audiences; hence, the proportion of serious cultural programming could be kept fairly high. *RAI* bought cheap American soap operas and other kinds of programs, and however banal its own quiz and variety shows, at least they were balanced by long hours devoted to the arts, history, and other educational programs. The approach was often conformist and uninspired, but no one could deny the cultural intent. Television was didactic in the Italian pedagogic manner and took relatively little account of audience tastes. Unfortunately, for a nation with such a talent for filmmaking, there was also a relatively high percentage of programs of low quality. The trouble here was that most of the top *RAI* executives, unlike their BBC counterparts, were not broadcasters but men brought in from the civil service or even from industry who were given the jobs for political reasons—few of them had any experience in or understanding of creative work, and they failed to set high standards.

The End of State Monopoly

Profound changes occurred in the 1970s. As a result of the tremors caused by the social unrest during 1968 and 1969, the Christian Democrats' hegemony started visibly to crumble. The Left began to elaborate a program of a decentralized broadcasting service, on a regional basis, and for internal reforms in *RAI*'s structure. This movement for decentralization was in line with the policy of devolution to the regions, envisaged in the Constitution of 1948 but not put into effect until 1970. Decentralization would mean, in broadcasting terms, reversing the trend that had dominated the *RAI* since 1946, for it entailed devolving decision-making about scheduling to the regional studios, greatly enhancing the latter as centers of production and as local news desks, dealing with regional and local realities, giving airtime to local groups (schools, unions, etc.), and enabling them to make programs using the *RAI's* technical and artistic expertise, equipment, and space.

At the same time as these changes were being proposed by the left, demands were also coming from the private broadcasting lobbies for a "liberalization of the airwaves." The privatizers wanted RAI's broadcasting monopoly to be declared unconstitutional on the grounds that it violated Article 21 of the Constitution, which states: "All people have the right to express their thoughts freely in speech, writing, or any other means of communication." What the private broadcasting lobbies were really interested in was not simply freedom of expression but freedom to exploit the lucrative advertising markets and attract revenues from local and national business clients. Their argument was convincing enough to sway the constitutional court and some sectors of public opinion.

In July 1976, a constitutional court decision not only abolished censorship, but also approved private broadcasting as long as it was not on a national scale. From that moment on, things developed rapidly, but along different lines from those originally envisaged by Parliament and the constitutional court. The court's decision opened a large loophole because precisely what "local" meant was not defined, while it was left to parliament to regulate the newly emergent private sector. The legal vacuum that developed also meant an absence of rules concerning several areas:

» the use of frequencies,
» the ratio of advertising to programming,
» the proportion of domestically produced to imported products,
» the construction and siting of transmitters, and
» the concentration of ownership and control.

On the one hand, *RAI* remained tightly regulated, because a legal ceiling was placed on advertising finance and the license fee was subject to the periodic decisions of parliament; on the other hand, the lack of regulation for competitors in the field of radio and television left open a rich field for commercial exploitation.

The ambiguities of the law turned out to favor not the decentralized building up of community-based alternatives to *RAI's* national channels but rather an accelerating tendency toward monolithic concentration. After the court's decision in 1976, a few thousand commercial radio stations and about one hundred television stations rapidly sprang to life; there are so many radio stations in Italy today that if you are driving with the radio on, you are switched automatically to a new station practically upon every turn of a corner. Since the 1980s Italy has had the highest number of television transmitters per capita of anywhere in the world. The passage from hyper-regulation to capitalist free-for-all was so abrupt that it did not allow for the crucial stage—experienced by other Western countries—of negotiation between television and state on how best to regulate the medium, and between television and its audiences over what service should entail.[3] Technological developments have made more complex the preservation of constitutional rights and the regulation of the communication system. The advent of satellite broadcasting has enabled the owners of a special aerial to watch hundreds of programs, which has further weakened public broadcasting and the control of the nation-state over television.

Television Conditioned by Market Culture

The judgment of the constitutional court in 1976 profoundly changed the general framework within which *RAI* had been accustomed to operate. Even if this did not immediately produce notable effects on the *RAI* agency, it did mean the beginning of competition between it and private operators; competition, furthermore, affected every area of its activity, from programming to the acquisition of copyrights, and from its relationship with its personnel and its audience to advertising. To better understand this picture, we need to remember the new type of television audience produced by the transformation of Italian society during the 1970s. It consisted of new viewers, most of whom had been freed from financial hardship, and who were better educated, more independent in their views, had more free time, and wanted a wider range of information, culture, and entertainment. Over a short period of time, therefore, *RAI* found itself operating in new and unforeseen political, social, and market conditions. The problem facing *RAI* was that of rethinking its relationship to political power, to its audience, and to its privately run competitors.

The new environment created a landscape that presented unexpected beauty and traps. For example, the political forces that imposed radical changes on the TV system and on the structure of *RAI* were not completely correct in their assessment of the impact of television on shaping the political views of spectators. With the liberalization of the medium, the ability to control the output of television news is necessarily very limited, primarily because political messages must be transformed by the media; in other words, the political parties are less and less an independent source of information; they tend to become mere items in an information system dominated by television. Moreover, overall mass behavior is affected by the entire information system and not just by television. Therefore, political control cannot be established over the totality of television output because it depends on the entire cultural industry. In fact, when in 1978 the Communist Party also acquired a voice by the establishment of *RAI 3,* the party did not register a significant change in the results at the polls. Thus, it should be stressed that there is no evidence that the media are able to influence the results of elections to any significant degree. There may be some influence over a small percentage of the population, which inevitably contributes to the small electoral swings. With a proportional representation system in place in Italy until 1994, these small swings could have affected the overall result and did affect the composition of the ruling majorities and the strength of the opposition.[4]

The major problem for *RAI* was its inability to organize a united response to the private sector, which from the very outset displaced *RAI* or created a new audience by filling the most important slots with entertainment programs—quiz shows, talk shows, and, above all, television movies, serials, and cartoons purchased on the international market.

Instead of opting for a course that differentiated public television from the private networks, by stressing its institutional role as a public service, *RAI* decided to challenge private television on the very ground that was most favorable to the latter, namely, in the area of entertainment, quiz shows, escapist amusements, and in the number of hours broadcast each day. It found itself in the contradictory situation of concentrating its financial resources on the purchase of foreign films, television movies, and serials (private television's most competitive genres), and thus diminishing the available resources for in-house production. One of the most absurd effects of this situation occurred in the early 1980s, when Italy became the world's principal importer of television programs from the U.S., Japan, and Brazil, and competition between *RAI* and the private networks for the rights to foreign programs caused a sharp rise in their prices.

A serious attempt to change this process was made in the early 1980s when *RAI* began a comeback strategy. That meant moving into an industrial phase of fiction production and training producers, directors, screenwriters, and actors for their new jobs. The aims of this strategy were, first, to put a check on the growing number of imported television movies, serials, and cartoons; second, to produce drama and serials whose content was more in keeping with national and European culture; and, third, to begin exporting these products, first of all to Europe, but then also to North America. These primary objectives were linked to the attempt at establishing greater cooperation throughout Europe based on the development of co-productions and on the creation of an efficient continental commercial network. *RAI* thus managed to become one of the principal Italian film producers.

Television as Mass Consumer Medium

In 1978 an important milestone took place: television, with just the *RAI* license fee, started to earn more revenue than the cinema. Thus, the crisis and restructuring in the entertainment industry generated a new framework in which the main player was clearly television. It is not that the consumption of entertainment fell overall; rather, it was distributed in a different manner. This period witnessed the defeat of the public place of entertainment by home-based entertainment, which had the not inconsiderable advantage of being spread around the entire country with fewer inequalities. Television became the most fertile ground for advertising investments; consequently, private broadcasters sprang up everywhere. The penetration of television as a mass consumer medium into the home, together with the rise of other forms of home-based leisure and cultural consumption, profoundly restructured the notion of community upon which traditional forms of collective political and religious participation depended. Also, the increase in television watching, together with other changes like mass literacy and mass post-primary education, helped make working-class people better educated and more aware of the political, social, and cultural issues, and thus less dependent on the party apparatus or the Church as sources of information and values. The media, through their focus on individuals and on dramatic rather than routine aspects of the political process, shifted the popular perception of politics away from party programs toward controversy, personalities, and spectacle. Moreover, the rise of the private networks freed the media from state protection and created in the people the idea that mass media would respond to the needs of all, free from political goals. By the end of the 1970s, public cultural manifestations and events intended for the masses no longer had a content that was packaged to contain a specific message but were organized to meet public satisfaction and appreciation.

From Mass to Segmented Audience

Today the Italian system is more open to the logic of industry and competition than to that of politics and cultural institutions. In the liberalization of broadcasting, what was revolutionary was an interactive use of the medium. Instead of being given information by studio experts about issues that often had little relevance to their lives, local people could themselves speak on radio and television and discuss questions of immediate importance to them, either by coming into the studio or by phoning in. With two or more telephone lines on the air simultaneously, people could talk not just to the presenter and to the audience but with one another. Radio and television were not only a means of distribution but also of communication. Instead of being the mouthpiece of a political group, they became the "platform" on which different voices could come together.

Therefore, television has had the most profound impact on the wider population. Television became fashionable, along with light entertainment and everything else that had once been so despised. This was a real cultural transformation. Television was perceived no longer as an educative instrument but as an integral part of the cultural industry, which could be run as a competitive business, thus leading, among other things, to market segmentation.

In all this, private television seems to better reflect the thinking of the general public. The distaste for long narratives, which according to Jean-Francois Lyotard (1924–98), the French philosopher, is the mark of our times, goes along with a greater capacity to grasp fragments, contradictions, differences, and redundancies:

> We can consider "postmodern" the skepticism towards certain types of narrative. The narrative function loses its actors, the great heroes, the great dangers, the great journeys and the great ends . . . Postmodern knowledge is not exclusively an instrument of power. It refines our sensibility for differences and strengthens our capacity to face the immeasurable.[5]

In the era of new media systems and new information and communication technologies that interact with new production systems and advertising markets, there is a decline in the notion of mass culture and mass communication. Technology and advertising have made broadcasting a segmented and targeted communication. Indeed, especially because of advertising, there has been a shift from mass audience to segmented audience, in Italy as elsewhere. There is a switch from broadcasting to "narrowcasting" or from mass communication to segmented communication. Firms can insert an advertisement where it will reach its target public, which need not be a "mass" public. A firm that manufactures personal computers or expensive cars is likely to be more interested in reaching 200,000 people in the right income and occupational bracket than 2 million whom it knows nothing about. "Italian commercial television, in the absence of any plan or legislation, did not develop on the classic model of the European broadcasting industries. It followed in the wake of advertising, it developed as an outgrowth of advertising messages and of the means of distribution and consumption specific to those messages."[6] It was the sponsors who determined the program content on the basis of attractiveness to advertisers, not the stations on the basis of any cultural policy or perceived public need or demand. The television system became geared almost entirely to the distribution end, with advertising "piggy-backed" onto prepackaged programs, rather than to the production end. The "product" that one sees on private television is determined by the power of money.

Competition for advertising dollars has also lowered standards. There are very few programs for schools on Italian television, and no exclusively cultural channel. The struggle for advertising produces gimmicks like the sudden stopping of a film at the most exciting part in a bid to hold viewers. Pornography, too, is used in advertising, as it is used on the covers of magazines.

Private television stations are vertically integrated with advertising agencies and main publishing groups. In the absence of regulation, three or four television groups emerged in the 1970s that eventually took control of the entire sector. Silvio Berlusconi, who became prime minister in 1994 (and again in 2001), in the 1970s built up a television conglomerate that not only dominates private television but also has overtaken the state network in advertising revenues and in viewers. Since 1984, after flattening the last of his major rivals, Berlusconi, through his highly diversified holding company, Fininvest, has dominated Italian private television. He controls the three principal private networks, *Canale 5, Italia 1* (1983), and *Rete 4* (1984).

The success of Berlusconi is a clear indication of how influential are advertising and a purely business approach to television. In 1981 Berlusconi first imported the Lorimar television series "Dallas" for around $20,000 an episode, to compete against *RAI*'s costly prime time in-house productions. Berlusconi's success had little to do with any media skills he may have possessed, although he was shrewd enough to open up previously untapped viewing slots. His background was in the construction business, unlike Rusconi *(Italia 1)* and Mondadori *(Rete 4)* who were publishers and would have seemed more natural media entrepreneurs based on the model of the multimedia tycoons elsewhere in Europe (such as Hachette, Murdoch, Maxwell, and Bertelsmann). Instead, Berlusconi's success had everything to do with his ability to sense potential advertising markets and to sell advertising space, confirming the point that it was advertising that drove the expansion of the networks.

Berlusconi was also able to target his products to specific kinds of viewers. In 1982 he began to use *Italia 1* in tandem with *Canale 5*, differentiating them for different markets. *Italia 1* was given a schedule that was oriented to a popular youth market, whereas *Canale 5* had a family-feminine profile. The two networks began to trail one another's programs in

1983, and Berlusconi shifted personnel and programs between them to try to secure maximum competitive advantage.

The emergence of private broadcasting had negative cultural consequences. In the absence of any form of effective state regulation (such as protective quotas or rules stipulating a certain proportion of in-house productions), and because it is much cheaper to import someone else's programs than to make your own, Italian television companies have increasingly become creatures of advertisers and importers of other countries' television. This domination of imports on Italian screens leads one to question the validity of traditional notions of a national cultural space, both popular and high culture, and consider its implications.

Impact of the Openness to Non-National Culture

Italy's history and its economic and policy choices have affected the flow of cultural goods into the country. Italy's regional fragmentation, late unification, late diffusion of the national language, and, very importantly, its low level of "national-popular" integration, that is to say, of voluntary participation by the mass of the people in the formation of the nation-state and in post-unification national culture—these have all had an imprint. The masses were alien to the nation-state; the unification was achieved without a revolution and without the masses' full participation. Italy may have been unified in a political and administrative sense in 1861, but outside the sphere of its ruling elite there was little or no shared cultural identity at the national level. This was partly because local and regional cultural traditions remained strong for a long time after unification and partly because the various attempts to construct and define a national culture from above were either restricted to an educated minority or were of a coercive, rhetorical kind.

In this respect, Italy's "openness" to non-Italian cultural material can be seen in part as a result of its relatively weak national-popular integration, its regional fragmentation, and possibly the "cosmopolitan" (or "non-national-popular") character of its intellectual elite.[7] However, it should also be said that imports were often cheaper to buy than Italian-made equivalents; as well, insofar as they had already been tried out on foreign markets, imports represented less risk for the cultural entrepreneur. Therefore, on one hand, the cultural dependency is a danger to the national character of the country, and on the other, Italy's openness to non-national culture could be seen as an index of cultural pluralism and vitality and a means by which diverse lifestyles have been absorbed and creatively reworked. It may be that while we wait for the "utopian" television of the future, in which the intermingling of national cultures will be generalized and intercultural viewing will be possible, Italy can offer us today the interesting spectacle of a system in transition.

Because of the nature of the medium, television has naturally become one of the cheaper forms of entertainment. After the expenditure on a set, installation, and servicing, it provides virtually unlimited material in the home at very low cost. In non-metropolitan areas with little or no book production and similarly limited book consumption (such as Marches, Abruzzi,

Calabria, Basilicata, and Sardinia), television is heavily consumed. By contrast, in the cities of the north, with more money and a greater diversity of available entertainment, viewing rates are slightly lower. Television programs must compete with more sophisticated forms of entertainment.

The popular view that television offers a proliferation of low-level mass entertainment is, in many respects, true. However, it should also be said that segments of the public who were either not previously catered to adequately by *RAI* (for instance, women, who constitute the majority of the audience, and youth) now are receiving proper attention. One could also say that a positive effect of the competition from the private networks has been not only to put better films on *RAI* at prime time but also to propel it to experiment with some imaginative entertainment shows. Moreover, private broadcasting has put an end to the monopoly of state-regulated broadcasting, which was frequently dull, patronizing, party-obsessed, and party-manipulated, while opening new ways of reaching the public. The importance given to the broadcasting of rock videos, low-intensity talk-shows ("Oprah" style), and variety programs, panel games, game shows, quizzes, cartoons, etc., while lowering the cultural level of broadcasting, shows the strong intent to make television profoundly democratic. It also shows that Italian television, like other television in the West, has become more an environmental medium than a representational or expressive one. The television set is becoming more and more like the radio, switched on and running permanently in the background. In the Italian household the television set is often not in the same room as the people, and as a consequence, the sound volume is turned up very high. Television has become a domestic companion.

So today the low quality of the programs in the entertainment, arts, and documentary genres is a much bigger problem than the old issue of political bias. Italian television may be more free and outspoken than in the old days, but it is even more culturally mediocre. Today the cultural output has dropped drastically. The new commercial rivalry between the networks has led to a non-stop struggle for high ratings and has pushed the companies into putting more stress on easy entertainment programs with a wide appeal. This would matter less if they were at least well done. But the competition has led the networks to rely heavily on cheap foreign products and reruns. As compared with 20% in Britain, over 50% of Italian TV material is imported, much of it American soap opera.

It is true that some good new work by talented people does reach the screen, but such programming is far too rare. For example, serial adaptations of classic novels rarely come near the quality of the best BBC work. When it comes to new television plays on modern subjects, the results are very disappointing.

In the matter of "morality," there has been a major relaxing of standards. Until the early 1980s TV drama was still influenced by the Catholic ethos. Italians have always been highly tolerant of all kinds of private behavior, so long as it remains private and is not aired in public, and television was a surviving bastion of this attitude toward public morality. However, new, freer values have reached the screen: nudity and sexually explicit scenes are now permitted on television almost as much as in cinema, and the Italian TV has even moved ahead (or behind!) of America with respect to the presence of sexually open programs.

The presence of private television networks has proven valid the fears of those who opposed the liberalization of television: fears of a further lowering of cultural standards, fears of the growth of powerful monopolies, and fears of political pressures of a new kind.

Technologically, Italian television is very advanced, in its way. It makes full use of the latest electronic news-gathering techniques, and it uses split-screen and montage effects with a virtuosity verging on gimmickry. But while the Italian government pours money into the subsidizing of theater companies and feature filmmaking, concerts, operas, and art exhibitions, and these activities draw good audiences, even so, in terms of sheer time devoted to it, most adults get most of their cultural exposure from television. It is a far more potent vehicle for the spreading of culture than any other, and, more than in most major European countries, the Italians are meagerly fed by that small screen.

Household cultural expenditure by domain: year 2000 (million euros) and % var. 1990–2000

Domains	2000	% Var. 00/90
Cultural goods and services	550.0	44.4
Museums and sites	149.8	124.6
Performing arts	400.2	27.4
Cultural industries	9,162.5	8.6
Press	2,482.1	−21.0
Books	2,870.0	14.9
Radio	131.2	7.3
Television	1,954.3	77.6
Cinema	529.4	17.5
Home Video-DVD	627.4	20.3
Recorded music	568.1	−6.5
Total	9,712.5	10.1

Source: ISTAT 2001

Dailies: Regionally Connected

The printed press too is uniquely Italian:

- » a predominance of regional over national papers;
- » historically low levels of readership therefore, the overall circulation has remained quite low;
- » a notable lack of independence of the press;

- » virtual nonexistence of a popular press
- » the existence of a group of daily "news"papers that are devoted solely to either sports, religious news, or other specialized topics.
- » most dailies, including almost all of the large ones, have piled up sizable deficits year after year;
- » the government controls newsstand prices, and
- » the advertising base covers a very small percentage of expenses.

It should also be noted that the Italian press industry is presently the most heavily subsidized in Europe. It is affected by falling reading rates, and, consequently, by falling income from the sale of newspapers and periodicals (–21% between 1990 and 2000) on one side, and growing competition with TV networks in attracting advertising income on the other side. In fact, the industry would not be able to survive without direct and indirect public financing to publishing houses provided for through the years by several laws, starting with Law 416/1891, establishing tax incentives for capital investments, loans, grants, and, mainly, postal tariff facilities, the latter substantially increased by Law 488/1999.

Italy lacks a national press as it is known in Britain and France. There is no equivalent of *Le Monde,* the *Times,* or the *Sun.* It is sufficient to compare this with the daily sales of 4.2 million of just one newspaper, the *Sun* in Britain, which has a similar population size. It is significant that Italy's newspaper market was, and has remained with a few exceptions, characteristically local or regional, not national, and the economic success of a daily paper was measured by how far it managed to dominate its particular market. Thus, in 2000 such major newspapers as *La Stampa* (400,000 copies, Piedmont), *La Nazione* (Tuscany), *Il Resto del Carlino* (Emilia), *Il Mattino* (Campania), and *La Gazzetta del Mezzogiorno* (Apulia) all still sold between 75% and 95% of their copies in their region of production. Even *Il Corriere della Sera,* then the only paper which could be said to have had a national presence, sold 66% of its copies in its native Lombardy. The paper with the most convincing national profile is *La Repubblica.* Launched in 1976 and based in Rome, it is not associated with a particular region or city, and it has carved a niche of readership among the younger generation. Although change of ownership and a more national orientation helped *Il Corriere della Sera* to reestablish itself as the leading paper in terms of sales and reputation, the regional bias remains. Apart from these pluri-regional or regional papers, each city or major town often has its own daily paper that is distributed in the surrounding province. Finally, there is a smaller provincial press that comes out once or twice a week and is exclusively local. The papers that, at least until recently, had the best national distribution over the peninsula were *L'Unità,* the daily of the former Communist Party (now the Democratic Party of the Left), and *L'Osservatore Romano,* the official paper of the Vatican. Probably the paper that has the most even distribution and sale across the country is *La Gazzetta dello Sport,* which is also the most-read daily! After all soccer plays an important part in the life of Italians *(See Box on p. 397).* What is also evident is that the Italian press has a strong regional character—provincial papers account for over two-thirds of the dailies' total sales—and that this continues to be the case.

Why doesn't Italy have a paper with a genuinely national readership, whose authority within the country is the basis for an international reputation? This localism is another confirmation of the strength of regional traditions. The strength of local identities is something the Catholic Church has long cultivated, celebrating the values of family and community. Regionalism derives in part from Italy's lack of a historical metropolitan capital comparable to London, Paris, or Berlin, from whose central position the rest of the country could be dominated. Whereas Rome is the political capital, Milan is the economic and cultural capital. Italy is a country of multiple urban centers that have not only maintained their identities but are currently reclaiming their distinctive traditions in the name of a greater degree of self-government. Because regions have become more powerful as centers of government and economic activity, the justification for this kind of press is enhanced. However, the strength of the regional and provincial press is not uniform throughout the peninsula. Because of the need for an advertising outlet for local business, the center and the north had a more vigorous press than the south and, as a result, Italian newspapers have endemic weaknesses of their own, both economic and editorial. One major problem is that the Italians by inclination have never been great newspaper readers and are becoming even less so with the emergence of electronic information systems.[8]

Causes of Low Readership

Today's relatively low readership in Italy is due to several factors. Because of historical, economical, and cultural reasons in Italy, only an elite readership was formed. In the second half of the twentieth century, when the majority of Italians became literate, the newspapers had ceased to have a monopoly of information, owing to radio and, above all, television. Language use is not a small drawback. Newspapers made no attempt to make themselves more accessible by using a "simpler" language. The lack of transparency and the high level of abstractness of bureaucratic and political discourse reproduced in journalism have not helped in breaking the barrier for a very high percentage of readers. The Italian journalistic establishment still considers the newspaper market a "quality" market. Newspapers and newspaper advertising are mostly targeted at a high-income, educated reading public, not a mass public. Sport not only is massively covered in the press with regional and local publications but enjoys coverage by three daily sports papers—*Corriere dello Sport*, *La Gazzetta dello Sport*, and *Tuttosport*. In fact, if sports papers and weekly magazines are included, the readership picture is not as bleak. Soccer, the most popular sport in Italy, attracts with equal enthusiasm fans from every social class and explains the higher sale of dailies on Sundays and Mondays. The absence of tabloids may be explained by the following facts:

» regional and local identity and their journalistic representation cut across the division of social class;

» popular issues such as sports and crime are covered by the Italian press in a different way—crime stories are covered by the national television news even when the individuals involved are not famous;

» the well-established large readership of weekly magazines remained faithful to their publications; and

» similar cultural functions appear to be fulfilled by weekly magazines.

These magazines have a very high total circulation owing to their strong visual element and in certain cases a typical tabloid content (scandal, sports, sex, television). But even this sector is not comparably popular because most Italians find them difficult to read. The effects of television on the press are described as uniformly deleterious. It is not just that television puts importance on entertainment values, making news into a spectacle for consumption, nor just that television has overtaken the press in speed of reporting, establishing itself as the chief source of news for the majority of Italians. The problem is that the press in Italy has allowed television to set its agendas so that anything in the *telegiornale* (TV evening news) has to be covered in the morning edition.[9] It has also tried to become more entertaining, symptomatically giving extensive coverage to television personalities and events.[10]

However, the most obvious explanation for the low level of readership is that Italy is a latecomer in the field of mass literacy and mass education. When this was finally achieved, the age of television had already come. It should also be noted that the newspapers are highly politicized and full of special vocabulary and esoteric language. All the newspapers are much more wordy than their equivalents in the English-language press. They are also more serious and probably go into the news in greater depth than their British or American equivalents. Since Italian universities did not offer degrees in journalism until very recently, journalists entered the profession without special training, usually coming from an academic background rich in classical studies. Moreover, Italian journalists belong to a "registered" profession with restricted entry and high salaries. As a result, newspapers cannot compete with news reporting on television, both for the cost and the ability to attract a large audience. Today the cost of dailies is set at one euro ($1.40 at the present exchange rate!)

The Italian press has shortcomings even when it tries to report assessments of national conditions. One of its editorial shortcomings as a whole, including *La Repubblica* and *Corriere della sera,* is that it has little tradition of the kind of fearless investigative reporting common in Britain and America. Papers are stronger on polemic or on mere news digest than on fully researched factual exposés when controversy is in the air. There are two underlying factors: first, Italian readers are generally more concerned with ideas and style than with facts; second, Italians are deferential toward not only the government but most power establishments as well. In this centralized and close-knit society, most journalists rely for their news sources on their personal links with people in positions of influence—be they ministers, civil servants, business tycoons, trade-union leaders, or leading politicians—and they are reluctant to prejudice these sources by making embarrassing revelations. Exceptions were rare until the fall of the First Republic and the national embarrassment caused by the *Tangentopoli* mega-scandal. Still, prudence is the watchword. The fact is that the press relies on millions of dollars' worth of assorted annual state aid in the form of newsprint subsidies.

The problem is also one of journalistic tradition and resources, or lack of them. As compared with the quality press in Britain or America, few Italian editors put the same insistence on factual accuracy or balanced judgments or instill these virtues in their staff. The better Italian journalism tries to combine two ingredients that often do not mix well: the brio of ideas and the substance of events; commentary and reporting; evaluation of themes and statement of facts. Moreover, it seems that the deductive methods of teaching used in Italy, whereby all schoolchildren are trained first to enunciate a thesis, then to parade facts to support it, are in no small part a cause of the way Italian journalists' minds work and even of their mixing of news and commentary. It is the reverse of the inductive British-American tradition, which likewise spills over from education into its journalism. Therefore, the Italian system, whatever its intellectual merits, is not the ally of objective inquiry.

The Press and Power Groups

Certainly the fact that the Italian press is not independent does not help either. Italian newspapers are strongly connected to centers of power: political institutions and political parties on the one hand and economic groups and forces on the other. The "party press," which has been in rapid decline since the end of the Cold War (*L'Unità's* circulation dropped from 500,000 in 1952 to 111,000 in 1997 to about 80,000 today) differs profoundly in its political orientation and therefore differs equally profoundly in the way it reports and interprets news. It is a press that is protected from the market in that it does not depend financially on sales and advertising; however, it is expected to respect the orthodoxy of the party and is subject to its censorship. Even so, the majority of influential newspapers were, and are, controlled by the business enterprises. Through newspapers, generations of Italian entrepreneurs have exercised strong influence on the economic and political affairs of the nation.

Although almost without exception newspapers are unprofitable and depend on government subsidies, this state of affairs has never unduly troubled the newspaper owners. Whether businessmen or other wealthy individuals, corporations or economic groups and associations, they do not look upon their journalistic holdings as money-making ventures. In a country where political influences are omnipresent, the corporate-controlled press is an important weapon, providing entrepreneurs with a means of influencing public opinion and the parties. They regard them as tools to protect and promote other, more important interests of their own through a complex combination and interplay of pressures and counter pressures, favors, and concessions involving the government and the political forces which share, or are expected to share soon, in running national or local affairs.

Indeed, a striking feature of Italian private industry is its role in the media. Virtually all the major daily newspapers are owned entirely or in part by corporate powers: *La Stampa* by Agnelli; *Il Messaggero* by Montedison; *Il Giornale Nuovo* by Berlusconi; *Il Sole 24 Ore* by Confindustria (the industrialists' organization); *Il Tempo* by Italmobiliare; *La Nazione, Il Resto del Carlino,* and

Il Piccolo, by Monti; and the *Corriere della* Sera by a consortium controlled by Agnelli, Pirelli, Bonomi, and Montedison. Agnelli, Monti, and Confindustria have absolute editorial control over their papers; the others have varying degrees of influence.

In spite of the connections between the press and the governing parties, much of the Italian press, particularly since the mid-1960s, tends to favor the parties of the center-Left. Ideologically the press tends to espouse various aspects of liberal tradition no matter who owns them.

La Repubblica is the best daily; during the first republic, it criticized the socialists or communists as much as the Christian Democrats. It is perhaps the most bulky newspaper in Italy with many long pieces and extensive cultural and financial sections; politicians also have an opportunity to express their views or answer points made against them, and there are sometimes long forums on the ills afflicting *Italia.*

Some of the changes, such as the greater proportion of women in journalism and the greater attention to social rather than narrow political issues, are positive. Newspapers are freer to focus on commentary and analysis of news that has already been delivered by the other media.

The Italian Press and the United States

In the 1970s America's Watergate scandal had provided encouragement and ammunition to all those bent on portraying America as a decadent and bumbling imperial power—one that was racist, corrupt, racked by domestic crises, and increasingly unable to face up to its adversaries or reward its allies in the international arena but still seeking greedily to promote its selfish interests at the expense of friends and foes. In the mid-1970s, carried away by all-out solidarity with the most militant "movement of liberation" in the Third World, Italy's Leftist newspapers vented their basic anti-American bias.

Toward the end of the 1970s, most of the Italian newspapers concentrated their fire on the "American Party" in Italy, the Christian Democratic Party. That is, the groups that were singled out for attack were ones that were perceived as bent on furthering the influence and wicked designs of America as well as their own selfish interests and privileges. For example, a determined and sustained effort was made to associate the United States (and more specifically, the CIA) with the kidnapping and murder of former premier and *DC* leader Aldo Moro in 1978. In the same breath, however, they used much more violent terms to denounce again the bombings, massacres, and corruption that in their opinion must be blamed on the Americans in Vietnam, Latin America, the Middle East, Greece, and elsewhere. Some radicals and left-wingers in Italy have admitted, more or less grudgingly, that some of their "evaluations and prophecies" about the nature and behavior of Communist regimes have turned out to be wrong. The anti-American slant was certainly more sustained and persistent in newspapers identified officially with political parties, especially *L'Unità,* the daily of the old Communist Party.

This anti-American bias was generally the fruit of a higher political education of the people. For example, in a series of articles appearing in 1979 in *Corriere della Sera,* the Italian writer Goffredo Parise could not be accused of mincing words in his critical assessment of American society. His invective was filled with such characterizations as: "The American people . . . have very little dignity and often no dignity at all. . . . The average American has undergone a sort of historical and political lobotomization and is not aware of his political identity, of the tremendous social and racial differentiations and discriminations that exist in the country. . . . Poverty in the U.S. is the blackest in the world."

In the 1960s and 1970s many of the same media and other Leftist journalists and "experts" sought to sell the idea that Italy had been a province, a most compliant and exploited province, of the "American empire." Film reviewers missed no opportunity to blame the troubles of the Italian movie industry on American colonization of the Italian market, and movie directors did likewise when their works received a bad reception. The same media displayed a marked bias in favor of Arab Leftists. It should be stressed, however, that this kind of mass-media practice took place in a country where the great majority of the population has a deep respect and admiration for the U.S., as we have seen in Chapter 4.

In the 1980s there was a changing trend. Some of the most militantly anti-American contributors left, while others trimmed their sails to the new trade winds and the press reflected more closely the sentiments of the Italian people toward America. That trend continues today and a more balanced picture is presented. Anti-American propaganda has gained a wider audience and had a greater impact since the U.S. interventions in Afghanistan and Iraq in 2001 and 2003.

Magazines: A Popular Commodity

The low readership in dailies has been balanced, to an extent, by the rise in popularity of the weekly news magazines that have become national publications. In a society that is becoming faster-paced, electronic news quickly makes printed news obsolete, and people are today less ready to find the time for reading a morning paper; news digests and feature material on the weekends has become more appealing. Consequently, news magazines have developed remarkably. Originally borrowing their formula from such publications as the American *Life* and *Look,* Italian weeklies have now become far more glossy than these, with thick shiny pages full of color ads; their content is much more newsy. By European standards their circulations are modest; nevertheless, these are prosperous for their owners owing to their high cover price (2 to 4 euros) and copious advertisements.

While the daily press remained stagnant, the weeklies went from 12.6 million sold each week in 1952 to 21 million in 1972 to about 28 million today. Published mostly by Rusconi and Mondadori, the weekly magazines are designed to appeal to everyone. One group follows the lines of the American *Time* magazine. The best known of these are *Panorama, L'Espresso,* and *Europeo.* They consist of articles on a wide range of subjects from politics to finance to cultural events. They are more accessible than newspapers on a number of counts:

>   their language is simpler;
>   their abundant use of photographs provides fast imagery reading to those with limited reading skills; and

» the content—stories about private lives of Hollywood stars—is sensationalized.

In fact, their specialty is research in depth, usually on sensational subjects dealt with in a serious way: drugs, homosexuality, where the Italians make love, and so forth. But they also deal with recurrent national problems: the crises in justice, housing, the health service, the economy, education. In summer, nudes appear on their covers to represent research into subjects such as "Torrid Summer: Causes, Effects, and Remedies," "Topless," and "On Holiday with Eros." Inside there is little or no suggestive material. After all, the cover may be a way of selling more copies, but at the same time these are subjects that are interesting in themselves. However, the abundant advertisements are very often quite suggestive, or they present products such as prophylactics with the same candidness as goods for a homey kitchen. These magazines have been astute in giving particular coverage to lifestyle matters, such as fashion and health. There is no doubt that major changes are taking place within the existing newspapers and magazines because of the growth of a female readership and affluence. New magazines have emerged above all in the areas of cooking and home design and décor.

Because Italian is not a world language like English, the Italian magazines do not sell internationally and therefore have a limited number of their own foreign correspondents, unlike *Time* and *Newsweek*. Although they are topical and are more concerned with research projects and comment, they get their news items secondhand and are not always completely up to date.

There are more family-oriented magazines that are widely read; three of these are *Oggi*, *L'Europeo,*and *Famiglia cristiana* and all three illustrate an important characteristic of the Italian press in general: the fact that they do not write for specific social groups but attempt in one publication to satisfy readers of every kind. There seems to be no differentiation between lowbrow and highbrow, perhaps because most Italians are not aware of this distinction them-selves. In either of these magazines one may get advice on *stitichezza* (constipation) in the same edition as an interview with the Italian prime minister, or a serious analysis of the inequities of the taxation system, along with a correspondence page, a horoscope, and two or three opinion pages on topical issues, whether the Mafia or the examination system. *Famiglia cristiana,*which has the highest sales of any magazine in Italy, as it may be expected, has an approach based on Catholic morality.

In addition to illustrated magazines, Italy also has high levels of consumption of comics (*fumetti*).*Topolino,* a magazine for children, has a wide readership and has surpassed its 2000th edition.

On the whole, then, the Italian press deals with any subject. It is conservative in that it has nothing sensational like *People,* has no tabloids, and displays on the whole a stolid format. It is written more in a literary style than a journalistic one, is rarely vulgar, and illustrates the general absence of divisions of class or of "intellectualism." It gives good coverage to foreign news. Much of the press is local, but it is rarely provincial. Despite or perhaps because of these reasons, it is not so widely read.

Media Geography System

Although the growth of television, especially through the private sector, represents an essential part of the "unification" of north and south on the language level, it has also created an increasingly polarized and uneven market for cultural goods. The structure of the information system is uneven between north and south. If we look at the written information we will notice a persistent gap: the south has 34% of the total population but publishes only 12% book titles a year, prints only 16 out of 87 daily papers (not one of which sells more than 100,000 daily copies in a country where there is no real national press), and buys only 10% of daily papers and 17% of periodicals. Moreover, whereas the bigger papers of the north are sold all over Italy and abroad, those in the south do not have the distribution structure to make this possible. And so, Italian newspapers that reach abroad do not have much in terms of southern news and issues.

If we examine the figures for television we see that there is virtually no consumption gap between north and south: 98% of the southern population owns a television set against a national average of 99%. There is, however, a production gap: most of the programs broadcast that are produced in Italy come from the north or the center. Southern culture has no outlet. The role of the south in this sector is that of consumer, a market for goods made elsewhere.

Although Italy displays a form of polycentrism in its media industry organization, there are no centers in the south. Rome, Florence, and Turin are home of some important book publishing houses, but their combined national impact is smaller than that of Milan. The publishing industry (above all book and magazine publishing) has Milan as its capital. Milan is the headquarters not only of some major book publishers (Mondadori, Rizzoli, and Garzanti) and distribution agencies but of almost all of the major periodicals. Because of its central role in publishing, Milan became also the national capital of advertising. However, Milan's pivotal role in the publishing sector is countered by a weakness in the other forms of mass communication. Until the advent of private television, Milan had a marginal role in film production.

Film production also began polycentrically, but it subsequently centered increasingly in Rome. With the creation first of the Istituto LUCE (1925) and then Cinecittà (1937), Rome became the capital of film production. The cinema industry was the first national cultural industry to have its production capital in the political capital. With the advent of television broadcasting through *RAI*, Rome became also the principal geographic area for TV production. This situation changed in a significant way after the arrival, well into the 1980s, of private television stations that made their home in Milan.

It is clear that Italy's cultural and communications industries are firmly rooted in central and northern Italy, in particular on the Rome-Milan axis. However, we cannot underplay the role of Naples in the south as a cultural center, for its important publishing houses, great opera house, prestigious university, and its vital role in the field of popular mass culture. As a national center of live variety theater, it has a tradition of theater in dialect with no equal in the nation, while as the national center of popular music, for many years it boasted the festival of popular music that enjoyed more popular interest than the one in the standard language in San Remo.[11] Until recently, its dialect enjoyed such a popularity that it had national appeal.

With the exception of Florentine, it was the only dialect that could safely be assumed to be understood from one end of the peninsula to the other. "It could be said, without forcing the analogy too much, that for a long time Naples was to Italian popular culture what the New Orleans-Nashville axis is to U.S. mass culture."[12] The iconography of the city—Vesuvius, the bay of Naples, the funicular—was an important part of a largely reinvented local tradition. The rise of more modern cultural forms and patterns of consumption associated with the north and center, most notably television, brought about the decline in the 1960s of Neapolitan song, and of Naples as a center of popular culture in Italy. The popularity of transnational music, the growth of interest in rock music, and the strong emergence of youth culture made regional culture less appealing.

In terms of the distribution of cultural power, then, the postindustrial era in Italy seems to be shaping up to look as bad as the industrial era. There may be a greater range of cultural goods on the market, and a greater variety in the means of distributing them. New audiences may have opened up and they may be responding to an increased supply of television in new ways. But access to the new media technologies and to the full range of cultural goods still depends on a very uneven spread of earnings and dispositions. Traditional inequalities between classes and regions are reinforced. Finally, the patterns of concentrated ownership that became established in the sixties and seventies show few signs of breaking up, and the major cultural industries are as far from any kind of democratic accountability and control as ever.

Homogenization and Different Forms of Culture

The advent of TV as a mass consumer medium coincided with the arrival of mass material wealth in Italy, and so it would be simplistic to say that a total "massification" of culture was brought about exclusively by TV. General material wealth created massification of culture and at same time distinctions in the creation of and interest in forming cultures, as distinctions are created by dispositions and competencies. People's cultural choices are shaped by several economic and ideological determinants:

» the amount of disposable income,
» sort of area they live in,
» social pressures to conform,
» the level of education, and
» family cultural dispositions.

Change in attitudes in goods consumption goes hand in hand with change in work attitudes and leisure patterns. Many of these are, of course, the result of rising living standards, for in the postwar period all social categories shared in the general rise in prosperity. In Italy, as in other Western countries, many consumer durables such as cars, which were luxury items owned by the privileged few before the war, became generalized to the mass of the population. Television sets, and, later, freezers, dishwashers, video-recorders, cellular phones, and computers, are all items that began as expensive luxuries and are now widely owned.

❀ SPIRIT

Traditions and Festivals

Italy is still very much attached to its traditions, and its rich tapestry of cultural diversity and heritage is evident in Italy's local festivals. Whether a festival honors a patron saint or remembers an important historic event or celebrates traditional local foods, Italians use the occasion to bring out the best in the community.

Everywhere in Italy the most important and strongest traditions are those based on the Catholic faith and its adherence to the calendar of saints' feast days. Some are small affairs held in the side streets, while others are huge celebrations complete with amusements and live performances, all illuminated by multi-colored lights hanging above the streets. Many of these festivals have been celebrated for hundreds of years. Their focal point usually is a particular saint significant to the community, be it a local patron saint or a saint dedicated to a local occupation. A large part of the veneration process, especially in small towns, includes an image of the saint, often a beautifully carved statue that is paraded through the streets and displayed at the local church or at an elaborately decorated temporary altar. Once the feast begins, festivities can range from solemn processions to boisterous parades, from music and games to a full-blown carnival. Some of the larger festivals have become annual tourist attractions, bringing in needed revenue to the communities that hold the events and often benefiting the city as a whole.

One of the most popular non-religious festivals is a costumed event that recalls old traditions associated with historical periods or events. One of these traditions is the *Palio* of Siena, in Tuscany, which celebrates the historic past of the town, captures the spirit of the people of the city, and reflects their strong *campanilismo.*

The *Palio di Siena* is a festival and horse race featuring medieval costumes and flag twirling. This celebration pits the various neighborhoods (*contrade*) in a traditional competition. Each *contrada* is united as a family in an effort to bring home *il Palio,* a banner of silk cloth with an effigy of the Virgin and Child.

The origins of this centuries-old festival, which is celebrated twice a year, on July 2 and August 16, are obscure. The celebration as we see it today was organized and given specific rules in 1632. Only ten of the seventeen *contrade* can compete in the horse race: seven by rotation and three by lottery.

While the *Palio di Siena* may be the best-known medieval pageant, other *Palio* contests take place in various Italian cities. In Arezzo, for example, people perform a medieval joust, the *Giostra del Saracino,* the first Sunday of September. The participating four *rioni* (neighborhoods) select two knights that will compete for the gold lance. The knights accumulate points by hitting a wooden effigy of a Saracen, a puppet with open arms. The puppet's left arm holds lead balls and the right arm a shield. The knights have to avoid being hit by the rotating metal balls while managing their horses and hitting the shield.

The *Palio Balestrieri* takes place the second Sunday in September in the town of Sansepolcro, near Arezzo. It is a crossbow shooting rivalry between archers of Gubbio and Sansepolcro dating back to 1461. In the city of Enna, Sicily, on August 13–14, the *Palio dei Normanni* features a horse race celebrating Sicily's liberation from the Arabs by the Norman count Ruggero d'Altavilla in 1091.

After the war the count gave a peace banner to Piazza Armerina. The city has celebrated this gift for centuries. Every year, on August 13, actors representing the count, his wife, and all his court (almost 300 actors wearing historical clothes) enter the city. They go to the main square where the most important personalities of Piazza Armerina present the count with the keys to the town. The next day, the townspeople put on a medieval contest with horses, lances, and Saracen-looking puppets.

Whatever their origin, festivals connect local peoples with an important part of the history of their city and provide an extraordinary occasion for human contact and civic life.

Therefore, what is relevant is not so much what people buy, but their different patterns of spending. Considerable differences have emerged over the past generation. Most striking is the fall in the percentage of income spent on food and on clothes. Conversely, the amounts spent on transport (including car purchases), on housing, and on vacation and recreational activities have all risen significantly. Obviously this does not mean that Italians are eating less well or are less well dressed. What it certainly indicates is that they have surplus income to devote to new kinds of spending.

As consumption patterns change, the traditional socioeconomic categories are crossed by other forms of stratification such as age and gender—groups like old people, young people, and women have significantly different consumption habits. Although many of the elderly today are affluent, they tend not to own cars; they spend less than other age groups on clothes, but they expend more on their domestic interior. The entry of women into the workforce has led to a marked increase in spending on restaurant meals in families where women work, while women now spend an astonishing 30% more on clothes than men in a context where overall spending on clothes has declined as a proportion of income. Young people are also a distinct consumer category. Young males, for example, spend up to 35% of their income on transportation—essentially on the purchase of a car and its maintenance—and as they are for the most part single, a great deal on eating out. Similarly, children have been identified both as significant consumers in their own right and as major influences on household spending decisions.

Domestic and Public Leisure

Perhaps the greatest change in the way people live in Italy today is in the expansion of leisure and the growth of leisure industries, especially the domestic leisure industries. At least in theory, Italians today have much more free time than their compatriots of the previous generations. This is partly a result of the enactment of legislation limiting hours of work, providing statutory paid holidays and earlier retirements. With more free time, people take more and/or longer vacations, and, if they can afford to do so, go away for the weekend and visit museums and sites of historical interest or natural beauty.[13] Not least important is the upsurge of interest in sports on the part of both practitioners and spectators.

By contrast, the expansion of the domestic leisure industries has affected virtually all Italian households; *la casa e' diventata la principale sala di spettacolo* (home has become the most important entertainment center). Besides television, most homes own VCRs, DVD players, and computers that are used both to record programs and to watch rented video material; the same is true of music centers or other means of listening to and recording music. The mass media and the domestic leisure industries have created both a degree of homogenization and different forms of stratification that have more to do with age than class, even though the category of the professional may stand apart for the amount it spends on culture.

However, the state supports culture and leisure activities in inverse proportion to their popularity, giving lots of money to the opera or the theater. Performances there are seen by few people compared to other forms of popular culture. There are attempts to decentralize cultural spending both by supporting and creating museums in smaller towns and encouraging local initiatives and workplace efforts. The regions have engaged in a political struggle with the central government that has been reluctant to relinquish its powers. The central government is gradually matching the decentralization of administrative functions with the decentralization of funding. Although the regions immediately understood the strong potential of cultural policy in enhancing their political identity, the development of regional cultural policies was a slow process because the central government was not eager to transfer funds to them.[14] Municipalities too understood the need for cultural policies and used them to achieve a variety of strategic objectives. "In an attempt to counteract trends toward social atomization and home-based cultural consumption, one of the aims of cultural policies was to reassert the function of the city center as a catalyst for civic identity and public sociability."[15] Open-air festivals and annual summer programs of cultural events are organized with the intent of pulling together people of different ages, sexes, social classes, and lifestyles. Municipalities of big and small towns sponsor a great variety of cultural events, especially in summertime, to entertain a large population, especially senior citizens.

Probably more than the public institutions but completely in a different way, stars have played a role in the way popular culture has evolved. The creation and serial production of star personalities for presentation and consumption of merchandise is clearly a feature of a social system whose economy is geared to mass production. The low level of national integration has meant that in place of formal institutions and official traditions, sports and entertainment have often been the principal sources of a shared set of national cultural symbols; thus stars within fields such as popular music, film, cycling, and soccer have been called upon to perform a function in terms of national mobilization. Since stars generally are of lower-class origin, they tend to be embraced by the average person, and hence their images are often used by cultural industries for advertising. Ever since the development of a consumer market of mass dimensions, this function has widened, and entertainment and sports stars have been involved in an ever greater range of promotion of food, drinks, cars, and household goods. They have become the leaders and illustrators of cultural trends, offering advice on all manner of topics, including beauty, diet, home furnishings, fashion, and voting choices.

The link with fashion is particularly important because it became Italy's most successful industry in the 1980s. Young Italian women of aristocratic background and many foreign models modeled their clothes. However, there has been a certain diffidence in Italian fashion

❁ **SPIRIT**

Masters in Soccer

Soccer is by far the most popular sport in Italy. Italy's parks are filled with both kids and adults playing soccer in leagues, as a family, and as a friendly pastime. In Italy, as in many other countries, soccer is practically the second official religion.

Soccer is played with very different styles and cultures, or "schools" as the Italians call them. Italians take soccer as life: creative, rational, and irrational at the same time: one never knows what's going to happen in a game. If one begins playing soccer at a young age, most likely one remains soaked in it for one's entire life. It can become a fever, which is why supporters are called in Italian *tifosi*, literally "typhus patients."

Every Italian city has a professional soccer team. Rome has two important clubs, Roma and Lazio, and an untreatable rivalry between the fans of the two. The most well-known and popular Italian teams are in northern Italy: Juventus, in Turin, Milan, and Inter (both in Milan).

Soccer's World Cup, held every four years, is practically a psychodrama for billions of fans around the globe. Italy has one of the top teams in international soccer and the second most successful national team in World Cup play, having won four World Cups (1934, 1938, 1982, 2006), just one fewer than Brazil. To this tally it can add one European championship (1968), and one Olympic Gold Medal (1936). Moreover, Italy's clubs have won 27 major European trophies, making the Italians the most successful soccer nation in Europe. The traditional color of the national team (as well as of all Italian teams and athletes, except in motor sports) is light blue (*azzurro*, in Italian); therefore national team members are nicknamed *Azzurri*.

The 2006 World Cup, in Berlin, was one of the most exciting world tournaments ever played. It was the most watched event in television history, garnering an estimated 30 billion viewers over the course of the tournament. The *Azzurri* won, defeating France on penalties in overtime.

circles toward domestic stars. Well-known designers such as Armani, Valentino, Ferragamo, Krizia, and Fendi court Hollywood stars and compete to dress them on occasions such as Oscar night. In the 1980s the designers themselves became international stars and within Italy they also have assumed something of the status of gurus on social and economic matters as well as questions of style and fashion.

The emphasis on appearance, combined with the wider importance of the media in social and economic relations, inevitably conditioned politics. Since the 1980s politicians have tended to present themselves as stars to some degree by paying attention to image and dress, and putting family and aspects of their personal lives on display. In the world of visual mass communication, politics and politicians do not escape the laws established by mass cultural consumption.

Therefore, in assessing cultural changes and their causes, one should consider an integrated cultural assessment that not only includes history of ideas and ideologies, sociology of culture (studies of audiences, markets, etc.), mass media research, analysis of cultural objects, and study of production-distribution-consumption, but that also takes into account modes of living. In fact, for a more complete understanding of cultural changes, it is essential that one try to see the

✺ SPIRIT

Carnevale

Carnevale in Italy is a huge winter festival celebrated with parades, masquerade balls, entertainment, music, and parties. It has roots in pagan festivals and traditions and was adapted to fit into Catholic ritual, as was often the case with traditional festivals. Although most of the festivities take place on Martedì Grasso, last day of the festival, the celebrations and parties go on for several weeks beginning in the third week of January. Coming in the depths of winter, during the dullest time of the year, what better excuse could there be to dress up and party? Carnevale is a time of excitement and merriment for all, a last fling before Ash Wednesday and the rigors of Lent. Hence the cry that accompanies the pranks, *A Carnevale Ogni Scherzo Vale!* (All's fair at Carnival). While children dress up in simple costumes, throw confetti at each other, and generally raise a ruckus, adults don sumptuous costumes and go out on the town.

The Carnevale is a great opportunity for people to put on a costume and forget who they are. There are no worries of social class. You can be whoever you want to be and enjoy the festivities to the fullest. The rich can mingle with the poor, and in some cases men and women go around and have sexual interludes with whomever they encounter without ever revealing their true identity.

The festival is celebrated differently throughout the peninsula and the islands even though masks, *maschere,* and customs are the common characteristic of the event. Masks became such an integral part that the artisans who created them were even recognized with their own guild in 1436. In Venice carnival masks are sold year round and can be found in many shops, ranging from cheap masks to elaborate and expensive masks. Walking through the streets of the city, it's a pleasure to view the variety of masks on display in shop windows. People also wear elaborate costumes for the festival, and there are costume or masquerade balls, both private and public.

Viareggio, on the Tuscan coast, has a very different Carnival tradition: A parade. The first was held at the beginning of the century, and featured floats pulled by oxen; now tractors have taken their place, and the floats are 50 feet high. Tuscans are famed for their sharp wit, and traditionally the floats of the Viareggini skewer politicians, soccer players, starlets, and other notables. As is the case with Venice's Carnevale, Viareggio's also lasts several days—the floats take a full year to prepare, and it would be impossible for everyone to see them in just one day. There are four parades, on the four weekends preceding Martedi Grasso, and a bash on Martedi Grasso itself.

The town of Oristano, in Sardinia, celebrates Carnevale with a costumed parade, horse races, and a re-enactment of a medieval jousting tournament. In the town of Lungro, in the southern Italian region of Calabria where there are Albanian settlements, there is a carnival parade of people in traditional Albanian costumes. The Carnival of Pollino in Castrovillari includes women dressed in intricate local costume and celebrates the Pollino wine of the region, *Lacrima di Castrovillari.* Also in northern Calabria, in Montalto Uffugo, there's an interesting wedding parade of men wearing women's dresses. They hand out sweets and tastes of Pollino wine. Following the parade, the kings and queens arrive for a night of dancing wearing costumes that include giant heads.

Pont St. Martin, in the Val d'Aosta region of northwestern Italy, celebrates carnival Roman style with nymphs and people dressed in togas; sometimes there's even a chariot race. On Shrove Tuesday Evening, festivities culminate by hanging and burning an effigy of the devil on the 2000-year-old bridge.

socio-cultural space as a whole; one cannot exclude many of the wider anthropological dimensions of culture, such as clothing styles, eating habits, social rituals, and mentalities. The view that "total" cultural change—including the assessment of the forms and sites of socialization and the consumption of particular kinds of goods, such as clothing, food, and drink—encouraged by the development of the mass media, brought about a re-evaluation of the function of the intellectual as producer of culture was rejected by young intellectuals.

Intellectuals sensed this phenomenon early on. By the end of the 1960s, therefore, the Gramscian historical paradigm—the desire to connect intellectual history (history of culture) with material history (politics and economics)—was undermined by three modes of critical thought: structuralism-semiotics, media studies, and studies of popular culture. Structuralism produced a new attention to the intrinsic qualities of the cultural artifact as a system of signification. Media studies brought, for the first time, mass cultural products within the purview of academic study. The field of cultural inquiry certainly widened and included areas that were not even included in the assessment of popular culture, in its rare cases of critical attention. The new work on popular culture (ethnography, ethnomusicology, dialectology) was frequently informed by a political commitment to reclaiming the culture of the subaltern social groups against the dominant culture reproduced by the education system.[16]

The early seventies, therefore, were certainly years rich in fermentation, but the challenges to traditional historicism did not come together to produce a new synthesis of cultural studies. Those who favored structuralism tended not just to be anti-historicist but to turn away from history altogether in an attempt to restore the intrinsic specificity of signification of cultural forms.[17] Media studies research was trying to establish its status as an autonomous discipline; in any case, it tended to be fiercely contemporary rather than historical in scope. Popular cultural studies, involving the recording or retrieval of increasingly marginalized traditional cultures, were generally conceived in polemical antithesis not only to the dominant elite culture, but also to mass culture.

The End of the Cultural Hegemony of the Left

These rapid cultural changes suffered a setback toward the beginning of the 1980s because of the terrorist activities that caused a drastic involution of the Left. The shift that took place away from the Left at the beginning of the 1980s was more than a temporary downturn; it was a swing of the electoral pendulum. What began to be undermined was the whole cultural legitimacy of the Left itself. Marxism had been throughout the 1950s, 1960s, and 1970s an unquestioned point of reference for most democratic intellectuals, but it began to go distinctly out of fashion at the beginning of the 1980s. It would be an exaggeration to talk of a Rightist cultural hegemony emerging at this point. Nothing as coherent as this seems to have arisen. But there is little doubt that the Left entered a serious crisis of cultural power since that moment.

By the end of the 1980s, a widespread deradicalization of intellectuals and students had set in. Intellectuals approached scholarly inquiries with an open mind or with tempered ideological views. Students "return[ed] to focus on studies," perhaps partly because of anxiety about employment prospects but also probably because of the general change of cultural mood. In 1993, the first election of a government of center-Right after WWII must be seen also in this context. In the process of modernization, Italy witnessed the growth of a consumer society and the weakening of Catholic culture and Leftist ideology.

Notes

1. In its initial years, tolerance of free discussion was not permitted, and frequently there was suppression of anti-government views in broadcasts or measures against hostile staff journalists. In those years, news material was edited to show the government in a positive light, while almost any program on a social or economic subject had to be censored in advance by the relevant ministry.

2. See Giorgio Grossi, *Rappresentanza e rappresentazione. Percorsi di analisi dell'interazione tra mass media e sistema politico in Italia* (Milan: Franco Angeli, 1985).

3. In several European countries, especially in Italy, the concept of broadcasting as a public service wholly or mainly financed by license-fee revenues and regulated by the state started to change in the seventies. Italy, in fact, has gone furthest of all in liberalizing from state control and the tacit approval of wildcat private broadcasting.

4. Franco Rositi, "Sistema politico, soggetti politici e sistema delle comunicazioni di massa," *Problemi del socialismo*, no 22, (1981): 88.

5. J.-F. Lyotard, *La condizione postmoderna* (Milan: Feltrinelli, 1982), 6–7.

6. Marigrazia Bruzzone, "Come la pubblicità ha influenzato l'evoluzione le TV private," *Problemi dell'Informazione*, 6, n. 4 (1981): 598–89.

7. Antonio Gramsci, *Selections from Cultural Writings,* eds. David Forgacs and Goffrey Nowell-Smith (London: Lawrence and Wishart, 1985), 209.

8. Whereas the ratio was one paper per 6.6 inhabitants in the north, it stood at one per 7.4 in the center and at one per 16 in the South. M. Olmi, *Il giornalismo in Italia* (Rome: Bulzoni, 1992), 96. Stefano Mauri, *Il libro in Italia. Geografia, produzione, consumo* (Milan: Hoepli, 1987), 75.

9. A. Papuzzi, *Manuale del giornalista* (Rome: Bulzoni, 1993)

10. Robert Lumley, *Italian Journalism: A Critical Anthology* (Manchester: Manchester UP, 1996).

11. The Festival of Piedigrotta, held annually in Naples on September 8, became the focus of a massive popularization of the Neapolitan song both in Italy and abroad which had reached its peak in the first half of the twentieth century.

12. Peppino Ortoleva, "Geography of the Media since 1945," in David Forgacs and Robert Lumley, eds., *Italian Cultural Studies* (Oxford: Oxford UP, 1996), 185–97.

13. Italians have much artistic treasure at their disposal. According to UNESCO, more than 50% of the world artistic heritage sites are located in Italy. In 1990 there were in Italy 710 state museums, galleries, historic

monuments, and archaeological sites, and about 2,300 museums owned by municipalities, foundations, the Church, and private individuals. This number is larger than in other European countries.

14.   It was urban local authorities, in the municipalities, rather than the regions, which developed high-profile cultural policies in response to interrelated processes of social, political, and cultural changes. *Comuni* understood much more clearly than the central government the need to respond to the growing, more differentiated, and sophisticated demand for cultural needs.

15.   F. Bianchini, M. Torrigiani and R. Cere, "Cultural Policy," in D. Forgacs and R. Lumley, eds., *Italian Cultural Studies* (Oxford: Oxford U. P., 1996), 296.

16.   For these challenges, see Lucio Colletti, *Il marxismo e Hegel* and *Ideologia e società,* both (Bari: Laterza, 1969); Roberto Guiducci, *Marx dopo Marx,* (Milan: Mondadori, 1971).

17.   See Filippo Bettini, "11 problema dello strutturalismo in Italia," in *Marxismo e strutturalismo nella critica letteraria italiana* (Rome: La Nuova Sinistra, 1974).

Bibliography

Allen, B. And Russo, M., (eds.), *Revisioning Italy. National Identity and Global Culture* (Minneapolis: University of Minnesota Press, 1997).

Baranski, Z. And Lumley, R., (eds.), *Culture of Conflict in Postwar Italy* (New York: St. Martin's, 1990).

Bedani, G. And Haddock, B., (eds.), *The Politics of Italian National Identity. A Multidisciplinary Perspective* (Cardiff: University of Wales Press, 2000).

Bruzzi, S., *Undressing Cinema. Clothing and Identity in the Movies* (London and New York, Routledge, 1997).

De Grazia, V. and Furlough, E. (eds.), *The Sex of Things. Gender and Consumption in Historical Perspective* (Berkeley: University of California Press, 1996).

Forgacs, D. and Lumley, R. (eds.), *Italian Cultural Studies* (Oxford: Oxford U. P., 1996)

Forgacs, D., *Italian Culture in the Industrial Era: 1880–1980* (Manchester: Manchester University Press, 1990.

Grossi, G., *Rappresentanza e rappresentazione. Percorsi di analisi dell'interazione tra mass media e sistema politico in Italia* (Milan: Franco Angeli, 1985).

Lumley, R., *Italian Journalism: A Critical Anthology* (Manchester: Manchester UP, 1996).

Malossi, G. (ed.) *Volare. The Icon of Italy in Global Pop Culture* (New York: Monacelli Press, 1999).

Papuzzi, A., *Manuale del giornalista* (Rome: Bulzoni, 1993).

When the second World War ended in 1945, Italian filmmakers were freed from the restrictions imposed by the fascist government and began to produce movies about real Italy (the devastation of the war, the difficulties of reconstruction, the poverty of their country, and the proletariat's world). The economic boom of postwar Italy pushed the cinema in new directions. In the late 1950s, Federico Fellini began to make films that clearly broke with the tradition. Fellini injected fantasy, dreams, and his own memories into his films, and broke many taboos. The cinematic world of sex became an area of great interest. Printed by courtesy of *Editions Soleil*.

CHAPTER 15

A MORE OPEN SOCIETY

A New Affluence

In the last 50 years Italy has become more industrial, more educated, more urban, and more secular. These changes have struck at the very heart and soul of the country. There used to be well-established ideas about compulsory public education, marriage, procreation, abortion, divorce, separation of Church and state, the relative responsibilities of spouses and their children, and the nature of work and leisure. But perhaps the most influential change has been Italy's new affluence.

The postwar rise in prosperity touched practically everyone, although in some areas the increases were somewhat fictitious because they were due only to a generous policy of public social programs. Today the upper middle class in particular lives better than it does in Britain and the United States, mainly because it rarely inflicts on itself the same burden of high private school tuition bills. Many families can thus afford expensive clothing, frequent dining out, a second home, and two long vacations each year. Surveys indicate that Italians have expanded their traveling habits; indeed, in the last 30 years the number of Italians going on vacation has increased from 28% in 1969 to 56% in 1991, to 69% in 2001. The trend today is to take two vacations a year, often abroad: 25% chose to go abroad in 2001 versus 15.3% in 1988. Among travelers, 43% take two vacations, while 21% take three or more vacations. In this as in so much else about Italy, the percentage of those going on vacation is still much higher in the north than in the south, 64% versus only 41%.

The Italians are less insular than they used to be; they have become more aware of other peoples and are curious about how they live. Many are now less interested in spending long weeks at the Italian seashore or in an Italian country villa; instead they go to Spain, Greece, the Balkans, France, Eastern Europe, and Asia. America especially is now popular, at least when the currency exchange is favorable. Among the middle and upper classes, the trend for some years has been toward more unusual, varied, and active kinds of vacations: a growing minority of people may opt for an archaeological dig in Mexico or a safari in Kenya.

Changes in the Social Classes

In the last 25 years Italy has experienced a socio-economic transformation as dramatic and profound as that of the "economic miracle" at the end of the 1950s and 1960s, though remarkably different from it in both content and consequences. The "miracle" created a big migration from south to north-west, from the countryside to the city, and transformed the country from an agricultural, backward nation to an advanced industrial and economic power. Workers, both those from the city and those coming from the countryside, made economic and social gains unequaled in the history of any nation. The situation began to change in the early 1980s mainly for the working class.

Fall 1980 saw the end of an era: the defeat of the divided working-class movement at Fiat was the beginning of profound changes in the blue-collar class. Breakthroughs in electronic research and their application to industry (which included the introduction of robots) and the world of communication initiated a new cycle in the global economy. The resulting revolution in modes of production and the organization of firms diminished the massed ranks of the industrial working class, offering those who remained an environment that had been radically transformed, both materially and ideologically.[1] Not only the number of blue-collar workers decreased, but their rate of affluence slowed down.

At this time, too, the service sector increased its dominion over employment and GDP, following the patterns of other advanced economies. The great majority of Italy's working population became service workers. In 1980 the service sector accounted for 48.3% of employment and 51.6% of added value; by 1995 these figures were 60.1% and 65%, respectively. In the second half of the 1980s, it seemed as if almost everyone in Italy, in social terms, was destined to flow upwards. In 1987 William Scobie, then *Observer* correspondent in Italy, caught the mood of the moment in this way:

Suddenly this is a land of upward mobility, of vital computerized industry, bustling young business managers and slick middle-aged tycoons who have abjured their sixties' ideals in the sacred cause of profit.[2]

Economic expansion, especially of the new tertiary services, elevated from the ranks of the lower bourgeoisie a new group that lacked inherited property but achieved significant affluence: sales and advertising executives and skilled technicians, together with shopkeepers, artisans, and small industrialists who modernized and moved with the times. This is an assertive status-seeking world of new social mobility that is immensely in love with material values.

The Middle Classes

In the 1980s the middle classes in Italian society expanded rapidly in both numerical and income terms. Intergenerational mobility was a commonplace. First, there was the passage from landless laborers or impoverished farmers to urban workers or artisans or shopkeepers; later on, there was the shift from urban blue-collar to white-collar employment or to small business. By the end of 1980s Italians had become accustomed to thinking of their country as a land of opportunity. However, in the 1990s there were increasing signs that these upward flows were drying up and that the absolute mobility of the previous decades was coming to an end.

The service economy brought a significant increase in the number of highly paid and qualified jobs; on the other hand, it created a large number of poorly paid and precarious jobs. This led to a division of work space and economic standards which had as a further consequence social fragmentation and weaker collective solidarity; gradually unemployment became again an individual fear and a collective concern. As in the U.S., this change affected the prosperity of the different social classes and increased the distance between them. Wealth as well as power and privileges started to flow more unevenly. At the end of the 20th century, Italy's social structure, like that of advanced capitalist countries, had become increasingly heterogeneous and more complex. The picture was very clear:

» Profound uncertainty and division created by the rapid advance of information technology and the service economy had reversed the process of social and economic equalization; and
» The weakening of institutions and ideologies that had previously formed identities and fostered cohesion (trade unions, political parties, the Church, etc.) were not offering solid support to stop or slow the slide.

Hence, in the urbanized Italian society, the middle classes remain the dominant social sector of the population, but it is a far from uniform social category because it includes people from many sectors of employment and the economy:

» One sector, heavily concentrated among small entrepreneurs and shopkeepers, is local, consumerist, strongly oriented both to self-interest and an overriding work ethic, and motivated by profit and the wish to make good, and

» The other sector, prevalent among those in education and the public/social services, is salaried, dependent, and operating more under the cloud of clientelism.

Overall, achieving prosperity has been more uneven for the middle classes. The less enterprising artisans and small traders, outclassed by the new consumer economy, are sliding into decline. The public servants—postal workers, clerks, and primary school teachers—have seen their wages rise more slowly than wages in the private sector. Their ranks have now been infiltrated by the sons and daughters of the poor farmers and the working class—young people who prefer soft jobs as clerks or typists to the drudgery of farm or factory.

The Working Class

The big growth of the tertiary sector and the concomitant introduction of electronic technology in the industrial sector profoundly changed the blue-collar working class. Once a strong and relatively united force, unusually class-conscious and capable of great actions of solidarity and mobilization, the blue-collar class suddenly fragmented and lost impetus. By the mid-1990s it could hardly be described as a class at all. Behind this transformation lay not so much a dramatic numerical decline as a fundamental change in its composition. In 1993 25% of the workforce was still industrial workers compared to 31% in 1971, but the big factories had ceased to be centers of working-class aggregation and political power.[3]

Traditional sectors like the metal and mechanical industries, chemical production, and textiles were most affected. Between 1980 and 1986, Fiat cut its workforce by nearly half. Those who remained had to rapidly learn a different organization of work and culture. Workers were asked to be knowledgeable, flexible, subjectively involved in what they were doing. Informality oiled the wheels of industrial relations, as did collective involvement in the fate of the firm.[4]

Head coach of the Italian team Marcello Lippi holds up the 2006 World Cup trophy after Italy won their final football match against France at Berlin's Olympic Stadium, July 9, 2006. Italy won 5–3 on penalties. AFP Photo/Odd Andersen.

Fewer workers, better trained, highly motivated, fully integrated into the firm was the trend. The change brought both great opportunities and great dangers. Skilled workers had more chance that their talent would be recognized, more possibilities for promotions and pay increases and professional mobility. They also enjoyed more independence and responsibility and much less routine and monotony.[5] On the other hand, their hours of work were long, especially in the small-sized family owned firms and the competitive stress considerable.

The situation was not any better in the small-family-owned firms, where neo-paternalism and neo-servilism in support of family neo-capitalism ruled. Many of the workers in Italy's small firms were linked by kinship ties to those who owned the firms. Many firms were directed by dominant male figures who assumed the old authoritarian and patriarchal position. As a result, the symbiosis of family and firm, of private and public, could be very oppressing. It can be easily stated that the working class has suffered big losses in the last twenty years: the link of work with collective organization has been drastically reduced and working conditions have become less secure and pleasant. Workers may become materially richer than ever before, but they seem poorer in terms of job security and collective identities. The arrival of immigrant workers has worsened the situation because of their propensity to accept lower pay and worse working conditions.

In all these changes, class divisions have been reduced, even though class-consciousness is still very much alive, especially in the south. It is another paradox of Italian life that the Italians are far more class-conscious than the Americans and French but are less class-divided. It is a psychological more than an economic division. In fact, except between families and groupings, there are few social barriers in Italy. Snobbishness exists, but playing a role is more important than any innate sense of superiority. A firm's boss will probably treat the employees in an authoritative way because he is in charge; however, when he is outside his firm that power is no longer present. There are no large number of prestigious private schools or universities that separate people socially.

The gap between the extremes of wealth and poverty has been reduced, unlike in the United States; however, Italians do not enjoy the same opportunity for social mobility. Certainly there is more mobility than before World War II, and children of all classes now mix in the same state schools until age 18; however, class divisions are still strong even though there has been a blurring of the outward distinctions between them. Under modern conditions, people's interests and habits have drawn closer. A skilled worker may own the same kind of car as a member of the bourgeoisie, and off duty he may dress much the same way; the new working generation has given up its old class "uniform" and is dressing like the middle class, so it becomes harder to tell them apart. A lot certainly has to do with the *bella figura* (the facade) that everyone wants to present to the outside world.

Bureaucracy: Twenty-First Century Baroque

If there is one "class" that all Italians could agree to despise, it is the bureaucratic class, *la burocrazia*. There persists a consensus that public officials do not work or, if they do, are not efficient. In Italy, the idea that any official organization is there to serve the citizen is not only unfamiliar, it is laughable. Most civil servants are neither "civil" nor "servants." It is a known fact that people join the bureaucracy not out of love for a certain kind of work or out of a calling for public service, but mainly because they want stable employment, a secure job, and no pressure from work. After all, most government and municipal offices are only open from 8:00 A.M. until 2:00 P.M.; there isn't another organization in the universe with such a schedule! Anyone who goes to an Italian consulate abroad can easily get a good taste of how things work in Italy. Government employees think more in terms of their own rights than their obligation to others. In an era dominated by services, to have public services that for the most part do not function at high efficiency is truly to cripple the nation from the outset.

The weakness of public administration and public service is a big national problem. Public administration, both nationally and locally, drains a lot of labor and expenditure, while generally offering a quality of service far below European norms. The reforming minister for the Civil Service in the 1993–94 government estimated that each Italian citizen lost an average of 15 to 20 working days a year in having to cope with the bureaucracy.[6] Today the situation is not much better. While productivity in industry doubled in the period 1978–92, in public administration it remained stationary; in the same period wages in the two sectors rose almost identically.

Such a situation engenders public frustration and a desire to circumvent the rules. Italians spend their lives devising ingenious rules and then finding equally cunning ways of evading them. Vertical loyalties of patron-client relations, present in other aspects of social and professional life, exist also in the realm of this kind of daily life; and clientelism is accompanied by widespread corruption.

Inefficiency and Public Ethics

Because it is impossible to get anything accomplished rapidly, this sprawling bureaucratic maze conceals all sorts of illegal and quasi-legal activities on both small and large scales. In requesting a driver's license or a permit to use public space, a citizen may easily be tempted to pay for speed or create a network of mutual favors. On a larger scale we need only look at the scandals in 1992–1993 that revealed wholesale kickback abuses, *tangenti,* in every sort of government control. The increase of scandals to the level of shameful obscenity finally turned public opinion against dishonesty in the public services, and magistrates did some clean-up by jailing hundreds of public officials, including major political personalities, since the "clean hands" (*mani pulite*) campaign of the 1990s.

Thus, it is not surprising that the public completely mistrusts the bureaucrats. The mask of anonymous authority stands between the two groups. No attempt has ever been made in Italy to personalize the employees' relations with the public, for example, by putting name-cards on desks as in the United States. Some change is taking place slowly in certain areas. The telephone service in particular has made a real effort to improve its relations with the public, and operators are now far more polite and helpful. Overall, however, the situation is still deplorable, and Italians dread those occasions when they must deal with governmental offices.

One basic problem in the bureaucratic system is the hiring process. Jobs in the wide Italian civil service are obtained by passing a generic *concorso* (competing exam) for which some workers need a college degree in any field. No attempt is made to use the vast surplus of college graduates and their academic training in an effective way.

Another problem in the bureaucratic system is the Italian concept of authority as an absolute entity. In Italy, there is much less delegation of power than in Britain or America. There is less sense of team responsibility: the head of an office or department will tend to concentrate the key work in his own hands rather than share the load. This extends even to relations between bosses and secretaries, for Italian managers tend to make inadequate use of their assistants. The reluctance to delegate is one more aspect of the Italian centralist tradition, which operates just as much within a firm or other small unit as on the wider levels of government. This reluctance has some unfortunate effects. It tends to create a gulf, more noticeable than in most countries, between the dynamic few at the top and the frustrated or time-serving many at more junior levels.

In the private sector the situation is not very different. When one compares the service and the cost of financial and bank services, car insurance, hotels, restaurants, laundry and dry cleaning, Italy and the U.S. are worlds apart. Italian banks are open until one in the afternoon, close for two hours, and then re-open at 3:00 for an additional forty-five minutes. Naturally, they are not open on Saturdays. The average citizen must take time off from work to go to the bank!

The country still suffers from some forms of feudal dominance. Some professions are fully controlled oligarchies that go back to the guilds of the Middle Ages. Public notaries (in Italy, lawyers specializing in real estate) are part of a very close-knit, restricted, extremely costly profession, marked by abundant nepotism. Pharmacists, too, belong to a similarly tightly controlled profession.

In the area of service, another failure is tourism, Italy's unparalleled resource and one the nation has not been able to capitalize enough on. Italy is a country of extraordinary beauty and immense cultural heritage, but the public services offered to its visitors are still grossly inadequate.

La Bella Figura

Notwithstanding the frustration Italians must face with poor public services and an atrocious bureaucracy, the nation is strikingly beautiful and people display an incredible flair for life. *La bella figura,* literally meaning 'the beautiful figure,' has to do with 'a good image.' In Italy, it really refers to a way of life that emphasizes beauty, aesthetics, and proper behavior.

Italy is a place of grandeur and elegance even in the details. For example, the uniforms of the Italian policemen, soldiers, and *carabinieri* (state police) are more stylish and elegant than those of neighboring countries. Even the road sweepers are more fashionable in their orange coveralls. Italian cars are known for their design and beauty. The art, history, architecture, fashion, and fine wines of Italy are undisputed. Italians have an inherent sense of appreciation for color, design, and form. Italy is the fashion center of the world and nearly everyone dresses the part. When the right combination

Models present outfit of Italian brand during the Italian Fashion Show at the European Style Conference Center in Chaoyang Park in Beijing, June 2, 2005. The fashion show was staged as part of the activities with a theme of Italy in the Park, a promotional event for the image of Italy in China, held by Italian Trade Commission. Source: Wikipedia.org of shoes, hat, accessories, and color come together, one is considered to have achieved 1*a bella figura.*

La bella figura is everywhere in Italian life. It rules the land, especially the south. Permutations can be seen in every shop window and on every magazine page. And it doesn't stop there. People are aware that every nuance of appearance, presentation, and behavior represents *la bella figura.* But it means more than merely dressing well and admiring fine art. It is an etiquette system as well. *La bella figura* also means acting properly, presenting oneself with, and being aware of, the proper nuances Italian society demands. It is knowing how to act and how to behave under particular circumstances. It is knowing what is appropriate and when, what is of high quality and taste versus what is too cheap. [7]

Fashion and clothing is an important industry in Italy. Some of the world's top designers are Italians: Armani, Gucci, Fendi, Valentino, Missoni, Ferragamo, and Krizia. As their counterparts have done in the car, furniture, and office machine industries, Italian fashion designers have been able to continue the long tradion of superb craftsmanship and combine it with high technology. From the archive of the author.

La bella figura is also loyalty. Italians have a strong sense of loyalty to their family, friends, neighbors, and business partners. Behaving properly, appropriately, and respectfully is crucial to maintaining the right air of *bella figura* both in family situations as well as in the business world. *La bella figura* is both a demureness and formality and is thoroughly entrenched in the culture of Italy. Italians believe that practicing *la bella figura* enhances beauty and peace in life.

The sense of beauty that you find everywhere in Italy has to do with the old cultural heritage, the breathtaking beauty of historical places wherever one goes. Italians don't need a stage to create movies. They live on a stage every day. This sense of beauty seems to reside even in the more insensitive Italians—the awareness of the right form, of colors, etc., is heightened. It expresses itself in design, art, and fashion. Not by chance have Italian design and fashion become well known and appreciated all over the world.

Italians have always been concerned about appearances, from the way they prepare their food to the way they dress. To most foreigners, Italian "style" often means extraordinary elegance and dignity. Italians lavish much attention to presenting a good appearance, and compliments in that regard are an ordinary practice. In fact, compliments are an essential part of a mutual admiration society. This tendency to comment on positive physical attributes partly explains the success of Italian men with northern women as well as the disappointment Italian women feel when they go to northern Europe, where compliments tend to be regarded either as insincere or as a way of playing on vanity.

This *bella figura* can be irritating. But of course it is the surface of personal living. Much of the attitude to fashion and *bella figura* comes originally from village life where everything is personal, one knows everyone, and one's appearance and behavior are important. That attitude was brought to the cities; today, only a small percentage of the people living in the city were born there, but, notwithstanding the profound changes, it is impossible to suddenly eradicate attitudes that are two thousand years old.

An interesting indication of the Italian sense of proportion and concern for *la bella figura* is that they rarely get drunk. Italians seem to know that alcohol, after all, does not generate exuberance, but rather it deadens the senses and makes people sloppy. Even at soccer celebrations most fans do not fall prey to the excesses of alcohol, contrary to what occurs in many other parts of Europe. Italians drink alcoholic beverages mainly at dinner time to complement a meal or at a *café* to enjoy a conversation with a friend *(See Box on p. 418)*.

Italian football fans at the Circo Massimo celebrating Italy's victory over France on July 9, 2006 in Rome, Italy. Italy defeated France 5-3 at the World Cup 2006 finals in Germany. Photograph by Franco Origlia/Getty Images.

The *bella figura* mode has been kept even with the new affluence and the Americanization of the Italian life style. Relatively speaking, Italians still place more emphasis on enjoyment, but their former reluctance to spend their money on useful possessions has waned sharply. During the boom years, the Italians steadily increased the share of their budget that went to their homes, not only on rent and mortgages but on comfort and equipment too.

With the growth of individual housing and the middle-class vogue for buying and restoring crumbling villas, castles, and old farm houses for weekend retreats, skilled hand work has also become a major pastime. For example, in the outskirts of many towns, one sees big new garden center supermarkets attracting a new generation of gardening enthusiasts. Even a respectable doctor no longer considers it undignified to be seen by his neighbors doing work around the house: today it is not a *butta figura* (ugly appearance) to do that kind of manual work.

Urbanization

The Italian concept of *la bella figura* was put to a severe test with internal migration, the moving of thousands of citizens from countryside to the city and from the south to the north. When people lived in areas where families had known each other for generations it required a certain appearance and behavior to maintain respect and esteem. When they moved into areas where they did not know anyone, the expectation existed that people might give up their concern for appearance and "etiquette behavior." The urban revolution steadily molded new lifestyles and new social attitudes. The many millions who moved from the farms or from slum districts to the new dwellings had to adapt, some times painfully, to very different needs and patterns of modern suburbia. Many people reacted by making a scared retreat into privacy, others by trying to form new clubs and associations—for sport or culture, for example, but even so they preserved the old concern for *bella figura*.

Slowly a new style of local community life is emerging in Italy, more informal and less institutional than that of the old urban bourgeois society but less warm and less relaxed than that of the old village or agrarian world. Among the cities' zestful, nervous crowded terrace-*café*, smart shop-windows, and frenzied *piazze*, these new citizens have had to get used to a new tempo *(See Box on p. 417)*. The congested narrow streets with their more aggressive and angry drivers are not easily acceptable to newcomers. Even Italophiles who spend a month or two in an Italian city, finding it fascinating and exciting, have difficulty adapting to the strains that cities such as Rome, Naples, and Milan present.

Urban Chaos

In all this process, a sense of aesthetic in architecture was lost immediately after WWII. When the country hurried to respond to the shortage of housing caused by the destruction of the war, the state and private sector gave up the traditional art form in architecture by allowing simple draftsmen (*geometri*) to project dwellings that could be built quickly. Unfortunately, that approach to construction lasted well in the 1960s. New high-rise buildings were erected often with little regard for aesthetics or amenities. Italy solved the housing shortage, but at a price.

In the mid-1950s only 10% of all Italian homes had a bath or shower and only 30% had flushing lavatories. The Italians used to live in overcrowded and often squalid conditions but cheaply. Since that time homes have been built for over half the population, and every town is ringed with modern blocks of flats, a common enough sight in the Western world. In many parts of the country, the new housing complexes built around cities, called *borgate* around Rome, were usually poorly planned. There were no meeting places, apart from the occasional *café*. Cafes, however, were reserved for men in the evenings, and the very few cinemas showed

only films of the lowest quality. There is a striking shortage of parks, hospitals, libraries, theaters, concerts halls, and sports centers relative to what is available just a few miles away.

Another feature of urban chaos is a distorted pattern of consumption. As in the fast-urbanizing capitalist countries, a burgeoning consumer goods sector goes hand in hand with inadequate social spending (for houses, roads, sanitation, hospitals, social services, etc.). It is characteristic of all capitalist

Since Italian cities were built before the advent of cars, most streets in the historic centers are narrow; therefore, scooters are more practical than cars. From the archive of the author.

societies in the course of their development that economic activity and the population it supports become polarized spatially. Wealth and people become concentrated in core regions, occupying a relatively small part of the territory, while the rest remains underdeveloped. According to recent statistics, 75% of Italians own their own homes, and many have purchased vacation homes as well.

But after the suburban high-rise boom of the 1970s (which, unfortunately, spoiled the old charm of Italian cities), the accent today is on much needed improvements to quality of life—more parks, fountains, traffic-free streets, reclaimed squares from traffic, rehabilitation of poorer districts, and so on.

Today, housing is far more plentiful and very comfortable, but prices have skyrocketed. The average share of family income devoted to rents or mortgage, plus basic charges, has risen since the war from the incredibly low figure of 3.4% to over 25%. But the burden is unevenly shared. State housing policy has made repeated U-turns since the war, and its complex bureaucratic system of controls and subsidies has relieved some injustices but created others.

Nevertheless, now that the Italians are well housed and freer to pick and choose the kind of homes they really want, that freedom has triggered some striking changes. Today, in all classes there is a steady trend towards buying rather than renting new property. This tendency satisfies the Italian's property-owning instincts, and it provides developers with quicker returns. The Italians have become quite "house-proud," and no longer do they readily reject home comfort in favor of food, vacations, or other pleasures. Their expectations have risen; they no longer tolerate the old overcrowding, and they want larger and better-built apartments and houses.

The housing urge has also expressed itself in the increased construction of second homes, and Italy is supposed to have more of these than any country in Europe. Some are ancient family houses deserted by migrants to the city who, once they were earning well, returned to modernize them and turn them into summer resorts. The houses that had been left to languish for forty years are being reclaimed by the grandchildren and restored with all the new amenities.

Foreigners are amazed by the type of first and second housing that even Italians with modest incomes are able to afford. In many cases the houses are inherited. As for the new housing, money comes through parents' sacrifice and personal *arrangiarsi* (being thrifty); with a poor farming background, Italians have maintained the habit of saving frugally for something they really want. However, the enthusiasm for second homes has tended to deaden some small towns. Moreover, many of the old houses are being bought by foreigners; parts of Tuscany have been referred to as "Chiantishire" because so many British own property there. But these second homes, whether owned by foreigners or by rich Italians, are occupied for only a few weeks a year, with the result that villages are losing their identity.

Speculation over land and property has for many years been a major cause of soaring rental and house prices. However, the tempo of new building has slackened considerably since the main needs have been met and the birthrate has been declining. Conversely, the new trend in modernizing old buildings instead of demolishing them has been strong. Especially for historic city centers, Italy has turned towards a policy of rehabilitation; regulations for rehabilitation of old housing in *centri storici* are very strict and detailed. The restoration of old housing is seen as the best human way to preserve Italy's architectural heritage and reanimate city centers. Any visitor is bound to be impressed by the way Italy cares for its "historical centers." And so today there are two trends, going in opposite directions. On the one hand, more people want to move back to city-center living when good housing is available; on the other hand, more people want their own homes, amid greenery, in the outskirts of the city or at least within commuter range. Both groups reject the sad high-rise apartments of the expansion years.

Italians tend to buy instead of leasing because living in dwellings for a short time is incompatible with the Italian idea of *domus,* which evokes solidity and permanence. And if Italians have a house, they normally do not sell it to buy a better one even as they become more prosperous. Instead, they keep the family home for their children, who were brought up in it, and they add to the home, if they can, when they need more room.

The Joy of Urban Preservation

There was a shift in priorities as an affluent society began to react against the negative aspects of too rapid urbanization. Italians demanded that their new individual prosperity be matched by better public amenities and by steps to make city life more tolerable. Since the late 1970s many town councils had shifted their emphasis from building monolithic housing projects to developments that paid more attention to ecological or aesthetic considerations. However, because of their *socialità* and love for nature, Italians always built housing that made for easy human relations, houses with balconies giving onto squares, and so forth. The new environmental trend took many forms and often was due to local or private, rather than state, initiative. Throughout the country there are new open-air or heated public swimming pools, well-equipped leisure and sports centers, advisory clinics, new homes for old people, renovated *palazzi* and castles, new museums and campaigns against noise and litter abound.

In this process, with skillful restoration techniques and a keen sense for beauty, Italians are succeeding in preserving the downtown of their cities by declaring them 'historic centers" that are subject to strict laws. While in the U.S. we don't always think twice about knocking down an old building to raise a skyscraper in its place, in Italy, cities play an important aesthetic part in the chain of human historic evolution.

Gastronomy as an Art Form

Italian aesthetic flair, as we know, is strong in the culinary art, gastronomy. Food is an extremely important part of Italian culture, history, and economy. Food certainly tells us a lot about any people, but in the case of Italy it exemplifies the character of its people and the diversity of its regions. Two popular sayings—*Il cibo é l'essenza della vita* (Food is the essence of life) and *Si vive per mangiare invece che mangiare per vivere* (One lives to eat instead of eating to live)— capture the value of food in life. For the Italians, food is a passion: many maintain that they live to eat, they don't eat to live.

Italy's culinary reputation dates back over two thousand years, declining after the fall of the Roman Empire. Food and its preparation were a very important part of the culture of the Roman Empire; the only surviving cookery book from the Classical period is Roman, a text known as *Apicius,* after the renowned Roman gourmet who lived in the first century BC. Although it is thought that the work itself is a compilation, constructed over many years by several contributors, it does indicate how important food was not only as culinary and alimentary tradition but for its cultural meaning and its significance in social change.[8] Today's extraordinary Italian culinary art is the product of many factors:

>   the historic development of different traditions and cultures;
>   the environment: the climate, the peninsula's topography, the sea;
>   colonization by Greeks, Arabs, Normans, and Spaniards;
>   recurring human migration and exploration;
>   agricultural interests; and
>   creative skills in using the available agricultural products.

Italian cooking is imbued with sunlight and draws its inspiration from the products of the land. Although Italy has been unified for over a century, and although modern storage, freezing methods, and shipping and transportation options are changing things worldwide, Italian food is still able to reflect regional and seasonal variations. To really discover Italian gastronomy, people must make their way down the whole boot of Italy, from Piedmont to Sicily, dawdling in each region, exploring the streets and alleys in order to better understand its roots. Every region has its own gastronomic traditions, cultural habits, and specialties, like so many individual signatures and perfumes.

Regional Food Delights

The islands of Sardinia and Sicily maintain the more traditional and simple cuisine styles, spit-roasting suckling pig pretty much as their ancestors did at the height of the Roman Empire, when Sicilian cooks enjoyed a certain amount of fame; producing soups and stews that draw upon the rich harvest from the Mediterranean: sardines (which share their name with the island of Sardinia), red mullet, swordfish, lobster, and anchovies. The Arab influence on the food of the south is very strong, and the two islands are no exception to this, especially in the areas of sweets and spices. Cassata, the famous Sicilian ice cream cake, takes its name from the Arabic *qas'at,* the name for a large, round bowl. The South also provides citrus fruits and creamy cheeses such as Ricotta, Mozzarella, and Provolone. However, the true mark of the southern style is in the use of the omnipresent tomato. The southerners, and the *Naplese* in particular, took the tomato to their hearts almost upon its arrival from the 'New World.' By marrying their fluffy flatbreads and creamy Mozzarella with the *Pomo D'Oro*, or golden apple (the first tomatoes were yellow), southerners created the famous open pie that has now been emulated worldwide: pizza.

The center and north of the peninsula contribute Tuscan beef, the excellent pork and dairy products of Parma, polenta, and, of course, the famous black truffles from the Marches. Naturally, the coastal areas have a wide variety of fish and seafood to draw upon: mussels, baby clams, squid, octopus, prawns, sardines, anchovies, and red mullet, along with many more, including the more exotic sea-dates, sea-truffles, and cuttlefish. Thus, all along the coasts of the peninsula and the islands, fish is king, all enhanced with the countless flavors of the Mediterranean.

Meat is cooked with great imagination: steak traditionally prevails in Tuscany (*bistecca alla fiorentina*); in the north roasts, *osso buco,* braised beef and game take pride of place; in the south, pork, goat, and veal—in Italy veal is slaughtered before it becomes beef. A platter of Italian cheese is impressive, constituting a festive meal all on its own. Cheese makes its way into countless dishes, sprinkled on a salad, melted and golden in a sauce or gratin, even forming some daring sweet alliances, elevating an array of desserts to the level of art, each one with an irresistible name, each an invitation to deliciously sinful indulgence.

Gelato—Variety of tastes and colors provides a feast for palates and eyes. From the archive of the author.

Pasta, synonymous with the term 'Italian food' for some, is found everywhere in all shapes, sizes, and colors, served with a variety of sauces that are limited only by the bounds of the imagination. One thing is sure, however, that no matter which region an Italian calls home, the same love of food prevails; most genuine Italian restaurants in the United States reflect this love. From the most humble *caffè* to the grander celebrity establishment, all offer the very best in food and delight in diners' appreciation and enjoyment of their efforts. The Italians' gastronomic zeal is not dying; however, Italians are increasingly channeling it toward the once or twice a week occasion out or into an experience to be had at home, with friends. There is a national style of cooking and an assortment of different regional styles that overflows into neighboring provinces. Pasta is certainly the common denominator of most cooking from one end of the peninsula to the other. And pasta comes with hundreds of names for hundreds of types: *spaghetti, tagliatelle, rigatoni, lasagne, orecchiette, ravioli, cannelloni, tortellini, linguine* are only the more obvious. Depending on the locale one may be offered *strangozzo, trenette, strozzaprete,* or dozens of other varieties. And then one may choose among the hundreds of possible rich flavorings and sauces: *all'arrabbiata, puttanesca, bolognese, carbonara, pesto,* and *napoletana,* to name just a few.

Trying to Hold onto Traditions

Home-cooking habits are not as consistent as they were just a couple of decades ago. Television, cars, foreign vacations, better housing, and other possessions all developed new rival claims on the average family's budget and interests and especially on the wife's time. In the middle class, far fewer wives now have servants than before the war, more have jobs, and life is more hectic. Some younger wives do not want to be a "slave" in the kitchen, nor have they the time to indulge in the preparation of elaborate recipes.

However, the Italian housewife still has a far wider variety of fresh foods to choose from than homemakers in most parts of Britain, Germany, and even France. After a long period of resistance her opposition to the idea of frozen foods is slowly thawing out. Even so, Italians eat less than half as much frozen produce as the British and the Americans, though the consumption figures are increasing each year, and frozen-food freezers in supermarkets have been lengthening. The main difference is that while in the U.S. the best-selling frozen foods are ordinary items, the Italians prefer much more complex and expensive deep-frozen pre-cooked dishes.

Other changes may be inevitable. It seems that Italians are starting to move over to the light-meal habit for at least one of their main meals of the day. It should be possible for the light snack and true gastronomy to coexist, each for its own occasion. Italy has long been a nation of people with too much stress set on the convention that a meal must contain three or four full courses. *A tavola non s'invecchia* (at the table one doesn't grow old), the saying goes.

Café   *La Piazza: A Stage for Everyone*

Leisure time is an important part of the Italian day. People congregate throughout the day in *la piazza* at the local *caffé* to have a cappuccino, espresso, or gelato. *La piazza* is the place for social encounters and the place for commercial activities; it is the heart of the town and is usually surrounded by the most important buildings: church, town hall theaters, caffés, shops. *La piazza* is above all the rendezvous for *la passeggiata* and the culminating point for the leisurely Italian stroll that is taken in *la sera* (early evening). This is the time when people come out to socialize, to discuss politics, domestic affairs, business, and sports. It is a time to gossip about neighbors and to boast and brag about one's own exploits or those of one's family. Italians are careful to select the styles and fashions of clothing that they will sport at the *passeggiata*, since all are aware of the impressions they will make on each other.

The *piazza* is the political arena for anyone seeking political exposure. It is the place for festivals, political rallies, religious processions, and parades; such events give *la piazza* its cheerful function in Italian life. *La piazza*, in many ways, is the nucleus of the Italian soul; it allows one to feel the pulse of the entire community and the essence of daily living; it never sleeps and therefore never closes.

☕ *Café*   *At the Bar*

In Italy, the bar is the center of social life. Patrons may visit their local bar several times in the morning for a *cappuccino* and a *cornetto* (croissant), again during the day for an espresso or a soft drink and perhaps a *panino* (*un panino* is one sandwich; two sandwiches are *due panini*), and another time in the early evening for an *aperitivo* or cocktail before dinner. In the larger bars, Italy's famous *gelato*, or ice cream (really more ice milk), may be served. People gather to settle the arguments of the day, ranging from politics to sports to personal matters—which are discussed, analyzed, and critiqued over a card game or the reading of newspapers. The bartender is a familiar figure who always seems to know everyone and everyone's affairs.

Usually the bar occupies a central location on the main avenues, in the piazzas, and on street corners. Outdoor chairs and tables with umbrellas signal its location: in the larger cities, and especially in the tourist centers, it costs more to sit at a table (sometimes even more if the table is outside) than it does to stand at the bar.

No question, coffee is the most popular drink consumed at bars. One can order a straight coffee (*un caffè*) any time of night or day. Italians tend to stay away from cappuccino after 11 P.M.

Coffee is served in many forms:

Caffè or simply espresso—a small cup of very strong coffee, topped with a caramel-colored foam called *crema*, a very important element.

Cappuccino—a shot of espresso in a larg(er) cup with steamed milk and foam.

Caffè Hag—a decaffeinated version. One can order a *decafinato* as well; Hag is the name of the largest producer of Italian decaf coffee and that's the way one will see it listed on many bar menu boards.

Caffè lungo—a long coffee. The water is poured from the machine until the coffee becomes weak and bitter. Also called a *Caffè Americano* or American coffee.

Caffè ristretto—a "restricted coffee" or one in which the stream of coffee is stopped before the normal amount. The essence of coffee, concentrated but not bitter.

Caffè con panna—espresso with sweet whipped cream.

Caffè corretto—coffee "corrected" with a drizzle of liquor. I like sambuca, but most prefer cognac or grappa.

Caffè macchiato—coffee "stained" with milk, usually just a bit of foam on top of the espresso.

Caffè latte—espresso with hot milk, a cappuccino without the foam, usually served in a glass. This is what you might call a "latte" in the US. In Italy, outside of tourist joints, you run the risk of getting what you asked for—milk, or worse yet, steamed milk.

Latte macchiato—Steamed milk "stained" with espresso, served in a glass.

Fortunately, being masters of the now-fashionable Mediterranean diet, Italians are on the average less obese than Americans. Nevertheless, with the nervous speeding-up of life, today far more care is being given to dieting.

Consequently, as in America and Britain, sales of cookbooks have soared; in Italy another reason for these sales is that after the war many middle-class urban mothers and grandmothers ceased handing on their culinary lore to their children and grandchildren, who are now having to learn it for themselves.

We have mentioned that Italians find it disgraceful to get drunk, but this self-restraint does not mean that good food goes unaccompanied by good wine. Italians have not made a religion of their wine-drinking: at dinner, an appropriate *vino* is an integral part of a good meal. There is an expression: "*un pranzo senza vino e' come un giorno senza sole,*" which translates as a meal without wine is like a day without sunshine. Today Italy produces and exports more wine than any other country, yet there is a suspicion that they keep the best for themselves. From cold, dry whites like *frascati, soave, pinot grigio,* and *verdicchio,* to smooth, hearty reds like *chianti, brunello, amarone, taurasi, aglianico,* and *barolo,* there is a *vino* to accompany any dish. To whet the appetite, there are dozens of *apperitivi,* and after the meal one might try a *digestivo.* Italian cordials are world famous *anisette, sambuca, amaretto, galliano, strega,* just to name a few although two fingers of *grappa* or *limoncello* might be a more usual way for an Italian to end a good meal.

Italy is a country of divinities, the land of Bacchus who, with his warm breath, made the vine grow from north to south and who imparted to the inhabitants of this boot stretching into the sea the secrets of making great spirits, wonderful nectars flavored with almonds, lemons, and other fruit. The country is constantly reinventing itself, enchanting young and old from all walks of life. As you sip an espresso or a cappuccino, allow yourself to be seduced by Italy and its rich menus.

Italians also like to spend some of their new wealth on eating. They spend as much as 38.8% of income on food, of which only about 5% goes for restaurant meals. Traditional Italian good eating has undergone many changes in the past decades and has come under various conflicting and complex pressures, pushing it simultaneously toward decline and recovery, and a foreign visitor may at first be baffled by what he sees, hears, and tastes. The tradition of multiple-course meals and the overall healthy eating habits of Italians are being threatened by the modern convenience of fast food. The Mediterranean diet, a healthy mix of pasta, beans, fruits, and vegetables with meats, seafoods, and olive oil, all served in small portions, is being threatened.

The Pressure from Fast Food

Although fast food restaurants have not yet made their way into many small towns and regions in Italy, they are easy to find in large cities. Fast-food places serving hot dogs, hamburgers, and pizza abound. These are crowded, cheerful places, popular with youngsters in the evening and office-workers at lunchtime, and they compare favorably with their American equivalents. The McDonald's in Rome is the most successful of the chain worldwide! Certainly, the social changes in Italy have affected eating habits. A modern nation in a hurry no longer has time or concern for serious daily cooking and eating: both at home and away from it, routine meals have become more simple, slapdash and utilitarian.

The growing fast food trend has prompted government officials in Italy to kick off a countrywide health education campaign. The campaign is aimed at both children and adults and focuses on teaching Italians to stick with their own traditions instead of going with fast food trends. In school, Italian children are taught that their diet is one of the healthiest in the world. Convincing young Italians that popular fast foods are not always the best foods for them is difficult, however, especially when many traditional foods take time to prepare, something people don't seem to have a lot of.

Italian Cuisine Creates an Important Industry

The high popularity of Italian cuisine around the world has led to one of the most startling developments in the Italian economy: the growth of large multi-national food companies in the agricultural sector. In 1980, of the top 100 Italian food companies, multi-nationals counted for only 4.9% of production and 3.6% of the employees. Just twelve years later (1992) these figures had shot up to 32.2% and 42.2% respectively. Today the figures are considerably higher. Nestlé-Italia has become Italy's largest food firm with over 8,000 employees; BSN, Unilever-Italia, and Kraft-Italia also figure prominently, along with the Italian Ferrero, Barilla, and Parmalat (until its collapse); by 1992 Unilever had become Italy's largest producer of olive oil and ice cream.[9]

The multi-nationals have been attracted to Italy as well by the large number of medium-sized farms that could be bought up at reasonable prices. Their control of all four phases of the agri-food system—production, transformation, distribution, and consumption—make them unbeatable competitors. Connected to this market, Italy has developed a big industry for the processing, canning, milling, and meatpacking sectors. Like tourism, this is a sector of the economy in which Italy could become extraordinarily big. As the standard of living increases, the desire to acquire good food and the necessity for new machinery to process food will increase. Italy is thus in the position to grow this industrial sector tremendously. State agencies and private enterprise should direct more energy and research so that the leadership can be maintained and consolidated.

Flair Also in Sexuality

Italian flair extends to sexual behavior and sexuality. Whether enjoying a good meal with friends or just greeting someone on the street, Italians are personal. It is often difficult for American and northern European visitors to accept the naturalness with which Italians touch

PROFILE

Italian Car Designers

Italian style has always been associated with creativity and elegance. One of the most success-ful areas of Italian design has been in automobiles. There are 10 top design firms for cars, all concentrated around Turin, the center of Italian auto manufacturing.

In Italy car manufacturers have from the very early days relied on external body design-ers, or coachbuilders (*carrozziere*), to design the bodies for their cars. It was not uncommon, particularly in the early part of the 20th century, for individual customers to ask a coachbuilder to do a one-off design for them, to be fitted to a standard chassis and engine supplied by a manufacturer. There are also several examples, again more the older than the newer cars, of different design houses producing different designs for the same model, both of which went into production. Some *carrozziere* have become major design houses now doing work for car manufacturers around the world, not just for Italian manufacturers.

The most prestigious car designer is Pininfarina S.p.A. (short for *Carozzeria Pininfarina*) founded in 1930 by automobile designer and builder Battista "Pinin" Farina (following the company, his family name became Pininfarina in 1961, as a result of combining his nickname and surname). Over the years Pininfarina has been employed by many automobile manu-facturers, notably Ferrari, Maserati, Cadillac, Citroen, Ford, Nash, Peugeot, Jaguar, Volvo, Alfa Romeo, and Lancia. Since the 1980s Pininfarina has also provided industrial design and interior design consultation to corporate clients. Today, Pininfarina is run by Battista's grandson. The Pininfarina Group employs more than 3,000 people in subsidiary company offices throughout Europe, as well as in Morocco and China.

Designers like Pininfarina have created works of art like the Ferrari and more down-to-earth cars like the Peugeot 205 and the Fiat Uno. In addition to cars, such firms design everything from forklifts to sailboats. Creativity has been applied to the bodywork, starting from the sheets that cover the frames, to the building of a limited quantity of prototypes, up to the project of the automobile. Very often, engineers' talent influences modern automobile design.

Concept cars have always demonstrated the designers' talent, the engineers' vision for style and safety, and the great potential of the Italian automobile industry. "Italian design has become a universal language of car design," says Lorenzo Ramaciotti, general manager of Pininfarina, which employs 2,000 people as modellers and engineers to support the tiny design team. "An American car is expected to be solid and a little flamboyant. An Italian car is expected to be aggressive, sportive and very sexy."

Like most of Italy's other designers, Turin car stylists prefer to work in small studios rather than in large corporate design centers. "I think we are delivering our best when the organization is not so huge," says Ramaciotti. "We're very individualistic people with taste rooted in the Renaissance. The stereotype of Italy as a land of creative people is true." Even if you haven't driven a Ferrari or worn a Versace lately, it's a difficult argument to refute.

each other. Usually it is simply an extension of the physical warmth and affection of the family. The way men embrace each other without self-consciousness can also be surprising to an Anglo-Saxon. The fact that the "northerners" recoil from touching or embracing each other is possibly due to excessive consciousness of sex. Certainly the fact that they are less demonstrative within their families could mean that for them touching is associated more with sex and less with warmth and spontaneous friendliness.

Despite strictures by the Vatican and the clergy, Italians have always had a reputation for sexual permissiveness, and foreign artists and writers, such as Goethe, Stendhal, Byron, Schopenhauer, and Tolstoy, learned much about the country from their Italian loves and praised the passionate nature of its women. The Italian lover, a movie cliché since Rudolph Valentino, is still an unadvertised asset of the Italian tourist business. The creation of Rudolph Valentino by Hollywood coincided with the beginning of the Roaring Twenties, when American society in general and women in particular were struggling to break free of hundred-year-old sexual, gender, and racial taboos. America needed a groundbreaker and the movies produced him: darkly handsome, muscular yet lithe and graceful, Valentino's on-screen persona represented long-forbidden eroticism to American women, and on his slender shoulders his fans hung the mantles of passionate lover, sex icon and exotic liberator of sexual mores. Nevertheless, the stir Valentino created helped Americans redefine the boundaries of acceptable romantic behavior. *Summertime,* in which Katharine Hepburn falls in love with the dashing Rossano Brazzi on her first visit to Venice, perhaps epitomize this romantic vision of Italy even more.

So much about Italy is part of this image: the gondolas, the songs, the wine, the sunglasses, the Ferraris *(See Box on p. 423), la dolce vita.* And the magic and romantic associations of names: Capri, Sorrento, Positano, Venice, Verona, the Trevi Fountain, the lakes. A number of women visitors to Italy seem to look forward to instant masculine attention and feed the notion that a lot of foreign women are coming to Italy in search of erotic adventures. Unquestionably, what is known as *caccia alle straniere* is also a pastime of young Italians to prove their virility and seductiveness. Italian playwright Mario Fratti created a well-known comedy on the skilful techniques used by Italian gigolos to seduce tourists.[10]

The most striking change in sexual behavior certainly happened with women. Today, the Italian woman expects the same degree of sexual freedom as a man and, conversely, the same degree of fidelity from a man. She no longer accepts that his peccadilloes are more forgivable than her own. Regarding Italian sexuality, it would be a fair assumption that Italian (and European) women are:

» by and large, more sexually liberated than American women, less concerned with sexual exploitation in the media, freer with their own sexuality;

» perhaps less concerned about being sexualized because men are sexualized equally; and have perhaps a stronger sense of self that allows them to be less contrived.

Sexuality is not taboo in Europe. It's acceptable conversation for the dinner table, and four-year-olds know the appropriate terms for and functions of all the body parts and have

PROFILE

Ferrari

Italy has been known for its flashy, sleek sport cars. Ferrari, Maserati, Lamborghini, Bugatti, and Ferrari are prestigious names in the history of car making.

Ferrari, based in Maranello (in Modena province, Northern Italy) and founded by Enzo Ferrari in 1929 as Scuderia Ferrari, sponsored drivers and manufactured race cars before moving into production of street vehicles in 1946 as Ferrari S.P.A. Ferrari is noted for its continued participation in racing, especially in Formula One, where it has enjoyed great success, especially during the 1950s, 1960s, 1970s, late 1990s, and 2000s. Off the race track, Ferrari's cars are among the most desirable of vehicles to own and drive, and they are one of the ultimate status symbols in the western world.

The latest Ferrari model for the road is the Enzo Ferrari, a 12-cylinder supercar named after the company's founder. It was built in 2003 using Formula One technology, including a carbon-fiber body, an F1-style sequential shift transmission, and carbon-ceramic brake discs.

The Enzo was introduced at the 2002 Paris Motor Show with a limited production run of 349 units and priced at $643,330. The company sent invitations to existing customers, specifically, those who had previously bought the Ferrari F40 and Ferrari F50. All 349 cars were sold in this way before production even began. Later, after numerous requests, Ferrari decided to build 50 more Enzos, bringing the total to 399.

On November 8, 2005, Ferrari announced that it would build one last Enzo to benefit survivors of the 2004 tsunami. The car was auctioned on June 28, 2005 for €950,000 ($1,274,229), almost twice its list price. Today, the Enzos typically trade above $1,000,000 at auction.

In 2005 Ferrari added two new models: the F430 and the limited-edition Superamerica. The F430 is a V8-powered, mid-engine replacement for the Ferrari 360, which has sold in three different versions to become the best-selling Ferrari of all time. Powered by a 490-horsepower 90-degree 4.3-liter V8 engine that is very light and compact, the F430 incorporates advancements in design, technology, and performance that promise acceleration from 0 to 60 mph in less than 4 seconds and a top speed of over 196 mph.

The Superamerica is a two-seat coupe that can covert to an open-top roadster. It has a tint-adjustable, electrochromic one-piece glass roof that rotates rearward and nests into a shallow storage area behind the seats. The completely power-operated process takes just ten seconds.

With a top speed of 200 mph, the Superamerica is the fastest production convertible in the world. The 540-horsepower 12-cylinder engine generates 434 lb-ft of torque and is mated to a 6-speed F1/manual gearbox. Ferrari plans to produce only 559 Superamericas.

seen mothers with uncovered breasts nursing their babies. In Italy, breasts are just another body part.

As late as the 1960s, all the evidence suggested that Italian unmarried girls as a whole, especially in the provinces, were among the most virginal in Europe. Well into the 1960s the old code of this Catholic society remained in force, at least on the surface. According to a survey in 1960, more than half of Italian mothers thought a girl should not be allowed out with a boy until she was 19, and many acted to enforce that belief. Less than one-third of girls said they approved of premarital sex even between engaged couples, while about 70% of married women under thirty claimed to have been virgins on their wedding night.

However, following the lead of the Nordic countries, sexual freedom began to spread. Parents became more willing to allow their daughters to go out with their boyfriends; young people had more leisure and money for going off together. In some student circles, relations had become very free by the mid-1960s. The 1970s saw further changes among the very young and their parents' attitudes toward them. This attitude change came from foreign influences, from the freeing of legal controls on contraception, from the steady decline in the role of the Church. Today at school teenage girls treat boys as sex objects in a free market, just as boys treat girls. However, lately there has been a swing away from promiscuity, mainly because of the fear of AIDS. In general, sexual freedom in Italy has now reached the same level as in France, Britain, Germany, and Sweden—and that, for this Catholic country, is quite a transformation. It would be wrong, however, to infer from the teenage revolution that every adult woman has become *leggera* overnight. Most women in their mid-twenties or older are still *serie* (serious) and will not give themselves except for love.

La Gioventù: Footloose but More Sincere

Naturally these changes in social behavior have had their effect on Italy's youth, its *gioventù*. Young people have their own consumer markets for music, clothes, and cars; they have their own world of rock groups and other singing idols. All enjoy far more freedom from parents than cloistered Italian youths had 30 years ago and far more sexual license, too.

Many of the most important changes in postwar Italy were due to a new generation rising against the standards of its elders. The postwar climate was very different from today's: more austere but also more open and adventurous. In the 1960s, a new generation, sipping its Coca-Cola and listening to pop music and singing American rock 'n' roll, was born. Quickly, Italian pop was born. At first the movement was highly derivative. Not only did the stars borrow American tunes, but several of them found it smart to adopt British and American names as well. Open-air concerts attracted tens of thousands of teenagers. These gatherings reflected the high sense of solidarity of the new generation. There was a tone of revolt in all this, but the revolution was purely one of music and rhythm, not morals and standards.

Through the 1960s youth remained very much under parental influence, leaving a dominant impression of docile reticence in society. Then, from the end of the 1960s, giving vent to frustrations that had lain beneath the surface, youth became almost an independent political and cultural force. This was the golden age of faith in ideologies and in the belief that a new generation could after all change society. Youth burst into action. But when the dust had settled, and society had not been changed very much, it soon became clear that the crisis between 1967 and 1969 had not turned all Italian youth into revolutionaries.

However, those years were not without their permanent legacy, notably in the way they modified relations between Italian youth and their elders. The old barriers of authority were broken, and this was true as much within families as in schools and universities. But, 25 years later, what use was made of this freedom by the ensuing generation? Italy's youth today are something of an enigma, and one that many adults find disquieting. Well, most of today's youngsters were born after those years of *contestazione,* protests and challenges For most of them those years of high ideals are history and are viewed with skepticism and passivity. Today's *gioventù* is not rebellious and is not fired with revolutionary ideals for trying to change society, very much in contrast to the seething youth of the late 1960s. Tolerant and reflective, today's young people seem curiously passive. Only rarely do they show much sense of public initiative.

Recently, whenever the youngsters have engaged in demonstrations, they have done so more in opposition to change, rather than as a constructive demand for change. They are much closer to their parents' interests and attitudes: rejecting ideologies and formal organizations, concerned with private pleasures and with "feathering the nest." The new Italian concern with an ethos of personal fulfillment and hedonism is even stronger among the young than among older people. It is easy to lament this apparent shift toward egotism and rejection of ideals of wider community service. Young people cling to their own trusted circle of family and friends and reject any wider allegiance.

One feature common to most young people in the past decade, even the more conformist ones, is that leisure and privacy have been replacing work as the essential paths to self-fulfillment. The young attitude to a job or career is frequently utilitarian. Work is seen as a means of ensuring the quality of their leisure lives, and only a minority shares the passionate work ethic that drove their elders to build the modern prosperous Italy. The country should, certainly, be concerned about the decline of the old dedicated work ethic. It seems, however, that there have been signs of a new swing of the pendulum among some very young people. Although very often individualistic and self-centered, they are more ambitious and are prepared to work harder. They have drive and initiative, but they do not challenge the system or seek to change it for the good of society as a whole; in fact, usually they would rather run their own business than work for a large organization or institution.

Idealism about a united Europe has also waned recently, for young people as much as their elders have grown cynical about the EU as an institution. Certainly, the setback caused by the failure to approve the constitution has dampened spirits. Yet, in a more general sense, Italians still feel "European," more so than the French, and much more so than the insular British. They have less sense of frontiers than the older generation. These young people not only are not racist, they take pride in showing solidarity with new immigrants, who are mostly of color, and they feel a strong concern toward the Third World.

Overall, *la gioventù* has won a new freedom from parents and teachers, but it has also lost its sure moral leadership. It cannot trust the values of an adult world that is corrupt and no longer offers certainties; hence, in the search for its own values it retreats into the private world.

Notes

1. M. Revelli, "Economia e modello sociale nel passaggio fra fordismo e toyotismo," in P. Ingrao and R. Rossanda (eds.), *Appuntamenti di fine secolo* (Roma: Transizioni, 1995), pp. 161–224.

2. W. Scobie, "La dolce vita," *Observer,* 15 November 1987.

3. A. Bagnasco, *L'Italia in tempi di cambiamenti politici* (Bologna: Il Mulino, 1996), 27.

4. M. Revelli, "Economia e modello sociale nel passaggio tra fordismo e toyotismo," in P. Ingrao and R. Rossanda (eds.), *Appuntamenti di fine secolo* (Roma: Transizioni, 1995), pp. 185 ff.

5. G. C. Cerruti and V. Rieser, *Fiat: qualità totale e fabbrica integrata* (Roma: Ediesse, 1991), 52–55.

6. Presidenza del Consiglio dei Ministri, dipartimento per la funzione pubblica, *Rapporto sulle condizioni delle pubbliche amministrazioni* (Roma, 1993), 13.

7. For a comprehensive study on "*Bella figura,*" see G. Nardini, *Che bella figura* (Albany: SUNY Press, 1999).

8. The first printed cookery book also came from Italy. Written by Bartolomeo Platina, the Vatican Librarian in 1475, his work *De Honesta Voluptate* drew largely from the manuscripts of an earlier 15th-century recipe writer, Maestro Martino of Como. After the collapse of the Roman Empire, Italy became fragmented, and the separate regions grew up as individual city states, each with their own identity, resources, and traditions.

9. P. De Castro and R. Deserti, "Imprese multinazionali, strategie di mercato e nuovi scenari del sistema agro-alimentare italiano," *Rivista di politica agraria,* vol. XIII (1995), no. 3, pp. 4–8.

10. M. Fratti, *L'accademia* (New York: S. French, 1964).

Bibliography

Bagnasco, A., *L'Italia in tempi di cambiamenti politici* (Bologna: Il Mulino, 1996).

Bonami, F., Frisa, M.L. and Tonchi, S. (eds.), *Uniform: Order and Disorder* (Milan: Charta, 2000).

Cerruti, G. C. And Rieser, V., *Fiat: qualità totale e fabbrica integrata* (Roma: Ediesse, 1991).

Garofoli, M. (ed.), *Le fibre intelligenti. Un secolo di storia e cinquant'anni di moda* (Milan: Electra, 1991)

Ingrao, P. and Rossanda, R. (eds.), *Appuntamenti di fine secolo* (Roma: Transizioni, 1995).

Nardini, G., *Che bella figura* (Albany: SUNY Press, 1999).

Ross, A. (ed.), *No Sweat. Fashion, Free Trade, and the Right of Garment Workers* (New York: Verso, 1997).

Severgnini, B., *La Bella Figura* ((New York: Broadway Books, 2006).

Steele, V., *Fashion, Italian Style* (New Haven: Yale University Press, 2003).

White, N., *Reconstructing Italian Fashion: America and the Development of the Italian Fashion Industry* (Oxford: Berg, 2000).

White, N. (ed.), *The Business of Fashion* (Oxford: Berg, 2001).

CHAPTER 16

CONCLUSION

A Country in Search of Equilibrium

The Elusive Citizen

Throughout this book we have demonstrated that Italy is alive, well, and thriving; that the Italian democratic system is very stable, despite its fractured political map; that Italian society is as lively as ever, paradoxically because problems often are not solved frontally, but by Italians' innate ability to "manage" whatever the situation.

Italy shares with the United States what political scientist Robert N. Putnam has identified as a low sense of civic community; indeed, Italy's problems are most serious in the least civic regions, where the horizontal bonds of collective reciprocity are missing. In these areas, a horizontally fractured community produces daily justification for feelings of exploitation, dependency, frustration, and, consequently, cynicism and alienation. In the less-civic regions nearly everyone expects everyone else to violate the rules; everyone expects everyone else to cheat.[1]

Therefore, while in most regions in the north citizens are engaged by public issues instead of by personality-driven or patron-client politics, and value solidarity, civic engagement, and cooperation, in the less civic regions of the south life is marked by hierarchy and clientelism.

However, a cynical attitude toward the government is equally strong in both the south and the north. To have an idea of what we mean, let's take a look at how the Italians deal with the many "crises," real and fictitious, that afflict the country. The average Italian is accustomed to associate with a crisis any problem encountered in daily activities. Very often minor or accidental problems are equated with national, regional, or local crises. In such a labyrinth, real crises cannot be disentangled from imagined ones, and the country appears to be constantly at the brink of chaos.

The average Italian faults the *classe politica* (the political class) and the *classe dirigente* (the administrative class) for such a nightmarish atmosphere. In fact, the political and the ruling classes are the culprits for everything that goes wrong. Here, too, it is difficult to identify what is real or who these classes really are. They are like an accordion; they can be expanded or contracted, depending on the nature of the crisis, who "sees" it, whether one is talking about a city or province or the whole nation, and so on. The *classe politica* is "they," those people, those incompetents and swindlers. It is certainly not "we" or "I" or any close friend who is of course heavily taxed and short-changed in all public service support. It is not uncommon to hear a "*prominente,*" a member of Italy's ruling class, excoriate the *classe politica* as if he or she were in no way responsible for the political, fiscal, and social crises of the country. There is much unintended irony and self-deception in all of this. One may argue that the Italian situation is nothing uncommon, that everyone likes to blame a scapegoat at one time or another, that we all tend to look elsewhere for the cause of those aspects of society, and of our own lives within it, that we find unpalatable.

But Italy does appear to be different, not only in the frequency of hostile references or attacks on the *classe politica* but also in the intensity with which each condemnation is expressed. The criticism is so ritualized, so well integrated into the citizens' role, so much part of Italian play-acting that it is difficult to tell how much of it is deeply felt. Italians love performance. Look at what happened at the end of the World Soccer Cup in 2006: Italy's victory became a national public celebration. Moreover, there is no persuasive evidence that these hostile attitudes toward the political class have negative or corrosive consequences on the Italian democracy; on the contrary, it seems that Italian democracy thrives on hostile criticism. Situations, conditions, and leaders are constantly reassessed.

Notwithstanding the self-criticism that at times is picked up also by the foreign press, in less than three decades Italy became an advanced industrial country, where the number of persons who work in agriculture was drastically reduced, and where, as in many other democracies, the so-called tertiary employment sector became the largest. Modern, well-off Italy got where it is because of the ideas, imagination, and hard work of its people. Progress was achieved not by chance or "miracle" but because the *classe politica* concocted political and economic formulas that the people accepted and that, when applied, worked. The *classe politica* has demonstrated how primary political rights and democratic processes can be used to improve the material and moral condition of the citizens. The Italians created a peculiar capitalism that does not fit any "ideal type" or rigid preconceived framework. It is rational, of course, and at the same time highly traditional, and while following universal rules it has never abandoned its firm original family base. It is a mixture, a cocktail of different attitudes and contradictory value orientations. Called "dynastic capitalism," it is recognized as a masterpiece of adaptation of traditional virtues and traits to modern functional requisites. For Italian capitalism the conventional concept of profit is too narrow, just as the current concept of productivity is too one-sided. Productivity and profit are not conceived only in terms of an individual productive unit. They are measured and assessed in terms of social stability and satisfactory performance of the system as a whole.

It would be wrong to overlook the social dimensions of Italian capitalism. It is less efficient but has less conspicuous waste; it allows for more individual self-expression and permits more conviviality. That is not necessarily bad; human beings desire and probably crave change but they also want and need stability. They might desire competition to vent their aggressiveness, but they also need cooperation, security, and the feeling of working together toward a reasonable goal.

In its leap into industrial prosperity, Italy has escaped the "flatness," the existential monotony that characterizes most other industrial countries. In such societies, life is dynamic, but it tends to be tedious and tasteless; things and people become gradually homogenized and interchangeable. Things are still different in Italy. The tempo of life can be irritatingly slow, especially in the south. Italians still prefer to do things leisurely. There seems always to be time for everything. Time, in Italy, is not a scarce raw material. One may occasionally find hurry and confusion, especially in a piazza or at a social function, but it is not a purposeful hurry.

Thus, people are usually late for their appointments. In Rome to be half an hour late for *un appuntamento* (an appointment) is not considered serious; it is commonly accepted. South of Rome, arriving on time may almost be regarded as an offensive behavior. Punctuality on the part of one person is viewed as a lack of trust in the other and a clear symptom of petty-mindedness. In some respects Italians' attitudes to leisure differ from those of Northern Europeans, notably in the way they like their free time divided up; for example, since World War II Italians have shown a preference for longer annual vacations rather than shorter working days. Italians take the longest vacations of all Europeans. Today, the strains of daily city life incite many people to take off for the country on the weekend, and most likely they will go neither to a hotel nor to relative's but to their own country cottage or villa, *la seconda casa*. Italians can boast of holding first place among Europeans in owning a second house. The race to the countryside is associated with both the new back-to-nature trend and the hedonistic—or perhaps spiritual—search for privacy. If weekends are now more important, lunches are less so. The leisurely two-hour family lunch, weekdays included, is one Italian tradition that is in decline, thanks to suburban commuting and changes in the economy. Lunch had habitually been the main meal of the day, with children coming home from school and husbands home from work—and so it still is, in many small towns and rural areas. But the cities have seen big changes.

The Art of *Arrangiarsi*, to Manage

The Italians "manage" their lives and their institutions in a manner that surprises even the most open-minded political science experts and the most informed sociologists. The area of politics is very revealing in this regard. Italy has one of the most active and participating electorates. If one assesses the strength of its democracy on the basis of public participation in the election process, the picture is very positive indeed. Even the high percentage of votes for the communists was something positive because the strong opposition to government provided a high level of checks and balances in the democratic process. Contrary to the general American belief that a vote for the Communist Party by Catholics was a sign of political pathology, the Italian vote was highly calibrated to keep a democratic system from falling under the control of groups with extreme ideologies. Now that the heat and the smoke of the Cold War have settled, it is easy to assess the political behavior of the Italians in those years. The fall of communism has led to a shift not only from the communists but also from the Christian Democrats—their traditional political enemies—to other political forces, creating a new political landscape which brings an end to *immobilismo*.

Italy's political behavior cannot be understood by the American mind that prefers everything in black and white. Matter-of-factness, which is usually and somewhat pompously referred to as "scientific habit of mind," has not trickled down to permeate the Italian mass mentality. Facts per se have no value; there is only interpretation of facts in Italian life. Everything is debatable. The activities in any Italian *caffe* reflect such Italian behavior. Luigi Pirandello and his relativistic view of life are the products of an Italian conception of existence. The Italian mind is still poetic, anthropomorphic, and unpredictable. This is why when the American tourists, who are fond of empirical details, ask questions such as "How tall is the Coliseum?" or "How wide is Piazza San Pietro?" the average Italian looks up surprised and a little amused at such questioning.

Foreigners are amazed by such a way of thinking and behavior. The question is always, why? According to Eduardo De Filippo, a postwar Italian actor and playwright, centuries of foreign domination have created a mind that subconsciously represses truth. In a hostile environment, truth was a luxury that few people could afford; invention at the individual level, a keen sense of life as a permanent theater, a profound and irreducible diversity, and a living challenge to the rules of logic became the normal behavior. Regardless of how tough a situation may be, Italians have learned to face life always with dignity and elegance. Needless to say, the end result of such efforts is the supreme value given to *bella figura*. *Bella figura* is more than simple make-shift or bombastic rhetoric. It has to do with an aesthetic ideal, and at the same time, it has to do with a question of survival.

Italians want it to be known that they are present; the fact that Italians are noisy and that Italy is a noisy country can be traced to this particular attitude. Noise can be nerve-wracking and, in terms of efficiency, time-consuming, but Italians seem to like noise. They regard it as a therapy against solitude. Noise is life, message, exchange, presence, *socialità*. And being sociable has remained a major Italian trait. With the advent of *progresso,* many social manifestations have not changed or become part of a rational notion of society, that is, of a functional society. In a functional society every major activity is planned toward a definite goal and is to be accounted for and evaluated in terms of costs-benefits analysis. In industrialized Italy, ceremonies are still for purely ceremonial purpose because people still have a love for ceremony.

Measuring Success

However, today Italy presents a confusing picture, for society appears to have evolved in certain respects but not in others. Personal attitudes and lifestyles have evolved rather more than the formal or official structures that dominate public life. These still tend to be impeded: by the survival of many out-of-date laws, regulations, and routine practices, and by the "stratified society" with its strong vested interests right across the board. Society is still too corporatist and compartmentalized, with each body protecting itself from its rivals, and still passionately regionalist.

Moreover, Italian society is still segmented and individualistic because loyalties are usually restricted to small groups held together by strong personal ties and loyalties. The family is the most important of these, but it is followed closely by the patron-client relationship, which is very strong and is by no means restricted to the south. Italians join associations with fellow-members of their own trade or social group but more for mutual self-defense than out of altruistic sentiment or a sense of civic duty.

This book has also attempted to trace the positive changes in attitudes and human relations—greater freedom for women and young people, the rise of social informality, the freer climate in education and in working life, and a small sign of a new cooperative spirit of self-help. All this might have led, one would suppose, to a waning of the old Italian traits built around mutual mistrust and to the rise of a less divided and, therefore, more civic-minded society. And in some ways it has. But there have been some failures. Some can be found in any capitalist society; some are merely part of the wider human condition—other nations, too, including Britain and the U.S., have their own full share of vested interests, corruption, and clumsy bureaucrats.

Italians have now modernized their country, or most of it, and have managed to adjust successfully without losing their essential Italianness. Anyone who travels around Italy today will find a country that is very modern, but in its own way, a blend of the new and the traditional, the native and the imported. Of course a highway or a skyscraper is much the same in any land, but the Italians add stylish innovative touches of their own. Inevitably the new Italy has lost some of the old's quaint picturesqueness, yet the Italians today show a flair for giving a phoenix-like rebirth to the picturesque.

The Italians are showing less success at reinventing the novel, the play, and the great painting. For some years now, Italian creative culture has remained at a low ebb. Intellectual life is more dazzle and frenzy than substance; the theater turns to brilliant gimmicks; and Italy still awaits the arrival of outstanding new talent among novelists, playwrights, painters, even filmmakers. But is this vacuum any deeper in Italy than elsewhere in Western Europe? The Italian cultural staleness is part of the staleness of the West in this age of technology and mass media. This is a time that favors individual creativity less than it does the disseminating of culture to new audiences; and here Italy is full of an impressive activity, notably in the world of museums.

It seems that in today's anxious world, the Italians have been searching for security, personal fulfillment, what can loosely be termed "quality of life." This could lead them as individuals to become more self-absorbed, more anti-social in a civic sense. Certainly there has been a new stress on personal initiative, ambition, and material success, especially among young people. This is certainly not a sign of passivity; it is somewhat egotistical rather than civic-oriented.

The issue is whether the Italians can harness their abundant energies to work together for new social goals or whether their old individualism will lead them down new entrepreneurial paths or whether as individuals they will relapse into the shuttered, mistrustful isolation that is one strong facet of their nature.

The Ills of Prosperity

In the last few decades, Italians have had experiences that have a strong American flavor. In the early 1960s, most Italians believed that prosperity would create the ultimate good society. As in the U.S. in the 1950s and 1960s, in the Italy of the 1960s and 1970s there was a general, fervent belief in the power of prosperity. Soon after the economic recovery, the Italians increasingly became accustomed to believing that they were entitled to a great deal: more opportunities, job security, better housing, better education, earlier retirement, rising living standards, a clean environment, and more. While family income grew rapidly, the quality of life improved in countless ways. In the process, their expensive notion of entitlement grew increasingly unrealistic.

When the fiscal and political crisis swept the country at the beginning of the 1990s, Italians felt a need to reassess their wants, needs, and moral attitudes. They started to answer some very basic questions: is upward mobility a birthright? Can the state continue to provide a high level of social and public assistance? Is prosperity going to continue? It seems that they started to learn what the Americans had already painfully learned, that prosperity can never satisfy all our expectations. Prosperity is not quite the social stabilizer that we thought it to be. Faith in prosperity is an infatuation, and like all infatuations, one is seduced by its pleasures and blinded to its shortcomings. Economic growth—the creation of new industries and technologies—can be disruptive: it may spawn excesses, overinvestment, speculation, too much borrowing, and recession. Moreover, not only are some social problems beyond prosperity's power to cure, but some social ills are the creation of prosperity.

Many Italians have been questioning the worth of such progress. In a book published in 1989, *Non siamo più povera gente* (We Are No Longer Poor People), Cesare Marchi lamented the cost of economic success. It was the follow-up to another book of his, *Quando eravamo povera gente* (When We Were Poor People), in which he had called to mind the Italy of poverty, while underlining the solid moral values of that society.[2] Is Marchi's lamentation symptomatic of a real situation, or is it part of the general Italian behavior to be critical of everything?

However, most Italians remain prey to the economy's euphoric expansions and dispiriting declines; they should realize that prosperity cannot be created at will and that is the most important term in the equation of the high achievements of a country. They must finally realize that even great amounts of prosperity won't solve all their social problems and that prosperity could bring moral decay. In fact, the prospect of a harmonious society is disfigured by huge blemishes—high unemployment, tension between south and north, budget deficits, an uncontrollable Mafia, corruption among public officials, the breakdown of moral values, an aging population, and a very low birth rate—that cannot continue to be overlooked.[3]

As the country grows in the twenty-first century, past progress has to be reconsidered. The sophisticated constitution has to be attuned to new political realities; the responsibilities of the state to the citizens and those of the citizens to the state have to be revalued. The "Italian behavior," while keeping its valuable traits, has to start to conform to that of a united Europe and of a shrinking world. With its unique cultural patrimony, artistic tradition, and creative strength—from Dante to Michelangelo, Giotto to Botticelli, Vivaldi to Verdi, Machiavelli to Gramsci, Volta to Fermi—it is unlikely that Italy will fail to contribute greatly to a Europe that may well be on the threshold of a radical new era. Italians have always known how to pair technical expertise with artistic genius, a tradition dating back at least as far as the Renaissance, when painters were also sculptors, architects, scientists, and men of letters. Italian design—the "made in Italy" trademark—has contributed to this tradition of uniting beauty with usefulness. The real challenge to Italy for the next century is how she is going to weld her two cultures, the Western European and the Mediterranean, and what role the presence of immigrants will play in shaping the future of the country.

How can we conclude and generalize about a people who in modern times have produced types as different as Mussolini and Pope John XXIII? Ever since they began to emerge as a nation, the Italians presented contrasting facets. Which is more typical of the national genius: Dante on his austere quest for truth and perfection or Boccaccio bubbling over with laughter at the human scene? Saint Francis with his love for nature and humankind or Machiavelli with his cynicism and "scientific art"? Which is the real Italy, the country that rose to a major economic power without natural resources or the nation struggling for fiscal responsibility? Both exist, both are real, and as things go, they are probably both eternal.

No other people over so long a history have shown a greater knack for survival and adaptability than the Italians and in a manner that is full of paradoxes. The national art of "arrangement"—dodging taxes, double-dealing, working only as hard as one must—is counteracted by Italian inventive genius, gusto for life, fierce individuality, and deep family ties, as well as animosity and a marvelously hedonistic sophistication. The Italians are a highly resilient, resourceful, and practical people and will keep a balance between work and leisure. Perhaps more than any other nation in Europe, the Italians bring a vast heritage of wisdom, taste, and humanism to the difficult task of preserving the best of the past in order to marry it with the future. They will do it by preserving a gusto for life.

Notes

1. Robert N. Putnam, *Making Democracy Work*, 111.

2. Cesare Marchi, *Non siamo piu' povera gente* (Milan: Rizzoli, 1989) and *Quando erevamo povera gente* (Milan: Rizzoli, 1989).

3. The picture is very bleak if the nation does not recognize the severity of the problem:

BIBLIOGRAPHY

General

Barzini, Luigi. *The Italians: A Full-Length Portrait Featuring Their Manners and Morals.* New York: Atheneum, 1964.

Braun, Michael. *L'Italia da Andreotti a Berlusconi. Rivolgimenti e prospettive politiche in un paese a rischio.* Milan: Feltrinelli, 1995.

Cassese, Sabino, ed. *Ritratto dell'Italia.* Bari: Laterza, 2001.

Chubb, Judith. *Patronage, Power and Poverty in Southern Italy.* Cambridge: Cambridge UP, 1982.

Curtis, M., Ammendola, G., et al., *Western European Government and Politics* (2nd Edition). New York: Longman Publishers, 2003.

Di Scala, Spencer M. *Italy. From Revolution to Republic, 1700 to the Present* (3rd Edition) Oxford: Westview Press, 2004.

Eurispes. *Rapporto Italia 2001.* Rome: Eurispes (Annual).

Forgacs, David and Lumley, Robert. *Italian Cultural Studies: An Introduction.* Oxford: Oxford University Press, 1996.

Ginsborg, Paul. *A History of Contemporary Italy: Society and Politics 1943–1988.* New York: Penguin Books, 1990.

Ginsborg, Paul, ed. *Stato dell'Italia.* Milan: Il Saggiatore Mondadori, 1994.

Ginsborg, Paul. *Italy and its Discontents—Family, Civil Society, State: 1980–2001.* New York: Palgrave Macmillan, 2003.

Gramsci, Antonio. *Selections from the Prison Notebooks,* edited by Q. Hoare and Nowell-Smith. London: Lawrence and Wishart, 1971.

Gribaudi, A. *Mondo operaio, mito operaio.* Turin: Einaudi, 1987.

Haycraft, John. *Italian Labyrinth: Italy in the 1980s.* London: Secker & Warburg, 1985.

Mammarella, Giuseppe. *Italy After Fascism: A Political History.* Notre Dame: Notre Dame UP, 1966.

Murray, William. *The Last Italian: Portrait of a People.* New York: Prentice Hall, 1991.

Pescosolido, Carl and Gleason, Pamela. *The Proud Italians.* Portland: Graphic Arts Center Publ., 1991

Rusconi, Gian Enrico and Scamuzzi, Sergio. *Italy Today: An Eccentric Society.* London: Sage, 1981.

Sassoon, Donald. *Contemporary Italy: Politics, Economy & Society Since 1945.* New York: Longman Inc., 1986.

Politics

Bull, Martin J. and Martin, Rhodes, eds. *Transition and Crisis in Italian Politics.* London: Cass, 1996.

D'Alberti, Marco and Finocchi, Renato, eds. *Corruzione e sistema istituzionale.* Bologna: Il Mulino, 1994.

Della Porta, Donatella and and Vannucci, Alberto. *Corruzione politica e amministrazione pubblica. Risorse, meccanismi, attori.* Bologna: Il Mulino, 1994.

Di Palma, Giuseppe. *Surviving Without Governing: The Italian Parties in Parliament.* Berkeley: University of California Press, 1977.

Galli, Giorgio and Prandi, Alfonso. *Patterns of Political Participation in Italy.* New Haven: Yale University Press, 1970.

Gozzini, Giovanni and Anderlini, Luigi, eds. *I partiti e lo stato.* Bari: De Donato, 1982.

Guidorossi, Giovanna. *Gli italiani e la politica.* Milan: Franco Angeli, 1984.

Kogan, Norman. *A Political History of Italy: The Postwar Years.* New York: Praeger Special Studies, 1983.

La Palombara, Joseph. *Democracy Italian Style.* New Haven: Yale University Press, 1987.

Mannheimer, Renato and Sani, Giacomo. *La rivoluzione elettorale. L'Italia tra la prima e la seconda repubblica.* Milan: Anabasi, 1994.

Pasquino, Gianfranco. *The End of Post-War Politics in Italy.* Boulder: Westview Press, 1993.

Spotts, Frederic and Wieser, Theodor. *Italy: A Difficult Democracy.* Cambridge: Cambridge University Press, 1986.

Treu, Tiziano, ed. *L'uso politico dello statuto dei lavoratori.* Bologna: Il Mulino, 1975.

Vacca, Giuseppe. *Quale democrazia?* Bari: De Donato, 1977.

Wollemborg, Leo J. *Stars, Stripes, and Italian Tricolor.* New York: Praeger, 1990.

Government

Amato, Giuliano. *Una politica riformare*. Bologna: Il Mulino, 1980.

Bobbio, Norberto. *Ideological Profile of Twentieth-Century Italy*. Princeton, N.J.: Princeton U. P., 1995.

Brosio, G. *Equilibri instabili*. Turin: Boringhieri, 1994.

Calandra, Piero. *Il governo della repubblica*. Bologna: Il Mulino, 1986.

Cassese, Sabino. *Esiste un governo in Italia?* Rome: Officina, 1988.

Cassese, Sabino and Franchini, C., eds. *L'amministrazione pubblica italiana. Un profilo*. Bologna: Il Mulino, 1994.

Cazzola, Giuliano. *Lo stato sociale tra crisi e riforme: il caso Italia*. Bologna: Il Mulino, 1994.

Certoma, G. L. *The Italian Legal System*. London: Butterworth, 1985.

Di Palma, Giuseppe. *Surviving Without Governing: The Italian Parties in Parliament*. Berkeley: University of California Press, 1977.

Ferrera, Maurizio. *Modelli di solidarietà: politica e riforme sociali nelle democrazie*. Bologna: Il Mulino, 1993.

Furlong, Paul. *Modern Italy. Representation and Reform*. London: Routledge, 1994.

Guarnieri, Carlo. *L'indipendenza della magistratura*. Padova: Cedam, 1981.

Leonardi, Robert and Nanetti, Raffaella Y. *The Regions and European Integration. The Case of Emilia-Romagna*. London: Pinter, 1991.

Rotelli, E. *Il martello e 1'incudine*. Bologna: Il Mulino, 1991.

Sales, O. *Leghisti e sudisti*. Roma-Bari: Laterza, 1993

SVIMEZ, *Rapporto sulla distribuzione Nord-Sud della spesa pubblica*. Bologna: Il Mulino, 1993.

Travaglio, Sergio, ed. *Come funziona 1'Italia*. Milan: Sperling and Kupfer, 1994.

Zannotti, F. *La magistratura. Un gruppo di pressione istituzionale*. Padova: Cedam, 1989.

Economy and Industry

Accornero, Aris. *La parabola del sindacato. Ascesa e declino di una cultura*. Bologna: Il Mulino, 1992.

Amato, Giuliano. *Economia, politica e istituzioni in Italia*. Bologna: Il Mulino, 1976.

Blim, Michael. *Made in Italy: Small Scale Industrialization and Its Consequences*. New York: Praeger, 1990.

Blum, Anna, et al., eds. *From Peasant to Entrepreneur*. Providence, RI: Berg, 1993.

Bruni, Michele and De Luca, Loretta. *Unemployment and Labor Market Flexibility*. Bologna: Il Mulino, 1994.

Cento Bull, Anna and Corner, P. *From Peasant to Entrepreneur. The Survival of the Family Economy in Italy*. Oxford: Oxford University Press, 1993.

Chubb, Judith. *Patronage, Power, and Poverty in Southern Italy*. Cambridge: Cambridge U. P., 1982.

Daneo, Camillo. *Breve storia dell'agricoltura italiana 1860–1970*. Milan: Mondadori, 1980.

D'Antonio, Mariano. *Sviluppo e crisi del capitalismo italiano 1951–1972.* Bari: De Donato, 1973.

Goodman, Edward and Bamford, Julia, eds. *Small Firms and Industrial Districts in Italy.* London: Routledge, 1991.

Holmstrom, Mark. *Industrial Democracy in Italy: Workers' Co-ops and the Self-Management Debate.* Aldershot: Averbury, 1989.

Lange, P. and Tarrow, S., eds. *Italy in Transition: Conflict and Consensus.* London: Frank Cass, 1980.

Lash, Scott and Urry, John. *The End of Organized Capitalism.* Cambridge: Polity, 1987.

Lazerson, Mark H. "Organizational Growth of Small Firms: An Outcome of Markets and Hierarchies?," *American Sociological Review,* 53 (June 1988).

Mershon, Carol. *The Micropolitics of Union Action: Industrial Conflict in Italian Factories,* Ph.D. diss., Yale University,1986.

Nannetti, Raffaella Y. *Growth and Territorial Policies: The Italian Model of Social Capitalism.* New York: Pinter, 1988.

Nannetti, Raffaella Y. and Robert Leonardi, eds., *The Regions and European Integration: The Case of Emilia-Romagna.* New York: Pinter, 1990.

Reu, Tiziano, ed. *L'uso politico dello statuto dei alvoratori.* Bologna: Il Mulino, 1975.

Sapelli, Giulio. *Sul capitalismo italiano. Trasformazione e declino.* Milan: Feltrinelli, 1993.

Trentin, Bruno. *Da sfruttati a produttori.* Bari: De Donato, 1977.

Triglia, Carlo. *Sviluppo senza autonomia.* Bologna: Il Mulino, 1992.

Valli, Vittorio. *L'economia e la politica economica italiana.* Milan: Etas Libri, 1979.

Valli, Vittorio. *Politica economica: I modelli, gli strumenti, l'economia italiana.* Rome: La Nuova Italia Scientifica, 1992.

Villari, L., ed. *Il capitalismo italiano del Novecento.* Bari: Laterza, 1975.

Weiss, Linda. *Creating Capitalism: the State and Small Business since 1945.* Oxford: Blackwell, 1988.

Society

Altan, Carlo Tullio. *L'altra Italia.* Milan: Feltrinelli, 1985.

Balbo, Laura. *Stato di famiglia.* Milan: 1976.

Balbo, Laura. *Women's Studies in Italy.* Old Westbury, N.Y.: Feminist Press, 1982.

Arlacchi, Pino. *Mafia Business.* New York: Verso, 1987.

Ascoli, U. and Catanzaro, R. *La società italiana degli anni ottanta.* Bari:Laterza, 1987.

Banfield, Edward. *The Moral Basis of a Backward Society.* Glencoe, Ill.: The Free Press, 1958.

Baranski, Zygmunt G. and Vinall, Shirley W., eds. *Women and Italy: Essays on Gender, Culture and History.* New York: St. Martin's Press, 1991.

Birnbaum, Lucia Chiavola. *Liberazione della donna: A Cultural History of the Contemporary Italian Women's Movement.* Middletown: Wesleyan UP, 1985.

Bono, Paola and Kemp, Sandra, eds. *Italian Feminist Thought: A Reader*. Oxford: Basil Blackwell, 1991.

Caldwell, Lesley. *Italian Family Matters*. London: Macmillan, 1991.

CENSIS. *Italy Today: Social Picture and Trends, 1985*. Milan: Franco Angeli, 1986.

Ceolin, Carlo, ed. *Università, cultura, terrorismo*. Milan: Franco Angeli, 1984.

Della Porta, Donatella, ed. *Terrorismi in Italia*. Bologna: Il Mulino, 1984.

Forgacs, David and Lumley, Robert, eds. *Introduction to Italian Cultural Studies*. Oxford: Oxford University Press, 1995.

Fraser, R. *1968: A Student Generation in Revolt*. New York: Pantheon Books, 1988.

Graziano, Luigi and Tarrow, Sidney, eds. *La crisi italiana*. Turin: Einaudi, 1979.

Gribaudi, A. *Mondo operaio, mito operaio*. Turin: Einaudi, 1987.

Hofmann, Paul. *That Fine Italian Hand*. New York: Henry Holt & Co., 1990.

Jeffries, Giovanna M., ed. *Feminine Feminists: Cultural Practices in Italy*. Minneapolis: University of Minnesota Press, 1994.

Kemp, Sandra and Bono, Paola. *The Lonely Mirror: Italian Perspectives on Feminist Theory*. London: Routledge, 1993.

Kertzer, David. *Sacrificed for Honor*. Boston: Beacon Press, 1993.

Labini, Paolo Sylos. *Le classi sociali negli anni 80*. Bari: Laterza, 1986.

Lumley, Robert. *States of Emergency: Cultures of Revolt in Italy from 1968 to 1978*. London; New York: Verso, 1990.

Lumley, Robert and Baranski, Zygmund G. *Culture and Conflict in Postwar Italy: Essays on Mass and Popular Culture*. London: Macmillan, 1990.

Lupri, E. ed. *The Changing Position of Women and Society: A Cross-National Comparison*. The Netherlands: Leiden-E. J. Brill, 1983.

Meyer, Donald. *Sex and Power: The Rise of Women in America, Russia, Sweden, and Italy*. Middletown: Wesleyan UP, 1987: 119–156, 445–491.

Pantaleone, Michele. *The Mafia and Politics*. London: Chatto and Windus, 1966.

Parks, Tim. *Italian Neighbors*. New York: Grove Weidenfeld, 1992.

Pivato, S. *Movimento operaio e istruzione popolare nell'Italia liberale*. Milan: Franco Angeli, 1986.

Richards, Charles. *The New Italians*. London: Penguin, 1995.

Servegnini, Beppe. *La Bella Figura*. New York: Broadway Books, 2006.

Turato, G. and Sasso, C. *I saccheggiatori*. Milan: Sperling and Kupfer, 1992.

Vertone, Saverio, ed. *La cultura degli italiani*. Bologna: Il Mulino, 1994.

Watson, James. *The Mafia and Clientelism: Roads to Rome in Post-War Calabria*. New York: Routledge, 1986.

Zuccotti, Susan. *The Italians and the Holocaust*. New York: Basic, 1987.

Arts, Intellectuals, Culture

Baranski, Zygmunt G. and Lumley, Robert. *Culture and Conflict in Postwar Italy.* London: The Macmillan Press LTD, 1990.

Bondanella, Peter. *Italian Cinema. From Neorealism to the Present.* New York: Frederick Ungar, 1983 (New York: Continuum, 2001).

Cortellazo, M. and Cardinale, V. *Dizionario di parole nuove: 1964–1984.* Turin: Einaudi, 1985.

De Mauro, Tullio. *Storia linguistica dell'Italia unita.* Bari: Laterza, 1976.

Forgacs, David. *Italian Culture in the Industrial Era 1880–1980.* Manchester: Manchester UP, 1990.

Grossi, Giorgio. *Rappresentanza e rappresentazione. Percorsi di analisi dell=interazione tra mass media e sistema politico in Italia.* Milan: Franco Angeli, 1985.

Inglehart, Ronald. *Culture Shift in Advanced Industrial Society.* Princeton: Princeton UP, 1990.

Jewell, Keala. *The Poiesis of History: Experimenting with Genre in Postwar Italy.* Ithaca: Cornell U.P., 1992.

Kerr, Paul ed. *The Hollywood Film Industry: A Reader. London:* Routledge and Kegan Paul, 1986.

Lanaro, Silvio. *L'Italia nuova. Identità e sviluppo 1861–1988.* Turin: Einaudi, 1988.

Mancini, Paolo. *Videopolitics: Telegiornali in Italia e in USA.* Turin: ERI, 1985.

Marcus, Millicent. *Italian Film in the Light of Neorealism.* Baltimore: The Johns Hopkins U.P., 2002.

Marletti, Carlo. *Media e politica.* Milan: Franco Agnelli, 1984.

Mauri, Stefano. *Il libro in Italia. Geografia, produzione, consumo.* Milan: Hoepli, 1987.

Michalczyk, John J. *The Italian Political Filmmakers.* Cranbury: Associated University Press, Inc., 1986.

Misler, Nicoletta. *La vita italiana al realismo. La politica culturale artistica del PCI dal 1944 al 1956.* Milan: Mazzotta, 1973.

Mondello, Elisabetta. *Gli anni delle riviste: Le riviste letterarie dal 1945 agli anni ottanta.* Lecce: Edizioni Milella, 1985.

Pansa, Gianpaolo. *Comprati e venduti: I giornali e il potere negli anni 70.* Milan: Bompiani, 1978.

———. *Carte false.* Milan: Rizzoli, 1986.

Pasolini, Pier Paolo. *Scritti corsari.* Milan: Garzanti, 1975.

———. *Letture luterane.* Turin: Einaudi, 1977.

Pinto, Francesco. *Intellettuali e tv negli anni 50.* Rome: Savelli, 1977.

Porter, William E. *The Italian Journalist.* Ann Arbor: University of Michigan Press, 1983.

Testa, Carlo. *Italian Cinema and Modern European Literature, 1945–2000.* Westport, CT: Praeger, 2002.

Vacca, Giuseppe. *L'informazione negli anni ottanta.* Rome: Riuniti, 1984.

INDEX

Index

Q